EUROPEAN ATLAS for travelers

PASSPORT BOOKS

Trade Imprint of National Textbook Company
Lincolnwood, Illinois U.S.A.

Atlas Scales

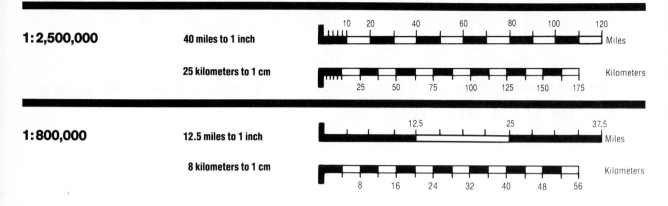

1:2,500,000

40 miles to 1 inch

25 kilometers to 1 cm

1:800,000

12.5 miles to 1 inch

8 kilometers to 1 cm

0-8442-9488-8

Contents

Legend for maps 1 : 2,500,000 · Abbreviations used in the maps	IV
Legend for maps 1 : 800,000	V
Europe · Main roads	VI–VII
Motor vehicle nationality letters	VIII

Europe 1 : 2,500,000

Key to maps	1
Maps	2– 32
Index	33– 56

Europe 1 : 800,000

Key to maps	57
Distance table	58
Southern Scandinavia: Key to maps	59
Maps	60– 84
Great Britain, Ireland: Key to maps	85
Maps	86–106
Germany: Key to maps	107
Maps	108–122
Switzerland, Austria: Key to maps	123
Maps	124–130
Benelux, France: Key to maps	131
Maps	132–160
Spain, Portugal: Key to maps	161
Maps	162–188
Italy: Key to maps	189
Maps	190–208
Yugoslavia: Key to maps	209
Maps	210–222
Greece: Key to maps	223
Maps	224–236

City maps

Oslo – Stockholm	238
Helsinki – Copenhagen	239
London	240
Berlin	241
Bonn – Munich	242
Vienna – Prague	243
Zurich – Bern	244
Amsterdam – Brussels	245
Paris	246
Luxembourg – Strasbourg	247
Madrid – Barcelona	248
Lisbon – Milan	249
Rome	250
Budapest – Bucharest	251
Athens – Istanbul	252

Legend to maps
1 : 2.500.000

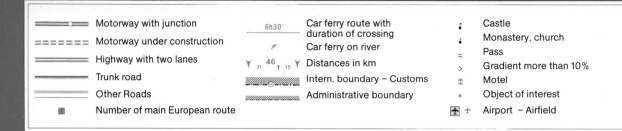

Motorway with junction	6h30'	Car ferry route with duration of crossing	⋮	Castle
Motorway under construction	⨍	Car ferry on river	⋮	Monastery, church
Highway with two lanes	31 46 15	Distances in km	≍	Pass
Trunk road		Intern. boundary – Customs	>	Gradient more than 10%
Other Roads		Administrative boundary	⌂	Motel
Number of main European route			*	Object of interest
			✈ +	Airport – Airfield

Abbreviations used in the maps

A.	Alp|en, -es, -i	-gr.	-gruppe	L°⁽ᵃ⁾	Lago(a)	Schw.	Schwarz|er, -e, -es
Agh.	Aghios	G!	Great	M.	Monte (at mountains	Sᵈ	Sound
Aig^lle(s)	Aiguille(s)	H.	Höhe		and towns);	Sd.; -sd.	Sund; -sund
Akr.	Akroterion	-h.	-höhe (at mountains)		Monasterio (at	Slav.	Slavonsk|i, -a, -o
Altop.	Altopiano		-hafen (at towns)		monasteries)	Sp.; -sp.	Spitze; -spitze
App.	Appennino	Hav.; -hav	Haven; -haven	Mal.	Mal|yj, -aja, -oje	S^ra(s)	Sierra(s)
B....	Bad	Hᵈ	Head	M^gne(s)	Montagne(s)	S^rra	Serra
...B.; -b.	Bach; -bach	-hfn.	-hofen	M^t(s)	Mont(s)	sˢ	sous
(-)B.	(-)Bucht, (-bucht)	hg.	hegység	M^t(s)	Mount(ains)	SSR	Socialist
Bf.	Bahnhof	-hgl.	-hügel	M^ti	Monti		Soviet Republic(s)
Bg.; -bg.	Berg; -berg	-hgn.	-hagen	nat.	national	S!	Saint
-b̆g.	-burg	(-)H.-I.	Halbinsel,	Naz.	Nazionale	St., S:t	Sankt
Bge.; -bge.	Berge; -berge		(-halbinsel)	Ndr.	Nieder, -er, -e, -es	-st.	-stadt (at towns)
-bgn.	-bergen	-hm.	-heim	Nw.	Now|o, -y, -a, -e		-stein (at mountains)
Bol.	Bol'š|oj, -aja, -oje,	-hⁿ	-horn	o.	ostrov	Št.	Šent
	-ije	-hⁿʳ	-hörner	Ö.	Öst|er, ra	Sta	Santa
Bos.	Bosansk|i, -a, -o	Hor.	Horní	Ob.	Ober, -er, -e, -es	Stat.	Station
-br(n).	-brück(en)	Hrv.	Hrvatsk|i, -a, -o	Or.	Oros	S^te	Sainte
C.	Cape	Hˢ	Hills	oz.	ozero	S^th	South
Can.	Canal	-hs(n).	-haus(en)	P.	Paß (at mountains)	-stⁿ	-stein
C^bo	Cabo	H^t(e)	Haut(e)		Port (at towns)	-stn.	-stetten
Ch^au	Château	Htr.	Hinter, -er, -e, -es	p.	potok	S^to	Santo
C^l(e)	Col(le) (at mountains)	-hvn.	-hoven	-p.	-paß	Str.	(German:) Straße
C^le	Castle (at towns)	I....	Isle	P^c(o)	Pic(o)		(English:) Strait
C^ma	Cima	...I.	Island	Pen.	Peninsula	-str.	-straße
C^no	Corno	(-)I.	(-)Insel), (-insel)	P^it(e)	Petit(e)	Sv.	Svet|i, -a, -o
Coll.ˢ	Collines	Î.	Île	pl^a	planina	T.	Tal
C^po	Capo	I^a(s)	Ilha(s)	Pl^au	Plateau	Unt.	Unter, -er, -e, -es
C^ro(s)	Cerro(s)	Ì^a	Ìsola	pl^e	planine	V.	Velik|i, -a, -o, -e
-df.	-dorf	Ì^e	Ìsole	poh.	pohorie	V^a	Vila
Dol.	Dolní	I^la(s)	Isla(s)	Poj.	Pojezierze	vdchr.	vodochranilišče
Ét^g	Étang	(-)I^n	(-)Inseln, (-inseln)	Pr.	Preußisch(-) (Prussian)	Vdr.	Vorder, -er, -e, es
-f^d	-field	I^s-Î^s	Islands; Îles	pr.	průsmyk	V^e	Valle
-fd(e).	-feld(e)	j.	joki	P^rto	Puerto	Vel(').	Vel(')k|ý, -á, -é
-fdn.	-felden	Jez.	Jezioro	P^so	Passo	V^la	Villa
F^ët	Forêt	K.; -k.	Kopf; -kopf	P^t	Point	W....	(German:) Weiß,
Fj.; -fj.	Fjord; -fjord	Kan.	(German:) Kanal;	P^ta	Punta		-er, -e, -es;
F^t(e)	Fort(e)		(Dutch:) Kanaal	P^te	Pointe		(English:) West
g.	gora	(-)kan.	(German:) (-)kanal;	P^to	Porto	...W.; -w.	Wald; -wald (at
G^a	Góra		(Dutch:) -kanaal	P^zo	Pizzo		mountains)
G^d(e)(es)	Grande(e)(es)	kap.	kapell	R.	Rio, Rio (Spanish,	-w.	-witz (at towns)
Geb.; -geb.	Gebirge; -gebirge,	-kch(n).	-kirch(en)		Portuguese;	-wd(e).	-wald(e)
	Gebiet	Kfl.; -kfl.	Kofel; -kofel		at rivers);	Whs.	Wirtshaus (Inn)
gesp.	gesperrt (closed)	Kfz	Kraftfahrzeug (motor car)		Rot|er, -e, -es (at	-wlr.	-weiler
G^fe; G^lo	Golfe; Golfo	Kgl.; -kgl.	Kogel; -kogel		mountains and rivers);		
Gft.	Grafschaft	Kl.	Klein, -er, -e, -es	R.	Ruine (at buildings)		
Gl.; -gl.	Gletscher;	Kol.	Kolonie	Rib^a	Ribeira		
	-gletscher	Kr.	Krasn|o, -yj, -aja,	Riv.	River		
-gn.	-ingen		-oje, -yje	S....	San		
Gr.	Groß, -er, -e, -es	-lbn.	-leben	(-)S.	(-)See; (-see)		
	(German)	(-)I^d(e)	(-)land(e)	-schd.	-scheid		
	Gran (Italian)	Lim.	Limni	Schl.; -schl.	Schloß; -schloß		

Legend to maps
1 : 800.000

Traffic

Bad Krozingen	Motorway with junction, filling station, restaurant
	(under construction – projected)
	Highway with two lanes (existing – under construction – projected)
	Trunk road (existing – under construction – projected)
	Main road
	Secondary road
	Other road
	Narrow road (with passing places)
	Cart-track
	Footpath
M4 8 5 A1	Number of motorway
7 N41 119 110	Numbers of trunk roads
E 18	Number of main European route
20 / 10 / 10	Distances on motorways in km
182 / 7 / 10 / 3 / 1	Distances on other roads in km
	Sealed
	Unsealed
	Very bad road
	Road under repair

Road condition

	Toll road
	Restricted traffic, road closed for motor traffic
XI-V	Road closed in winter (from – to)
XI-V	Mountain pass closed in winter (from – to)
15%	Gradient – Gradient less than 20% – more than 20% (in Greece only)
	Closed for caravans – Not suitable for caravans
	Tourist route
	Road with fine scenery
	Railway with station, tunnel
	Railway closed down
	Rack railway
	Cable lift
	Chair-lift or T-bar
	Shipping route
	Car ferry route
	Railway ferry
	Airport – Airfield

Places of interest

GRANADA	Place of particular interest
Belle-Ile	Place of interest
★ Arco de Barà ★ Ponts de Cubzac	Other object of interest – Medieval town (in France only)
	Nationalpark
	Tower – Lighthouse – View-point
	Castle, manor house – Ruin – Moorish castle – Ruin
	Church – Monastery – Hermitage
	German military cemetery
	Church or monastery (byzantine) (in Greece only)
	Mosque – Former mosque – Mosque, converted to church
∴ DELPHI	Archaeological excavation
	Buildings or excavations:
	Prehistoric
	Celtic, celtic-Iberian
	Greek – Punic
	Roman
	Cave with prehistoric paintings
	Menhirs und dolmens
✕	Battle-field
	Gorge – Cave – Waterfall

Other information

⊕	Village with church (in Scandinavia only)
	Holiday bungalows – Winter sports resort
	Motel – Country hotel or inn
A H P E	Albergue, Hostal, Parador, Pousada, Estalagem (hotels and restaurants in Spain and Portugal)
■ □ △	Hamlet, isolated building – open in summer only – Lapp settlement
	Youth hostel – Mountain hut, tourist or club hut
△ ▲ △	Camping site – Campingsite permanent – seasonal (in Italy only)
Alfame	Spa
	Beach
φ (φ)	Underwater fishing – prohibited
	International boundary – Border crossing point (customs)
	Administrative boundary
· 2029)((734)	Summit – Pass (hight in metres)

0   10   20   30   40   50 km

Europa · Eurooppa · Europe · Ελρώπη · Avrupa

Motor vehicle nationality letters

The motor vehicle nationality letters are usually abbreviations of the country names.

A	–	Austria	GBM	–	Isle of Man	RCB	–	Congo
ADN	–	Southern Yemen	GBZ	–	Gibraltar	RCH	–	Chile
AL	–	Albania	GCA	–	Guatemala	RH	–	Haiti
AND	–	Andorra	GH	–	Ghana	RI	–	Indonesia
AUS	–	Australia	GR	–	Greece	RIM	–	Mauretania
			GUY	–	Guyana	RL	–	Lebanon
B	–	Belgium				RM	–	Madagascar
BD	–	Bangla Desh	H	–	Hungary	RMM	–	Mali
BDS	–	Barbados	HK	–	Hong Kong	RN	–	Niger
BG	–	Bulgaria				RO	–	Romania
BH	–	Belize	I	–	Italy	ROK	–	South Korea
BR	–	Brazil	IL	–	Israel	ROU	–	Uruguay
BRN	–	Bahrain	IND	–	India	RP	–	Philippines
BRU	–	Brunei	IR	–	Iran	RSM	–	San Marino
BS	–	Bahamas	IRL	–	Ireland	RWA	–	Rwanda
BUR	–	Burma	IRQ	–	Iraq			
			IS	–	Iceland	S	–	Sweden
C	–	Cuba				SD	–	Swaziland
CDN	–	Canada	J	–	Japan	SF	–	Finland
CH	–	Switzerland	JA	–	Jamaica	SGP	–	Singapore
CI	–	Ivory Coast	JOR	–	Jordan	SME	–	Surinam
CL	–	Sri Lanka (Ceylon)				SN	–	Senegal
CO	–	Colombia	K	–	Cambodia	SP	–	Somalia
CR	–	Costa Rica	KWT	–	Kuwait	SU	–	Soviet Union
CS	–	Czechoslavakia				SY	–	Seychelles
CY	–	Cyprus	L	–	Luxembourg	SYR	–	Syria
			LAO	–	Laos			
D	–	Federal Republic of Germany	LAR	–	Libya	T	–	Thailand
			LS	–	Lesotho	TG	–	Togo
DDR	–	German Democratic Republic				TN	–	Tunisia
			M	–	Malta	TR	–	Turkey
DK	–	Denmark	MA	–	Morocco	TT	–	Trinidad and Tobago
DOM	–	Dominica	MAL	–	Malaysia			
DY	–	Benin	MC	–	Monaco	USA	–	Unites States of America
DZ	–	Algeria	MEX	–	Mexico			
			MS	–	Mauritius	V	–	Vatican City
E	–	Spain	MW	–	Malawi	VN	–	Vietnam
EAK	–	Kenya				WAG	–	Gambia
EAT	–	Tanzania	N	–	Norway	WAL	–	Sierra Leone
EAU	–	Uganda	NA	–	Netherlands Antilles	WAN	–	Nigeria
EC	–	Equador	NIC	–	Nicaragua	WD	–	Dominica
ES	–	El Salvador	NL	–	Netherlands	WG	–	Grenada
ET	–	Egypt	NZ	–	New Zealand	WL	–	Saint Lucia
ETH	–	Ethiopia				WS	–	Samoa
			P	–	Portugal	WV	–	Saint Vincent
F	–	France and overseas territories	PA	–	Panama			
			PAK	–	Pakistan	YU	–	Yugoslavia
FJI	–	Fiji	PE	–	Peru	YV	–	Venezuela
FL	–	Liechtenstein	PL	–	Poland			
FR	–	Faeroe Islands	PY	–	Paraguay	Z	–	Zambia
						ZA	–	South Africa
GB	–	Great Britain and Northern Ireland	RA	–	Argentina	ZRE	–	Zaire
			RB	–	Botswana	ZW	–	Zimbabwe
GBA	–	Alderney	RC	–	Taiwan (Nationalist China)			
GBG	–	Guernsey				CC	–	Consular corps
GBJ	–	Jersey	RCA	–	Central African Republic	CD	–	Corps diplomatiques

Europa · Eurooppa · Europe · Ευρώπη · Avrupa
1 : 2.500.000

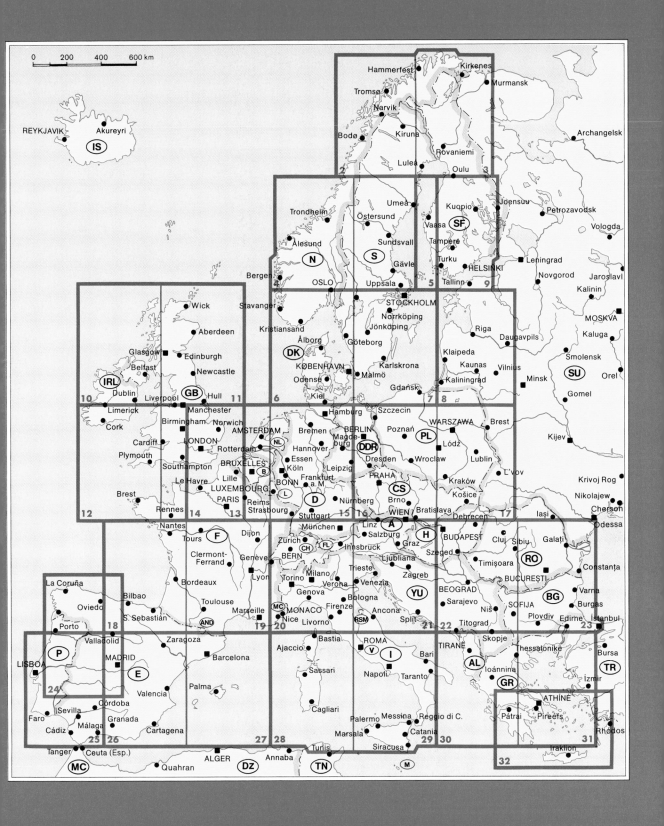

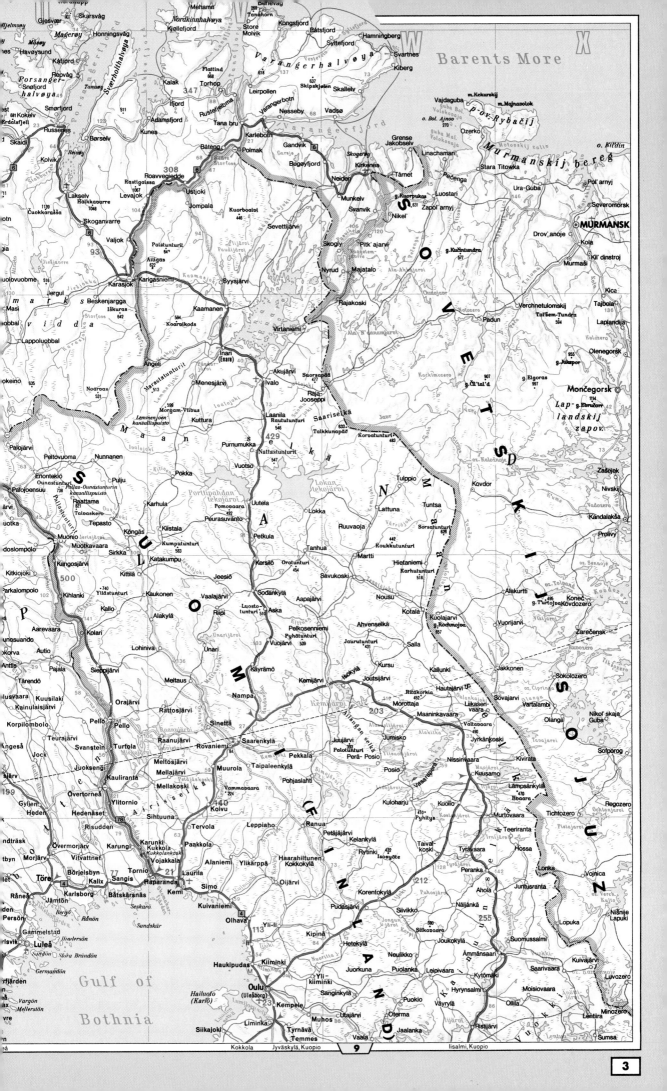

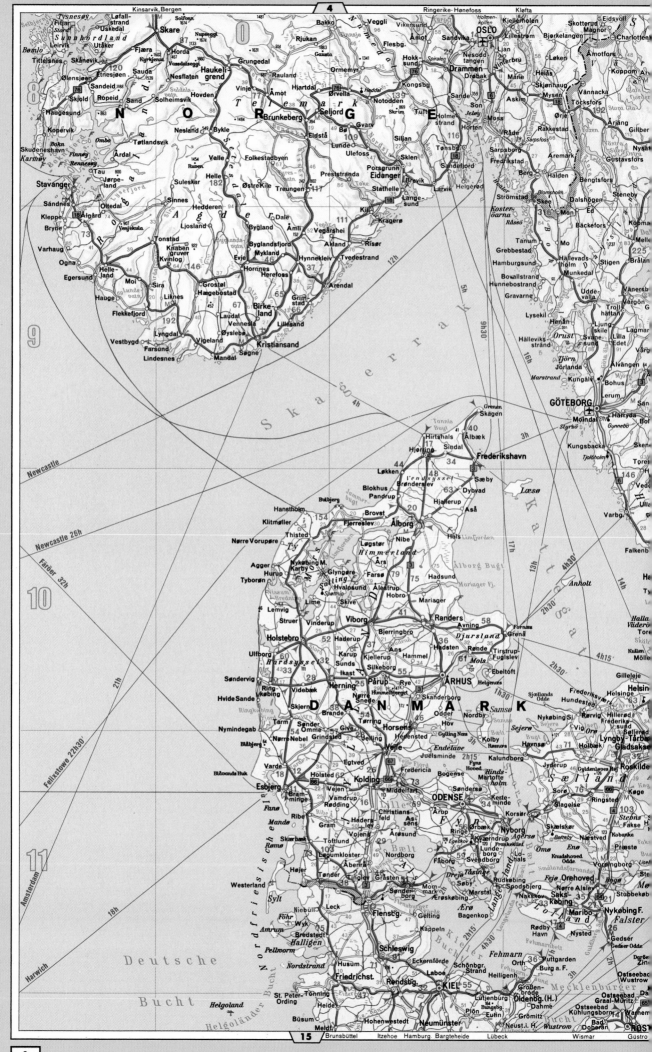

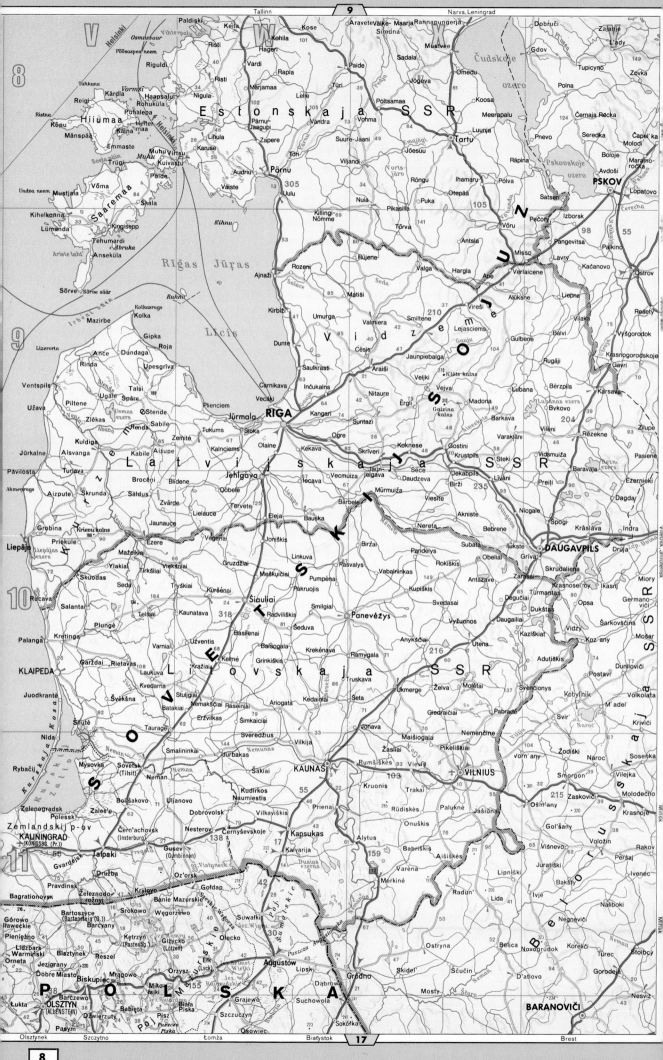

V

W

8

9

10

11

Helsinki

Hiiumaa
Saaremaa

Estonskaja SSR

Rīgas Jūras

Līcis

Vidzeme

Latvijskaja SSR

RIGA
Jūrmala

Jelgava

Liepāja

Sovetskaja

Klaipeda

Sovietskaja

Liovovskaja SSR

KAUNAS

VILNIUS

KALININGRAD
(KÖNIGSBG. (Pr.))

Zemlandskijp-ov

POLSKA

OLSZTYN
(ALLENSTEIN)

PSKOV

Čudskoje
ozero

Pskovskoje
ozero

Tartu

DAUGAVPILS

Beloruusskaja SSR

BARANOVIČI

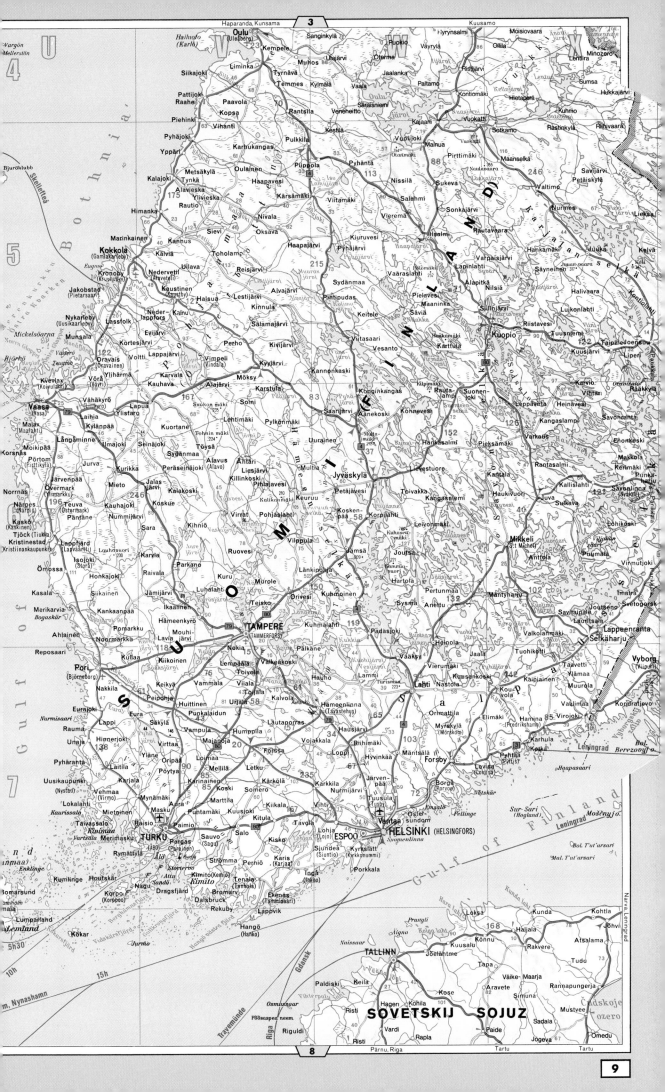

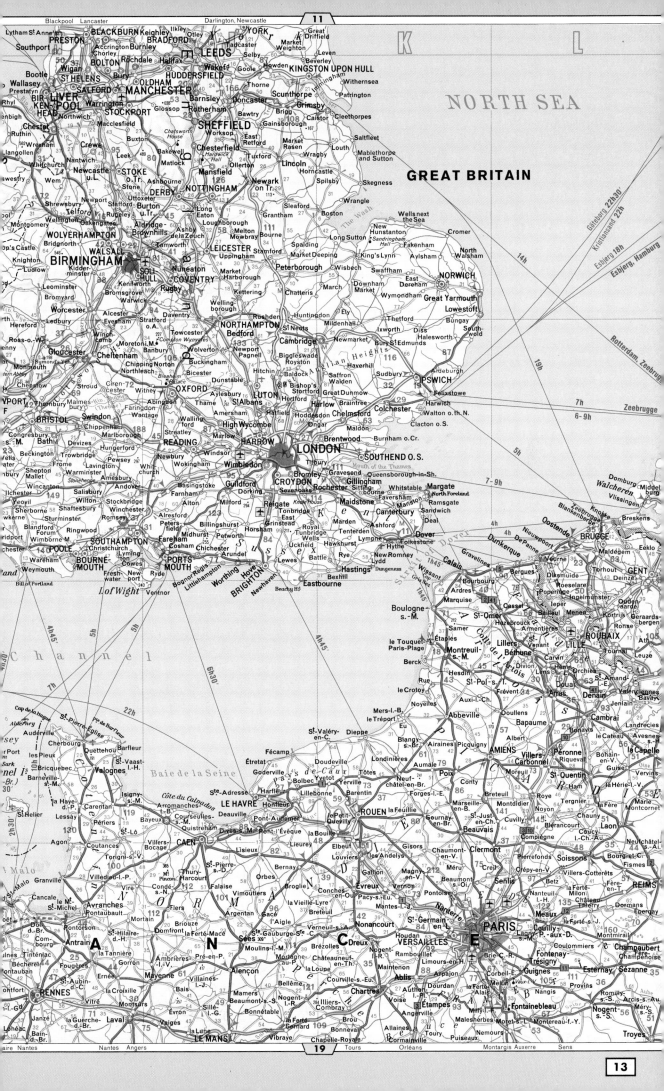

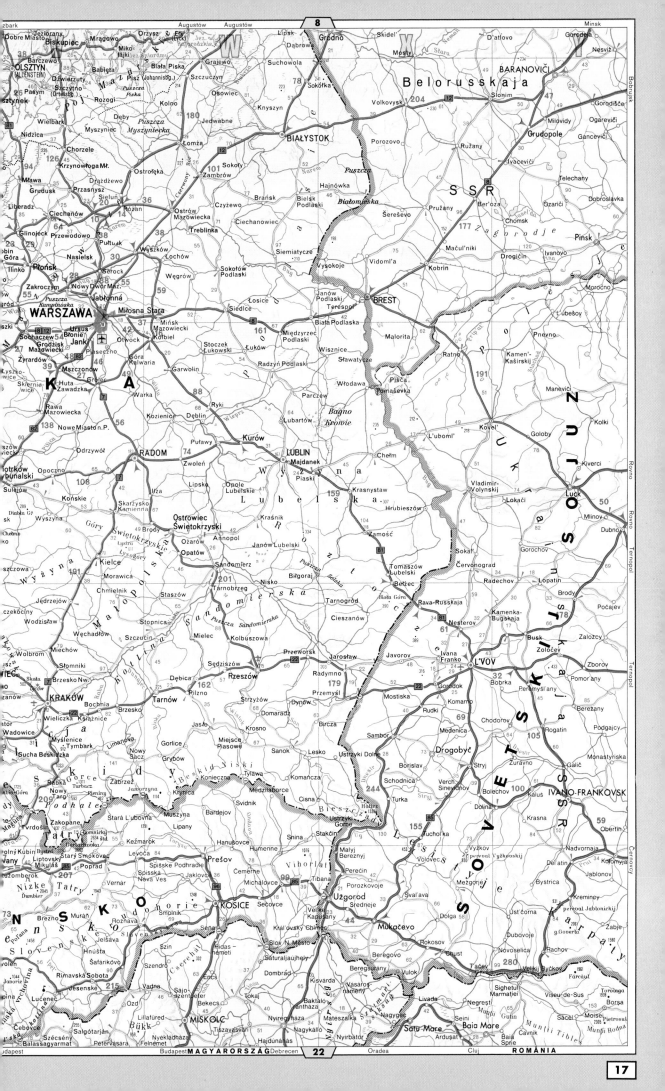

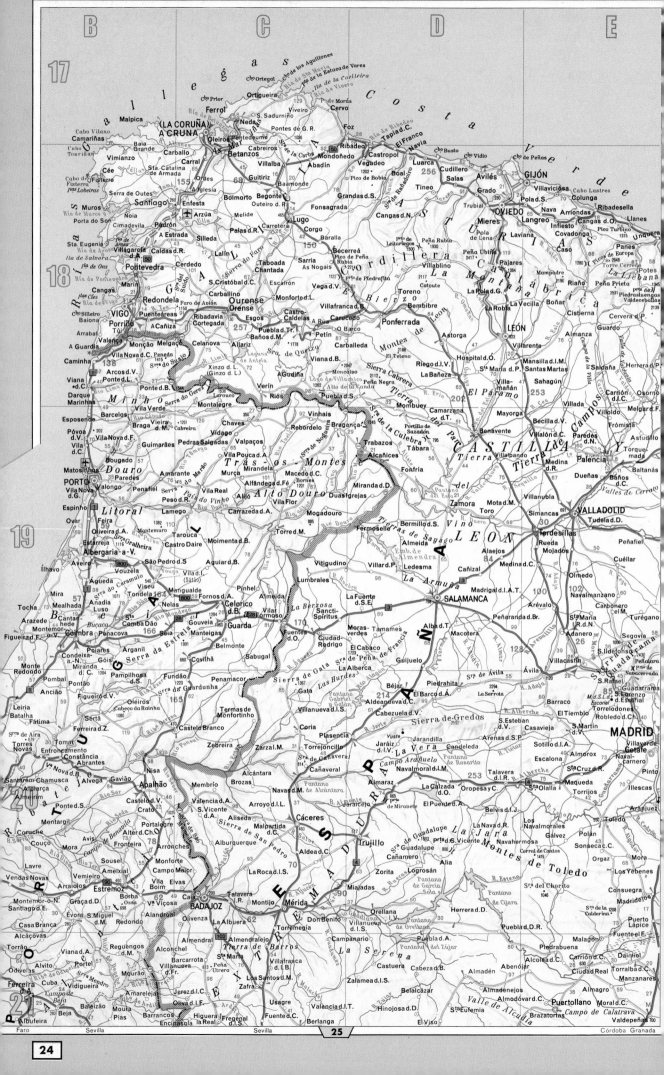

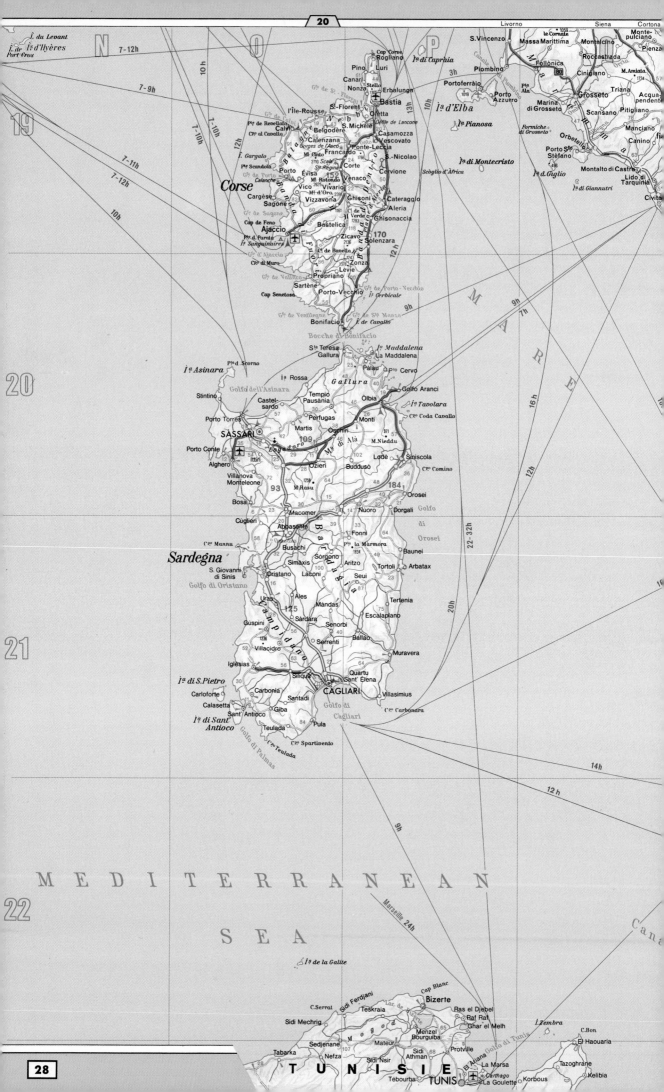

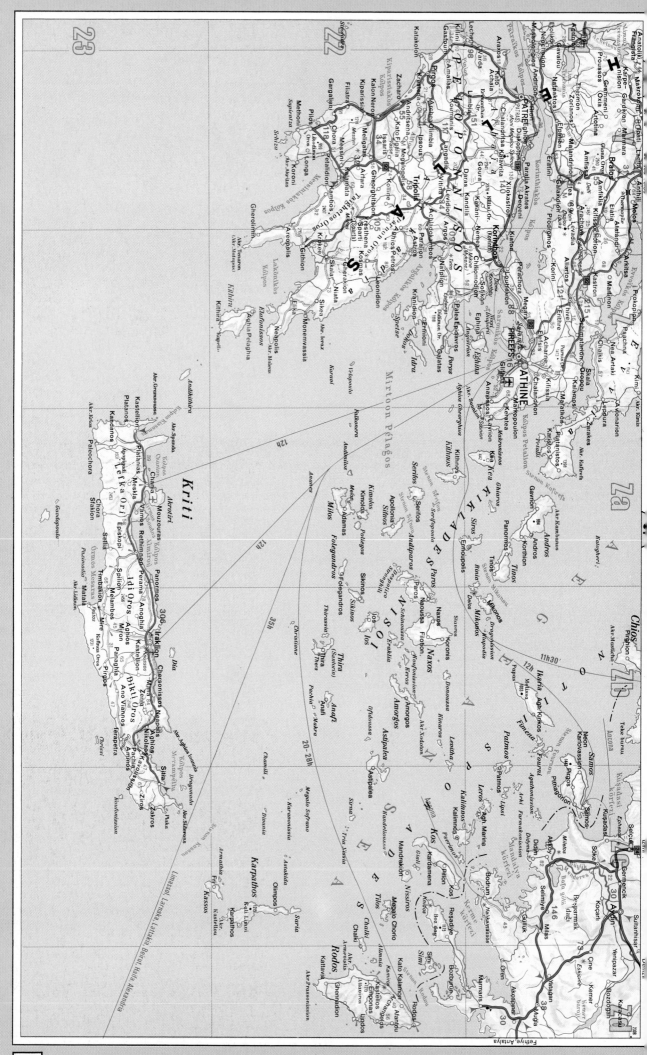

Register · Hakemisto · Index · Namenverzeichnis
Register · Index · Índice · Elenco dei nomi
1:2.500.000

Anvisningar till registrets användning.

Namnförteckningen omfattar alla på kartan förekommande namn i oavkortad form.

Ovanliga bokstäver på främmande språk eller bokstäver med accenter behandlas som vanliga bokstäver, ex-vis ä=a, æ=ae, č=c, ø=o, ß=ss, osv.

Geografiska namn känns igen på de symboler ≈ (floder, sjör etc), eller △ (berg, öar, landskap) som placeras före namnen.

Efter varje namn anges inom parentes statstillhörighet genom användande av de internationella registreringsbokstäverna. De efterföljande siffrorna hänvisa till sida resp. positionsangivelse på sidan.

Ohjeita hakemiston käyttäjälle

Kartassa esiintyvät nimet ovat hakemistossa aakkosjärjestyksessä lyhentämättömässä muodossa. Erikoiskirjaimet, kuten kaksoisvokaalit, vieraskieliset kirjaimet ja aksenttikirjaimet, on järjestetty normaalien aakkosten tapaan; ä=a, æ=ae, č=c, ł=l, ø=o, ß=ss jne.

Hakemistossa, kuten kartoissakin, esiintyvät paikalliset nimet, viralliset rinnakkaisnimet (esimerkiksi Helsingfors = Helsinki) sekä perinteiset saksankieliset nimet (esimerkiksi Danzig = Gdańsk). Suurten vuoristojen, alueiden, merien jne. kohdalla mainitaan ainoastaan saksankielinen nimi.

Luonnonmaantieteelliset kohteet osoitetaan merkeillä, kuten ≈ (joki, järvi, meri jne.) tai △ (vuori, vuoristo, saari jne.)

Jokaisen nimen perässä on hakasuluissa mainittu maatunnus. Sen jäljessä oleva kirjain-numeroyhdistelmä ilmoittaa kartan sivun ja karttalehden ruudun, jossa nimi esiintyy.

How to use the index

The index includes all names appearing in the maps in their unabbreviated form.

Special letters of foreign languages or letters with diacriticals are arranged as regular letters: ä=a; æ=ae; č=c; ø=o; ß=ss etc.

Geographical names are marked with the following symbols preceding the names ≈ = (rivers, lakes, seas etc.,) or △ = (mountain ranges, mountains, islands, regions etc.) Names not identified by a symbol are place names.

After each name, its country is indicated by means of motor vehicle nationality letters.

The numbers and letters following refer to the map pages and the grid containing the name.

Hinweise zur Benutzung des Registers

Das Namenverzeichnis umfaßt alle in den Karten vorkommenden Namen in ungekürzter Form.

Sonderbuchstaben fremder Sprachen oder Buchstaben mit Akzenten sind wie normale Buchstaben eingeordnet: ä=a; æ=ae; č=c; ø=o; ß=ss usw.

Geographische Namen sind durch die Signaturen ≈ (Flüsse, Seen, Meere usw.) oder △ (Berge, Gebirge, Inseln, Landschaften usw.) gekennzeichnet, die den Namen vorangestellt sind.

Hinter jedem Namen folgt in eckigen Klammern die Angabe der Staatszugehörigkeit durch die internationalen Autokennzeichen.

Die danach folgenden Lagehinweise geben die Seite und das Suchfeld an, in dem der Name zu finden ist.

Hoe het register te gebruiken

Het register bevat alle plaatsnamen en geografische benamingen die voorkomen op de kaarten in onverkorte vorm.

Speciale letters en leestekens hebben op de alfabetische volgorde geen invloed, bijv.: ä=a; æ=ae; č=c; ø=o; ß=ss.

Geografische namen worden aangeduid door de symbolen ≈ (rivier, meer, zee, enz.) of △ (berg, gebergte, eiland, landschap, enz.) en zijn vóór de namen geplaatst.

Achter elke plaatsnamen volgt tussen haakjes de aanduiding van de nationaliteit door middel van de bij het motorverkeer internationaal bekend zijnde nationaliteitsplaatjes.

De letters en cijfers, die tevens in de marge van de kaarten zijn aangebracht, geven het zoekveld aan waar de plaats is te vinden.

Utilisation de l'index

Cet index comprend tous les noms – non abrégés – cités sur les cartes.

Les lettres spécifiques à certaines langues, ainsi que celles qui sont accentuées, sont classées dans l'ordre alphabétique normal (par exemple: ä=a; æ=ae; č=c; ø=o; ß=ss; etc.).

Les noms géographiques sont précédés par les symboles ≈ (fleuves, rivières, lacs, etc.) ou △ (montagnes, collines, îles, etc.).

A la suite de chaque nom figure, entre crochets, le pays (sous la forme de sa plaque minéralogique de nationalité), puis la page sur laquelle il se trouve, ainsi que ses coordonnées.

Instrucciones para el uso del índice alfabético de topónimos

El índice alfabético de topónimos incluye, sin abreviaturas, cuantos topónimos figuran en los mapas.

Las letras especiales o con signos diacríticos se hallan ordenadas como letras corrientes; así: ä=a; æ=ae; č=c; ł=l; ø=o; ß=ss; etc.

También la ch y la ll figuran en el índice ordenados como letras simples, no como letras dobles: ch = c + h; ll = l + l.

Los topónimos de geografía física aparecen precedidos de los signos ≈ (ríos, lagos, mares, etc.) o △ (montes, cordilleras, islas, comarcas, etc.).

Detrás de cada nombre figura, entre corchetes [ ], el distintivo nacional para automóviles del estado a que corresponde. Las cifras que siguen indican la página y la cuadrícula en que figura el nombre.

Istruzioni per l'uso dell'elenco dei nomi.

L'elenco comprende in forma integrale tutti i nomi che compaiono sulle carte.

Le lettere particolari delle lingue straniere o le lettere con accento sono classificate come lettere normali: ä=a; æ=ae; č=c; ø=o; ß=ss, ecc.

I nomi fisico-geografici sono contrassegnati con i segni ≈ (fiumi, laghi, mari, ecc.) o △ (monti, isole, paesaggi, ecc.) anteposti ai nomi.

Ad ogni nome segue, tra parentesi quadra, l'indicazione dello Stato di appartenenza espressa con la targa automobilistica internazionale.

Le successive indicazioni si riferiscono alla pagina ed al riquadro nel quale si trova il nome.

A

Å [N] 2 Q 3
Aachen [D] 15 N 14
Aalen [D] 15 P 15
Aalst [B] 14 M 14
Aalten [NL] 15 N 13
Äänekoski [SF] 9 W 6
Aapajärvi [SF] 3 V 3
Aarau [CH] 20 O 16
≈ Aare [CH] 20 O 16
Aareavaara [S] 3 U 3
Aarschot [B] 14 M 14
Abadín [E] 24 C 18
Abanilla [E] 26 G 21
Abano Terme [I] 20 Q 17
≈ Abava [SU] 8 V 9
Abbasanta [I] 28 O 21
Abbekås [S] 7 R 11
Abbeville [F] 14 K 14
Abbeyleix [IRL] 10 F 12
Abbiategrasso [I] 20 O 17
Abborrträsk [S] 2 T 4
Abelvær [N] 4 Q 5
Abenójar [E] 26 E 21
Åbenrå [DK] 6 P 11
≈ Åbenrå Fjord [DK] 6 P 11
Abensberg [D] 15 Q 15
Aberaeron [GB] 12 G 12
Aberdare [GB] 12 G 13
Aberdeen [GB] 11 J 9
Aberfeldy [GB] 11 H 10
Aberfoyle [GB] 11 H 10
Abergavenny [GB] 13 H 13
Aberystwyth [GB] 12 G 12
Δ Abetone [I] 20 Q 18
Abingdon [GB] 13 J 13
Abington [GB] 11 H 10
Abisko [S] 2 S 2
Δ Abisko nationalpark [S] 2 S 2
Abla [E] 26 E 22
Ablis [F] 14 K 15
Abony [H] 22 V 16
Åbo = Turku [SF] 9 V 7
Aboyne [GB] 11 J 9
Abrantes [P] 25 B 20
Abrets, les — [F] 19 M 17
Abrud [RO] 22 X 16
Δ Abruka [SU] 8 V 9
Δ Abruzzese, Appennino — [I] 29 R 19
Δ Abruzzo, Parco Nationale d' — [I] 29 S 19
Åbyn [S] 3 U 4
Accrington [GB] 11 H 11
Δ Achaïa [GR] 30 Y 21
Acharne [GR] 31 Z 21
≈ Acheloos [GR] 30 X 21
Δ Achill Head [IRL] 10 D 11
Δ Achill Island [IRL] 10 D 11
Achladochorion [GR] 31 Z 19
Achladokampos [GR] 30 Y 22
Achnalea [GB] 10 G 9
Achnasheen [GB] 11 H 9
Acireale [I] 29 T 22
Acquapendente [I] 28 Q 19
Acri [I] 29 U 21
Acsa [H] 22 V 15
Ada [YU] 22 W 17
≈ Adaja, Río — [E] 26 E 19
Adak [S] 2 S 4
Adakgruvan [S] 2 S 4
Adalsliden [S] 5 S 5
Adamas [GR] 31 Za 22
Adamsfjord [N] 3 V 1
Adanero [E] 26 E 19
Adaševci [YU] 22 V 17
≈ Adda [I] 20 P 17
Adelboden [CH] 20 N 16
Δ Ademello [I] 20 P 17
Ademuz [E] 26 G 20
Adenau [D] 15 N 14
≈ Adige [I] 20 Q 17
Adjud [RO] 23 Za 16
Admont [A] 21 S 16
Adolfsström [S] 2 S 4
Adony [H] 22 V 16
Adorf [DDR] 15 Q 14
≈ Adour [F] 18 G 18
Adovščina [YU] 21 S 17
Adra [E] 26 E 22
Adrano [I] 29 T 22
Adria [I] 20 Q 17
Δ Adula [CH] 20 O 17
Adutiškis [SU] 8 Y 10
Δ Ærø [DK] 6 P 11
Ærøskøbing [DK] 6 P 11
Aetos [GR] 30 X 20
Afantou [GR] 32 Zd 22
Åfarnes [N] 4 O 6
Åfjord [N] 4 P 5
≈ Åfjord [N] 4 N 7
Δ Africa, Scoglio d' — [I] 28 P 19
Δ Afsluitdijk [NL] 14 M 12
Afumaţi [RO] 23 Za 17
Δ Agathonission [GR] 31 Zd 21
Agde [F] 19 L 18
Δ Agder [N] 6 O 9
Agen [F] 19 J 18
Δ Agenais [F] 19 J 18
Δ Agersø [DK] 6 Q 11
Agger [DK] 6 O 10
Aghia [GR] 30 Y 20
Aghia Anna [GR] 31 Z 21
Aghia Evfimia [GR] 30 X 21
Aghia Pelaghia [GR] 31 Z 22
Aghios Efstratios [GR] 31 Za 20
Δ Aghios Efstratios [GR] 31 Za 20
Δ Aghios Gheorghios [GR] 32 Z 22
Δ Aghios Ioannis, Akrotirion — [GR] 32 Zb 23
Aghios Kirikos [GR] 31 Zb 21
Aghios Marina [GR] 31 Zc 21
Aghios Mattheos [GR] 30 W 21
Aghios Miron [GR] 32 Zb 23
Aghios Nikolaos [GR] 31 Z 20
Aghios Nikolaos [GR] 32 Zb 23
Aghios Petros [GR] 30 X 21
Aghios Petros [GR] 30 Y 22
Agighiol [RO] 23 Zb 16
Agira [I] 29 S 22
Agnanda [GR] 30 X 21
Agnanderon [GR] 30 Y 20
Agnita [RO] 22 Y 16
Δ Ago [S] 5 S 7
Agon [F] 13 H 15
Agordo [I] 20 Q 17
≈ Agra, Río — [E] 18 G 19
Ágreda [E] 26 G 19
≈ Agri [I] 29 U 20
Agrigento [I] 29 S 22
Agrinion [GR] 30 X 21
Δ Agro Pontino [I] 29 R 20
≈ Aguas Vivas, Río — [E] 26 H 19
Águeda [P] 25 B 19
≈ Águeda, Río — [E] 25 C 19
Aguiar da Beira [P] 25 C 19
Aguilar [E] 25 D 21
Aguilar de Campóo [E] 24 E 18
Águilas [E] 26 F 22
Δ Aguillones, Cabo de los — [E] 24 C 17
Ahaus [D] 15 N 13
Åheim [N] 4 N 6
Ahlainen [SF] 9 U 6
Ahmetli [TR] 31 Zc 20
Ahola [SF] 3 W 4
≈ Ahr [D] 15 N 14
Ähtäri [SF] 9 V 6
≈ Ähtärinjärvi [SF] 9 V 6
Ahun [F] 19 K 17
Åhus [S] 7 R 10
Δ Ahvenanmaa = Åland [SF] 5 T 7
Ahvenselkä [SF] 3 W 3
Aibar [E] 18 G 19
Aich [D] 21 R 15
Aichach [D] 15 Q 15
Aigle [CH] 20 N 17
Aigle, l' — [F] 14 J 15
Δ Aigna [SU] 9 W 8
Δ Aigoual, l' — [F] 19 L 18
Aigre [F] 19 J 17
Aiguebelle [F] 20 N 17
Aigues-Mortes [F] 19 L 18
≈ Aigues-Mortes, Golfe d' — [F] 19 L 18
Δ Aiguille, Monte — [F] 19 M 18
Δ Aiguille, Pointe de l' — [F] 18 H 16
Aiguilles [F] 20 N 18
Aiguillon [F] 19 J 18
Aigurande [F] 19 K 16
Δ Ailangan selkä [SF] 3 W 3
Δ Ailigas [N] 3 U 1
≈ Ain [F] 19 M 17
Ainsa [E] 26 H 19
Δ Aira, Serra de — [P] 25 A 20
Airaines [F] 14 K 14
Airdrie [GB] 11 H 10
Aire, Isla del — [E] 27 L 21
Aire-sur-l'adour [F] 18 H 18
Airolo [CH] 20 O 16
Aišiškės [SU] 8 X 11
≈ Aisne [F] 14 L 15
Δ Aitana [E] 26 G 21
Aiud [RO] 22 Y 16
≈ Aiveekste [SU] 8 X 9
Aix-en-Provence [F] 19 M 18
Aixe-sur-Vienne [F] 19 J 17
Aix-les-Bains [F] 19 M 17
Aizenay [F] 18 H 16
Aizpute [SU] 8 V 10
Aizupe [SU] 8 V 9
Ajaccio [F] 28 O 19
≈ Ajaccio, Golfo d' — [F] 28 O 19
Ajtos [BG] 23 Zb 18
≈ Akasjoki [SF] 3 U 3
Akçapinar [TR] 32 Zd 21
Δ Ak dağ [TR] 31 Zb 21
Akhisar [TR] 31 Zc 20
Δ Akka [S] 2 S 3
≈ Akkajaure [S] 2 S 3
Akkarfjord [N] 2 T 1
Akköy [TR] 31 Zc 21
Akland [N] 6 P 9
Δ Akmenrags [SU] 8 V 10
Akniste [SU] 8 X 10
Δ Akrathos, Akrotirion — [GR] 31 Z 20
Δ Akritas, Akritirion — [GR] 30 Y 22
Δ Akrotiri [GR] 32 Za 23
Åkujärvi [SF] 3 V 2
Åkullsjön [S] 5 T 5
Ala [I] 20 Q 17
Δ Alà, Monti di — [I] 28 O 20
Δ Ala, Punta — [I] 20 Q 19
≈ Ala-Akkajarvi [SU] 3 W 1
Alaejos [E] 25 D 19
Alagna Valsésia [I] 20 O 17
Alagón [E] 26 G 19
≈ Alagón, Río — [E] 25 C 20
Alajärvi [SF] 9 V 6
≈ Alakitka [SF] 3 W 3
Alakurtti [SU] 3 X 3
Alakyla [SF] 3 V 3
≈ Ala-N'aanamjarvi [SU] 3 W 2
Alanäs [S] 5 R 5
Δ Åland [SF] 5 T 7
Alandroal [P] 25 B 20
≈ Ålands hav 5 T 8
Alaniemi [SF] 3 V 4
Alapitkä [SF] 9 W 5
Alarcón [E] 26 F 20
≈ Alarcón, Pantano de — [E] 26 F 20
Alassio [I] 20 O 18
≈ Alasuolijärvi [SF] 3 W 3
Alatri [I] 29 R 20
Δ Álava, Concha de — [E] 18 F 18
Alaveteli = Nedervetil [SF] 9 V 5
Alavieska [SF] 9 V 5
Alavo = Alavus [SF] 9 V 6
Alavus [SF] 9 V 6
Alayor [E] 27 L 21
Alba [I] 20 O 18
Albac [RO] 22 X 16
Albacete [E] 26 F 21
Alba de Tormes [E] 25 D 19
Albæk [DK] 6 P 9
Alba Iulia [RO] 22 Y 16
Alban [F] 19 K 18
Δ Albani, Monti — [I] 29 R 20
Δ Albarracín, Sierra de — [E] 26 G 20
Albatera [E] 26 G 21
≈ Albegna [I] 28 Q 19
Albenga [I] 20 O 18
Albens [F] 19 M 17
Alberca, La — [E] 25 D 19
≈ Alberche, Río — [E] 25 D 20
Albergaria-a-Velha [P] 25 B 19
Alberique [E] 26 G 21
Alberobello [I] 29 U 20
Albert [F] 14 L 14
Albertirsa [H] 22 V 16
≈ Albertkanaal [B] 14 M 13
Albertville [F] 20 N 17
Albeşti Paleologu [RO] 23 Za 17
Albi [F] 19 K 18
Δ Albigenois [F] 19 K 18
Albino [I] 20 P 17
Albiţa [RO] 23 Za 15
Ålborg [DK] 6 P 10
≈ Ålborg Bugt [DK] 6 P 10
Albox [E] 26 F 22
≈ Albret, Pay d' — [F] 18 H 18
Albstadt [D] 20 O 15
Albuera, La — [E] 25 C 20
Albufeira [P] 25 A 21
≈ Albufera, La — [E] 26 H 21
Albujón [E] 26 G 22
Albuñol [E] 26 E 22
Alburquerque [E] 25 C 20
Alcácer do Sal [P] 25 A 20
Alcáçovas [P] 25 B 21
Alcalá de Chivert [E] 26 H 20
Alcalá de Guadaira [E] 25 C 21
Alcalá de Henares [E] 26 F 20
Alcalá de los Gazules [E] 25 C 22
Alcalá del Río [E] 25 C 21
Alcalá la Real [E] 26 E 22
Álcamo [I] 29 R 22
≈ Alcanadre, Río — [E] 26 H 19
Alcanede [P] 25 A 20
Alcañices [E] 25 D 19
Alcañiz [E] 26 H 20
Alcántara [E] 25 C 20
Alcantarilla [E] 26 G 21
≈ Alcántaro, Pantano de — [E] 25 C 20
Alcaracejos [E] 25 D 21
Alcaraz [E] 26 F 21
Δ Alcaraz, Sierra de — [E] 26 F 21
≈ Alcarrache, Ribeira — [P] 25 B 21
Alcarraz [E] 26 H 19
Δ Alcarria, La — [E] 26 F 20
Alcaucín [E] 25 D 22
Alcaudete [E] 26 E 21
Alcazar de San Juan [E] 26 E 20
Alcazares, Los — [E] 26 G 22
Alceda [E] 18 F 18
Alcester [GB] 13 H 12
Alcira [E] 26 G 21
Alcobaça [P] 25 A 20
Alcocer [E] 26 F 20
Alcochete [P] 25 A 20
Alcolea de Calatrava [E] 26 E 21
Alcolea del Pinar [E] 26 F 19
Alconchel [E] 25 B 21
Alcorisa [E] 26 H 20
Alcoutim [P] 25 B 21
Alcoy [E] 26 G 21
Alcsútdoboz [H] 21 U 16
Alcubierre [E] 26 H 19
Δ Alcubierre, Sierra de — [E] 26 H 19
Alcublas [E] 26 G 20
Alcudia [E] 27 K 21
≈ Alcudia, Bahía de — [E] 27 K 21
Δ Alcudia, Valle de — [E] 25 D 21
Aldea del Cano [E] 25 C 20
Aldeanueva de Abro [E] 26 G 19
Aldeanueva del Camino [E] 25 D 20
Aldeburgh [GB] 13 K 13
Aldeia Nova de São Bento [P] 25 B 21
Aldekerk [D] 15 N 13
Δ Alderney [GB] 13 H 14
Δ Aldra [N] 2 Q 4
Aldridge-Brownhills [GB] 13 H 12
Aleksandrovac [YU] 22 X 18
Aleksandrovo [BG] 23 Z 18
Aleksandrów Łodzki [PL] 16 U 13
Aleksinac [YU] 22 X 18
Ålem [S] 7 S 10
Alemdal [E] 25 C 21
Alemdralejo [E] 25 C 21
Alençon [F] 14 J 15
Alenia [F] 28 P 19
Δ Alentejo [P] 25 B 21
Δ Aleria, Plaine d' — [F] 28 P 19
Alès [F] 19 L 18
Ales [I] 28 O 21
Aleşd [RO] 22 X 16
Alessándria [I] 20 O 18
Ålestrup [DK] 6 P 10
Ålesund [N] 4 N 6
Δ Aletschgletscher [CH] 20 N 17
Δ Aletschhorn [CH] 20 O 17
Alexandria [GR] 30 Y 20
Alexandria [RO] 23 Z 17
Alexandroupolis [GR] 31 Za 19
Alf [D] 15 N 14
Alfajarín [E] 26 H 19
Alfambra [E] 26 G 20
Alfândega da Fé [P] 25 C 19
Alfaro [E] 26 G 19
Alfarràs [E] 26 H 19
Alfatar [BG] 23 Zb 17
Alfeld (Leine) [D] 15 P 13
≈ Alfios [GR] 30 Y 22
Alfonsine [I] 20 Q 18
Alford [GB] 11 J 9
Δ Ålfotbre [N] 4 N 7
Alfta [S] 5 S 7
Ålgård [N] 6 N 9
Δ Algarrobo [E] 26 G 22
Δ Algarve [P] 25 A 21
Algeciras [E] 25 C 22
≈ Algeciras, Bahía de — [E] 25 C 22
Algete [E] 26 E 20
Alghero [I] 28 O 20
Alghult [S] 7 S 10
Alginet [E] 26 G 21
Algodonales [E] 25 C 22
≈ Algodor, Río — [E] 26 E 20
Algora [E] 26 F 20
Algorta [E] 18 F 18
Algoz [P] 25 A 21
Alhama de Aragón [E] 26 G 19
Alhama de Granada [E] 25 D 22
Alhama de Murica [E] 26 G 22
Alhambra [E] 26 E 21
Alhaurín el Grande [E] 25 D 22
Ålhus [N] 4 N 7
Alía [E] 25 D 20
Aliağa [TR] 31 Zc 20
≈ Aliakmon [GR] 30 Y 20
Aliartos [GR] 31 Z 21
≈ Alibej, ozero — [SU] 23 Zc 16
Alibunar [YU] 22 W 17
Alicante [E] 26 G 21
Δ Alice, Punta — [I] 29 U 21
Δ Alicudi, Isalo — [I] 29 S 22
Alife [I] 29 S 20
Alijó [P] 25 C 19
Δ Alimnia [GR] 32 Zd 22
Alingsås [S] 6 Q 9
Aliseda [E] 25 C 20
≈ Aliste, Río — [E] 25 D 19
Alistrati [GR] 31 Z 19
Aljezur [P] 25 A 21
Aljubarrota [P] 25 A 20
≈ Aljucén, Río — [E] 25 D 20
Aljustrel [P] 25 B 21
Alkmaar [NL] 14 M 12
Allaines [F] 14 K 15
Ållåluokta [S] 2 T 3
Allariz [E] 24 C 18
Δ Alleberg [S] 7 R 9
Allejaur [S] 2 S 4
Allendorf (Eder) [D] 15 O 14
Allenstein = Olsztyn [PL] 8 V 12
Allepuz [E] 26 G 20
≈ Aller [D] 15 P 13
Alleuze [F] 19 L 17
Allevard [F] 19 M 17
Δ Allgäuer Alpen [D] 20 P 16
≈ Allier [F] 19 L 16
Allinge-Sandvig [DK] 7 S 11
≈ Allones, Río — [E] 24 B 17
Allos [F] 20 N 18
Almacellas [E] 26 H 19
Almada [P] 25 A 20
Almadén [E] 25 D 21
Almadenejos [E] 25 D 21
Almagro [E] 26 E 21
Almansa [E] 26 G 21
Almansil [P] 25 A 21
Almanza [E] 24 E 18
≈ Almanzora, Río — [E] 26 F 22
≈ Almar, Río — [E] 25 D 19
Almaraz [E] 25 D 20
Almarcha, La — [E] 26 F 20
Almarza [E] 26 F 19
Δ Almăş, Munţii — [RO] 22 X 17
Almazán [E] 26 F 19
Almeboda [S] 7 S 10
Almeida [E] 25 D 19
Almeida [P] 25 C 19
Almeirim [P] 25 B 20
Almelo [NL] 15 N 13
Almenar [E] 26 H 19
Almenara [E] 26 H 20
Δ Almenara, Cerro de — [E] 26 F 21
Δ Almenara, Pico de — [E] 26 G 19
Δ Almenara, Sierra — [E] 26 F 22
Almenar de Soria [E] 26 G 19
≈ Almería, Golfo de — [E] 26 F 22
Δ Almería, Llanos de — [E] 26 E 22
Almhult [S] 7 R 10
Δ Almina, Punta — [E] 25 C 22
Almiros [GR] 30 Y 21
≈ Almirou, Kolpos — [GR] 32 Za 23
Almodôvar [P] 25 B 21
Almodóvar del Campo [E] 26 E 21
Almodóvar del Río [E] 25 D 21
Almonacid de Zorita [E] 26 F 20
Almonte [E] 25 C 21
≈ Almonte, Río — [E] 25 C 20
Almorox [E] 26 E 20
Almudébar [E] 26 H 19
Almuñécar [E] 26 E 22
Almunge [S] 5 T 8
Almunica de Doña Godina, La — [E] 26 G 19
Almvik [S] 7 S 9
Alness [GB] 11 H 9
Alnmouth [GB] 11 J 10
Δ Alnö [SF] 9 V 7
Alnwick [GB] 11 J 10
Alonnissos [GR] 31 Z 21
Δ Alonnissos [GR] 31 Z 20
Álora [E] 25 D 22
Alpe-d'Huez, l' — [F] 19 M 17
Alpens [E] 27 K 19
Alphen aan de Rijn [NL] 14 M 13
Alpiarça [P] 25 B 20
Δ Alpilles, Chaîne des — [F] 19 M 18
Δ Alpujarras, Las — [E] 26 E 22
Alresford [GB] 13 J 13
Δ Als [DK] 6 P 11
Δ Alsace [F] 20 N 16
Alsasua [E] 18 G 18
Alsfeld [D] 15 P 14
Alstahaug [N] 2 Q 4
Δ Alsten [N] 2 Q 4
Alsterbro [S] 7 S 10
Alston [GB] 11 J 11
Alsvanga [SU] 8 V 9
Alta [N] 2 T 1
≈ Altaelv [N] 3 U 2
≈ Altafjord [N] 2 T 1
Δ Altamira, Cueva de — [E] 18 F 18
Altamura [I] 29 U 20
Altdorf [CH] 20 O 16
Altea [E] 26 H 21
Altenberg [DDR] 16 R 14
Altenburg [DDR] 15 Q 14
Altenkirchen [DDR] 7 R 11
Altenkirchen (Westerwald) [D] 15 O 14
Altenmarkt an der Alz [D] 21 R 16
Altenmarkt bei Sankt Gallen [A] 21 S 16
Altenstadt an der Waldnaab [D] 15 Q 14
Altentreptow [DDR] 16 R 12
Alter do Chão [P] 25 B 20
≈ Altevatn [N] 2 S 2
Altheim [A] 21 R 15
Altkirch [F] 20 N 16
Δ Altmark [DDR] 15 Q 13
≈ Altmühl [D] 15 Q 15
Altnaharra [GB] 11 H 8
Alton [GB] 13 J 13
Altötting [D] 21 R 15
Alūksne [SU] 8 X 9
Ålund [S] 2 T 4
Alunda [S] 5 T 8
Alvajärvi [SF] 9 V 5
≈ Alvajärvi [SF] 9 V 5
Alvängen [S] 6 Q 9
Alvastra [S] 7 R 9
Alvdal [N] 4 P 6
Älvdalen [S] 5 R 7
Δ Alvdalen [S] 4 Q 7
Alvega [P] 25 B 20
Alversund [N] 4 N 7
Alvesta [S] 7 R 10
Alvito [P] 25 B 21
Älvkarleby [S] 5 S 7
Alvros [S] 5 R 6
Alvsbacka [S] 5 R 8
Älvsbyn [S] 2 T 4
Alytus [SU] 8 X 11
≈ Alz [D] 21 R 15
Alzey [D] 15 O 14
Alzonne [F] 19 K 18
Δ Amager [DK] 6 Q 11
Åmål [S] 6 Q 8
Amalfi [I] 29 S 20
Amalias [GR] 30 Y 22
Amándola [I] 21 R 19
Amantea [I] 29 U 21
Amarante [P] 25 B 19
Amărăştii de Jos [RO] 23 Z 17
Amareleja [P] 25 B 21
Δ Amaro, Monte — [I] 29 S 19
Amberg [D] 15 Q 15
Ambérieu-en-Bugey [F] 19 M 17
Ambert [F] 19 L 17
Amboise [F] 19 J 16
Ambrières-les-Vallées [F] 14 J 15
Ameixial [P] 25 B 20
Ameixial [P] 25 B 21
Δ Ameland [NL] 15 N 12
Amélia [I] 29 R 19
Ameria [E] 26 F 22
Amersfoort [NL] 14 M 13
Amersham [GB] 13 J 13
Amesbury [GB] 13 H 13
Amfiklia [GR] 30 Y 21
Amfilochia [GR] 30 X 21
Amfissa [GR] 30 Y 21
Δ Amiata, Monte — [I] 20 Q 19
Amiens [F] 14 K 14
Amindeon [GR] 30 X 20
Åmli [N] 6 O 9
Amlwch [GB] 10 G 12
Ammänsaari [SF] 3 W 4
Δ Ammarfjället [S] 2 R 4
Ammarnäs [S] 2 R 4
Δ Ammerån [S] 5 R 6
≈ Ammersee [D] 20 Q 6
Amorebieta [E] 18 F 18
Amorgos [GR] 31 Zb 22
Δ Amorgos [GR] 31 Zb 22
Åmot [N] 4 P 8
Åmot [N] 6 O 8
Åmot [S] 5 S 7
Åmotfors [S] 4 Q 8
Δ Amøy [N] 2 Q 3
Ampelos [GR] 32 Za 23
Ampolla [E] 26 H 20
Amposta [E] 26 H 20
Δ Ampurdán, El — [E] 27 K 19
Ampurias [E] 27 K 19
Δ Amrum [D] 6 O 11
Amsele [S] 5 T 5
Amsterdam [NL] 14 M 13
Amstetten [A] 21 S 15
≈ Amungen [S] 5 S 7
Amurrio [E] 18 F 18
≈ Amvrakikos Kolpos [GR] 30 X 21
Anadia [P] 25 B 19
Anafi [GR] 31 Zb 22
Δ Anafi [GR] 31 Zb 22
Δ Anåfjället [S] 4 Q 6
Åndalsnes [N] 4 O 6
Δ Ananes [GR] 31 Za 22
Δ Anarisfjällen [S] 4 Q 6
Anäset [S] 5 U 5
Anatoliki Frangista [GR] 30 Y 21
Δ Anatoliki Rodopi [GR] 31 Za 19
≈ Anättijärvi [SF] 3 X 4
Anavissos [GR] 31 Z 21
An Bóthar Buidhe = Innfield [IRL] 10 F 11
An Cabhán = Cavan [IRL] 10 F 11
An Caisleán nua = Newcastle West [IRL] 12 D 12
An Caisleán Riabhach = Castlerea [IRL] 10 E 11
Ance [SU] 8 V 9
Ancenis [F] 18 H 16
Ancião [P] 25 B 20
An Clochán = Clifden [IRL] 10 D 11
An Clochán Liath = Dungloe [IRL] 10 E 10
An Cóf = Cobh [IRL] 12 E 12
Ancona [I] 21 R 18
An Craoslach = Creeslough [IRL] 10 F 10
Δ Andalucía [E] 26 E 22
Andartikon [GR] 30 X 20
Andelot [F] 19 M 15
Andelys, les — [F] 14 K 15
Andenes [N] 2 R 2
Andermatt [CH] 20 O 16
Andernach [D] 15 O 14
Δ Andévalo, Sierra de — [E] 25 B 21
Δ Andia, Sierra de — [E] 18 G 18
Δ Andimilos [GR] 32 Za 22
Δ Andiparos [GR] 31 Za 22
Δ Andipaxi [GR] 30 X 21
Δ Andipsara [GR] 31 Za 21
Andirrion [GR] 30 Y 21
Andoain [E] 18 G 18
Δ Andøly [N] 2 R 2
Δ Andørja [N] 2 S 2
Andorra la Vella [AND] 27 J 19
Andover [GB] 13 H 13
Andraitx [E] 27 K 21
Ándria [I] 29 U 20
Andrijevica [YU] 22 W 19
Andritsena [GR] 30 Y 22
Andros [GR] 30 Za 21
Δ Andros [GR] 31 Za 21
Andselv [N] 2 S 2
≈ Andsfjord [N] 2 R 2
Andújar [E] 26 E 21
Anduze [F] 19 L 16
Δ Aneto, Pico de — [E] 27 J 19
Änettu [SF] 9 W 6
Ånge [S] 5 S 6
Δ Angèle, Mont d' — [F] 19 M 18
Δ Angeles, Cerro de los — [E] 26 E 20
Ängelholm [S] 7 R 10
Angeli [SF] 3 U 2
Angeoulême [F] 19 J 17
≈ Ångermanälven [S] 5 S 5
Δ Ångermanland [S] 5 S 6
Angermünde [DDR] 16 R 12
Angern [A] 21 T 15
Angers [F] 18 H 16
Angerville [F] 14 K 15
Angeså [S] 3 U 3
≈ Angesån [S] 3 U 3
Δ Angesön [S] 5 U 5
Δ Angistrion [GR] 31 Z 21
Anglès [E] 27 K 19
Δ Anglesey [GB] 10 G 12
An Gort = Gort [IRL] 10 E 11
Δ Angoumois [F] 19 J 17
Ångsö [S] 5 S 8
Anguès [E] 26 H 19
Angvik [N] 4 O 6
Δ Anholt [DK] 6 Q 10
Δ Anie, Pic d' — [F] 18 H 18
Anina [RO] 22 X 17
≈ Anjan [S] 4 Q 5
Δ Anjosvarden [S] 5 R 7
Δ Anjou [F] 18 H 15
Ankarede kapell [S] 5 R 5
Ankerlia [N] 2 T 2
Anklam [DDR] 16 R 12
An Móta = Moate [IRL] 10 E 11
An Muileann Cearr = Mullingar [IRL] 10 F 11
Ånn [S] 4 Q 6
Annaberg-Buchholz [DDR] 16 R 14
Annan [GB] 11 H 11
Annecy [F] 20 N 17
≈ Annecy, Lac d' — [F] 20 N 17
Annemasse [F] 20 N 17
Annonay [F] 19 M 17
Annopol [PL] 17 W 13
Annot [F] 20 N 18
Anoghia [GR] 32 Zb 23
Ano Viannos [GR] 32 Zb 23
Ans [DK] 6 P 10
Ansbach [D] 15 P 15
An Sciobairín = Skibbereen [IRL] 12 D 12
Antazave [SU] 8 X 10
≈ Antela, Laguna de — [E] 24 C 18
Antequera [E] 25 D 22
Anthili [GR] 30 Y 21
Antibes [F] 20 N 18
Δ Antibes, Cap d' — [F] 20 N 18
An tInbhear Mór = Arklow [IRL] 12 F 12
≈ Antioche, Pertuis d' — [F] 18 H 16
Antipatra [AL] 30 W 20
Antnäs [S] 3 U 4
Antrain [F] 13 H 15
Antrim [GB] 10 G 11
Δ Antrim Mountains [GB] 10 G 10
Antrodoco [I] 29 R 19
Antsma [SU] 8 X 9
An tSnaidhm = Sneem [IRL] 12 D 12
Anttis [S] 3 U 3
Anttola [SF] 9 X 6
Antwerpen [B] 14 M 13
An Uaimh = Navan [IRL] 10 F 11
Anykščiai [SU] 8 X 10
Anzánigo [E] 26 H 19
Anzio [I] 29 R 20
Aonach Urmhumhan = Nenagh [IRL] 10 E 12
Aosta [I] 20 N 17
Δ Aosta, Val d' — [I] 20 N 17
Apahida [RO] 22 Y 16
Apalhão [P] 25 B 20
Apatin [YU] 22 V 17
Ape [SU] 8 X 9
Apeldoorn [NL] 15 N 13
Apolda [DDR] 15 Q 14
Apollonia [AL] 30 W 20
Apollonia [GR] 31 Z 20
Apollonia [GR] 31 Za 22
Δ Apopigadi [GR] 32 Za 23
Appenzell [CH] 20 P 16
Appiano [I] 20 Q 17
Appleby [GB] 11 H 11
Apricena [I] 29 T 19
Apt [F] 19 M 18
Δ Apuseni, Munţii — [RO] 22 X 16
Aquila, L' — [I] 29 R 19
Aquiléia [I] 21 R 17
Aquincum [H] 22 V 16
Aqui Terme [I] 20 O 18
Arabba [I] 20 R 17
Aracena [E] 25 C 21
Δ Aracena, Sierra de — [E] 25 C 21
Arachova [GR] 30 Y 21
≈ Arachthos [GR] 30 X 21
Arad [RO] 22 W 16
Aradu Nou [RO] 22 W 16
Aragnouet [F] 18 H 19
≈ Aragón, Río — [E] 26 G 19
Δ Aragoncillo [E] 26 G 20
Arahal, El — [E] 25 C 22
Aranda de Duero [E] 26 F 19
Arandjelovac [YU] 22 W 18
Δ Aran Island [IRL] 10 E 10
Δ Aran Islands [IRL] 10 D 11
Aranjuez [E] 26 E 20
Δ Aran Mawddwy [GB] 12 G 12
Δ Arañuelo, Campo — [E] 25 D 20
Araši [SU] 8 X 9
Aravete [SU] 8 W 8
Araxos [GR] 30 Y 21
Δ Araz, Monte — [E] 18 G 18
Arazede [P] 25 B 19
≈ Arba, Río — [E] 26 G 19
Arbatax [I] 28 P 21
Arboga [S] 7 S 8
≈ Arbogaån [S] 7 S 8
Arbois [F] 19 M 16
Arbrås [S] 5 S 7
Arbresle, l' — [F] 19 M 17
Arbroath [GB] 11 J 10
≈ Arc [F] 20 N 17
Arcachon [F] 18 H 17
≈ Arcachon, Bassin d' — [F] 18 H 17
Archangelos [GR] 32 Zd 22
Archea Olimbia [GR] 30 Y 22
Archiac [F] 18 H 17
Archidona [E] 25 D 22
Arcis-sur-Aube [F] 14 L 15
Arco [I] 20 Q 17
≈ Arconce [F] 19 L 16
Arcos, Los — [E] 18 G 19
Arcos de la Frontera [E] 25 C 22
Arcos de Valdevez [P] 24 B 18
Arcriz [SU] 23 Zb 16
Årdal [N] 6 N 8

≈ Årdalsfjord [N] 4 O 7
Årdalstangen [N] 4 O 7
Ardanion [GR] 31 Zb 19
≈ Ardèche [F] 19 L 18
Δ Ardèche, Canyon de l' — [F] 19 L 18
Ardee [IRL] 10 F 11
≈ Ardennes, Canal des — [F] 14 L 15
Δ Ardennes [B,F] 14 M 14
≈ Ardila, Río — [E] 25 C 21
≈ Ardila, Ribeira de — [P] 25 B 21
Ardino [BG] 23 Za 19
Ardres [F] 14 K 13
Ardrossan [GB] 10 G 10
Δ Ards Peninsula [GB] 10 G 11
Ardușat [RO] 17 X 15
Åre [S] 4 Q 6
Δ Arefjället [S] 2 R 4
Δ Årefjell [N] 2 R 4
Δ Årekjølen [N] 4 Q 7
Aremark [N] 6 Q 8
Arén [E] 27 J 19
Arenas de San Pedro [E] 25 D 20
Arendal [N] 6 O 9
Arenys de Mar [E] 27 K 19
Areopolis [GR] 30 Y 22
Arès [F] 18 H 17
Δ Åreskutan [S] 4 Q 6
≈ Arevalillo, Río — [E] 26 E 19
Arévalo [E] 26 E 19
Arezzo [I] 20 Q 18
Arfa [E] 27 J 19
Arfara [GR] 30 Y 22
Argalasti [GR] 31 Z 21
Arganda [E] 26 E 20
Arganil [P] 25 B 19
Argelès-sur-Mer [F] 27 K 19
≈ Argens [F] 19 M 18
Argenta [I] 20 Q 18
Argentan [F] 14 J 15
Argentat [F] 19 K 17
Δ Argentera [I] 20 N 18
Argenton-Château [F] 18 H 16
Argenton-sur-Creuse [F] 19 K 16
Argent-sur-Sauldre [F] 19 K 16
≈ Argeș [RO] 23 Z 17
Argnage [F] 19 J 15
≈ Argolikos Kolpos [GR] 31 Z 22
Δ Argonne [F] 14 M 15
Argos [GR] 31 Z 22
Argos Orestikon [GR] 30 X 20
Argostolion [GR] 30 X 21
Argyrion [AL] 30 W 20
Århus [DK] 6 P 10
Ariane, El — [TN] 28 P 22
Ariano Irpino [I] 29 T 20
Ariano nel Polesina [I] 20 Q 17
Aridea [GR] 30 Y 20
≈ Ariège [F] 19 J 18
Arilje [YU] 22 W 18
Ariogata [SU] 8 W 10
≈ Ariste laht [SU] 8 V 9
Aritzo [I] 28 O 21
Ariza [E] 26 G 19
Årjäng [S] 6 Q 8
Arjeplog [S] 2 S 4
Arjona [E] 26 E 21
Δ Arkadia [GR] 30 Y 22
Δ Arki [GR] 31 Zc 21
Arkitsa [GR] 31 Z 21
Arklow [IRL] 12 F 12
Δ Arkö [S] 7 S 9
Arkösund [S] 7 S 9
Arlanc [F] 19 L 17
≈ Arlanza, Río — [E] 26 E 19
Arlanzón [E] 18 F 19
≈ Arlanzón, Río — [E] 24 E 19
Δ Arlberg [A] 20 P 16
Arles [F] 19 L 18
Arlon [B] 15 N 14
Armadala [GB] 10 G 9
Armagh [GB] 10 F 11
Δ Armagnaç [F] 18 H 18
≈ Armançon de Bourgogne [F] 19 L 15
Δ Armathia [GR] 31 Zc 22
Armeniș [RO] 22 X 17
Armentières [F] 14 L 14
Δ Armevistis, Akrotirion — [GR] 32 Zd 22
Δ Armuña, La — [E] 25 D 19
Armuña de Tajuña [E] 26 F 20
Arnay-le-Duc [F] 19 M 16
Arnea [GR] 31 Z 20
Arnedo [E] 26 G 19
Årnes [N] 4 Q 8
Arnheim [NL] 15 N 13
≈ Arno [I] 20 Q 18
Δ Arnøy [N] 2 T 1
Arnsberg [D] 15 O 13
Arnstadt [DDR] 15 Q 14
Aroche [E] 25 B 21
Δ Aroche, Picos de — [E] 25 B 21
Arolsen [D] 15 O 13
Arona [I] 20 O 17
≈ Arosa, Río de — [E] 24 B 18
Δ Arosa, Isla de — [E] 24 B 18
Årosjåkk [S] 2 S 3
Årøsund [DK] 6 P 11
Arpajon [F] 14 K 15
Arquillos [E] 26 E 21
Arraiolos [P] 25 B 20
Δ Arran [GB] 10 G 10
Arras [F] 14 L 14
Arreau [F] 18 H 19
Δ Arrée, Monts d' — [F] 12 F 15
≈ Arresø [DK] 6 Q 10
Arriondas [E] 24 E 18
Arrochar [GB] 11 H 10
Arromanches-les-Bains [F] 14 J 14
Arronches [P] 25 C 20
Arroyo de la Luz [E] 25 C 20
Års [DK] 6 P 10
Årsand [N] 4 Q 5
Ars-en-Ré [F] 18 H 16
Arsoli [I] 29 R 19
Artá [E] 27 K 21
Arta [GR] 30 X 21
Δ Artá, Cuevas de — [E] 27 K 21
Artenay [F] 19 K 15
Artesa de Segre [E] 27 J 19
Δ Arthos (Halbinsel) [GR] 31 Z 20
Δ Artois [F] 14 K 14
Δ Artois, Collines de l' — [F] 14 K 14
Artotina [GR] 30 Y 21
Arundel [GB] 13 J 13
Årup [DK] 6 P 11
Arvidsjaur [S] 2 T 4
Årvik [N] 4 N 6
Arvika [S] 4 Q 8
Arviksand [N] 2 T 1
Arzúa [E] 24 C 18
As [B] 14 M 14
Aš [CS] 15 Q 14
Åsa [DK] 6 P 10
Åsa [S] 7 R 10
Åsarna [S] 5 R 6
Åsarum [S] 7 S 10
Aschaffenburg [D] 15 P 14
Aschersleben [DDR] 15 Q 13
Δ Asco, Gorges de l' — [F] 28 O 19
Ascoli, Piceno [I] 21 S 19
Ascoli Satriano [I] 29 T 20
Åseda [S] 7 S 10
Åsele [S] 5 S 5
Δ Åsele Lappmark [S] 5 R 5
Åsen [N] 4 Q 6
Åsen [S] 5 R 7
≈ Åsenfjord [N] 4 P 6
Asenovgrad [BG] 23 Z 19
Ashbourne [GB] 13 J 12
Ashby de la Zouch [GB] 13 J 12
Åsheim [N] 4 Q 7
Ashford [GB] 13 K 13
Asiago [I] 20 Q17
≈ Asinara, Golfo di — [I] 28 O 20
Δ Asinara, Isola [I] 28 O 20
Aska [SF] 3 V 3
Åskersund [S] 7 R 6
Åskilje [S] 5 S 5
Askim [N] 6 Q 8
Δ Askön [S] 7 T 8
Asköping [S] 7 S 8
Askvoll [N] 4 N 7
≈ Åsnen [S] 7 R 10
≈ Aso [I] 21 S 19
Asola [I] 20 P 17
Aspach-le-Bas [F] 20 N 16
Aspet [F] 19 J 18
Δ Aspö [S] 7 S 10
Aspres-sur-Buech [F] 19 M 18
Δ Aspromonte [I] 29 T 22
Assen [NL] 15 N 12
Assens [DK] 6 P 11
Assiros [GR] 30 Y 20
Assissi [I] 21 R 19
Assos [GR] 30 X 21
Asswieler [D] 15 N 15
≈ Åsta [N] 4 P 7
Astaffort [F] 19 J 18
≈ Astafjord [N] 2 S 2
Δ Astakida [GR] 31 Zc 22
Astakos [GR] 30 X 21
Δ Astarac [F] 18 H 18
Asti [I] 20 O 18
Astillero, El — [E] 18 F 18
Astipalea [GR] 31 Zb 22
Astipalea [GR] 31 Zc 22
Astorga [E] 24 D 18
Åstorp [S] 7 R 10
Åsträsk [S] 5 T 5
Astudillo [E] 24 E 19
Δ Asturias [E] 24 D 18
≈ Åsunden [S] 7 S 9
Aszód [H] 22 V 16
Atalandi [GR] 31 Z 21
Δ Atalayasa [E] 27 J 21
Atarfe [E] 26 E 22
Ateca [E] 26 G 19
Atessa [I] 29 S 19
Ath [B] 14 L 14
Áth Cinn = Headford [IRL] 10 E 11
Áth Fhirdia = Ardee [IRL] 10 F 11
Áth Í = Athy [IRL] 10 F 12
Athine [GR] 31 Z 21
Athlone [IRL] 10 E 11
Áth Luain = Athlone [IRL] 10 E 11
Áth na nUrlainn = Urlingford [IRL] 12 E 12
Δ Athos (Berg) [GR] 31 Z 20
Athy [IRL] 10 F 12
Atienza [E] 26 F 19
Atina [I] 29 S 20
≈ Atna [N] 4 P 7
Atnaoset [N] 4 P 7
Δ Atøy [N] 4 N 7
Åtran [S] 7 R 10
≈ Åtran [S] 7 R 10
Atri [I] 29 S 19
Atsalama [SU] 9 X 8
Δ Attaviros [GR] 32 Zd 22
Attersee [A] 21 R 16
Attigny [F] 14 M 15
Δ Attu [SF] 9 V 7
Åtvidaberg [S] 7 S 9
Aubagne [F] 19 M 19
≈ Aube [F] 14 L 15
Aubenas [F] 19 L 18
Aubiet [F] 19 J 18
Aubin [F] 19 K 18
Δ Aubrac, Monts d' — [F] 19 K 18
Aubusson [F] 19 K 17
Auch [F] 19 J 18
Auderville [F] 13 H 14
Audierne [F] 12 F 15
Audriu [SU] 8 W 8
Aue [DDR] 16 R 14
Auerbach in der Oberpfalz [D] 15 Q 14
Auer = ora [I] 20 Q 17
Aughnacloy [GB] 10 F 11
Augsburg [D] 20 Q 15
Augusta [I] 29 T 22
≈ Augusta, Golfo di — [I] 29 T 22
Augustów [PL] 8 W 11
Auktsjaur [S] 2 T 4
Aulanko [SF] 9 V 7
Aulla [I] 20 P 18
Aulnay [F] 18 H 16
Aumale [F] 14 K 14
Aumetz [F] 15 N 15
Aumont-Aubrac [F] 19 L 18
Δ Aunis [F] 18 H 16
Aups [F] 20 N 18
Aura [SF] 9 V 7
≈ Aurajoki [SF] 9 V 7
Auray [F] 18 G 15
Aurdal [N] 4 P 7
≈ Aurejärvi [SF] 9 V 6
Aurich [D] 15 O 12
Aurignac [F] 19 H 18
Aurillac [F] 19 K 17
≈ Aurlandsfjord [N] 4 O 7
Auronzo di Cadore [I] 21 R 16
≈ Aursunden [N] 4 Q 6
Δ Aurunci, Monti — [I] 29 S 20
Auschwitz = Oświęcim [PL] 17 V 14
Ausejo [E] 26 G 19
Δ Austvågøy [N] 2 R 2
Auterive [F] 19 J 18
Authon-la-Plaine [F] 14 K 15
Autio [S] 3 U 3
Autun [F] 19 L 16
Δ Auvergne [F] 19 K 17
Auxerre [F] 19 L 16
Auxi-le-Château [F] 14 K 14
Auxon [F] 19 L 15
Auxonne [F] 19 M 16
Auzances [F] 19 K 17
Δ Avala [YU] 22 W 17
Avalon [F] 19 L 16
Avaviken [S] 2 S 4
Avdoši [SU] 8 Y 8
≈ Ave, Rio — [P] 24 B 19
Aveiro [P] 25 B 19
Avellino [I] 29 S 20
Δ Aven Armand [F] 19 L 18
Δ Averøy [N] 4 O 6
Aversa [I] 29 S 20
Avesnes-sur-Helpe [F] 14 L 14
Avesta [S] 5 S 8
≈ Aveyron [F] 19 J 18
Avezzano [I] 29 R 19
Aviemore [GB] 11 H 9
Avigliano [I] 29 T 20
Avignon [F] 19 M 18
Ávila [E] 26 E 20
Δ Ávila, Sierra de — [E] 25 D 20
Avilés [E] 24 D 18
Aving [DK] 6 P 10
Δ Avión, Faro de — [E] 24 C 18
Avionarion [GR] 31 Z 21
Aviz [P] 25 B 20
Avola [I] 29 T 22
Avradsberg [S] 5 R 8
Avramov [BG] 23 Za 18
Avranches [F] 13 H 15
Avrig [RO] 22 Y 16
Δ Avsa adası [TR] 31 Zb 19
Avtovac [YU] 22 V 18
≈ Awe, Loch — [GB] 10 G 10
Δ Axenstein [CH] 20 O 16
≈ Axios [GR] 30 Y 20
Ax-les-Thermes [F] 19 J 19
Axmarsbruk [S] 5 S 7
Axminster [GB] 13 H 13
Ayamonte [E] 25 B 21
Aydın [TR] 31 Zc 21
Ayerbe [E] 26 H 19
Aylesbury [GB] 13 J 13
Ayllón [E] 26 F 19
Δ Aylón, Sierra de — [E] 26 F 19
Aylsham [GB] 13 K 12
Ayora [E] 26 G 21
Ayr [GB] 10 G 10
Δ Ayre, Point of — [GB] 10 G 11
≈ Ayrolle, Étang de l' — [F] 19 K 19
Ayvacık [TR] 31 Zb 20
Ayvalık [TR] 31 Zb 20
Aywaille [B] 15 N 14
Δ Azahar, Costa del — [E] 26 H 21
Azaila [E] 26 H 19
Azambuja [P] 25 A 20
Azay-le-Rideau [F] 19 J 16
Azuaga [E] 25 C 21
≈ Azuer, Río — [E] 26 E 21

B

Baamonde [E] 24 C 18
Baarle-Nassau [NL] 14 M 13
Baarn [NL] 7 M 13
Δ Baba burnu [TR] 31 Zb 20
Babadag [RO] 23 Zb 16
Babaeski [TR] 23 Zb 19
Băbeni-Bistrița [RO] 22 Y 17
Δ Babia Góra [PL] 17 V 14
Δ Babička gora [YU] 22 X 16
Babięta [PL] 8 V 12
Babino Poljye [YU] 21 U 19
Babriškis [SU] 8 X 11
Δ Babuna [YU] 30 X 19
Babušnica [YU] 22 Y 18
Bač [YU] 22 V 17
Bacău [RO] 23 Za 16
Băcești [RO] 23 Za 15
Δ Bačka [YU] 22 V 17
Bačka Palanka [YU] 22 V 17
Bačka Topola [YU] 22 V 17
Backe [S] 5 S 5
Bäckerfors [S] 6 Q 9
Bäckhammar [S] 7 R 8
Bácsalmás [H] 22 V 16
Δ Badacsony [H] 21 U 16
Bad Aibling [D] 20 Q 16
Badajoz [E] 25 C 20
Badalona [E] 27 K 20
Bad Aussee [A] 21 R 16
Bad Bergzabern [D] 15 O 15
Bad Berka [DDR] 15 Q 14
Bad Berneck im Fichtelgebirge [D] 15 Q 14
Bad Brambach [DDR] 15 Q 14
Bad Bramstedt [D] 15 P 12
Bad Brückenau [D] 375 P 14
Bad Doberan [DDR] 15 Q 12
Bad Düben/Mulde [DDR] 16 R 13
Bad Dürkheim [D] 15 O 15
Baddusò [I] 28 P 20
Baden [A] 21 T 15
Baden [CH] 20 O 16
Baden-Baden [D] 15 O 15
Baderna [YU] 21 S 17
Bad Freienwalde [DDR] 16 R 12
Badgastein [A] 21 R 16
Bad Gleichenberg [A] 21 T 16
Bad Godesberg [D] 15 N 14
Bad Harzburg [D] 15 P 13
Bad Hersfeld [D] 15 P 14
Bad Homburg vor der Höhe [D] 15 O 14
Badia Polèsine [I] 20 Q 17
Bad Ischl [A] 21 R 16
Bad Kissingen [D] 15 P 14
Bad Kreuznach [D] 15 O 14
Bad Langensalza [DDR] 15 P 14
Bad Leonfelden [A] 21 S 15
Bad Liebenwerda [DDR] 16 R 13
Badljevina [YU] 21 U 17
Bad Meinberg [D] 15 O 13
Bad Mergentheim [D] 15 P 15
Bad Muskau [DDR] 16 S 13
Bad Neuenahr [D] 15 N 14
Bad Neustadt an der Saale [D] 15 P 14
Bad Oeynhausen [D] 15 O 13
Bad Oldesloe [D] 15 P 12
Bad Pyrmont [D] 15 P 13
Bad Reichenhall [D] 21 R 16
Bad Schandau [DDR] 16 R 14
Bad Schmiedeberg [DDR] 16 R 13
Bad Schwalbach [D] 15 O 14
Bad Segeberg [D] 15 P 12
Bad Soden-Allendorf [D] 131 P 13
Bad Sülze [DDR] 6 Q 12
Bad Tölz [D] 20 Q 16
Bad Waldsee [D] 20 P 16
Bad Wildungen [D] 15 P 14
Bad Zwischenahn [D] 15 O 12
Δ Bæččegal-Haldde [N] 2 T 2
Baena [E] 25 D 21
Baeza [E] 26 E 21
≈ Bafa gölü [TR] 31 Zc 21
Bagenkop [DK] 6 P 11
≈ Bages et de Sigean, Étang de — [F] 19 K 19
Bagheria [I] 29 S 22
Bagnara Càlabra [I] 29 T 22
Bagnères-de-Bigorre [F] 18 H 18
Bagnères-de-Luchon [F] 19 J 19
Bagni di Lucca [I] 20 P 18
Bagno di Romagna [I] 20 Q 18
Δ Bagno Krowie [PL] 17 X 13
Bagnols-sur-Cèze [F] 19 L 18
Bagrationovsk [SU] 8 V 11
Δ Bagur, Cabo — [E] 27 K 19
Bahnea [RO] 22 Y 16
Baia Mare [RO] 17 X 15
Baia Sprie [RO] 17 Y 15
Baigneux-les-Juifs [F] 19 M 16
Baile an Ródhba = Ballinrobe [IRL] 10 E 11
Baile Átha Cliath = Dublin [IRL] 10 F 11
Baile Brigin = Balbriggan [IRL] 10 F 11
Baile Chaislean Bhéarra = Castletown Bearhaven [IRL] 12 D 12
Băile Govora [RO] 22 Y 17
Băile Herculane [RO] 22 X 17
Baile Locha Riach = Loughrea [IRL] 10 E 11
Baile Mhathamhna = Ballymahon [IRL] 10 E 11
Baile Mhistéala = Mitchelstown [IRL] 12 E 12
Bailén [E] 26 E 21
Băile Slănic [RO] 23 Z 16
Băilești [RO] 22 Y 17
Baileul [F] 14 L 14
Bain-de-Bretagne [F] 18 H 15
Bais [F] 14 J 15
Baisogala [SU] 8 W 10
Baja [H] 22 V 16
Bajánsenye [H] 21 T 16
Bajina Bašta [YU] 22 V 18
Bajmok [YU] 22 V 17
Bak [H] 21 T 16
Bakewell [GB] 13 J 12
≈ Bakır çayı [TR] 31 Zc 20
Bakkejord [N] 2 S 2
Bakko [N] 4 P 8
Δ Bakony [H] 21 U 16
Bakšty [SU] 8 Y 11
Baktalórántháza [H] 17 W 15
B'ala [BG] 23 Za 18
Bălăbanești [RO] 23 Za 16
Balaci [RO] 23 Z 17
Bălăcița [RO] 22 Y 17
Bala-de-Aramă [RO] 22 X 17
Δ Balagne [F] 28 O 19
Balaguer [E] 27 J 19
Balassagyarmat [H] 22 V 15
≈ Balaton [H] 21 U 16
Balatonalmádi [H] 21 U 16
Balatonboglár [H] 21 U 16
Balatonföldvár [H] 21 U 16
Balatonkeresztúr [H] 21 U 16
Bălăușeri [RO] 22 Y 16
Balazote [E] 26 F 21
Balbriggan [IRL] 10 F 11
Bălcești [RO] 22 Y 17
Balčik [BG] 23 Zb 17
Baldoch [GB] 13 J 13
Δ Baleares, Islas — [E] 27 J 21
Δ Baleines, Pointe des — [F] 18 H 16
Baleizão [P] 25 B 21
Bălgarski Izvor [BG] 23 Z 18
Balıkesir [TR] 31 Zc 20
Balina [IRL] 10 E 11
Bälinge [S] 7 R 10
Balingen [D] 20 O 15
Balinț [RO] 22 X 17
Ballachulish [GB] 10 G 9
Ballaghaderren [IRL] 10 E 11
Ballangen [N] 2 R 2
Ballantrae [GB] 10 G 10
Ballao [I] 28 P 21
Ballater [GB] 11 J 9
Ballinamore [IRL] 10 F 11
Ballinasloe [IRL] 10 E 11
Ballinrobe [IRL] 10 E 11
Ballycastle [GB] 10 G 10
Ballyhaunis [IRL] 10 E 11
Ballymahon [IRL] 10 E 11
Ballymena [GB] 10 G 10
Ballymoney [GB] 10 F 10
Ballyshannon [IRL] 10 E 11
Balmazújvaros [H] 22 W 15
Balmoral Castle [GB] 11 H 9
Balneario de Panticosa [E] 18 H 19
Balș [RO] 22 Y 17
Balsareny [E] 27 J 19
≈ Balsfjord [N] 2 S 2
Balsièges [F] 19 L 18
Balsorano [I] 29 S 19
Balta [RO] 22 X 17
Baltanás [E] 26 E 19
Baltijsk [SU] 7 U 11
Δ Baltrum [D] 15 O 12
Balvan [BG] 23 Za 18
≈ Balvatn [N] 2 R 3
Balvi [SU] 8 Y 9
Balya [TR] 31 Zc 24
Bamberg [D] 15 Q 14
Bampton [GB] 12 G 13
Ban'a [BG] 23 Z 18
Ban'a [BG] 23 Z 19
Δ Baña, Punta de la — [E] 26 H 20
Bañalbufar [E] 27 K 21
Δ Banat [RO, YU] 22 W 17
Δ Banatului, Munții — [RO] 22 X 17
Banbridge [GB] 10 F 11
Banbury [GB] 13 J 13
Banchory [GB] 11 J 9
Δ Banda di Dentro [F] 28 P 20
Δ Banda di Fuori [F] 28 O 19
≈ Bandak [N] 6 O 8
Bandırma [TR] 31 Zc 19
Bandol [F] 19 M 19
Bandon [IRL] 12 D 12
Bañeza, La — [E] 24 D 18
Banff [GB] 11 J 9
Bangor [GB] 10 G 11
Bangor [GB] 12 G 12
Bangsund [N] 4 Q 5
Banie Mazurskie [PL] 8 W 11
Banja Luka [YU] 21 U 17
Banjska [YU] 22 W 18
Bannalec [F] 12 G 15
Bañolas [E] 27 K 19
Banon [F] 19 M 18
Baños de Cerrato [E] 26 E 19
Baños de Moglas [E] 24 C 18
Banovići [YU] 22 V 18
Banská Bystrica [CS] 17 V 15
Banská Štiavnica [CS] 17 V 15
Bantry [IRL] 12 D 12
≈ Bantry Bay [IRL] 12 D 12
Bapaume [F] 14 L 14
Bar [YU] 30 V 19
Baracaldo [E] 18 F 18
Δ Bărăganu [RO] 23 Za 17
Baraganul [RO] 23 Zb 17
Barahona [E] 26 F 19
Δ Barania Góra [PL] 16 U 14
Δ Baranja-lolga, gora — [SU] 000 X 2
Baranoviči [SU] 8 Y 12
Baraolt [RO] 23 Z 16
Δ Baraolt, Munții — [RO] 23 Z 16
Baraque-de-Fraiture [B] 15 N 14
Baravaja [SU] 8 Y 9
Barbadillo de Herreros [E] 26 F 19
Barbaros [TR] 31 Zb 19
Barbastro [E] 26 H 19
≈ Barbate, Río — [E] 25 C 22
Barbate de Franco [E] 25 C 22
Bărbele [SU] 8 W 10
Barbezieux [F] 18 H 17
Bărbovo [BG] 23 Za 19
Barcarrota [E] 25 C 21
Barcellona Pozzo di Gotto [I] 29 T 22
Barcelona [E] 27 K 20
Barcelonne-du-Gers [F] 18 H 18
Barcelonnette [F] 20 N 18
Barcelos [P] 24 B 19
Barcin [PL] 16 T 12
Barcino [PL] 7 T 11
Barco, El — [E] 24 C 18
Barco de Ávila, El — [E] 25 D 20
Barcs [H] 21 U 17
Barcyany [PL] 8 V 11
Barczewo [PL] 8 V 12
Δ Bardagia [I] 28 O 21
Bardejov [CS] 17 W 14
Δ Bárdenas, Las — [E] 26 G 19
Bardi [I] 20 P 18
Δ Bardsey [GB] 12 G 12
Bardu [N] 2 S 2
Barentin [F] 14 K 14
≈ Barents More [SU] 3 W 1
Barfleur [F] 13 H 14
Barfleur, Pointe de — [F] 13 H 14
Barga [I] 20 P 18
Bargteheide [D] 15 P 12
Bari [I] 29 U 20
Barière-de-Champlan [B] 14 M 14
Barjols [F] 19 M 18
Barkava [SU] 8 X 9
Bar-le-Duc [F] 14 M 15
Barles [F] 20 N 18
Barlette [I] 29 T 20
Barmouth [GB] 12 G 12
Barnard Castle [GB] 11 J 11
Barneveld [NL] 15 N 13
Barneville-sur-Mer [F] 13 H 14
Barnsley [GB] 13 J 12
Barnstaple [GB] 12 G 13
Δ Barøy [N] 2 R 2
Barr [F] 20 N 15
Δ Barra [GB] 10 F 9
Barracas [E] 26 G 20
Barraco [E] 26 E 20
Δ Barra Head [GB] 10 F 9
Δ Barra Islands [GB] 10 F 9
Barranco do Velho [P] 25 B 21
Barrancos [P] 25 B 21
Barranda [E] 26 F 21
Barrax [E] 26 F 21
Barreio [P] 25 A 20
Barreiros [E] 24 C 17
Barrême [F] 20 N 18
Barrhead [GB] 11 H 10
Δ Barros, Tierra de — [E] 25 C 21
≈ Barrow, River — [IRL] 12 F 12
Barrow-in-Furness [GB] 11 H 11
Barry [GB] 12 G 13
Bar-sur-Aube [F] 19 M 15
Bar-sur-Seine [F] 19 M 15
Bartenstein (Ostpreußen) = Bartoszyce [PL] 8 V 11
Barth [DDR] 7 R 11
Bartoszyce [PL] 8 V 11
Barvas [GB] 10 G 8
Barwice [PL] 7 T 12
≈ Barycz [PL] 16 T 13
Bašaid [YU] 22 W 17
Basel [CH] 20 O 16
Basella [E] 27 J 19
≈ Basento [I] 29 U 20
Basilenai [SU] 8 W 10
≈ Basilicata [I] 29 T 20
Basingtoke [GB] 13 J 13
Baška [YU] 21 S 17
Båsmoen [N] 2 R 4
Bassano del Grappa [I] 20 Q 17
Bassum [D] 15 O 12
Båstad [S] 7 R 10
Bastelica [F] 28 O 19
Bastenaken = Bastogne [B] 15 N 14
Bastia [F] 28 P 19
Bastogne [B] 15 N 14
Basturäsk [S] 5 T 5
Batajnica [YU] 22 W 17
Batak [BG] 23 Z 19
Batakiai [SU] 8 W 10
Batalha [P] 25 B 20
≈ Bataška planina [BG] 23 Z 19
Bátaszék [H] 22 V 16
Batea [E] 26 H 20
Båteng [N] 3 V 1
Bath [GB] 13 H 13
≈ Batlava jezero [YU] 22 X 18
Båtsfjord [N] 3 V 1
Båtsjaur [S] 2 S 4
Båtskärsnäs [S] 3 U 4
Battipàglia [I] 29 T 20
Battle [GB] 13 K 13
Battonya [H] 22 W 16
Δ Batz, Ile de — [F] 12 G 15
Baud [F] 12 G 15
Baugé [F] 19 J 16
Baule-Escoublac, la — [F] 18 G 16
Baume-les-Dames [F] 20 N 16
Baume-les-Messieurs [F] 19 M 16
Baumholder [D] 15 N 14
Baunei [I] 28 P 21
Bauska [SU] 8 W 10
Bautzen [DDR] 16 S 13
Bavay [F] 14 L 14
Δ Bavella, Col de — [F] 28 P 19
≈ Båven [S] 7 S 8
Bawtry [GB] 13 J 12
Δ Bayerische Alpen [D] 20 Q 16
Bayerisch Eisenstein [D] 16 R 15
Δ Bayerischer Wald [D] 15 Q 15
Bayeux [F] 14 J 14
Bayındır [TR] 31 Zc 21
Bayo [E] 24 B 18
Bayon [F] 15 N 15
Bayona [E] 24 B 18
Bayonne [F] 18 G 18
Bayramiç [TR] 31 Zb 20
Bayreuth [D] 15 Q 14
Baza [E] 26 E 22
Δ Baza, Sierra de — [E] 26 E 22
Δ Bazadois [F] 18 H 18
Bazas [F] 18 H 18
Δ Beachy Head [GB] 13 J 14
Bealach an Doirin = Ballaghadereen [IRL] 10 E 11
Béal an Átha = Ballina [IRL] 10 E 11
Béal an Átha Móir = Ballinamore [IRL] 10 F 11
Béal an Mhuirthid = Belmullet [IRL] 10 D 11
Béal Átha hArnhais = Ballyhaunis [IRL] 10 E 11
Béal Átha na Sluagh = Ballinasloe [IRL] 10 E 11
Béal Átha Seanaigh = Ballyshannon [IRL] 10 E 11
Beanntraighe = Bantry [IRL] 12 D 12
Δ Béarn [F] 18 H 18
Beasain [E] 18 G 18
Beas de Segura [E] 26 F 21
Beaucaire [F] 19 L 18
Δ Beauce [F] 14 K 15
Beauduc, Golfe de — [F] 19 L 18
Beaugency [F] 19 K 15
Δ Beaujolais [F] 19 L 17
Δ Beaujolais, Monts du — [F] 19 L 17
Beaulieu-sur-Dordogne [F] 19 K 17
Beauly [GB] 11 H 9
Beaumaris [GB] 12 G 12
Beaumont [B] 14 M 14
Δ Beaumont [F] 19 M 18
Beaumont-de-Lomagne [F] 19 J 18
Beaumont-du-Périgord [F] 19 J 17
Beaumont-sur-Oise [F] 14 K 15
Beaumont-sur-Sarthe [F] 14 J 15
Beaune [F] 19 M 16
Beaupreau [F] 19 H 16
Beauraing [B] 14 M 14
Beaurepaire [F] 19 M 17
Beauvais [F] 14 K 14
Beauvoir-sur-Mer [F] 18 G 16
Bebra [D] 15 P 14
Bebrene [SU] 8 X 10
Δ Beca, Punta — [E] 27 K 21
Bečej [YU] 22 W 17
Beceni [RO] 23 Za 16
Becerreá [E] 24 C 18
Bécherel [F] 13 H 15
Bechetu [RO] 22 Y 18
Becilla de Valderaduey [E] 24 E 19
Beciu [RO] 23 Z 17
Beckington [GB] 13 H 13
Beckum [D] 15 O 13
Beclean [RO] 22 Y 15
Bécon-les-Granits [F] 18 H 16
Bečov nad Teplou [CS] 16 R 14
Bédarieux [F] 19 K 18
Bederkesa [D] 15 O 12
Bedford [GB] 13 J 13
Będzin [PL] 16 U 14
Beelitz [DDR] 16 R 13
Beeskow [DDR] 16 R 13
Begelly [GB] 12 G 13
Begndal [N] 4 P 7
Begonte [E] 24 C 18
Béhobie [F] 18 G 18
Beian [N] 4 P 5
Beiarn [N] 2 R 3
Beilen [NL] 15 N 12
Beilngries [D] 15 Q 15
Δ Beira [P] 25 B 19
≈ Beitstadfjord [N] 4 P 5
Beiuș [RO] 22 Y 16
Beja [P] 25 B 21
Δ Beja, Campo de — [P] 25 B 21
Béjar [E] 25 D 20
Bekecs [H] 17 W 15
Békés [H] 22 W 16
Békéscsaba [H] 22 W 16
Bela Crkva [YU] 22 X 17
Δ Bel Air [F] 12 G 15
Bela Palanka [YU] 22 X 18
Δ Belasica [BG, YU] 30 Y 19
Bełchatów [PL] 16 U 13
Belchite [E] 26 H 19

Beled [H] 21 T 16
Belém, Lisboa — [P] 25 A 20
Belfast [GB] 10 G 11
≈ Belfast Lough [GB] 126 G 11
Belford [GB] 11 J 10
Belfort [F] 20 N 16
Belgard (Persante) = Białogard [PL] 7 S 12
Belgodère [F] 28 O 19
Belgorod Dnestrovskij [SU] 23 Zc 15
Belica [SU] 8 X 11
≈ Beli Drim [YU] 22 W 19
Beli Manastir [YU] 22 V 17
Belin [F] 18 H 17
Beliş [RO] 22 X 16
Δ Beljanica [YU] 22 X 18
Bellac [F] 19 J 17
Bellágo [I] 20 P 17
Bellano [I] 20 P 17
Δ Belledonne, Chaîne de — [F] 19 M 17
Bellegard-du-Loiret [F] 19 K 15
Bellegarde-sur-Valserine [F] 135 M 17
Δ Belle Ile [F] 18 G 15
Bellême [F] 14 J 15
Belley [F] 19 M 17
Bellinzona [CH] 20 O 17
Bell-Lloch [E] 27 J 19
Belluno [I] 20 Q 17
Bélmez [E] 25 D 21
Belmonte [P] 25 C 19
Belmullet [IRL] 10 D 11
Belogradčik [BG] 22 Y 18
Δ Belorusskaja SSR [SU] 8 Y 11
Beluša [CS] 16 U 15
Belušić [YU] 22 X 18
Belvedere Marittimo [I] 29 T 21
Belvès [F] 19 J 17
Belvis de la Jara [E] 25 D 20
Bełżec [PL] 17 X 13
Belzig [DDR] 16 R 13
≈ Bembézar, Pantano del — [E] 25 D 21
≈ Bembézar, Río — [E] 25 D 21
Bembibre [E] 24 D 18
Benabarre [E] 26 H 19
Benalcázar [E] 25 D 21
Benamejí [E] 25 D 22
Benavente [E] 24 D 19
Benavente [P] 25 A 20
Δ Benavila, Campo de — [P] 25 B 20
Δ Benbecula [GB] 10 G 9
Bendery [SU] 23 Zb 15
Bendorf [D] 15 O 14
Benesat [RO] 22 X 15
Benešov [CS] 16 S 14
Benevento [I] 29 S 20
Bengtfors [S] 6 Q 8
Benicartó [E] 26 H 20
Benicasim [E] 26 H 20
Benidorm [E] 26 H 21
Δ Benidorm, Isla de — [E] 26 H 21
Benisa [E] 26 H 21
Benkovac [YU] 21 T 18
Bensersiel [D] 15 O 12
Bensheim [D] 15 O 14
Beograd [YU] 22 W 17
Berat [AL] 30 W 20
Δ Berberia, Punta — [E] 27 J 21
Bercel [H] 22 V 15
Berceto [I] 20 P 18
Berching [D] 15 Q 15
Berchtesgaden [D] 21 R 16
Berck [F] 14 K 14
Berdún [E] 18 H 19
Beregovo [SU] 17 X 15
Beregsurány [H] 17 X 15
Berettyóújfalu [H] 22 W 16
Berežany [SU] 17 Y 14
Berg [N] 6 Q 8
Berg [S] 5 R 6
Berga [E] 27 J 19
Berga [S] 123 R 10
Bergama [TR] 31 Zc 20
Bèrgamo [I] 20 P 17
Bergen [N] 4 N 8
Bergenac [F] 19 J 17
Bergen op Zoom [NL] 14 M 13
Bergen/Rügen [DDR] 7 R 11
≈ Berghamnsfjärd [SF] 9 U 8
Bergheim [D] 15 N 14
Bergisch Gladbach [D] 15 N 14
Δ Bergö [S] 3 U 4
Bergshamra [S] 5 T 8
Bergsjö [S] 5 S 6
Δ Bergslagen [S] 5 R 8
Bergues [F] 14 L 13
≈ Bergviken [S] 5 S 7
Berja [E] 26 E 22
Berkåk [N] 4 P 6
Berkovica [BG] 22 Y 16
Berkovići [YU] 22 V 18
Berlanga [E] 25 C 21
Δ Berlenga, Ilha — [P] 25 A 20
Berlevåg [N] 3 V 1
Berlinek [PL] 16 S 12
Berlin (Ost) [DDR] 16 R 13
Berlin (West) [D] 16 R 13
Bermeo [E] 18 F 18
Bermillo de Sayago [E] 25 D 19
Bern [CH] 20 N 16
Bernalda [I] 29 U 20
Bernartice [CS] 16 S 15
Bernau bei Berlin [DDR] 16 R 12
Bernay [F] 14 J 15
Bernberg/Saale [DDR] 15 Q 13
Berndorf [A] 21 T 15
Δ Berner Alpen [CH] 20 N 17
Δ Bernina [CH, I] 20 P 17
Δ Berninapass [CH] 20 P 17
Bernkastel-Kues [D] 15 N 14
Bernstein [A] 21 T 16
Beronovo [BG] 23 Za 18
Beroun [CS] 16 R 14
≈ Berounka [CS] 16 R 14
Berovo [YU] 30 Y 19
Ber'oza [SU] 17 X 12
≈ Berre, Etang de — [F] 19 M 18
Δ Berry [F] 19 K 16
Bersenbrück [D] 15 O 13
Berwick-upon-Tweed [GB] 11 J 10
Berzasca [RO] 22 X 17
Δ Berzosa, La — [E] 25 C 19
Bērzpils [SU] 8 Y 9
Besalú [E] 27 K 19
Besançon [F] 20 N 16
Beskenjargga [N] 3 U 2
Δ Beskid Niski [PL] 17 W 14
Δ Beskidy [PL] 17 V 14
Besna Kobila [YU] 22 X 19
Δ Beşparmak dağı [TR] 31 Zc 21
Bessarabka [SU] 23 Zb 16
Bessines-sur-Gartempe [F] 19 K 17
Δ Bessou, Mont — [F] 19 K 17
Best [NL] 130 M 13
Betanzos [E] 24 C 18
≈ Betanzos, Ría de — [E] 24 C 17
≈ Betarsjön [S] 5 S 5
Δ Bétharram, Grotte de — [F] 18 H 18
Béthune [F] 14 L 14
Bettna [S] 7 S 6
Bettyhill [GB] 11 H 8
Betws-y-Coed [GB] 12 G 12
Betz [F] 14 L 15
Beuthen (Oberschlesien) = Bytom [PL] 16 U 14
Beverley [GB] 11 J 12
Bexhill [GB] 13 K 13
Bezau [A] 20 P 16
Béziers [F] 19 K 18
Biagoevgrad [BG] 22 Y 19
≈ Biała [PL] 17 W 14
Δ Biała Góra [PL] 17 X 14
Biała Piska [PL] 8 W 12
Biała Podlaska [PL] 17 W 12
Białogard [PL] 7 S 12
Biały Bór [PL] 7 T 12
Białystok [PL] 17 W 12
Biarritz [F] 18 G 18
Biasca [CH] 20 O 17
Bibbiena [I] 20 Q 18
Biberach an der Riß [D] 20 P 15
Bibione [I] 21 R 17
Bicaj [AL] 30 W 19
Bicaz [RO] 23 Z 15
Bicester [GB] 13 J 13
Bichl [D] 20 Q 16
Bicske [H] 21 U 16
Bideford [GB] 12 G 13
≈ Biebrza [PL] 8 W 12
Biel [CH] 20 N 16
Bielawy [PL] 17 V 13
Bielefeld [D] 15 O 13
≈ Bieler See [CH] 20 N 16
Biella [I] 20 O 17
Bielsa [E] 26 H 19
Bielsk [PL] 17 V 12
Bielskobiała [PL] 16 U 14
Bielsk Podlaski [PL] 17 W 12
Bienne = Biel [CH] 20 N 16
Δ Bierzo, El — [E] 24 C 18
Biescas [E] 18 H 19
Δ Bieszcady [PL] 17 X 14
Bieżuń [PL] 17 V 12
Biga [TR] 31 Zb 19
Biganos [F] 18 H 17
Biggar [GB] 11 H 10
Biggeluobbal [N] 3 U 2
Biggleswade [GB] 13 J 13
Bignasco [CH] 20 O 17
Δ Bignone, Monte — [I] 20 O 18
Bihać [YU] 21 T 17
Biharea [RO] 22 X 16
Δ Bihor [RO] 22 X 16
Δ Bihor, Munţii — [RO] 22 X 16
Bijeljina [YU] 22 V 17
Bílá [CS] 16 U 14
Bilbao [E] 18 F 18
Bilbilis [E] 26 G 19
Bileća [YU] 22 V 19
Δ Bílé Karpaty [CS] 16 U 15
Biłgoraj [PL] 17 W 13
Bilisht [AL] 30 X 20
Bilje [YU] 22 V 17
Billingshurst [GB] 13 J 13
Billom [F] 19 L 17
Δ Bilo gora [YU] 21 T 17
Bilto [N] 2 T 2
Bilzen [B] 14 M 14
Binas [F] 19 K 15
Binche [B] 14 M 14
≈ Bindalsfjord [N] 4 Q 4
Binéfar [E] 26 H 19
Bingen [D] 15 O 14
Binz [DDR] 7 R 11
Biograd [YU] 21 T 18
Δ Biokovo [YU] 21 U 18
Biorra = Birr [IRL] 10 E 11
Biot, le — [F] 20 N 17
Bircza [PL] 17 W 14
Δ Bîrgău, Munţii — [RO] 22 Y 15
Birkeland [N] 6 O 9
Birkenfeld [D] 15 N 14
Birkenhead [GB] 13 H 12
Birkfeld [A] 21 T 16
Bîrlad [RO] 23 Za 16
≈ Bîrlad [RO] 23 Za 16
Birmingham [GB] 13 H 12
Birr [IRL] 10 E 11
Biržai [SU] 8 X 10
Birzebbuga [M] 30 V 22
Birži [SU] 8 X 10
Bisbal, La — [E] 27 K 19
≈ Biscarrosse et de Parentis, Étand de — [F] 18 H 17
Biscarrosse-Plage [F] 18 H 17
Biscéglie [I] 29 U 20
Bischofshofen [A] 21 R 16
Bischofswerda [DDR] 16 R 13
Δ Biševo [YU] 21 T 19
≈ Biševski kanal [YU] 21 T 19
Bishop Auckland [GB] 11 J 11
Bishop's Castle [GB] 13 H 12
Bishop's Stortford [GB] 13 J 13
Biskupiec [PL] 8 V 11
Bismark [DDR] 15 Q 13
Bispfors [S] 5 S 6
Bispo [P] 25 A 21
≈ Bistra [RO] 22 X 17
Bistreţu [RO] 22 Y 18
Bistriţa [RO] 22 Y 15
Bisztynek [PL] 8 V 11
Bitburg [D] 15 N 14
Bitche [F] 15 N 15
Δ Bitihorn [N] 4 P 7
Bitola [YU] 30 X 20
Bitonto [I] 29 U 20
Δ Bitovnja [YU] 21 U 18
Bitterfeld [DDR] 15 Q 13
Bizerte [TN] 28 P 22
≈ Bizerte, Lac de — [TN] 28 P 22
Bizovac [YU] 22 V 17
Δ Bjarkøy [N] 2 R 2
Bjästa [S] 5 T 6
Δ Bjelasica [YU] 22 W 19
Δ Bjelašnica [YU] 21 U 18
Δ Bjelašnica [YU] 22 V 18
Δ Bjelašnica [YU] 22 V 19
Δ Bjelolasica [YU] 21 S 17
Bjelovar [YU] 21 T 17
Bjerkvik [N] 2 S 2
Bjerringbro [DK] 6 P 10
Bjøberg [N] 4 O 7
Bjøllånes [N] 2 R 4
Björbo [S] 5 R 7
Bjørkåsen [N] 2 S 2
Björkberg [S] 5 S 5
Bjørkelangen [N] 4 Q 8
Δ Björkfjället [S] 2 S 4
Björkfors [S] 2 R 4
Δ Björkö [S] 5 T 8
Δ Björkö [SF] 9 U 5
Björköby [S] 7 R 9
Björksele [S] 5 S 4
≈ Björkvattnet [S] 2 R 4
Björna [S] 5 T 5
≈ Bjørnafjord [N] 4 N 8
Björneborg = Pori [SF] 9 U 7
Bjørnfjell [N] 2 S 2
Björnlunda [S] 7 S 8
Δ Bjørntoppen [N] 2 S 3
Björsarv [S] 5 S 6
Bjurberget [S] 4 Q 7
Bjurholm [S] 5 T 5
Δ Bjuröklubb [S] 5 U 5
Bjursås [S] 5 S 7
Δ Blåbjerg [DK] 6 O 11
Blace [YU] 22 X 18
Blackburn [GB] 11 H 11
Blackpool [GB] 11 H 11
Blackstad [S] 7 S 9
≈ Blackwater, River — [IRL] 12 E 12
Δ Blåfjell [N] 2 Q 4
Δ Blåfjell [N] 4 Q 5
Blaiken [S] 2 S 4
Δ Blaikfjället [S] 5 S 5
Blain [F] 18 H 15
Blairgowrie [GB] 11 H 10
Blaj [RO] 22 Y 16
Δ Blåmanen [N] 2 S 2
Δ Blåmansisen [N] 2 R 3
Δ Blanc, Cap — [TN] 28 P 22
Blancos, Los — [E] 26 G 22
Blandford Forum [GB] 13 H 13
Blanes [E] 27 K 19
Blangy-sur-Bresle [F] 14 K 14
Blankenberge [B] 14 L 13
Blankenburg [DDR] 15 Q 13
Blankenheim (Ahr) [D] 15 N 14
Blanzy [F] 19 M 16
Δ Blåskavl [N] 4 O 7
Błaszki [PL] 16 U 13
Blatná [CS] 16 R 15
Blatnica [BG] 23 Zb 17
Blattnicksele [S] 2 S 4
Blaubeuren [D] 20 P 15
Blaufelden [D] 15 P 15
Δ Blåvands Huk [DK] 6 O 11
Blaye [F] 18 H 17
Bled [YU] 21 S 17
Bleik [N] 2 R 2
Bleikvassli [N] 2 R 4
Δ Blekinge [S] 7 S 10
Blenheim Palace [GB] 13 J 13
Blérancourt [F] 14 L 14
Bléré [F] 19 J 16
Blīdene [SU] 8 W 10
Δ Blidö [S] 5 T 8
Blinisht [AL] 30 W 19
Blnac, le — [F] 19 J 16
Blois [F] 19 K 16
Blokhus [DK] 6 P 10
Blomsholm [N] 6 Q 8
Błonie [PL] 17 V 13
Bludenz [A] 20 P 16
Blyth [GB] 11 J 11
Bø [N] 6 P 8
Boal [E] 24 D 18
Bòbbio [I] 20 P 18
Δ Bobia, Pico de — [E] 24 D 18
Böblingen [D] 15 O 15
Bobovdol [BG] 22 Y 19
≈ Bóbr [PL] 16 S 13
Bobrka [SU] 17 Y 14
Bochnia [PL] 17 V 14
Bocholt [D] 15 N 13
Bochum [D] 15 N 13
Bockara [S] 7 S 9
Bocşa Romînă [RO] 22 X 17
Bocsig [RO] 22 X 16
Boda [S] 5 R 7
Böda [S] 7 T 9
Boden [S] 3 U 4
≈ Bodensee [A, CH, D] 20 P 16
Bodenwerder [D] 15 P 13
Bodmin [GB] 12 F 13
Bodø [N] 2 R 3
Bodom [TR] 31 Zc 21
Bodsjö [S] 5 R 6
Bodträskfors [S] 2 T 4
Bodum [S] 5 S 5
Bodzanów [PL] 17 V 12
Boën [F] 19 L 17
Bogas [TR] 31 Zc 19
Δ Bogaskär [SF] 9 U 6
Δ Bogdan [BG] 23 Z 18
Bogen [N] 2 S 2
Bogense [DK] 6 P 11
Bognes [N] 2 R 3
Bognor Regis [GB] 13 J 13
Δ Bogø [DK] 6 Q 11
Bogøy [N] 2 R 3
Bohain-en-Vermandois [F] 14 L 14
Bohdaneč [CS] 16 S 14
Bohinjska Bistrica [YU] 21 S 17
Δ Böhmerwald [CS, D] 16 R 15
Böhönye [H] 21 U 16
Δ Bohor [YU] 21 T 17
Bohus [S] 6 Q 9
Δ Bohuslän [S] 6 Q 9
Boimorto [E] 24 C 18
Boire [E] 24 B 18
Δ Bois, le — [F] 18 H 17
Boizenburg/Elbe [DDR] 15 Q 12
Bojano [I] 29 S 20
Boka [YU] 22 W 17
Δ Bokn [N] 6 N 8
≈ Boknfjord [N] 6 N 8
Bol [YU] 21 U 18
Bol'arovo [BG] 23 Zb 18
Bolbec [F] 14 J 14
Bölebyn [S] 3 U 4
Bolechov [SU] 17 X 14
Boleslawiec [PL] 16 S 13
Bolgrad [SU] 23 Zb 16
Boljaniči [YU] 20 B 18
Boljevac [YU] 22 X 18
Bolków [PL] 16 T 14
Bollden [S] 5 T 4
Bollebygd [S] 6 Q 9
Bollène [F] 19 M 18
Bollnäs [S] 5 S 7
Bollstabruk [S] 5 S 6
Bollullos par del Condado [E] 25 C 21
≈ Bolmen [S] 7 R 10
Bolmsö [S] 7 R 10
Bologna [I] 20 Q 18
Boloje [SU] 8 Y 8
≈ Bol'šaja Volokovaja, guba — [SU] 3 W 1
Bol'šakovo [SU] 8 V 11
≈ Bolsena, Lago di — [I] 28 Q 19
Δ Bol'šoj Ajnov, ostrov — [SU] 3 W 1
Δ Bol'šoj Tut'arsari [SU] 9 X 7
Boltaña [E] 26 H 19
Bolton [GB] 11 H 12
Bóly [H] 22 V 17
Bolzano [I] 20 Q 16
Bomarsund [SF] 9 U 7
Δ Bømlo [N] 4 N 8
Bomsund [S] 5 S 6
Δ Bon, Cap — [TN] 28 Q 22
Bonaduz [CH] 20 P 16
Boñar [E] 24 E 18
Bonarbridge [GB] 11 H 9
Bonares [E] 25 C 21
Bonavis [F] 14 L 14
Bondeno [I] 20 Q 18
Bonete [E] 26 G 21
Δ Bonette, Col de la — [F] 20 N 18
Bonifacio [F] 28 O 20
≈ Bonifacio, Bocche di — [E] 28 O 20
Bonn [D] 15 N 14
Bonnasjsøen [N] 2 R 3
Bonnat [F] 19 K 16
Bonnétable [F] 14 J 15
Bonneuil-Matours [F] 19 J 16
Bonneval [F] 14 K 15
Bonneville [F] 20 N 17
Bonny-sur-Loire [F] 19 L 16
Bons [F] 20 N 17
Bónyhád [H] 22 V 16
Bootle [GB] 11 H 12
Bor [CS] 16 R 14
Bor [YU] 22 X 18
Borås [S] 7 R 9
Δ Bora Tucholskie [PL] 16 T 12
Borba [P] 25 B 20
Bordeaux [F] 18 H 17
Bordes, les — [F] 19 K 16
Bordighera [I] 20 N 18
≈ Boren [S] 7 S 9
Borensberg [S] 7 S 9
Borg [D] 15 N 15
Borgå [SF] 9 W 7
Borgafjell [S] 5 R 5
Δ Børgefjell [N] 5 R 4
Borger [NL] 15 N 12
Borgholm [S] 7 S 10
Borgomanero [I] 20 O 17
Borgo San Dalmazzo [I] 20 N 18
Borgo San Lorenzo [I] 20 Q 18
Borgosesia [I] 20 O 17
Borgo Val di Taro [I] 20 P 18
Borgo Valsugana [I] 20 Q 17
Borgsjö [S] 5 S 5
Borgsjö [S] 5 S 6
Borgund [N] 4 O 7
Borgvattnet [S] 5 S 6
Borislav [SU] 17 X 14
Borja [E] 26 G 19
Δ Borja [YU] 21 U 18
Borjas Blancas [E] 27 J 19
Börjelsbyn [S] 3 U 4
Borken [D] 15 N 13
Δ Borkum [D] 15 N 12
Borlänge [S] 5 S 7
Borlaug [N] 4 O 7
Bòrmio [I] 20 P 17
Borna [DDR] 16 R 14
Δ Bornes [P] 25 C 19
Δ Bornholm [DK] 7 S 11
Bornholmsgattet [DK] 7 R 11
Boronów [PL] 16 U 14
Borovan [BG] 22 Y 18
Borovec [BG] 22 Y 19
Borów [PL] 16 S 13
Δ Borowa Góra [PL] 17 V 13
Borrby [S] 7 R 11
Borreby [DK] 6 Q 11
Borredà [E] 27 K 19
Δ Borronar, Punta del — [E] 27 J 21
Börrum [S] 7 S 9
Borşa [RO] 17 Y 15
Børselv [N] 3 U 1
Bort-les-Orgues [F] 19 K 17
Börtnan [S] 5 R 6
Boruganeuf [F] 19 K 17
Δ Börzsöny [H] 22 V 15
Bosa [I] 28 O 20
Bosanska Gradiška [YU] 21 U 17
Bosanska Kupa [YU] 21 T 17
Bosanski Brod [YU] 21 U 17
Bosanski Šamac [YU] 22 V 17
Bosansko Grahovo [YU] 21 T 18
Boscastle [GB] 12 G 13
Bosilegrad [YU] 22 Y 19
Boskovice [CS] 16 T 14
≈ Bosna [YU] 21 U 17
Δ Bosna [BG] 23 Zb 18
Δ Bosna [YU] 21 T 18
Bosnaski Novi [YU] 21 T 17
Bosnaski Petrovac [YU] 21 T 16
Bosost [E] 19 J 19
Boston [GB] 13 K 12
Boteå [S] 5 S 6
Δ Botev [BG] 23 Z 18
Botevgrad [BG] 22 Y 18
Δ Bothnia, Gulf of — [S] 5 T 7
Botnhamn [N] 2 S 2
Botsmark [S] 5 T 5
Bottnaryd [S] 7 R 9
Bottrop [D] 15 N 13
Bouaye [F] 18 H 16
Δ Boubín [CS] 16 R 15
Boucau [F] 18 G 18
Bougado [P] 25 B 19
Bouille, la — [F] 14 K 14
Bouillon [B] 14 M 14
Boulogne-sur-Gesse [F] 19 J 18
Boulogne-sur-Mer [F] 14 K 14
Δ Boumort, Sierra de — [E] 27 J 19
Bourbon-Lancy [F] 19 L 16
Bourbon-l'Archambault [F] 19 L 16
Bourbonne-les-Bains [F] 19 M 16
Bourboule, la — [F] 19 K 17
Bourbourg [F] 14 L 13
Bourg-Argental [F] 19 M 17
Bourg-de-Péage [F] 19 M 17
Bourg-en-Bresse [F] 19 M 17
Bourges [F] 19 K 16
Bourget, le — [F] 19 M 17
≈ Bourget, Lac du — [F] 19 M 17
Bourg-et-Comin [F] 14 L 15
≈ Bourgneuf, Baie de — [F] 18 G 16
Bourgneuf-en-Retz [F] 18 H 16
Δ Bourgogne [F] 19 L 16
Bourgoin-Jallieu [F] 19 M 17
Bourg-Saint-Andéol [F] 19 L 18
Bourg-Saint-Maurice [F] 20 N 17
Bourne [GB] 13 J 12
Bournemouth [GB] 13 H 13
Boussac [F] 19 K 16
Bova [I] 29 U 22
Bovalino [I] 29 U 22
Bovallstrand [S] 6 Q 9
Bova Marina [I] 29 U 22
Bøverdal [N] 4 O 7
Boxholm [S] 7 S 9
Boxmeer [NL] 15 N 13
Boyle [IRL] 10 E 11
Bozburun [TR] 32 Zd 22
Δ Bozca ada [TR] 31 Zb 20
Δ Boz dağ [TR] 31 Zc 22
Bozdoğan [TR] 32 Zd 21
Bozen = Bolzano [I] 20 Q 16
Bozouls [F] 19 K 18
Bra [I] 20 O 18
Brabova [RO] 22 Y 17
Δ Brač [YU] 21 T 18
Bracadale [GB] 10 G 9
Bracciano [I] 29 R 19
≈ Bracciano, Lago di — [I] 29 R 19
Bräcke [S] 5 R 6
≈ Brački kanal [YU] 21 U 18
Brad [RO] 22 X 16
Bradford [GB] 11 J 11
Braedownie [GB] 11 H 9
Braemar [GB] 11 H 9
Braga [P] 24 B 19
Bragança [P] 24 C 19
Brăila [RO] 23 Zb 16
Δ Brăilei, Baltă — [RO] 23 Zb 17
Braintree [GB] 13 K 13
Brakel [D] 15 P 13
Brake (Unterweser) [D] 15 O 12
Brålanda [S] 6 Q 9
Bralos [GR] 30 Y 21
Bramminge [DK] 6 O 11
Δ Brämön [S] 5 S 6
Brampton [GB] 11 H 11
Bramsche [D] 15 O 13
Δ Bran, Pasul — [RO] 23 Z 16
Δ Brand Ballon [F] 20 N 16
Brandbu [N] 4 P 8
Brande [DK] 6 P 10
Brandenburg/Havel [DDR] 16 R 13
Δ Brandfjell [N] 4 Q 5
Δ Brandon Mountain [IRL] 12 D 12
Brandvoll [N] 2 S 2
Brandýs nad Labem [CS] 16 S 14
Braniewo [PL] 7 U 11
Brannica [BG] 23 Za 19
Brännland [S] 5 T 5
Branov [RO] 23 Zc 16
Brańsk [PL] 17 W 12
Brantôme [F] 19 J 17
Brasov [RO] 23 Z 16
Brassus, le — [CH] 20 N 16
Břasy [CS] 16 R 14
Bratai [AL] 30 W 20
Bratislava [CS] 21 T 15
Bratten [S] 5 S 5
Brattvåg [N] 4 O 6
Bratunac [YU] 22 V 18
Braunau am Inn [A] 21 R 15
Braunlage [D] 15 P 13
Braunschweig [D] 15 P 13
≈ Bråviken [S] 7 S 9
Bray [IRL] 10 F 12
Brazatortas [E] 26 E 21
Brčko [YU] 22 V 17
≈ Brda [PL] 16 T 12
Δ Brdy [CS] 16 R 14
Breared [S] 7 R 14
Breaza [RO] 23 Z 17
Brebeni [RO] 23 Z 17
Brechin [GB] 11 J 10
Břeclav [CS] 16 T 15
Brecon [GB] 12 G 13
Δ Brecon Beacons [GB] 12 G 13
Breda [NL] 14 M 13
Bredaryd [S] 7 R 10
Bredbyn [S] 5 S 5
Bredsel [S] 2 T 4
Bredstedt [D] 6 O 11
Bredstrup [DK] 6 P 10
Bredträsk [S] 5 T 5
Bree [B] 15 N 13
≈ Bregalnica [YU] 30 Y 19
Bregenz [A] 20 P 16
Bregovo [BG] 22 Y 18
Δ Bréhat, Ile de — [F] 12 G 15
≈ Breimsvatn [N] 4 N 7
Breisach am Rhein [D] 22 O 16
Breitengüßbach [D] 15 Q 14
Breitenhees [D] 15 P 12
Δ Breitind [N] 2 S 2
Breivikbotn [N] 2 T 1
Brekke [N] 4 N 7
Brekken [N] 4 Q 6
Brekkvasselv [N] 4 Q 5
Δ Bremangerland [N] 4 N 7
Bremen [D] 15 O 12
Bremerhaven [D] 15 O 12
Bremervörde [D] 15 P 12
Bremsnes [N] 4 O 6
Δ Brenner [A, I] 20 Q 16
Breno [I] 20 P 17
Brentwood [GB] 13 K 13
Brèscia [I] 20 P 17
Breskens [NL] 14 L 13
Breslau = Wrocław [PL] 16 T 13
Bressanone [I] 20 Q 16
Δ Bresse [F] 19 M 17
Bressuire [F] 18 H 16
Brest [F] 12 F 15
Brest [SU] 17 X 12
Brestova [YU] 21 S 17
Brestovačka Banja [YU] 22 X 18
Δ Bretagne [F] 12 G 15
Bretenoux [F] 19 K 17
Breteuil [F] 14 K 14
Breteuil [F] 14 K 15
≈ Breton, Pertuis — [F] 18 H 16
Bretten [D] 15 O 15
Brevik [N] 6 P 8
Brežice [YU] 21 T 17
Breznik [BG] 22 Y 18
Brezno [CS] 17 V 15
Brezoi [RO] 22 Y 17
Brézolles [F] 14 K 15
Brezovo [BG] 23 Z 18
Briançon [F] 20 N 18
Briare [F] 19 L 16
Bri Chualann = Bray [IRL] 10 F 12
Bricquebec [F] 13 H 14
Bridgend [GB] 12 G 13
Bridgnorth [GB] 13 H 12
Bridgwater [GB] 13 H 13
Bridlington [GB] 11 K 11
Bridport [GB] 13 H 13
Δ Brie [F] 14 L 15
Briec [F] 12 F 15
Brie-Comte-Robert [F] 14 L 15
Brieg = Brzeg [PL] 16 T 14
Brienne-le-Château [F] 14 M 15
Brienz [CH] 20 O 16
Brienza [I] 29 T 20
≈ Brienzer See [CH] 20 O 16
Briey [F] 15 N 15
Brig [CH] 20 O 17
Brigg [GB] 13 J 12
Brighton [GB] 13 J 13
Brignogan-Plage [F] 12 F 15
Brignoles [F] 19 M 18
Brihuega [E] 26 M 18
Δ Brijuni [YU] 21 S 17
Δ Briksvær [N] 2 R 3
Brilon [D] 15 O 13
Brimmes [N] 4 O 8
Brindisi [I] 30 V 20
Brioni = Brijuni [YU] 21 S 17
Brioude [F] 19 L 17
Brioux-sur-Boutonne [F] 18 H 16
Briouze [F] 14 J 15
Brisighella [I] 20 Q 18
Brissac [F] 19 J 16
Bristol [GB] 13 H 13
≈ Bristol Channel [GB] 12 G 13
Brive-la-Gaillarde [F] 19 K 17
Briviesca [E] 18 F 18
Brixen = Bressanone [I] 20 Q 16
Brixham [GB] 12 G 14
Brno [CS] 16 T 15
Bro [S] 7 T 9
Broadford [GB] 10 G 9
Δ Broad Law [GB] 11 H 10
Broby [S] 7 R 10
Broceni [SU] 8 V 10
Δ Brocken [DDR] 15 P 13
Brod [YU] 30 X 19
Brodarevo [YU] 22 W 18
Broddebo [S] 7 S 9
Brodica [YU] 22 X 17
Brodick [GB] 10 G 10
Brodnica [PL] 16 U 12
Brody [PL] 17 W 13
Brody [SU] 17 Y 14
Broglie [F] 14 J 15
Bromarv [SF] 9 V 7
Bromley [GB] 13 J 13
Δ Brommö [S] 7 R 9
Brömsebro [S] 7 S 10
Bromsgrove [GB] 13 H 12
Bromyard [GB] 13 H 12
Brønderslev [DK] 6 P 10
Brønnøysund [N] 2 Q 4
Bronte [I] 29 T 22
Bronzani Majdan [YU] 21 U 17
≈ Broom, Loch — [GB] 11 H 9
Broons [F] 13 H 15
Brora [GB] 11 H 9
Brøstadbotn [N] 2 S 2
Broşteni [RO] 22 Y 17
Broşteni [RO] 23 Z 15
Broto [E] 26 H 19
Brou [F] 14 K 15
Brough [GB] 11 J 11
Brovst [DK] 6 P 10
Brozas [E] 25 C 20
Bruchsal [D] 15 O 15
Bruck an der Großglocknerstraße [A] 21 R 16
Bruck an der Leitha [A] 21 T 15
Bruck an der Mur [A] 21 S 16
Δ Brücke [NL] 14 L 13
Bruck in der Oberpfalz [D] 15 Q 15
Brüel [DDR] 15 Q 12
≈ Brufjord [N] 4 N 7
Brugg [CH] 20 O 16
Brugge [B] 14 L 13
Brühl [D] 15 N 14
Δ Brújula, Puerto de la — [E] 18 F 19
Brumath [F] 15 O 15
Brumunddal [N] 4 Q 7
Bruneck = Brunico [I] 20 Q 16
Brunflo [S] 5 R 6
Brunico [I] 20 Q 16
Brunkeberg [N] 6 O 8
Brunsbuttel [D] 15 P 12
Bruntál [CS] 16 T 14
Δ Brurskanken [N] 2 R 4
Brus [YU] 22 X 18
Brussel = Bruxelles [B] 14 M 14
Brusy [PL] 7 T 12
Bruxelles [B] 14 M 14
Bruyères [F] 20 N 15
Bryggja [N] 4 N 7
Bryne [N] 6 N 9
Brza Palanka [YU] 22 X 17
Brzeg [PL] 16 T 14
Brześć Kujawski [PL] 16 U 12
Brzesko [PL] 17 V 14

Brzesko Nowe [PL] 17 V 14
Brzeżnica [PL] 16 U 13
Brzózka [PL] 16 S 13
Δ Buçaco [P] 25 B 19
Bucău [RO] 23 Za 16
Buccino [I] 29 T 20
Δ Bucegi, Munţii — [RO] 23 Z 17
Buchholz in der Nordheide [D] 15 P 12
Buchloe [D] 20 Q 16
Buchs [CH] 20 P 16
Bückeburg [D] 15 P 13
Buckhaven [GB] 11 H 10
Buckie [GB] 11 J 9
Buckingham [GB] 13 J 13
Δ Bucklige Welt [A] 21 T 16
Bückwitz [DDR] 15 Q 12
Bučovice [CS] 16 T 15
Bud [N] 4 O 6
Δ Budacu, Munţii — [RO] 23 Z 15
Budăicasa [RO] 23 Za 16
Δ Budai hegység [H] 22 V 16
Budapest [H] 22 V 16
Budeşti [RO] 23 Za 17
Bude-Stratton [GB] 12 G 13
Budva [YU] 30 V 19
Buenache de Alarcón [E] 26 F 20
≈ Buendia, Pantano de — [E] 26 F 20
≈ Bufjord [N] 4 N 7
≈ Bug [PL, SU] 17 W 12
Δ Bugac [H] 22 V 16
Δ Bugarach, Pech de — [F] 19 K 19
Δ Bugey [F] 19 M 17
Bugojno [YU] 21 U 18
Bugøyfjord [N] 3 W 1
Bugue, le — [F] 19 J 17
Buhuşi [RO] 23 Za 16
Builth Wells [GB] 13 H 12
Buis-les-Baronnies, le — [F] 19 M 18
Buitrago de Lozoya [E] 26 E 19
Bujalance [E] 25 D 21
Bujanovac [YU] 22 X 19
Bujaraloz [E] 26 H 19
Buje [YU] 21 R 17
Buk [PL] 16 T 13
Δ Bükk [H] 17 W 15
Δ Bukovica [YU] 21 T 18
Bukureşti [RO] 23 Za 17
Δ Bulbjerg [DK] 6 P 10
Bulkowo [PL] 17 V 12
Bullas [E] 26 R 21
Bulle [CH] 20 N 16
Bumbeşti-Jiu [RO] 22 Y 17
Bun an Phobail = Moville [IRL] 10 F 10
Bunclody [IRL] 12 F 12
Bun Clóidi = Bunclody [IRL] 12 F 12
Buncrana [IRL] 10 F 10
Bun Crannaighe = Buncrana [IRL] 10 F 10
Bun Dobhráin = Bundoran [IRL] 10 E 11
Bundoran [IRL] 10 E 11
Bungay [GB] 13 K 12
Δ Bungsberg [D] 6 P 12
Δ Bunnerfjällen [S] 4 Q 6
Bunzlau = Boleslawiec [PL] 16 S 13
≈ Búrdalo, Río — [E] 25 C 20
Bure, Pic de — [F] 19 M 18
Bureå [S] 5 U 5
Δ Bureba, La — [E] 18 F 18
Buresjön [S] 2 S 4
Burfjord [N] 2 T 1
Burg, Den — [NL] 14 M 12
Burgas [BG] 23 Zb 18
Burg auf Fehmarn [D] 6 Q 11
Burg bei Magdeburg [DDR] 15 Q 13
Burgdorf [CH] 20 O 16
Burgdorf [D] 15 P 13
Δ Burgenland [A] 21 T 16
Δ Burgfjället [S] 5 R 5
Burghausen [D] 21 R 15
Burghead [GB] 11 H 9
Burgo de Osna, El — [E] 26 F 19
Burgos [E] 18 F 19
Burg Schlitz [DDR] 15 Q 12
Burgsvik [S] 7 T 10
Burhaniye [TR] 31 Zb 20
Burjasot [E] 26 G 21
Burnham on Crouch [GB] 13 K 13
Burnley [GB] 11 H 11
Burrel [AL] 30 W 19
Burriana [E] 26 H 20
Bürstadt [D] 15 O 14
Burton upon Trent [GB] 13 J 12
Burträsk [S] 5 T 5
Bury [GB] 11 H 12
Bury Saint Edmunds [GB] 13 K 13
Busachi [I] 28 O 21
Busca [I] 20 N 18
Bushat [AL] 30 W 19
Bushmills [GB] 10 F 10
Busk [SU] 17 Y 14
Busovača [YU] 21 U 18
Bussang [F] 20 N 16
Busseto [I] 20 P 17
Bussum [NL] 14 M 13
Buşteni [RO] 23 Z 16
Δ Busto, Cabo — [E] 24 D 18
Busto Arsizio [I] 20 O 17
Büsum [D] 6 O 12
Buteni [RO] 22 X 16
Butrint [AL] 30 W 20
Δ Butt of Lewis [GB] 10 G 8
Butzbach [D] 15 O 14
Bützow [DDR] 15 Q 12
Buxtehude [D] 15 P 12
Buxton [GB] 13 J 12
Büyük Cekmece [TR] 23 Zc 19
Büyük Karıştıran [TR] 23 Zb 19
Δ Büyük Mahya [TR] 23 Zb 18
≈ Büyük Menderes nehri [TR] 31 Zc 21
Buzançais [F] 19 K 16
≈ Bužau [RO] 23 Za 16
Buziaş [RO] 22 X 17
Bydgoszcz [PL] 16 T 12
Bygdeå [S] 5 U 5
Bygdin [N] 4 Q 7
≈ Bygdin [N] 4 O 7
Bygdsiljum [S] 5 T 5
Bygland [N] 6 O 9
Byglandsfjord [N] 6 O 9
≈ Byglandsvatn [N] 6 O 9
Bykle [N] 6 O 8
Bykovo [SU] 8 Y 9
Bykse [S] 5 U 4
Δ Bystrá [CS] 17 V 15
Bystrica [SU] 17 Y 15
Bystřice nad Perňstejnem [CS] 16 T 14
Bystřice pod Hostýnem [CS] 16 U 14
Bystrzyca Ktodzka [PL] 16 T 14
Bytča [CS] 16 U 15
Bytom [PL] 16 U 14
Bytów [PL] 7 T 11
Byxelkrok [S] 7 T 9

C

Cabaco, El — [E] 25 D 19
Δ Caballería, Cabo de — [E] 27 L 20
Δ Cabañas [E] 26 E 21
Çabanes [E] 27 H 20
Čabar [YU] 21 S 17
Cabeza del Buey [E] 25 D 21
Cabezas de San Juan, Las — [E] 25 C 22
Cabezón de la Sal [E] 24 E 18
Cabezuela del Valle [E] 25 D 20
Δ Cabo Blanco [E] 27 K 21
Cabra [E] 25 D 22
Δ Cabre, Col de — [F] 19 M 18
Δ Cabreira [P] 24 C 19
Cabreiros [E] 24 C 18
Δ Cabrera, Isla — [E] 27 K 21
Δ Cabrera, Sierra — [E] 24 D 18
Δ Çabrito, Puerto del — [E] 25 C 22
Δ Čabulja [YU] 21 U 18
Čačak [YU] 22 W 18
Càccamo [I] 29 S 22
Cáceres [E] 25 C 20
Çachopo [P] 25 B 21
Čadca [CS] 16 U 14
Δ Cadena, Pueto de la — [E] 26 G 22
Cadenet [F] 19 M 18
Δ Cadi, Sierra de — [E] 27 J 19
Cádiz [E] 25 C 22
≈ Cádiz, Bahía de — [E] 25 C 22
≈ Cádiz, Golfo de — [E] 25 B 21
Čadyr-Lunga [SU] 23 Zb 16
Caen [F] 14 J 14
Caernarvon [GB] 12 G 12
Caerphilly [GB] 13 H 13
Çağiş [TR] 31 Zc 20
Cagli [I] 21 R 18
Càgliari [I] 28 O 21
≈ Càgliari, Golfo di — [I] 28 O 21
Cagnes-sur-Mer [F] 20 N 18
Cahersiveen [IRL] 12 D 12
Cahir [IRL] 12 E 12
Cahors [F] 19 J 18
Caia [P] 25 C 20
Caiazzo [I] 29 S 20
Δ Caimodorro [E] 26 G 20
Cairnryan [GB] 10 G 10
Càiro Montenotte [I] 20 O 18
Caiseal = Cashel [IRL] 12 E 12
Caislean a'Bharraigh = Castlebar [IRL] 10 E 11
Caistor [GB] 13 J 12
Çajarc [F] 19 K 18
Čajetina [YU] 22 W 18
Çajka [BG] 23 Zb 18
Çajniče [YU] 22 V 18
Čakovec [YU] 21 T 16
Cala [E] 25 C 21
Δ Calabrese, Appennino — [I] 29 U 22
Δ Calàbria [I] 29 U 22
Calac [F] 12 G 15
Calaceite [E] 26 H 20
Calaf [E] 27 J 19
Calafat [RO] 22 Y 18
Δ Cala Figuera, Cabo de — [E] 27 K 21
Calahorra [E] 26 G 19
Calais [F] 14 230
Calamocha [E] 26 G 20
Calañas [E] 25 B 21
Δ Calanche [F] 28 O 19
Calanda [E] 26 H 20
Călăraşi [RO] 23 Zb 17
Calasetta [I] 28 O 21
Calasparra [E] 26 E 21
Calatañazor [E] 26 F 19
Calatayud [E] 26 G 19
Δ Calatrava, Campo de — [E] 26 E 21
Δ Calavà, Capo — [I] 29 T 22
Calbach [D] 15 O 15
Calbe/Saale [DDR] 15 Q 13
Caldas da Rainha [P] 25 A 20
Caldas de Mombúy [E] 27 K 19
Caldas de Reyes [E] 24 B 18
Δ Caldeirão, Serra do — [P] 25 A 21
Calderas [E] 27 J 19
Δ Calderina, Sierra de la — [E] 26 E 20
Calenzana [F] 28 D 19
Δ Căliman, Munţii — [RO] 22 Y 15
Călineşti [RO] 22 Y 17
Çalitri [I] 29 T 20
Čaljina [YU] 21 U 18
Callander [GB] 11 H 10
Callington [GB] 12 G 13
Callosa de Segura [E] 26 G 21
≈ Călmăjutiu [RO] 23 Za 17
≈ Calniştea [RO] 23 Z 17
Caltagirone [I] 29 S 22
Caltanissetta [I] 29 S 22
Caltavuturo [I] 29 S 22
Δ Calvados, Côte du — [F] 14 J 14
Calvi [F] 28 O 19
≈ Calvi, Golfe de — [F] 28 O 19
Calvörde [DDR] 15 Q 13
Calw [D] 15 O 15
Calzada de Oropesa [E] 25 D 20
Camaiore [I] 20 P 18
Camaret-sur-Mer [F] 12 F 15
Camargo [E] 18 F 18
Δ Camargue [F] 19 L 18
Camariñas [E] 24 B 17
Camarzana de Tera [E] 24 D 19
Camas [E] 25 C 21
Cambo-les-Bains [F] 18 G 18
Cambrai [F] 14 L 14
Δ Cambrian Mountains [GB] 12 G 12
Cambridge [GB] 13 K 13
Cambrils [E] 27 J 20
Camelford [GB] 12 G 13
Camerino [I] 21 R 19
Δ Camerros, Sierra de — [E] 26 F 19
Caminha [P] 24 B 18
Caminreal [E] 26 G 20
Campagna [I] 29 T 20
Campan [F] 18 H 18
Campanario [E] 25 D 21
Δ Campània [I] 29 S 20
Δ Campano, Appennino — [I] 29 S 20
Camp de Criptana [E] 26 F 20
Campello [E] 26 G 21
Campeltown [GB] 10 G 10
Δ Campidano [I] 28 O 21
Campillos [E] 25 D 22
Δ Campiña [E] 26 F 20
Δ Campiña, La — [E] 25 D 21
Campisábalos [E] 26 F 19
Campo [E] 26 H 19
Campobasso [I] 29 S 20
Campo Maior [P] 25 C 20
Camporeale [I] 29 R 22
Δ Campos, Tierra de — [E] 24 D 19
Campos del Puerto [E] 27 K 21
Camprodón [E] 27 K 19
Can [TR] 31 Zb 20
Çanakkale [TR] 31 Zb 20
≈ Çanakkale boğazi [TR] 31 Za 20
≈ Canal du Midi [F] 19 K 18
Cañamero [E] 25 D 20
Canari [F] 28 P 19
Cañaveral [E] 25 C 20
Δ Cañaveral, Sierra de — [E] 25 C 20
Cañaveras [E] 26 F 20
Cancale [F] 13 H 15
Cancon [F] 19 J 18
Δ Canda, Portillo de la — [E] 24 C 18
Candarlı körfezi [TR] 31 Zb 20
Candé [F] 18 H 15
Candela [I] 29 T 20
Candeleda [E] 25 D 20
Cañete [E] 26 G 20
Canfranc [E] 18 H 19
Cangas [E] 24 B 18
Cangas de Narcea [E] 24 D 18
Cangas de Onis [E] 24 E 18
Canha [P] 25 A 20
Canicatti [I] 29 S 22
≈ Canigou, Mont [F] 27 K 19
Caniles [E] 26 F 22
Canino [I] 28 Q 19
Cañiza, La — [E] 24 B 18
Cañizal [E] 25 D 19
Canjáyar [E] 26 E 22
Δ Canna [GB] 10 G 9
Cannae [I] 29 T 20
Cannes [F] 20 N 18
Cannòbio [I] 20 O 17
Canosa di Pìglia [I] 29 T 20
Canossa [I] 20 P 18
Canourgue, la — [F] 19 L 18
Δ Cantabria, Sierra de — [E] 18 F 18
Δ Cantábrica, Cordillera — [E] 24 C 18
Δ Cantal [F] 19 K 17
Δ Cantal, Plomb du — [F] 19 K 17
Canterbury [GB] 13 K 13
Cantillana [E] 25 C 21
Cantoria [E] 26 F 22
Cantú [I] 20 O 17
Càorle [I] 21 R 17
Capáccio [I] 29 T 20
Caparroso [E] 26 G 19
Capbreton [F] 18 G 18
Cap-D'Agde [F] 19 L 18
Capdepera [E] 27 K 21
Δ Cape Clear [IRL] 12 D 12
Čapel'ka [SU] 8 Y 8
Capelle, la — [F] 14 L 14
Capestang [F] 19 K 18
Δ Capitanata [I] 29 T 19
Caple [E] 26 H 21
Δ Cap Noir, [MA] 25 C 22
Δ Capràia, Isola di — [I] 20 P 19
Caprara, Isola — [I] 29 T 19
Capri [I] 29 S 20
Δ Capri, Isola di — [I] 29 S 20
Captieux [F] 18 H 18
Càpua [I] 29 S 20
Capurso [I] 29 U 20
Caracal [RO] 23 Z 17
Cara Droma Rúisc = Carrick-on-Shannon [IRL] 10 E 11
Caràglio [I] 20 N 18
Caraman [F] 19 J 18
Δ Caramulo, Serra do — [P] 25 B 19
Caransebeş [RO] 22 X 17
Caravaca [E] 26 F 21
Caravàggio [I] 20 P 17
Δ Carba, Sierra de la — [E] 24 C 17
Carballeda [E] 24 C 18
Carballino [E] 24 C 18
Carballo [E] 24 B 18
Δ Carbonara, Capo — [I] 28 P 21
Carboneras de Guadazaón [E] 26 G 20
Carbonero el Mayor [E] 26 E 19
≈ Carbones, Rio — [E] 25 D 22
Carbònia [I] 28 O 21
Carbonne [F] 19 J 18
≈ Carcans, Étang de — [F] 18 H 17
Carcassonne [F] 19 K 18
Carcastillo [E] 26 G 19
Cardiff [GB] 13 H 13
Cardigan [GB] 12 G 12
≈ Cardigan Bay [GB] 12 G 12
Cardona [E] 27 J 19
Carei [RO] 22 X 15
Carentan [F] 13 H 14
Cargèse [F] 28 O 19
Carignano [I] 20 O 18
Cariñena [E] 26 G 19
Carini [I] 29 R 22
Cârkva [BG] 22 Y 18
Carlentini [I] 29 T 22
Carlet [E] 26 G 21
Carliste [GB] 11 H 11
Carloforte [I] 28 O 21
Carlota, La — [E] 25 D 21
Carlow [IRL] 12 F 12
Carmagnola [I] 20 O 18
Carmarthen [GB] 12 G 12
≈ Carmarthen Bay [GB] 12 G 13
Carmaux [F] 19 K 18
Δ Carmel Head [GB] 10 G 12
Carmona [E] 25 C 21
Carnac [F] 18 G 15
Carn Domhnaigh = Carndonagh [IRL] 10 F 10
Carndonagh [IRL] 10 F 10
Δ Carn Eige [GB] 11 H 9
Carnforth [GB] 11 H 11
Carnikava [SU] 8 W 9
Δ Carnsore Point [IRL] 12 F 12
Δ Caroche, Pico — [E] 26 G 21
Carolina, La — [E] 26 E 21
Carolinensiel [D] 15 O 12
Carona [I] 20 P 17
Δ Carpaţii Meridionali [RO] 22 X 17
Δ Carpaţii Orientali [RO] 23 Z 15
Carpentras [F] 19 M 18
Carpi [I] 20 Q 18
Cărpiniş [RO] 22 W 17
Carpio, El — [E] 25 D 21
Carraig Mhachaire Rois = Carrickmacross [IRL] 10 F 11
Carral [E] 24 C 18
Carrara [I] 20 P 18
Carrascosa del Campo [E] 26 F 20
Δ Carrauntoohil [IRL] 12 D 12
Carrazeda de Anciães [P] 25 C 19
Carrbridge [GB] 11 H 9
Carregado [P] 25 A 20
Carrickmacross [IRL] 10 F 11
Carrick-on-Shannon [IRL] 10 E 11
≈ Carrión, Río — [E] 24 E 18
Carrión de Calatrava [E] 26 E 21
Carrión de los Condes [E] 24 E 18
Carsoli [I] 29 R 19
Carsphairn [GB] 11 H 10
Cartagena [E] 26 G 22
Cartaxo [P] 25 A 20
Cartaya [E] 25 B 21
Carthago [TN] 28 P 22
Carthaix-Plouguer [F] 12 G 15
Carucedo [E] 24 D 18
Carùnchio [I] 29 S 19
Carvin [F] 14 L 14
Δ Carvoeiro, Cabo — [P] 25 A 20
Casa Branca [P] 25 B 20
Casacalenda [I] 29 S 19
Casale Monferrato [I] 20 O 17
Casalmaggiore [I] 20 P 17
Casalpusterlengo [I] 20 P 17
Casamàssima [I] 29 U 20
Casamozza [F] 28 P 19
Casarano [I] 30 V 20
Casarsa della Delizia [I] 21 R 17
Casas Ibáñez [E] 26 G 21
Casavieja [E] 26 E 20
Cascais [P] 25 A 20
Cascante [E] 26 G 19
Δ Casentino [I] 20 Q 18
Casere [I] 20 Q 16
Caserta [I] 29 S 20
Casetas [E] 26 G 19
Cashel [IRL] 12 E 12
Çasinos [E] 26 G 20
Čáslav [CS] 16 S 14
Caso [E] 24 E 18
Càsoli [I] 29 S 19
Caspe [E] 26 H 20
Cassagnes-Bégonhès [F] 19 K 18
Cassano al lònio [I] 29 U 21
Cassano d'Adda [I] 20 P 17
Cassel [F] 14 L 14
Cassino [I] 29 S 20
Cassis [F] 19 M 19
Castèggio [I] 20 O 17
Δ Castejón, Montes des — [E] 26 G 19
Castejón des Sos [E] 27 J 19
Castelbuono [I] 29 S 22
Castel de Ferro [E] 26 E 22
Castel del Monte [I] 29 T 20
Castel di Sangro [I] 29 S 19
Castelfiorentino [I] 20 Q 18
Castelfranco Emilia [I] 20 Q 18
Castelfranco Vèneto [I] 20 Q 17
Castel Gandolfo [I] 29 R 20
Casteljaloux [F] 18 H 18
Castellabate [I] 29 T 20
≈ Castellammare, Golfo di — [I] 29 R 22
Castellammare del Golfo [I] 29 R 22
Castellammare di Stàbia [I] 29 S 20
Castellane [F] 20 N 18
Castellaneta [I] 29 U 20
Δ Castellar, El — [E] 26 G 19
Castell'Arquato [I] 20 P 18
Castelló de Ampurias [E] 27 K 19
Castellón de la Plana [E] 26 H 20
Castelnaudary [F] 19 K 18
Castelnau-de-Médoc [F] 18 H 17
Castelnau-Magnoac [F] 19 H 18
Castelnovo ne' Monti [I] 22 P 18
Castelo Branco [P] 25 C 20
Castelo de Vide [P] 25 B 20
Castelsardo [I] 28 O 20
Castelsarrasin [F] 19 J 18
Casteltèrmini [I] 29 S 22
Castelvetrano [I] 29 R 22
Castéra-Verduzan [F] 19 J 18
Castets [F] 18 H 18
Castielfabib [E] 26 G 20
Castiglione di Sicilia [I] 29 T 22
Castiglion Fiorentino [I] 20 Q 19
Δ Castilla, Playa de — [E] 25 B 21
Δ Castilla la Nueva [E] 26 E 21
Δ Castilla la Vieja [E] 18 F 19
Castillo de las Guardas, El — [E] 25 C 21
Castillon-la-Bataille [F] 18 H 17
Castillonnès [F] 19 J 17
Castlebar [IRL] 10 E 11
Castlebay [GB] 10 F 9
Castlederg [GB] 10 F 10
Castle Douglas [GB] 11 H 11
Castleisland [IRL] 12 D 12
Castlerea [IRL] 10 E 11
Castletown [GB] 10 G 11
Castletown Bearhaven [IRL] 12 D 12
Castres [F] 19 K 18
Castro-Caldelas [E] 24 C 18
Castro Daire [P] 25 B 19
Castro del Río [E] 25 D 21
Castro Marim [P] 25 B 21
Castropol [E] 24 D 18
Castro-Urdiales [E] 18 F 18
Castro Verde [P] 25 B 21
Castrovillari [I] 29 U 21
Castuera [E] 25 D 21
Catalca [TR] 23 Zc 19
Δ Cataluña [E] 27 J 20
Catanhede [P] 25 B 19
Catània [I] 29 T 22
≈ Catània, Golfo di — [I] 29 T 22
Catanzaro [I] 29 U 21
Catanzaro Lido [I] 29 U 21
Catarroja [E] 26 G 21
Cateau, le — [F] 14 L 14
Cateraggio [F] 28 P 19
Cathair Dún Jascaigh = Cahir [IRL] 12 E 12
Cathair na Mart = Westport [IRL] 10 E 11
Δ Catoute [E] 24 D 18
Δ Càtria, Monte — [I] 21 R 18
Càttaro = Kotor [YU] 22 V 19
Cattòlica [I] 21 R 18
Cattòlica Eraclea [I] 29 S 22
Cătunu [RO] 23 Z 17
Caudé [E] 26 G 20
Cauldcleuch Head [GB] 11 H 10
Caulnes [F] 13 H 15
Caulònia [I] 29 U 22
Caunes-Minervois [F] 19 K 18
Caussade [F] 19 J 18
Δ Causses [F] 19 K 18
Cauterets [F] 18 H 18
Δ Caux, Pay de — [F] 14 J 14
≈ Cávado, Río — [P] 24 B 19
Cavaillon [F] 19 M 18
Cavalese [I] 20 Q 17
Δ Cavallo, Capo al — [F] 28 O 19
Δ Cavallo, Île de — [F] 28 P 20
Cavan [IRL] 10 F 11
Cavàrzere [I] 20 Q 17
Cavnic [RO] 17 Y 15
Cavtat [YU] 22 V 19
Caylar, le — [F] 19 L 18
Caylus [F] 19 K 18
Δ Cayolle, Col de la — [F] 20 N 18
Cazalla de la Sierra [E] 25 C 21
Căzăneşti [RO] 23 Za 17
≈ Cazaux et de Sanguinet, Étang de — [F] 18 H 17
Caze, la — [F] 19 L 18
Çazin [YU] 21 T 17
Čazma [YU] 21 T 17
Cazorla [E] 26 E 21
Δ Cazorla, Sierra de — [E] 26 E 21
≈ Cea, Río — [E] 24 E 19
Ceannanas = Kells [IRL] 10 F 11
Ceann Átha Gad = Kinnegad [IRL] 10 F 11
Ceatharlach = Carlow [IRL] 12 F 12
Δ Cebollera, La — [E] 26 F 19
Čebovce [CS] 17 V 15
Ceccano [I] 29 R 20
Çece [H] 22 V 16
Čechtice [CS] 16 S 14
Δ Čechty [CS] 16 S 15
Cècina [I] 20 P 19
≈ Cècina [I] 20 Q 19
≈ Cècita, Lago di — [I] 29 U 21
Cedègolo [I] 20 P 17
≈ Cedrón, Río — [E] 26 E 20
Cedynia [PL] 16 R 12
Cée [E] 24 B 18
Cefalù [I] 29 S 22
≈ Cega, Río — [E] 26 E 19
Cegléd [H] 22 V 16
Cèglie Messàpica [I] 29 U 20
Çehegin [E] 26 F 21
Čejč [CS] 16 T 15
Celano [I] 29 S 19
Çelanova [E] 24 C 18
Čelić [YU] 22 V 17
Celje [YU] 21 S 17
Celldömöl [H] 21 U 16
Celle [D] 15 P 13
Çelorico da Baira [P] 25 C 19
Čemerne [CS] 17 W 15
Δ Čemernica [YU] 21 U 18
≈ Cenajo, Pantano del — [E] 26 F 21
Cenei [RO] 22 W 17
Cenicero [E] 18 F 19
Çenon [F] 18 H 17
Čenta [YU] 22 W 17
Centallo [I] 20 N 18
Çento [I] 20 Q 18
Čepinci [BG] 22 Y 18
Δ Cer [YU] 22 V 17
Cerbère [F] 27 K 19
Δ Cerbère, Cabo — [F] 27 K 19
Δ Cerbicale, Îles — [F] 28 P 20
Cercal [P] 25 A 20
Cercal [P] 25 A 21
Cercy-la-Tour [F] 19 L 16
Δ Cerdaña, La — [E] 27 J 19
Cerdedo [E] 24 B 18
≈ Çère [F] 19 K 17
≈ Čerecha [SU] 8 Y 8
Čerepovo [BG] 23 Za 19
Cères [I] 20 N 17
Céret [F] 27 K 19
Cerignola [I] 29 T 20
Cérilly [F] 19 K 16
Cerisiers [F] 19 L 15
Cerkezköy [TR] 23 Zc 19
Cerknica [YU] 21 S 17
Cermei [RO] 22 X 16
Cerna [RO] 23 Zb 16
Cerna [YU] 22 V 17
≈ Cerna [RO] 22 Y 17
Δ Cerna, Munţii — [RO] 22 X 17
Čern'achovsk [SU] 8 V 11
Çernaja Rěcka [SU] SU 224
Δ Černatica [BG] 23 Z 19
Cernavoda [RO] 23 Zb 17
≈ Cerni Lom [BG] 23 Za 18
Çernoočene [BG] 23 Za 19
Çernozemen [BG] BG 239
Černyševskoje [SU] 8 W 11
Δ Cerrato, Valles de — [E] 26 E 19
Çerrik [AL] 30 W 20
Certosa di Pavia [I] 20 O 17
Δ Cervelle, Montagne de la — [F] 19 M 18
Červená Voda [CS] 16 T 14
Cervera [E] 27 J 19
Cervera de Pisuerga [E] 24 E 18
Cèrvia [I] 21 R 18
Cervignano del Friuli [I] 21 R 17
Cervione [F] 28 P 19
Çervo [E] 24 C 17
Çervonoarmejskoje [SU] 23 Zb 16
Červonograd [SU] 17 X 13
Cesena [I] 21 R 18
Cesenàtico [I] 21 R 18
Cësis [SU] 8 X 9
Česká Kamenice [CS] 16 S 14
Česká Lipa [CS] 16 S 14
Çeské Budějovice [CS] 16 S 15
Δ Českomoravske mezihoří [CS] 16 T 14
Český Brod [CS] 16 S 14
Český Krumlov [CS] 16 S 15
Český Těšín [CS] 16 U 14
Česma [YU] 21 T 17
Çeşme [TR] 31 Zb 21
Cetate [RO] 22 Y 18
≈ Cetina [YU] 21 U 18
Cetinje [Yu] 30 V 19
Cetraro [I] 29 T 21
Cette = Sète [F] 19 L 18
Ceuta [E] 25 C 22
Ceva [I] 20 O 18
Δ Cévennes [F] 19 L 18
Δ Chaasia Ori [GR] 30 X 20
Chabanais [F] 19 J 17
Chabeuil [F] 19 M 17
Δ Chablais [F] 20 N 17
Chablis [F] 19 L 16
≈ Chadžibejskij liman [SU] 23 Zc 15
Chagny [F] 19 M 16
Chaise-Dieu, la — [F] 19 L 17
Chalais [F] 19 J 17
Chalandrion [GR] 31 Z 21
Chalandritsa [GR] 30 Y 21
Chalki [GR] 31 Zc 22
Δ Chalki [GR] 31 Zc 22
Δ Chalkidiki [GB] 30 Y 20
Chalkidon [GR] 30 Y 20
Chalkis [GR] 31 Z 21
Challans [F] 18 H 16
Châlon-sur-Marne [F] 14 M 15
Châlon-sur-Saône [F] 19 M 16
Δ Chalosse [F] 18 H 18
Châlus [F] 19 J 17
Cham [CH] 20 O 16
Cham [D] 16 R 15
Chamberet [F] 19 K 17
Chambéry [F] 19 M 17
Chambon-sur-Voueize [F] 19 K 17
Chambord [F] 19 K 16
Chamborêt [F] 19 J 17
Chamboulive [F] 19 K 17
Δ Chamili [GR] 31 Zc 22
Chamonix-Mont-Blanc [F] 20 N 17
Champagne-Mouton [F] 19 J 17
Champagnole [F] 19 M 16
Champaubert [F] 14 L 15
Champlitte-et-le-Prélot [F] 19 M 16
Δ Champsaur, Massif du — [F] 20 N 18
Chamusca [P] 25 B 20
≈ Chança, Rio — [P] 25 B 21
Chania [GR] 32 Za 23
≈ Chanion, Kolpos — [GR] 32 Za 23
Δ Channel Islands [GB] 13 H 14
Chantada [E] 24 C 18
Chantonnay [F] 18 H 16
Chaource [F] 19 L 15
Δ Chapagne [F] 19 L 15
Chapelle-d'Angillon, la — [F] 19 K 16
Chapelle-Glain, la — [F] 18 H 15
Chapelle-Royale [F] 14 K 15
Charavgi [GR] 30 Y 20
Chard [GB] 13 H 13
≈ Charente [F] 18 H 17
Charité-sur-Loire, la — [F] 19 L 16
Charleroi [B] 14 M 14
Charleville [IRL] 12 E 12
Charleville-Mézières [F] 14 M 14
Charlieu [F] 19 L 17
Charlottenberg [S] 4 Q 8
Charmes [F] 20 N 15
Δ Charolais, Monts du — [F] 19 L 17
Charolles [F] 19 L 16
Chartres [F] 14 K 15
Chartre-sur-le-Loir, la — [F] 19 J 15
Chasseneuil-sur-Bonnieure [F] 19 J 17
Chătaigneraie, la — [F] 18 H 16
Château-Arnoux [F] 19 M 18
Châteaubriant [F] 18 H 15
Château-Chinon [F] 19 L 16
Château-d'Oex [CH] 20 N 17
Château-d'Oléron, le — [F] 18 H 17
Château-du-Loir [F] 19 J 15
Châteaudun [F] 19 K 15
Château-Gontier [F] 18 H 15
Château-la-Vallière [F] 19 J 16
Châteaulin [F] 12 F 15
Châteaumeillant [F] 19 K 16
Châteauneuf-de-Randon [F] 19 L 18
Châteauneuf-du-Faou [F] 12 G 15
Châteauneuf-du-Pape [F] 19 M 18
Châteauneuf-en-Thymerais [F] 14 K 15
Châteauneuf-la-Forět [F] 19 K 17
Châteauneuf-sur-Charente [F] 19 J 17
Châteauneuf-sur-Cher [F] 19 K 16
Châteauneuf-sur-Loire [F] 19 K 15
Châteauneuf-sur-Sarthe [F] 19 J 15
Château-Renault [F] 19 J 16
Châteauroux [F] 19 K 16
Château-Salins [F] 15 N 15
Château-Thierry [F] 14 L 15
Châteauvillain [F] 19 M 15
Châtelguyon [F] 19 L 17
Châtellerault [F] 19 J 16
Châtillon [I] 20 O 17
Châtillon-Coligny [F] 19 L 16
Châtillon-sur-Chalaronne [F] 19 M 17
Châtillon-sur-Indre [F] 19 J 16
Châtillon-sur-Seine [F] 19 M 16
Châtillon-sur-Sevre [F] 18 H 16
Châtre, la — [F] 19 K 16
Chatsworth House [GB] 13 J 12
Chatteris [GB] 13 J 12
Chaudes-Aigues [F] 19 K 17
Chauffailles [F] 19 L 17
Chaumont-en-Bassigny [F] 19 M 15
Chaumont-en-Vexin [F] 14 K 15
Chaumont-sur-Loire [F] 19 K 16
Chauny [F] 14 L 14
Chauvigny [F] 19 J 16
Chaux-de-Fonds, la — [CH] 20 N 16
Chaves [P] 24 C 19
Chazelles-sur-Lyon [F] 19 L 17

Cheb [CS] 15 Q 14
Chef-Boutonne [F] 19 J 16
Chełm [PL] 17 X 13
Δ Chełmińskie, Pojezierze — [PL] 16 U 12
Chełmno [PL] 16 U 12
Δ Chełmo [PL] 17 V 13
Chelmsford [GB] 13 K 13
Chełmża [PL] 16 U 12
Cheltenham [GB] 13 H 13
Chemillé [F] 19 H 16
Chemnitz = Karl-Marx-Stadt [DDR] 16 R 14
Chenonceaux [F] 19 J 16
Chepstow [GB] 13 H 13
≈ Cher [F] 19 K 16
Cherbourg [F] 13 H 14
Chersonissos [GR] 32 Zb 33
Chert [E] 26 H 20
Chesne, le — [F] 14 M 14
Chessy-les-Prés [F] 19 L 15
Chester [GB] 13 H 12
Chesterfield [GB] 13 J 12
Δ Cheviot, the — [GB] 11 J 10
Δ Cheviot Hills [GB] 11 H 10
Cheylard, le — [F] 19 L 17
Δ Chianti, Monti del — [I] 20 Q 18
Chiaravalle Centrale [I] 29 U 21
Chiari [I] 20 P 17
Chiàvari [I] 20 P 18
Chiavenna [I] 20 P 17
Chichester [GB] 13 J 13
Δ Chiclana, Loma de — [E] 26 E 21
Chiclana de la Frontera [E] 25 C 22
Chiechanów [PL] 17 V 12
Chiechanowiec [PL] 17 W 12
≈ Chiemsee [D] 21 R 16
≈ Chienti [I] 21 R 19
Δ Chies, Islas — [E] 24 B 18
Chieszyn [PL] 16 U 14
Chieti [E] 26 E 21
Chieti [I] 29 S 19
≈ Chilia, Bratul — [RO] 23 Zc 16
Chilia Veche [RO] 23 Zc 16
Chiliomodion [GR] 31 Z 21
Chimarros [GR] 30 Y 19
Chimay [B] 14 M 14
Δ Chimino, Monte — [I] 29 R 19
Δ Chinchilla, Altos de — [E] 26 G 21
Chinchilla de Monte Aragón [E] 26 F 21
Chinon [F] 19 J 16
≈ Chio, Stenon — [GR] 31 Zb 21
Chiógia [I] 21 R 17
Chionata [GR] 30 X 21
Chios [GR] 31 Zb 21
Δ Chios [GR] 31 Zb 21
Chipiona [E] 25 C 22
Chippenham [GB] 13 H 13
Chipping Norton [GB] 13 J 13
Chiril [RO] 23 Z 15
Chirivel [E] 26 F 22
Chişineu-Criş [RO] 22 W 16
Δ Chituc, Insula — [RO] 23 Zb 17
Chiusa [I] 20 Q 16
Chiusa Sclàfani [I] 29 S 22
Chivasso [I] 20 O 17
Chlumec nad Cidlinou [CS] 16 S 14
Chmielnik [PL] 17 V 14
Choccìwel [PL] 16 S 12
Chodez [PL] 16 U 12
Chodorov [SU] 17 Y 14
Chodzież [PL] 16 T 12
Chojna [PL] 16 S 12
Chojnice [PL] 16 T 12
Cholet [F] 18 H 16
Chomsk [SU] 17 Y 12
Chomutov [CS] 16 R 14
Chora [GR] 30 Y 22
Chora Sfakion [GR] 32 Za 23
Chorges [F] 20 N 18
Chorin [DDR] 16 R 12
Δ Chorito, Sierra del — [E] 26 E 20
Chorley [GB] 11 H 12
Chorzele [PL] 17 V 1
Chorzów [PL] 16 U 18
Choszczno [PL] 16 S 12
Chřiby [CS] 16 T 15
Δ Chrissi [GR] 32 Zb 23
Chrissoupolis [GR] 31 Z 19
Christchurch [GB] 13 H 13
Δ Christiane [GR] 31 Zb 22
Christiansfeld [DK] 6 P 11
Δ Christiansø [DK] 7 S 11
Chrudim [CS] 16 T 14
Chrzanów [PL] 17 V 14
Chur [CH] 20 P 16
Chust [SU] 17 X 15
≈ Chutojavr [SU] 3 W 1
Ciano d'Enza [I] 20 P 18
Δ Ćićarija [YU] 21 S 17
Ćićevac [YU] 22 X 18
Cieszanów [PL] 17 X 14
Cieza [E] 26 G 21
Cifuentes [E] 26 F 20
≈ Cijara, Pantano de — [E] 25 D 20
Cill Airne = Killarny [IRL] 12 D 12
Cillas [E] 26 G 20
Cill Bheagáin = Kilbeggan [IRL] 10 F 11
Cill Chainnigh = Kilkenny [IRL] 12 E 12
Cill Chaoidhe = Kilkee [IRL] 10 D 12
Cill Dara = Kildare [IRL] 10 F 11
Cilleruelo de Bezana [E] 18 F 18
Cill Mhanntáin = Wicklow [IRL] 12 F 12
Cill Ruis = Kilrush [IRL] 10 D 12
Δ Cil'tal'd, gora — [SU] 3 W 2
Cimpeni [RO] 22 X 16
Cîmpina [RO] 23 Z 17
Cîmpul lui Neag [RO] 22 Y 17
Cîmpulung [RO] 23 Z 17
Cîmpulung Moldovenesc [RO] 23 Z 15
≈ Cinca, Río — [E] 26 H 19
Δ Cincer [YU] 21 U 18
Δ Cinco Villas, Las — [E] 26 G 19
Cindeşti Deal [RO] 23 Z 17
Δ Cîndrelu [RO] 22 Y 17
Çine [TR] 32 Zd 21
Ciney [B] 14 M 14
Cîngoli [I] 21 R 18
Cinigiano [I] 20 Q 19
Δ Cinto, Mont — [F] 28 O 19
Cintruénigo [E] 26 G 19
Ciorani [RO] 23 Za 17
Ciotat, la — [F] 19 M 19
Δ Ćiovo [YU] 21 T 18
Cipău [RO] 22 Y 16
≈ Cipringa, ozero — [SU] 3 X 3
Ciprovci [BG] 22 Y 18
Δ Circeo, Monte — [I] 29 R 20
Δ Circeo, Parco Nazionale del — [I] 29 R 20
Cirencester [GB] 13 H 13
Ciria [E] 26 G 19
Ciriè [I] 20 N 17
Cîrlibaba [RO] 22 Y 15
Cirò [I] 29 U 21
Cirpan [BG] 23 Za 18
Δ Cisa, Passo della — [I] 20 P 18
Čisimšlija [SU] 23 Zb 15
Cislău [RO] 23 Za 16
Cisna [PL] 17 W 14
Cisnădie [RO] 22 Y 16
Čista [YU] 21 U 18
Cisterna di Latina [I] 29 R 20
Cistierna [E] 24 E 18
Cittadella [I] 20 Q 17
Città di Castello [I] 21 R 18
Città Pieve [I] 20 Q 19
Δ Ciuc, Munţii — [RO] 23 Z 16
Δ Ciucas [RO] 23 Z 16
Ciucea [RO] 22 X 16
Ciucurova [RO] 23 Zb 16
Ciudadela [E] 27 L 21
Δ Ciudad Encantada [E] 26 F 20
Ciudad Real [E] 26 E 21
Ciudad Rodrig [E] 25 C 19
Ciumeghiu [RO] 22 W 16
Ciutadilla [E] 27 J 19
Cividale del Friuli [I] 21 R 17
Civita Castellana [I] 29 R 19
Civitanova Marche [I] 21 S 19
Civitavècchia [I] 28 Q 19
Civray [F] 19 J 16
Clacton on Sea [GB] 13 K 13
≈ Clain [F] 19 J 16
Clamecy [F] 19 L 16
Clar Chlainne Mhuiris = Claremorris [IRL] 10 E 11
Δ Clare Island [IRL] 10 D 11
Claremorris [IRL] 10 E 11
Claudy [GB] 10 F 10
Clausthal-Zellerfeld [D] 15 P 13
Clayette, la — [F] 19 L 17
Cleethorpes [GB] 13 K 12
Clemont [F] 14 L 15
Clemont-en-Argonne [F] 14 M 15
Clemont-Ferrand [F] 19 L 17
Clemont-l'Hérault [F] 19 L 18
Cles [I] 20 Q 17
Clevedon [GB] 13 H 13
Clifden [IRL] 10 D 11
Δ Clisham [GB] 10 G 8
Clisson [F] 18 H 16
Clitheroe [GB] 11 H 11
Cloch na gCoillte = Clonakilty [IRL] 12 D 12
Clonakilty [IRL] 12 D 12
Clonmel [IRL] 12 E 12
Cloppenburg [D] 15 O 12
Cluain Meala = Clonmel [IRL] 12 E 12
Cluj [RO] 22 Y 16
Cluny [F] 19 M 16
Cluses [F] 20 N 17
Clusone [I] 20 P 17
Δ Clyde, Firth of — [GB] 10 G 10
Clydebank [GB] 11 H 10
≈ Coa, Rio — [P] 25 C 19
Cobadin [RO] 23 Zb 17
Cobh [IRL] 12 E 12
Coburg [D] 15 Q 14
Cochem [D] 15 N 14
Cockermouth [GB] 11 H 11
Δ Coda Cavallo, Capo — [I] 28 P 20
Codlea [RO] 23 Z 16
Codogno [I] 20 P 17
Codròipo [I] 21 R 17
Δ Codru, Munţii — [RO] 22 X 16
Δ Coellèria, Isla — [E] 24 C 17
Coesfeld [D] 15 N 13
Coevorden [NL] 15 N 13
Cofrentes [E] 26 G 21
Cogealac [RO] 23 Zb 17
Cognac [F] 18 H 17
Cogolin [F] 20 N 19
Coimbra [P] 25 B 19
Coin [E] 25 D 22
≈ Coirib, Loch — [IRL] 10 E 11
Čoka [YU] 22 W 17
Colares [P] 25 A 20
Colchester [GB] 13 K 13
Coldstream [GB] 11 J 10
Coleraine [GB] 10 F 10
Cólico [I] 20 P 17
Δ Coll [GB] 10 G 9
Coll de Nargo [E] 27 J 19
Colle di Val d'Elsa [I] 20 Q 18
Collesalvetti [I] 20 P 18
Δ Colline Metallifere [I] 20 Q 19
Collonges [F] 19 K 17
Collooney [IRL] 10 E 11
Colmar [F] 20 N 15
Colmars [F] 20 N 18
Colmenar [E] 25 D 22
Coloneşti [RO] 23 Z 17
Δ Colonne, Capo delle — [I] 29 U 21
Δ Colonsay [GB] 10 G 10
Δ Columbretes, Islas — [E] 26 H 20
Colunga [E] 24 E 18
Colwyn Bay [GB] 13 H 12
≈ Comàcchio, Valli di — [I] 21 R 18
Comakovci [BG] 23 Z 18
Comăneşti [RO] 23 Z 16
Combeaufontaine [F] 19 M 16
Combourg [F] 13 H 15
Δ Comino, Capo — [I] 28 P 20
Δ Comino [M] 30 V 22
Cómiso [I] 29 T 22
Commàcchio [I] 20 Q 18
Commentry [F] 19 K 16
Commercy [F] 14 M 15
Δ Comminges [F] 19 H 18
Como [I] 20 O 17
≈ Como, Lago di — [I] 20 P 17
Compiègne [F] 14 L 14
Compton Wynyates [GB] 13 J 13
Comrie [GB] 11 H 10
Concarneau [F] 12 F 15
Conceição [P] 25 B 21
Conches-en-Ouche [F] 14 K 15
Condat [F] 19 K 17
Condeixa-a-Nova [P] 25 B 19
Condé-sur-Noireau [F] 14 J 15
Condom [F] 19 J 18
Conegliano [I] 21 R 17
Δ Conejera, Isla — [E] 27 K 21
Δ Cònero, Monte — [I] 21 R 18
Δ Conflent [F] 27 K 19
Confolens [F] 19 J 17
Congresbury [GB] 13 H 13
Conil [E] 25 C 22
Δ Connacht [IRL] 10 E 11
Conop [RO] 22 X 16
Conques [F] 19 K 18
Conquet, le — [F] 12 F 15
Δ Conserans [F] 19 J 19
Constância [P] 25 B 20
Constanţa [RO] 23 Zb 17
Constantina [E] 25 C 21
Consuegra [E] 26 E 20
Contres [F] 19 K 16
Contrexéville [F] 20 N 15
Controne [I] 29 U 21
Conty [F] 14 K 14
Conway [GB] 12 G 12
Cookstown [GB] 10 F 11
Δ Cope, Cabo — [E] 26 F 22
Copertino [I] 30 V 20
Çöpköy [TR] 31 Zb 19
Copparo [I] 20 Q 18
Copşa Mică [RO] 22 Y 16
Corabia [RO] 23 Z 18
Corato [I] 29 U 20
Corbeil-Essones [F] 14 K 15
Δ Corbières [F] 19 K 19
Corbigny [F] 19 L 16
Corcaigh = Cork [IRL] 12 E 12
Cordes [F] 19 K 18
Córdoba [E] 25 D 21
Δ Córdoba, Sierra de — [E] 25 D 21
Corfu = Kerkira [GR] 30 W 21
Δ Corfu = Kerkira [GR] 30 W 21
Corgo [E] 24 C 18
Coria [E] 25 C 20
Coria del Río [E] 25 C 21
Corigliano Càlabro [I] 29 U 21
Coripe [E] 25 C 22
Cork [IRL] 12 E 12
Corlay [F] 12 G 15
Corleone [I] 29 S 22
Corleto Perticara [I] 29 T 20
Corlu [TR] 23 Zc 19
Cormainville [F] 19 K 15
Δ Cornate, le — [I] 20 Q 19
Cornăţel [RO] 22 Y 16
Corneşti [RO] 23 Z 17
Δ Cornouaille [F] 22 F 15
Δ Cornwall [GB] 12 F 14
Çorovodë [AL] 30 W 20
Corral de Almaguer [E] 26 F 20
Δ Corral de Cantos [E] 26 E 20
Corrales de Buelna, Los — [E] 18 F 18
Δ Corse [F] 28 O 19
Δ Corse, Cap — [F] 28 P 19
Corte [F] 28 O 19
Cortegada [E] 24 C 18
Cortegana [E] 25 C 21
Cortemilia [I] 20 O 18
Cortes [E] 26 G 19
Cortina d'Ampezzo [I] 20 Q 16
Cortona [I] 20 Q 19
Coruche [P] 25 B 20
Coruña, La — [E] 24 C 17
Cosenza [I] 29 U 21
Cosham [GB] 13 J 13
Cosne-Cours-sur-Loire [F] 19 L 16
Cospicua [M] 30 V 22
Cossonay [CH] 20 N 16
Δ Costa Blanca [E] 26 G 22
Δ Costa Brava [E] 27 K 19
Costache Negri [RO] 23 Za 16
Δ Costa de la Luz [E] 25 B 21
Δ Costa del Sol [E] 25 C 22
Δ Costa Dorada [E] 27 J 20
Costa Levantina [E] 27 K 20
Δ Costa Verde [E] 24 D 17
Costeşti [RO] 23 Za 17
Coştuleni [RO] 23 Za 15
Coswig [DDR] 15 Q 13
Δ Côte d'Argent [F] 18 G 18
Δ Côte d'Azur [F] 20 N 19
Δ Cotentin [F] 13 H 14
Côte-Saint-André, la — [F] 19 M 17
Cotmeana, Mănăstire — [RO] 23 Z 17
Δ Cotswold Hills [GB] 13 H 13
Cottbus [DDR] 16 S 13
Δ Coubre, Pointe de la — [F] 18 H 17
Couches [F] 19 M 16
Couço [P] 25 B 20
Coucy-le-Château-Auffrique [F] 14 L 14
Couëron [F] 18 H 16
Couhé [F] 19 J 16
Couilly-Pont-aux-Dames [F] 14 L 15
Couiza [F] 19 K 19
Coulommiers [F] 14 L 15
Coupar Angus [GB] 11 H 10
Couronne, la — [F] 19 J 17
Cours [F] 19 L 17
Coursan [F] 19 K 18
Courseulles-sur-Mer [F] 14 J 14
Courson-les-Carrières [F] 19 L 16
Courtenay [F] 19 L 15
Courtine, la — [F] 19 K 17
Courville-sur-Eure [F] 14 K 15
Coutances [F] 13 H 15
Couvin [B] 14 M 14
Coux-et-Bigaroque [F] 19 J 17
Covadonga [E] 24 E 18
Covasna [RO] 23 Z 16
Coventry [GB] 13 J 12
Covilhã [P] 25 C 19
Cowes [GB] 13 H 13
Δ Cozie, Alpi — [F] 20 N 18
Craieşti [RO] 23 Za 16
Craigavon [GB] 10 F 11
Craigellachie [GB] 11 J 9
Crailheim [D] 15 P 15
Craiova [RO] 22 Y 17
Craon [F] 18 H 15
Craponne-sur-Arzon [F] 19 L 17
Crasna [RO] 23 Za 16
≈ Crasna [RO] 22 X 15
Δ Crasna, Munţii — [RO] 22 X 16
Crathie [GB] 11 H 9
Crato [P] 25 B 20
Δ Crau [F] 19 M 18
Crediton [GB] 12 G 13
Creeslough [IRL] 10 F 10
Creil [F] 14 L 15
Crema [I] 20 P 17
Cremona [I] 20 P 17
Crepaja [YU] 22 W 17
Crépy-en-Valois [F] 14 L 15
Cres [YU] 21 S 17
Δ Cres [YU] 21 S 18
Crest [F] 19 M 18
Δ Creus, Cabo — [E] 27 K 19
≈ Creuse [F] 18 J 16
Creusot, le — [F] 19 M 16
Crevedia Mare [RO] 23 Z 17
Crevillente [E] 26 G 21
Crewe [GB] 13 H 12
Crewkerne [GB] 13 H 13
Crianlarich [GB] 11 H 10
Criccieth [GB] 12 G 12
Crieff [GB] 11 H 10
Crikvenica [YU] 21 S 17
Crimmitşchau [DDR] 15 Q 14
Δ Crişana [RO] 22 X 16
Cristuru Secuiesc [RO] 23 Z 16
≈ Crişul Alb [RO] 22 X 16
Crivitz [DDR] 15 Q 12
≈ Crna gora [YU] 22 X 19
Δ Crna Gora [YU] 22 V 19
≈ Crna reka [YU] 30 X 19
Crna Rijeka [YU] 21 U 18
Crna Trava [YU] 22 X 18
Črnimelj [YU] 21 S 17
Δ Croisette, Cap — [F] 19 M 19
Croisic, le — [F] 18 G 16
Croisière, la — [F] 19 K 16
Croix-de-Vie [F] 18 G 16
Croixille, la — [F] 13 H 15
Cromer [GB] 13 K 12
Crook [GB] 11 S 11
Crotone [I] 29 U 21
Crotoy, le — [F] 14 K 14
Croydon [GB] 13 J 13
Crozon [F] 12 F 15
Crucea [R] 23 Zb 17
Δ Crvanj [YU] 22 V 18
Δ Cserhát [H] 22 V 15
Csongrád [H] 22 V 18
Csorna [H] 21 U 16
Csorvás [H] 22 W 16
Cuarte de Huerva [E] 26 G 19
Cuba [P] 25 B 21
Δ Cucalón, Sierra de — [E] 26 G 20
Cudillero [E] 24 D 18
≈ Čudskoje ozero [SU] 8 X 8
Cuenca [E] 26 F 20
Δ Cuenca, Serrania de — [E] 26 F 20
≈ Cuerda del Pozo, Pandano — [E] 26 F 19
Cuétlar [E] 26 E 19
Cuevas de Almudén [E] 26 G 20
Cuevas del Almanzora [E] 26 F 22
Cuevas de Vinromá [E] 26 H 20
Cùglieri [I] 28 O 21
Cuisery [F] 19 M 16
Cujmir [RO] 22 Y 17
Culan [F] 19 R 8
Δ Culebra, Sierra de la — [E] 24 D 19
Culemborg [NL] 14 M 13
Cúllar de Baza [E] 26 F 22
Cullera [E] 26 H 21
Δ Cullin Hills [GB] 10 G 9
≈ Cullin Sound [GB] 10 G 9
Cullompton [GB] 12 G 13
Cúl Mhuine = Collooney [IRL] 10 E 11
Culoz [F] 19 M 17
Δ Cumberland [GB] 11 H 11
Δ Cumbrian Mountains [GB] 11 H 11
Cumnock [GB] 11 H 10
Cúneo [I] 20 N 18
Δ Cunillera, Isla — [E] 27 J 21
Cunlhat [F] 19 F 17
Δ Čuokkarašša [N] 3 U 1
Çupar [GB] 11 H 10
Ćuprija [YU] 22 X 18
Cure, la — [CH] 20 N 16
Curtea de Arges [RO] 23 Z 17
Cushendall [GB] 10 G 10
Cusset [F] 19 L 17
Cutro [I] 29 U 21
Cuvilly [F] 14 L 14
Cuxhaven [D] 15 O 12
Czaplinek [PL] 16 S 12
Czarlin [PL] 7 U 11
Czarnków [PL] 16 T 12
Δ Czerehát [H] 17 W 15
Czersk [PL] 16 T 12
Δ Czerwony Bór [PL] 17 W 12
Częstochowa [PL] 16 U 14
Człopa [PL] 16 S 12
Czyżewo [PL] 17 W 12

D

Dąbie [PL] 16 U 13
Dąbrowa [PL] 8 W 11
Dăbuleni [RO] 23 Z 18
Dachau [D] 20 Q 15
Δ Dachstein [A] 21 R 16
Dačice [CS] 16 S 15
Dad [H] 21 U 16
Dädesjö [S] 7 S 10
Dagali [N] 4 O 8
Dagda [SU] 8 Y 10
Dahme [D] 6 Q 12
Daia [RO] 23 Za 17
Daimiel [E] 26 E 21
Dajkanvik [S] 5 S 4
Dala-Järna [S] 5 R 7
≈ Dalälven [S] 5 S 7
Δ Dalarna [S] 5 R 7
Dalarö [S] 7 T 8
Dalasjö [S] 5 S 5
Dalbeattie [GB] 11 H 11
Δ Dalbosjön [S] 6 Q 9
Dalby [S] 4 Q 7
Dalby [S] 7 R 11
Dale [N] 4 N 7
Dale [N] 6 O 9
Dalfors [S] 5 R 7
Dalj [YU] 22 V 17
Dalkeith [GB] 11 H 10
Dallías [E] 26 E 22
Δ Dalmacija [YU] 21 T 18
Dalmally [GB] 10 G 10
Dalmellington [GB] 11 H 10
Δ Dal'n'aja, gora — [SU] 3 X 1
Dalry [GB] 10 G 10
Dalsbruck [SF] 9 V 7
≈ Dalsfjord [N] 4 N 7
Dalshögen [S] 6 Q 8
Δ Dalsland [S] 6 Q 9
Δ Dalsnibba [N] 4 O 6
Dalton-in-Furness [GB] 11 H 11
Δ Daluis, Gorges de — [F] 20 N 18
Dalwhinnie [GB] 11 H 9
Damuc [RO] 23 Z 16
Dancharia [F] 18 G 18
Dăneasa [RO] 23 Z 17
Danilovgrad [YU] 22 V 19
Dannenberg (Elbe) [D] 15 Q 12
Danzig = Gdańsk [PL] 17 U 11
≈ Dão, Rio — [P] 25 B 19
Daoulas [F] 12 F 15
Daras [GR] 30 Y 22
Dardhë [AL] 30 X 20
Δ Dardon, Mont — [F] 19 L 16
Darfo [I] 20 P 17
Darlington [GB] 11 J 11
Darłowo [PL] 7 S 11
Darmstadt [D] 15 O 14
Darney [F] 20 N 15
Daroca [E] 26 G 20
Darque [P] 24 B 18
Δ Darß [DDR] 6 Q 11
Δ Darßer Ort [DDR] 6 Q 11
Δ Dartmoore Forrest [GB] 12 G 13
Dartmouth [GB] 12 G 14
Dartowo [PL] 7 S 11
Δ Dartuch, Cabo — [E] 27 L 21
Darú = Durrow [IRL] 12 E 12
Daruvar [YU] 21 U 17
Dasburg [D] 15 N 14
≈ Dăsnăţuiu [RO] 22 Y 17
Dassow [DDR] 15 Q 12
D'atlovo [SU] 8 X 11
Daudzeva [SU] 8 X 10
Daugailiai [SU] 8 X 10
≈ Daugava [SU] 8 X 10
Daugavpils [SU] 8 Y 10
Δ Dauphiné [F] 19 M 17
Daventry [GB] 13 J 12
Davos [CH] 20 P 16
Dax [F] 18 H 18
Deal [GB] 13 K 13
Δ Dealului, Munţii — [RO] 22 X 16
Δ Dearg, Beinn — [GB] 11 H 9
Deauville [F] 14 J 14
Debăr [BG] 23 Za 19
Debar [YU] 30 W 19
Dębica [PL] 17 W 14
Dęblin [PL] 17 W 13
Debrc [YU] 22 W 17
Debrecen [H] 22 W 15
Debrzno [PL] 16 T 12
Dęby [PL] 17 V 12
Dečani [YU] 22 W 19
Decazeville [F] 19 K 18
Děčín [CS] 16 S 13
Decize [F] 19 L 16
≈ Dee, River — [GB] 11 J 9
≈ Dee, River — [GB] 13 H 12
≈ Degebe, Ribeira de — [P] 25 B 21
≈ Degerfjärden [S] 5 T 5
Degerfors [S] 7 R 8
Degerselet [S] 3 U 4
Deggendorf [D] 16 R 15
Degučiai [SU] 8 X 10
Deinze [B] 14 L 14
Dej [RO] 22 Y 16
Δ Dejës, Mali i — [AL] 30 W 19
Delary [S] 7 R 10
Del'atin [SU] 17 Y 15
Delčevo [YU] 30 Y 19
Delémont [CH] 20 N 16
≈ Delet [SF] 9 U 7
Delfi [GR] 30 Y 21
Delfzijl [NL] 15 N 12
Deliblato [YU] 22 W 17
Deliblatska peščara [YU] 22 W 17
Delitzsch [DDR] 15 Q 13
Delle [F] 20 N 16
Delmenhorst [D] 15 O 12
Delnice [YU] 21 S 17
Delos [GR] 31 Zb 21
Delsbo [S] 5 S 7
Delvinakion [GR] 30 X 20
Delvinë [AL] 30 W 20
Demir Kapija [YU] 30 Y 19
Demirköy [TR] 23 Zb 18
Demmin [DDR] 16 R 12
Δ Demoiselles, Grotte des — [F] 19 L 18
Demonte [I] 20 N 18
Denain [F] 14 L 14
Denbigh [GB] 13 H 12
Dendermonde [B] 14 M 13
Denia [E] 26 H 21
Derby [GB] 13 J 12
Derecske [H] 22 W 16
≈ Derg, Lough — [IRL] 10 E 11
Dermanci [BG] 23 Z 18
Derval [F] 18 H 15
Derveni [GR] 30 Y 21
Derventa [YU] 21 U 17
Desenzano del Garda [I] 20 P 17
Deskati [GR] 30 X 20
Δ Despeñaperros, Puerto de — [E] 26 E 21
Δ Despotiko [GR] 31 Za 22
Despotovac [YU] 22 X 18
Dessau [DDR] 15 Q 13
Deta [RO] 22 W 17
Detmold [D] 15 O 13
Deurne [NL] 15 N 13
≈ Deutsche Bucht6 N 11
Deutsch Krone = Wałcz [PL] 16 T 12
Deutschlandsberg [A] 21 S 16
Deva [E] 18 G 18
Deva [RO] 22 X 16
Deventer [NL] 15 N 13
Δ Devět skal [CS] 16 T 14
Devin [BG] 23 Z 19
Devín [CS] 21 T 15
Devizes [GB] 13 H 13
≈ Devoll [AL] 30 W 20
Δ Devoluy [F] 19 M 18
Δ Devon [GB] 12 G 13
Dezzo di Scalve [I] 20 P 17
Δ Dia [GR] 32 Zb 23
Δ Diabła Góra [PL] 17 V 13
Diakopton [GR] 30 Y 21
Δ Diaporii, Nissi — [GR] 31 Z 21
Diavata [GR] 30 Y 20
≈ Diavlos Oreon [GR] 30 Y 21
≈ Diavlos Thassou [GR] 31 Z 19
Dicomano [I] 20 Q 18
Didim [TR] 31 Zc 21
Δ Didimon Oros [GR] 31 Z 22
Didimotichon [GR] 31 Zb 19
Didyma [TR] 31 Zc 21
Die [F] 19 M 18
Diekirch [L] 15 N 14
≈ Diemel [D] 15 O 13
Diepholz [D] 15 O 13
Dieppe [F] 14 K 14
Dießen am Ammersee [D] 20 Q 16
Diest [B] 14 M 14
Dieulefit [F] 19 M 18
Dieuze [F] 15 N 15
Digne [F] 20 N 18
Digoin [F] 19 L 16
Dijon [F] 19 M 16
Dikanäs [S] 5 R 4
Dikili [TR] 31 Zb 20
Diksmuide [B] 14 L 13
Δ Dikti Oros [GR] 32 Zb 23
Δ Dilij [YU] 21 U 17
Dillenburg [D] 15 O 14
Dillingen an der Donau [D] 15 P 15
≈ Dimbovita [RO] 23 Z 17
Dimitrovgrad [BG] 23 Za 19
Dimitrovgrad [YU] 22 Y 18
Dimovo [BG] 22 Y 18
Dinan [F] 13 H 15
Dinant [B] 14 M 14
Δ Dinara [YU] 21 T 18
Δ Dinara [YU] 21 T 18
Dinard [F] 13 H 15
Dinas-Mawddwy [GB] 12 G 12
Dingle [IRL] 12 D 12
≈ Dingle Bay [IRL] 12 D 12
Dingli [M] 30 V 22
Dingolfing [D] 16 R 15
Dingwall [GB] 11 H 9
Dinkelsbühl [D] 15 P 15
Dipotama [GR] 31 Z 19
Disentis [CH] 20 O 16
Diss [GB] 13 K 13
Ditrău [RO] 23 Z 16
Dives-sur-Mer [F] 14 J 14
≈ Dividal [N] 2 S 2
Divin [SU] 17 X 12
Divion [F] 14 L 14
≈ Divor, Rio — [P] 25 B 20
Δ Divunia [GR] 31 Zc 22
Djakovia [YU] 22 W 19
Djakovo [YU] 22 V 17
Djedeida [TN] 28 P 22
Δ Djerdap [YU] 22 X 17
Δ Djulica [YU] 22 X 18
Djurakovac [YU] 22 W 19
Djuramåla [S] 7 S 10
Djurås [S] 5 R 7
Djurdjevac [YU] 21 U 17
Djursholm [S] 7 T 8
Δ Djursland [DK] 6 P 10
≈ Dnestr [SU] 17 Y 14
Dnestrovsk [SU] 23 Zc 15
≈ Dnestrovskij Liman [SU] 23 Zc 15
Dobbiaco [I] 20 Q 16
Dobele [SU] 8 W 10
Döbeln [DDR] 16 R 14
Dobersberg [A] 21 S 15
Dobiegniew [PL] 16 S 12
Doboj [YU] 21 U 17
Dobra [YU] 22 X 17
≈ Dobra [YU] 21 T 17
Dobre Miasto [PL] 8 V 11
Dobreta Turnu Severin [RO] 22 X 17
Dobřís [CS] 16 S 14
Dobrodzień [PL] 16 U 14
Δ Dobrogea [BG, R] 23 Zb 17
Dobroslavka [SU] 17 Y 12
Dobrovolsk [SU] 8 W 11
Dobruči [SU] 8 Y 8
Dobrzyń nad Wisłą [PL] 16 U 12
Doctor Petru Groza [RO] 22 X 16
≈ Dödafjallet [S] 5 S 6
Doetinchem [NL] 15 N 13
Dogliani [I] 20 O 18
≈ Doïranis, Limni — [GR] 30 Y 19
Dokka [N] 4 P 7
≈ Dokka [N] 4 P 7
Dokkas [S] 2 T 3
Dokkum [NL] 15 N 12
Δ Dokos [GR] 31 Z 22
Doksy [CS] 16 S 14
Dölbach [D] 15 P 14
Dol-de-Bretagne [F] 13 H 15
Dôle [F] 19 M 16
Dolen Bliznak [BG] 23 Zb 18
Δ Dolenjski [YU] 21 S 17
Δ Dolent, Mont — [CH, I] 20 N 17
Dolga [SU] 17 X 15
Dolgellan [GB] 12 G 12
Dolina [SU] 17 X 14
Dolna Dikan'a [BG] 22 Y 19
Dolní Dvořiště [CS] 16 S 15
Dolní Kralovice [CS] 16 S 14
Dolni Lom [BG] 22 Y 18
Dolní Žd'ar [CS] 16 R 14
Dolný Kubín [CS] 17 V 15
Δ Dolomiti [I] 20 Q 17
Δ Dom [CH] 20 O 17
Domaradz [PL] 17 W 14
Δ Domaşnea, Poarta — [RO] 22 X 17
Domažlice [CS] 16 R 15
Dombås [N] 4 P 6
Δ Dombes [F] 19 M 17
Dombóvár [H] 21 U 16
Dombrád [H] 17 W 15
Domburg [NL] 14 L 13
Δ Dôme, Puy de — [F] 19 L 17
Domfront [F] 14 J 15
Dömitz [DDR] 15 Q 12
Domme [F] 19 J 17
Domneşti [RO] 23 Z 17
Domodossola [I] 20 O 17
Domokos [GR] 30 Y 21
Dompierre-sur-Besbre [F] 19 L 16

Domrémy-la-Pucelle [F] 14 M 15
Domsjö [S] 5 T 6
Domžale [YU] 21 S 17
≈ Don, River — [GB] 11 J 9
Donaghadee [GB] 10 G 11
Δ Doñana, Coto de — [E] 25 C 22
Δ Donard, Slieve — [GB] 10 G 11
≈ Donau [D] 16 R 15
Donaueschingen [D] 20 O 16
Donauwörth [D] 15 Q 15
Don Benito [E] 25 C 20
Doncaster [GB] 13 J 12
Donegal [IRL] 10 E 10
≈ Donegal Bay [IRL] 10 E 10
Donji Miholjac [YU] 21 U 17
Donji Milanovac [YU] 22 X 17
Donji Vakuf [YU] 21 U 18
Donjon, le — [F] 19 L 16
Δ Dønna [N] 2 Q 4
Dønnes [N] 2 Q 4
Δ Donoussa [GR] 31 Zb 22
Donzenac [F] 19 K 17
Donzère [F] 19 M 18
Donzy [F] 19 L 16
≈ Dora Bâltea [I] 20 O 17
≈ Dora Ripària [I] 20 N 17
Dorat, le — [F] 19 J 16
Dorchester [GB] 13 H 13
Dordives [F] 19 L 15
≈ Dordogne [F] 18 H 17
Dordrecht [NL] 14 M 13
≈ Dore [F] 19 L 17
Δ Dore, Mont — [F] 19 K 17
Dores [GB] 11 H 9
Dorgali [I] 28 P 20
Dorking [GB] 13 J 13
Dormans [F] 14 L 15
Dornbirn [A] 20 P 16
Dornecy [F] 19 L 16
Dornoch [GB] 11 H 9
≈ Dornoch Firth [GB] 11 H 9
Dorog [H] 21 U 15
Dorotea [S] 5 S 5
Dorpat = Tartu [SU] 8 X 8
Dorsten [D] 15 N 13
Dortmund [D] 15 O 13
≈ Dortmund-Ems-Kanal [D] 15 O 13
Dos Hermanas [E] 25 C 21
Dospat [BG] 31 Z 19
≈ Dosse [DDR] 15 Q 12
Douai [F] 14 L 14
Douarnenez [F] 12 F 15
Δ Double [F] 19 J 17
≈ Doubs [F] 19 M 16
Douchy [F] 19 L 15
Doudeville [F] 14 K 14
Doué-la-Fontaine [F] 19 J 16
Douglas [GB] 10 G 11
Douglas Mill [GB] 11 H 10
Doullens [F] 14 L 14
Dourdan [F] 14 K 15
≈ Douro, Rio — [P] 25 C 19
Δ Douro Litoral [P] 25 B 19
≈ Douze [F] 18 H 18
Douzy [F] 14 M 14
Dover [GB] 13 K 13
≈ Dover, Strait of — 13 K 13
Δ Dovrefjell [N] 4 P 6
Downham Market [GB] 13 K 12
Downpatrick [GB] 10 G 11
Doxaton [GR] 31 Z 19
Δ Drach, Cuevas del — [E] 27 K 21
Drachten [NL] 15 N 12
Dračvo [YU] 30 X 19
Dragalina [RO] 23 Za 17
≈ Dragan [S] 5 R 5
Drăgăneşti Vlaşca [RO] 23 Z 17
Drăgăşani [RO] 22 Y 17
Dragnes [N] 2 R 2
Dragodol [YU] 30 X 19
Dragomireşti [RO] 23 Za 16
Δ Dragonada [GR] 32 Zc 23
Δ Dragonera, Isla — [E] 27 J 21
Δ Dragonission [GR] 31 Zb 21
Dragsfjärd [SF] 9 V 7
Draguignan [F] 20 N 18
Drăguşeni [RO] 23 Z 15
Δ Drahanská vrchovina [CS] 16 T 14
Drama [GR] 31 Z 19
Drammen [N] 4 P 8
Drängsmark [S] 5 T 4
Dr'anovo [BG] 23 Za 18
≈ Drau [A] 21 R 16
≈ Drava [YU] 22 V 17
Dravograd [YU] 21 S 16
≈ Drawko, Jezioro — [PL] 16 S 12
Drawno [PL] 16 S 12
Drawsko Pomorskie [PL] 16 S 12
Drążdżewo [PL] 17 V 12
Δ Drejø [DK] 6 P 11
Δ Dren [YU] 30 X 19
Δ Drepanon, Akrotirion — [GR] 31 Z 20
Dresden [DDR] 16 R 14
Dreux [F] 14 K 15
Drevsjø [N] 4 Q 7
Drezdenko [PL] 16 S 12
≈ Drin [AL] 30 W 19
≈ Drina [YU] 22 V 17
Δ Drina kanjon [YU] 22 V 18
≈ Drinit, Gjiri i — [AL] 30 W 19
Drniš [YU] 21 T 18
Drøbak [N] 6 P 8
Drobin [PL] 17 V 12
Drogheda [IRL] 10 F 11
Drogičin [SU] 17 Y 12
Drogobyč [SU] 17 X 14
Droichead Atha = Drogheda [IRL] 10 F 11
Droichead na Bandan = Bandon [IRL] 12 D 12
≈ Drôme [F] 19 M 18
Dronero [I] 20 N 18
≈ Dronne [F] 18 H 17
≈ Dropt [F] 19 J 17
Δ Dropull [AL] 30 W 20
Drottningholm [S] 7 T 8
Drov'anoje [SU] 3 X 1
Druja [SU] 8 Y 10
Drumevo [BG] 23 Zb 18
Drummore [GB] 10 G 11
Drumnadrochit [GB] 11 H 9
Δ Drumochter, Pass of — [GB] 11 H 9
Družba [BG] 23 Zb 18
Družba [SU] 8 V 11
Drvar [YU] 21 T 18
Drvenik [YU] 21 U 18
Drymen [GB] 11 H 10
Duas Igreias [P] 25 D 19
Dubica [YU] 21 U 17
Dublin [IRL] 10 F 11
Dubno [SU] 17 Y 13
Dubovac [YU] 21 U 17
Dubovoje [SU] 17 Y 15
Dubrovnik [YU] 22 V 19
Duderstadt [D] 15 P 13
Dueñas [E] 26 E 19
Δ Dueodde [DK] 7 S 11
≈ Duero, Rio — [E] 25 F 19
Dufftown [GB] 11 J 9
Duga Poljana [YU] 22 W 18
Δ Dugi Otok [YU] 21 S 18
Duisburg [D] 15 N 13
Dukštas [SU] 8 Y 10
Dülmen [D] 15 N 13
Δ Dumba [N] 4 N 7
Dumbarton [GB] 11 H 10
Δ Ďumbier [CS] 17 V 15
Dumfries [GB] 11 H 11
≈ Dümmer [D] 15 O 13
≈ Duna [H] 22 V 16
Dunaalmás [H] 21 U 16
Dunaföldvár [H] 22 V 16
≈ Dunaj [CS] 21 U 15
≈ Dunajec [PL] 17 V 14
Dunajská Streda [CS] 21 U 15
Dunakeszi [H] 22 V 16
Dú na nGall = Donegal [IRL] 10 E 10
≈ Dunărea [RO] 22 X 17
≈ Dunărea [RO] 23 Zb 17
≈ Dunărea Veche [RO] 23 Zb 17
Δ Dunării, Cîmpia — [RO] 22 Y 17
Δ Dunării, Delta — [RO] 23 Zc 16
Dunaújváros [H] 22 V 16
≈ Dunav [BG] 23 Za 17
≈ Dunav [YU] 22 V 17
Dunavci [BG] 22 Y 18
Dunbar [GB] 11 J 10
Dunblane [GB] 11 H 10
Δ Duncansby Head [GB] 11 J 8
Dundaga [YU] 8 V 9
Dundalk [IRL] 10 F 11
Dún Dealgan = Dundalk [IRL] 10 F 11
Dundee [GB] 11 H 10
Δ Dundret [S] 2 T 3
Dunfermline [GB] 11 H 10
Dungannon [GB] 10 F 11
Dún Garbháin = Dungarvan [IRL] 12 E 12
Dungarvan [IRL] 12 E 12
Δ Dungeness [GB] 13 K 13
Dungiven [GB] 10 F 10
Dungloe [IRL] 10 E 10
Dunilovići [SU] 8 Y 10
Dunkeld [GB] 11 H 10
Δ Dunkelsteiner Wald [A] 21 S 15
Dunkerque [F] 14 L 13
Dún Laoghaire = Kingstown [IRL] 10 F 11
Dun—le—Palestel [F] 19 K 16
Dunluce Castle [GB] 10 F 10
Δ Dunnet Head [GB] 11 J 8
Dunnottar Castle [GB] 11 J 9
Dunoon [GB] 10 G 10
Dunrobin Castle [GB] 11 H 9
Duns [GB] 11 J 10
Dunstable [GB] 13 J 13
Dun-sur-Auron [F] 19 K 16
Dun-sur-Meuse [F] 14 M 15
Dunte [SU] 8 W 9
Dunvegan Castle [GB] 10 G 9
≈ Durance [F] 19 M 18
Durango [E] 18 F 18
Duras [F] 19 J 17
Durazzo = Durrës [AL] 30 W 20
Dúrcal [E] 26 E 22
Düren [D] 15 N 14
Durham [GB] 11 J 11
Δ Durmitor [YU] 22 V 18
Durness [GB] 11 H 8
Durrës [AL] 30 W 20
Durrow [IRL] 12 E 12
Δ Dursey Head [IRL] 12 D 12
Durtal [F] 19 J 15
≈ Dusios ezeras [SU] 8 W 11
Düsseldorf [D] 15 N 13
Duved [S] 4 Q 6
Duvno [YU] 21 U 18
Dvor [YU] 21 T 17
Dybvad [DK] 6 P 10
≈ Dyje [CS] 16 T 15
Δ Dylewska Gora [PL] 16 U 12
Dynów [PL] 17 W 14
Dyrnesvågen [N] 4 O 6
Δ Dyrøy [N] 2 S 2
Działdowo [PL] 17 V 12
Dzierzgoń [PL] 7 U 12
Dźwierzuty [PL] 8 V 12

E

Éadan Doire = Edenderry [IRL] 10 F 11
Eani [GR] 30 Y 20
Easingwold [GB] 11 J 11
Δ East Anglian Heights [GB] 13 J 13
Eastbourne [GB] 13 J 13
East Dereham [GB] 13 K 12
East Grinstead [GB] 13 J 13
East Retford [GB] 13 J 12
Eauze [F] 18 H 18
Ebeleben [DDR] 15 P 13
Ebeltoft [DK] 6 P 10
Eberbach [D] 15 O 15
Eberndorf [A] 21 S 16
Ebersbach [DDR] 16 S 14
Eberstein [A] 21 S 16
Eberswalde [DDR] 16 R 12
Eboli [I] 29 T 20
≈ Ebro, Pantano del — [E] 18 F 18
≈ Ebro, Rio — [E] 26 H 19
Δ Ebro, Delta del — [E] 27 J 20
Δ Ebrucorr, gora — [SU] 3 X 2
Δ Ebručorr, gora — [SU] 3 X 2
Ebstorf [D] 15 P 12
Eceabat [TR] 31 Zb 20
Echarri — Aranaz [E] 18 G 18
Δ Echinades Nissi [GR] 30 X 21
Echinos [GR] 31 Za 19
Echt [GB] 11 J 9
Echternach [L] 15 N 14
Ecija [E] 25 D 21
Eckartsberga [DDR] 15 Q 14
Eckernförde [D] 6 P 11
Eckerö [SF] 5 T 7
Δ Eckerö [SF] 5 T 7
Écommoy [F] 19 J 15
Δ Ecrins [F] 20 N 17
Ed [S] 5 S 6
Ed [S] 6 Q 8
Edam [NL] 14 M 13
Ede [NL] 15 N 13
Edefors [S] 2 T 4
Edenderry [IRL] 10 F 11
Edessa [GR] 30 Y 20
Edgeworthstown = Mostrim [IRL] 10 F 11
Edinburgh [GB] 11 H 10
Edirne [TR] 23 Zb 19
Edolo [I] 20 P 17
≈ Edøyfjord [N] 4 O 6
Edremit [TR] 31 Zb 20
≈ Edremit körfezi [TR] 31 Zb 20
Edsbro [S] 5 T 8
Edsbruck [S] 7 S 9
Edsbyn [S] 5 S 7
Edsele [S] 5 S 6
Eeklo [B] 14 L 13
Eferding [A] 21 S 15
≈ Efjord [N] 2 R 2
Eforie Nord [RO] 23 Zb 17
Eforie Sud [RO] 23 Zb 17
Efpalion [GR] 30 Y 21
Δ Egadi, Isole — [I] 29 R 22
Egea de los Caballeros [E] 26 G 19
Egeln [DDR] 15 Q 13
Eger [H] 22 V 15
Egersund [N] 6 N 9
Egeskov [DK] 6 P 11
Eggenburg [A] 21 T 15
Eggenfelden [D] 21 R 15
Eghina [GR] 31 Z 21
Δ Eghina [GR] 31 Z 21
Eghinion [GR] 30 Y 20
Eghion [GR] 30 Y 21
Egiertowo [PL] 7 T 11
Egletons [F] 19 K 17
Egremont [GB] 11 H 11
Egtved [DK] 6 P 11
Ehingen (Donau) [D] 20 P 15
Eibar [E] 18 G 18
Eichstätt [D] 15 Q 15
Eidanger [N] 6 P 8
Eide [N] 4 O 6
≈ Eider [D] 6 P 11
Eidfjord [N] 4 O 8
≈ Eidfjord [N] 4 O 7
Eidskog [N] 4 Q 8
Eidstå [N] 6 O 8
Eidsvåg [N] 4 O 6
Eidsvoll [N] 4 Q 8
Δ Eifel [D] 15 N 14
Δ Eigg [GB] 10 G 9
Eilenburg [DDR] 16 R 13
Eina [N] 4 P 7
Einbeck [D] 15 P 13
Eindhoven [NL] 14 M 13
Einöd [D] 15 N 15
Einsiedeln [CH] 20 O 16
Eisenach [DDR] 15 P 14
Eisenberg [DDR] 15 Q 14
Eisenhüttenstadt [DDR] 16 S 13
Eisenstadt [A] 21 T 16
Eisfeld [DDR] 15 Q 14
Eisleben [DDR] 15 Q 13
Ekenäs [SF] 9 V 7
Δ Eknö [S] 7 S 9
Ekolsund [S] 5 T 8
Ekshärad [S] 5 R 8
Eksjö [S] 7 S 9
Δ Elafonissos [GR] 31 Z 22
Elasson [GR] 30 Y 20
Elatia [GR] 30 Y 21
Δ Elba, Isola d' — [I] 28 P 19
Elbasan [AL] 30 W 20
≈ Elbe [D, DDR] 15 Q 13
≈ Elbe — Havel — Kanal [DDR] 15 Q 13
Elbeuf [F] 14 K 14
Elbing = Elbląg [PL] 7 U 11
Elbląg [PL] 7 U 11
Elche [E] 26 G 21
Elche de la Sierra [E] 26 F 21
Elda [E] 26 G 21
≈ Elde [DDR] 15 Q 12
Elefsis [GR] 31 Z 21
Eleftheroupolis [GR] 31 Z 19
Eleja [SU] 8 W 10
Elek [H] 22 W 16
Elena [BG] 23 Za 18
Elgå [N] 4 Q 6
Δ Elgåhogna [N] 4 Q 6
Δ Elgepiggen [N] 4 Q 6
Elgin [GB] 11 J 9
Elgol [GB] 10 G 9
Δ Elgoras, gora — [SU] 3 X 2
Elhovo [BG] 23 Zb 18
Elie [GB] 11 J 10
Elika [GR] 31 Z 22
Elimäki [SF] 9 W 7
Elizondo [E] 18 G 18
Ełk [PL] 8 W 11
Elkefjord [N] 4 N 7
Ellecom [NL] 15 N 13
Ellingen [D] 15 Q 15
Ellon [GB] 11 J 9
Ellwangen (Jagst) [D] 15 P 15
Elmshorn [D] 15 P 12
Elmsta [S] 5 T 8
Elne [F] 19 K 19
Elsfjord [N] 2 Q 4
≈ Elster [DDR] 15 Q 14
Elsterwerda [DDR] 16 R 13
Elvas [P] 25 C 20
Elven [F] 18 G 15
Elverum [N] 4 Q 7
Ely [GB] 13 K 12
Elz [D] 15 O 14
Emådalen [S] 5 R 7
≈ Emajõgi [SU] 8 X 8
≈ Emån [S] 7 S 9
Embouchure-de-l'Aude, l' — [F] 19 K 18
Embrun [F] 20 N 18
Emden [D] 15 O 12
Δ Emine, nos — [BG] 23 Zb 18
Emlichheim [D] 15 N 13
Emmaboda [S] 7 S 10
Emmaste [SU] 8 V 8
Emmeloord [NL] 15 N 12
Emmen [NL] 15 N 12
Emmerich [D] 15 N 13
Empoli [I] 20 Q 18
Emponas [GR] 32 Zd 22
≈ Ems [D] 15 O 13
Δ Emsalö [SF] 9 W 7
Δ Emsland [D] 15 N 13
Enånger [S] 5 S 7
Enare = Inari [SF] 3 V 2
≈ Enare = Inari [SF] 3 V 2
Encinasola [E] 25 C 21
Encs [H] 17 W 15
Δ Endelave [DK] 6 P 11
Enden [N] 4 P 7
Δ Enderrocat, Cabo — [E] 27 K 21
Enez [TR] 31 Za 19
Enfesta [E] 24 C 18
Engelberg [CH] 20 O 16
Engelhartszell [A] 21 R 15
Δ Engeløy [N] 2 R 3
Engen [D] 20 O 16
Engerdalsætra [N] 4 Q 7
≈ Engeren [N] 4 Q 7
Engerneset [N] 4 Q 7
Δ England [GB] 11 J 11, J 12
≈ English Channel 12 G 14
Enkhuizen [NL] 14 M 12
Δ Enklinge [SF] 9 U 7
Enköping [S] 5 S 8
Enna [I] 29 S 22
Ennis [IRL] 10 E 12
Enniscorthy [IRL] 12 F 12
Enniskillen [GB] 10 F 11
Ennistimon [IRL] 10 D 11
Enns [A] 21 S 15
≈ Enns [A] 21 S 16
Δ Enø [DK] 6 Q 11
Enonkoski [SF] 9 X 6
Enontekiö [SF] 3 U 2
Enschede [NL] 15 N 13
Δ Entinas, Punta de las — [E] 26 E 22
Entrains-sur-Nohain [F] 19 L 16
Entraygues-sur-Truyère [F] 19 K 18
≈ Entrepeñas, Pantano de — [E] 26 F 20
Entrevaux [F] 20 N 18
Entroncamento [P] 25 B 20
≈ Enz [D] 15 O 15
Enzlar [D] 15 P 14
≈ Eo, Rio — [E] 24 D 18
Eochaill = Youghal [IRL] 12 E 12
Epanomi [GR] 30 Y 20
Epe [NL] 15 N 13
Épernay [F] 14 L 15
Ephesos [TR] 31 Zc 21
Epidavros [GR] 31 Z 22
Épinal [F] 20 N 15
Episkopi [GR] 32 Za 23
Eppan = Appiano [I] 20 Q 17
Δ Eraklia [GR] 31 Zb 22
Eratini [GR] 30 Y 21
Erba [I] 20 P 17
Erbalunga [F] 28 P 19
Ercolano [I] 29 S 20
Ercsi [H] 22 V 16
Érd [H] 22 V 16
Erdek [TR] 31 Zc 19
≈ Erdek körfezi [TR] 31 Zb 19
Erding [D] 20 Q 15
≈ Erei, Monti — [I] 29 S 22
Δ Erfjället [S] 5 R 5
≈ Erft [D] 15 N 14
Erfurt [DDR] 15 Q 14
≈ Ergene nehri [TR] 23 Zb 19
≈ Erges, Rio — [P] 25 C 20
Ergli [SU] 8 X 9
≈ Eria, Rio — [E] 24 D 18
Ericeira [P] 25 A 20
Eriksmåla [S] 7 S 10
Δ Erimanthos Oros [GR] 30 Y 21
Eringsboda [S] 7 S 10
Erithre [GR] 31 Z 21
Erize-la-Petite [F] 14 M 15
≈ Erken [S] 5 T 8
Erlangen [D] 15 Q 15
Erlsbach [A] 21 R 16
Ermelo [NL] 15 N 13
Ermidas [P] 25 A 21
Ermioni [GR] 31 Z 22
Ermoupolis [GR] 31 Za 21
≈ Erne, Lower Lough — [GB] 10 F 11
Ernée [F] 13 H 15
Ernei [RO] 22 Y 16
Ernstbrunn [A] 21 T 15
Erquelinnes [B] 14 M 14
Δ Errigal Mount [IRL] 10 F 10
Δ Erris Head [IRL] 10 D 10
Erro [E] 18 G 18
Ersekë [AL] 30 X 20
Ersfjordbotn [N] 2 S 2
Δ Ertvågøy [N] 4 O 6
Erwitte [D] 15 O 13
Δ Erzgebirge [CS, DDR] 16 R 14
Eržvilkas [SU] 8 W 10
Esbjerg [DK] 6 O 11
Escala, La— [E] 27 K 19
Escalada [E] 18 F 18
Escalaplano [I] 28 P 21
Δ Escaliers, les — [F] 18 H 18
Escalona [E] 26 E 20
Δ Escandorgue, l' — [F] 19 K 18
Esch [D] 15 O 14
Escholzmatt [CH] 20 O 16
Esch-sur-Alzette [L] 15 N 14
Eschwege [D] 15 P 13
≈ Ésera, Rio — [E] 26 H 19
Esgos [E] 24 C 18
≈ Esgueva, Rio — [E] 26 E 19
≈ Ésino [I] 21 R 18
Eskiçine [TR] 32 Zd 21
Eskilstuna [S] 7 S 8
≈ Esla, Canal de — [E] 24 D 19
≈ Esla, Pantano del — [E] 25 D 19
≈ Esla, Rio — [E] 24 E 18
Δ Espadán [E] 26 H 20
Espalion [F] 19 K 18
Δ Espalmador, Isla del — [E] 27 J 21
Δ Espardell, Isla del — [E] 27 J 21
Esparraguera [E] 27 J 19
Espejo [E] 25 D 21
Espelkamp [D] 15 O 13
Espiel [E] 25 D 21
Espinho [P] 25 B 19
Espinosa de los Monteros [E] 18 F 18
Espluga de Francolí [E] 27 J 20
Δ Espochel, Cabo de — [P] 25 A 20
Espoo [SF] 9 W 7
Esposende [P] 24 B 19
Δ Espuña, Sierra de — [E] 26 F 22
Esrange [S] 2 T 3
Essen [D] 15 N 13
Essen (Oldenburg) [D] 15 O 12
Essimi [GR] 31 Za 19
Esslingen am Neckar [D] 15 P 15
Δ Estaca de Vares, Punta de la — [E] 24 C 17
Estagel [F] 19 K 19
Δ Estales, Ilhas — [P] 25 A 20
Estarreja [P] 25 B 19
Δ Estats, Pico d' — [E,F] 27 J 19
Este [I] 20 Q 17
Estella [E] 18 G 18
≈ Estena, Rio — [E] 25 D 20
Estepa [E] 25 D 22
Estépar [E] 18 E 19
Estepona [E] 25 D 22
Δ Estérel [F] 20 N 18
Esternay [F] 14 L 15
Esterri de Aneo [E] 27 J 19
Estivella [E] 26 H 20
Estoi [P] 25 B 21
Δ Estonskaja SSR [SU] 8 W 8
Estoril [P] 25 A 20
Estrada, La — [E] 24 B 18
Δ Estrela, Serra da — [P] 25 B 19
Δ Estrella [E] 26 E 21
Δ Estremadura [E] 25 C 21
Δ Estremadura [P] 25 A 20
Estremoz [P] 25 B 20
Esztergom [H] 21 U 15
Étain [F] 14 M 15
Étampes [F] 14 K 15
Étaples [F] 14 K 14
Δ Etna, Monte — [I] 29 T 22
Etnesjøen [N] 4 N 8
Etolikon [GR] 30 X 21
Étretat [F] 14 J 14
Etropole [BG] 23 Z 18
Ettelbruck [L] 15 N 14
Ettlingen [D] 15 O 15
Eu [F] 14 K 14
Δ Euboea = Evvia [GR] 31 Z 21
Δ Euganei [I] 20 Q 17
Δ Eugmo [SF] 9 U 5
Eupen [B] 15 N 14
Eura [SF] 9 U 7
Eurajoki [SF] 9 U 7
≈ Eurajoki [SF] 9 U 7
Δ Europa, Picos de — [E] 24 E 18
Δ Europa, Punta de — [GB] 25 C 22
Europoort [NL] 14 M 13
Euskirchen [D] 15 N 14
Eutin [D] 6 P 12
Eutzsch [DDR] 16 R 13
Evanger [N] 4 N 7
Évaux-les-Bains [F] 19 K 17
Evertsberg [S] 5 R 7
Evesham [GB] 13 H 13
Évian-les-Bains [F] 20 N 17
Evijärvi [SF] 9 V 5
Evisa [F] 28 O 19
Evje [N] 6 O 9
Évora [P] 25 B 20
Évreux [F] 14 K 15
Évron [F] 14 J 15
≈ Evrotas [GR] 31 Z 22
Δ Evvia [GR] 31 Z 21
≈ Evvoikos Kolpos [GR] 31 Z 21
Evzoni [GR] 30 Y 19
Exaplatanos [GR] 30 Y 20
Excideuil [F] 19 J 17
Exeter [GB] 12 G 13
Δ Exmoor Forest [GB] 12 G 13
Exmouth [GB] 12 G 13
Exochi [GR] 31 Z 19
Eygurande [F] 19 K 17
Eymet [F] 19 J 17
Eymoutiers [F] 19 K 17
Eyzies-de-Tayac-Sireuil, les — [F] 19 J 17
Ezere [SU] 8 V 10
Ezernieki [SU] 8 Y 10
Ezine [TR] 31 Zb 20

F

Fåberg [N] 4 O 7
Fåberg [N] 4 P 7
Fåborg [DK] 6 P 11
Fabriano [I] 21 R 19
Faenza [I] 20 Q 18
Făgăraş [RO] 23 Z 16
Δ Făgăraş, Munţii — [RO] 22 Y 16
Fågelsjö [S] 5 R 7
Fagernes [N] 2 S 2
Fagernes [N] 4 P 7
Fagersta [S] 5 S 8
Făget [RO] 22 X 16
Δ Făget, Munţii — [RO] 22 X 15
≈ Fahijska reka [BG] 23 Zb 18
Faing = Foynes [IRL] 12 D 12
Fairlie [GB] 10 G 10
Fakenham [GB] 13 K 12
Fakse [DK] 6 Q 11
≈ Fakse Bugt [DK] 6 Q 11
Falaise [F] 14 J 15
Falconara Marittima [I] 21 R 18
Falerna [I] 29 U 21
Falkenau = Sokolov [CS] 16 R 14
Falkenberg [S] 6 Q 10
Falkensee [DDR] 16 R 13
Falkirk [GB] 11 H 10
Δ Falkonera [GR] 32 Za 22
Falköping [S] 7 R 9
Fällfors [S] 2 T 4
Falmouth [GB] 12 F 14
Falset [E] 27 J 20
Δ Falster [DK] 6 Q 11
Falsterbo [S] 7 R 11
Δ Falterona, Monte — [I] 20 Q 18
Fălticeni [RO] 23 Z 15
Δ Faludden [S] 7 T 10
Falun [S] 5 S 7
Δ Fångö [S] 7 S 9
Fano [I] 21 R 18
Δ Fanø [DK] 6 O 11
Faouët, le — [F] 12 G 15
Δ Fărcăul [RO] 17 Y 15
≈ Fardes, Rio — [E] 26 E 22
Fareham [GB] 13 J 13
Δ Farihões, Ilhas — [P] 25 A 20
Faringdon [GB] 13 H 13
Färjestaden [S] 7 S 10
Δ Farmakonission [GR] 31 Zc 21
Farnham [GB] 13 J 13
Faro [P] 25 B 21
Δ Faro, Sierra del — [E] 24 C 18
Δ Faro, Punta del — [I] 29 T 22
Δ Fårön [S] 7 U 9
Fårösund [S] 7 T 9
Farsala [GR] 30 Y 21
Farsø [DK] 6 P 10
Farsund [N] 6 N 9
Fasano [I] 29 U 20
Fátima [P] 25 B 20
Fättjaur [S] 5 R 4
Δ Fau, Col du — [F] 19 M 17
Δ Faucilles, Monts — [F] 19 M 16
Făurei [RO] 23 Za 16
Fauske [N] 2 R 3
Faverges [F] 20 N 17
Faversham [GB] 13 K 13
Δ Favignana, Isola — [I] 29 R 22
≈ Faxälven [S] 5 S 6
Fayl-Billot [F] 19 M 16
Fécamp [F] 14 J 14
≈ Fedjefjord [N] 4 N 7
Fegen [S] 7 R 10
≈ Fegen [S] 7 R 10
Δ Fehmarn [D] 6 Q 11
≈ Fehmarnbelt [D,DK] 6 Q 11
≈ Fehmarnsund [D] 6 Q 11
Feira [P] 25 B 19
Δ Fejø [DK] 6 Q 11
Felanitx [E] 27 K 21
Feldbach [A] 21 T 16
Δ Feldberg [D] 20 O 16
Feldkirch [A] 20 P 16
Feldkirchen in Kärnten [A] 21 S 16
Felixstowe [GB] 13 K 13
Felletin [F] 19 K 17
Felnac [RO] 22 W 16
Felnémet [H] 17 V 15
Feltre [I] 20 Q 17
≈ Femund [N] 4 Q 6
Fenestrelle [I] 20 N 17
Fénétrange [F] 15 N 15
Δ Fengari [GR] 31 Za 20
Δ Feno, Cap de — [F] 28 O 19
Δ Fenouillèdes [F] 19 K 19
≈ Fensfjord [N] 4 N 7
Feolin Ferry [GB] 10 G 10
≈ Feragen [N] 4 Q 6
Fère, la — [F] 14 L 14
Fère-Champenoise [F] 14 L 15
Δ Feredeu, Obcina — [RO] 23 Z 15
Fère-en-Tardenois [F] 14 L 15
≈ Feren [N] 4 Q 6
Ferentino [I] 29 R 20
Ferlach [A] 21 S 16
Fermo [I] 21 S 19
Fermoselle [E] 25 D 19
Fermoy [IRL] 12 E 12
Fernán-Núñez [E] 25 D 21
Ferrals-les-Corbières [F] 19 K 18
Ferrara [I] 20 Q 18
Ferreira de Zêzere [P] 25 B 20
Ferreira do Alentejo [P] 25 B 21
Ferreras, Acueducto de las — [E] 27 J 20
Ferrerías [E] 27 L 21
Δ Ferret, Cap — [F] 18 H 17
Ferrol del Caudillo, El — [E] 24 C 17
Ferté-Alais, la — [F] 14 K 15
Ferté-Bernard, la — [F] 14 J 15
Ferté-Macé, la — [F] 14 J 15
Ferté-Milon, la — [F] 14 L 15
Ferté-Saint-Aubin [F] 19 K 16
Ferté-sous-Jouarre, la — [F] 14 L 15
Fertőszentmiklós [H] 21 T 16
Festos [GR] 32 Zb 23
Feteşti [RO] 23 Zb 17
Feuchtwangen [D] 15 P 15
Feuille, la — [F] 14 K 14
Feurs [F] 19 L 17
Δ Fichtelgebirge [D] 15 Q 14
Fidenza [I] 20 P 18
Fieberbrunn [A] 21 R 16
Fier [AL] 30 W 20
Fiera di Primiero [I] 20 Q 17
Fiesch [CH] 20 O 17
Δ Fife Ness [GB] 11 J 10
Figeac [F] 19 K 18
Figeholm [S] 7 S 9
Figline Valdarno [I] 20 Q 18
Figueira da Foz [P] 25 B 19
Figueiras [E] 27 K 19
Figueró dos Vinhos [P] 25 B 20
Δ Filabres, Sierra de los — [E] 26 E 22
Filey [GB] 11 K 11
Δ Filfla [M] 30 V 22
Filiaşi [RO] 22 Y 17
Filiatra [GR] 30 Y 22
Δ Filicudi, Isola — [I] 29 S 21
Filipovo [BG] 31 Z 19
Filippias [GR] 30 X 21
Filipstad [S] 5 R 8
Filotion [GR] 31 Zb 22
Filx [E] 26 H 20
Δ Fimena [GR] 31 Zb 21
Fimo [I] 29 U 21
Finale Ligure [I] 20 O 18
Findrol [F] 20 N 17
Fines [N] 4 P 5
Finisterre [E] 24 B 18
Δ Finisterre, Cabo de — [E] 24 B 18
≈ Finland, Gulf of — 9 W 7
Δ Finnkneet [N] 2 Q 4
Δ Finnmarksvidda [N] 3 U 2
Δ Finnö [S] 7 S 9
Δ Finnøy [N] 6 N 8
Finnskog [N] 4 Q 7
Δ Finnskogene [N,S] 4 Q 7
Finnsnes [N] 2 S 2
Δ Finnvelden [S] 7 R 10
Δ Finnvollhei [N] 4 P 5

Finspång [S] 7 S 9
Δ Finsteraarhorn [CH] 20 O 16
Finsterwalde [DDR] 16 R 13
Fionphort [GB] 10 G 10
Fiorenzuola d'Arda [I] 20 P 18
Firenze [I] 20 Q 18
Firenzuola [I] 20 Q 18
Fîrliug [RO] 22 X 17
Fir Maighe = Fermoy [IRL] 12 E 12
Firminy [F] 19 L 17
Δ Fischbacher Alpen [A] 21 S 16
Fishguard u. Goodwick [GB] 12 G 12
Fiskardon [GR] 39 X 21
Fismes [F] 14 L 15
Fitjar [N] 4 N 8
Fiume = Rejeka [YU] 21 S 17
Fivizzano [I] 20 P 18
Fjæra [N] 4 N 8
≈ Fjærlandsfjord [N] 4 O 7
Δ FjällfjällenS [S] 5 R 4
Fjällnäs [S] 4 Q 6
≈ Fjällsjöälven [S] 5 S 5
Δ Fjärdhundra [S] 5 S 8
Fjellbu [N] 2 S 3
Fjerreslev [DK] 6 P 10
Flå [N] 4 P 8
Δ Flakstadøy [N] 2 Q 3
Δ Flamborough Head [GB] 11 K 11
Δ Fläming [DDR] 15 Q 13
Δ Flandre [F] 13 L 14
Δ Flannan Isles [GB] 10 G 8
≈ Fläsjön [S] 5 R 5
Flatow = Złotów [PL] 16 T 12
Δ Flattind [N] 3 V 1
Flèche, la — [F] 19 J 15
Fleetwood [GB] 11 H 11
Flekkefjord [N] 6 N 9
Flen [S] 7 S 8
Flensburg [D] 6 P 11
≈ Flensburger Förde [D] 6 P 11
Flensungen [D] 15 O 14
Flers [F] 14 J 15
Flesberg [N] 4 P 8
Flesnes [N] 2 R 2
Fleurance [F] 19 J 18
Fleuré [F] 19 J 16
Flirey [F] 15 N 15
Flisa [N] 4 Q 7
Flora [N] 4 N 7
Florac [F] 19 L 18
Florenville [B] 14 M 14
Florìdia [I] 29 T 22
Florina [GR] 30 X 20
Flötningen [S] 4 Q 7
Fluberg [N] 4 P 7
≈ Fluvia, Rio — [E] 27 K 19
Flyinge [S] 7 R 11
Foça [TR] 31 Zb 21
Foča [YU] 22 V 18
Fochabers [GB] 11 J 9
Focşani [RO] 23 Za 16
Δ Fogdön [S] 7 S 8
Fòggia [I] 29 T 20
Fohnsdorf [A] 21 S 16
Δ Föhr [D] 6 O 11
Δ Foia [P] 25 A 21
Foix [F] 19 J 19
≈ Folda [N] 2 R 3
Foldereid [N] 4 Q 5
Folegandros [GR] 31 Za 22
Δ Folegandros [GR] 31 Za 22
Δ Folgefonni [N] 4 N 8
Foligno [I] 21 R 19
Folkestad [N] 4 N 6
Folkestadbyen [N] 6 O 8
Folkestone [GB] 13 K 13
≈ Folla [N] 4 P 6
Follafoss [N] 4 Q 5
Folldalsverk [N] 4 P 6
Föllinge [S] 5 R 5
Follònica [I] 20 Q 19
Folteşti [RO] 23 Zb 16
Fondi [I] 29 R 20
Fonfria [E] 25 D 19
Δ Fongen [N] 4 Q 6
Fonni [I] 28 P 21
Fonsagrada [E] 24 D 18
Fontainebleau [F] 14 L 15
Fontenay [F] 19 M 16
Fontenay-le-Comte [F] 18 H 16
Fonteny-Trésigny [F] 14 L 15
Fontevrault [F] 19 J 16
Fonyód [H] 21 U 16
≈ Fora [N] 4 P 6
Forcalquier [F] 19 M 18
Forchheim [D] 15 Q 14
Ford [GB] 10 G 10
Førde [N] 4 N 7
≈ Førdefjord [N] 4 N 7
Fordon [PL] 16 U 12
Δ Forelhogna [N] 4 P 6
Δ Forez, Monts du — [F] 19 L 17
Forfar [GB] 11 J 10
Forges-les-Eaux [F] 14 K 14
Forlì [I] 20 Q 18
Formazza [I] 20 O 17
Δ Formentera [E] 27 J 21
Δ Formentor, Cabo — [E] 27 K 21
Fòrmia [I] 29 S 20
Formigine [I] 20 Q 18
Formofoss [N] 4 Q 5
Δ Fornæs [DK] 6 Q 10
Fornos de Algodres [P] 25 C 19
Fornovo di Taro [I] 20 P 18
Forres [GB] 11 H 9
Forså [N] 2 R 2
Forsby [SF] 9 W 7
Forshaga [S] 7 R 8
Forsnäs [S] 2 S 4
Forsnes [N] 4 O 6
Forssa [SF] 9 V 7
Forst/Lausitz [DDR] 16 S 13
Fort Augustus [GB] 11 H 9
≈ Forth, Firth of — [GB] 11 H 10
Fortun [N] 4 O 7
Fortuna [E] 26 G 21
Fort William [GB] 11 H 9
Forvik [N] 2 Q 4
Fos [F] 19 J 19
Δ Fosna [N] 4 P 5
Fossano [I] 20 O 18
Fosse [B] 14 M 14
Fossombrone [I] 21 R 18
Fos-sur-Mer [F] 19 M 18
Fougères [F] 13 H 15
Fountains Abbey [GB] 11 J 11
Δ Fourni [GR] 31 Zb 21
≈ Fournou-Stenon [GR] 31 Zb 21
Fousseret, le — [F] 19 J 18
Foustani [GR] 30 Y 19
Fowey [GB] 12 F 13
≈ Foxen [S] 6 Q 8
≈ Foyle, Lought — [GB] 10 F 10
Foynes [IRL] 12 D 12
Foz [E] 24 C 17
Fræna [N] 4 O 6
Fraga [E] 26 H 19
Francardo [F] 28 O 19
Francavilla al Mare [I] 29 S 19
Francavilla Fontana [I] 29 U 20
Δ Franche Comté [F] 19 M 16
Franco, El — [E] 24 D 18
Francofonte [I] 29 T 22
Frankeklint [DK] 6 Q 11
Δ Franken [D] 15 P 14
Frankenberg (Eder) [D] 15 O 14
Frankfurt am Main [D] 15 O 14
Frankfurt/Oder [DDR] 16 S 13
Δ Fränkische Alb [D] 15 Q 15
Frankrikeg [S] 5 R 5
Fränsta [S] 5 S 6
Franzburg [DDR] 7 R 12
Frascati [I] 29 R 19
Fraserburgh [GB] 11 J 9
Frasne [F] 20 N 16
Frauenfeld [CH] 20 O 16
Frayssinet-le-Gélat [F] 19 J 17
Frechen [D] 15 N 14
Fredericia [DK] 6 P 11
Frederiksberg [S] 5 R 8
Frederikshavn [DK] 6 P 9
Frederikssund [DK] 6 Q 10
Frederiksværk [DK] 6 Q 10
Fredrika [S] 5 T 5
Fredrikshamn = Hamina [SF] 9 X 7
Fredrikstad [N] 6 Q 8
Fregenal de la Sierra [E] 25 C 21
Fregene [I] 29 R 19
Δ Fréhel, Cap — [F] 13 H 15
Δ Frei [N] 4 O 6
Freiberg [DDR] 16 R 14
Freiburg = Fribourg [CH] 20 N 16
Freiburg im Breisgau [D] 20 O 16
Freihung [D] 15 Q 14
Freiland [A] 21 S 15
Freilassing [D] 21 R 16
Freising [D] 20 Q 15
Freistadt [A] 21 S 15
Freital [DDR] 16 R 14
Fréjus [F] 20 N 18
Frenštát pod Radhoštěm [CS] 16 U 14
Freshwater [GB] 13 H 13
Δ Fresvikbre [N] 4 O 7
Fréteval [F] 19 K 15
Δ Freu, Cabo del — [E] 27 K 21
Freudenstadt [D] 15 O 15
Frévant [F] 14 L 14
Freyburg/Unstrut [DDR] 15 Q 13
Fri [GR] 31 Zc 22
Fribourg [CH] 20 N 16
Fridhem [S] 7 S 9
Friedberg (Hessen) [D] 15 O 14
Friedland [DDR] 16 R 12
Friedrichshafen [D] 20 P 16
Friedrichstadt [D] 6 P 11
Friesoythe [D] 15 O 12
Friggesund [S] 5 S 6
Frihetsli [N] 2 S 2
Fritzlar [D] 15 P 14
Friuli [I] 21 R 17
Frohnleiten [A] 21 S 16
Frome [GB] 13 H 13
Frómista [E] 24 E 19
Fronteira [P] 25 B 20
Frontenhausen [D] 16 R 15
Frontignan [F] 19 L 18
Frosinone [I] 29 R 20
Frøskeland [N] 2 R 2
Froso [S] 5 R 6
Frosta [N] 4 P 6
Δ Frostisen [N] 2 S 2
≈ Frostviken [S] 5 R 5
Δ Frøya [N] 4 N 7
Δ Frøya [N] 4 O 5
Δ Frøyningsfjell [N] 4 Q 5
Frumoasa [RO] 23 Z 16
Δ Fruška gora [YU] 22 V 17
Frutigen [CH] 20 O 16
Frýdek-Místek [CS] 16 U 14
Frýdlant [CS] 16 S 14
Fucécchio [I] 20 Q 18
Fuencaliente [E] 25 D 21
Fuengirola [E] 25 D 22
≈ Fuensanta, Pantano de la — [E] 26 F 21
Fuente de Cantos [E] 25 C 21
Fuente de San Esteban, La — [E] 25 D 19
Fuente el Fresno [E] 26 E 20
Fuente Ovejuna [E] 25 D 21
Fuentes de Ebro [E] 26 H 19
Fuentes de Jiloca [E] 26 G 19
Fuentes de Oñora [E] 25 C 19
Δ Fugløy [N] 2 Q 3
Δ Fugløy [N] 2 S 1
Fulda [D] 15 P 14
≈ Fulda [D] 15 P 14
Fulnek [CS] 16 U 14
Δ Fulufjället [S] 4 Q 7
Fulunäs [S] 4 Q 7
Fumel [F] 19 J 18
Funäsdalen [S] 4 Q 6
Fundão [P] 25 C 20
Fundulea [RO] 23 Za 17
Furculeşti [RO] 23 Z 17
Δ Furkapass [CH] 20 O 16
Furstenau [D] 15 O 13
Fürstenberg/Havel [DDR] 16 R 12
Fürstenfeld [A] 21 T 16
Fürstenfeldbruck [D] 20 Q 15
Fürstenwalde/Spree [DDR] 16 R 13
Fürstenzell [D] 16 R 15
Fürth [D] 15 Q 15
Furudal [S] 5 R 7
Furusund [S] 5 T 8
Furuvik [S] 5 S 7
Fusa [N] 4 N 8
Fushë-Muhur [AL] 30 W 19
Fusio [CH] 20 O 17
Füssen [D] 20 P 16
Δ Futa, La — [I] 20 Q 18
Δ Fyn [DK] 6 P 11
Δ Fyns Hoved [DK] 6 P 11
≈ Fyresvatn [N] 6 O 8

G

Gabia la Grande [E] 26 E 22
≈ Gabriel y Galán, Pantano de — [E] 25 D 20
Gabrovo [BG] 23 Z 18
Gacé [F] 14 J 15
Gäddede [S] 5 R 5
Gadebusch [DDR] 15 Q 12
Gádor [E] 26 F 22
Δ Gádor, Sierra de — [E] 26 E 22
Gaël [F] 13 H 15
Găeşti [RO] 23 Z 17
Gaeta [I] 29 S 20
≈ Gaeta, Golfo di — [I] 29 R 20
Gagliano del Capo [I] 30 V 21
Gailac [F] 19 K 18
Gaildorf [D] 15 P 15
Gaillimh = Galway [IRL] 10 E 11
Gaillon [F] 14 K 15
Δ Gailtaler Alpen [A] 21 R 16
Gainsborough [GB] 13 J 12
Gairloch [GB] 10 G 9
Δ Gaizina Kalns [SU] 8 X 9
Galanta [CS] 16 U 15
Galashiels [GB] 11 H 10
Galatas [GR] 31 Z 22
Galati [RO] 23 Zb 16
Galatina [I] 30 V 20
Galatista [GR] 31 Z 20
Galàtone [I] 30 V 20
Δ Galatzó [E] 27 K 21
Galaxidion [GR] 30 Y 21
Δ Galdhøppigen [N] 4 O 7
Galera [E] 26 F 22
Δ Galibier, Col du — [F] 20 N 17
Galič [SU] 17 Y 14
Galicea Mare [RO] 22 Y 17
Δ Galicia [E] 24 B 18
Δ Galicja [PL] 17 V 14
Δ Galite, Iles de la — [TN] 28 O 22
Gallarate [I] 20 O 17
≈ Gállego, Rio — [E] 26 H 19
Galliate [I] 20 O 17
≈ Gallikos [GR] 30 Y 20
Gallipoli [I] 30 V 20
Gallipoli = Gelibolu [TR] 31 Zb 19
Gällivare [S] 2 T 3
Gällö [S] 5 R 6
≈ Gallo, Rio — [E] 26 G 20
Δ Galloway [GB] 10 G 11
Δ Galloway, Mull of — [GB] 10 G 11
Δ Gallura [I] 28 O 20
Gálvez [E] 26 E 20
Galway [IRL] 10 E 11
≈ Galway Bay [IRL] 10 D 11
Gambatesa [I] 29 T 20
Gamlakarleby = Kokkola [SF] 9 U 5
Gamleby [S] 7 S 9
Gammelstad [S] 3 U 4
Gamvik [N] 3 V 1
Gancevići [SU] 17 Y 12
Gandesa [E] 26 H 20
Gandia [E] 26 H 21
Gandvik [N] 3 V 1
Ganges [F] 19 L 18
Gangi [I] 29 S 22
Gannat [F] 19 L 17
Gänserndorf [A] 21 T 15
Gaoth Dobhair = Gweedore [IRL] 10 F 10
Gap [F] 19 M 18
≈ Garcia Sola, Pantano de — [E] 25 D 20
Gard, Pont du — [F] 19 L 18
≈ Gard [F] 19 L 18
Garda [I] 20 Q 17
≈ Garda, Lago di — [I] 20 P 17
Gardanne [F] 19 M 18
Garde, la — [F] 18 H 17
Gardelegen [DDR] 15 Q 13
Δ Gardfjället [S] 2 R 4
Gardikion [GR] 30 X 20
Gardikion [GR] 30 Y 21
Gardone Riviera [I] 20 P 17
Gärdsjö [S] 5 R 7
Gårdsjö [S] 7 R 8
Garelochhead [GB] 10 G 10
Gargaliani [GR] 30 Y 22
Δ Gargalo, Ile — [F] 28 O 19
Δ Gargano [I] 29 T 19
Δ Gargano, Testa del — [I] 29 T 19
Gargejaure [S] 2 S 4
Gargia [N] 3 U 1
Gargnano [I] 20 Q 17
Gargnäs [S] 2 S 4
Garlasco [I] 20 O 17
Garmisch-Partenkirchen [D] 20 Q 16
≈ Garonne [F] 18 H 17
Garray [E] 26 F 19
Δ Garrigues [F] 19 L 18
Garrucha [E] 26 F 22
≈ Garsjø [N] 3 V 1
Garvān [RO] 23 Zb 16
Garve [GB] 11 H 9
Garwolin [PL] 17 W 13
Garždai [SU] 8 V 10
≈ Gascogne, Golfe de — [F] 18 F 17
Δ Gascogne [F] 18 H 18
Gastouni [GR] 30 X 22
Δ Gastrikland [S] 5 S 7
Gata [E] 25 C 20
Δ Gata, Cabo de — [E] 26 F 22
Δ Gata, Sierra de — [E] 25 C 20
Δ Gata, Sierra de — [E] 26 F 22
Gătaia [RO] 22 W 17
Gateshead [GB] 11 J 11
Δ Gâtinais [F] 19 K 15
Δ Gâtine, Hauteurs de — [F] 18 H 16
Gattendorf [A] 21 T 15
Gaucín [E] 25 C 22
≈ Gauja [SU] 8 W 9
≈ Gaula [N] 4 Q 6
Δ Gauldal [N] 4 P 6
≈ Gaulfoss [N] 4 P 6
Gaupne [N] 4 O 7
≈ Gausa [N] 4 P 7
Δ Gausta [N] 4 O 8
Gausvik [N] 2 R 2
≈ Gautan [S] 2 R 4
Gavalou [GR] 30 Y 21
Δ Gavarnie, Cirque de — [F] 18 H 19
Δ Gavdopoula [GR] 32 Za 23
Gavdos [GR] 32 Za 23
Gavião [P] 25 B 20
Gävle [S] 5 S 7
≈ Gävlebukten [S] 5 S 7
Gavri [SU] 8 Y 9
Gavrion [GR] 31 Za 21
Gävunda [S] 5 R 7
Gdańsk [PL] 7 U 11
≈ Gdańska, Zatoka — [PL] 7 U 11
Gdov [SU] 8 Y 8
Gdynia [PL] 7 U 11
≈ Gediz nehri [TR] 31 Zc 20
Gedser [DK] 6 Q 1
Δ Gedser Odde [DK] 6 Q 11
Geesthacht [D] 15 P 12
Geilenkirchen [D] 15 N 14
Geilo [N] 4 O 7
Geiranger [N] 4 O 6
Geisingen [D] 20 O 16
Geislingen an der Steige [D] 15 P 15
Gela [I] 29 S 22
≈ Gela, Golfo di — [I] 29 S 22
Geldern [D] 15 N 13
Gelibolu [TR] 31 Zb 19
Gelsdorf [D] 15 N 14
Gelsenkirchen [D] 15 N 13
Gelting [D] 6 P 11
Gembloux [B] 14 M 14
Gemona del Friuli [I] 21 R 17
Gençay [F] 19 J 16
≈ Generalísimo, Pantano del — [E] 26 G 20
General Nikolaevo [BG] 23 Z 18
General Toševo [BG] 23 Zb 17
Genève [CH] 20 N 17
≈ Genil, Rio — [E] 25 D 21
Genk [B] 14 M 14
Genlis [F] 19 M 16
Gennep [NL] 15 N 13
Gènova [I] 20 O 18
≈ Gènova, Golfo di — [I] 20 O 18
Gent [B] 14 L 13
Genthin [DDR] 15 Q 13
Gera [DDR] 15 Q 14
Geraardsbergen [B] 14 L 14
Gérardmer [F] 20 N 15
Δ Gerecse [H] 21 U 16
Δ Gerez, Serra do — [P] 24 B 18
Δ Gerlachovka [CS] 17 V 14
Δ Germandön [S] 3 U 4
Germanoviči [SU] 8 Y 10
Germencik [TR] 31 Zc 21
Gerona [E] 27 K 19
≈ Gers [F] 19 J 18
Gersfeld [D] 15 P 14
Gersthofen [D] 15 Q 15
Geseke [D] 15 O 13
Gesunda [S] 5 R 7
≈ Gesunden [S] 5 S 6
Geta [SF] 9 U 7
Getafe [E] 26 E 20
Δ Getic, Podisul — [RO] 22 Y 17
Gevgelija [YU] 30 Y 19
Gex [F] 20 N 17
Ghar el Melh [TN] 28 P 22
Ghefira [GR] 30 Y 20
Ghennadion [GR] 32 Zd 22
Gheorghe-Gheorghiu-Dej [RO] 23 Za 16
Gheorghieni [RO] 23 Z 16
Gheorghitsion [GR] 30 Y 22
Gherakini [GR] 31 Z 21
Gherakion [GR] 31 Z 22
Δ Gherghiu, Munţii — [RO] 23 Z 15
Gherla [RO] 22 Y 16
Gherolimin [GR] 31 Z 22
Ghiannitsa [GR] 30 Y 20
Δ Ghiaros [GR] 31 Za 21
Δ Ghioura [GR] 31 Z 20
Ghisonaccia [F] 28 P 19
Ghisoni [F] 28 P 19
Δ Giali [GR] 31 Zc 22
Δ Giannutri, Isola di — [I] 28 Q 19
Δ Giant's Causeway [GB] 10 F 10
Giarre [I] 29 T 22
Giat [F] 19 K 17
Giba [I] 28 O 21
Gibellina [I] 29 R 22
Gibostad [N] 2 S 2
Gibraleón [E] 25 B 21
Gibraltar [GB] 25 C 22
≈ Gibraltar, Estrecho de — 25 C 22
Gideå [S] 5 T 5
Giedraičiai [SU] 8 X 10
Gien [F] 19 K 16
Giens [F] 19 M 19
Giera [RO] 22 W 17
Gießen [D] 15 O 14
Gieten [NL] 15 N 12
Gifhorn [D] 15 P 13
Gigen [BG] 23 Z 18
Δ Gigha [GB] 10 G 10
Δ Giglio, Isola del — [I] 28 Q 19
Gignac [F] 19 L 18
Gijón [E] 24 E 18
Gilău [RO] 22 X 16
Gildeskål [N] 2 R 3
Δ Giljeva [YU] 22 W 18
Gillberga [S] 6 Q 8
Gilleleje [DK] 6 Q 10
Gillhovs kapell [S] 5 R 6
Gillingham [GB] 13 K 13
Gillisnuole [S] 2 S 4
Gimo [S] 5 T 8
Gimont [F] 19 J 18
Δ Gimsøy [N] 2 R 3
Gineta, La — [E] 26 F 21
Ginosa [I] 29 U 20
Ginzo de Limia [E] 24 C 18
≈ Giòia, Golfo di — [I] 29 T 21
Giòia del Colle [I] 29 U 20
Giòia Tàuro [I] 29 T 22
Δ Giona Oros [GR] 30 Y 21
Giornico [CH] 20 O 17
Δ Giovi, Passo dei — [I] 20 O 18
Gipka [SU] 8 V 9
Δ Girjastjåkko [S] 2 R 4
Gîrlau [RO] 22 Y 15
≈ Gironde [F] 18 H 17
Gironella [E] 27 J 19
≈ Girou [F] 19 J 18
Girov [RO] 23 Z 15
Girvan [GB] 10 G 10
≈ Girvas [SU] 3 W 2
Gislaved [S] 7 R 10
Gisors [F] 14 K 15
Githion [GR] 31 Z 22
Giulianova [I] 21 S 19
Δ Giùlie, Alpi — [I, YU] 21 R 17
Giurgeni [RO] 23 Zb 17
Giurgiu [RO] 23 Za 17
Give [DK] 6 P 10
Givors [F] 19 M 17
Givry-en-Argonne [F] 14 M 15
Giżycko [PL] 8 V 11
Δ Gjalicës, Mali i — [AL] 30 W 19
Δ Gjeitfjell [N] 4 Q 5
Gjemnes [N] 4 O 6
Gjesvær [N] 3 U 1
≈ Gjevilvatn [N] 4 P 6
Gjirokastër [AL] 30 W 20
Gjøra [N] 4 P 6
Gjøvik [N] 4 P 7
Δ Gjuhës, Kep i — [AL] 30 W 20
Gladsakse [DK] 6 Q 11
Gladstad [N] 2 Q 4
Glamis Castle [GB] 11 J 10
Glamoč [YU] 21 U 18
Δ Glamočko polje [YU] 21 U 18
Glåmos [N] 4 Q 6
≈ Glan [D] 15 O 14
Δ Glarner Alpen [CH] 20 O 16
Glarus [CH] 20 O 16
Glasgow [GB] 11 H 10
Glastonbury [GB] 13 H 13
Glatz = Kłodzko [PL] 16 T 14
Glauchau [DDR] 16 R 14
Glavan' [SU] 23 Zb 16
≈ Glavsfjorden [S] 6 Q 8
Gleisdorf [A] 21 T 16
Gleiwitz = Gliwice [PL] 16 U 14
Glenarm [GB] 10 G 10
Glenfinnan [GB] 10 G 9
Glenties [IRL] 10 E 10
Glifada [GR] 31 Z 21
Glina [YU] 21 T 17
≈ Glina [YU] 21 T 17
Glinojeck [PL] 17 V 12
Δ Glittertind [N] 4 O 7
Gliwice [PL] 16 U 14
Gloggnitz [A] 21 T 16
Głogów [PL] 16 T 13
Głogówek [PL] 16 U 14
Glomfjord [N] 2 R 3
Glomma [N] 6 Q 7
Glommersträsk [S] 2 T 4
Glossop [GB] 13 J 12
Gloucester [GB] 13 H 13
Głowno [PL] 17 V 13
Głubczyce [PL] 16 U 14
Glückstadt [D] 15 P 12
Glyngøre [DK] 6 O 10
Gmajn Tuffiema [M] 30 V 22
Gmarb [M] 30 V 22
Gmünd [A] 21 R 16
Gmünd [A] 21 S 15
Gmunden [A] 21 R 16
Gnarp [S] 5 S 6
Gniechowice [PL] 16 T 13
Gniew [PL] 7 U 12
Gniezno [PL] 16 T 12
Gnjilane [YU] 22 X 19
Gnoien [DDR] 16 R 12
Goce Delčev [BG] 31 Z 19
Goch [D] 15 N 13
Δ Godeanu, Vîrful — [RO] 22 X 17
Goderville [F] 14 J 14
Godętowo [PL] 7 T 11
Gödöllő [H] 22 V 16
Godziszewo [PL] 7 U 11
Δ Goeree [NL] 14 M 13
Goes [NL] 14 M 13
Göhren [DDR] 7 R 11
Góis [P] 25 B 19
Gojan [AL] 30 W 19
Gol [N] 4 P 7
Golčův Jeníkov [CS] 16 S 14
Gołdap [PL] 8 W 11
Goldberg [DDR] 15 Q 12
Δ Golden Vale [IRL] 12 E 12
Δ Golema planina [BG] 22 Y 18
Golemo Konare [BG] 23 Z 19
Golemo Selo [YU] 22 X 18
Goleniów [PL] 16 S 12
Δ Goleš [YU] 22 V 18
Golfo Aranci [I] 28 P 20
Δ Golija [YU] 22 V 18
Δ Golija [YU] 22 W 18
Golina [PL] 16 U 13
Golling an der Salzach [A] 21 R 16
Gölmarmara [TR] 31 Zc 20
≈ Golo [F] 28 P 19
Goloby [SU] 17 Y 13
Gol'šany [SU] 8 Y 11
Golspie [GB] 11 H 9
Golßen [DDR] 16 R 13
Golubac [YU] 22 X 17
Goma Or'ahovica [BG] 23 Za 18
Δ Gondo [CH] 20 O 17
Gönen [TR] 31 Zc 20
Gonni [GR] 30 Y 20
Gönyü [H] 21 U 16
Goole [GB] 11 J 12
≈ Gopło, Jezioro — [PL] 16 U 12
Göppingen [D] 15 P 15
Góra [PL] 16 T 13
Góra [PL] 17 V 12
Góra Kalwaria [PL] 17 V 13
Goransko [YU] 22 V 18
Goražde [YU] 22 V 18
Δ Gorce [PL] 17 V 14
Gördalen [S] 4 Q 7
Δ Gorenjsko [YU] 21 S 17
Gorey [IRL] 12 F 12
Δ Gorgona, Isola di — [I] 20 P 18
Gorizia [I] 21 R 17
Δ Gorjanci [YU] 21 T 17
Gorlice [PL] 17 W 14
Görlitz [DDR] 16 S 13
Gornji Milanovac [YU] 22 W 18
Gornji Vakuf [YU] 21 Y 13
Gorochov [SU] 17 Y 13
Gorodeja [SU] 8 Y 11
Gorodišče [SU] 17 Y 12
Gorodok [SU] 17 X 14
Górowo Iławeckie [PL] 8 V 11
Gorron [F] 13 H 15
Gort [IRL] 10 E 11
Δ Gorumna Island [IRL] 10 D 11
Gorzów Wielkopolski [PL] 16 S 12
Gorzyń [PL] 16 S 13
Gosau [A] 21 R 16
Gos e Madhe [AL] 30 W 20
Goslar [D] 15 P 13
Gospić [YU] 21 T 18
Δ Gossa [N] 4 O 6
Gostini [SU] 8 X 9
Gostivar [YU] 30 X 19
Gostków [PL] 16 U 13
Göstling an der Ybbs [A] 21 S 16
Gostomia [PL] 16 T 12
Gostyń [PL] 16 T 13
Gostynin [PL] 16 U 12
Goszcz [PL] 16 T 13
≈ Göta älv [S] 6 Q 9
≈ Götakanal [S] 7 S 9
Δ Götaland [S] 6 Q 9
Göteborg [S] 6 Q 9
Götene [S] 7 R 9
Gotha [DDR] 15 P 14
Gothem [S] 7 T 9
Δ Gotland [S] 7 T 9
Δ Gotska Sandön [S] 7 U 9
Göttingen [D] 15 O 14
Göttingen [D] 15 P 13
Gottwaldov [CS] 16 U 15
Götzis [A] 20 P 16
Goulette, La — [TN] 28 P 22
Goumenissa [GR] 30 Y 20
Goura [GR] 30 Y 21
Gourdon [F] 19 J 17
Gournay-en-Bray [F] 14 K 14
Gournia [GR] 32 Zb 23
Gouveia [P] 25 C 19
Gouzon [F] 19 K 17
Δ Goverla, gora — [SU] 17 Y 15
Δ Gower Peninsula [GB] 12 G 13
Δ Gozna, Vîrful — [RO] 22 X 17
Δ Gozo [M] 30 V 22
Grabow [DDR] 15 Q 12
Grabów nad Prosną [PL] 16 U 13
Gračac [YU] 21 T 18
Graça do Divor [P] 25 B 20
Gračanica [YU] 22 V 17
Gradac [YU] 21 U 19
Gradačac [YU] 22 V 17
Gradara [I] 21 R 18
Gradec [BG] 23 Za 18
Δ Gradeška planina [YU] 30 Y 19
Grado [E] 24 D 18
Grado, El — [E] 26 H 19
Grado [I] 21 R 17
Gradsko [YU] 30 X 19
Δ Gråhø [N] 4 O 6
Grahovo [YU] 22 V 19
Δ Graie, Alpi — [F] 20 N 17
Grajewo [PL] 8 W 12
Δ Gralheira, Serra — [P] 25 B 19
Gram [DK] 6 P 11
Gramat [F] 19 K 17
Grammeni Oxia [GR] 30 Y 21
Δ Grammos Oros [GR] 30 X 20
Δ Grampian Mountains [GB] 11 H 10
Gramsh [AL] 30 W 20
Δ Gramvoussa, Akrotirion — [GR] 32 Za 23
Gramzow [DDR] 16 R 12
Granada [E] 26 E 22
Granadella [E] 26 H 20
Grandas de Salime [E] 24 D 18
Grand-Bourg, le — [F] 19 K 17
≈ Grand Canal [IRL] 10 E 11
Grand' Combe, la — [F] 19 L 18
Δ Grande Chartreuse [F] 19 M 17
Grande-Motte, la — [F] 19 L 18
Δ Grandes Rousses [F] 20 N 17
Grândola [P] 25 A 21
Δ Grândola, Serra de — [P] 25 A 21
Δ Grand Saint Bernard, Col du — [CH,I] 20 N 17
Grandson [CH] 20 N 16
Grane [N] 2 Q 4
Gran = Esztergom [H] 21 U 15
Grange [GB] 11 H 11
Grängesberg [S] 5 R 8
Graninge [S] 5 S 6
≈ Graningesjön [S] 5 S 6
Granja de Torrehermosa [E] 25 D 21
Grankullavik [S] 7 T 9
Gränna [S] 7 R 9
Grannäs [S] 2 S 4
Granollers [E] 27 K 19
Granön [S] 5 T 5
Δ Gran Paradiso [I] 20 N 17
Δ Gran Sasso d'Itàlia [I] 29 R 19
Gransee [DDR] 16 R 12
Grantham [GB] 13 J 12
Grantown-on-Spey [GB] 11 H 9
Grantshouse [GB] 11 J 10
Granville [F] 13 H 15
Δ Gråsö [S] 5 T 7
Grasse [F] 20 N 18
Gråsten [DK] 6 P 11
Grästorp [S] 6 Q 9
Gratangen [N] 2 S 2
Gråträsk [S] 2 T 4
Δ Graubünden [CH] 20
Grau-du-Roi, le — [F] 19 L 18
Graulhet [F] 19 K 18
Graus [E] 26 H 19
Gravarne [S] 6 Q 9
Grave, la — [F] 20 N 17
Grave [NL] 15 N 13
Δ Grave, Pointe de — [F] 18 H 17
Gravelines [F] 14 K 13
Gravenhage, 's — [NL] 14 M 3
Δ Graves [F] 18 H 17
Gravesend [GB] 13 K 13
Gravina in Pùglia [I] 29 U 20
≈ Gravone [F] 28 O 19
Gray [F] 19 M 16
Graz [A] 21 S 16
Grdelica [YU] 22 X 18
Greaca [RO] 23 Za 17
Great Driffield [GB] 11 J 11
Great Dunmow [GB] 13 K 13
Great Torrington [GB] 12 G 13
Great Yarmouth [GB] 13 K 12
Grebbestad [S] 6 Q 9
Δ Gredos, Sierra de — [E] 25 D 20
Greenock [GB] 10 G 10
Greifswald [DDR] 7 R 12
≈ Greifswalder Bodden [DDR] 7 R 11
Δ Greifswalder Oie [DDR] 7 R 11
Grein [A] 21 S 15

Greiz [DDR] 15 Q 14
Grenå [DK] 6 P 10
Grenade-sur-Garonne [F] 19 J 18
Grenade-sur-l'Adour [F] 18 H 18
Grenchen [CH] 20 N 16
Δ Grenen [DK] 6 P 9
Grenoble [F] 19 M 17
Grense Jakobselv [N] 3 W 1
Gresten [A] 21 S 15
Gretna Green [GB] 11 H 11
Greve [I] 20 Q 18
Greven [D] 15 O 13
Grevena [GR] 30 X 20
Grevenbrück [D] 15 Q 14
Grevenmacher [L] 15 N 14
Grevesmühlen [DDR] 15 Q 12
Δ Gribës, Mali i — [AL] 30 W 20
Grillefjord [N] 2 R 2
Grimma [DDR] 16 R 13
Grimmen [DDR] 7 R 12
Grimsby [GB] 13 K 12
Grimslöv [S] 7 R 10
Grimstad [N] 6 O 9
Grindelwald [CH] 20 O 16
Grindsted [DK] 6 O 11
Grinkiškis [SU] 8 W 10
Gripenberg [S] 7 R 9
Gripsholm [S] 7 S 8
Δ Gris Nez, Cap — [F] 14 K 14
Grisolles [F] 19 J 18
Grisslehamn [S] 5 T 8
Griva [SU] 8 Y 10
Grivica [BG] 23 Z 18
Griviţa [RO] 23 Za 17
Δ Grmeč [YU] 21 T 17
Grobina [SU] 8 V 10
Gröbming [A] 21 S 16
Grodków [PL] 16 T 14
Grodno [SU] 8 X 11
Grodzewo [PL] 16 S 13
Grodzisk Mazowiecki [PL] 17 V 13
Grodzisk Wielkopolski [PL] 16 T 13
Groenlo [NL] 15 N 13
Δ Groix, Île de — [F] 18 G 15
Grójec [PL] 17 V 13
Grömitz [D] 6 Q 12
Gronau in Westfalen [D] 15 N 13
Grong [N] 4 Q 5
Groningen [NL] 15 N 12
Grönskåra [S] 7 S 10
Gropeni [RO] 23 Zb 16
Gropniţa [RO] 23 Za 15
Δ Grosa, Punta — [E] 27 J 21
Großenbrode [D] 6 Q 11
Großenhain [DDR] 16 R 13
Δ Große Rachel [D] 16 R 15
Δ Großer Arber [D] 16 R 15
Δ Großer Beerberg [DDR] 15 Q 14
Grosseto [I] 28 Q 19
Δ Grosseto, Formiche di — [I] 28 Q 19
Groß-Gerau [D] 15 O 14
Großgerungs [A] 21 S 15
Δ Großglockner [A] 21 R 16
Großpetersdorf [A] 21 T 16
Großweikersdorf [A] 21 T 15
Grostøl [N] 6 O 9
Grotli [N] 4 O 7
Δ Grøtøy [N] 2 S 1
≈ Grøtsund [N] 2 S 1
Grottaglie [I] 29 U 20
Δ Grouin du Cou, Pointe du — [F] 18 H 16
Grovfjord [N] 2 S 2
Grudopole [SU] 17 Y 12
Grudovo [BG] 23 Zb 18
Grudusk [PL] 17 V 12
Grudziądz [PL] 16 U 12
Gruissan [F] 19 K 19
Grumo Appula [I] 29 U 20
Grums [S] 7 R 8
Grünberg in Schlesien = Zielona Góra [PL] 16 S 13
Grundsjö [S] 5 S 6
Grundsunda [S] 5 T 5
Grundträsk [S] 3 U 4
Grungedal [N] 4 O 8
Gruvberget [S] 5 S 7
Gruyères [CH] 20 N 16
Gruža [YU] 22 W 18
Gruzdžiai [SU] 8 W 10
Grybów [PL] 17 W 14
Gryfice [PL] 16 S 12
Gryfino [PL] 16 S 12
Gryfów Śląski [PL] 16 S 14
Gryt [S] 7 S 9
Δ Grytøy [N] 2 R 2
Guadalajara [E] 26 F 20
≈ Guadalaviar, Río — [E] 26 G 20
Guadalcanal [E] 25 C 21
≈ Guadalete, Río — [E] 25 C 22
≈ Guadalhorce, Río — [E] 25 D 22
≈ Guadalimar, Río — [E] 26 E 21
≈ Guadalmellato, Pantano de — [E] 25 D 21
≈ Guadalmena, Río — [E] 26 F 21
≈ Guadalope, Río — [E] 26 H 20
≈ Guadalquivir, Río — [E] 25 C 21
Guadalupe [E] 25 D 20
Δ Guadalupe, Sierra de — [E] 25 D 20
≈ Guadamez, Río — [E] 25 C 21
Guadarrama [E] 26 E 20
≈ Guadarrama, Río — [E] 26 E 20
Δ Guadarrama, Sierra la — [E] 26 E 20
≈ Guadiana, Río — [E, P] 25 B 21
≈ Guadiaro, Río — [E] 25 C 22
≈ Guadiato, Río — [E] 25 D 21
≈ Guadiela, Río — [E] 26 F 20
Guadix [E] 26 E 22
Guaire = Gorey [IRL] 12 F 12
Gualdo Tadino [I] 21 R 19
Δ Guara, Sierra de — [E] 26 H 19
Guarda [P] 25 C 19
Guardamar del Segura [E] 26 G 21
Guardia, La — [E] 24 B 18
Guardia, La — [E] 26 E 20
Guardiagrele [I] 29 S 19
Guardo [E] 24 E 18
Δ Guardunha, Serra da — [P] 25 B 20
Guarromán [E] 26 E 21
Guastalla [I] 20 P 18
Gubbio [I] 21 R 19
Guben [DDR] 16 S 13
Guča [YU] 22 W 18
Δ Gúdar, Sierra de — [E] 26 G 20
Δ Gudbrandsdal [N] 4 P 6
≈ Gudenå [DK] 6 P 10
Gudhjem [DK] 7 S 11
≈ Gudín, Río — [E] 25 D 19
Gudiña, La — [E] 24 C 18
Gudvangen [N] 4 O 7
Guecho = Algorta [E] 18 F 18
Guémené-Penfao [F] 18 H 15
Guémené-sur-Scorff [F] 12 G 15
Guer [F] 13 H 15
Guérande [F] 18 G 16
Guerche-de-Bretagne, la — [F] 13 H 15
Guerche-sur-l'Aubois, la — [F] 19 L 16
Guéret [F] 19 K 17
Guernica y Luno [E] 18 F 18
Δ Guernsey [GB] 12 G 14
Gueugnon [F] 19 L 16
Guglionesi [I] 29 S 19
Guignes [F] 14 L 15
Guijuelo [E] 25 D 19
Guildford [GB] 13 J 13
Guillaumes [F] 20 N 18
Guillestre [F] 20 N 18
Guimarães [P] 25 B 19
Guimiliau [F] 12 G 15
Guingamp [F] 12 G 15
Guisborough [GB] 11 J 11
Guise [F] 14 L 14
Guitiriz [E] 24 C 18
Gul'anci [BG] 23 Z 18
Gulbene [SU] 8 X 9
≈ Guldborg Sund [DK] 6 Q 11
Guldsmedshyttan [S] 5 R 8
Δ Gullkronafjärd [SF] 9 V 8
≈ Gullmarsfjord [S] 6 Q 9
Gullspång [S] 7 R 8
Güllük [TR] 31 Zc 21
Gulsele [S] 5 S 5
Gumbinnen = Gusev [SU] 8 W 11
Gumiel de Hizán [E] 26 F 19
Gummersbach [D] 15 O 14
Gunnarn [S] 5 S 5
Gunnarsnes [N] 3 U 1
Gunnebo [S] 6 Q 9
Gunnilbo [S] 5 S 8
Günselsdorf [A] 21 T 15
Guntín [E] 24 C 18
Günzburg [D] 15 P 15
Gunzenhausen [D] 15 Q 15
Gurahonţ [RO] 22 X 16
Gura Humorului [RO] 23 Z 15
Gura Teghii [RO] 23 Za 16
Δ Gurghiu, Munţii — [RO] 23 Z 16
Guriezo [E] 18 F 18
Gur i Zi [AL] 30 W 19
Gurk [A] 21 S 16
Gurkovo [BG] 23 Za 18
Gusev [SU] 8 W 11
Gusinje [YU] 22 W 19
Guspini [I] 28 O 21
Güssing [A] 21 T 16
Gußwerk [A] 21 S 16
Gustavsberg [S] 7 T 8
Gustavsfors [S] 6 Q 8
Güstrow [DDR] 15 Q 12
Gutenstein [A] 21 T 16
Gütersloh [D] 15 O 13
Δ Gutin, Munţii — [RO] 17 X 15
Δ Guverte [S] 2 R 4
Δ Guyenne [F] 19 J 17
Gvardejsk [SU] 8 V 11
Gvarv [N] 6 P 8
Gweedore [IRL] 10 F 10
Δ Gwennap Head [GB] 12 F 14
Gy [F] 19 M 16
Δ Gyldenløves Høj [DK] 6 Q 11
Gyljen [S] 3 U 3
Δ Gylling Næs [DK] 6 P 11
Gyoma [H] 22 W 16
Gyöngyös [H] 22 V 15
Győr [H] 21 U 16
Gysinge [S] 5 S 8
Gyula [H] 22 W 16

H

Haag, Den - = 's-Gravenhage [NL] 14 M 13
Haag in Oberbayern [D] 20 Q 15
Haapajärvi [SF] 9 V 5
≈ Haapajärvi [SF] 9 W 5
Δ Haapasaari [SF] 9 X 7
≈ Haapaselkä [SF] 9 X 6
Haapavesi [SF] 9 V 5
Haapsalu [SU] 8 V 8
Δ Haardt [D] 15 O 15
Haarlem [NL] 14 M 13
Habo [S] 7 R 9
Hackås [S] 5 R 6
Hacksjö [S] 5 S 5
Haddington [GB] 11 J 10
Δ Hadeland [N] 4 P 8
Haderslev [DK] 6 P 11
Haderup [DK] 6 P 10
Δ Hadseløy [N] 2 R 2
Hadsten [DK] 6 P 10
Hadsund [DK] 6 P 10
Hægebostad [N] 6 O 9
Hagen [D] 15 O 13
Hagenow [DDR] 15 Q 12
Hageri [SU] 9 W 8
Hagetmau [F] 18 H 18
Hagfors [S] 5 R 8
Häggenås [S] 5 R 6
Häggsjön [S] 5 R 5
≈ Hagiu Orus, Kolpos — [GR] 31 Z 20
Δ Hague, Cap de la — [F] 13 H 14
Haguenau [F] 15 O 15
Hahót [H] 21 T 16
Δ Hailuoto [SF] 3 V 4
Hainburg an der Donau [A] 21 T 15
Hainichen [DDR] 16 R 14
Hajdúböszörmény [H] 22 W 15
Hajdúhadház [H] 22 W 15
Hajdúnánás [H] 22 W 15
Δ Hajdúság [H] 22 W 15
Hajdúszoboszló [H] 22 W 15
Hajnówka [PL] 17 X 12
Håkafot [S] 5 R 5
Hakkas [S] 2 T 3
Halberstadt [DDR] 15 Q 13
Halden [N] 6 Q 8
Haldensleben [DDR] 15 Q 13
Halesworth [GB] 13 K 13
Halifax [GB] 11 J 12
Halikarnassos [TR] 31 Zc 21
Halivaara [SF] 9 X 5
Haljala [SU] 9 X 8
Δ Halkkavarre [N] 3 U 1
Hälla [S] 5 S 5
Δ Halland [S] 6 Q 10
Δ Hallandsåsen [S] 7 R 10
Δ Hallands Väderö [S] 6 Q 10
Hällefors [S] 5 R 8
Hallein [A] 21 R 16
Hallen [S] 5 R 6
Halle/Saale [DDR] 15 Q 13
Hällesjö [S] 5 S 6
Hällestad [S] 7 S 9
Hälleviksstrand [S] 6 Q 9
Δ Halligen [D] 6 O 11
Δ Hallingdal [N] 4 P 7
Hällnäs [S] 5 T 5
Hallsberg [S] 7 R 8
Hallviken [S] 5 R 5
Halmstad [S] 7 R 10
Hals [DK] 6 P 10
Halsanaustan [N] 4 O 6
Δ Hälsingland [S] 5 R 7
Halsua [SF] 9 V 5
Haltdalen [N] 4 Q 6
Haltern [D] 15 N 13
Δ Haltiatunturi [SF] 2 T 2
Ham [F] 14 L 14
Hamar [N] 4 Q 7
Hamburg [D] 15 P 12
Hamburgsund [S] 6 Q 9
Δ Häme [SF] 9 V 7
Hämeenkyrö [SF] 9 V 6
Hämeenlinna [SF] 9 W 7
Δ Hämeen selkä [SF] 9 V 6
Hameln [D] 15 P 13
Hamidiye [TR] 31 Zb 19
Hamilton [GB] 11 H 10
Hamina [SF] 9 X 7
Hamm [D] 15 O 13
Hammarland [SF] 9 U 7
Hammel [DK] 6 P 10
Hammelburg [D] 15 P 14
Hammerdal [S] 5 R 5
Hammerfest [N] 3 U 1
Hammershus [DK] 7 S 11
Hamneidet [N] 2 T 1
Hamningberg [N] 3 W 1
Hamra [S] 5 R 7
Hamrånge [S] 5 S 7
Δ Haná [CS] 16 T 15
Hanau [D] 15 O 14
Handen [S] 7 T 8
Δ Handnesøy [N] 2 Q 4
Hanfthal [A] 21 T 15
Hangö [SF] 9 V 8
≈ Hangö västra fjärd [SF] 9 V 8
Hankamäki [SF] 9 X 5
Hankasalmi [SF] 9 W 6
Hanko = Hangö [SF] 9 V 8
Hannover [D] 15 P 13
Hannut [B] 14 M 14
Δ Hanö [S] 7 S 10
≈ Hanöbukten [S] 7 R 10
Han Pijesak [YU] 22 V 18
Δ Hanság [H] 21 T 16
Hansnes [N] 2 S 1
Hanstholm [DK] 6 O 10
Hanu [RO] 23 Za 16
Hanušovce [CS] 17 W 14
Haouaria, El — [TN] 28 Q 22
Haparanda [S] 3 U 4
Harads [S] 2 T 4
≈ Hara laht [SU] 9 W 7
Δ Harana, Sierra — [E] 26 E 22
≈ Hardangerfjord [N] 4 N 8
Δ Hardangerjøkulen [N] 4 O 7
Δ Hardangervidda [N] 4 O 8
Harderwijk [NL] 15 N 13
Δ Hardsyssel [DK] 6 O 10
Hardwick Hall [GB] 13 J 12
Hareid [N] 4 N 6
Harfleur [F] 14 J 14
Harglá [SU] 8 X 9
≈ Härjån [S] 5 R 7
Δ Härjedalen [S] 4 Q 6
Δ Härjehågna [N, S] 4 Q 7
Harkány [H] 21 U 17
Harlech Castle [GB] 12 G 12
Harlingen [NL] 15 N 12
Harlow [GB] 13 J 13
Härlunda [S] 7 R 10
Hărman [RO] 23 Z 16
Harmånger [S] 5 S 6
Harmanli [BG] 23 Za 19
Härnösand [S] 5 S 6
Haro [E] 18 F 19
Harran [N] 4 Q 5
Δ Harris [GB] 10 G 9
Harrogate [GB] 11 J 11
Harrow [GB] 13 J 13
Härryda [S] 6 Q 9
Harsprånget [S] 2 T 3
Harstad [N] 2 R 2
Harsvik [N] 4 P 5
Hartberg [A] 21 T 16
Δ Hårteigen [N] 4 O 8
Hartlepool [GB] 11 J 11
Hartola [SF] 9 W 6
Harwich [GB] 13 K 13
Δ Harz [D, DDR] 15 P 13
Harzebrouck [F] 14 L 14
Harzgerode [DDR] 15 Q 13
Haselünne [D] 15 O 13
Haskovo [BG] 23 Za 19
Haslach im Kinzigtal [D] 20 O 15
Hasle [DK] 7 S 11
Hassel [S] 5 S 6
Hassela [S] 5 S 6
Hässelholm [S] 7 R 10
Δ Hasselö [S] 7 S 9
Hasselt [B] 14 M 14
Haßfurt [D] 15 P 14
Hastings [GB] 13 K 13
Hasvik [N] 2 T 1
Haţeg [RO] 22 X 17
Hatfield [GB] 13 J 13
Hatherleigh [GB] 12 G 13
Δ Haticz [PL] 17 X 14
Hattfjelldal [N] 2 R 4
Hatvan [H] 22 V 15
Haudères, les — [CH] 20 N 17
Haugastøl [N] 4 O 7
Hauge [N] 6 N 9
Haugesund [N] 6 N 8
Hauho [SF] 9 W 7
Haukeligrend [N] 4 O 8
Haukipudas [SF] 3 V 4
≈ Haukivesi [SF] 9 X 6
Haukivuori [SF] 9 X 6
Haurida [S] 7 R 9
Hausjärvi [SF] 9 W 7
Hautajärvi [SF] 3 W 3
Hautefort [F] 19 J 17
≈ Havel [DDR] 15 Q 13
Havelberg [DDR] 15 Q 12
Δ Havelland [DDR] 11 J 11
Haverfordwest [GB] 12 G 12
Haverhill [GB] 13 K 13
Haverö [S] 5 R 6
Havlíčkův Brod [CS] 16 S 14
Havnsø [DK] 6 Q 11
Havøysund [N] 3 U 1
Havre, le — [F] 14 J 14
Havsa [TR] 23 Zb 19
Hawes [GB] 11 J 11
Hawick [GB] 11 H 10
Hawkhurst [GB] 13 K 13
Hayange [F] 15 N 15
Haye-Descartes, la — [F] 19 J 16
Haye-du-Puits, la — [F] 13 H 14
Hayle [GB] 12 F 13
Hayrabolu [TR] 31 Zb 19
Hažlach [PL] 16 U 14
Headford [IRL] 10 E 11
≈ Hebrides, Sea of the — [GB] 10 H 9
Δ Hebrides [GB] 10 F 9
Heby [S] 5 S 8
Hechingen [D] 20 O 15
Hechtel [B] 14 M 13
Hedberg [S] 2 T 4
Heddal [N] 6 P 8
Hedderen [N] 6 O 9
Hede [S] 5 R 6
Hedemora [S] 5 S 8
Heden [S] 3 U 3
Hedenäset [S] 3 U 3
Hedenstedt [DK] 6 P 11
Hedesunda [S] 5 S 7
≈ Hedesundafjärden [S] 5 S 8
Δ Hedmark [N] 4 Q 7
Heemstede [NL] 14 M 3
Heerenveen [NL] 15 N 12
Heerlen [NL] 15 N 14
Hegra [N] 4 Q 6
Hegyeshalom [H] 21 T 15
Δ Hegyhát [H] 21 U 16
Heiås [N] 4 Q 8
Δ Heidalsmuen [N] 4 P 7
Heide [D] 6 P 12
Heidelberg [D] 15 O 15
Heidenheim an der Brenz [D] 15 P 15
Heilbronn [D] 15 P 15
Heiligenblut [A] 21 R 16
Heiligenhafen [D] 6 Q 11
Δ Heimdalshaugan [N] 4 Q 5
Heinävesi [SF] 9 X 6
Heinola [SF] 9 W 6
Hejde [S] 7 T 9
Hel [PL] 7 U 11
Δ Helagsfjället [S] 4 Q 6
Helder, Den — [NL] 14 M 12
≈ Helgeån [S] 7 R 10
Δ Helgenæs [DK] 6 P 10
Helgerød [N] 6 P 8
Δ Helgoland [D] 6 O 12
≈ Helgoländer Bucht [D] 15 O 12
Δ Helgøy [N] 2 S 1
Δ Helgøy [N] 4 Q 7
Hella [N] 4 O 7
Δ Hellberge [DDR] 15 Q 13
Δ Helldalisen [N] 2 R 3
Helle [N] 6 O 8
Helleland [N] 6 N 9
Hellesylt [N] 4 O 6
Hellevoetsluis [NL] 14 M 13
Δ Helligvær [N] 2 Q 3
Hellín [E] 26 F 21
Helmond [NL] 15 N 13
Helmsdale [GB] 11 H 9
Helmsley [GB] 11 J 11
Helmstedt [D] 15 Q 13
Δ Helpter Berg [DDR] 16 R 12
Helsingborg [S] 6 Q 10
Helsinge [DK] 6 Q 10
Helsingfors = Helsinki [SF] 9 W 7
Helsingør [DK] 6 Q 10
Helsinki [SF] 9 W 7
Helston [GB] 12 F 14
Heltermaa [SU] 8 V 8
Heming [F] 15 N 15
Hemmingsmark [S] 3 U 4
Hemnesberget [N] 2 Q 4
Hemse [S] 7 T 9
Hemsedal [N] 4 O 7
Δ Hemsedalsfjella [N] 4 O 7
Δ Hemsö [S] 5 T 6
Henån [S] 6 Q 9
≈ Henares, Río — [E] 26 F 20
Hendaye [F] 18 G 18
Hengelo [NL] 15 N 13
Hénin-Liétard [F] 14 L 14
Hennebont [F] 12 G 15
Hennef (Sieg) [D] 15 N 14
Heradsbygd [N] 4 Q 7
Herborn [D] 15 O 14
Herby Śląskie [PL] 16 U 14
Hercegnovi [YU] 22 V 19
Δ Hercegovina [YU] 22 V 19
Hereford [GB] 13 H 13
Herefors [N] 6 O 9
Herencia [E] 26 E 20
Hérépian [F] 19 K 18
Herford [D] 15 O 13
Héric [F] 18 H 16
Héricourt [F] 20 N 16
Hérie-la-Viéville, la — [F] 14 L 14
Herisau [CH] 20 P 16
Δ Herm [GB] 13 H 14
Hermannsburg [D] 15 P 12
Hermanverk [N] 4 O 7
Hermeskeil [D] 15 N 14
≈ Hernád [H] 17 W 15
Herne [D] 15 N 13
Herning [DK] 6 P 10
Herrenberg [D] 15 O 15
Herrera [E] 25 D 22
Herrera del Duque [E] 25 D 20
Herrera de Pisuerga [E] 24 E 18
Hersbruck [D] 15 Q 15
Hertford [GB] 13 J 13
Hertogenbosch, 's — [NL] 14 M 13
Herzberg am Harz [D] 15 P 13
Herzberg/Elster [DDR] 16 R 13
Hesdin [F] 14 K 14
Hesel [D] 15 O 12
Δ Hestmona [N] 2 Q 4
Hetekylä [SF] 3 W 4
Hettstedt [DDR] 15 Q 13
Heves [H] 22 V 15
Hévíz [H] 21 U 16
Hexham [GB] 11 J 11
Hidasnemeti [H] 7 W 15
Δ Hiddensee [DDR] 7 R 11
Hieflau [A] 21 S 16
Hietaniemi [SF] 3 W 3
Hietapera [SF] 9 X 4
Δ High Willhays [GB] 12 G 13
High Wycombe [GB] 13 J 13
Δ Higuera, Punta de la — [E] 26 E 22
Higuera la Real [E] 25 C 21
Δ Hiiumaa [SU] 8 V 8
Hijar [E] 26 H 20
Hildesheim [D] 15 P 13
Hillerød [DK] 6 Q 10
Hillesøy [N] 2 S 2
Hilmanka [SF] 9 V 5
Hilversum [NL] 14 M 13
Himarë [AL] 30 W 20
Δ Himmelbjerget [DK] 6 P 10
Δ Himmerland [DK] 6 P 10
Δ Hindersön [S] 3 U 4
Δ Hindsholm [DK] 6 P 11
Hinnerjoki [SF] 9 U 7
Δ Hinnøy [N] 2 R 2
Hinojosa del Duque [E] 25 D 21
≈ Hinterrhein [CH] 20 P 17
Hirlău [RO] 23 Za 15
Hirschberg im Riesengebirge = Jelenia Góra [PL] 16 S 14
Hirson [F] 14 M 14
Hirşova [RO] 23 Zb 17
Δ Hîrtibaciului, Dealurile — [RO] 22 Y 16
Hirtshals [DK] 6 P 9
Hisar'a [BG] 23 Z 18
Hitchin [GB] 13 J 13
Δ Hitra [N] 4 O 6
Hjallerup [DK] 6 P 10
≈ Hjälmaren [S] 7 S 8
Hjältanstorp [S] 5 S 6
Hjartdal [N] 6 O 8
Δ Hjartfjell [N] 2 R 4
Hjelle [N] 4 O 7
Hjellnes [N] 2 T 1
Δ Hjelmsøy [N] 3 U 1
≈ Hjeltefjord [N] 4 N 7
Hjerkinn [N] 4 P 6
Δ Hjerttind [N] 2 S 2
Hjo [S] 7 R 9
Hjørring [DK] 6 P 9
Hjortkvarn [S] 7 S 8
Hlebarovo [BG] 23 Za 18
Hlohovec [CS] 16 U 15
Hluboká nad Vltavou [CS] 16 S 15
Hnúšťa [CS] 17 V 15
Hobro [DK] 6 P 10
Δ Hoburg [S] 7 T 10
Δ Hochlantsch [A] 21 S 16
Hochosterwitz [A] 21 S 16
Hochspeyer [D] 15 O 15
Hockeroda [DDR] 15 Q 14
Hoddesdon [GB] 13 J 13
Hódmezővásárhely [H] 22 W 16
Hodonín [CS] 16 T 15
Hoek van Holland [NL] 14 M 13
Hof [D] 15 Q 14
Hofors [S] 5 S 7
Hofstad [N] 4 P 5
Δ Hogland = Sur Sari [SU] 9 X 7
Högsby [S] 7 S 10
Δ Høgtind [N] 2 R 3
Δ Høgtuvbre [N] 2 Q 4
Hőgyész [H] 21 U 16
Hohenau an der March [A] 21 T 15
Hohenwestedt [D] 6 P 12
Δ Hohe Tauern [A] 20 Q 16
Højer [DK] 6 O 11
Hokksund [N] 4 P 8
Hol [N] 4 O 7
Holbæk [DK] 6 Q 11
Holešov [CS] 16 U 15
Holíč [CS] 16 T 15
Hollabrunn [A] 21 T 15
Höllevadsholm [S] 6 Q 9
Holm [S] 5 S 6
Holmen [N] 4 P 7
Holmenkollen [N] 4 P 8
Holmestrand [N] 6 P 8
Holmfors [S] 2 S 4
Holmön [S] 5 U 5
Δ Holmön [S] 5 U 5
≈ Holmsjön [S] 5 R 6
≈ Holmsjön [S] 5 S 6
Holmsund [S] 5 T 5
Holmsveden [S] 5 S 7
Δ Holmudden [S] 7 U 9
Hølonda [N] 4 P 6
Δ Holsnøy [N] 4 N 7
Holstebro [DK] 6 O 10
Holsted [DK] 6 O 11
Holsworthy [GB] 12 G 13
Holwerd [NL] 15 N 12
Holyhead [GB] 10 G 12
Δ Holy Island [GB] 10 G 12
Holzminden [D] 15 P 13
Homburg [D] 15 N 15
Δ Hommelfjell [N] 4 Q 6
Δ Homolje [YU] 22 X 18
Δ Homoljske planine [YU] 22 X 17
Homps [F] 19 K 18
Honfleur [F] 14 J 14
Honiton [GB] 12 G 13
Honkajoki [SF] 9 U 6
Δ Honkamäki [SF] 9 W 5
Honningsvåg [N] 3 U 1
Honrubia [E] 26 F 20
Hoogeveen [NL] 15 N 12
Hoogezand-Sappemeer [NL] 15 N 12
Höör [S] 7 R 10
Hoorn [NL] 14 M 12
Δ Hope, Ben — [GB] 11 H 8
Horažďovice [CS] 16 R 15
Horb am Neckar [D] 20 O 15
Hörby [S] 7 R 10
Horda [N] 4 O 8
Horezu [RO] 22 Y 17
Horgen [CH] 20 O 16
Hořice [CS] 16 S 14
Horka u Staré Paky [CS] 16 S 14
Δ Hormigas, Isla — [E] 26 G 22
Horn [A] 21 T 15
Horn [S] 7 S 9
≈ Hornavan [S] 2 S 4
Horncastle [GB] 13 J 12
Horndal [S] 5 S 8
Hörnefors [S] 5 T 5
Horní Bousov [CS] 16 S 14
Horní Lideč [CS] 16 U 15
Hornindal [N] 4 O 7
≈ Hornindalsvatn [N] 4 N 7
Hornnes [N] 6 O 9
Hornos [E] 26 F 21
Δ Hornslandet [S] 5 S 7
Horred [S] 6 Q 10
Horsens [DK] 6 P 10
Horsham [GB] 13 J 13
Horšovský Týn [CS] 16 R 15
Horten [N] 6 P 8
Hortlax [S] 3 U 4
≈ Hortobágy [H] 22 W 16
Δ Hortobágy [H] 22 W 16
Hörvik [S] 7 S 10
Hospital de Órbigo [E] 24 D 18
Hospitalet [E] 27 J 20
Hospitalet del Infante [E] 27 J 20
Hospitalet-Prés-l'Andorre, l' — [F] 19 J 19
Hossa [SF] 3 X 4
Hotagen [S] 5 R 5
≈ Hotagen [S] 5 R 5
Hoting [S] 5 S 5
Houdan [F] 14 K 15
Hourtin [F] 18 H 17
≈ Hourtin, Étang d' — [F] 18 H 17
Houtskär [SF] 9 U 7
Hov [DK] 6 P 10
Hov [N] 4 P 6
Hovden [N] 6 O 8
Hove [GB] 13 J 13
Hovmantorp [S] 7 S 10
Howden [GB] 11 J 12
Höxter [D] 15 P 13
Δ Hoy [GB] 11 J 8
Δ Hoya, La — [E] 26 H 19
Høyanger [N] 4 N 7
Hoyerswerda [DDR] 16 R 13
Høylandet [N] 4 Q 5
≈ Höytiäinen [SF] 9 X 5
Hradec [CS] 16 U 14
Hradek Králové [CS] 16 T 14
Hranice [CS] 16 U 14
≈ Hron [CS] 21 U 15
Hrubieszów [PL] 17 X 13
Δ Hrvatska [YU] 21 T 17
Hrvatska Kostajnica [YU] 21 T 17
Huben [A] 21 R 16
Huddersfield [GB] 11 J 12
Hudiksvall [S] 5 S 7
≈ Hudiksvallsfjärden [S] 5 S 7
≈ Huebra, Río — [E] 25 C 19
Huelgoat [F] 12 G 15
Huelva [E] 25 B 21
≈ Huelva, Río de — [E] 25 C 21
Huéneja [E] 26 E 22
Huércal-Overa [E] 26 F 22
Huerta del Rey [E] 26 F 19
Δ Huertas, Cabo de las — [E] 26 G 21
Huesca [E] 26 H 19
Huéscar [E] 26 F 21
≈ Hufteren [N] 4 N 8
Hugh Town [GB] 12 E 14
Δ Hugla [N] 2 Q 4
Huittinen [SF] 9 V 7
Hukkajärvi [SF] 9 X 4
Hulín [CS] 16 U 15
Hulst [NL] 14 M 13
Hultanäs [S] 7 S 10
Hultsfred [S] 7 S 9
≈ Humber, River — [GB] 13 J 12
Humenne [CS] 17 W 15
Δ Humina [YU] 21 U 18
Δ Hümmling [D] 15 O 12
Humpolec [CS] 16 S 14
Humppila [SF] 9 V 7
Hundested [DK] 6 Q 10
Hunedoara [RO] 22 X 16
Hünfeld [D] 15 P 14
Hungerford [GB] 13 H 13
Hunnebostrand [S] 6 Q 9
Δ Hunsrück [D] 15 N 14
≈ Hunte [D] 15 O 13
Huntingdon [GB] 13 J 12
Huntley [GB] 11 J 9
Hurdalssjø [N] 4 Q 8
Δ Hurdes, Las — [E] 25 C 20
Hurezani [RO] 22 Y 17
Δ Hurrungane [N] 4 O 7
Hursovo [BG] 23 Zb 17
Hurup [DK] 6 O 10
Husbondliden [S] 5 T 5
Husby [S] 5 S 7
Huşi [RO] 23 Za 15
Huskvarna [S] 7 R 9
Hustopeče [CS] 16 T 15
Husum [D] 6 P 11
Husum [S] 5 T 6
Huta Zawadzka [PL] 17 V 13
Huy [B] 14 M 14
Δ Hvaler [N] 6 P 8
Hvalpsund [DK] 6 P 10
Hvar [YU] 21 T 19
Δ Hvar [YU] 21 U 19
≈ Hvarski kanal [YU] 21 U 18
Hvide Sande [DK] 6 O 10
Hvojna [BG] 23 Z 19
Hyen [N] 4 N 7
Hyères [F] 19 M 19
≈ Hyères, Rade d' — [F] 19 M 19
Δ Hyères, Îles d' — [F] 20 N 19
Hyltebruck [S] 7 R 10
Hynnekleiv [N] 6 O 9
≈ Hyrynjärvi [SF] 3 W 4
Hyrynsalmi [SF] 3 W 4

Hythe [GB] 13 K 13
Hyvinkää [SF] 9 W 7

I

Iacobeni [RO] 23 Z 15
≈ Ialomiţa [RO] 23 Za 17
Δ Ialomiţei, Baltă — [RO] 23 Zb 17
Ianca [RO] 23 Za 16
Iaşi [RO] 23 Za 15
Iballë [AL] 30 W 19
≈ Ibar [YU] 22 W 18
Ibbenbüren [D] 15 O 13
Δ Iberica, Cordillera — [E] 26 G 19
Ibestad [N] 2 S 2
Ibiza [E] 27 J 21
Δ Ibiza [E] 27 J 21
Δ Iblei, Monti — [I] 29 T 22
Idar-Oberstein [D] 15 N 14
Δ Idiazábal, Puerto de — [E] 18 G 18
Δ Idi Oros [GR] 32 Za 23
Idivuoma [S] 2 T 2
Δ Idra [GR] 31 Z 22
Idre [S] 4 Q 7
Idrija [YU] 21 S 17
Iecava [SU] 8 W 10
Ieper [B] 14 L 14
Ierapetra [GR] 32 Zb 23
Δ Ierax, Akrotírion — [GR] 31 Z 22
Ierissos [GR] 31 Z 20
Ièsolo [I] 21 R 17
Δ Ifach, Punta de — [E] 26 H 21
Ifjord [N] 3 V 1
Igal [H] 21 U 16
Igalo [YU] 22 V 19
Iggesund [S] 5 S 7
Iglésias [I] 28 O 21
Iglesuela del Cid, La — [E] 26 H 20
Iğneada [TR] 23 Zc 18
Igoumenitsa [GR] 30 X 21
Igualada [E] 27 J 19
Ihamaru [SU] 8 X 8
Ihtiman [BG] 23 Z 18
Ii [SF] 3 V 4
≈ Iijärvi [SF] 3 V 1
≈ Iijärvi [SF] 3 W 3
≈ Iijärvi [SF] 3 W 4
≈ Iijoki [SF] 3 V 4
≈ Iijoki [SF] 3 W 4
Iisalmi [SF] 9 W 5
Δ Iivaara [SF] 3 X 3
≈ IJssel [NL] 15 N 13
≈ IJsselmeer [NL] 14 M 12
Ikaalinen [SF] 9 V 6
Δ Ikaria [GR] 31 Zb 21
Ikasnj [SU] 8 Y 10
Ikast [DK] 6 P 10
Ilanz [CH] 20 P 16
Ilava [CS] 16 U 15
Ilchester [GB] 13 H 13
Île-Bouchard, l' — [F] 19 J 16
Δ Île de France [F] 14 K 15
Île-Rousse, l' — [F] 28 O 19
Ílhavo [P] 25 B 19
Ilia [RO] 22 X 16
Ilidža [YU] 22 V 18
Ilinko [PL] 17 V 12
Ilirska Bistrica [YU] 21 S 17
Ilkley [GB] 11 J 11
≈ Iller [D] 20 P 16
Illertissen [D] 20 P 15
Illescas [E] 26 E 20
Ille-sur-Têt [F] 19 K 19
Ilfracombe [GB] 12 G 13
Illiers - Combray [F] 14 K 15
Ilmajoki [SF] 9 U 6
Ilmenau [DDR] 15 Q 14
Ilminster [GB] 13 H 13
Δ Ilovik [YU] 21 S 18
Ilūkste [SU] 8 X 10
Iłża [PL] 17 W 13
Imatra [SF] 9 X 6
Immenstadt im Allgäu [D] 20 P 16
Immingham [GB] 13 J 12
Imola [I] 20 Q 18
Imotski [YU] 21 U 18
Impèria [I] 20 O 18
Imphy [F] 19 L 16
Imroz [TR] 31 Za 20
Δ Imroz adası [TR] 31 Za 20
Imst [A] 20 Q 16
Inari [SF] 3 V 2
≈ Inari [SF] 3 V 2
≈ Inarijoki [SF] 3 U 2
Inca [E] 27 K 21
Inchnadamph [GB] 11 H 9
Inčukalns [SU] 8 W 9
Indal [S] 5 S 6
≈ Indalsälven [S] 4 Q 6
≈ Indalsälven [S] 5 S 6
Indjija [YU] 22 W 17
Indra [SU] 8 Y 10
≈ Indre [F] 19 J 16
≈ Indre Foldafjord [N] 4 Q 5
Δ Indre Solund [N] 4 N 7
Inece [TR] 23 Zb
Ineu [RO] 22 X 16
Infantes [E] 26 E 21
Infiesto [E] 24 E 18
Δ Infreschi, Punta d' — [I] 29 T 21
Ingå [SF] 9 W 7
Ingatorp [S] 7 S 9
Ingelmunster [B] 14 L 14
Ingelstd [S] 7 S 10
Ingolstadt [D] 15 Q 15
Δ Ingøy [N] 3 U 1
Ingulsvatn [N] 4 Q 5
≈ Iniönaukko [S] 9 U 7
Inis Coirthe = Enniscorthy [IRL] 12 F 12
Inis Díomáin = Ennistimon [IRL] 10 D 11
Inis = Ennis [IRL] 10 E 12
Δ Inishowen [IRL] 10 F 10
Δ Inishturk [IRL] 10 D 11
Inkoo = Ingå [SF] 9 W 7
≈ Inn [DA] 21 R 15
Inndyr [N] 2 R 3
≈ Inner Sound [GB] 10 G 9
Innertkirchen [CH] 20 O 16
Innfield [IRL] 10 F 11
Innhavet [N] 2 R 3
Δ Innherad [N] 4 Q 5
Innsbruck [A] 20 Q 16
Innset [N] 2 S 2
≈ Innviksfjord [N] 4 N 7
Δ Inoussai [GR] 31 Zb 21
Inowrocław [PL] 16 U 12
Insterburg = Čern'achovsk [SU] 8 V 11
Interlaken [CH] 20 O 16
Întorsura Buzăului [RO] 23 Z 16
Inverary [GB] 10 G 10
Inverbervie [GB] 11 J 9
Inverkeithing [GB] 11 H 10
Invermoriston [GB] 11 H 9
Inverness [GB] 11 H 9
Inverurie [GB] 11 J 9
Ioannina [GR] 30 X 20
Ioneşti [RO] 23 Z 17
Δ Ionioi Nisoi [GR] 30 W 21
Ios [GR] 31 Zb 22
Δ Ios [GR] 31 Zb 22
Ipati [GR] 30 Y 21
≈ Ipel [CS] 17 V 15
Δ Ipel'ská kotlina [CS] 17 V 15
Δ Ipiros [GR] 30 X 21
Ipsala [TR] 31 Zb 19
Ipsarion Oros [GR] 31 Z 19
Ipsous [GR] 30 Y 22
Ipswich [GB] 13 K 13
Iraklia [GR] 30 Y 19
Iraklion [GR] 32 Zb 23
≈ Irbeni väin [SU] 8 V 9
≈ Irish Sea10 G 11
≈ Irnijärvi [SF] 3 W 4
Irşina [I] 29 U 20
Irún [E] 18 G 18
Irurzun [E] 18 G 18
Irvine [GB] 10 G 10
Isaccea [RO] 23 Zb 16
Işalniţa [RO] 22 Y 17
≈ Isar [D] 15 Q 15
Ìschia [I] 29 S 20
Δ Ìschia, Ìsola d' — [I] 29 S 20
≈ Isefjord [DK] 6 Q 10
≈ Iseo, Lago d — [I] 20 P 17
Δ Iseran, Col de l' — [F] 20 N 17
≈ Isère [F] 19 M 17
Iserlohn [D] 15 O 13
Isèrnia [I] 29 S 20
Isigny-sur-Mer [F] 13 H 14
≈ Iskar [BT] 23 Z 18
≈ Iskŭr [BG] 22 Y 18
Isla-Cristina [E] 25 B 21
Δ Islay [GB] 10 G 10
≈ Isle [F] 19 J 17
Isle-en-Dodon, l' — [F] 19 J 18
Isle-Jourdain, l' — [F] 19 J 16
Isle-Jourdain, l' — [F] 19 J 18
Isle-sur-la-Sorgue, l' — [F] 19 M 18
Ismaning [D] 20 Q 15
Isnetotten [N] 2 T 1
≈ Isojärvi [SF] 9 U 6
Isojoki [SF] 9 U 6
Isokylä [SF] 3 W 3
Ìsola della Scala [I] 20 Q 17
Ìsola del Liri [I] 29 S 20
Ìsola di Capo Rizzuto [I] 29 U 21
≈ Iso Lamujärvi [SF] 9 W 5
Ìsola Rossa [I] 28 O 20
Isona [E] 27 J 19
Δ Isosyöte [SF] 3 W 4
Isperih [BG] 23 Za 17
Ìspica [I] 29 T 22
Issaris [GR] 30 Y 22
Isselburg [D] 15 N 13
Issoire [F] 19 L 17
Issoudun [F] 19 K 16
Is-sur-Tille [F] 19 M 16
Δ Ist [YU] 21 S 18
İstanbul [TR] 23 Zc 19
≈ Isteren [N] 4 Q 6
Istha [D] 15 P 13
Istiea [GR] 31 Z 21
Istok [YU] 22 W 19
Δ Istra [YU] 21 S 17
Δ Istranca dağlari [TR] 23 Zb 18
Istres [F] 19 M 18
Istria [RO] 23 Zb 17
Itálica, Ruinas de — [E] 25 C 21
Itea [GR] 30 Y 21
Ithaki [GR] 30 X 21
Δ Ithaki [GR] 30 X 21
Ìttiri [I] 28 O 20
Itzehoe [D] 15 P 12
Ivaceviči [SU] 17 Y 12
Ivajlovgrad [BG] 23 Za 19
Ivalo [SF] 3 V 2
≈ Ivalojoki [SF] 3 V 2
Ivana Franko [SU] 17 X 14
Ivanec [YU] 21 T 17
Ivangrad [YU] 22 W 19
Ivanić-Grad [YU] 21 T 17
Ivanjica [YU] 22 W 18
Ivanjska [YU] 21 U 17
Ivano Frankovsk [SU] 17 Y 14
Ivanovo [SU] 17 Y 12
Ivenec [SU] 8 Y 11
Iveşti [RO] 23 Za 16
Ivje [SU] 8 Y 11
Ivrea [I] 20 O 17
Ivrindi [TR] 31 Zc 20
Ixworth [GB] 13 K 13
Izbica [PL] 7 T 11
Izborsk [SU] 8 Y 9
Izmail [SU] 23 Zb 16
İzmir [TR] 31 Zc 21
≈ İzmir körfezi [TR] 31 Zb 21
≈ Iznajar, Pantano de — [E] 25 D 22
Iznalloz [E] 26 E 22
Izsák [H] 22 V 16
Izvor [YU] 30 X 19

J

Jaala [SF] 9 W 7
Jaalanka [SF] 3 W 4
≈ Jääsjärvi [SF] 9 W 6
≈ Jabalón, Río — [E] 26 E 21
Jablanac [YU] 21 S 18
Jablanica [YU] 21 U 18
Jablonec nad Nisou [CS] 16 S 14
Jablonica [CS] 16 U 15
Δ Jablonickij, pereval — [SU] 17 Y 15
Jabłonna [PL] 17 V 11
Jablonné v Podještědí [CS] 16 S 14
Jablonov [SU] 17 Y 15
Jabłonowo [PL] 16 U 12
Δ Jablunkovský průsmyk [VS] 16 U 14
Δ Jabuka [YU] 21 T 19
Jaca [E] 26 H 19
Jäckvik [S] 2 S 4
≈ Jade [D] 15 O 12
≈ Jadebusen [D] 15 O 12
Δ Jadovnik [YU] 22 W 18
Δ Jægervasstind [N] 2 S 1
Jaén [E] 26 E 21
Δ Jagodnja [YU] 22 V 18
≈ Jagst [D] 15 P 15
Δ Jahorina [YU] 22 V 18
Jajce [YU] 21 U 18
Jakimovo [BG] 22 Y 18
Jakkonen [SU] 3 X 3
Jaklovce [CS] 17 W 15
Jakobstad [SF] 9 U 5
Δ Jakupica [YU] 30 X 19
Jalasjärvi [SF] 9 V 6
≈ Jállas, Río — [E] 24 B 18
≈ Jalón, Río — [E] 26 F 19
≈ Jalpug, ozero — [SU] 23 Zb 16
Jambol [BG] 23 Za 18
Jämijärvi [SF] 9 V 6
Jämjöslätt [S] 7 S 10
≈ Jammerbugt [DK] 6 P 10
Jämsä [SF] 9 W 6
Δ Jämtland [S] 4 Q 6
Jämtlands-Sikås [S] 5 R 5
Jämtön [S] 3 U 4
≈ Janda, Laguna de la — [E] 25 C 22
≈ Jándula, Río — [E] 26 E 21
Janja [YU] 22 V 17
Janjevo [YU] 22 X 19
Janki [PL] 17 V 13
Janoshalma [H] 22 V 16
Jánosháza [H] 21 U 16
Janów Lubelski [PL] 17 W 13
Janów Podlaski [PL] 17 W 12
Δ Janson, Bois — [F] 19 M 16
Jantarnyj [SU] 7 U 11
≈ Jantra [BG] 23 Z 18
Janzé [F] 13 H 15
Δ Jara, La — [E] 25 D 20
Jaraco [E] 26 H 21
Jaraicejo [E] 25 D 20
Jaráiz de la Vera [E] 25 D 20
≈ Jarama, Río — [E] 26 E 20
Jarandilla [E] 25 D 20
Järbo [S] 5 S 7
Jaren [N] 4 P 8
Jargara [SU] 23 Zb 16
Jargeau [F] 19 K 15
Järkvissle [S] 5 S 6
Jarmen [DDR] 16 R 12
Jarnac [F] 18 H 17
Järnäshamm [S] 5 T 5
Δ Järnäsudden [S] 5 T 5
Järnforsen [S] 7 S 9
Jarny [F] 15 N 15
Jarocin [PL] 16 T 13
Jaroměř [CS] 16 T 14
Jaroměřice nad Rokytnou [CS] 16 T 15
Jarosław [PL] 17 X 14
Järpen [S] 5 R 6
Järvenpää [SF] 9 U 6
Järvenpää [SF] 9 W 7
Järvsö [S] 5 S 7
Jaša Tomić [YU] 22 W 17
≈ Jasel'da [SU] 17 Y 12
Jasen [BG] 23 Z 18
Jašiūnai [SU] 8 X 11
Jáskisér [H] 22 V 16
Jasło [PL] 17 W 14
Δ Jastrebac [YU] 22 X 18
Jastrebarsko [YU] 21 T 17
Jastrowie [PL] 16 T 12
Jászapáti [H] 22 V 16
Jászárokszállás [H] 22 V 15
Jászberény [H] 22 V 16
Δ Jászság [H] 22 V 16
Játiva [E] 26 G 21
Jaunauce [SU] 8 V 10
Jaunjelgava [SU] 8 X 9
Jaunpiebalga [SU] 8 X 9
Δ Jaurutunturi [SF] 3 W 3
Δ Javalambre [E] 26 G 20
Δ Javor [YU] 22 V 18
Δ Javor [YU] 22 W 18
Δ Javorice [SU] 16 S 15
Δ Javorie [CS] 17 V 15
Δ Javorníky [CS] 16 U 15
Javorov [SU] 17 X 14
≈ Javr [SU] 3 W 2
Jävre [S] 3 U 4
Jawor [PL] 16 T 13
Jaworzno [PL] 17 V 14
Δ Jaworzyna [PL] 17 V 14
Jebel [RO] 22 W 17
Jedburgh [GB] 11 J 10
Δ Jedovnik [YU] 21 T 18
Jędrzejów [PL] 17 V 14
Jedwabne [PL] 17 W 12
Jeesiö [SF] 3 V 3
≈ Jeesiöjoki [SF] 3 V 3
Jehlgava [SU] 8 W 10
Jekabpils [SU] 8 X 9
Jelenia Góra [PL] 16 S 14
Jeleniów [PL] 16 S 13
Δ Jelica [YU] 22 W 18
Jelling [DK] 6 P 11
Δ Jeløy [N] 6 P 8
Jelsa [YU] 21 U 19
Jelšava [CS] 17 V 15
Jemnice [CS] 16 S 15
Jena [DDR] 15 Q 14
≈ Jena [SU] 3 X 2
Jenbach [A] 20 Q 16
Jenlain [F] 14 L 14
Jerez de la Frontera [E] 25 C 22
Jerezde los Caballeros [E] 25 C 21
Jergul [N] 3 U 2
Jerka [PL] 16 T 13
≈ Jerte, Río — [E] 25 D 20
Δ Jersey [GB] 13 H 14
Jesenice [YU] 21 S 16
Δ Jesenik [CS] 16 T 14
Jesenské [CS] 17 V 15
Jesi [I] 21 R 18
Jessheim [N] 4 Q 8
Δ Jetnamsklumpen [N] 5 R 4
≈ Jeziorak, Jezioro — [PL] 7 U 12
Jeziorany [PL] 8 V 11
Jibou [RO] 22 X 15
Jičín [CS] 16 S 14
Δ Jiekkevarre [N] 2 S 2
≈ Jiešjavrre [N] 3 U 1
≈ Jiešjokka [N] 3 U 2
Jihlava [CS] 16 S 15
≈ Jihlava [CS] 16 T 15
Jijona [E] 26 G 21
Jilava [RO] 23 Za 17
≈ Jiloca, Río — [E] 26 G 20
Jimbolia [RO] 22 W 17
Jimena de la Frontera [E] 25 C 22
Jindřichuv Hradec [CS] 16 S 15
Jitaru [RO] 23 Z 17
≈ Jiu [RO] 22 Y 17
≈ Jizera [CS] 16 S 14
Jnaži [SU] 8 W 9
Δ Jøa [N] 4 Q 5
Jobbágyi [H] 22 V 15
Jock [S] 3 U 3
Jódar [E] 26 E 21
Jõelähtme [SU] 9 W 8
Joensuu [SF] 9 X 5
Jõesuu [SU] 8 X 8
Jõgeva [SU] 8 X 8
John Groat's [GB] 11 J 8
Jõhv [SU] 9 X 8
Joigny [F] 19 L 15
Joinville [F] 14 M 15
Δ Jøkeleggja [N] 4 O 7
Jokkmokk [S] 2 T 3
≈ Jølstervatn [N] 4 N 7
Δ Jomafjell [N] 5 R 5
Jomata [SF] 9 U 8
Jompala [SF] 3 V 1
Jonava [SU] 8 X 10
≈ Jongunjärvi [SF] 3 W 4
≈ Jongun joki [SF] 9 X 5
Joniškis [SU] 8 W 10
Jönköping [S] 7 R 9
Jordet [N] 4 Q 7
Jorgucat [AL] 30 W 20
Jörlanda [S] 6 Q 9
Jörn [S] 5 T 4
Jörpeland [N] 6 N 8
Jošanička Banja [YU] 22 W 18
Josipdol [YU] 21 T 17
Josselin [F] 12 G 15
Jøssund [N] 4 P 5
Jostedal [N] 4 O 7
Δ Jostedalsbre [N] 4 O 7
Δ Jostefonn [N] 4 O 7
Δ Jotunheimen [N] 4 O 7
Joukokylä [SF] 3 W 4
Joutsa [SF] 9 W 6
Joutseno [SF] 9 X 6
Joutsijärvi [SF] 3 W 3
Joyeuse [F] 19 L 18
Judenburg [A] 21 S 16
Juelsminde [DK] 6 P 11
Δ Jugoiztočni Rodopi [BG] 31 Z 19
Jugon-les-Lacs [F] 13 H 15
Juillac [F] 19 J 17
Δ Juist [D] 15 N 12
Jukkasjärvi [S] 2 T 3
Δ Jukspoor, gora — [SU] 3 X 2
≈ Juktån [S] 2 S 4
Jülich [D] 15 N 14
Δ Julierpass [CH] 20 P 17
Jumilla [E] 26 G 21
≈ Jumilla, Río — [E] 26 G 21
Jumisko [SF] 3 W 3
Δ Jungfrau [CH] 20 O 17
Δ Jungfrun(nationalpark) [S] 7 S 9
Δ Junkerdalen [N] 2 R 3
Junosuando [S] 3 U 3
Junsele [S] 5 S 5
Juntusranta [SF] 3 X 4
Juodkrantė [SU] 8 V 10
≈ Juojärvi [SF] 9 X 5
Juoksengi [S] 3 U 3
Juorkuna [SF] 3 W 4
≈ Jura, Sound of — [GB] 10 G 10
≈ Jura [SU] 8 V 10
Δ Jura [CH] 20 N 16
Δ Jura [GB] 10 G 10
Δ Jura Krakowska [PL] 17 V 14
Juratiški [SU] 8 Y 11
Jurbakas [SU] 8 W 11
Jūrkalne [SU] 8 V 9
Jūrmala [SU] 8 W 9
Δ Jurmo [SF] 9 U 8
Jurva [SF] 9 U 6
Jüterbog [DDR] 16 R 13
Δ Juuan vaara [SF] 9 X 5
Juujärvi [SF] 3 W 3
Juuka [SF] 9 X 5
≈ Juurusvesi [SF] 9 X 5
Juva [SF] 9 X 6
≈ Južna Morava [YU] 22 X 18
Jyderup [DK] 6 Q 11
Δ Jylland [DK] 6 P 11
Jyväskylä [SF] 9 W 6

K

≈ Kaalasjärvi [S] 2 S 3
Kaamanen [SF] 3 V 2
≈ Kaamasjoki [SF] 3 V 1
Kaaresuvanto [SF] 2 T 2
Kåbdalis [S] 2 T 4
Δ Kabhegy [H] 21 U 16
Kabile [SU] 8 V 9
Kačanik [YU] 22 X 19
Kačanovo [SU] 8 Y 9
Kacelovo [BG] 23 Za 18
≈ Kackimozero [SU] 3 W 2
Kadaň [CS] 16 R 14
Kadarkút [H] 21 U 17
≈ Kafirefs, Stenon — [GR] 31 Za 21
Δ Kafirefs, Akrotírion — [GR] 31 Za 21
Kåfjordbotn [N] 2 T 2
Kåge [S] 5 T 4
Δ Kågen [N] 2 T 1
Kagul [SU] 23 Zb 16
≈ Kagul, ozero — [SU] 23 Zb 16
Δ Kahler Asten [D] 15 O 13
Kaina [SU] 8 V 8
Kaindorf [A] 21 T 16
Kainu [SF] 9 V 5
Kainulaisjärvi [S] 3 U 3
Δ Kainuun selkä [SF] 3 W 4
Kaipiainen [SF] 9 X 7
Kaiserslautern [D] 15 O 15
Δ Kaiserstuhl [D] 20 O 15
≈ Kaitum älv [S] 2 T 3
≈ Kaitumjaure [S] 2 S 3
Kajaani [SF] 9 W 5
Kakanj [YU] 21 U 18
Δ Kalabak [YU, AL] 30 W 19
Kalajoki [SF] 9 V 5
≈ Kalajoki [SF] 9 V 5
Kalak [N] 3 V 1
Kalakoski [SF] 9 V 6
Kalamata [GR] 30 Y 22
Kalambaka [GR] 30 X 20
Kalamos [GR] 31 Z 21
Δ Kalamos [GR] 30 X 21
Kalandra [GR] 31 Z 20
Kalaras [SU] 23 Za 15
Kälarne [S] 5 S 6
Kalavrita [GR] 30 Y 21
Kalce [YU] 21 S 17
Kaldenkirchen [D] 15 N 13
Kalenić [YU] 22 W 18
Kalentzion [GR] 30 X 21
Δ Kaliakra, nos — [BG] 23 Zb 17
Kaliani [GR] 30 Y 21
Δ Kalikanmäki [SF] 9 V 6
Δ Kali Limvi [GR] 31 Zc 22
Kalimnos [GR] 31 Zc 22
Δ Kalimnos [GR] 31 Zc 22
Kalindria [GR] 30 Y 19
Kaliningrad [SU] 8 V 11
Kalinovik [YU] 22 V 18
Kalisz [PL] 16 U 13
Kalisz Pomorski [PL] 16 S 12
Kalix [S] 3 U 4
≈ Kalix älv [S] 3 U 3
Kall [S] 4 Q 6
Δ Kållandsö [S] 7 R 9
≈ Kallavesi [SF] 9 X 5
Källeryd [S] 7 R 9
Kallislahti [SF] 9 X 6
Kallo [SF] 3 U 3
Kalloni [GR] 31 Zb 20
Kallsedet [S] 4 Q 5
≈ Kallsjön [S] 4 Q 5
Kallunki [SF] 3 W 3
Kalmar [S] 7 S 10
≈ Kalmarsund [S] 7 S 10
Kálna [CS] 16 U 15
≈ Kalnica [BG] 23 Za 18
Kalniciems [SU] 8 W 9
Δ Kalnik [YU] 21 T 17
Kalocsa [H] 22 V 16
Kalon Neron [GR] 30 Y 22
≈ Kaložnoje, ozero — [SU] 3 X 2
Kalundborg [DK] 6 Q 11
Kaluš [SU] 17 Y 14
Kalvarija [SU] 8 W 11
Kälviä [SF] 9 V 5
Kalvola [SF] 9 V 7
Kalvträsk [S] 5 T 5
Kalwang [A] 21 S 16
Kám [H] 21 T 16
Δ Kambanos, Akrotirion — [GR] 31 Za 21
Kambos [GR] 30 Y 22
≈ Kamčija [BG] 23 Zb 18
Kamen [D] 15 O 13
Kamenica [YU] 22 W 18
Δ Kamenjak, Rt — [YU] 21 S 18
Kamenka [SU] 23 Zc 15
Kamenka-Bugskaja [SU] 17 X 14
Kamen'-Kašširskij [SU] 17 Y 13
Kamenz [DDR] 16 R 13
Kames [GB] 10 G 10
Kamienna Góra [PL] 16 T 14
Kamień Pomorski [PL] 7 S 12
Kamieńsk [PL] 17 V 13
Kamiros [GR] 32 Zd 22
Δ Kammiovuori [SF] 9 W 6
Kamnik [YU] 21 S 17
Kampen [NL] 15 N 13
Kanalion [GR] 30 X 21
Kandalakša [SU] 3 X 2
Kandanos [GR] 32 Za 23
Kandel [D] 15 O 15
Δ Kandeloussa [GR] 31 Zc 22
Kandila [GR] 30 Y 22
Kangari [SU] 8 W 9
Kangaslampi [SF] 9 X 6
Kangasniemi [SF] 9 W 6
Kangaz [SU] 23 Zb 16
Kangos [S] 3 U 3
Kangosjärvi [SF] 3 U 3
Kanjiža [YU] 22 W 16
Kankaanpää [SF] 9 U 6
Kånna [S] 7 R 10
Kannonkoski [SF] 9 W 5
Kannus [SF] 9 V 5
Kantala [SF] 9 X 6
Δ Kap Arkona [DDR] 7 R 11
Δ Kapela [YU] 21 S 17
Kapelln [A] 21 T 15
Δ Kapello [GR] 31 Z 22
Kapfenberg [A] 21 S 16
Δ Kapıdağı yarımadası [TR] 31 Zc 19
≈ Kapos [H] 21 U 16
Kaposvár [H] 21 U 16
Kapp [N] 4 P 7
Kappeln [D] 6 P 11
Kappelshamn [S] 7 T 9
Kappelskär [S] 5 T 8
Kapsukas [SU] 8 W 11
Kapuvár [H] 21 T 16
Karabiga [TR] 31 Zb 19
Karaburun [TR] 31 Zb 21
Δ Karaburun [AL] 30 W 20
Δ Kara burun [TR] 31 Zb 21
Karacabey [TR] 31 Zc 19
Karacaköy [TR] 23 Zc 19
Karacasu [TR] 32 Zd 21
≈ Karadeniz boğazi [TR] 23 Zc 19
Karasjok [N] 3 U 1
≈ Karasjokka [N] 3 U 2
≈ Karatj [S] 2 S 3
Δ Karavi [GR] 32 Z 22
Δ Karavonissia [GR] 31 Zc 22
Δ Karawanken [A,I,YU] 21 S 16
Kårböle [S] 5 R 6
Karby [DK] 6 O 10
Karcag [H] 22 W 16
Kardamena [GR] 31 Zc 22
Kardamila [GR] 31 Zb 21
Karditsa [GR] 30 Y 21
Kärdla [SU] 8 V 8
Kărdžali [BG] 23 Za 19
Karesuando [S] 2 T 2
≈ Karhijärvi [SF] 9 V 6
Karhukangas [SF] 9 V 5
Karhula [SF] 3 U 2
Karhula [SF] 9 X 7
Δ Karhutunturi [SF] 3 W 3
Karia [GR] 30 X 21
Kariaa = Karis [SF] 9 V 7
Karie [GR] 31 Z 20
Karigasniemi [SF] 3 U 1
Karinainen [SF] 9 V 7
Karis [SF] 9 V 7
Karistos [GR] 31 Za 21
Karjala [SF] 9 V 7
Δ Karjalan selkä [SF] 9 X 5
Karkkila [SF] 9 W 7
Kärkölä [SF] 9 V 7
Δ Karkonosze [PL] 16 S 14
Karlebotn [N] 3 V 1
Karlino [PL] 7 S 12
Karl-Marx-Stadt [DDR] 16 R 14
Karlobag [YU] 21 S 18
Δ Karlö = Hailuoto [SF] 3 V 4
Karlovac [YU] 21 T 17
Karlovo [BG] 23 Z 18
Karlovy Vary [CS] 16 R 14
Karlsborg [S] 3 U 4
Karlsborg [S] 7 R 9
Karlshafen [D] 15 P 13
Karlshamn [S] 7 S 10
Karlskoga [S] 7 R 8
Karlskrona [S] 7 S 10
Δ Karlsøy [N] 2 S 1
Karlsruhe [D] 15 O 15
Karlstad [S] 7 R 8
Karlstadt [D] 15 P 14
Karlstadt = Karlovac [YU] 21 T 17
Karlštejn [CS] 16 S 14
Karlstift [A] 21 S 15
Karlsvik [S] 3 U 4
Δ Karmøy [N] 6 N 8
Kărnare [BG] 23 Z 18
Δ Karnische Alpen [A, I] 21 R 16
Karnobat [BG] 23 Zb 18
Δ Kärnten [A] 21 R 16
Karoussades [GR] 30 W 20
Karow [DDR] 15 Q 12
Karpathos [GR] 31 Zc 22
Δ Karpathos [GR] 31 Zc 22
Karpenision [GR] 30 Y 21
Karperon [GR] 30 X 20
Kärsämäki [SF] 9 W 5
Δ Kårsåtjåkko [S] 2 S 3
Kårsava [SU] 8 Y 9
Karstula [SF] 9 V 6
Karttula [SF] 9 W 5
Kartuzy [PL] 7 T 11
Karungi [S] 3 U 4
Karunki [SF] 3 U 4
Karup [DK] 6 P 10
Karuse [SU] 8 W 8
Karvala [SF] 9 V 5
Karvia [SF] 9 V 6
Karviná [CS] 16 U 14
Karvio [SF] 9 X 5
Kasala [SF] 9 U 6
Kasern = Casere [I] 20 Q 16
Δ Kaskasatjåkko [S] 2 S 3
Kasker [S] 2 S 4
Kaskinen = Kaskö [SF] 9 U 6
Kaskö [SF] 9 U 6
Δ Kassandra [GR] 31 Z 20
≈ Kassandras, Kolpos — [GR] 31 Z 20
Δ Kassandras, Akrotirion — [GR] 31 Z 20
Kassel [D] 15 P 13
Δ Kassos [gR] 31 Zc 22
≈ Kassou, Stenon — [GR] 32 Zd 22
Kastaneai [GR] 23 Za 19
Kastelholm [SF] 9 U 7
Kastellion [GR] 32 Za 23
Kastellos [GR] 32 Zd 22
Δ Kastellou, Akrotirion — [GR] 31 Zc 22
Kasterlee [B] 14 M 13
Kastoria [GR] 30 X 20
Kastron [GR] 31 Z 21
Δ Kaszuby [PL] 7 T 11
Katakolon [GR] 30 Y 22
Katakumpu [SF] 3 V 3
Katerini [GR] 30 Y 20
≈ Katlabuch, ozero — [SU] 23 Zb 16
Katlanovo [YU] 30 X 19
Kato Achaïa [GR] 30 Y 21
Kato Figalia [GR] 30 Y 22
Δ Katogheri [GR] 31 Za 21
Kato Kalamon [GR] 32 Zd 22
Kato Nevrokopion [GR] 31 Z 19
Katowice [PL] 16 U 14
Katrineholm [S] 7 S 8
Kattavia [GR] 32 Zd 22
≈ Kattegat6 Q 10
Katthammarsvik [S] 7 T 9
Kattisavan [S] 5 S 5
Katwijk aan Zee [NL] 14 M 3
Katzbach [A] 21 S 15
Kaufbeuren [D] 20 P 16
Kauhajoki [SF] 9 U 6
Kauhava [SF] 9 V 5
Kaukonen [SF] 3 U 3
Kauliranta [SF] 3 U 3
Kaunas [SU] 8 W 11
Kaunatava [SU] 8 W 10
Kaupanger [N] 4 O 7
Δ Kaurissalo [SF] 9 U 7
Kaušany [SU] 23 Zb 15
Kaustby = Kaustinen [SF] 9 V 5
Kaustinen [SF] 9 V 5
Kautokeino [N] 3 U 2
Kavajë [AL] 30 W 20
Kavak [TR] 31 Zb 19
Kavala [GR] 31 Z 19
≈ Kavalas, Kolpos — [GR] 31 Z 19
Kavarna [BG] 23 Zb 17
Kavoussion [GR] 32 Zb 23
Kaxås [S] 5 R 6
Kaytamo [SF] 3 V 3
Kazanlăk [BG] 23 Za 18
Δ Kaz dağ [TR] 31 Zb 20
Kazlškiat [SU] 8 X 10
Kcynia [PL] 16 T 12
Kea [GR] 32 Za 21
Δ Kea [GR] 32 Za 21

Keady [GB] 10 F 11
Δ Kebnekajse [S] 2 S 3
Kecel [H] 22 V 16
Kecskemét [H] 22 V 16
Kedainiai [SU] 8 W 10
Kedros [GR] 30 Y 21
Kędzierzyn [PL] 16 U 14
Δ Kefallinia [GR] 30 X 21
Kehl [D] 15 O 15
Keighley [GB] 11 J 11
Keikyä [SF] 9 V 7
Keila [SU] 8 W 8
Keitele [SF] 9 W 5
Keith [GB] 11 J 9
Kekava [SU] 8 W 9
Δ Kékes [H] 22 V 15
Δ Kekurskij, mys — [SU] 3 W 1
Këlcyrë [AL] 30 W 20
Δ Kelečský Javornik [CS] 16 U 14
Kelenkylä [SF] 3 W 4
Kelheim [D] 15 Q 15
Kelibia [TN] 8 Q 22
Kells [IRL] 10 F 11
≈ Kellvjärvi [SF] 9 X 4
Kelmė [SU] 8 W 10
Kelvä [SF] 9 X 5
Δ Kemeneshát [H] 21 T 16
Kemer [TR] 32 Zd 21
≈ Kemer barajı [TR] 32 Zd 21
Kemi [SF] 3 V 4
Kemijärvi [SF] 3 W 3
≈ Kemijärvi [SF] 3 V 3
≈ Kemijoki [SF] 3 V 3
≈ Kemijoki [SF] 3 W 2
Kemiö = Kimito [SF] 9 V 7
Kemnath [D] 15 Q 14
Kempele [SF] 3 V 4
Kempten (Allgäu) [D] 20 P 16
Kemptthal [CH] 20 O 16
Kendal [GB] 11 H 11
Kenilworth [GB] 13 J 12
Kenmare [IRL] 12 D 12
≈ Kenmare River [IRL] 12 D 12
Δ Kent [GB] 13 K 13
Kępno [PL] 16 U 13
Δ Keprník [CS] 16 T 14
Kepsut [TR] 31 Zc 20
Keramia [GR] 31 Zb 20
Keramitsa [GR] 30 X 20
Keramoti [GR] 31 Z 19
Keratea [GR] 31 Z 21
Kerecsend [H] 22 V 15
Kerimäki [SF] 9 X 6
Kerion [GR] 30 X 22
Δ Kerkini Oros [GR] 30 Y 19
≈ Kerkinis, Limni — [GR] 30 Y 19
Kerkira [GR] 30 W 21
Δ Kerkira [GR] 30 W 21
≈ Kermajärvi [SF] 9 X 6
≈ Kerme körfezi [TR] 31 Zc 21
Kermen [BG] 23 Za 18
Δ Keros [GR] 31 Zb 22
Kersilö [SF] 3 V 3
Kerstinbo [S] 5 S 8
Kerteminde [DK] 6 P 11
Keşan [TR] 31 Zb 19
Kesarevo [BG] 23 Za 18
Kesh [GB] 10 F 11
Kestilä [SF] 9 W 5
Keswick [GB] 11 H 11
Keszthely [H] 21 U 16
Kętrzyn [PL] 8 V 11
Kettering [GB] 13 J 12
Kęty [PL] 17 V 14
Keuruu [SF] 9 V 6
≈ Keuruun selkä [SF] 9 V 6
Kežmarok [CS] 17 V 14
≈ Kiantajärvi [SF] 3 X 4
Kiaton [GR] 31 Z 21
Kiberg [N] 3 W 1
Kica [SU] 3 X 1
Kičevo [YU] 30 X 19
Kidderminster [GB] 13 H 12
Kidwelly [GB] 12 G 13
Kiel [D] 6 P 11
Kielce [PL] 17 V 13
Kieleczka [PL] 16 U 14
≈ Kieler Bucht [D] 6 P 11
Kifino Selo [YU] 22 V 18
Kifissia [GR] 31 Z 21
Kifissochorion [GR] 30 Y 21
Kihelkonna [SU] 8 V 9
Kihlanki [SF] 3 U 3
Kihniö [SF] 9 V 6
Δ Kihnu [SU] 8 W 9
≈ Kihti = Skiftet [SF] 9 U 7
Kiikala [SF] 9 V 7
Kiikoinen [SF] 9 V 7
Kiiminki [SF] 3 V 4
Kiistala [SF] 3 V 2
Kikinda [YU] 22 W 17
Δ Kiklades Nisoi [GR] 31 Za 21
Kil [N] 6 P 9
Kil [S] 7 R 8
Kila [S] 7 S 9
Kilafors [S] 5 S 7
Kilbeggan [IRL] 10 F 11
Kildare [IRL] 10 F 11
Δ Kil'din, ostrov — [SU] 3 X 1
Kil'dinstroj [SU] 3 X 1
Kilifarevo [BG] 23 Za 18
Kilija [SU] 23 Zb 16
Kilkee [IRL] 10 D 12
Kilkeel [GB] 10 F 11
Kilkenny [IRL] 12 E 12
Kilkis [GR] 30 Y 19
Killarney [IRL] 12 D 12
Δ Killiecrankie, Pass of — [GB] 11 H 9
Killikoski [SF] 9 V 6
Killin [GB] 11 H 10
Killingi-Nõmme [SU] 8 W 9
Killini [GR] 30 X 22
Δ Killini Oros [GR] 30 Y 21
Killybegs [IRL] 10 E 10
Kilmarnock [GB] 11 H 10
Kilmelford [GB] 10 G 10
Δ Kilpimäki [SF] 9 W 6
Kilpisjärvi [SF] 2 T 2
≈ Kilpisjärvi [S, SF] 2 T 2
Kilrenny [GB] 11 J 10
Kilrush [IRL] 10 D 12
Kilyos [TR] 23 Zc 19
Kimi [GR] 31 Z 21
Δ Kimis, Akrotirion — [GR] 31 Z 21
Kimito [SF] 9 V 7
Δ Kimito [SF] 9 V 7
Kimolos [GR] 31 Za 22
Δ Kimolos [GR] 31 Za 22
Δ Kinaros [GR] 31 Zb 22
Kinbrace [GB] 11 H 8
Kindberg [A] 21 S 16
Kingisepp [SU] 8 V 9
Kingsbridge [GB] 12 G 14
King's Lynn [GB] 13 K 12
Kingston upon Hull [GB] 11 J 12
Kingstown [IRL] 10 F 11
Kingussie [GB] 11 H 9
Kınık [TR] 31 Zc 20
Kinlochleven [GB] 11 H 9
Kinloch Rannoch [GB] 11 H 9
Δ Kinnaird's Head [GB] 11 J 9
Δ Kinnarodden = Nordkinn [N] 3 V 1
Kinnegad [IRL] 10 F 11
Δ Kinnekulle [S] 7 R 9
Kinnula [SF] 9 V 5
Kinross [GB] 11 H 10
Kinsarvik [N] 4 O 8
Δ Kintyre [GB] 10 G 10
Kionion [GR] 30 X 21
Kiparissia [GR] 30 Y 22
≈ Kiparissiakos Kolpos [GR] 30 Y 22
Kipinä [SF] 3 W 4
Δ Kira Panaghia [GR] 31 Z 20
Kirbiži [SU] 8 W 9
Kirchberg an der Pielach [A] 21 S 15
Kirchheim unter Teck [D] 15 P 15
Kirchschlag [A] 21 T 16
Kırkağaç [TR] 31 Zc 20
Kirkbean [GB] 11 H 11
Kirkby Lonsdale [GB] 11 H 11
Kirkby Stephen [GB] 11 H 11
Kirkcaldy [GB] 11 H 10
Kirkcudbright [GB] 11 H 11
Kirkenær [N] 4 Q 8
Kirkenes [N] 3 W 1
Kirkkonummi = Kyrkslätt [SF] 9 W 7
Kirklareli [TR] 23 Zb 19
Kirkwall [GB] 11 J 8
Kirnyĉki [SU] 23 Zb 16
Kirriemuir [GB] 10 J 10
Kiruna [S] 2 T 3
Δ Kirunavaara [S] 2 T 3
Kisa [S] 7 S 9
Δ Kisalföld [H] 21 T 16
Kisbér [H] 21 U 16
Kiseljak [YU] 21 U 18
Kišin'ov [SU] 23 Zb 15
Kisko [SF] 9 V 7
Kiskőrös [H] 22 V 16
Kiskunfélegyháza [H] 22 V 16
Kiskunhalas [H] 22 V 16
Kiskunlacháza [H] 22 V 16
Kiskunmajsa [H] 22 V 16
Δ Kiskúnság [H] 22 V 16
Kismarja [H] 22 W 16
≈ Kissamou, Kolpos — [GR] 32 Za 23
Kistanje [YU] 21 T 18
Kistelek [H] 22 V 16
Kisújszallas [H] 22 W 16
Kisvárda [H] 17 W 15 23
≈ Kitaj, ozero — [SU] 23 Zb 16
Δ Kithira [GR] 31 Z 22
Kithnos [GR] 32 Za 22
Δ Kithnos [GR] 32 Za 22
≈ Kitinen [SF] 3 V 3
Δ Kitka [YU] 22 X 19
Kitkiöjoki [S] 3 U 3
Kitros [GR] 30 Y 20
Kittelfjäll [S] 5 R 4
Kittilä [SF] 3 U 3
Kitula [SF] 9 V 7
Kitzbühel [A] 21 R 16
Kitzingen [D] 15 P 14
Kiuruvesi [SF] 9 W 5
Kiverci [SU] 17 Y 13
Kivijärvi [SF] 9 V 5
≈ Kivijärvi [SF] 9 V 5
≈ Kivijärvi [SF] 9 X 6
Δ Kivimaa [SF] 9 U 7
Kivirata [SF] 3 X 3
Kıyıköy [TR] 23 Zc 19
Kjeldebotn [N] 2 R 2
Δ Kjelelvtinden [N] 2 S 2
Kjellerholen [N] 4 Q 8
Kjellerup [DK] 6 P 10
Kjerningvåg [N] 4 P 5
Δ Kjølhaugene [N] 4 Q 6
Kjøllefjord [N] 3 V 1
Kladanj [YU] 22 V 18
Kladno [CS] 16 S 14
Kladovo [YU] 22 X 17
Klagenfurt [A] 21 S 16
Klaipėda [SU] 8 V 10
Klarabro [S] 4 Q 7
≈ Klarälven [S] 4 Q 7
Klatovy [CS] 16 R 15
Klaus an der Pyhrnbahn [A] 21 S 16
Klausen = Chiusa [I] 20 Q 16
Kleczew [PL] 16 U 13
Kleppe [N] 6 N 9
Δ Klēts kalns [SU] 8 X 9
Kleve [D] 15 N 13
Δ Klibreck, Ben — [GB] 11 H 8
Klimpfjäll [S] 5 R 5
Klingenthal/Sachsen [DDR] 16 R 14
Δ Klínovec [CS] 16 R 14
Klintehamn [S] 7 T 9
Klisa [YU] 21 U 17
Klisura [BG] 23 Z 18
Klitmøller [DK] 6 O 10
Δ Ključ [YU] 22 X 17
Kłodawa [PL] 16 U 13
Kłodzko [PL] 16 T 14
Kløfta [N] 4 Q 8
Klokkarvik [N] 4 N 8
Klosters [CH] 20 P 16
Klövsjö [S] 5 R 6
Kluczbork [PL] 16 U 13
Kmeťovce [CS] 16 U 15
Knabengruver [N] 6 O 9
Knaften [S] 5 T 5
Knäred [S] 7 R 10
Knäsjö [S] 5 S 5
Kn'ažaja Guba [SU] 0 X 3
Kneža [BG] 23 Z 18
Knidos [TR] 31 Zc 22
Knighton [GB] 13 H 12
Knin [YU] 21 T 18
Knislinge [S] 7 R 10
Knittelfeld [A] 21 S 16
Knjaževac [YU] 22 X 18
Knokke [B] 14 L 13
Knole House [GB] 13 J 13
Knossos [GR] 32 Zb 23
Δ Knudshoved Odde [DK] 6 Q 11
Δ Knutshø [N] 4 P 6
Δ Knutsholtind [N] 4 O 7
Knyszyn [PL] 17 W 12
Δ Koarvikods [SF] 3 V 2
Δ Kobanke [DK] 6 Q 11
Kobarid [YU] 21 R 17
København [DK] 6 Q 11
Koblenz [CH] 20 O 16
Koblenz [D] 15 O 14
Kobrin [SU] 17 X 12
Kobyl'nik [SU] 8 Y 10
≈ Koca çayı [TR] 31 Zc 20
Kočani [YU] 30 Y 19
Koçarlı [TR] 31 Zc 21
Koceljevo [YU] 22 W 18
Kočerniovo [BG] 22 Y 19
Kočevje [YU] 21 S 17
≈ Kocher [D] 15 P 15
Δ Kociewie [PL] 7 T 10
Kočmar [BG] 23 Zb 17
Kodyma [SU] 0 Zb 14
Δ Kofinas Oros [GR] 32 Zb 23
Köflach [A] 21 S 16
Køge [DK] 6 Q 11
≈ Køge Bugt [DK] 6 Q 11
Kohila [SU] 9 W 8
Kohtla [SU] 9 X 8
Koivu [SF] 3 V 3
Koivulahti = Kvevlax [SF] 9 U 6
Kökar [SF] 9 U 8
≈ Kökarsfjärd [SF] 9 U 8
Kokelv [N] 3 U 1
≈ Kokemäenjoki [SF] 9 U 7
Kokkokylä [SF] 3 V 4
Kokkola [SF] 9 U 5
Koknese [SU] 8 X 9
≈ Kokonselkä [SF] 9 X 6
Kola [SU] 3 X 1
≈ Kola [SU] 3 X 1
Kołacin [PL] 17 V 13
Kolari [SF] 3 U 3
Kolašin [YU] 22 W 19
Kolbäck [S] 5 S 8
Kolberg = Kołobrzeg [PL] 7 S 11
Kolbuszowa [PL] 17 W 14
Kolby [DK] 6 P 11
Kolding [DK] 6 P 11
Koler [S] 2 T 4
≈ Kolga laht [SU] 9 W 8
Δ Koli [SF] 9 X 5
≈ Kolimajärvi [SF] 9 W 5
Kolín [CS] 16 S 14
Kolka [SU] 8 V 9
Δ Kolkasrags [SU] 8 V 9
Kolki [SU] 17 Y 13
Kolline [GR] 30 Y 22
Kollnbrunn [A] 21 T 15
Köln [D] 15 N 14
Kolno [PL] 17 W 12
Koło [PL] 16 U 13
Kołobrzeg [PL] 7 S 11
Kolomyja [SU] 17 Y 15
≈ Kolozero [SU] 3 X 2
≈ Kol'skij zaliv [SU] 3 X 1
Kolsva [S] 5 S 8
Koltveit [N] 4 N 8
Kolvereid [N] 4 Q 5
Kolvik [N] 3 U 1
Komańcza [PL] 17 W 14
Komárno [CS] 21 U 15
Komarno [SU] 17 X 14
Komárom [H] 21 U 16
Kombotion [GR] 30 X 21
Komiža [YU] 21 T 19
Komotini [GR] 31 Za 19
Kompelusvaara [S] 3 U 3
Komrat [SU] 23 Zb 16
Komunari [BG] 23 Zb 18
Konare [BG] 23 Zb 17
Δ Kon'avska planina [BG] 22 Y 19
Kondratjevo [SU] 9 X 7
Koneč Kovdozero [SU] 3 X 3
Köngäs [SF] 3 U 2
Konginkangas [SF] 9 W 6
Δ Kongsbakktinden [N] 2 S 2
Kongsberg [N] 6 P 8
Kongsfjord [N] 3 V 1
Kongsmoen [N] 4 Q 5
Kongsvinger [N] 4 Q 8
Konice [CS] 16 T 14
Koniecna [PL] 17 W 14
Königsberg (Preußen) = Kaliningrad [SU] 8 V 11
Königsbrück [DDR] 16 R 13
Königssee [D] 21 R 16
Königs Wusterhausen [DDR] 16 R 13
Konin [PL] 16 U 13
Konispol [AL] 30 W 20
Konitsa [GR] 30 X 20
Konjic [YU] 21 U 18
Δ Konjuh [YU] 22 V 18
≈ Könkämä älv [S] 2 T 2
Könnern [DDR] 15 Q 13
Konnevesi [SF] 9 W 6
≈ Konnevesi [SF] 9 W 5
Könnu [SU] 9 W 8
Konotop [PL] 16 S 13
Końskie [PL] 17 V 13
Konstanz [D] 20 P 16
Kontiolahti [SF] 9 X 5
Kontiomäki [SF] 9 W 4
Kontopoulion [GR] 31 Za 20
Konuš [BG] 23 Za 19
Koosa [SU] 8 X 8
Δ Kopaonik [YU] 22 W 18
Koper [YU] 21 R 17
Kopervik [N] 6 N 8
Köping [S] 7 S 8
Koplik i Sipërm [AL] 30 W 19
Köpmanholmen [S] 5 T 6
Köpmannebro [S] 6 Q 9
Koppang [N] 4 Q 7
Kopparberg [S] 5 R 8
Koppom [S] 4 Q 8
Koprivnica [YU] 21 T 17
Kopsa [SF] 9 V 4
Kõpu [SU] 8 V 8
Δ Korab [YU, AL] 30 W 19
Δ Koralpe [A] 21 S 16
Korbach [D] 15 O 13
Korbous [TN] 28 Q 22
Korçë [AL] 30 X 20
Korčula [YU] 21 U 19
Δ Korčula [YU] 21 U 19
≈ Korčulanski kanal [YU] 21 U 19
Koreliči [SU] 8 Y 11
Korentokylä [SF] 3 W 4
Korgen [N] 2 R 4
Korini [GR] 31 Z 21
≈ Korinthiakos Kolpos [GR] 30 Y 21
Korinthos [GR] 31 Z 21
≈ Korinthou, Diorx — [GR] 31 Z 21
Δ Kőrishegy [H] 21 U 16
Körmend [H] 21 T 16
Δ Kornat [YU] 21 T 18
Korneuburg [A] 21 T 15
Koroni [GR] 30 Y 22
Koronis [GR] 31 Zb 22
Koronowo [PL] 16 T 12
≈ Körös [H] 22 W 16
≈ Korpijärvi [SF] 9 X 6
≈ Korpijoki [SF] 3 W 4
Korpilahti [SF] 9 W 6
Korpilombolo [S] 3 U 3
Korpo [SF] 9 U 7
Korppoo = Korpo [SF] 9 U 7
≈ Korsfjord [N] 4 N 8
Korskrogen [S] 5 S 7
Korsmo [N] 4 Q 8
Korsnäs [S] 5 S 7
Korsnäs [SF] 9 U 6
Korsør [DK] 6 Q 11
Kortesjärvi [SF] 9 V 5
Korthion [GR] 31 Za 21
Kortrijk [B] 14 L 14
Δ Korvatunturi [SF, SU] 3 W 2
Kos [GR] 31 Zc 22
Δ Kos [GR] 31 Zc 22
Kościan [PL] 16 T 13
Kościerzyna [PL] 7 T 11
Kose [SU] 8 W 8
Košetice [CS] 16 S 14
Košice [CS] 17 W 15
Kosjerić [YU] 22 W 18
Koskenpää [SF] 9 W 6
Koski [SF] 9 V 7
Koskue [SF] 9 V 6
Koskullskulle [S] 2 T 3
Köslin = Koszalin [PL] 7 S 11
Δ Kosmaj [YU] 22 W 17
Kosmas [GR] 31 Z 22
Δ Kosovo polje [YU] 22 X 18
Kosovska Mitrovica [YU] 22 W 18
Kostelec nad Černými Lesi [CS] 16 S 14
Kostenec [BG] 23 Z 19
Δ Kosteröarna [S] 6 Q 9
Kostinbrod [BG] 22 Y 18
Kostolac [YU] 22 W 17
≈ Kostonjärvi [SF] 3 W 3
Kostrzyn [PL] 16 S 13
Koszalin [PL] 7 S 11
Koszęcin [PL] 16 U 14
Kőszeg [H] 21 T 16
Kotala [SF] 3 W 3
Δ Kotari [YU] 21 T 18
Köthen/Anhalt [DDR] 15 Q 13
Kotka [SF] 9 X 7
Δ Kotlina Sandomierska [PL] 17 V 14
Kotor [YU] 22 V 19
≈ Kotorska, Boka — [YU] 30 V 19
Kotor Varoš [YU] 21 U 18
Kotovsk [sw. Kišin'ov] [SU] 23 Zb 15
Kötschach-Mauthen [A] 21 R 16
Δ Koufonission [GR] 31 Zb 22
Δ Koufonission [GR] 32 Zc 23
Δ Koukkutunturi [SF] 3 W 2
Koumanis [GR] 30 Y 22
Kouvola [SF] 9 X 7
Kovačica [YU] 22 W 17
Kovdor [SU] 3 W 2
≈ Kovdozero [SU] 3 X 3
Kovel' [SU] 17 X 13
Kovin [YU] 22 W 17
Kowal [PL] 16 U 12
Kowalewo Pomorskie [PL] 16 U 12
Kowary [PL] 16 S 14
Kozani [GR] 30 Y 20
Koz'any [SU] 8 Y 10
Δ Kozara [YU] 21 T 17
Kozarac [YU] 21 U 17
Kozar Belene [BG] 23 Z 18
Kozienice [PL] 17 W 13
Kózle [PL] 16 U 14
Kozloduj [BG] 22 Y 18
Koźmin [PL] 16 T 13
Kożuchów [PL] 16 S 13
Δ Kožuf [YU] 30 Y 19
Kräckelbäcken [S] 5 R 7
Kragerø [N] 6 P 9
Kraguljevac [YU] 22 W 18
Δ Krajina [YU] 21 T 17
Δ Krajina [YU] 22 X 18
Δ Krajište [YU] 22 Y 19
Krakberget [N] 2 R 2
Kraków [PL] 17 V 14
Králíky [CS] 16 T 14
Kraljevica [YU] 21 S 17
Kraljevo [YU] 22 W 18
Kral'ovany [CS] 17 V 15
Kralovice [CS] 16 R 14
Kráľovský Chlmec [CS] 17 W 15
Kramfors [S] 5 S 6
Kranidion [GR] 31 Z 22
Kranj [YU] 21 S 17
Krapina [YU] 21 T 17
Krapkowice [PL] 16 U 14
Δ Kras [I, YU] 21 R 17
Krāslava [SU] 8 Y 10
Krasna [SU] 17 Y 14
Kraśnik [PL] 17 W 13
Krasnogorodskoje [SU] 8 Y 9
Krasnoje [SU] 8 Y 11
Krasnosel'cy [SU] 8 Y 10
Krasnystaw [PL] 17 X 13
Kratovo [YU] 22 Y 19
Kražiai [SU] 8 W 10
Krefeld [D] 15 N 13
Krekenava [SU] 8 W 10
Křelovice [CS] 16 S 14
Δ Kremen [YU] 21 T 18
Kremenica [YU] 30 X 20
Kremincz [SU] 17 Y 15
≈ Kremnaston, Limni — [GR] 30 X 21
Kremnica [CS] 16 U 15
Krems an der Donau [A] 21 S 15
Krepoljin [YU] 22 X 18
Krestena [GR] 30 Y 22
Kretinga [SU] 8 V 10
Δ Krievu kalns [SU] 8 V 10
Krikovo [SU] 23 Zb 15
Krimml [A] 20 Q 16
Kriničnoje [SU] 23 Zb 16
Δ Krios, Akrotirion — [GR] 32 Za 23
Kristdala [S] 7 S 9
Kristiansand [N] 6 O 9
Kristianstad [S] 7 R 10
Kristiansund [N] 4 O 6
Kristiinankaupunki = Kristinestad [SF] 9 U 6
Kristineberg [S] 5 S 4
Kristinehamn [S] 7 R 8
Kristinestad [SF] 9 U 6
Δ Kriti [GR] 32 Za 23
≈ Krivaja [YU] 22 V 18
Kriva Palanka [YU] 22 Y 19
Kriviči [SU] 8 Y 10
Krivi Vir [YU] 22 X 18
Krivodol [BG] 22 Y 18
Križevci [YU] 21 T 17
Krk [YU] 21 S 17
Δ Krk [YU] 21 S 17
≈ Krka [YU] 21 T 18
Krnov [CS] 16 U 14
Krøderen [N] 4 P 8
≈ Krøderen [N] 4 P 8
Krokee [GR] 31 Z 22
Kroken [N] 2 R 4
Krokhaug [N] 4 P 6
Krokom [S] 5 R 6
Krokowo [PL] 7 T 11
Kroměříž [CS] 16 T 15
Kronach [D] 15 Q 14
Kronoby [SF] 9 U 5
≈ Kronoby [SF] 9 U 5
Krośniewice [PL] 16 U 13
Krosno [PL] 17 W 14
Krosno Odrzańkie [PL] 16 S 13
Krotoszyn [PL] 16 T 13
Δ Krrabë [AL] 30 W 20
Krško [YU] 21 T 17
Krujë [AL] 30 W 19
Krumbach (Schwaben) [D] 20 P 15
Krumovgrad [BG] 31 Za 19
Kruonis [SU] 8 X 11
Krupac [YU] 22 Y 18
Krupina [CS] 17 V 15
Δ Krupinská vrchovina [CS] 17 V 15
Krušari [BG] 23 Zb 17
Kruščica [YU] 21 T 18
Kruševac [YU] 22 X 18
Kruševo [YU] 30 X 19
Krustpils [SU] 8 X 9
Kruunupyy = Kronoby [SF] 9 U 5
Krylbo [S] 5 S 8
Krylovo [SU] 8 V 11
Krynica [PL] 17 W 14
Krynowłoga Mała [PL] 17 V 12
Książnice [PL] 17 V 14
Δ Ktapodia [GR] 31 Zb 21
Kubbe [S] 5 S 5
Küblis [CH] 20 P 16
Kubrat [BG] 23 Za 17
Δ Kučaj [YU] 22 X 18
Kučevo [YU] 22 X 17
Δ Kučintundra, gora — [SU] 3 W 1
Kuçove = Qytet Stalin [AL] 30 W 20
Kudirkos [SU] 8 W 11
Kudirkos Naumiestis [SU] 8 W 11
Kudowa Zdrój [PL] 16 T 14
Kuenes [N] 3 U 1
Kufstein [A] 20 Q 16
Δ Kuhasenmäki [SF] 9 W 6
Kuhmalahti [SF] 9 V 6
Kuhmo [SF] 9 X 4
Kuhmoinen [SF] 9 W 6
Kuivajärvi [SF] 3 X 4
≈ Kuivajoki [SF] 3 V 4
Kuivaniemi [SF] 3 V 4
Kuivastu [SU] 8 V 8
≈ Kujal'nickij liman [SU] 23 Zc 15
Δ Kujawy [PL] 16 U 12
Kukes [AL] 30 W 19
≈ Kukkiajärvi [SF] 9 W 6
Kukkola [SF] 3 U 4
≈ Kukkolankoski [SF] 3 U 4
Kula [BG] 22 X 18
Kula [YU] 22 V 17
Kulata [BG] 30 Y 19
Kuldīga [SU] 8 V 9
Kulen Vakuf [YU] 21 T 18
Kullaa [SF] 9 U 7
Δ Kullen [S] 6 Q 10
Kulmbach [D] 15 Q 14
Kuloharju [SF] 3 W 3
≈ Kultsjön [S] 5 R 5
Kumanovo [YU] 22 X 19
≈ K'ume [SU] 3 X 2
Kumla [S] 7 R 8
Kumlinge [SF] 9 U 7
Δ Kumputunturi [SF] 3 V 2
Kumrovec [YU] 21 T 17
Kunda [SU] 9 X 8
≈ Kunda laht [SU] 9 X 7
Kungälv [S] 6 Q 9
Kungsbacka [S] 6 Q 9
Kungsör [S] 7 S 8
Kunhegyes [H] 22 W 16
Kunmadaras [H] 22 W 16
Kunszentmárton [H] 22 W 16
Kunszentmiklós [H] 22 V 16
≈ Kuohijärvi [SF] 9 W 7
Kuolajarvi [SU] 3 W 3
≈ Kuolimojärvi [SF] 9 X 6
Kuolio [SF] 3 W 3
Kuopio [SF] 9 X 5
Δ Kuorboaivi [SF] 3 V 1
Δ Kuormakka [S] 2 T 3
Δ Kuorpukas, gora — [SU] 3 W 1
Kuortane [SF] 9 V 6
Kuosanen [S] 2 T 3
Kuouka [S] 2 T 3
Δ Kuoutatjärro [S] 2 T 2
≈ Kupa [YU] 21 S 17
≈ Kupa [YU] 21 T 17
Kupari [YU] 22 V 19
Kupiškis [SU] 8 X 10
Kupres [YU] 21 U 18
Kurikka [SF] 9 U 6
Kurort Schmalkalden [DDR] 15 P 14
Kurów [PL] 17 W 13
Kurravaara [S] 2 T 3
Kuršenai [SU] 8 W 10
Δ Kurskaja Kosa [SU] 8 V 11
≈ Kurskij zaliv [SU] 8 V 11
Kursu [SF] 3 W 3
Kuršumlija [YU] 22 X 18
Kuru [SF] 9 V 6
Δ Kurzeme [SU] 8 V 10
Kuşadası [TR] 31 Zc 21
≈ Kuşadası körfezi [TR] 31 Zc 21
Kušnierz [PL] 16 U 12
Δ Kustarakajse [S] 2 S 3
K'ustendil [BG] 22 Y 19
Küstrin = Kostrzyn [PL] 16 S 13
Kutina [YU] 21 T 17
Kutná Hora [CS] 16 S 14
Kutno [PL] 16 U 13
Kuttura [SF] 3 V 2
Kúty [CS] 16 T 15
Kuusalu [SU] 9 W 8
Kuusamo [SF] 3 W 3
Kuusankoski [SF] 9 X 7
Kuusilaki [S] 3 U 3
Kuusjärvi [SF] 9 X 5
Kuusjoki [SF] 9 V 7
≈ Kvænangen [N] 2 T 1
Kvænangsbotn [N] 2 T 1
Kværndrup [DK] 6 P 11
Δ Kvaløy [N] 2 S 2
Δ Kvaløy [N] 3 U 1
Kvaløysletta [N] 2 S 2
Kvalsund [N] 3 U 1
Kvam [N] 4 Q 5
Kvanndal [N] 4 O 7
Kvanne [N] 4 O 6
Kvarnberg [S] 5 R 7
≈ Kvarner [YU] 21 S 18
≈ Kvarnerić [YU] 21 S 17
Kvedarna [SU] 8 V 10
Kvevlax [SF] 9 U 6
Δ Kvia [N] 4 P 7
Kvidja [SF] 9 V 7
Δ Kvigtind [N] 5 R 4
Kvikkjokk [S] 2 S 3
Kvikne [N] 4 P 6
Kvinlog [N] 6 O 9
Kvisvik [N] 4 O 6
Kwidzyn [PL] 16 U 12
Δ Kyffhäuser [DDR] 15 Q 13
Kyjov [CS] 16 T 15
Kylänpää [SF] 9 U 6
Kyle of Lochalsh [GB] 10 G 9
Kylmälä [SF] 9 W 4
Kymbo [S] 7 R 9
≈ Kymijoki [SF] 9 X 7
≈ Kynsivesi [SF] 9 W 6
Kyritz [DDR] 15 Q 12
Kyrkas [S] 5 R 6
Δ Kyrkjenut [N] 4 N 8
Kyrksæterøra [N] 4 P 6
Kyrkslätt [SF] 9 W 7
≈ Kyrönjoki [SF] 9 U 6
≈ Kyrösjärvi [SF] 9 V 6
Kytömäki [SF] 3 W 4
Kyyjärvi [SF] 9 V 5
≈ Kyyvesi [SF] 9 X 6

L

Laage [DDR] 15 Q 12
≈ Laakajärvi [SF] 9 W 5
Laanila [SF] 3 V 2
Laasphe [D] 15 O 14
Labastide-Murat [F] 19 J 17
≈ Labe [CS] 16 S 14
Łabiszyn [PL] 16 T 12
Laboe [D] 6 P 11
Labouheyre [F] 18 H 18
Δ Labourd [F] 18 G 18
Labrit [F] 18 H 18
Labruguière [F] 19 K 18
Lacanau [F] 18 H 17
≈ Lacanau, Étang de — [F] 18 H 17
Lacanau-Océan [F] 18 H 17
Lacaune [F] 19 K 18
Δ Lacaune, Monts de — [F] 19 K 18
Łack [PL] 16 U 12
Läckeby [S] 7 S 10
Läckö [S] 7 R 9
Laconi [I] 28 O 21
Lacq [F] 18 H 18
Ląd [PL] 16 U 13
Ladek Zdrój [PL] 16 T 14
L'ady [SU] 8 Y 8
Lærdalsøyri [N] 4 O 7
Δ Læsø [DK] 6 Q 10
Lafrançaise [F] 19 J 18
Δ Laga, Monti della — [I] 29 R 19
≈ Lagan [S] 7 R 10
Lage [D] 15 O 13
≈ Lågen [N] 4 O 8
≈ Lågen [N] 4 P 7
≈ Lågen [N] 6 P 8
Lagg [GB] 10 G 10
Łagiewniki [PL] 16 T 14
Lagmansered [S] 6 Q 9
Lagny-sur-Marne [F] 14 L 15
Lagôa [P] 25 A 21
≈ Lago Maggiore [I] 20 O 17
Lagos [P] 25 A 21
≈ Lagos, Baía de — [P] 25 A 21
Laguiole [F] 19 K 18
≈ Lahn [D] 15 O 14
Laholm [S] 7 R 10
≈ Laholmsbukten [S] 6 Q 10
Lahr [D] 20 O 15
Lahti [SF] 9 W 7
Laignes [F] 19 M 16
Laihia [SF] 9 U 6
Lainio [S] 2 T 3
≈ Lainio älv [S] 2 T 3
Lairg [GB] 11 H 9
≈ Laisälven [S] 2 S 4
Laissac [F] 19 K 18
Laisvall [S] 2 S 4
Laitila [SF] 9 U 7
Lajkovac [YU] 22 W 18
Lakaträsk [S] 2 T 4
Lakka [GR] 30 W 21
≈ Lakonikos Kolpos [GR] 31 Z 22
≈ Laksefjord [N] 3 V 1
Lakselv [N] 3 U 1
≈ Laksfoss [N] 2 Q 4
Laktaši [YU] 21 U 17
Lalapaşa [TR] 23 Zb 19
Lalín [E] 24 C 18

alinde [F] 19 J 17
alm [N] 4 P 7
amastre [F] 19 M 17
ambach [A] 21 R 15
amballe [F] 12 G 15
Δ Lambay Island [IRL] 10 F 11
ambia [GR] 30 Y 21
amborn [S] 5 S 7
amego [P] 25 C 19
amézia Terme [I] 29 U 21
amia [GR] 30 Y 21
ammhult [S] 7 R 10
ammi [SF] 9 W 7
≈ Lamone [I] 20 Q 18
amotte-Beuvron [F] 19 K 16
ampeter [GR] 12 G 12
ämpsänkylä [SF] 3 X 3
ana [I] 20 Q 16
anaja [E] 26 H 19
anark [GB] 11 H 10
ancaster [GB] 11 H 11
anciano [I] 29 S 19
Δ Lancone, Défilé de — [F] 28 P 19
andau an der Isar [D] 16 R 15
andau in der Pfalz [D] 15 O 15
andeck [A] 20 P 16
Δ Landegode [N] 2 R 3
anderneau [F] 12 F 15
Δ Landes [F] 18 H 18
≈ Landösjön [S] 5 R 5
andquart [CH] 20 P 16
andrecies [F] 14 L 14
andsberg am Lech [D] 20 Q 15
andsberg (Warthe) = Gorzów Wielkopolski [PL] 16 S 12
Δ Land's End [GB] 12 F 14
andshut [D] 15 O 15
andskrona [S] 7 R 10
Δ Landsort [S] 7 T 8
ångå [S] 4 Q 6
≈ Langada, Limni — [GR] 30 Y 20
angadas [GR] 30 Y 20
anga de Duero [E] 26 F 19
angadia [GR] 30 Y 22
ångåminne [SF] 9 U 6
≈ Långan [S] 5 R 6
angeac [F] 19 L 17
angeais [F] 19 J 16
Δ Langeland [DK] 6 P 11
≈ Langelands Bælt [DK] 6 Q 11
≈ Längelmävesi [SF] 9 V 6
ängenfeld [A] 20 Q 16
angenhagen [D] 15 P 13
angenthal [CH] 20 O 16
Δ Langeoog [D] 15 O 12
angesund [N] 6 P 8
Δ Langfjället [S] 4 Q 6
≈ Langfjord [N] 3 V 1
≈ Langfjord [N] 4 O 6
angfjordbotn [N] 2 T 1
Δ Langfjordjøkelen [N] 2 T 1
ångflon [S] 4 Q 7
≈ Långhalsen [S] 7 S 8
angholm [GB] 11 H 11
angnau im Emmental [CH] 20 O 16
Δ Långö [S] 7 T 8
angogne [F] 19 L 18
angon [F] 18 H 17
Δ Langøy [N] 2 R 2
angreo [E] 24 D 18
angres [F] 19 M 16
angres, Plateau de — [F] 19 M 16
ångsele [S] 5 R 5
≈ Långseleån [S] 5 R 5
angstrand [N] 2 T 1
ångsträsk [S] 2 S 4
ångsträsk [S] 2 T 4
Δ Languedoc [F] 19 K 18
≈ Langvatn [N] 2 R 4
ångvattnet [S] 5 S 4
anietą [PL] 16 U 12
anjarón [E] 26 E 22
änkipohja [SF] 9 W 6
annemezan [F] 19 H 18
annion [F] 12 G 15
anouaille [F] 19 J 17
Δ Lans, Montagne de — [F] 19 M 17
anselbourg-Mont-Cenis [F] 20 N 17
ansjärv [S] 3 U 3
≈ Lanterne [F] 20 N 16
anz [E] 18 G 18
anzo Torinese [I] 20 N 17
aon [F] 14 L 14
apalisse [F] 19 L 17
apinlahti [SF] 9 W 5
aplandija [SU] 3 X 2
Δ Laplandskij zapovednik [SU] 3 X 2
apovo [YU] 22 W 18
appajärvi [SF] 9 V 5
≈ Lappajärvi [SF] 9 V 5
äppe [S] 7 S 8
appeenranta [SF] 9 X 6
appfjärd [SF] 9 U 6
appi [SF] 9 U 7
Δ Lappland [S. SF. SU] 2 S 4
appvik [SF] 9 V 7
apqoluobdal [N] 3 U 2
apseki [TR] 31 Zb 19
apua [SF] 9 V 6
≈ Lapuanjoki [SF] 9 U 5
Δ Lăpuș, Munții — [RO] 22 X 15
Lapușna [RO] 23 Z 16
apušna [SU] 23 Zb 15
apväärtti = Lappfjärd [SF] 9 U 6
Laragne-Montéglin [F] 19 M 18
ärbro [S] 7 T 9
arche [F] 20 N 18
Δ Larche, Col de — [F, I] 20 N 18
aredo [E] 18 F 18
argentière [F] 19 L 18
args [GB] 10 G 10
Larino [I] 29 S 19
Larissa [GR] 30 Y 20
arkhall [GB] 11 H 10
arne [GB] 10 G 11
Δ Larouco [P] 24 C 18
Larraun [E] 18 G 18
Larressingle [F] 19 J 18
Laruns [F] 18 H 18
Larvik [N] 6 P 8
Δ Lascaux, Grotte de — [F] 19 J 17
Łasin [PL] 16 U 12
Lask [PL] 16 U 13
Lassfolk [SF] 9 U 5
Δ Lastovčići [YU] 21 U 19
Lastovo [YU] 21 U 19
Δ Lastovo [YU] 21 U 19
≈ Lastovski kanal [YU] 21 U 19
Δ Lastres, Cabo de — [E] 24 E 18
≈ Lätäseno [SF] 2 T 2
Laterza [I] 29 U 20
Latheron [GB] 11 J 9
Latikberg [S] 5 S 5
Latina [I] 29 R 20
Lattuna [SF] 3 W 2
Δ Latvijskaja SSR [SU] 8 V 9
Lauban = Lubań [PL] 16 S 13
Lauchhammer [DDR] 16 R 13
Laudal [N] 6 O 9
Lauder [GB] 11 H 10
Lauenburg/Elbe [D] 15 P 12
Lauf an der Pegnitz [D] 15 Q 15
Laufen [CH] 20 N 16
Laufen [D] 21 R 16
Δ Lauhavuori [SF] 9 U 6
Laujar de Andarax [E] 26 E 22
Lauker [S] 2 T 4
Δ Laukøy [N] 2 T 1
Laukslettа [N] 2 T 1
Laukuva [SU] 8 V 10
Launceston [GB] 12 G 13
Laupheim [D] 20 P 15
Δ Lauragais [F] 19 J 18
Laureano di Borello [I] 29 U 21
Laurenzana [I] 29 T 20
Laurila [SF] 3 V 4
Lauritsala [SF] 9 X 6
Lausanne [CH] 20 N 16
Δ Lausitzer Gebirge [CS] 16 S 14
≈ Lausitzer Neiße [DDR] 16 S 13
Lautaporras [SF] 9 V 7
Lauterbach [D] 15 P 14
Lauterecken [D] 15 O 14
Lautrec [F] 19 K 18
Lauzerte [F] 19 J 18
Laval [F] 13 H 15
Δ Lavall, Gorges de — [F] 27 K 19
Lavamünd [A] 21 S 16
Lavandou, le — [F] 20 N 19
Lavardac [F] 19 J 18
≈ Lävasjokk [S] 2 S 3
Lavaur [F] 19 K 18
Lavelanet [F] 19 J 19
Lavello [I] 29 T 20
Laveno-Mombello [I] 20 O 17
Lavia [SF] 9 V 6
Laviana [E] 24 E 18
Lavik [N] 4 N 7
Lavington [GB] 13 H 13
Lavre [P] 25 B 20
Lavrion [GR] 31 Za 21
Lavry [SU] 8 Y 9
Δ Lawers, Ben — [GB] 11 H 10
Laxå [S] 7 R 8
Laxbäcken [S] 5 S 5
Laxsjö [S] 5 R 5
Lazarevac [YU] 22 W 18
Δ Lázio [I] 29 R 19
Łeba [PL] 7 T 11
Lebach [D] 15 N 15
Lebane [YU] 22 X 18
Lębork [PL] 7 T 11
Lebrija [E] 25 C 22
≈ Łebsko, Jezioro — [PL] 7 T 11
Lecce [I] 30 V 20
Lecco [I] 20 P 17
Lécera [E] 26 H 20
≈ Lech [D] 15 Q 15
Lechena [GR] 30 X 21
Lechovice [CS] 16 T 15
Δ Lechtaler Alpen [A] 20 P 16
Leck [D] 6 P 11
Lectoure [F] 19 J 18
Łęczyca [PL] 16 U 13
Ledbury [GB] 13 H 13
Ledesma [E] 25 D 19
Leeds [GB] 11 J 11
Leek [GB] 13 H 12
Leer (Ostfriesland) [D] 15 O 12
Leeuwarden [NL] 15 N 12
Δ Lefka Ori [GR] 32 Za 23
Lefkas [GR] 30 X 21
Δ Lefkas [GR] 30 X 21
Lefkimmi [GR] 30 W 21
Lefkon [GR] 31 Z 19
Lege [F] 18 H 16
Legnano [I] 20 O 17
Legnano [I] 20 Q 17
Legnica [PL] 16 T 13
Lehčevo [BG] 22 Y 18
Lehliu [RO] 23 Za 17
Lehrte [D] 15 P 13
Lehtimäki [SF] 9 V 6
Leibnitz [A] 21 T 16
Leicester [GB] 13 J 12
Leiden [NL] 14 M 3
Leikanger [N] 4 N 6
≈ Leine [D, DDR] 15 P 13
Leinefelde [DDR] 15 P 13
Δ Leinster [IRL] 10 F 11
Leinstrand [N] 4 P 6
Leipivaara [SF] 3 W 4
Leipzig [DDR] 15 Q 13
Leira [N] 4 P 7
Leirâmo [N] 2 R 3
Leirbotn [N] 2 T 1
Leirfjord [N] 2 Q 4
Leiria [P] 25 B 20
Leirpollen [N] 3 V 1
Leirvik [N] 4 N 7
Leirvik [N] 4 N 8
Δ Leitariegos, Puerto de — [E] 24 D 18
Leith [GB] 11 H 10
Δ Leithagebirge [A] 21 T 15
Leithbhear = Lifford [IRL] 10 F 10
Leitir Ceannainn = Letterkenny [IRL] 10 F 10
Leivonmäki [SF] 9 W 6
Lejasciems [SU] 9 X 9
≈ Lek [NL] 14 M 13
Δ Leka [N] 4 Q 5
Leksand [S] 5 R 7
≈ Leksdalsvatn [N] 4 Q 5
Lekvattnet [S] 4 Q 8
≈ Lelången [S] 6 Q 8
Δ Lelija [YU] 22 V 18
Lelle [SU] 8 W 8
≈ Léman [CH] 20 N 17
Lemdes [F] 19 L 17
Lemgo [D] 15 O 13
Δ Lemland [SF] 9 U 8
Δ Lemmenjoen Kansallispuisto [SF] 3 U 2
≈ Lemmenjoki [SF] 3 V 2
Lemmer [NL] 15 N 12
Lempäälä [SF] 9 V 7
Lemvig [DK] 6 O 10
Lena [E] 24 D 18
Lencloître [F] 19 J 16
Lend [A] 21 R 16
Lendava [YU] 21 T 16
≈ Lenglingen [N] 5 R 5
Lenhovda [S] 7 S 10
Lenk im Simmental [CH] 20 N 17
Lens [F] 14 L 14
Lensvik [N] 4 P 6
Lentini [I] 29 T 22
Lentjira [SF] 3 X 4
≈ Lentua [SF] 9 X 4
Leoben [A] 21 S 16
Leominster [GB] 13 H 12
León [E] 24 D 18
Léon [F] 18 G 18
Δ León [E] 24 D 19
Δ León, Montañas de — [E] 24 D 18
Δ Léon, Pays de — [F] 12 F 15
Leonberg [D] 15 O 15
Leonessa [I] 29 R 19
Leonforte [I] 29 S 22
Leonidion [GR] 31 Z 22
Leopoldsburg [B] 14 M 13
Lepe [E] 25 B 21
Lepenski vir [YU] 22 X 17
Lepoura [GR] 31 Z 21
Leppävirta [SF] 9 X 6
Leppiaho [SF] 3 V 4
Lepsény [H] 21 U 16
Leptokaria [GR] 30 Y 20
Lequeitio [E] 18 G 18
Lercara Friddi [I] 29 S 22
Lérici [I] 20 P 18
Lérida [E] 26 H 19
Lerín [E] 18 G 19
≈ Leringen [S] 5 S 6
Δ Lérins, Iles de — [F] 20 N 18
Lerma [E] 26 F 19
Lermoos [A] 20 Q 16
Δ Leros [GR] 31 Zc 21
Lerum [S] 6 Q 9
Leș [RO] 22 W 16
≈ Lèsina, Lago di — [I] 29 T 19
Δ Lesistyje Karpaty [SU] 17 X 15
Lesjaskog [N] 4 O 6
Lesko [PL] 17 W 14
Leskovac [YU] 22 X 18
Leskovik [AL] 30 X 20
Lesneven [F] 12 F 15
Lešnica [YU] 22 V 17
Lesnoje [SU] 23 Zb 15
Lesnovo [YU] 22 Y 19
Lesparre-Médoc [F] 18 H 17
Lessay [F] 13 H 14
Lestijärvi [SF] 9 V 5
≈ Lestijärvi [SF] 9 V 5
≈ Lestijoki [SF] 9 V 5
Δ Lesvos [GR] 31 Zb 20
Leszno [PL] 16 T 13
≈ Letälven [S] 7 R 8
Letea [RO] 23 Zb 16
Letenye [H] 21 T 16
Letku [SF] 9 V 7
Letterkenny [IRL] 10 F 10
Leu [RO] 22 Y 17
≈ Leucate ou de Salces, Étang de — [F] 19 K 19
Leucate-Plage [F] 19 K 19
Leuna [DDR] 15 Q 13
Leušeny [SU] 23 Zb 15
Leutkirch im Allgäu [D] 20 P 16
Leuven [B] 14 M 14
Leuze [B] 14 L 14
Levadia [GR] 31 Z 21
Levajok [N] 3 U 1
Δ Levant, Ile du — [F] 20 N 19
Δ Levante, Riviera di — [I] 20 O 18
Lèvanto [I] 20 P 18
Δ Levanzo, Isola di — [I] 29 R 22
Leven [GB] 11 J 12
Levene [S] 6 Q 9
Leverkusen [D] 15 N 14
Δ Levezou [F] 19 K 18
Levidion [GR] 30 Y 22
Levie [F] 28 O 20
Levier [F] 20 N 16
Δ Levitha [GR] 31 Zb 2
Levoča [CS] 17 V 15
Levroux [F] 19 K 16
Levski [BG] 23 Z 18
Lewes [GB] 13 J 13
Δ Lewis, Isle of — [GB] 10 G 8
≈ Leyre [F] 18 H 17
Lézardrieux [F] 12 G 15
Lezay [F] 19 J 16
Lezhë [AL] 30 W 19
Lézignan-Corbières [F] 19 K 18
Δ Lezirias [P] 25 A 20
Lezoux [F] 19 L 17
Liart [F] 14 M 14
Liatorp [S] 7 R 10
Libavá Město [CS] 16 U 14
Liberadz [PL] 17 V 12
Liberec [CS] 16 S 14
Libos [F] 19 J 18
Libourne [F] 18 H 17
Librazhd [AL] 30 W 20
Librilla [E] 26 G 22
Licata [I] 29 S 22
Lichtenau [A] 21 S 15
Lichtenfels [D] 15 Q 14
Δ Ličko polje [YU] 21 T 18
Lida [SU] 8 X 11
Liden [S] 5 S 6
Lidhult [S] 7 R 10
Δ Lidingö [S] 7 T 8
Δ Lidinon, Akrotirion — [GR] 32 Za 23
Lidköping [S] 7 R 9
Δ Lidnatjärro [S] 2 T 2
Lido [I] 21 R 17
Lido di Òstia [I] 29 R 20
Lido di Tarquinia [I] 28 Q 19
Lidzbark [PL] 16 U 12
Lidzbark Warmiński [PL] 8 V 11
Δ Liébana, La — [E] 24 E 18
Lieberose [DDR] 16 S 13
Lieboch [A] 21 S 16
Liège [B] 14 M 14
Liegnitz = Legnica [PL] 16 T 13
Lieksa [SF] 9 X 5
Lielauce [SU] 8 W 10
≈ Lielupe [SU] 8 W 10
Liendo [E] 18 F 18
Lienz [A] 21 R 16
Liepāja [SU] 8 V 10
≈ Liepājas ezers [SU] 8 V 10
Liepna [SU] 8 Y 9
Lier [B] 14 M 13
Liesjärvi [SF] 9 V 6
≈ Lietvesi [SF] 9 X 6
Lieurey [F] 14 J 15
Lievestuore [SF] 9 W 6
Liezen [A] 21 S 16
Liffol-le-Grand [F] 19 M 15
Lifford [IRL] 10 F 10
Lignano Sabbiadoro [I] 21 R 17
Lignières [F] 19 K 16
Ligny-en- Barrois [F] 14 M 15
Δ Ligure, Appennino — [I] 20 O 18
Δ Liguri, Alpi — [I] 20 O 18
Δ Ligùria [I] 20 O 18
Lihula [SU] 8 W 8
Liikasenvaara [SF] 3 W 3
Likenes [N] 6 O 9
Δ Likodimon Oros [GR] 30 Y 22
Lilla Edet [S] 6 Q 9
Lillafüred [H] 17 W 15
Δ Lilla Karlsö [S] 7 T 9
≈ Lilla Lule älv [S] 2 T 3
Lille [F] 14 L 14
≈ Lille Bælt [DK] 6 P 11
Lillebonne [F] 14 J 14
Lilleeidet [N] 2 Q 3
Lillehammer [N] 4 P 7
Lillers [F] 14 L 14
Lillesand [N] 6 O 9
Lillestrøm [N] 4 Q 8
Lillhärdal [S] 5 R 7
Lillholmsjön [S] 5 R 5
Lillkågeträsk [S] 5 T 4
Lillkyro = Vähäkyrö [SF] 9 U 6
≈ Lim [YU] 22 W 18
Lima [S] 5 R 7
≈ Lima, Rio — [P] 24 B 18
Limanova [PL] 17 V 14
Limavady [GB] 10 F 10
Limburg (Lahn) [D] 15 O 14
Lime [DK] 6 O 10
Limenaria [GR] 31 Z 20
Limerick [IRL] 12 E 12
≈ Limfjorden [DK] 6 P 10
≈ Limia, Rio — [E] 24 C 18
≈ Limingen [N] 4 Q 5
Liminka [SF] 9 V 4
Limni [GR] 31 Z 21
Δ Limnos [GR] 31 Za 20
Limoges [F] 19 J 17
Limogne-en-Quercy [F] 19 K 18
Limone Piemonte [I] 20 N 18
Limours-en-Hurepoix [F] 14 K 15
Δ Limousin [F] 19 J 17
Limoux [F] 19 K 19
Lin [AL] 30 X 20
≈ Lina älv [S] 2 T 3
Linachamari [SU] 3 W 1
Linares [E] 26 E 21
Δ Linaro, Capo — [I] 28 Q 19
Lincoln [GB] 13 J 12
Lindau (Bodensee) [D] 20 P 16
Δ Linderödsåsen [S] 7 R 10
Lindesberg [S] 5 S 8
Lindesnes [N] 6 O 9
Lindos [GR] 32 Zd 22
Linea, La — [E] 25 C 22
Lingen (Ems) [D] 15 O 13
Linköping [S] 7 S 9
Linkuva [SU] 8 W 10
Linlithgow [GB] 11 H 10
Linnes [N] 4 Q 7
Linn of Dee [GB] 11 H 9
Linsell [S] 5 R 6
Linthal [CH] 20 O 16
Linz [A] 21 S 15
≈ Lion, Golfe du — [F] 19 L 19
Lion-d'Angers, le — [F] 18 H 15
Lipany [CS] 17 W 14
Lipari [I] 29 T 22
Δ Lipari, Isola — [I] 29 T 22
Δ Lipari, Isole — [I] 29 S 21
Liperi [SF] 9 X 5
Lipiany [PL] 16 S 12
Lipik [YU] 21 U 17
Lipka [PL] 16 T 12
Lipljan [YU] 22 X 19
Lipnica [PL] 16 U 12
Lipník nad Bečvou [CS] 16 U 14
Lipniško [SU] 8 X 11
Lipno [PL] 16 U 12
Lipno nad Vltavou [CS] 16 S 15
Lipova [RO] 22 X 16
Δ Lipovei, Dealurile — [RO] 22 X 16
≈ Lippe [D] 15 O 13
Lippstadt [D] 15 O 13
Liprovsky Mikuláš [CS] 17 V 15
Δ Lipsi [GR] 31 Zc 21
Lipsk [PL] 8 W 11
Lipsko [PL] 17 W 13
Δ Lisac [YU] 22 X 18
Δ Lisa planina [BG] 23 Za 18
Lisboa [P] 25 A 20
Lisburn [GB] 10 G 11
Liselund [DK] 6 Q 11
Lisieux [F] 14 J 15
Liskeard [GB] 12 G 13
Lisskogsåsen [S] 5 R 7
Lištica [YU] 21 U 18
Lit [S] 5 R 6
Lit-et-Mixe [F] 18 H 18
Litija [YU] 21 S 17
Litochoron [GR] 30 Y 20
Litoměřice [CS] 16 R 14
Litomyšl [CS] 16 T 14
Δ Litovskaja SSR [SU] 8 V 10
Littehampton [GB] 13 J 13
≈ Little Minch [GB] 10 G 9
≈ Liva [SU] 3 X 2
Livada [RO] 17 X 15
Līvāni [SU] 8 X 10
Δ Livanjsko polje [YU] 21 T 18
Liverpool [GB] 13 H 12
Livno [YU] 21 U 18
≈ Livojoki [SF] 3 W 4
Livorno [I] 20 Q 18
Δ Livradois, Monts du — [F] 19 L 17
Lixourion [GR] 30 X 21
Lizard [GB] 12 F 14
Δ Lizard Point [GB] 12 F 14
Δ Lizerorta [SU] 8 V 9
Ljan [N] 4 P 8
Ljig [YU] 22 W 18
Ljosland [N] 6 O 9
Ljubija [YU] 21 T 17
Ljubljana [YU] 21 S 17
Ljubovija [YU] 22 V 18
Δ Ljubuša [YU] 21 U 18
Ljubuški [YU] 21 U 18
≈ Ljugaren [S] 5 R 7
Ljugarn [S] 7 T 9
Ljung [S] 7 R 9
≈ Ljungan [S] 5 S 6
Ljungby [S] 7 R 10
Ljungdalen [S] 4 Q 6
Ljungskile [S] 6 Q 9
Ljusdal [S] 5 S 7
≈ Ljusnan [S] 4 R 6
Ljusne [S] 5 S 7
Δ Ljusterö [S] 5 T 8
Ljutomer [YU] 21 T 16
Llagostera [E] 27 K 19
Llandeilo [GB] 12 G 13
Llandovery [GB] 12 G 12
Llandrindod Wells [GB] 13 H 12
Llandudno [GB] 12 G 12
Llanelly [GB] 12 G 13
Llanes [E] 24 E 18
Llangollen [GB] 13 H 12
Llansá [E] 27 K 19
Llavorsí [E] 27 J 19
Llerena [E] 25 C 21
Δ Lleyn Peninsula [GB] 12 G 12
Llinás [E] 27 K 19
Llodio [E] 18 F 18
Lluchmayor [E] 27 K 21
Loano [I] 20 O 18
Loarre [E] 26 H 19
Löbau [DDR] 16 S 13
Δ Lobeiras, Islas — [E] 24 B 18
Löbnitz [DDR] 7 R 11
Locarno [CH] 20 O 17
Lochaline [GB] 10 G 9
Lochboisdale [GB] 10 G 9
Lochem [NL] 15 N 13
Loches [F] 19 J 16
Loch Garman = Wexford [IRL] 12 F 12
Lochgilphead [GB] 10 G 10
Lochinver [GB] 11 H 8
Lochmaddy [GB] 10 G 9
Δ Lochnagar [GB] 11 H 9
Lochów [PL] 17 W 12
Lockerbie [GB] 11 H 11
Locminé [F] 12 G 15
Locorotondo [I] 29 U 20
Locri [I] 29 U 22
Δ Lodalskåpa [N] 4 O 7
Lodè [I] 28 P 20
Lodève [F] 19 L 18
Lodi [I] 20 P 17
Lødingen [N] 2 R 2
Lodosa [E] 18 G 19
Łódź [PL] 16 U 13
Loen [N] 4 O 7
Løfallstrand [N] 4 N 8
Lofer [A] 21 R 16
Δ Lofoten [N] 2 Q 3
Lofsdalen [S] 4 Q 6
≈ Lofsen [S] 5 R 6
Loftahammar [S] 7 S 9
Lofthus [N] 4 O 8
Lögdeå [S] 5 T 5
Logroño [E] 18 F 19
Logrosán [E] 25 D 20
Δ Logudoro [I] 28 O 20
Løgumkloster [DK] 6 P 11
Lohals [DK] 6 Q 11
Lohéac [F] 13 H 15
Lohikoski [SF] 9 X 6
Lohiniva [SF] 3 V 3
Lohja [SF] 9 W 7
≈ Lohjanjärvi [SF] 9 V 7
Lohr am Main [D] 15 P 14
Loimaa [SF] 9 V 7
≈ Loir [F] 19 J 15
≈ Loire [F] 19 K 16
≈ Loisach [D] 20 Q 16
Loja [E] 25 D 22
Lojo [SF] 9 W 7
Lokači [SU] 17 Y 13
Lokalahti [SF] 9 U 7
≈ Lokan tekojärvi [SF] 3 V 2
Løken [N] 4 Q 8
Lokeren [B] 14 M 13
Lokka [SF] 3 V 2
Løkken [DK] 6 P 10
Loksa [SU] 9 W 8
Δ Lolland [DK] 6 Q 11
Lom [BG] 22 Y 18
Lom [N] 4 O 7
≈ Lom [BG] 22 Y 18
Δ Lomagne [F] 19 J 18
Δ Lombardia [I] 20 P 17
Δ Lomnický štít [CS] 17 V 14
≈ Lomond, Loch — [GB] 11 H 10
Δ Lomseggja [N] 4 O 7
Lomselenäs [S] 5 S 4
Lomsjö [S] 5 S 5
Łomża [PL] 17 W 12
Londinières [F] 14 K 14
London [GB] 13 J 13
Londonderry [GB] 10 F 10
Δ Lønehorgi [N] 4 N 7
Longa [GR] 30 Y 22
Longarone [I] 21 R 17
Long Eaton [GB] 13 J 12
Longeau [F] 19 M 16
Longford [IRL] 10 E 11
Longobucco [I] 29 U 21
Longphort = Longford [IRL] 10 E 11
Long Sutton [GB] 13 K 12
Longtown [GB] 11 H 11
Longué-Jumelles [F] 19 J 16
Longuyon [F] 14 M 15
Longwy [F] 15 N 15
Lonigo [I] 20 Q 17
Löningen [D] 15 O 12
Δ Lonjsko Polje [YU] 21 T 17
Lonka [SU] 3 X 4
Lonsboda [S] 7 R 10
Lønsdal [N] 2 R 3
Δ Lønsdal [N] 2 R 4
Lønset [N] 4 O 6
Lons-le-Saunier [F] 19 M 16
Looe [GB] 12 G 13
Δ Loop Head [IRL] 10 D 12
Lopar [YU] 21 S 17
Lopatin [SU] 17 Y 14
Lopatovo [SU] 8 Y 8
Δ Loppa [N] 2 T 1
≈ Lopphavet [N] 2 T 1
Loppi [SF] 9 W 7
Δ Lopud [YU] 22 V 19
Lopuka [SU] 3 X 4
Δ Lora, La — [E] 18 E 18
Lora del Río [E] 25 C 21
Lorås [S] 5 R 6
Lorca [E] 26 F 22
Loreto [I] 21 R 18
Lorient [F] 12 G 15
Loriol-sur-Drôme [F] 19 M 18
≈ Lorne, Firth of — [GB] 10 G 10
Δ Lorraine [F] 14 M 15
Los [S] 5 R 7
Łosice [PL] 17 W 12
Δ Lošinj [YU] 21 S 18
Łosino [PL] 7 T 11
Lossiemouth [GB] 11 J 9
Løstør [DK] 6 P 10
Lostwihiel [GB] 12 F 13
≈ Lot [F] 19 J 18
Lotovel [CS] 16 T 14
Δ Lotru, Munții — [RO] 22 Y 17
≈ Lotta [SU] 3 W 2
Lötzen = Giżycko [PL] 8 V 11
Louargat [F] 12 G 15
Loudéac [F] 12 G 15
≈ Loudias [GR] 30 Y 20
Loudun [F] 19 J 16
≈ Loue [F] 19 M 16
≈ Loue, Source de la — [F] 20 N 16
Loughborough [GB] 13 J 12
Loughrea [IRL] 10 E 11
Louhans [F] 19 M 16
Loulé [P] 25 B 21
Louny [CS] 16 R 14
Loupe, la — [F] 14 K 15
Lourdes [F] 18 H 18
Loures [P] 25 A 20
Lourinha [P] 25 A 20
Louros [GR] 30 X 21
Louth [GB] 13 K 12
Loutra [GR] 31 Z 20
Loutra Edipsou [GR] 31 Z 21
Loutrakion [GR] 31 Z 21
Loutropighi [GR] 30 Y 21
Louvain = Leuven [B] 14 M 14
Louviers [F] 14 K 15
Lövånger [S] 5 U 5
Lövberga [S] 5 R 5
Δ Lovćen [YU] 30 V 19
Loveč [BG] 23 Z 18
Lòvere [I] 20 P 17
Lövestad [S] 7 R 11
Loviisa = Lovisa [SF] 9 W 7
Lovisa [SF] 9 W 7
Lövő [H] 21 T 16
Lovosice [CS] 16 R 14
Lovran [YU] 21 S 17
Lovrin [RO] 22 W 16
Lövstabruk [S] 5 T 7
Lövstad [S] 7 S 9
Löwenberg/Mark [DDR] 16 R 12
Lowestoft [GB] 13 K 12
Łowicz [PL] 17 V 13
Δ Lowlands [GB] 11 H 10
Lozen [BG] 23 Z 19
Δ Lozère [F] 19 L 18
Loznica [YU] 22 V 17
Lozoyuela [E] 26 E 19
Luarca [E] 24 D 18
Lubań [PL] 16 S 13
Lubana [SU] 8 X 9
≈ Lubānas ezers [SU] 8 Y 9
Lubartów [PL] 17 W 13
Lubawa [PL] 16 U 12
Lübbecke [D] 15 O 13
Lübbenau/Spree [DDR] 16 R 13
Lübben/Spree [DDR] 16 R 13
Lübeck [D] 15 P 12
≈ Lübecker Bucht [D] 15 Q 12
Δ Lubéron, Montagne du — [F] 19 M 18
Lubersac [F] 19 J 17
L'ubešov [SU] 17 Y 12
Lubień Kujawski [PL] 16 U 12
L'ubimec [BG] 23 Za 19
Lubin [PL] 16 T 13
Lublin [PL] 17 W 13
Lubliniec [PL] 16 U 14
L'ubomľ [SU] 17 X 13
Luboń [PL] 16 T 13
Łubsko [PL] 16 S 13
Łuby [PL] 16 U 12
Luc, le — [F] 20 N 18
Lucainena de las Torres [E] 26 F 22
Δ Lucano, Appennino — [I] 29 T 20
Lucca [I] 20 P 18
Lucena [E] 25 D 22
Lučenec [CS] 17 V 15
Lucera [I] 29 T 20
≈ Luchena, Río — [E] 26 F 22
Lüchow [D] 15 Q 12
Luck [SU] 17 Y 13
Luckau [DDR] 16 R 13
Luckenwalde [DDR] 16 R 13
Luco de Jiloca [E] 26 G 20
Luçon [F] 18 H 16
≈ Luda Kamčija [BG] 23 Za 18
Ludbreg [YU] 21 T 17
Lude, le — [F] 19 J 15
Lüdenscheid [D] 15 O 13
Lüdinghausen [D] 15 O 13
Ludlow [GB] 13 H 12
Δ Ludogorie [BG] 23 Za 17
Δ Ludogorsko plato [BG] 23 Za 17
Luduș [RO] 22 Y 16
Ludvika [S] 5 R 8
Ludwigsburg [D] 15 P 15
Ludwigshafen am Rhein [D] 15 O 15
Ludwigslust [DDR] 15 Q 12
Lugano [CH] 20 O 17
≈ Lugano, Lago di — [CH, I] 20 O 17
Lugnvik [S] 5 S 6
Lugo [E] 24 C 18
Lugo [I] 20 Q 18
Lugoj [RO] 22 X 17
Luhačovice [CS] 16 U 15

Luhalahti [SF] 9 V 6
Luik = Liège [B] 14 M 14
Luikonlahti [SF] 9 X 5
Luimneach = Limerick [IRL] 12 E 12
Luino [I] 20 O 17
≈ Luirojoki [SF] 3 V 2
Luisiana, La — [E] 25 D 21
Lukovit [BG] 23 Z 18
Lukovo [YU] 21 S 18
Łuków [PL] 17 W 13
Łukta [PL] 8 V 12
Luleå [S] 3 U 4
≈ Luleälv [S] 2 T 4
Lüleburgaz [TR] 23 Zb 19
Δ Lule Lappmark [S] 2 S 3
Lümanda [SU] 8 V 9
Lumbier [E] 18 G 19
Lumbrales [E] 25 C 19
≈ Lumijoen selkö [SF] 3 V 4
Lumparland [SF] 9 U 8
≈ Luna, Río — [E] 24 D 18
Lunca-de-Jos [RO] 23 Z 16
Lund [S] 7 R 11
Lunda [S] 5 T 8
Lunde [N] 6 P 8
Lunde [S] 5 S 6
Lundeborg [DK] 6 P 11
≈ Lundevatn [N] 6 N 9
Δ Lundøy [N] 2 R 3
Lundsjön [S] 5 R 6
Δ Lundy Island [GB] 12 G 13
Lune, la — [F] 14 J 15
Lüneburg [D] 15 P 12
Δ Lüneburger Heide [D] 15 P 12
Lunel [F] 19 L 18
Lünen [D] 15 O 13
Lunéville [F] 15 N 15
Lungsjön [S] 5 S 6
Δ Lunjevača [YU] 21 T 18
Lunz am See [A] 21 S 16
≈ Luodon selkä [SF] 3 V 4
≈ Luontari [SF] 9 X 6
Luostari [SU] 3 W 1
Δ Luostotunturi [SF] 3 V 3
Lupeni [RO] 22 Y 17
Lupşanu [RO] 23 Za 17
Lure [F] 20 N 16
Δ Lure, Montagne de — [F] 19 M 18
Lurgan [GB] 10 F 11
Luri [F] 28 P 19
≈ Luru [N] 4 Q 5
Lushnjë [AL] 30 W 20
Lusignan [F] 19 J 16
Luso [P] 25 B 19
Lussac-les-Châteaux [F] 19 J 16
≈ Lusterfjord [N] 4 O 7
Lutherstadt Wittenberg [DDR] 16 R 13
Lütjenburg [D] 6 P 11
Luton [GB] 13 J 13
≈ Luttojoki [SF] 3 V 2
Lututów [PL] 16 U 13
Luunja [SU] 8 X 8
Luvozero [SU] 3 X 4
Luxembourg [L] 15 N 14
Luxeuil-les-Bains [F] 20 N 16
Luz [P] 25 B 21
Luzern [CH] 20 O 16
≈ Lužnice [CS] 16 S 15
Luz-Saint-Sauveur [F] 18 H 19
Luzy [F] 19 L 16
L'vov [SU] 17 X 14
Lwówek Śląski [PL] 16 S 13
Lybester [GB] 11 J 9
Lychen [DDR] 16 R 12
Lyckeby [S] 7 S 10
Lyck = Ełk [PL] 8 W 11
Lycksele [S] 5 T 5
Δ Lycksele Lappmark [S] 2 R 4
Lydd [GB] 13 K 13
Lye [S] 7 T 9
≈ Lyme Bay [GB] 12 G 13
Lyme Regis [GB] 13 H 13
Lymington [GB] 13 H 13
Lympne [GB] 13 K 13
Lyngby-Tårbæk [DK] 6 Q 11
Lyngdal [N] 6 O 9
≈ Lyngenfjord [N] 2 T 2
Δ Lyngstuva [N] 2 S 1
Lynton [GB] 12 G 13
Lyon [F] 19 M 17
Δ Lyonnais, Monts du — [F] 19 L 17
Δ Łysa Góra [PL] 16 T 13
Δ Lysá hora [CS] 16 U 14
≈ Lysefjord [N] 6 N 8
Lysekil [S] 6 Q 9
Δ Łysica [PL] 17 V 13
Δ Łysogóry [PL] 17 V 13
Lysvik [S] 5 R 8
Łyszkowice [PL] 17 V 13
Lytham Saint Anne's [GB] 11 H 11

M

Maalahti = Malax [SF] 9 U 6
Maaninka [SF] 9 W 5
Maaninkavaara [SF] 3 W 3
Maanselkä [SF] 9 X 5
Δ Maan selkä [SF] 3 U 2
Δ Maan Selkä [SF, SU] 3 W 2
Maarheeze [NL] 15 N 13
Maarianhamina = Mariehamn [SF] 9 U 8
≈ Maas [NL] 15 N 13
Maaseik [B] 15 N 14
Maassluis [NL] 14 M 13
Maastricht [NL] 15 N 14
Mablethorpe and Sutton [GB] 13 K 12
≈ Maçãs, Rio — [P] 25 D 19
Macclesfield [GB] 13 H 12
Δ Macdhui, Ben — [GB] 11 H 9
Macedo de Cavaleiros [P] 25 C 19
Macerata [I] 21 R 19
Δ Machichaco, Cabo — [E] 18 F 18
Machrihanish [GB] 10 G 10
Machynlleth [GB] 12 G 12
Măcin [RO] 23 Zb 16
Δ Măcin, Munţii — [RO] 23 Zb 16
Mackmyra [S] 5 S 7
Macomer [I] 28 O 20
Mâcon [F] 19 M 17
Macotera [E] 25 D 19
Macroom [IRL] 12 D 12
Mačul'niki [SU] 17 X 12
Δ Mačva [YU] 22 V 17
Madan [BG] 31 Za 19
Maddalena, La — [I] 28 P 20
Δ Maddalena, Isola — [I] 28 P 20
Maddaloni [I] 29 S 20
M'adel' [SU] 8 Y 10
Δ Madeleine, Montagne de la — [F] 19 L 17
Madona [SU] 8 X 9
Madone d'Utelle [F] 20 N 18
Δ Madonie [I] 29 S 22
Δ Madra daği [TR] 31 Zc 20
Madrid [E] 26 E 20
Madridejos [E] 26 E 21
Madrigal de las Altas [E] 25 D 19
Δ Madrona, Sierra — [E] 26 E 21
Maella [E] 26 H 20
Măeruş [RO] 23 Z 16
Δ Maestrazgo, El — [E] 26 H 20
Mafra [P] 25 A 20
Δ Mafrovouni [GR] 30 Y 20
Magadino [CH] 20 O 17
Magdeburg [DDR] 15 Q 13
Magenta [I] 20 O 17
Δ Mageride, Monts de la — [F] 19 L 17
Δ Magerøy [N] 3 U 1
Maggia [CH] 20 O 17
Δ Maggiorasca, Monte — [I] 20 P 18
Magh Chromtha = Macroom [IRL] 12 D 12
Maghera [GB] 10 F 10
Δ Mágina, Sierra de — [E] 26 E 21
Magione [I] 21 R 19
Maglaj [YU] 21 U 18
Màglie [I] 30 V 20
Magnor [N] 4 Q 8
Magny-en-Vexin [F] 14 K 15
≈ Magro, Río — [E] 26 G 21
Măgureni [RO] 22 Y 17
Mahón [E] 27 L 21
Mahora [E] 26 G 21
Măicăneşti [RO] 23 Za 16
Maîche [F] 20 N 16
Màida [I] 29 U 21
Maidstone [GB] 13 K 13
Δ Mailhebiau [F] 19 K 18
Mailly-le-Camp [F] 14 M 15
≈ Main [D] 15 P 14
Mainburg [D] 15 Q 15
Δ Maine [F] 18 H 15
Mainistir Laoise = Abbeyleix [IRL] 10 F 12
Mainistirna Búille = Boyle [IRL] 10 E 11
Δ Mainland [GB] 11 J 8
Maintenon [F] 14 K 15
Mainua [SF] 9 W 5
Maišiogala [SU] 8 X 11
Maitum [S] 2 T 4
≈ Majaceite, Río — [E] 25 C 22
Majaki [SU] 23 Zc 15
Majanoja [SF] 9 V 7
Majatalo [SU] 3 W 1
Majavatn [N] 4 Q 4
≈ Majavatn [N] 4 Q 4
Majdanek [PL] 17 W 13
Majdanpek [YU] 22 X 17
Δ Majevica [YU] 22 V 17
Δ Majnavolok, mys — [SU] 3 X 1
Makarska [YU] 21 U 18
Δ Makedonia [GR] 30 X 20
Δ Makedonija [YU] 30 X 19
Makkola [SF] 9 X 6
Makó [H] 22 W 16
Makov [CS] 16 U 14
Δ Makra [GR] 31 Zb 22
Makri [GR] 31 Za 19
Makrokomi [GR] 30 Y 21
Δ Makronissos [GR] 31 Za 21
Malacky [CS] 16 T 15
Δ Maladeta [E] 27 J 19
Δ Malá Fatra [CS] 16 U 15
Malaga [E] 25 D 22
Malagón [E] 26 E 21
≈ Malagón, Río — [E] 25 B 21
≈ Malaja Volokovaja, guba — [SU] 3 W 1
Malaješty [SU] 23 Zb 15
Δ Mala Kapela [YU] 21 T 17
Malakassion [GR] 30 X 20
Mala Krsna [YU] 22 W 17
Mala = Mallow [IRL] 12 E 12
≈ Malån [S] 5 T 4
Malandrinon [GR] 30 Y 21
Malangen [N] 2 S 2
≈ Malangen [N] 2 S 2
≈ Mälaren [S] 7 S 8
Malåträsk [S] 2 T 4
Malax [SF] 9 U 6
Malbork [PL] 7 U 11
Malcèsine [I] 20 Q 17
Malchin [DDR] 16 R 12
Malchow [DDR] 15 Q 12
Maldegem [B] 14 L 13
Maldon [GB] 13 K 13
Malè [I] 20 Q 17
Δ Maleas, Akrotirion — [GR] 31 Z 22
Δ Malé Karpaty [CS] 16 T 15
Målerås [S] 7 S 10
Δ Maleševske planine [YU] 30 Y 19
Malesherbes [F] 14 K 15
Malestroit [F] 12 G 15
≈ Malgomaj [S] 5 S 5
Malgrat [E] 27 K 19
Malia [GR] 32 Zb 23
Målilla [S] 7 S 9
Mali Lošinj [YU] 21 S 18
Malines = Mechelen [B] 14 M 14
Malingsbo [S] 5 S 8
Δ Malin Head [IRL] 10 F 10
Maliq [AL] 30 X 20
Δ Maljen [YU] 22 W 18
Δ Maljovica [BG] 22 Y 19
Malkara [TR] 31 Zb 19
Malko-Tarnovo [BG] 23 Zb 18
Mallaig [GB] 10 G 9
Mâlles Venosta [I] 20 P 16
Mallnitz [A] 21 R 16
Δ Mallorca [E] 27 K 21
Mallow [IRL] 12 E 12
Malm [N] 4 Q 5
Malmberget [S] 2 T 3
Malmédy [B] 15 N 14
Malmesbury [GB] 13 H 13
Malmköping [S] 7 S 8
Malmö [S] 7 R 11
Δ Malojapass [CH] 20 P 17
Δ Małopolska [PL] 17 V 14
Malorita [SU] 17 X 13
Malpartida de Cáceres [E] 25 C 20
Malpica de Bergantiños [E] 204 B 17
Mals = Mâlles Venosta [I] 20 P 16
Målsnes [N] 2 S 2
Δ Malta [M] 30 V 22
Malton [GB] 11 J 11
Malung [S] 5 R 7
Malungen [S] 5 S 6
Malvik [N] 4 P 6
≈ Malý Dunaj [CS] 21 U 15
Malyi Bereznij [SU] 17 X 15
Δ Malyj Tut'arsari [SU] 9 X 7
Mamaia [RO] 23 Zb 17
Mamers [F] 14 J 15
Δ Mampodre [E] 24 E 18
≈ Mamry, Jezioro — [PL] 8 V 11
Δ Man, Isle of — [GB] 10 G 11
Manacor [E] 27 K 21
Δ Manamansalo [SF] 9 W 4
Manasija [YU] 22 X 18
Δ Mancha, La — [E] 26 E 21
Mancha Real [E] 26 E 21
Manchester [GB] 13 H 12
Manciano [I] 28 Q 19
Mandal [N] 6 O 9
≈ Mandalya körfezi [TR] 31 Zc 21
Màndas [I] 28 O 21
Δ Mandø [DK] 6 O 11
Mandrakion [GR] 31 Zc 22
Mandùria [I] 30 V 20
Manèrbio [I] 20 P 17
Manevići [SU] 17 Y 13
Manfredònia [I] 29 T 19
≈ Manfredònia, Golfo di — [I] 29 T 20
Mangalia [RO] 23 Zb 17
Mångsbodarna [S] 5 R 7
Mangualde [P] 25 B 19
Δ Manhartsberg [A] 21 T 15
Maniago [I] 21 R 17
Manisa [TR] 31 Zc 20
Δ Manjača [YU] 21 U 18
Mannheim [D] 15 O 15
Δ Mannu, Capo — [I] 28 O 21
Manosque [F] 19 M 18
Manresa [E] 27 J 19
Mans, le — [F] 19 J 15
Mansfeld [DDR] 15 Q 13
Mansfield [GB] 13 J 12
Mansilla de las Mulas [E] 24 D 18
Mansle [F] 19 J 17
Mänspää [SU] 8 V 8
Manston [GB] 13 K 13
Manteigas [P] 25 C 19
Mantes-la-Jolie [F] 14 K 15
Màntova [I] 20 Q 17
Mäntsälä [SF] 9 W 7
Mänttyharju [SF] 9 X 6
Manyas [TR] 31 Zc 20
≈ Manyas gölü [TR] 31 Zc 19
Manzanares [E] 26 E 21
Maqueda [E] 26 E 20
Maramoročka [SU] 8 Y 8
Maranchón [E] 26 F 19
Marans [F] 18 H 16
Δ Marão, Serra do — [P] 25 B 19
Mărăşeşti [RO] 23 Za 16
Δ Marastatunturit [SF] 3 V 2
Maratea [I] 29 T 21
Marateca [P] 25 A 20
Marathon [GR] 31 Z 21
Marbella [E] 25 D 22
Marburg (Lahn) [D] 15 O 14
Marcali [H] 21 U 16
Marcaria [I] 20 P 17
Marcenat [F] 19 K 17
March [GB] 13 K 12
Δ Marche [F] 19 J 16
Δ Marche, Plateau de la — [F] 19 K 17
Marche-en-Famenne [B] 14 M 14
Marchena [E] 25 C 21
Δ Marchfeld [A] 21 T 15
Marcigny [F] 19 L 17
Marcillac-la-Croisille [F] 19 K 17
Marden [GB] 13 K 13
Mårdsel [S] 2 T 4
Δ Mare, Dealul — [RO] 23 Za 17
≈ Maree, Loch — [GB] 11 H 9
Δ Maremma [I] 28 Q 19
Marennes [F] 18 H 17
Δ Marèttimo, Isola — [I] 29 R 22
Mareuil [F] 19 J 17
Mareuil-sur-Lay-Dissais [F] 18 H 16
Marfa [M] 30 V 22
Margarition [GR] 30 X 21
Margate [GB] 13 K 13
Margherita di Savòia [I] 29 T 20
Marghita [RO] 22 X 15
Margonin [PL] 16 T 12
Maria [E] 26 F 22
Δ Maria, Sierra de — [E] 26 F 22
Mariager [DK] 6 P 10
≈ Mariager Fjord [DK] 6 P 10
Mariannelund [S] 7 S 9
Mariánské-Lázně [CS] 16 R 14
Mariazell [A] 21 S 16
Maribo [DK] 6 Q 11
Maribor [YU] 21 T 16
Marica [BG] 23 Za 19
Marie [N] 4 Q 8
Mariefred [S] 7 S 8
Mariehamn [SF] 9 U 8
Marieholm [S] 7 R 10
Marienberg [DDR] 16 R 14
Marienburg (Westpreußen) = Malbork [PL] 7 U 11
Mariestad [S] 7 R 9
Δ Marijovo [YU] 30 X 20
Marín [E] 24 B 18
Marina di Grosseto [I] 28 Q 19
Marina di Ravenna [I] 21 R 18
Δ Mariñas, Las — [E] 24 C 18
Marinha Grande [P] 25 A 20
Marinhas [P] 24 B 18
Marinka [BG] 23 Zb 18
Marinkainen [SF] 9 V 5
Δ Marismas, Las — [E] 25 C 22
Δ Marismas, Puerto de las — [E] 25 C 21
Δ Marittime, Alpi — [F, I] 20 N 18
Märjamaa [SU] 8 W 8
Markabygt [N] 4 Q 5
Markaryd [S] 7 R 10
Δ Marken [NL] 14 M 13
Market Deeping [GB] 13 J 12
Market Harborough [GB] 13 J 12
Market Rasen [GB] 13 J 12
Market Weighton [GB] 11 J 12
Markkina [SF] 2 T 2
Markkleeberg [DDR] 15 Q 13
Markopoulon [GR] 31 Z 21
Δ Markotjåkko [S] 2 S 3
Markovac [YU] 22 W 18
Markranstädt [DDR] 15 Q 13
Marktoberndorf [D] 20 P 16
Markt Piesting [A] 21 T 16
Marktredwitz [D] 15 Q 14
Markt Sankt Florian [A] 21 S 15
Markt Weyer [A] 21 S 16
Marlborough [GB] 13 H 13
Marle [F] 14 L 14
Marlow [GB] 13 J 13
Marma [S] 5 S 7
Marmande [F] 19 J 17
Marmara [GR] 30 Y 21
Marmara [TR] 31 Zb 19
Δ Marmara adası [TR] 31 Zc 19
≈ Marmara denizi [TR] 31 Zb 19
Marmaraereğlisi [TR] 31 Zc 19
Marmaris [TR] 32 Zd 21
≈ Mar Menor [E] 26 G 22
Δ Marmolada [I] 20 Q 17
Δ Màrmora, Punta la — [I] 28 P 21
Marnay [F] 19 M 16
≈ Marne [F] 14 M 15
≈ Marne au Rhin, Canal de la — [F] 15 N 15
Mårnes [N] 2 R 3
Marnheim [D] 15 O 14
Maronia [GR] 31 Za 19
≈ Maronne [F] 19 K 17
≈ Maros [H] 22 W 16
Marquise [F] 14 K 14
Marradi [I] 20 Q 18
Δ Marroquí, Punta — [E] 25 C 22
Marsa, La — [TN] 28 P 22
Marsala [I] 29 R 22
Δ Marsan [F] 18 H 18
Marsaxlokk [M] 30 V 22
Marsciano [I] 21 R 19
Marseille [F] 19 M 19
Marseille-en-Beauvaisis [F] 14 K 14
Δ Marsfjället [S] 5 R 4
Màrsico Nuovo [I] 29 T 20
Mars-la-Tour [F] 15 N 15
Marstal [DK] 6 P 11
Δ Marstrand [S] 6 Q 9
Martano [I] 30 V 20
Δ Martano, Monte — [I] 21 R 19
Δ Martés, Sierra — [E] 26 G 21
Martigné-Ferchaud [F] 18 H 15
Martigny [CH] 20 N 17
Martigues [F] 19 M 18
Martin [CS] 16 U 15
≈ Martín, Río — [E] 26 H 20
Martina Franca [I] 29 U 20
Martín del Río [E] 26 G 20
Martinon [GR] 31 Z 21
Martis [I] 28 O 20
Martofte [DK] 6 P 11
Martorell [E] 27 J 20
Martos [E] 26 E 21
Martres-Tolosane [F] 19 J 18
Martti [SF] 3 W 2
Marttila [SF] 9 V 7
Marvejols [F] 19 L 18
Maryport [GB] 11 H 11
Masamagrell [E] 26 H 21
Masham [GB] 11 J 11
Masi [N] 3 U 2
Masku [SF] 9 V 7
Δ Måsøy [N] 3 U 1
Massa [I] 20 P 18
Massafra [I] 29 U 20
Massa Marittima [I] 20 Q 19
Massat [F] 19 J 19
Masseube [F] 19 J 18
Massiac [F] 19 L 17
Δ Massif Central [F] 19 K 17
Δ Masticho, Akrotirion — [GR] 31 Zb 21
Masugnsbyn [S] 2 T 3
Maszewo [PL] 16 S 12
Maszewo Lęborskie [PL] 7 T 11
≈ Mat [AL] 30 W 19
≈ Matachel, Río — [E] 25 C 21
Δ Matapas, Akrotirion — = Akrotirion Tenaron [GR] 31 Z 22
Mataró [E] 27 K 19
Mataruška Banja [YU] 22 W 18
Matejče [YU] 30 X 19
Matera [I] 29 U 20
Mateševo [YU] 22 W 19
Mátészalka [H] 17 X 15
Mateur [TN] 28 P 22
Matfors [S] 5 S 6
Matha [F] 18 H 17
Matiši [SU] 8 W 9
Matlock [GB] 13 J 12
Matočina [BG] 23 Zb 19
Δ Mator [BG] 23 Za 18
Matosinhos [P] 25 B 19
Δ Mátra [H] 22 V 15
Δ Mátraalja [H] 22 V 15
Matre [N] 4 N 7
Matrei in Osttirol [A] 21 R 16
Δ Matterhorn [CH, I] 20 O 17
Mattersburg [A] 21 T 16
Mattighofen [A] 21 R 15
Mattmar [S] 5 R 6
Mattsmyra [S] 5 R 7
Δ Maubermé, Pic de — [F] 19 J 19
Maubeuge [F] 14 M 14
Maubourguet [F] 18 H 18
Mauchline [GB] 11 H 10
Δ Maun [YU] 21 S 18
Δ Maures, Monts des — [F] 20 N 19
Mauriac [F] 19 K 17
Mauron [F] 12 G 15
Maurs [F] 19 K 17
Maurvangen [N] 4 P 7
Mautendorf [A] 21 R 16
Mauthausen [A] 21 S 15
Mauvezin [F] 19 J 18
Mauzé-sur-le-Mignon [F] 18 H 16
≈ Mavrovsko jezero [YU] 30 X 19
Mavrovë [AL] 30 W 20
Maybole [GB] 10 G 10
Mayen [D] 15 N 14
Mayenne [F] 14 J 15
≈ Mayenne [F] 18 H 15
Mayorga [E] 24 E 19
Mayrhofen [A] 20 Q 16
Mazagón [E] 25 B 21
Mazagran [F] 14 M 15
Mazamet [F] 19 K 18
Δ Mazara, Val di — [I] 29 R 22
Mazara del Vallo [I] 29 R 22
Mazarrón [E] 26 G 22
≈ Mazarrón, Golfo de — [E] 26 G 22
Mažeikiai [SU] 8 V 10
Mazirbe [SU] 8 V 9
Δ Mazowsze [PL] 17 V 13
Δ Mazurskie, Pojezierze — [PL] 17 V 12
Mazzarino [I] 29 S 22
Mealhada [P] 25 B 19
Meathas Troim = Mostrim [IRL] 10 F 11
Meaux [F] 14 L 15
Mechelen [B] 14 M 14
Mecidiye [TR] 31 Zb 19
≈ Mecklenburger Bucht [DDR] 6 Q 11
Δ Mecsek [H] 21 U 17
Mede [I] 20 O 17
Δ Medelpad [S] 5 S 6
Δ Medelser Schlucht [CH] 20 O 16
Medenica [SU] 17 X 14
Medevi [S] 7 R 9
Medgidia [RO] 23 Zb 17
Mediaş [RO] 22 Y 16
Medinaceli [E] 26 F 19
Medina del Campo [E] 26 E 19
Medina de Pomar [E] 18 F 18
Medina de Rioseco [E] 26 E 19
Medina-Sidonia [E] 25 C 22
Δ Médoc [F] 18 H 17
Δ Médous, Grotte de — [F] 18 H 18
Medvedja [YU] 22 X 18
Medzilaborce [CS] 17 W 14
Meerane [DDR] 16 R 14
Meerapalu [SU] 8 X 8
Mées, le — [F] 19 M 18
Mega Derion [GR] 31 Za 19
Megalo Chorio [GR] 31 Zc 22
Megalonission [GR] 31 Zb 20
Megalopolis [GR] 30 Y 22
Δ Megalo Sofrano [GR] 31 Zc 22
Megalou Spileou, Moni — [GR] 30 Y 21
Δ Meganission [GR] 30 X 21
Megara [GR] 31 Z 21
Mehadia [RO] 22 X 17
Mehamn [N] 3 V 1
Δ Mehedinţi, Munţii — [RO] 22 X 17
Meillerie [F] 20 N 17
Meiningen [DDR] 15 P 14
Meißen [DDR] 16 R 13
Melambes [GR] 32 Zb 23
Melbu [N] 2 R 2
Meldorf [D] 6 P 12
Melegnano [I] 20 P 17
Melenci [YU] 22 W 17
Melfi [I] 29 T 20
≈ Melfjord [N] 2 Q 4
Melgaço [P] 24 B 18
Melgar de Fernamental [E] 24 E 18
Melhus [N] 4 P 6
Meligalas [GR] 30 Y 22
Melineşti [RO] 22 Y 17
Δ Melissa [GR] 31 Zb 21
Melissopetra [GR] 30 X 20
Mèlito di Porto Salvo [I] 29 T 22
Melk [A] 21 S 15
Δ Melkfjell [N] 2 R 4
Mellajärvi [SF] 3 V 3
Mellakoski [SF] 3 V 3
≈ Mellanfryken [S] 5 R 8
Mellansel [S] 5 T 5
Melle [F] 19 J 16
Δ Mellerstön [S] 3 U 4
Mellerud [S] 6 Q 9
Mellid [E] 24 C 18
Melliema [M] 30 V 22
Mellilä [SF] 9 V 7
Mellrichstadt [D] 15 P 14
Mělník [CS] 16 S 14
Melos [GR] 31 Za 22
Δ Meløy [N] 2 Q 3
Melrose Abbey [GB] 11 J 10
Melsungen [D] 15 P 14
Meltaus [SF] 3 K 3
≈ Meltausjoki [SF] 3 V 3
Melton Mowbray [GB] 13 J 12
Meltosjärvi [SF] 3 V 3
Melun [F] 14 L 15
Melvich [GB] 11 H 8
Mélykút [H] 22 V 16
Membrio [E] 25 C 20
Membrolle-sur-Choisille, la — [F] 19 J 16
≈ Mēmele [SU] 8 X 10
Memmingen [D] 20 P 16
Mende [F] 19 L 18
Δ Mendro, Serra — [P] 25 B 21
Menemen [TR] 31 Zc 21
Menen [B] 14 L 14
Menesjärvi [SF] 3 V 2
Menfi [I] 29 R 22
Mengíbar [E] 26 E 21
Menhire [F] 18 G 15
Δ Menorca [E] 27 L 20
Mens [F] 19 M 18
Menton [F] 20 N 18
Menzel Bourguiba [TN] 28 P 22
Meppel [NL] 15 N 12
Meppen [D] 15 O 12
≈ Mequinenza, Pantano de — [E] 26 H 19
Meråker [N] 4 Q 6
≈ Merampellou, Kolpos — [GR] 32 Zb 23
Meran = Merano [I] 20 Q 16
Merano [I] 20 Q 16
Mercadal [E] 27 L 21
Mercato San Severino [I] 29 S 20
Mercato Saraceno [I] 21 R 18
Merdrignac [F] 12 G 15
≈ Merenkurkku5 U 5
≈ Meriç nehri [TR] 31 Zb 19
Mérida [E] 25 C 20
Merikarvia [SF] 9 U 6
Merimasku [SF] 9 U 7
Merkinė [SU] 8 X 11
Mernye [H] 21 U 16
Δ Merrick [GB] 10 G 10
Mersch [L] 15 N 14
Merseburg [DDR] 15 Q 13
Mers-les-Bains [F] 14 K 14
Merthyr Tydfil [GB] 12 G 13
Mértola [P] 25 B 21
Méru [F] 14 K 15
Mervans [F] 19 M 16
Méry-sur-Seine [F] 14 L 15
Merzig [D] 15 N 15
Δ Mesa de Roldán, Punta de la — [E] 26 F 22
Mesagne [I] 30 V 20
≈ Mesaras, Ormos — [GR] 32 Za 23
Meschede [D] 15 O 13
Meselefors [S] 5 S 5
Meskla [GR] 32 Za 23
Meškuičiai [SU] 8 W 10
Mesocco [CH] 20 P 17
Mèsola [I] 21 R 18
Messaure [S] 2 T 3
Messene = Messini [antike Stätte] [GR] 30 Y 22
Messina [I] 29 T 22
≈ Messina, Stretto di — [I] 29 T 21
≈ Messiniakos Kolpos [GR] 30 Y 22
Messini [antike Stätte] [GR] 30 Y 22
Messini [Ort] [GR] 30 Y 22
Meßkirch [D] 20 P 16
Messochorion [GR] 30 Y 20
Messolongion [GR] 30 Y 21
≈ Mesta [BG] 31 Z 19
Mestre [I] 21 R 17
Δ Metalici, Munţii — [RO] 22 X 16
Metaponto [I] 29 U 20
≈ Metauro [I] 21 R 18
Meteora [GR] 30 X 20
Methoni [GR] 30 Y 22
Metkvić [YU] 21 U 19
Metlika [YU] 21 T 17
Δ Metohija [YU] 22 W 19
Metsäkylä [SF] 9 V 5
Metsovon [GR] 30 X 20
Metz [F] 15 N 15
Metzingen [D] 15 P 15
Meung-sur-Loire [F] 19 K 15
≈ Meuse [F] 14 M 14
Meximieux [F] 19 M 17
Meymac [F] 19 K 17
Meyrueis [F] 19 L 18
Mezdra [BG] 22 Y 18
Mèze [F] 19 L 18
Mézel [F] 20 N 18
Δ Mézenc, Mont — [F] 19 L 17
Δ Mezes, Munţii — [RO] 22 X 16
Mežgorje [SU] 17 X 15
Mézières-en-Brenne [F] 19 J 16
Mézières-sur-Issoire [F] 19 J 17
Mezőberény [H] 22 W 16
Δ Mezőföld [H] 21 U 16
Mezőkövesd [H] 22 W 15
Mezőtúr [H] 22 W 16
Mezzolombardo [I] 20 Q 17
Mgarr [M] 30 V 22
Miajadas [E] 25 C 20
Mianowice [PL] 7 T 11
Miastko [PL] 7 T 12
Micfalău [RO] 23 Z 16
Michalovce [CS] 17 W 15
Michelstadt [D] 15 O 14
Δ Mickelsöarna [SF] 9 U 5
Mičurin [BG] 23 Zb 18
Middelburg [NL] 14 L 13
Middelfart [DK] 6 P 11
Middlesbrough [GB] 11 J 11
Middleton [GB] 11 J 11
Midhurst [GB] 13 J 13
Δ Midi de Bigorre, Pic du — [F] 18 H 18
Δ Midi d'Ossau, Pic du — [F] 18 H 18
≈ Midour [F] 18 H 18
≈ Midskogsforsen [S] 5 R 6
Δ Midžor [YU, BG] 22 Y 18
Miechów [PL] 17 V 14
Miecno [PL] 16 T 13
Międzyrzec Podlaski [PL] 17 W 13
Miedzyrzecz [PL] 16 S 13
Miejsce Piastowe [PL] 17 W 14
≈ Miekojärvi [SF] 3 U 3
Miélan [F] 18 H 18
Mielec [PL] 17 W 14
Miercurea Ciuc [RO] 23 Z 16
Mieres [E] 24 D 18
Mierzeja Wislana [PL] 7 U 11
Miesbach [D] 20 Q 16
Miesjka Górka [PL] 16 T 13
Mieszków [PL] 16 T 13
Mieto [SF] 9 U 6
Mietoinen [SF] 9 U 7
Mifol [AL] 30 W 20
Migai [SU] 23 Zc 15
Migliarino [I] 20 Q 18
Mihăeşti [RO] 23 Z 17
Mihăileşti [RO] 23 Za 17
Mihai-Viteazu [RO] 23 Zb 17
Mihajlovgrad [BG] 22 Y 18
Mihalkovo [BG] 23 Z 19
≈ Mijares, Río — [E] 26 H 20
Δ Mijas, Sierra de — [E] 25 D 22
Mikine [GR] 31 Z 22
Mikkeli [SF] 9 X 6
Mikkelvik [N] 2 S 1
Mikolajki [PL] 8 V 11
Mikołów [PL] 16 U 14
Mikonos [GR] 31 Zb 21
Δ Mikonos [GR] 31 Zb 21
≈ Mikonou, Stenon — [GR] 31 Za 21
≈ Mikra Prespa, Limni — [GR] 30 X 20
Mikron Derion [GR] 31 Za 19
Mikulov [CS] 16 T 15
Miłakowo [PL] 8 V 11
Milano [I] 20 P 17
Milas [TR] 31 Zc 21
Milazzo [I] 29 T 22
Mildenhall [GB] 13 K 13
Δ Milejewska Góra [PL] 7 U 11
Mileševo [YU] 22 W 18
Miletkovo [YU] 30 Y 19
Miletos [TR] 31 Zc 21
Milevsko [CS] 16 S 15
Milford [GB] 13 J 13
Milford Haven [GB] 12 G 13
Milicz [PL] 16 T 13

illas [F] 19 K 19
illau [F] 19 K 18
Millevaches, Plateau de — [F] 19 K 17
illom [GB] 11 H 11
illy-la-Forêt [F] 14 K 15
ilna [YU] 21 T 18
Milos [GR] 31 Za 22
ilosna Stara [PL] 17 V 11
ilot [AL] 30 W 19
ilovidy [SU] 17 Y 12
iltenberg [D] 15 P 14
imizan [F] 18 H 18
imoň [CS] 16 S 14
ina de São Domingos [P] 25 B 21
Minas de Riotinto [E] 25 C 21
Minăstiria [RO] 23 Za 17
Minaya [E] 26 F 21
Mindelheim [D] 20 P 16
Minden [D] 15 O 13
Mîndra, Vîrful — [RO] 22 Y 17
Minehead [GB] 12 G 13
Minèrbio [I] 20 Q 18
Minervino Murge [I] 29 T 20
Minglanilla [E] 26 G 20
Minho [P] 24 B 18
Minićevo [YU] 22 X 18
≈ Miño, Río — [E] 24 B 18
Minozero [SU] 3 X 4
Mińsk Mazowiecki [PL] 17 W 12
Minturno [I] 29 S 20
Miory [SU] 8 Y 10
Mira [I] 20 Q 17
Mira [P] 25 B 19
≈ Mira, Rio — [P] 25 A 21
Miramar [E] 27 K 21
Miramas [F] 19 M 18
Mirambeau [F] 18 H 17
Miramont-de-Guyenne [F] 19 J 17
Miranda de Ebro [E] 18 F 18
Miranda do Corvo [P] 25 B 19
Miranda do Douro [P] 25 D 19
Mirande [F] 19 J 18
Mirandela [P] 25 C 19
Mirándola [I] 20 Q 18
Miravet [E] 26 H 20
∆ Miravete, Puerto de — [E] 25 D 20
Mire [GR] 32 Zb 23
Mirebeau [F] 19 J 16
Mirebeau [F] 19 M 16
Mirecourt [F] 20 N 15
Mirepoix [F] 19 K 18
Miribel [F] 19 M 17
Mirina [GR] 31 Za 20
Mirosławiec [PL] 16 S 12
≈ Mirtoon Pelagos [GR] 31 Z 22
Misilmeri [I] 29 S 22
Miskolc [H] 17 W 15
Misso [SU] 8 Y 9
Mistelbach an der Zaya [A] 21 T 15
Misterbianco [I] 29 T 22
Mistras [GR] 30 Y 22
Mistretta [I] 29 S 22
Mitchelstown [IRL] 12 E 12
Mithimna [GR] 31 Zb 20
Mitikas [GR] 30 X 21
Mitilini [GR] 31 Zb 20
≈ Mitilinis, Stenon — [GR] 31 Zb 20
Mittelberg [A] 20 P 16
∆ Mittelfranken [D] 15 P 15
≈ Mittellandkanal [DDR] 15 Q 13
Mittenwald [D] 20 Q 16
Mitterding [A] 21 R 15
Mittersill [A] 21 R 16
Mitterteich [D] 15 Q 14
∆ Mizen Head [IRL] 12 D 12
Mizil [RO] 23 Za 17
Mjölby [S] 7 S 9
≈ Mjörn [S] 6 Q 9
≈ Mjøsa [N] 4 P 7
Mladá Boleslav [CS] 16 S 14
Mladá Vožice [CS] 16 S 14
Mladenovac [YU] 22 W 17
Mława [PL] 17 V 12
Mliništa [YU] 21 U 18
Mlinov [SU] 17 Y 13
∆ Mljet [YU] 21 U 19
≈ Mljetski kanal [YU] 21 U 19
Młodasko [PL] 16 T 13
Mnichovo Hradiště [CS] 16 S 14
Mo [S] 6 Q 9
Moate [IRL] 10 E 11
Mochy [PL] 16 T 13
Möckern [DDR] 15 Q 13
Modane [F] 20 N 17
Mòdena [I] 20 Q 18
Mòdica [I] 29 T 22
Modriča [YU] 22 V 17
Moelv [N] 4 P 7
Moffat [GB] 11 H 10
Mogadouro [P] 25 C 19
∆ Mogod [TN] 28 O 22
Moguer [E] 25 B 21
Mohács [H] 22 V 17
Mohelnice [CS] 16 T 14
Moi [N] 6 N 9
Moikipää [SF] 9 U 6
Moimenta da Beira [P] 25 C 19
Moineşti [RO] 23 Za 16
Mo i Rana [N] 2 R 4
Moirans-en-Montagne [F] 19 M 17
Moisdon-la-Rivière [F] 18 H 15
Moisei [RO] 17 Y 15
Moisiovaara [SF] 3 X 4
Moissac [F] 19 J 18
∆ Möja [S] 5 T 8
Mojácar [E] 26 F 22
Mojados [E] 26 E 19
Mojkovac [YU] 22 W 18
∆ Mokra gora [YU] 22 W 18
Mokrin [YU] 22 W 17
Möksy [SF] 9 V 5
Mol [B] 14 M 13
∆ Mola, La — [E] 27 J 21
Mola di Bari [I] 29 U 20
Molar, El — [E] 26 E 20
∆ Molat [YU] 21 S 18
Molde [N] 4 O 6
≈ Moldova [RO] 23 Z 15
∆ Moldova [RO] 23 Z 15
Moldova Nouă [RO] 22 X 17
∆ Moldoveanu [RO] 23 Z 16
Molėtai [SU] 8 X 10
Molfetta [I] 29 U 20
Molières [F] 19 J 18
Molina [E] 26 G 20
Molina de Segura [E] 26 G 21
Molkom [S] 7 R 8
∆ Molla [N] 2 R 3
Mölle [S] 6 Q 10
Molledo [E] 18 F 18
Mollerusa [E] 27 J 19
Mollina [E] 25 D 22
Mölln [D] 15 P 12
Mölltorp [S] 7 R 9
Mölndal [S] 6 Q 9
Molodečno [SU] 8 Y 11
Molodi [SU] 8 Y 8
Molos [GR] 30 Y 21
Møløy [N] 4 N 7
∆ Mols [DK] 6 P 10
Molsheim [F] 15 N 15
Mombuey [E] 24 D 19
Momčilgrad [BG] 23 Za 19
Mommark [DK] 6 P 11
Mon [S] 6 Q 9
∆ Mön [DK] 6 Q 11
∆ Monach Islands [GB] 10 F 9
Monaco [MC] 20 N 18
∆ Monadhliath Mountains [GB] 11 H 9
≈ Monåfjärd [SF] 9 U 5
Monaghan [IRL] 10 F 11
Monastier-sur-Gazeille, le — [F] 19 L 17
Monastyriska [SU] 17 Y 14
Moncada y Reixach [E] 27 K 20
Moncalieri [I] 20 O 17
Moncalvo [I] 20 O 17
∆ Moncalvo [E] 24 C 18
Monção [P] 24 B 18
∆ Moncayo, Sierra del — [E] 26 G 19
Mončegorsk [SU] 3 X 2
≈ Mončeozero [SU] 3 X 2
Mönchdorf [A] 21 S 15
Mönchen-Gladbach [D] 15 N 13
∆ Mönchgut [DDR] 7 R 11
Mönchhof [A] 21 T 15
Monchique [P] 25 A 21
∆ Monchique, Serra de — [P] 25 A 21
Moncontour [F] 12 G 15
≈ Mondego, Rio — [P] 25 B 19
∆ Mondego, Cabo — [P] 25 B 19
Mondello [I] 29 S 22
Mondoñedo [E] 24 C 18
Mondoubleau [F] 19 J 15
Mondovì [I] 20 O 18
Mondragon [F] 19 M 18
Mondragone [I] 29 S 20
Mondsee [A] 21 R 16
∆ Monduber [E] 26 H 21
∆ Monegros, Los — [E] 26 H 19
Monemvassia [GR] 31 Z 22
Monesterio [E] 25 C 21
Monfalcone [I] 21 R 17
∆ Monferrato [I] 20 O 18
Monflanguin [F] 19 J 18
Monforte [P] 25 B 20
Monforte del Cid [E] 26 G 21
Monforte de Lemos [E] 24 C 18
∆ Mongó [E] 26 H 21
Moniaive [GB] 11 H 10
Moni Lavras [GR] 31 Z 20
Monmouth [GB] 13 H 13
∆ Monné, Mont — [F] 19 J 19
Monòpoli [I] 29 U 20
Monor [H] 22 V 16
Monor [RO] 22 Y 16
Monóvar [E] 26 G 21
Monplaisir [F] 19 J 15
Monreal [E] 18 G 19
Monreal del Campo [E] 26 G 20
Monreale [I] 29 S 22
Monroyo [E] 26 H 20
Mons [B] 14 L 14
Monschau [D] 15 N 14
Monsèlice [I] 20 Q 17
∆ Møns Klint [DK] 6 Q 11
Montagnac [F] 19 L 18
Montagnana [I] 20 Q 17
∆ Montagne Noire [F] 19 K 18
∆ Montagut [E] 27 J 20
Montaigu [F] 18 H 16
Montaigu-de-Quercy [F] 19 J 18
Montalbán [E] 26 G 20
Montalbo [E] 26 F 20
Montalcino [I] 20 Q 19
Montalegre [P] 24 C 18
Montalto di Castro [I] 28 Q 19
Montalto Uffugo [I] 29 U 21
∆ Montaña, La — [E] 24 D 18
Montargis [F] 19 L 15
Montauban [F] 13 H 15
Montauban [F] 19 J 18
Montbard [F] 19 M 16
Montbazon [F] 19 J 16
Montbéliard [F] 20 N 16
∆ Mont Blanc [F] 20 N 17
Montblanch [E] 27 J 20
Montbrison [F] 19 L 17
Montceau-les-Mines [F] 19 L 16
∆ Mont Cenis, Col du — [F] 20 N 17
Montcornet [F] 14 L 14
Montcuq [F] 19 J 18
Mont-de-Marsan [F] 18 H 18
Montdidier [F] 14 L 14
Mont-Dore, le — [F] 19 K 17
Montebelluna [I] 20 Q 17
Monte-Carlo [MC] 20 N 18
∆ Monte Caro [E] 26 H 20
Montecassino [I] 29 S 20
Montecatini Terme [I] 20 Q 18
Montech [F] 19 J 18
Montech [F] 19 J 18
∆ Montecristo, Isola di — [I] 28 P 19
Montefiascone [I] 28 Q 19
Montefiorino [I] 20 P 18
Montélimar [F] 19 M 18
Montella [I] 29 T 20
Montemor-o-Novo [P] 25 B 20
Montemor-o-Velho [P] 25 B 19
∆ Montemuro [P] 25 B 19
Montendre [F] 18 H 17
∆ Monte Perdido [E] 26 H 19
Montepulciano [I] 20 Q 19
Montereau-faut-Yonne [F] 14 L 15
Monte Redondo [P] 25 B 20
Monteroni d'Àrbia [I] 20 Q 19
∆ Monte Rosa [CH, I] 20 O 17
∆ Monte Saçro [I] 29 T 20
Monte Sant'Angelo [I] 29 T 19
Montesàrchio [I] 29 S 20
Montevarchi [I] 20 Q 18
Montfaucon-en-Velay [F] 19 L 17
Montfort [F] 13 H 15
∆ Mont Genèvre, Col du — [F, I] 20 N 17
Montgomery [GB] 13 H 12
Monti [I] 28 P 20
Montichiari [I] 20 P 17
∆ Montiel, Campo de — [E] 26 E 21
Montignac [F] 19 J 17
Montigny-le-Roi [F] 19 M 15
Montijo [E] 25 C 20
Montijo [P] 25 A 20
Montilla [E] 25 D 21
Mont-Louis [F] 19 K 19
Montluçon [F] 19 K 16
Montmarault [F] 19 L 16
Montmédy [F] 14 M 15
Montmirail [F] 14 L 15
Montmoreau [F] 19 J 17
Montoire-sur-le-Loir [F] 19 J 15
Montoncel, Puy de — [F] 19 L 17
Montoro [E] 25 D 21
Montpellier [F] 19 L 18
∆ Montpellier le Vieux [F] 19 K 18
Montpon-sur-l'Isle [F] 19 J 17
Montréal [F] 19 K 18
∆ Montrecon [F] 19 L 16
Montréjeau [F] 19 H 18
Montreuil-Bellay [F] 19 J 16
Montreux [CH] 20 N 17
Montreux-sur-Mer [F] 14 K 14
Montrevel-en-Bresse [F] 19 M 17
Montrichard [F] 19 K 16
Montrillon [F] 19 J 16
Montrose [GB] 11 J 10
Mont-Saint-Michel, le — [F] 13 H 15
∆ Montsech, Sierra de — [E] 27 J 19
∆ Montseny [E] 27 K 19
Montserrat, Monasterio de — [E] 27 J 19
∆ Montsia [E] 26 H 20
Mont-sous-Vaudrey [F] 19 M 16
Montsûrs [F] 14 J 15
∆ Montuez [F] 19 M 17
Montuiri [E] 27 K 21
Monza [I] 20 P 17
Monzón [E] 26 H 19
Moosburg an der Isar [D] 20 Q 15
Mór [H] 21 U 16
Mora [E] 26 E 20
Mora [P] 25 B 20
Mora [S] 5 R 7
Morača [YU] 22 V 19
Mora de Ebro [E] 26 H 20
Mora de Rubielos [E] 26 G 20
Morąg [PL] 7 U 11
Moral de Calatrava [E] 26 E 21
Morăreşti [RO] 23 Z 17
∆ Morás, Cabo — [E] 24 C 17
Morasverdes [E] 25 D 19
Moratalla [E] 26 F 21
≈ Morava [A, CS] 16 T 15
≈ Morava [YU] 22 X 18
∆ Morava [CS] 16 T 15
Moraviţa [RO] 22 W 17
∆ Moravská brana [CS] 16 U 14
Moravské Budějovice [CS] 16 T 15
∆ Moravský Kras [CS] 16 T 15
Moravský Krumlov [CS] 16 T 15
Morawica [PL] 17 V 13
≈ Moray Firth [GB] 11 H 9
Morbach [D] 15 N 14
Morbegno [I] 20 P 17
Mörbylånga [S] 7 S 10
Morcone [I] 29 S 20
∆ More, Ben — [Island of Mull] [GB] 10 G 10
∆ More, Ben — [North Uist] [GB] 10 G 9
∆ More, Ben — [Schottland] [GB] 11 H 10
∆ More, Glen — [GB] 11 H 9
∆ More Assynt, Ben — [GB] 11 H 9
≈ Morecambe Bay [GB] 11 H 11
Morecambe & Heysham [GB] 11 H 11
Morella [E] 26 H 20
∆ Morella [E] 27 J 20
Moreni [RO] 23 Z 17
Moretonhampstead [GB] 12 G 13
Moreton in Marsh [GB] 13 H 13
Moret-sur-Loing [F] 14 L 15
Moreuil [F] 14 L 14
Morez [F] 20 N 16
∆ Morgam-Viibus [SF] 3 V 2
Morgat [F] 12 F 15
Morges [CH] 20 N 16
Morhange [F] 15 N 15
Morjärv [S] 3 U 4
∆ Mörkö [S] 7 T 8
Mörkret [S] 4 Q 7
Morlaix [F] 12 G 15
Mormanno [I] 29 T 21
≈ Mornos [GR] 30 Y 21
Moročno [SU] 17 Y 12
Morón de la Frontera [E] 25 C 22
Morottaja [SF] 3 W 3
∆ Moroy [E] 27 K 21
∆ Morozov [BG] 23 Z 18
Morpeth [GB] 11 J 11
≈ Mörrumsån [S] 7 R 10
∆ Mors [DK] 6 O 10
Mörsil [S] 5 R 6
Mörskom = Myrskylä [SF] 9 W 7
Mortagne-au-Perche [F] 14 J 15
Mortagne-sur-Sèvre [F] 18 H 16
Mortain [F] 13 H 15
Mortara [I] 20 O 17
Morteau [F] 20 N 16
Mortenslund [N] 4 Q 5
∆ Morvan [F] 19 L 16
Mošar [SU] 8 Y 10
Mosbach [D] 15 P 15
∆ Moščnyj ostrov [SU] 9 X 7
≈ Mosel [D] 15 N 14
≈ Moselle [F] 15 N 15
Mosjøen [N] 2 Q 4
∆ Mosken [N] 2 Q 3
∆ Moskenesøy [N] 2 Q 3
≈ Moskenesstraumen [N] 2 Q 3
Moskog [N] 4 N 7
Moskosel [S] 2 T 4
∆ Moslavačka gora [YU] 21 T 17
∆ Moslavina [YU] 21 T 17
Mosonmadyaróvár [H] 21 U 15
∆ Mosor [YU] 21 U 18
Moss [N] 6 P 8
Most [CS] 16 R 14
Mosta [M] 30 V 22
Mostar [YU] 21 U 18
Mostiska [SU] 17 X 14
Mostrim [IRL] 10 F 11
Mosty [SU] 8 X 12
≈ Møsvatn [N] 4 O 8
Mosza [PL] 16 U 14
Mota del Cuervo [E] 26 F 20
Mota del Marqués [E] 25 D 19
∆ Motajica [YU] 21 U 17
Motala [S] 7 R 9
Mothe-Achard, la — [F] 18 H 16
Motherwell & Wishaw [GB] 11 H 10
Mothe-Saint-Héray, la — [F] 19 J 16
Motilla del Palancar [E] 26 F 20
≈ Motovskij zaliv [SU] 3 W 1
Motril [E] 26 E 22
Mòttola [I] 29 U 20
Mouchard [F] 19 M 16
∆ Mouchet, Mont — [F] 19 L 17
Moudon [CH] 20 N 16
Moudros [GR] 31 Za 20
Mouhijärvi [SF] 9 V 6
Moulins [F] 19 L 16
Moulins-Engilbert [F] 19 L 16
Moulins-la-Marche [F] 14 J 15
Moulins-lès-Metz [F] 15 N 15
Moura [P] 25 B 21
Mourão [P] 25 B 21
∆ Mourtzeflos [GR] 31 Za 20
Moustheni [GR] 31 Z 19
Moustiers-Sainte-Marie [F] 20 N 18
Moutier [CH] 20 N 16
Moûtiers [F] 20 N 17
Moux [F] 19 K 18
Mouzouras [GR] 32 Za 23
Moville [IRL] 10 F 10
Moy [GB] 11 H 9
Moya [E] 27 K 19
Moyenvic [F] 15 N 15
∆ Møysalen [N] 2 R 2
Mragowo [PL] 8 V 11
Mrkonjićgrad [YU] 21 U 18
Mrzeżyno [PL] 7 S 12
Mszczonów [PL] 17 V 13
∆ Mu [P] 25 B 21
∆ Muck [GB] 10 G 9
∆ Muddus nationalpark [S] 2 T 3
Muel [E] 26 G 19
Muela, La — [E] 26 G 19
Muge [P] 25 A 20
Muğla [TR] 32 Zd 21
Mühlen [A] 21 S 16
Mühlhausen/Thüringen [DDR] 15 P 13
Muhos [SF] 3 V 4
Muhu [SU] 8 V 8
∆ Muhu [SU] 8 V 8
Muineachán = Monaghan [IRL] 10 F 11
Muirkirk [GB] 11 H 10
Mukačevo [SU] 17 X 15
Mula [E] 26 G 21
≈ Mulde [DDR] 16 R 13
∆ Mulhacén [E] 26 E 22
Mülheim an der Ruhr [D] 15 N 13
Mulhouse [F] 20 N 16
∆ Mull, Island of — [GB] 10 G 9
Mullingar [IRL] 10 F 11
Mullsjö [S] 7 R 9
Mulstrand [N] 2 R 3
∆ Multamäki [SF] 9 W 6
Multia [SF] 9 V 6
Mumbles [GB] 12 G 13
Münchberg [D] 15 Q 14
Müncheberg [DDR] 16 R 13
München [D] 20 Q 15
Münden [D] 15 P 13
Mundheim [N] 4 N 8
≈ Mundo, Río — [E] 26 F 21
∆ Munëllës, Mali i — [AL] 30 W 19
Munera [E] 26 F 21
Muniesa [E] 26 G 20
Munilla [E] 26 G 19
Munkedal [S] 6 Q 9
Munkelv [N] 3 W 1
Munkfors [S] 5 R 8
Munsala [SF] 9 U 5
∆ Munsfjällét [S] 5 R 5
Münsingen [CH] 20 O 16
Munster [D] 15 P 12
Munster [F] 20 N 16
∆ Munster [IRL] 12 D 12
Münster (Westfalen) [D] 15 O 13
∆ Muntele Mare [RO] 22 X 16
∆ Muntenia [RO] 23 Z 17
Muodoslompolo [S] 3 U 2
≈ Muojärvi [SF] 3 W 3
Muonio [SF] 3 U 2
≈ Muonio älv [S] 3 U 2
≈ Muoniojoki [SF] 3 U 3
Muotkavaara [SF] 3 U 2
≈ Mur [A] 21 T 16
≈ Mura [YU] 21 T 16
Muradiye [TR] 31 Zc 20
Muran [CS] 17 V 15
Murat [F] 19 K 17
Muratlı [TR] 31 Zb 19
Murat-sur-Vèbre [F] 19 K 18
Murau [A] 21 S 16
Muravera [I] 28 P 21
Murça [P] 25 C 19
Murcia [E] 26 G 21
Mur-de-Barrez [F] 19 K 17
Mûr-de-Bretagne [F] 12 G 15
Mure, la — [F] 19 M 17
Mürefte [TR] 31 Zb 19
≈ Mureş [RO] 22 X 16
Mureşenii Bîrgăului [RO] 22 Y 15
Muret [F] 19 J 18
Murfatlar [RO] 23 Zb 17
≈ Murg [D] 15 O 15
∆ Murge, Le — [I] 29 T 20
Murgeni [RO] 23 Za 16
Murighiol [RO] 23 Zc 16
Murillo de Gállego [E] 26 H 19
≈ Müritz [DDR] 16 R 12
Murjek [S] 2 T 3
Murmansk [SU] 3 X 1
∆ Murmanskij bereg [SU] 3 X 1
Murmaši [SU] 3 X 1
Mūrmuiža [SU] 8 X 10
Murnau [D] 20 Q 16
∆ Muro, Capo di — [F] 28 O 20
Muro del Alcoy [E] 26 G 21
Murole [SF] 9 V 6
Muro Lucano [I] 29 T 20
Muros [E] 24 B 18
≈ Muros y Noya, Ría de — [E] 24 B 18
Murowana Goślina [PL] 16 T 12
∆ Murro di Porco, Capo — [I] 29 T 22
Murska Sobota [YU] 21 T 16
Murta [RO] 22 Y 18
Murten [CH] 20 N 16
Murter [YU] 21 T 18
∆ Murter [YU] 21 T 18
Murtovaara [SF] 3 W 3
≈ Mürz [A] 21 S 16
Mürzzuschlag [A] 21 T 16
∆ Muselle, la — [F] 19 M 17
∆ Muskö [S] 7 T 8
Musselburgh [GB] 11 H 10
Mussidan [F] 19 J 17
Mustjala [SU] 8 V 8
Mustvee [SU] 8 X 8
Muszyna [PL] 17 W 14
≈ Muurasjärvi [SF] 9 V 5
Muurola [SF] 3 V 3
Muurola [SF] 9 X 7
Muy, le — [F] 20 N 18
∆ Muzhllit të Skëndërbeut [AL] 30 W 19
Muzillac [F] 18 G 15
Myckelgensjö [S] 5 S 5
Mykene = Mikine [GR] 31 Z 22
Mykland [N] 6 O 9
Mynämäki [SF] 9 U 7
Myra [n. Tromsø] [N] 2 S 2
Myre [n. Dragnes] [N] 2 R 2
Myre [w. Dragnes] [N] 2 R 2
Myrheden [S] 2 T 4
Myrskylä [SF] 9 W 7
Mysen [N] 6 Q 8
Myślenice [PL] 17 V 14
Myślibórz [PL] 16 S 12
Myślowice [PL] 16 U 14
Mysovka [SU] 8 V 9
Myszyniec [PL] 17 V 12

N

≈ Naab [D] 15 Q 15
Naas [IRL] 10 F 11
≈ Näätämöjoki [SF] 3 V 1
Na Cealla Beaga = Killybegs [IRL] 10 E 10
Náchod [CS] 16 T 14
Nacka [S] 7 T 8
Nădlac [RO] 22 W 16
Nadur [M] 30 V 22
Nadvornaja [SU] 17 Y 15
Næsved [DK] 6 Q 11
Näfels [CH] 20 O 16
Nafpaktos [GR] 30 Y 21
Nafplion [GR] 31 Z 22
Nagis [F] 14 L 15
Na Gleanntaí = Glenties [IRL] 10 F 10
Nagu [SF] 9 V 7
Nagyatád [H] 21 U 17
Nagybaracska [H] 22 V 17
Nagygec [H] 17 X 15
Nagyigmánd [H] 21 U 16
Nagykálló [H] 17 W 15
Nagykanizsa [H] 21 U 16
Nagykáta [H] 22 V 16
Nagykőrös [H] 22 V 16
∆ Nagykunság [H] 22 W 16
Nagyléta [H] 22 W 16
∆ Nagy Magyar Alföld [H, YU] 22 V 17
Nagyszénás [H] 22 W 16
≈ Nahe [D] 15 N 14
Naimakka [S] 2 T 2
Nairn [GB] 11 H 9
∆ Naissaar [SU] 9 W 8
Najac [F] 19 K 18
Nájera [E] 18 F 19
Nakkila [SF] 9 U 7
Nakło nad Notecią [PL] 16 T 12
Nakskov [DK] 6 Q 11
Nälden [S] 5 R 6
Naliboki [SU] 8 Y 11
Näljänkä [SF] 3 W 4
≈ Nalón, Río — [E] 24 E 18
∆ Namdal [N] 4 Q 5
Namdalseid [N] 4 Q 5
Námestovo [CS] 17 V 14
≈ Nämforsen [S] 5 S 6
Namnå [N] 4 Q 7
Nampa [SF] 3 V 3
≈ Namsen [N] 4 Q 5
Namsos [N] 4 Q 5
Namsskogan [N] 4 Q 5
≈ Namsvatn [N] 5 R 5
Namur [B] 14 M 14
Namysłów [PL] 16 U 13
Nancy [F] 15 N 15
Năneşti [RO] 23 Za 16
Nant [F] 19 L 18
Nanterre [F] 14 K 15
Nantes [F] 18 H 16
Nanteuil-le-Haudouin [F] 14 L 15
Nantua [F] 19 M 17
Nantwich [GB] 13 H 12
∆ Nao, Cabo de la — [E] 26 H 21
Naoussa [GR] 30 Y 20
Naoussa [GR] 31 Zb 22
Nàpoli [I] 29 S 20
≈ Nàpoli, Golfo di — [I] 29 S 20
Narbonne [F] 19 K 18
≈ Narcea, Río — [E] 24 D 18
≈ Narew [PL] 17 V 12
≈ N'aris [SU] 8 X 11
∆ Närke [S] 7 R 8
Narni [I] 29 R 19
Naroč [SU] 8 Y 11
≈ Naroč, ozero — [SU] 8 Y 10
Närpes [SF] 9 U 6
Närpiö = Närpes [SF] 9 U 6
Narta [YU] 21 T 17
Narvik [N] 2 S 2
≈ Narvskij zaliv [SU] 9 X 7
∆ Nasafjell [N] 2 R 4
Năşăud [RO] 22 Y 15
Nasavrky [CS] 16 T 14
Našice [YU] 21 U 17
Nasielsk [PL] 17 V 11
≈ Näsijärvi [SF] 9 V 6
Nás = Naas [IRL] 10 F 11
Nassereith [A] 20 Q 16
Nässjö [S] 7 R 9
Nästansjö [S] 5 S 5
Nastola [SF] 9 W 7
∆ Nattastunturit [SF] 3 V 2
Nattavara [S] 2 T 3
Nattavara by [S] 2 T 3
Nauen [DDR] 16 R 13
∆ Naulavaara [SF] 9 X 5
Naumburg/Saale [DDR] 15 Q 14
Naustbukta [N] 4 Q 5
Naustdal [N] 4 N 7
Nava [E] 24 E 18
≈ Nava, Lago de — [E] 26 E 19
∆ Nava, Colle di — [I] 20 O 18
∆ Navacerrada, Puerto de — [E] 26 E 19
Nava de Ricomalillo, La — [E] 25 D 20
Navahermosa [E] 26 E 20
Navalcarnero [E] 26 E 20
Navalmanzano [E] 26 E 19
Navalmoral de la Mata [E] 25 D 20
Navalmorales, Los — [E] 26 E 20
Navan [IRL] 10 F 11
∆ Navarra [E] 18 G 19
Navascués [E] 18 G 19
Navas de Madroño [E] 25 C 20
Navelli [I] 29 S 19
≈ Naver, River — [GB] 11 H 8
Navia [E] 24 D 18
≈ Navia, Río — [E] 24 D 18
≈ N'avki [SU] 3 X 2
Navodari [RO] 23 Zb 17
Naxos [GR] 31 Zb 22
∆ Naxos [GR] 31 Zb 22
Nazaré [P] 25 A 20
≈ Nea [N] 4 Q 6
Nea Artaki [GR] 31 Z 21
≈ Neagh, Lough — [GB] 10 F 11
Nea Kallikratia [GR] 30 Y 20
Nea Moudania [GR] 31 Z 20
Neapolis [GR] 30 X 20
Neapolis [GR] 31 Z 22
Neapolis [GR] 32 Zb 23
Nea Sanda [GR] 31 Za 19
Neath [GB] 12 G 13
Nea Zichni [GR] 31 Z 19
∆ Nebbio [F] 28 O 19
∆ Nebrodi, Monti — [I] 29 S 22
≈ Neckar [D] 15 O 15
Neda [E] 24 C 17
Nederlappfors [SF] 9 V 5
Nedervetil [SF] 9 V 5
Nedre Soppero [S] 2 T 2
≈ Nedre Storfoss [N] 3 V 1
Nefyn [GB] 2 G 12
Nefza [TN] 28 O 22
Negades [GR] 30 X 20
Negnevići [SU] 8 Y 11
Negotin [YU] 22 X 17
Negotino [YU] 30 Y 19
Négrepelisse [F] 19 J 18
Negreşti [RO] 17 X 15
Negru Voda [RO] 23 Zb 17
Nehoiaşu [RO] 23 Za 16
Neiden [N] 3 W 1
Neidenburg = Nidzica [PL] 17 V 12
Neidín = Kenmare [IRL] 2 D 12
Neira de Jusa [E] 24 C 18
Neisse = Nysa [PL] 16 T 14
Nejdek [CS] 16 R 14
Neksø [DK] 7 S 11
≈ Nela, Río — [E] 18 F 18
Nelas [P] 25 B 19
Nemakščiai [SU] 8 W 10
Neman [SU] 8 V 11
≈ Neman [SU] 8 V 11
≈ Neman [SU] 8 Y 11
Nemea [GR] 30 Y 21
Nemenčine [SU] 8 X 11
Nemours [F] 14 L 15
≈ Nemunas [SU] 8 W 11
≈ Nemunas [SU] 8 X 11
Nenagh [IRL] 10 E 12
Neochorion [GR] 30 X 21
Neon Karlovassion [GR] 31 Zc 21
∆ Nephin [IRL] 10 E 11
Nepomuk [CS] 16 R 15
Neptun [RO] 23 Zb 17
≈ Ner [PL] 16 U 13
Nérac [F] 19 J 18
Nereta [SU] 8 X 10
≈ Neretljanski kanal [YU] 21 U 19
≈ Neretva [YU] 21 U 18
Néris-les-Bains [F] 19 K 16
Nerja [E] 26 E 22
Nerva [E] 25 C 21
Nervi [I] 20 O 18
Nes [N] 4 P 7
Nes [N] 4 Q 8
Nesbyen [N] 4 P 7
Nesebar [BG] 23 Zb 18
Nesflatn [N] 6 O 8
Nesland [N] 6 O 8
Nesna [N] 2 Q 4
Nesoddtangen [N] 4 P 8
∆ Nesøy [N] 2 Q 4
≈ Nesque [F] 19 M 18
≈ Ness, Loch — [GB] 11 H 9
Nesseby [N] 3 V 1
Nesterov [SU] 17 X 14
Nesterov [SU] 8 W 11
Nestorion [GR] 30 X 20
≈ Nestos [GR] 31 Z 19
Nesttun [N] 4 N 8
Nesviž [SU] 8 Y 11
Nettuno [I] 29 R 20
Neubrandenburg [DDR] 16 R 12
Neuburg an der Donau [D] 15 Q 15
Neuchâtel [CH] 20 N 16
≈ Neuchâtel, Lac de — [CH] 20 N 16
Neudau [A] 21 T 16
Neudorf [D] 15 O 15
Neuenburg [D] 20 O 16
Neuf-Brisach [F] 20 O 16
Neufchâteau [B] 14 M 14
Neufchâteau [F] 19 M 15
Neufchâtel-en-Bray [F] 14 K 14
Neufchâtel-sur-Aisne [F] 14 L 15
Neuhaus am Grimming [A] 21 S 16
Neuillé — Pont-Pierre [F] 19 J 16

Neulengbach [A] 21 T 15
Neulikko [SF] 3 W 4
Neulise [F] 19 L 17
Neumarkt in der Oberpfalz [D] 15 Q 15
Neumünster [D] 15 P 12
Neung — sur — Beuvron [F] 19 K 16
Neunkirchen [A] 21 T 16
Neunkirchen/Saar [D] 15 N 15
Neuötting [D] 21 R 17
Neupölla [A] 21 S 15
Neuruppin [DDR] 16 R 12
Neusalz (Oder) = Nowa Sól [PL] 16 S 13
Neuses am Sand [D] 15 P 14
Neusiedl am See [A] 21 T 16
≈ Neusiedler See [A, H] 21 T 16
Neuss [D] 15 N 13
Neustadt an der Aisch [D] 15 P 15
Neustadt an der Donau [D] 15 Q 15
Neustadt an der Rheda = Wejherowo [PL] 7 T 11
Neustadt an der Weinstraße [D] 15 O 15
Neustadt in Holstein [D] 6 Q 12
Neustadt/Orla [DDR] 15 Q 14
Neustettin = Szczecinek [PL] 16 T 12
Neustrelitz [DDR] 16 R 12
Neu-Ulm [D] 20 P 15
Neuvic [F] 19 K 17
Neuville-sur-Saône [F] 19 M 17
Neuvy-Saint-Sépulchre [F] 19 K 16
Neuvy-sur-Barangeon [F] 19 K 16
Neuvy-sur-Loire [F] 19 L 16
△ Neuwerk [D] 15 O 12
Neuwied [D] 15 O 14
△ Neverfjell [N] 4 P 17
Nevers [F] 19 L 16
Nevesinje [YU] 22 V 18
Nevestino [BG] 22 Y 19
≈ Nevežis [SU] 8 W 10
△ Nevis, Ben — [GB] 11 H 9
Newark on Trent [GB] 13 J 12
Newbiggin-by-the-Sea [GB] 11 J 11
Newburgh [GB] 11 J 9
Newbury [GB] 13 J 13
Newby Bridge [GB] 11 H 11
Newcastle [GB] 10 G 11
Newcastle Emlyn [GB] 12 G 12
Newcastle under Lyme [GB] 13 H 12
Newcastle upon Tyne [GB] 11 J 11
Newcastle West [IRL] 12 D 12
New Deer [GB] 11 J 9
New Galloway [GB] 11 H 10
Newhaven [GB] 13 J 13
New Hunstanton [GB] 13 K 12
Newmains [GB] 11 H 10
Newmarket [GB] 13 K 13
Newport [England] [GB] 13 H 12
Newport [Isle of Wight] [GB] 13 H 13
Newport Pagnell [GB] 13 J 13
Newport [Wales] [GB] 13 H 13
Newquay [GB] 12 F 13
New Quay [GB] 12 G 12
New Romney [GB] 13 K 13
New Ross [IRL] 12 F 12
Newry [GB] 10 F 11
Newton Abbot [GB] 12 G 13
Newtonstewart [GB] 10 F 10
Newton Stewart [GB] 10 G 11
Newtown [GB] 13 H 12
Newtownards [GB] 10 G 11
Newtownbutler [GB] 10 F 11
Nexon [F] 19 J 17
Niata [GR] 31 Y 22
Nibe [DK] 6 P 10
Nice [F] 20 N 18
Nicgale [SU] 8 X 10
Nicosia [I] 29 S 22
Nida [SU] 8 V 11
Nidda [D] 15 O 14
≈ Nidelv [N] 6 O 9
△ Nidže [YU] 30 X 20
Nidzica [PL] 17 V 12
Nieddu, Monte — [I] 28 P 20
△ Niederbayern [D] 15 Q 15
△ Niedere Tauern [A] 21 R 16
△ Niederlausitz [DDR] 16 R 13
Nienburg (Weser) [D] 15 P 13
△ Nieras [S] 3 S 3
≈ Niers [D] 15 N 13
Niesky [DDR] 16 S 13
Nieuwpoort [B] 14 L 13
Nigrita [GR] 31 Y 19
Nigula [SU] 8 W 8
≈ Niinivesi [SF] 9 W 5
Nijar [E] 26 F 22
△ Nijar, Campo de — [E] 26 F 22
Nijmegen [NL] 15 N 13
Nikea [GR] 30 Y 20
Nikel' [SU] 3 W 1
Niki [GR] 30 X 20
Nikiforos [GR] 31 Z 19
Nikkaluokta [S] 2 S 3
Nikopol [BG] 23 Za 18
Nikšić [YU] 22 V 19
≈ Nilakka [SF] 9 W 5
Nilivaara [S] 2 T 3
Nilsiä [SF] 9 X 5
Nîmes [F] 19 L 18
Ninove [B] 14 M 14
Niort [F] 18 H 16
Niš [YU] 22 X 18
Nisa [P] 25 B 20
Niscemi [I] 29 S 22
Niška Banja [YU] 22 X 18
Nisko [PL] 17 W 14
Nišinje Lapuki [SU] 3 X 4
≈ Nissan [S] 7 R 10
Nissan-les-Enserune [F] 19 K 18
≈ Nisser [N] 6 O 8
Nissilä [SF] 9 W 5
Nitaure [SU] 8 X 9
Nitra [CS] 16 U 15
Nitrianske Pravno [CS] 16 U 15
≈ Niva [SU] 3 X 2
Nivala [SF] 9 V 5
Nivelles [B] 14 M 14
△ Nivernais [F] 19 L 16
Nivskij [SU] 3 X 2
△ Nizke Tatry [CS] 17 V 15

△ Nižnij Trajanov val [SU] 23 Zb 16
Nizza di Sicilia [I] 29 T 22
Nizza Monferrato [I] 20 O 18
△ Njarggavarre [N] 2 T 2
≈ Njegoš [YU] 22 V 19
△ Njunjespkar [S] 4 Q 7
≈ Njunjes [N] 2 S 2
△ Njunjes [N] 2 S 2
Njurunda [S] 5 S 6
△ Njutånger [S] 5 S 6
Noain [E] 18 G 18
≈ Noarvas [N] 3 U 2
≈ Noasca [I] 20 N 17
Nocera Umbra [I] 21 R 19
Nogales, Los — [E] 24 C 18
Nogara [I] 21 Q 17
Nogaro [F] 18 H 18
△ Nogent-le-Roi [F] 14 K 15
≈ Nogent-le-Rotrou [F] 14 J 15
Nogent-sur-Seine [F] 14 L 15
△ Nogueira, Serra de — [P] 24 C 19
≈ Noguera Pallaresa, Río — [E] 27 J 19
Noirétable [F] 19 L 17
△ Noirmoutier, Île de — [F] 18 G 16
Noirmoutier-en-l'Île [F] 18 G 16
Nokia [SF] 9 V 6
Nola [I] 29 S 20
Nolay [F] 19 M 16
Nonancourt [F] 14 K 15
Nontron [F] 19 J 17
Nonza [F] 28 P 19
Noordoostpolder [NL] 15 N 12
Noormarkku [SF] 9 U 6
Nora [S] 7 R 8
≈ Norberg [S] 5 S 8
△ Norbotten [S] 2 T 4
Nòrcia [I] 21 R 19
Nordanas [S] 5 S 5
Nordberg [N] 4 O 7
Nordborg [DK] 6 P 11
Nordby [DK] 6 P 10
Norden [D] 15 O 12
Nordenham [D] 15 O 12
△ Norderney [D] 15 O 12
Nordfjordeid [N] 4 N 7
△ Nordfolda [N] 2 R 3
△ Nordfolda [N] 2 R 3
△ Nordfriesische Inseln [D] 6 O 11
Nordhausen [DDR] 15 Q 13
△ Nordhordland [N] 4 N 7
Nordhorn [D] 15 N 13
△ Nordhuet [N] 4 O 7
△ Nordjord [N] 4 N 7
△ Nordkapp [N] 3 U 1
△ Nordkinn [N] 3 V 1
△ Nordkinnhalvøya [N] 3 V 1
Nordkiosbotn [S] 2 S 2
△ Nordli [N] 5 R 5
Nördlingen [D] 15 P 15
Nordmaling [S] 5 T 5
Nordmark [S] 5 R 8
△ Nordmøre [N] 4 O 6
Nordnes [N] 2 T 1
≈ Nord-Ostsee-Kanal [D] 15 P 12
△ Nordøyane [N] 4 N 6
Nordreisa [N] 2 T 1
△ Nordre Kvaløy [N] 2 S 1
Nordre Osen [N] 4 Q 7
Nordsjö [S] 5 S 7
≈ Nordsjø [N] 6 P 8
△ Nordstrand [D] 6 O 11
△ Nore, Pic de — [F] 19 K 18
≈ Norefjell [N] 4 P 8
Norheimsund [N] 4 N 8
△ Norische Alpen [A] 21 S 16
△ Normandie [F] 13 H 15
≈ Norra Barken [S] 5 S 8
Norra Bergnäs [S] 2 S 4
△ Norra Bredåker [S] 2 T 4
≈ Norra Dellen [S] 5 S 6
Norra Finnskoga [S] 4 Q 7
≈ Norra Gloppet [S] 9 U 5
Norråker [S] 5 R 5
Norra Ny [S] 5 R 8
△ Norra Storfjället [S] 2 R 4
Norra Tresund [S] 5 S 5
Norra Unnaryd [S] 7 R 9
Norrby [S] 5 S 5
Norrbyn [S] 5 T 5
Nørre Alslev [DK] 6 Q 11
Nørre Nebel [DK] 6 O 11
Nørre Snede [DK] 6 P 10
Nørre Vorupøre [DK] 6 O 10
Norrfjärden [S] 3 U 4
Norrfors [S] 5 T 5
Norrhult [S] 7 S 10
Norrköping [S] 7 S 9
△ Norrland [S] 5 R 5
Norrnäs [SF] 9 U 6
Norrtälje [S] 5 T 8
Norsholm [S] 7 S 9
Norsjö [S] 5 T 4
≈ Norsjön [S] 5 S 5
Nörten-Hardenberg [D] 15 P 13
Northallerton [GB] 11 J 11
Northampton [GB] 13 J 12
North Berwick [GB] 11 J 10
≈ North Channel [GB] 10 F 10
Northeim [D] 15 P 13
≈ Northern Ireland [GB] 10 F 11
△ North Foreland [GB] 13 K 13
Northleach [GB] 13 H 13
≈ North Minch [GB] 10 G 9
△ North Rona [GB] 11 H 8
△ North Ronaldsay [GB] 11 J 8
△ North Uist [GB] 11 F 9
North Walsham [GB] 13 K 12
△ Northwest Highlands [GB] 10 G 9
Northwich [GB] 13 H 12
Nort-sur-Erdre [F] 18 H 16
Norwich [GB] 13 K 12
≈ Nota [SU] 3 W 2
≈ Noteć [PL] 16 T 12
△ Notii Sporades [GR] 31 Za 21
Noto [I] 29 T 22
≈ Noto, Golfo di — [I] 29 T 22
≈ Noto, Val di — [I] 29 S 22
Notodden [N] 6 P 8
≈ Notozero [SU] 3 W 2
Notranjsko [YU] 21 S 17
Nottingham [GB] 13 J 12
Nouans-les-Fontaine [F] 19 K 16
Nousu [SF] 3 X 3
Novaci [RO] 22 Y 17
Nova Crnja [YU] 22 V 17
Nova Gorica [YU] 21 R 17
Nova Gradiška [YU] 21 U 17

Novara [I] 20 O 17
Novate Mezzola [I] 20 P 17
Nova Varoš [YU] 22 W 18
Nová Ves [CS] 16 T 14
Nova Zagora [BG] 23 Za 18
Novelda [E] 26 G 21
Novellara [I] 20 P 17
Nové Město nad Vahom [CS] 16 U 15
Nové Zámky [CS] 21 U 15
Novi Bečej [YU] 22 W 17
Novi Han [BG] 22 Y 18
Novi Ligure [I] 20 O 18
Novi Pazar [BG] 23 Zb 18
Novi Pazar [YU] 22 X 18
Novi Sad [YU] 22 V 17
Novi Vinodolski [YU] 21 S 17
Novo Brdo [YU] 22 X 19
Novogrudok [SU] 8 Y 11
Novo Mesto [YU] 21 S 17
Novoselci [BG] 23 Zb 18
Novoselica [SU] 17 Y 15
Novska [YU] 21 U 17
Nový Bor [CS] 16 S 14
Novyj Aneny [SU] 23 Zb 15
Nowa Karczma [PL] 7 T 11
Nowa Ruda [PL] 16 T 14
Nowa Sól [PL] 16 S 13
Nowe [PL] 16 U 12
Nowe Miasto Lubawskie [PL] 16 U 12
Nowe Miasto nad Piliçą [PL] 17 V 13
Nowe Warpno [PL] 16 R 12
Nowogród Bobrzański [PL] 16 S 13
Nowy Dwór Gdański [PL] 7 U 11
Nowy Dwór Mazowiecki [PL] 17 V 11
Nowy Sacz [PL] 17 V 14
Nowy Staw [PL] 7 U 11
Nowy Targ [PL] 16 T 13
Nowy Targ [PL] 17 V 14
Nowy Tomyśl [PL] 16 T 13
Noya [E] 24 B 18
Noyant [F] 19 J 16
Noyelles [F] 14 K 14
Noyers [F] 19 L 16
Noyon [F] 14 L 14
Nozay [F] 18 H 15
≈ Nuasjärvi [SF] 9 W 4
Nucet [RO] 22 X 16
Nuia [SU] 8 X 8
Nuits-Saint-Georges [F] 19 M 16
Nules [E] 26 H 20
Numantia [E] 26 F 19
△ Numedal [N] 4 P 8
Nummijärvi [SF] 9 U 6
Nuneaton [GB] 13 J 12
Nunnamen [SF] 3 U 2
≈ Nuorittajoki [SF] 3 W 4
Nùoro [I] 28 P 20
△ Nuppevarre [N] 2 T 1
△ Nupseggi [N] 4 O 8
Nurmes [SF] 9 X 5
Nurmijärvi [SF] 9 W 7
△ Nurmisaari [SF] 9 U 7
Nürnberg [D] 15 Q 15
Nus [I] 20 N 17
Nyåker [S] 5 T 5
Nybergsund [N] 4 Q 7
Nyborg [DK] 6 Q 11
Nybro [S] 7 S 10
Nydala [S] 7 R 9
Nykládháza [H] 17 W 15
Nyhammar [S] 5 R 8
Nyhem [S] 5 R 6
Nyiradony [H] 22 W 15
Nyírbátor [H] 17 X 15
Nyíregyháza [H] 17 W 15
△ Nyírség [H] 17 W 15
Nykarleby [SF] 9 U 5
Nykøbing Falster [DK] 6 Q 11
Nykøbing Mors [DK] 6 O 10
Nykøbing Sjælland [DK] 6 Q 10
Nyköping [S] 7 S 8
Nykroppa [S] 5 R 8
≈ Nyland = Uusimaa [SF] 9 W 7
Nymburk [CS] 16 S 14
Nymindegab [DK] 6 O 10
Nynäshamn [S] 7 T 8
Nyon [CH] 20 N 17
Nyons [F] 19 M 18
Nyrud [N] 3 W 1
Nysa [PL] 16 T 14
≈ Nysa Kłodzka [PL] 16 T 14
Nysäter [S] 5 R 8
Nyslott = Savonlinna [SF] 9 X 6
Nystad = Uusikaupunki [SF] 9 U 7
Nysted [DK] 6 Q 11

Novate Mezzola — section continues

Ocresa, Ribeira — [P] 25 B 20
Odda [N] 4 O 8
Odder [DK] 6 P 10
Odeleite [P] 25 B 21
Odemira [P] 25 B 21
Odensbacken [S] 7 S 8
Odense [DK] 6 P 11
Odenwald [D] 15 O 15
≈ Oder [DDR, PL] 16 S 13
△ Oderbruch [DDR] 16 R 12
Oderzo [I] 21 R 17
Odeshög [S] 7 R 9
Odessa [SU] 23 Zc 15
≈ Odiel, Rio — [E] 25 B 21
Odivelas [P] 25 B 21
≈ Odivelas, Ribeira de — [P] 25 B 21
△ Ödmården [S] 5 S 7
≈ Odobeşti [RO] 23 Za 16
Odorheiul Secuiesc [RO] 23 Z 16
≈ Odra [P] 16 S 13
Odrzywół [PL] 17 V 13
Odžaci [YU] 22 V 17
Odžak [YU] 22 V 17
Oebisfelde [DDR] 15 Q 13
≈ Ofanto [I] 29 T 20
≈ Ofanto [I] 29 T 20
Offenbach am Main [D] 15 O 14
Offenburg [D] 15 O 15
Offerdal [S] 5 R 5
Offida [I] 21 S 19
△ Ofidoussa [GR] 31 Zb 22
≈ Ofotfjord [N] 2 R 2
Oftringen [CH] 20 O 16
Ogareviči [SU] 17 Y 12
≈ Oglio [I] 20 P 17
Ogna [N] 6 N 9
≈ Ognon [F] 19 M 16
≈ Ogosta [BG] 22 Y 18
△ Ogražden [BG, YU] 30 Y 19
Ogre [SU] 8 W 9
Ogulin [YU] 21 S 17
Ohlau = Oława [PL] 16 T 14
Ohrdruf [DDR] 15 P 14
≈ Ohře [CS] 16 R 14
Ohrid [YU] 30 X 20
≈ Ohridsko jezero [YU] 30 X 20
Öhringen [GB] 15 P 15
≈ Ohrit, Liqeni i — [AL] 30 X 20
Oijärvi [SF] 9 W 4
Oileán Ciarraighe = Castleisland [IRL] 12 D 12
≈ Oise [F] 14 L 15
≈ Ojan [S] 5 R 5
Ojców [PL] 17 V 14
△ Ojców [PL] 17 V 14
Oje [S] 5 R 7
△ Ojesjön [S] 5 R 7
Öjung [S] 5 S 7
Öjvallberget [S] 4 Q 7
Okehampton [GB] 12 G 13
Oksava [S] 7 S 9
Øksfjord [N] 2 T 1
≈ Øksfjordjøkelen [N] 2 T 1
Øksna [N] 4 Q 7
Øksneshamn [N] 2 R 2
△ Okstindane [N] 2 R 4
Olaine [SU] 8 W 9
△ Oland [S] 7 S 10
≈ Örbigo, Río — [E] 24 D 18
Orchies [F] 14 L 14
Orchomenos [GR] 31 Z 21
≈ Orcia [I] 20 Q 19
Orcières [F] 20 N 18
≈ Orco [I] 20 N 17
Ördenes [E] 24 C 18
△ Ordesa, Parque Nacional de — [E] 26 H 19
Orduña [E] 18 F 18
≈ Ore alv [S] 5 R 7
△ Ore alv [S] 5 R 7
Orebić [YU] 21 U 19
Orebro [S] 7 S 8
△ Oldfjallen [S] 5 R 5
Oldham [GB] 11 H 12
Oldisleben [DDR] 15 Q 13
Oldmeldrum [GB] 11 J 9
Olecko [PL] 8 W 11
Oleiros [E] 24 C 17
Oleiros [P] 25 B 20
Olenegorsk [SU] 3 X 2
Ølensjøen [N] 6 N 8
△ Oléron, Ile d' — [F] 18 H 17
Oleśnica [PL] 16 T 13
Olesno [PL] 16 U 13
Oletta [F] 28 P 19
≈ Øljeelv [N] 2 R 3
△ Ølfjell [N] 2 R 3
Olhão [P] 25 B 21
Olhava [SF] 9 V 4
Oliana [E] 27 J 19
△ Olib [YU] 21 S 18
Olimbia [GR] 30 Y 22
△ Olimbos, Oros — [GR] 30 Y 20
Olimpos [GR] 31 Zc 22
Olingskog [S] 5 R 7
Olite [E] 26 G 19
Oliva [E] 26 H 21
Oliva [PL] 7 U 11
△ Oliva [E] 26 G 21
Oliva de la Frontera [E] 25 C 21
Olivares de Júcar [E] 26 F 20
Oliveira de Azeméis [P] 25 B 19
Olivenza [E] 25 C 20
Olkusz [PL] 17 V 14
Ollerton [GB] 13 J 12
Ollila [SF] 3 X 4
Olmedo [E] 26 E 19
Olmillos de Sasamón [E] 18 E 19
Olofström [S] 7 R 10
Olomouc [CS] 16 T 14
Oloneşty [SU] 23 Zc 15
Olonne-sur-Mer [F] 18 H 16
≈ Oloron, Gave d' — [F] 18 H 18
Oloron-Sainte-Marie [F] 18 H 18
Olot [E] 27 K 19
Olovo [YU] 22 V 18
Olpe [D] 15 O 14
Olsborg [N] 2 S 2
Olseröd [S] 7 R 10
Olsztyn [PL] 8 V 12
Olsztynek [PL] 17 V 12
≈ Olt [RO] 22 Y 17
≈ Olt [RO] 22 Y 17
△ Oltenia [RO] 22 Y 17
Olteni [RO] 23 Za 17
Olteniţa [RO] 23 Za 17
≈ Olteţ [RO] 22 Y 17

Ólvega [E] 26 G 19
Olvera [E] 25 D 22
Olympia = Olimbia [GR] 30 Y 22
△ Olymp = Oros Olimbos [GR] 30 Y 20
Omagh [GB] 10 F 11
≈ Omañas, Río — [E] 24 D 18
≈ Omberg [S] 7 R 9
≈ Ombo [N] 6 N 8
≈ Ombrone [I] 28 Q 19
Omedu [SU] 9 X 8
Omegna [I] 20 O 17
Omiš [YU] 21 U 18
Omišalj [YU] 21 S 17
Ommen [NL] 15 N 13
≈ Omø [DK] 6 Q 11
△ Omodeo, Lago — [I] 28 O 21
△ Ömossa [SF] 9 U 6
Omurtag [BG] 23 Za 18
Oña [E] 18 F 18
Ondara [E] 26 H 21
Ondárroa [E] 18 G 18
≈ Ondava [CS] 17 W 14
Ongar [GB] 13 K 13
≈ Onkivesi [SF] 9 W 5
Ontaniente [E] 26 G 21
Ontojärvi [SF] 9 X 4
Onuškis [SU] 8 X 10
△ Oostelijk Flevoland [NL] 15 N 13
Oostende [B] 14 L 13
Oostmalle [B] 14 M 13
Opatija [YU] 21 S 17
Opatów [PL] 17 V 13
Opava [CS] 16 U 14
Opoczno [PL] 17 V 13
Opole [PL] 16 U 14
Opole Lubielskie [PL] 17 W 13
Oppdal [N] 4 P 6
Oppeln = Opole [PL] 16 U 14
Oppenheim [D] 15 O 14
Oppido Mamertina [I] 29 U 22
△ Oppland [N] 4 O 7
Opsa [SU] 8 Y 10
△ Or, Côte d' — [F] 19 M 16
Ora [I] 20 Q 17
Oradea [RO] 22 X 16
Oradour-sur-Vayres [F] 19 J 17
Orahovac [YU] 22 W 19
Or'ahovo [BG] 22 Y 18
Oraison [F] 19 M 18
Orajärvi [SF] 3 U 3
Orange [F] 19 M 18
Oranienburg [DDR] 16 R 12
≈ Oranmore [IRL] 10 E 11
Orán Mór = Oranmore [IRL] 10 E 11
Orăştie [RO] 22 Y 17
△ Oratunturi [SF] 3 V 3
≈ Orava [CS] 17 V 14
Oravainen = Oravais [SF] 9 U 5
Oravais [F] 9 U 5
△ Oravisalo [SF] 9 X 6
Oravița [RO] 22 X 17
△ Oravská Magura [CS] 17 V 14
Ørbæk [DK] 6 P 11
Orbes [F] 14 J 15
Orbetello [I] 28 Q 19
△ Orbieu [F] 19 K 19
≈ Ørbigo, Río — [E] 24 D 18
Orchies [F] 14 L 14
Orchomenos [GR] 31 Z 21
≈ Orcia [I] 20 Q 19
Orcières [F] 20 N 18
≈ Orco [I] 20 N 17
Ørdenes [E] 24 C 18
△ Ordesa, Parque Nacional de — [E] 26 H 19
Orduña [E] 18 F 18
≈ Ore alv [S] 5 R 7
△ Ore alv [S] 5 R 7
Orebić [YU] 21 U 19
Orebro [S] 7 S 8
Öregrund [S] 5 T 7
△ Öregrunds grepen [S] 5 T 7
Orehoved [DK] 6 Q 11
△ Orellana, Pantano de — [E] 25 D 20
Orellana la Vieja [E] 25 D 20
Orense [TR] 32 Zd 21
Orense [E] 24 C 18
Orestias [BG] 23 Zb 19
≈ Øresund [DK] 6 Q 10
≈ Orfanu, Kolpos — [GR] 31 Z 20
△ Orfjäll [S] 2 S 4
△ Orgaña [E] 27 J 19
Orgaz con Arisgotas [E] 26 E 20
Orgelet [F] 19 M 16
Ørgenvik [N] 4 P 8
△ Orgnac, Aven d' — [F] 19 L 18
△ Orhy, Pico de — [E, F] 18 H 18
△ Oriambre, Cabo — [E] 24 E 18
Orihuela [E] 26 G 21
Orimattila [SF] 9 W 7
Oriolo [I] 29 U 20
Oripää [SF] 9 V 7
△ Oristano [I] 28 O 21
≈ Oristano, Golfo di — [I] 28 O 21
Orivesi [SF] 9 V 6
≈ Orivesi [SF] 9 X 6
△ Orje [N] 6 Q 8
Orjiva [E] 26 E 22
Orkanger [N] 4 P 6
△ Orkdal [N] 4 P 6
Örkelljunga [S] 7 R 10
Örkény [H] 22 V 15
≈ Orkla [N] 4 P 6
△ Orkney [GB] 11 J 8
△ Orlando, Capo d' — [I] 29 T 22
△ Oréanais [F] 19 K 16
Orléans [F] 19 K 15
△ Orlické hory [CS] 16 T 14
Orma [GR] 30 Y 20
△ Ormanság [H] 21 U 17
Ormea [I] 20 O 18
Ormemyr [N] 4 P 8
Ormsjö [S] 5 S 5
≈ Ornans [F] 20 N 16
≈ Orne [F] 14 J 15
≈ Ornö [S] 5 T 8
△ Ornsköldsvik [S] 5 T 6
△ Orø [DK] 6 Q 11
△ Oro, Monte d' — [F] 28 O 19
△ Oropesa, Cabo de — [E] 26 H 20
Oropesa y Corchuela [E] 25 D 20

Orosei [I] 28 P 20
≈ Orosei, Golfo di — [I] 28 O 20
Orosháza [H] 22 W 16
Oroso [E] 24 C 18
Orsa [S] 5 R 7
△ Orsaro, Monte — [I] 20 P 18
≈ Orsasjön [S] 5 R 7
Örsjö [S] 7 S 10
≈ Orsjön [S] 5 S 7
△ Örskär [S] 5 T 7
Orşova [RO] 22 X 17
Ørsta [N] 4 N 7
Örsundsbro [S] 5 S 8
Orta Nova [I] 29 T 20
Orte [I] 29 R 19
△ Ortegal, Cabo — [E] 24 C 17
Ortelsburg = Szczytno [PL] 17 V 12
Orth [D] 6 Q 11
Orthez [F] 18 H 18
Ortigueira [E] 24 C 17
△ Ortler = Ortles [I] 20 P 17
△ Ortles [I] 20 P 17
Ortona [I] 29 S 19
Örträsk [S] 5 T 5
△ Orust [S] 6 P 8
Orvieto [I] 28 Q 19
Orzinuovi [I] 20 P 17
Orzysz [P] 8 W 11
Os [N] 2 R 3
Os [N] 4 Q 6
≈ Osâm [BG] 23 Z 18
Osby [S] 7 R 10
Oschatz [DDR] 16 R 13
Oschersleben/Bode [DDR] 15 Q 13
Oschiri [I] 28 O 20
Osečina [YU] 22 V 18
Osen [N] 4 P 5
Osenovec [BG] 23 Za 17
Osera [E] 26 H 19
Osie [PL] 16 U 12
Osijek [YU] 22 V 17
Ôsimo [I] 21 R 18
Oskarshamn [S] 7 S 9
≈ Oslava [S] 16 T 15
Oslo [N] 4 P 8
≈ Oslofjord [N] 6 P 8
Os'm'any [SU] 8 Y 11
≈ Osmo [S] 7 T 8
△ Osmussaar [SU] 8 V 8
Osnabrück [D] 15 O 13
△ Osogovska planina [YU] 22 Y 19
Osor [YU] 21 S 18
Osorno [E] 24 E 18
Osowiec [PL] 9 W 11
Osøyra [N] 4 N 8
Oss [NL] 14 N 13
△ Ossa [S] 25 B 20
Ossa del Montiel [E] 26 F 21
△ Ossa Oros [GR] 30 Y 20
Ossiou Louka, Moni — [GR] 30 Y 21
≈ Ossjø [S] 2 S 4
Ostansjö [S] 2 S 4
Ostavall [S] 5 S 6
≈ Oste [D] 15 P 12
△ Österbotten = Pohjanmaa [SF] 9 V 5
Osterburg/Altmark [DDR] 15 Q 12
Österbybruk [S] 5 T 8
Österbymo [S] 7 S 9
△ Österdalälven [S] 5 R 7
△ Østerdalen [N] 4 P 7
≈ Osterems [D] 15 N 12
Österfärnebo [S] 5 S 8
△ Osterfjord [N] 4 N 7
Osterforse [S] 5 S 6
△ Östergarns holme [S] 7 U 9
△ Östergötland [S] 7 S 9
△ Östergraninge [S] 5 S 6
Osterholz-Scharmbeck [D] 16 O 12
Österkorsberga [S] 7 S 10
△ Östermark = Teuva [SF] 9 U 6
Osterode in Ostpreußen = Ostróda [PL] 7 U 12
△ Osterøy [N] 4 N 8
△ Österreichische Alpen [A] 21 S 16
Österskär [S] 5 T 8
Östersund [S] 5 R 6
Ostersundom [SF] 9 W 7
△ Ostfriesische Inseln [D] 15 N 12
Osthammar [S] 5 T 7
Ostia Antica [I] 29 R 20
Ostiglia [I] 20 Q 17
Ostmark [S] 4 Q 8
△ Ostpreußen [PL] 7 U 12
Ostra Ed [S] 7 S 9
Östra Frölunda [S] 7 R 10
≈ Östra Gloppet [SF] 9 U 5
≈ Östra Kvarken = Merenkurkku5 U 5
≈ Östra Lägern [S] 7 S 9
△ Östra Silen [S] 6 Q 8
Ostrava [CS] 16 U 14
△ Ostredok [CS] 17 V 15
Østre Kile [N] 6 O 8
Ostróda [PL] 7 U 12
Ostróg [SU] 22 V 19
Ostrołęka [PL] 17 V 12
Ostrov [SU] 8 Y 9
△ Ostrov [CS] 21 U 15
Ostrowiec Swiętokrzyski [PL] 17 W 13
Ostrów Mazowiecka [PL] 17 W 12
Ostrów Wielkopolski [PL] 16 U 13
Ostrowy Brdowskie [PL] 16 U 13
Ostrzeszów [PL] 16 U 13
Ostryna [SU] 8 X 11
Ostseebad Graal-Müntz [DDR] 6 Q 11
Ostseebad Kühlungsborn [DDR] 6 Q 12
Ostuni [I] 29 U 20
≈ Osum [AL] 30 X 20
Osuna [E] 25 D 22
Oswestry [GB] 13 H 12
Oświęcim [PL] 17 V 14
△ Otanmäki [SF] 9 W 5
△ Otava [CS] 16 R 15
Otawa [PL] 16 T 14
Otepää [SU] 8 X 8
Oterma [S7] 3 W 4
Otero del Rey [E] 24 C 18
Oteševo [YU] 30 X 20
△ Othe, Forêt d' — [F] 19 L 15
△ Othoni [GR] 30 W 20
△ Othris Oros [GR] 30 Y 21
Otley [GB] 11 J 11

Otočac [YU] 21 T 17
≈ Otra [N] 6 O 9
Otranto [I] 30 V 20
≈ Otranto, Canale d' — 30 V 20
Δ Otranto, Capo d' — [I] 30 V 20
Δ Otscher [A] 21 S 16
Otta [N] 4 P 7
≈ Otta [N] 4 P 7
Ottenby [S] 7 S 10
Ottenschlag [A] 21 S 15
Otterburn [GB] 11 J 11
Otterøy [N] 4 Q 5
Δ Otterøy [N] 4 O 6
Ottone [I] 20 P 18
Ottsjön [S] 5 R 5
Ottweiler [D] 15 N 15
Otwock [PL] 17 V 13
Δ Ötztal [A] 20 Q 16
Δ Ötztaler Alpen [A, I] 20 Q 16
Oucques [F] 19 K 15
Ouddorp [NL] 14 M 13
Oudenaarde [B] 14 L 14
Δ Ouessant, Île d' — [F] 12 F 15
Oughterard [IRL] 10 E 11
Oulainen [SF] 9 V 5
Oullins [F] 19 M 17
Oulu [SF] 3 V 4
≈ Oulujärvi [SF] 9 W 4
Oulx [I] 20 N 17
≈ Ounasjoki [SF] 3 U 2
Δ Ounastunturi [SF] 3 U 2
Ourique [P] 25 A 21
Δ Ourique, Campos de — [P] 25 A 21
≈ Ourthe [B] 14 M 14
≈ Ouse, River — [GB] 11 J 11
≈ Oust [F] 12 G 15
Δ Outer Hebrides [GB] 10 F 9
Outes [E] 24 B 18
≈ Ouvèze [F] 19 M 18
Ovar [P] 25 B 19
Ovaro [I] 21 R 16
Δ Ovče [YU] 30 X 19
Överhogdal [S] 5 R 6
Överhörnäs [S] 5 T 6
Övermark [SF] 9 U 6
Övermorjärv [S] 3 U 4
Övernäs [S] 2 S 4
Överstbyn [S] 3 U 4
Övertorneå [S] 3 U 3
Överturingen [S] 5 R 6
Överum [S] 7 S 9
≈ Överuman [S] 2 R 4
Ovidijopol' [SU] 23 Zc 15
Oviedo [E] 24 D 18
Oviken [S] 5 R 6
Δ Oviksfjällen [S] 5 R 6
Ovra [S] 5 S 5
Øvre Årdal [N] 4 O 7
≈ Øvre Fryken [S] 4 Q 8
Øvre Rendal [N] 4 Q 7
Övre Soppero [S] 2 T 2
Övre Svartlå [S] 2 T 4
Oxelösund [S] 7 S 9
Oxford [GB] 13 J 13
Oy [D] 20 P 16
Oya [E] 24 B 18
Øye [N] 4 O 6
≈ Øyeren [N] 4 Q 8
Oyonnax [F] 19 M 17
Øyslebø [N] 6 O 9
Ozariči [SU] 17 Y 12
Ożarów [PL] 17 W 13
Ózd [H] 17 V 15
Ozerka [SU] 3 W 1
Ozieri [I] 28 O 20
Ozłuchów [PL] 16 T 12
Ozorków [PL] 16 U 13
Oz'orsk [SU] 8 V 11
Δ Ozren [YU] 21 U 18
Δ Ozren [YU] 22 V 18
Δ Ozren [YU] 22 X 18

P

Paadarjärvi [SF] 3 V 2
≈ Pääjärvi [SF] 9 V 6
Paakkola [SF] 3 V 4
Paavola [SF] 9 V 4
Pabianice [PL] 16 U 13
Pabradė [SU] 8 X 10
Paca, La — [E] 26 F 21
Pacaudière, la — [F] 19 L 17
Δ Pachia [GR] 31 Zb 22
Pachia Ammos [GR] 32 Zb 23
Pachino [I] 29 T 22
Pacov [CS] 16 S 15
Pacy-sur-Eure [F] 14 K 15
Paczków [PL] 16 T 14
Padasjoki [SF] 9 W 6
Paderborn [D] 15 O 13
Δ Padeşul [RO] 22 X 17
Padirac [F] 19 K 17
Δ Padjelanta [S] 2 S 3
Pàdova [I] 20 Q 17
Padrón [E] 24 B 18
Padroñeras, Las — [E] 26 F 20
Δ Padrosa, Coma — [AND, E, F] 27 J 19
Padstow [GB] 12 F 13
Padul [E] 26 E 22
Padun [SU] 3 W 2
Paestum [I] 29 T 20
Pag [YU] 21 S 18
Δ Pag [YU] 21 S 18
≈ Pagasitikos Kolpos [GR] 31 Z 21
≈ Pàglia [I] 20 Q 19
Paide [SU] 9 W 8
Paignton [GB] 12 G 13
≈ Päijänne [SF] 9 W 6
Paimbœuf [F] 18 H 16
Paimio [SF] 9 V 7
Paimpol [F] 12 G 15
Paisley [GB] 11 H 10
Δ Paistunturit [SF] 3 V 1
Paittasjärvi [S] 3 U 2
≈ Paiva, Rio — [P] 25 B 19
Pajala [S] 3 U 3
Pajanosas, Las — [E] 25 C 21
Pajares [E] 24 D 18
Δ Paklenica [YU] 21 T 18
Pakosławice [PL] 16 T 14
Pakosze [PL] 7 U 11
Pakruojis [SU] 8 W 10
Paks [H] 22 V 16
Palacios y Villafranca, Los — [E] 25 C 22
Palagonia [I] 29 T 22
Palais, le — [F] 18 G 15
Δ Palakarija [BG] 22 Y 19
Palamas [GR] 30 Y 20
Palamós [E] 27 K 19
≈ Palancia, Río — [E] 26 H 20
Palanga [SU] 8 V 10
Palas del Rey [E] 24 C 18
Pålau [I] 28 P 20
Palazzolo Acrèide [I] 29 T 22
Palazzolo sull'Oglio [I] 20 P 17
Paldiski [SU] 8 W 8
Palea Epidavros [GR] 31 Z 22
Palencia [E] 26 E 19
Paleochora [GR] 32 Za 23
Paleokastritsa [GR] 30 W 21
Palermo [I] 29 S 22
≈ Palermo, Golfo di — [I] 29 S 22
Paleros [GR] 30 X 21
Palestrina [I] 29 R 19
Δ Paliourion, Akrotirion — [GR] 31 Z 20
Palkäne [SF] 9 V 7
Palkino [SU] 8 Y 9
Δ Pallas-Ounastunturin kansallispuisto [SF] 3 U 2
Δ Pallastunturit [SF] 3 U 2
Δ Pallemtjåkko [S] 2 S 2
Δ Pallës, Bishti i — [AL] 30 W 19
Palma [E] 27 K 21
≈ Palma, Bahía de — [E] 27 K 21
Palma del Condado, La — [E] 25 C 21
Palma del Río [E] 25 D 21
Palma di Montechiaro [I] 29 S 22
≈ Palmas, Golfo di — [I] 28 O 21
Palmi [I] 29 T 22
Palojärvi [SF] 3 U 2
Palojoensuu [SF] 3 U 2
Palokorva [S] 3 U 3
Palombara Sabina [I] 29 R 19
Δ Palomera [E] 26 G 20
Δ Palos, Cabo de — [E] 26 G 22
Palos de la Frontera [E] 25 B 21
Δ Palotunturi [SF] 3 W 3
Paltamo [SF] 9 W 4
Păltinoasa [RO] 23 Z 15
Δ Påltsa [S] 2 T 2
Paluknė [SU] 8 X 11
Pamhagen [A] 21 T 16
Pamiers [F] 19 J 18
Pampilhosa da Serra [P] 25 B 20
Pamplona [E] 18 G 18
Panaghia [GR] 32 Zb 23
Panagjurište [BG] 23 Z 18
Δ Panarea, Isola — [I] 29 T 21
≈ Panaro [I] 20 Q 18
Pančevo [YU] 22 W 17
Panciu [RO] 23 Za 16
Pancorbo [E] 18 F 18
Pandelys [SU] 8 X 10
Pandrup [DK] 6 P 10
Panes [E] 24 E 18
Panevėžys [SU] 8 X 10
Pangevitsa [SU] 8 Y 9
Panissières [F] 19 L 17
Paniza [E] 26 G 19
Δ Paniza, Puerto — [E] 26 G 19
Panne, De — [B] 14 L 13
Panormos [GR] 31 Za 21
Panormos [GR] 32 Za 23
Pantäne [SF] 9 U 6
Pantelleria [I] 29 R 22
Δ Pantelleria, Isola di — [I] 29 R 22
Pàola [I] 29 T 21
≈ P'aozero [SU] 3 X 3
Pápa [H] 21 U 16
Paparzyn [PL] 16 U 12
Δ Papas [GR] 31 Zb 21
Papenburg [D] 15 O 12
Δ Papikion Oros [GR] 31 Za 19
Δ Papuk [YU] 21 U 17
Paraćin [YU] 22 X 18
Parainen = Pargas [SF] 9 V 7
Paralia Akrates [GR] 30 Y 21
Paralion Astros [GR] 31 Z 22
Paramithia [GR] 30 X 21
Δ Páramo, El — [E] 24 D 18
Paranestion [GR] 31 Z 19
Paras [N] 2 T 2
Δ Paras [N] 2 T 2
Δ Parate, Pointe de — [F] 28 O 19
Paray-le-Monial [F] 19 L 16
Parchim [DDR] 15 Q 12
Parczew [PL] 17 W 13
Pardilla [E] 26 E 19
Pardubice [CS] 16 S 14
Paredes [P] 25 B 19
Paredes de Nava [E] 24 E 19
Parentis-en-Born [F] 18 H 18
Parga [GR] 30 X 21
Pargas [SF] 9 V 7
Paris [F] 14 K 15
Parkalompolo [S] 3 U 3
Parkano [SF] 9 V 6
Parma [I] 20 P 18
Pàrnica [CS] 17 V 15
Δ Parnis Oros [GR] 31 Z 21
Δ Parnon Oros [GR] 30 Y 22
Pärnu [SU] 8 W 8
≈ Pärnu [SU] 8 W 8
Pärnu-Jaagupi [SU] 8 W 8
Paros [GR] 31 Za 22
Δ Paros [GR] 31 Za 22
≈ Parsęta [PL] 7 S 12
Partanna [I] 29 R 22
Δ Pårtefjällen [S] 2 S 3
Parthenay [F] 19 J 16
Partinico [I] 29 R 21
Partizánske [CS] 16 U 15
Pårup [DK] 6 P 10
Påryd [S] 7 S 10
Paşcani [RO] 23 Z 15
Pasewalk [DDR] 16 R 12
Pasiene [SU] 8 Y 9
Påskallavik [S] 7 S 10
Pasłek [PL] 7 U 11
Δ Pašman [YU] 21 T 18
Passau [D] 16 R 15
Δ Pàssero, Capo — [I] 29 T 22
Pasvalys [SU] 8 W 10
Pasym [PL] 8 V 12
Pásztó [H] 22 V 15
Pataias [P] 25 A 20
Patay [F] 19 K 15
Pateley Bridge [GB] 11 J 11
Paternion [A] 21 R 16
Paternò [I] 29 T 22
Patmos [GR] 31 Zc 21
Δ Patmos [GR] 31 Zb 21
Patos [AL] 30 W 20
≈ Patraikos Kolpos [GR] 30 X 21
Patras = Patre [GR] 30 Y 21
Patre [GR] 30 Y 21
Patrington [GB] 13 K 12
Patterdale [GB] 11 H 11
Patti [I] 29 T 22
≈ Patti, Golf di — [I] 29 T 22
Pattijoki [SF] 9 V 4
Pau [F] 18 H 18
≈ Pau, Gave de — [F] 18 H 18
≈ Paudijärvi [SF] 3 V 1
Pauillac [F] 18 H 17
Paulhaguet [F] 19 L 17
Păuliş [RO] 22 W 16
≈ Pauranki [S] 2 T 3
Pauträsk [S] 5 S 5
Pavia [I] 20 O 17
Pāvilosta [SU] 8 V 10
Pavlikeni [BG] 23 Z 18
Pavlovac [YU] 21 U 17
Pavullo nel Frignano [I] 20 Q 18
Paxi [GR] 30 X 21
Δ Paxi [GR] 30 W 21
Δ Paximadia [GR] 32 Za 23
Payerne [CH] 20 N 16
Pazardžik [BG] 23 Z 19
Pazin [YU] 21 S 17
≈ Pčinja [YU] 22 X 19
Péage, le — [F] 19 M 17
Peal de Becerro [E] 26 E 21
Peć [YU] 22 W 19
≈ Peca [SU] 3 X 2
Pečenga [SU] 3 W 1
≈ Pečenga [SU] 3 W 1
Pecica [RO] 22 W 16
Pećinci [YU] 22 W 17
Pecka [YU] 22 V 18
Pečory [SU] 8 Y 9
Pécs [H] 21 U 17
Pedaso [I] 21 S 19
≈ Pedja [SU] 8 X 8
Pedras Salgadas [P] 24 C 19
Δ Pedroches, Los — [E] 25 D 21
Peebles [GB] 11 H 10
Peel [GB] 10 G 11
≈ Peene [DDR] 16 R 12
Pegalajar [E] 26 E 21
Peggau [A] 21 S 16
Δ Pègla, Monte — [I] 21 R 19
Pegnitz [D] 15 Q 14
≈ Pegnitz [D] 15 Q 15
Pego [E] 26 H 21
Δ Peguera, Pico — [E] 27 J 19
Pehčevo [YU] 30 Y 19
Peine [D] 15 P 13
Peipohja [SF] 9 V 7
≈ Peipussee [SU] 8 X 8
Peiting [D] 20 Q 16
Peitz [DDR] 16 S 13
Pekkala [SF] 3 V 3
Δ Pelagonija [YU] 30 X 19
Pelasghia [GR] 30 Y 21
Δ Pelat, Mont — [F] 20 N 18
Δ Peleaga [RO] 22 X 17
Pelhřimov [CS] 16 S 15
Δ Pelineon [GR] 31 Zb 21
Δ Pelister [YU] 30 X 20
Δ Peljekajse nationalpark [S] 2 S 4
Δ Pelješac [YU] 21 U 19
Pelkosenniemi [SF] 3 V 3
Δ Pellinge [SF] 9 W 7
Pello [S] 3 U 3
Pello [SF] 3 U 3
Δ Pellworm [D] 6 O 11
Δ Peloponnisos [GR] 30 Y 22
Δ Peloritani, Monti — [I] 29 T 22
Peltovuoma [SF] 3 U 2
Δ Pelvoux, Massif du — [F] 20 N 17
Pembroke [GB] 12 G 13
Δ Peña, Sierra de la — [E] 26 H 19
Penacova [P] 25 B 19
Δ Peña de Francia, Sierra de — [E] 25 D 19
Peñafiel [E] 26 E 19
Penafiel [P] 25 B 19
Peñaflor [E] 25 D 21
Δ Peñagolosa [E] 26 H 20
Δ Peñalara [E] 26 E 19
Peñalba [E] 26 H 19
Penamacor [P] 25 C 20
Δ Peña Negra [E] 24 D 18
Δ Peña Prieta [E] 24 E 18
Peñaranda de Bracamonte [E] 25 D 19
Δ Peñarroya [E] 26 G 20
Peñarroya-Pueblonuevo [E] 25 D 21
Δ Peña Rubia [E] 24 D 18
Δ Peña Rubia, Pico de — [E] 24 D 18
Δ Peñas, Cabo de — [E] 24 D 18
Δ Peña Vieja [E] 24 E 18
Pendalofos [GR] 30 X 20
Δ Peneda [P] 24 B 18
Δ Penibética, Cordillera — [E] 26 E 22
Peniche [P] 25 A 20
Penicuik [GB] 11 H 10
Peñíscola [E] 26 H 20
Penmarch [F] 12 F 15
Δ Penmarch, Pointe de — [F] 12 F 15
Δ Penna, Punta della — [I] 29 S 19
Pennabilli [I] 21 R 18
Penne [I] 29 S 19
Δ Pennines [GB] 11 J 11
Penrith [GB] 11 H 11
≈ Pentland Firth [GB] 11 J 8
Penzance [GB] 12 F 14
Peqin [AL] 30 W 20
Perachora [GR] 31 Z 21
Perales de Tajuña [E] 26 E 20
Peralta [E] 26 G 19
Perama [GR] 32 Za 23
Peranka [SF] 3 W 4
Perä-Posio [SF] 3 W 3
Peräseinäjoki [SF] 9 V 6
Δ Perche [F] 14 J 15
Δ Percoraro, Monte — [I] 29 U 21
Perdika [GR] 30 X 21
Perečin [SU] 17 X 15
Perelló [E] 26 H 20
Peremysl'any [SU] 17 Y 14
Perfugas [I] 28 O 20
Pergamon [TR] 31 Zb 20
Pèrgine Valsugana [I] 20 Q 17
Pèrgola [I] 21 R 18
Perho [SF] 9 V 5
≈ Perhonjoki [SF] 9 V 5
Periam [RO] 22 W 16
Périers [F] 13 H 14
Δ Périgord [F] 19 J 17
Périgueux [F] 19 J 17
Perithorion [GR] 31 Z 19
Perl [D] 15 N 15
Perleberg [DDR] 15 Q 12
Perlez [YU] 22 W 17
Përmet [AL] 30 W 20
Pernik [BG] 22 Y 18
Perniö [SF] 9 V 7
Pernštejn [CS] 16 T 14
Péronne [F] 14 L 14
Perosa Argentina [I] 20 N 17
Pérouges [F] 19 M 17
Perpignan [F] 19 K 19
Perros-Guirec [F] 12 G 15
Peršaj [SU] 8 Y 11
Persön [S] 3 U 4
Perstorp [S] 7 R 10
Perth [GB] 11 H 10
Δ Perthus, Collado de — [E, F] 27 K 19
Pertoulion [GR] 30 X 20
Pertuis [F] 19 M 18
Pertunmaa [SF] 9 W 6
Perùgia [I] 21 R 19
Perušić [YU] 21 T 18
Pèsaro [I] 21 R 18
Pescara [I] 29 S 19
≈ Pescara [I] 29 S 19
Pèschici [I] 29 T 19
Peschiera del Garda [I] 20 Q 17
Peshkopi [AL] 30 W 19
Pesočani [YU] 30 X 19
Peso da Régua [P] 25 C 19
Pessac [F] 18 H 17
Δ Pessiniki [S] 2 T 2
Peşteana-Jiu [RO] 22 Y 17
Peštera [BG] 23 Z 19
Petäiskylä [SF] 9 X 5
Petäjäjärvi [SF] 3 W 4
Petäjävesi [SF] 9 W 6
Petalidion [GR] 30 Y 22
Δ Petalii [GR] 31 Za 21
≈ Petalion, Kolpos — [GR] 31 Za 21
Peterborough [GB] 13 J 12
Peterculter [GB] 11 J 9
Peterhead [GB] 11 J 9
Petersfield [GB] 13 J 13
Pétervására [H] 17 V 15
Petilia Policastro [I] 29 U 21
Petín [E] 24 C 18
Petit-Quevilly, le — [F] 14 K 14
Δ Petit Saint Bernard, Col du — [F, I] 20 N 17
Petkula [SF] 3 V 2
Petra [GR] 31 Zb 20
Petrades [GR] 23 Zb 19
Petrana [GR] 30 Y 20
Petrič [BG] 30 Y 19
Petrila [RO] 22 Y 17
Petrinja [YU] 21 T 17
Δ Petrohanski prohod [BG] 22 Y 18
Petroşeni [RO] 22 Y 17
Petrovac [YU] 22 X 17
Petrovac [YU] 30 V 19
Petworth [GB] 13 J 13
Peurasuvanto [SF] 3 V 2
Pewsey [GB] 13 H 13
Peyruis [F] 19 M 18
Pézenas [F] 19 L 18
Pezinok [CS] 16 U 15
Pfaffenhofen an der Ilm [D] 15 Q 15
Pfarrkirchen [D] 16 R 15
Pforzheim [D] 15 O 15
Pfullingen [D] 20 P 15
Phalsbourg [F] 15 N 15
Philippeville [B] 14 M 14
Piacenza [I] 20 P 17
Piàdena [I] 20 P 17
Pianoro [I] 20 Q 18
Δ Pianosa, Isola — [I] 28 P 19
Δ Pianosa, Isola — [I] 29 T 19
Pias [P] 25 B 21
Piaseczno [PL] 17 V 13
Piaski [PL] 17 W 13
Piątek [PL] 16 U 13
Piatra Neamţ [RO] 23 Z 15
≈ Piave [I] 21 R 17
Piazza Armerina [I] 29 S 22
Piazza Bremo [I] 20 P 17
Δ Picardie [F] 14 K 14
Picerno [I] 29 T 20
Pickering [GB] 11 J 11
Δ Pic Long [F] 18 H 19
Pico [I] 29 S 20
Δ Pico Grande [E] 26 F 19
Picquigny [F] 14 K 14
Δ Piedade, Ponta da — [P] 25 A 21
Piedra, Monasterio de — [E] 26 G 19
Piedrabuena [E] 26 E 21
Δ Piedrafita, Puerto de — [E] 24 C 18
Piedrahita [E] 25 D 20
Δ Piedrasluengas, Puerto de — [E] 24 E 18
Piehinki [SF] 9 V 4
Pieksämäki [SF] 9 W 6
Pielavesi [SF] 9 W 5
≈ Pielavesi [SF] 9 W 5
≈ Pielinen [SF] 9 X 5
≈ Pielisjoki [SF] 9 X 5
Δ Piemonte [I] 20 N 18
Pieniężno [PL] 8 V 11
Δ Pieniny [PL] 17 V 14
Pienza [I] 20 Q 19
Δ Pieria Ori [GR] 30 Y 20
Pierrefonds [F] 14 L 15
Pierrelatte [F] 19 M 18
Δ Pierre sur Haute [F] 19 L 17
Piešťany [CS] 16 U 15
Pietarsaari = Jacobstad [SF] 9 U 5
Pietra Lìgure [I] 20 O 18
Pietrasanta [I] 20 P 18
Pietreni [RO] 23 Zb 17
Δ Pietrii, Vîrful — [RO] 22 X 17
Δ Pietrosul [RO] 17 Y 15
Pieux, les — [F] 13 H 14
Pieve di Cadore [I] 21 R 17
Pieve di Teco [I] 20 O 18
Pihlajavesi [SF] 9 V 6
Pihtipudas [SF] 9 W 5
Piippola [SF] 9 W 5
Pikasilla [SU] 8 X 8
Pikeliškiai [SU] 8 X 11
Piła [PL] 16 T 12
Δ Pila [E] 26 G 21
Pilas [E] 25 C 21
≈ Pilica [PL] 17 V 13
Pilion [GR] 31 Zc 22
Δ Pilion Oros [GR] 31 Z 20
Piliscsaba [H] 22 V 16
Pilisszentkereszt [H] 22 V 16
Pillau = Baltijsk [SU] 7 U 11
Δ Pillon, Col du — [CH] 20 N 17
Pilos [GR] 30 Y 22
Piltene [SU] 8 V 9
Pilzno [PL] 17 W 14
≈ Pina [SU] 17 Y 12
Δ Piná, Cabo des — [E] 27 K 21
Piñar [E] 26 E 22
Δ Pinar, Cabo del — [E] 27 K 21
Pınarhisar [TR] 23 Zb 19
Δ Pincon, Mont — [F] 14 J 15
Pîncota [RO] 22 X 16
Δ Pindos [GR] 30 X 20
Pinerolo [I] 20 N 18
Pinggau [A] 21 T 16
Pinhel [P] 25 C 19
≈ Pinios [GR] 30 Y 20
≈ Pinios [GR] 30 Y 21
Pinneberg [D] 15 P 12
Pino [F] 28 P 19
Pinoso [E] 26 G 21
Pinsk [SU] 17 Y 12
Pinto [E] 26 E 20
Δ Pinzgau [A] 21 R 16
Pinzolo [I] 20 Q 17
Piombino [I] 20 P 19
≈ Piombino, Canale di — [I] 28 P 19
Piotrków Trybunalski [PL] 17 V 13
Δ Piottinoschlucht [CH] 20 O 17
Piove di Sacco [I] 20 Q 17
Δ Piperion [GR] 31 Z 20
Piqeras [AL] 30 W 20
Δ Piqueras, Puerto de — [E] 26 F 19
Piran [YU] 21 R 17
Pireefs [GR] 31 Z 21
Pirghetos [GR] 30 Y 20
Pirghi [GR] 30 X 20
Pirghion [GR] 31 Zb 21
Pirgos [GR] 30 Y 22
Pirgos [GR] 31 Zc 21
Pirgos [GR] 32 Zb 23
Piriac-sur-Mer [F] 18 G 15
Δ Pirin [BG] 30 Y 19
Δ Pirineos [E, F] 18 G 18
Pirmasens [D] 15 O 15
Pirna [DDR] 16 R 14
Pirot [YU] 22 Y 18
Pirsoghianni [GR] 30 X 20
Pirttikylä = Pörtom [SF] 9 U 6
Pirttimäki [SF] 9 W 5
Pisa [I] 20 P 18
Pišča [SU] 17 X 13
Pisciotta [I] 29 T 20
Písek [CS] 16 S 15
Pissos [F] 18 H 18
≈ Pistajarvi [SU] 3 X 4
Pisticci [I] 29 U 20
Pistòia [I] 20 O 18
Pisz [PL] 8 V 12
Piteå [S] 3 U 4
≈ Pite älv [S] 2 T 4
Δ Pite Lappmark [S] 2 S 4
Piteşti [RO] 23 Z 17
Pithagorion [GR] 31 Zc 21
Pithiviers [F] 19 K 15
Pitigliano [I] 28 Q 19
Pitk'ajarvi [SU] 3 W 1
Pitlochry [GB] 11 H 10
≈ Piva [YU] 22 V 18
Pivka [YU] 21 S 17
Pizarra [E] 25 D 22
Δ Plačkovica [YU] 30 Y 19
Δ Plaine [F] 18 H 16
Δ Plaka [GR] 32 Zc 23
Δ Plaka, Akrotirion — [GR] 31 Za 20
Planá [CS] 16 R 14
Plana [YU] 22 V 19
Δ Plana Tabarca, Isla — [E] 26 G 21
Plancoët [F] 13 H 15
Plandište [YU] 22 W 17
Plasencia [E] 25 D 20
Δ Plasencia, Llano de — [E] 26 G 19
Plasencia de Jalón [E] 26 G 19
Plaški [YU] 21 T 17
Plassen [N] 4 Q 7
Platanias [GR] 32 Za 23
Platanistos [GR] 31 Za 21
Platanos [GR] 32 Za 23
Platanoussa [GR] 30 X 21
Platikambos [GR] 30 Y 20
Plattling [D] 16 R 15
Płaty [PL] 16 S 12
Plau [DDR] 15 Q 12
Plauen [DDR] 15 Q 14
Plav [YU] 22 W 19
Δ Plavnik [YU] 21 S 17
Pleaux [F] 19 K 17
≈ Pleiße [DDR] 16 R 14
Plélan-le-Grand [F] 13 H 15
Pléneuf [F] 12 G 15
Δ Pleşul [RO] 22 X 16
Pleszew [PL] 16 T 13
Pleven [BG] 23 Z 18
Pleyben [F] 12 F 15
Plienciem [SU] 8 W 9
Plitvice [YU] 21 T 17
≈ Plitvička jezera [YU] 21 T 17
Δ Plješevica [YU] 21 T 17
Pljevlja [YU] 22 V 18
Δ Ploča, Rt — [YU] 21 T 18
Ploče [YU] 21 U 19
Płock [PL] 16 U 12
Ploëmeur [F] 12 G 15
Ploërmel [F] 12 G 15
Plogoff [F] 12 F 15
Ploieşti [RO] 23 Za 17
Plomarion [GR] 31 Zb 20
Plombières [F] 20 N 16
Plön [D] 6 P 12
Płońsk [PL] 17 V 12
Ploştina [RO] 22 Y 17
Ploudalmézeau [F] 12 F 15
Ploumanac'h [F] 12 G 15
Plovdiv [BG] 23 Z 19
Plozévet [F] 12 F 15
Plunge [SU] 8 V 10
≈ Pl'ussa [SU] 8 Y 8
Plymouth [GB] 12 G 13
Plzeň [CS] 16 R 14
Pnevno [SU] 17 Y 13
Pnevo [SU] 8 Y 8
Pniewy [PL] 16 T 13
≈ Po [I] 20 P 17
Pobla de Segur [E] 27 J 19
Poblet, Monasterio de — [E] 27 J 20
Pobo de Dueñas, El — [E] 26 G 20
Počajev [SU] 17 Y 14
Δ Pocerina [YU] 22 V 17
Pocking [D] 21 R 15
Poddębice [PL] 16 U 13
Poděbrady [CS] 16 S 14
Podgajcy [SU] 17 Y 14
Δ Podgorina [YU] 22 V 18
≈ Podgorski kanal [YU] 21 S 17
Δ Podhale [PL] 17 V 14
Podkova [BG] 31 Za 19
Δ Podlasie [PL] 17 W 13
Δ Podlužje [YU] 22 W 17
Podplat [YU] 21 T 17
Δ Podravina [YU] 21 T 17
Podravska Slatina [YU] 21 U 17
Δ Podrima [YU] 22 W 19
Podromanija [YU] 22 V 18
Podujevo [YU] 22 X 18
Podu Iloaiei [RO] 23 Za 15
Δ Podunajská nížina [CS] 21 U 15
Podu Turcului [RO] 23 Za 16
Δ Poel [DDR] 15 Q 12
Poggibonsi [I] 20 Q 18
Pòggio Rusco [I] 20 Q 17
Pogoanele [RO] 23 Za 17
Pogradec [AL] 30 X 20
Δ Pohjanmaa [SF] 9 V 5
Pohjaslahti [SF] 3 V 3
Pohjaslahti [SF] 9 V 6
Pohořelice [CS] 16 T 15
Δ Pohorje [YU] 21 S 16
Poiana Mare [RO] 22 Y 18
Δ Poiana Ruscă, Munţii — [RO] 22 X 17
Poiana-Stampei [RO] 22 Y 15
Poiana Teiului [RO] 23 Z 15
Poiares [P] 25 B 19
Poide [SU] 8 W 8
Poitiers [F] 19 J 16
Δ Poitou [F] 18 H 16
Poix [F] 14 K 14
Poix-Terron [F] 14 M 14
Δ Pojezierze Suwalskie [PL] 8 W 11
Pokka [SF] 3 V 2
Pola de Gordón, La — [E] 24 D 18
Pola de Siero [E] 24 E 18
Polán [E] 26 E 20
Δ Pol'ana [CS] 17 V 15
Polanów [PL] 7 T 11
Pol'arnyj [SU] 3 X 1
Δ Polarssirkelsstøtte [N] 2 R 4
Połczyn Zdrój [PL] 16 S 12
Polesella [I] 20 Q 17
Δ Polèsine [I] 20 Q 17
Δ Polesje [SU] 17 Y 13
Polessk [SU] 8 V 11
Polgar [H] 22 W 15
Poliçan [AL] 30 W 20
≈ Policastro, Golfo di — [I] 29 T 21
Polichnitos [GR] 31 Zb 20
Polička [CS] 16 T 14
Δ Poliegos [GR] 31 Za 22
Poligiros [GR] 31 Z 20
Polignano a Mare [I] 29 U 20
Poligny [F] 19 M 16
Polikastron [GR] 30 Y 19
Polistena [I] 29 U 22
Polkowice [PL] 16 T 13
Polla [I] 29 T 20
Pollensa [E] 27 K 21
Pòllica [I] 29 T 20
Δ Pollino [I] 29 U 21
Polmak [N] 3 V 1
Polna [SU] 8 Y 8
Δ Polog [YU] 30 X 19
Δ Pölomäki [SF] 9 W 5
Polski Trambeš [BG] 23 Za 18
Põltsamaa [SU] 8 X 8
Põlva [SU] 8 X 8
Δ Półwysep Hel [PL] 7 U 11
Pomarkku [SF] 9 U 6
Pombal [P] 25 B 20
≈ Pommersche Bucht [DDR, PL] 7 R 12
Pomor'any [SU] 17 Y 14
Pomorie [BG] 23 Zb 18
Δ Pomorze [PL] 7 T 11
Δ Pomovaara [SF] 3 V 2
Pompadour [F] 19 J 17
Pompei [I] 29 S 20
≈ Ponča [SU] 3 X 3
Δ Ponente, Riviera di — [I] 20 O 18
Ponferrada [E] 24 D 18
Δ Poniente, Costa de — [E] 27 J 20
Pons [E] 27 J 19
Pons [F] 18 H 17
≈ Ponsul, Rio — [P] 25 C 20
Pont, le — [CH] 20 N 16
Pontailler-sur-Saône [F] 19 M 16
Pont-à-Mousson [F] 15 N 15
Pontão [P] 25 B 20
Pontarion [F] 19 K 17
Pontarlier [F] 20 N 16
Pontaubault [F] 13 H 15
Pont-Audemer [F] 14 J 14
Pontaumur [F] 19 K 17
Pont-Canavese [I] 20 N 17
Pontchâteau [F] 18 H 15
Pont-d'Ain [F] 19 M 17
Pont-de-Beauvoisin, le — [F] 19 M 17
Pont-de-Roide [F] 20 N 16
Pont-de-Salars [F] 19 K 18
Pont-de-Vaux [F] 19 M 16
Pont-de-Veyle [F] 19 M 17
Pont-du-Château [F] 19 L 17
Pontebba [I] 21 R 16
Pontecorvo [I] 29 S 20
Ponte de Barca [P] 24 B 18
Pontedera [I] 20 P 18
Ponte de Sor [P] 25 B 20
Ponte di Legno [I] 20 P 17
Ponte do Lima [P] 24 B 18

Ponteland [GB] 11 J 11
Ponte-Leccia [F] 28 P 19
Ponte nell'Alpi [I] 21 R 17
Pontenx-les-Forges [F] 18 H 18
Pontevedra [E] 24 B 18
≈ Pontevedra, Ría de — [E] 24 B 18
Pontivy [F] 12 G 15
Pont-l'Abbé [F] 12 F 15
Pont-l'Évêque [F] 14 J 14
Pontoise [F] 14 K 15
Pontorson [F] 13 H 15
Pontrèmoli [I] 20 P 18
Pontrieux [F] 12 G 15
Pont-Saint-Esprit [F] 19 L 18
Ponts-de-Cé, les — [F] 18 H 16
Δ Ponza, Isola di — [I] 29 R 20
Δ Ponziane [I] 29 R 20
Poole [GB] 13 H 13
Δ Põõsaspea neem [SU] 8 V 8
Popeni [RO] 23 Za 16
Poperinge [B] 14 L 14
Pòpoli [I] 29 S 19
Popovica [BG] 23 Z 19
Popovo [BG] 23 Za 18
Poppenhausen [D] 15 P 14
Poprad [CS] 17 V 15
Popsko [BG] 23 Za 19
Porąbka [PL] 17 V 14
Porceşti [RO] 22 Y 16
Porcuna [E] 25 D 21
Pordenone [I] 21 R 17
Poreč [YU] 21 R 17
Pori [SF] 9 U 7
Porjus [S] 2 T 3
Porkkala [SF] 9 W 7
Pornic [F] 18 G 16
Δ Poros [GR] 31 Z 22
Porozina [YU] 21 S 17
Porozkovoje [SU] 17 X 15
Porozovo [SU] 17 X 12
Δ Porquerolles, Île de — [F] 19 M 19
Porrentruy [CH] 20 N 16
Porretta Terme [I] 20 Q 18
Porriño [E] 24 B 18
≈ Porsangerfjord [N] 3 U 1
Δ Porsangerhalvøya [N] 3 U 1
Porsgrunn [N] 6 P 8
Portaferry [GB] 10 G 11
Portalegre [P] 25 B 20
Δ Portas, Punta — [E] 27 J 21
Port Ascaig [GB] 10 G 10
Port-Bou [F] 27 K 19
Δ Port Cros, Île de — [F] 20 N 19
Port-de-Bouc [F] 19 M 18
Portel [P] 25 B 21
Port Ellen [GB] 10 G 10
Port Erin [GB] 10 G 11
Porthmadog [GB] 12 G 12
Δ Porţile de Fier [Donau] [RO] 22 X 17
Δ Porţile de Fier [Munţii Ţarcu] [RO] 22 X 17
Portimão [P] 25 A 21
≈ Portiţii, Gura — [RO] 23 Zc 17
Port-Joinville [F] 18 G 16
Port Láirge = Waterford [IRL] 12 E 12
Δ Portland [GB] 13 H 13
Δ Portland, Bill of — [GB] 13 H 13
Port-la-Nouvelle [F] 19 K 19
Port Laoise [IRL] 10 F 12
Port-Leucate-Barcarès [F] 19 K 19
Port Louis [F] 12 G 15
Portnacroish [GB] 10 G 9
Portnahaven [GB] 10 G 10
Porto [F] 28 O 19
Porto [P] 25 B 19
≈ Porto, Golfe de — [F] 28 O 19
Porto Azzurro [I] 28 P 19
Porto Cervo [I] 28 P 20
Porto Conte [I] 28 O 20
Porto Empèdocle [I] 29 S 22
Portoferràio [I] 28 P 19
Δ Portofino Vetta [I] 20 O 18
Port of Ness [GB] 10 G 8
Portogruaro [I] 21 R 17
Pörtom [SF] 9 U 6
Portomaggiore [I] 20 Q 18
Port Omna = Portumna [IRL] 10 E 11
Porto Recanati [I] 21 S 18
Porto Santo Stéfano [I] 28 Q 19
Porto Tolle [I] 21 R 17
Porto Tórres [I] 28 O 20
Porto-Vecchio [F] 28 P 20
≈ Porto-Vecchio, Golfe de — [F] 28 P 20
Portpatrick [GB] 10 G 11
Portree [GB] 10 G 9
Portrush [GB] 10 F 10
Port-Sainte-Marie [F] 19 J 18
Port-Saint-Louis-du-Rhône [F] 19 M 18
Portsmouth [GB] 13 J 13
Port Talbot [GB] 12 G 13
≈ Porttipahdan tekojärvi [SF] 3 V 2
Portugalete [E] 18 F 18
Portumna [IRL] 10 E 11
Port-Vendres [F] 27 K 19
Port William [GB] 10 G 11
Porvoo = Borgå [SF] 9 W 7
≈ Porvoon joki [SF] 9 W 7
Posadas [E] 25 D 21
Δ Posavina [YU] 21 T 17
Δ Posets [E] 26 H 19
Poshnjë [AL] 30 W 20
Posio [SF] 3 W 3
Positano [I] 29 S 20
Postavi [SU] 8 Y 10
Postojna [YU] 21 S 17
Posušje [YU] 21 U 18
Potami [GR] 31 Z 19
Potenza [I] 29 T 20
Potes [E] 24 E 18
Potsdam [DDR] 16 R 13
Pouancé [F] 18 H 15
Pouilly-en-Auxois [F] 19 M 16
Pouilly-sur-Loire [F] 19 L 16
Δ Pourri, Mont — [F] 20 N 17
Pouzauges [F] 18 H 16
Δ Považský Inovec [CS] 16 U 15
Δ Povlen [YU] 22 W 18
Póvoa de Varzim [P] 24 B 19
Poysdorf [A] 21 T 15
Pöytya [SF] 9 V 7
Poza de la Sal [E] 18 F 18
Pozallo [I] 29 T 22
Požarevac [YU] 22 W 17
Požega [YU] 22 W 18
Δ Požeška gora [YU] 21 U 17
Poznań [PL] 16 T 13
Pozo Alcón [E] 26 E 22
Pozoblanco [E] 25 D 21
Pozo Cañada [E] 26 F 21
Pozzuoli [I] 29 S 20
Prabuty [PL] 7 U 12
Δ Pradales, Sierra de — [E] 26 E 19
Δ Praděd [CS] 16 T 14
Pradelles [F] 19 L 17
Prades [F] 19 K 19
Præstø [DK] 6 Q 11
Praha [CS] 16 S 14
Prahovo [YU] 22 X 17
Praia a Mare [I] 29 T 21
Praid [RO] 23 Z 16
Δ Prangli [SU] 9 W 8
Prasetin [CS] 16 S 15
Δ Prassonission, Akrotirion — [GR] 32 Zd 22
Praszka [PL] 16 U 13
Prato [I] 20 Q 18
Prats-de-Mollo-la-Preste [F] 27 K 19
Pravdinsk [SU] 8 V 11
Δ Prawle Point [GB] 12 G 14
Prazzo [I] 20 N 18
Preajba [RO] 23 Z 17
Predazzo [I] 20 Q 17
Predeal [RO] 23 Z 16
Δ Predel [BG] 30 Y 19
Pré-en-Pail [F] 14 J 15
Pregarten [A] 21 S 15
≈ Pregol'a [SU] 8 V 11
Preiļi [SU] 8 Y 10
Preljina [YU] 22 W 18
Přelouč [CS] 16 S 14
Prémery [F] 19 L 16
Δ Premuda [YU] 21 S 18
Δ Prenj [YU] 21 U 18
Prenzlau [DDR] 16 R 12
Přerov [CS] 16 U 14
Pré-Saint-Didier [I] 20 N 17
Δ Presanella, Cima — [I] 20 P 17
Preševo [YU] 22 X 19
Presicce [I] 30 V 20
Preslav [BG] 23 Za 18
Prešov [CS] 17 W 15
≈ Prespansko jezero [YU] 30 X 20
≈ Prespës, Liqeni i — [AL] 30 X 20
Prestatyn [GB] 13 H 12
Přeštice [CS] 16 R 14
Preston [GB] 11 H 11
Preststranda [N] 6 P 8
Prestwick [GB] 10 G 10
Preveza [GR] 30 X 21
Pribinić [YU] 21 U 18
Priboj na Limu [YU] 22 V 18
Příbram [CS] 16 R 14
Priego de Córdoba [E] 25 D 22
Priekule [SU] 8 V 10
Prienai [SU] 8 W 11
Prievidza [CS] 16 U 15
Δ Prignitz [DDR] 15 Q 12
Prijedor [YU] 21 T 17
Prijepolje [YU] 22 W 18
Prilep [YU] 30 X 19
Δ Prilepsko polje [YU] 30 X 19
Primaube, la — [F] 19 K 18
Primolano [I] 20 Q 17
Primorsk [SU] 7 U 11
Primorsko [BG] 23 Zb 18
Primošten [YU] 21 T 18
Δ Prior, Cabo — [E] 24 C 17
≈ Prip'at' [SU] 17 X 13
Prisoje [YU] 21 U 18
Priština [YU] 22 X 19
Pritzier [DDR] 15 Q 12
Pritzwalk [DDR] 15 Q 12
Privas [F] 19 L 18
Priverno [I] 29 R 20
Prizren [YU] 22 W 19
Prizzi [I] 29 S 22
Prnjavor [YU] 21 U 17
Prochowice [PL] 16 T 13
Δ Pròcida, Isola di — [I] 29 S 20
Prodromos [GR] 31 Z 21
Prokopion [GR] 31 Z 21
Prokuplje [YU] 22 X 18
Prolivy [SU] 3 X 2
Propriano [F] 28 O 20
Prosenik [BG] 23 Zb 18
Prosjek [YU] 22 V 18
≈ Prosna [PL] 16 T 13
Prostějov [CS] 16 T 14
Protville [TN] 28 P 22
Proussos [GR] 30 Y 21
Provadija [BG] 23 Zb 18
≈ Provadijska reka [BG] 23 Zb 18
Δ Provence [F] 19 M 18
Provencio, El — [E] 26 F 21
Δ Provincias Vascongadas [E] 18 F 18
Provins [F] 14 L 15
Prozor [YU] 21 U 18
Prudnik [PL] 16 U 14
Prüm [D] 15 N 14
Prusak [PL] 16 U 13
Pruszcz [PL] 16 T 12
Pruszcz Gdański [PL] 7 U 11
Prut [SU] 23 Zb 16
Prutz [A] 20 P 16
Pružany [SU] 17 X 12
Przasnysz [PL] 17 V 12
Przemków Chocianów [PL] 16 S 13
Przemyśl [PL] 17 X 14
Przewodowo [PL] 17 V 11
Przeworsk [PL] 17 W 14
Przewóz [PL] 16 S 13
Δ Przylądek Rozewie [PL] 7 T 11
Psachna [GR] 31 Z 21
Psara [GR] 31 Zb 21
Δ Psara [GR] 31 Za 21
Δ Psathoura [GR] 31 Z 20
Δ Pserimos [GR] 31 Zc 22
Pskov [SU] 8 Y 8
≈ Pskova [SU] 8 Y 8
≈ Pskovskoje ozero [SU] 8 Y 8
Δ Psunj [YU] 21 U 17
Pszczyna [PL] 16 U 14
Pteleos [GR] 31 Z 21
Ptolemaïs [GR] 30 X 20
Ptuj [YU] 21 T 16
Puchberg am Schneeberg [A] 21 T 16
Puciosa [RO] 23 Z 17
Pudarica [YU] 21 S 18
Pudasjärvi [SF] 3 W 4
Puebla, La — [E] 27 K 21
Puebla de Alcocer [E] 25 D 21
Puebla de Almoradiel, La — [E] 26 F 20
Puebla de Arganzón, La — [E] 18 F 18
Puebla de Cazalla, La — [E] 25 D 22
Puebla de Don Fadrique [E] 26 F 21
Puebla de Don Rodrigo [E] 25 D 20
Puebla de Guzmán [E] 25 B 21
Puebla del Caramiñal [E] 24 B 18
Puebla de Sanabria [E] 24 D 18
Puebla de Trives [E] 24 C 18
Puebla de Valverde, La — [E] 26 G 20
Puenteáreas [E] 24 B 18
Puente del Arzobispo, El — [E] 25 D 20
Puentedeume [E] 24 C 17
Puente-Genil [E] 25 D 22
Puente la Reina [E] 18 G 19
Puentes de García Rodríguez [E] 24 C 17
Puente-Viesgo [E] 18 F 18
Puerto de Santa María, El — [E] 25 C 22
Puerto de San Vicente [E] 25 D 20
Puerto de Sóller [E] 27 K 21
Puerto-Lápice [E] 26 E 20
Puertollano [E] 26 E 21
Puerto Lumbreras [E] 26 F 22
Puerto Mazarrón [E] 26 G 22
Puerto Pollensa [E] 27 K 21
Puerto Real [E] 25 C 22
Puget-Théniers [F] 20 N 18
Δ Pùglia [I] 29 T 20
Pühalepa [SU] 8 V 8
≈ Puhosjärvi [SF] 3 W 4
Puieşti [RO] 23 Za 16
Puigcerdà [E] 27 J 19
Δ Puig Mayor [E] 27 K 21
Puigreig [E] 27 J 19
Puiseaux [F] 19 K 15
Puisserguier [F] 19 K 18
Puka [SU] 8 X 8
Pukavik [S] 7 R 10
≈ Pukaviksbukt [S] 7 S 10
Pukë [AL] 30 W 19
Pula [I] 28 O 21
Pula [YU] 21 S 18
Puławy [PL] 17 W 13
Pulju [SF] 3 U 2
≈ Pulkau [A] 21 T 15
Pulkkila [SF] 9 V 5
Pułtusk [PL] 17 V 11
Pumpėnai [SU] 8 W 10
Punkaharju [SF] 9 X 6
Δ Punkaharju [SF] 9 X 6
Punkalaidun [SF] 9 V 7
Puntamäki [SF] 9 V 7
Puokio [SF] 3 W 4
Puolanka [SF] 3 W 4
Purchena [E] 26 F 22
Purkersdorf [A] 21 T 15
Purnumukka [SF] 3 V 2
≈ Puruvesi [SF] 9 X 6
Püspökladány [H] 22 W 16
Pustec [AL] 30 X 20
Δ Puszcza Augustowska [PL] 8 W 11
Δ Puszcza Białowieska [PL] 17 X 12
Δ Puszcza Kampinoska [PL] 17 V 12
Δ Puszcza Myszyniecka [PL] 17 V 12
Δ Puszcza Piska [PL] 17 V 12
Δ Puszcza Sandomierska [PL] 17 W 14
Δ Puszcza Solska [PL] 17 W 13
Putignano [I] 29 U 20
Putineiu [RO] 23 Za 17
Puttgarden [D] 6 Q 11
≈ Puulavesi [SF] 9 W 6
Puumala [SF] 9 X 6
Puy, le — [F] 19 L 17
Puy-Guillaume [F] 19 L 17
Puylaurens [F] 19 K 18
Puy-l'Évêque [F] 19 J 18
Δ Puymorens, Col de — [F] 19 J 19
Puyoô-Bellocq-Ramous [F] 18 H 18
Pwllheli [GB] 12 G 12
Pyhäjärvi [SF] 9 W 5
≈ Pyhäjärvi [SF] 9 V 7
≈ Pyhäjärvi [SF] 9 W 5
≈ Pyhäjärvi [SF] 9 W 6
≈ Pyhäjärvi [SF] 9 W 7
Pyhäjoki [SF] 9 V 5
≈ Pyhäjoki [SF] 9 V 5
Pyhäntä [SF] 9 W 5
Pyhäranta [SF] 9 U 7
≈ Pyhäselkä [SF] 9 X 5
Δ Pyhätunturi [SF] 3 V 3
Δ Pyhitys [SF] 3 W 4
Δ Pyhrnpaß [A] 21 S 16
Pyhtää [SF] 9 X 7
Δ Pyla, Dune de — [F] 18 H 17
Pylkönmäki [SF] 9 V 6
Pyrzyce [PL] 16 S 12
Pyskowice [PL] 16 U 14
Δ Pytteggja [N] 4 O 6
Pyttis = Pyhtää [SF] 9 X 7
Pyzdry [PL] 16 T 13

Q

Quakenbrück [D] 15 O 13
Quartu Sant'Elena [I] 28 P 21
Quatre-Chemins, les — [F] 18 H 16
Quedlinburg [DDR] 15 Q 13
Δ Queija, Sierra de — [E] 24 C 18
Δ Quejo, Cabo — [E] 18 F 18
Δ Quercy [F] 19 J 18
Querfurt [DDR] 15 Q 13
Quesada [E] 26 E 21
Quettehou [F] 13 H 14
Quiberon [F] 18 G 15
Quillan [F] 19 K 19
Quimper [F] 12 F 15
Quimperle [F] 12 G 15
Quintanar de la Orden [E] 26 F 20
Quintanar del Rey [E] 26 F 21
Quintin [F] 12 G 15
Quissac [F] 19 L 18
Quistreham [F] 14 J 14
Qytet Stalin [AL] 30 W 20

R

Raabs an der Thaya [A] 21 S 15
Raahe [SF] 9 V 4
Rääkylä [SF] 9 X 6
Raanujärvi [SF] 3 V 3
≈ Raanujärvi [SF] 3 V 3
Δ Raasay [GB] 10 G 9
Raattama [SF] 3 U 2
Rab [YU] 21 S 18
Δ Rab [YU] 21 S 18
≈ Rába [H] 21 U 16
≈ Raba [PL] 17 V 14
Rabac [YU] 21 S 17
≈ Rabaçal, Rio — [P] 24 C 19
Răbăgani [RO] 22 X 16
Δ Rábaköz [H] 21 U 16
Rabat [M] 30 V 22
Rabat = Victoria [M] 30 V 22
Råberg [S] 5 S 5
Rábida, La — [E] 25 B 21
Rabka [PL] 17 V 14
Răcăciuni [RO] 23 Za 16
Racalmuto [I] 29 S 22
Răcăşdia [RO] 22 X 17
Racconigi [I] 20 O 18
Rachov [SU] 17 Y 15
Raciąż [PL] 17 V 12
Racibórz [PL] 16 U 14
Δ Radan [YU] 22 X 18
Radanovo [BG] 23 Za 18
Råde [N] 6 P 8
Radeberg [DDR] 16 R 13
Radechov [SU] 17 Y 13
Radkersburg [A] 21 T 16
Δ Rådmansö [S] 5 T 8
Radnevo [BG] 23 Za 18
Radolfzell am Bodensee [D] 20 O 16
Radom [PL] 17 V 13
Radomir [BG] 22 Y 18
Radomsko [PL] 17 V 13
Radoviš [YU] 30 Y 19
Δ Radøy [N] 4 N 7
Radstadt [A] 21 R 16
Radun' [SU] 8 X 11
Radviliškis [SU] 8 W 10
Radymno [PL] 17 X 14
Radziejów [PL] 16 U 12
Radzyń Chełmiński [PL] 16 U 12
Radzyń Podlaski [PL] 17 W 13
Raffadali [I] 29 S 22
Raf Raf [TN] 28 P 22
Rafsbotn [N] 3 U 1
≈ Raftsund [N] 2 R 2
Ragunda [S] 5 S 6
Ragusa [I] 29 T 22
Ragusa = Dubrovnik [YU] 22 V 19
Δ Rainha, Cabeço da — [P] 25 B 20
Δ Raippaluoto [SF] 9 U 5
Δ Raisduoddarhaldde [N] 2 T 2
Raisio [SF] 9 V 7
Raisjavrre [N] 2 T 2
Raivala [SF] 9 V 6
Raja-Jooseppi [SF] 3 V 2
Rajakoski [SU] 3 W 2
≈ Rajgrodski, Jezioro — [PL] 8 W 11
Δ Rajinac [YU] 21 S 18
Rajka [H] 21 U 15
Δ Rakisvaara [S] 2 T 2
Rakkestad [N] 6 Q 8
Rákos [H] 22 W 16
Rakov [SU] 8 Y 11
Rakovník [CS] 16 R 14
Råkvåg [N] 4 P 5
Rakvere [SU] 9 X 8
Ramacca [I] 29 T 22
Ramales de la Victoria [E] 18 F 18
Ramberg [N] 2 Q 3
Rambervillers [F] 20 N 15
Rambouillet [F] 14 K 15
Ramnäs [S] 5 S 8
Ramsay [GB] 10 G 11
Ramsberg [S] 5 S 8
Ramsele [S] 5 S 5
Ramsgate [GB] 13 K 13
Ramsjö [S] 5 S 6
Ramygala [SU] 9 X 10
≈ Rana [N] 2 R 4
Δ Rana [N] 2 R 4
Δ Rañadoiro, Sierra de — [E] 24 D 18
≈ Ranafjord [N] 2 Q 4
Δ Randa [E] 27 K 21
Randan [F] 19 L 17
Randazzo [I] 29 T 22
≈ Rånden [S] 4 Q 6
Randers [DK] 6 P 10
≈ Randijaur [S] 2 S 3
Δ Randon, Mont — [F] 19 L 18
≈ Randsfjord [N] 4 P 7
Randsverk [N] 4 P 7
Råneå [S] 3 U 4
Ranemsletta [N] 4 Q 5
Rannapungerja [SU] 8 X 8
Rannoch Station [GB] 11 H 9
Δ Rånön [S] 3 U 4
Rantasalmi [SF] 9 X 6
Rantsila [SF] 9 V 4
Ranua [SF] 3 V 4
Raon-l'Étape [F] 20 N 15
Rapallo [I] 20 P 18
Rapina [SU] 8 Y 8
Rapla [SU] 9 W 8
Rapperswil [CH] 20 O 16
Raša [YU] 21 S 17
Raseiniai [SU] 8 W 10
Ras el Djebel [TN] 28 P 22
Raška [YU] 22 W 18
Δ Raso, Cabo — [P] 25 A 20
Δ Rässö [S] 6 Q 9
Rastatt [D] 15 O 15
Rastede [D] 15 O 12
Rastenburg = Kętrzyn [PL] 8 V 11
Δ Rastigaissa [N] 3 U 1
Rastinkylä [SF] 9 X 5
Δ Råsto [S] 2 T 2
Răstoci [RO] 22 X 15
≈ Råstojaure [S] 2 T 2
Δ Rasu, Monte — [I] 28 O 20
Rätansbyn [S] 5 R 6
Rathenow [DDR] 15 Q 13
Rathfriland [GB] 10 F 11
Δ Rathlin Island [GB] 10 G 10
Ráth Loirc = Charleville [IRL] 12 E 12
Ratibor = Racibórz [PL] 16 U 14
Δ Rätikon [A, CH, FL] 20 P 16
Δ Rätische Alpen [CH] 20 P 16
Ratno [SU] 17 X 13
Rattosjärvi [SF] 3 V 3
Rättvik [S] 5 R 7
Ratzeburg [D] 15 P 12
Rauland [N] 4 O 8
Rauma [SF] 9 U 7
≈ Rauma [N] 4 O 6
Rautalampi [SF] 9 W 6
≈ Rautasjaure [S] 2 S 3
Rautavaara [SF] 9 X 5
≈ Rautavesi [SF] 9 V 7
Rautio [SF] 9 V 5
Δ Raututunturi [SF] 3 V 2
Ravanica [YU] 22 X 18
Rava-Russkaja [SU] 17 X 14
Ravenglass [GB] 11 H 11
Ravenna [I] 21 R 18
Ravensburg [D] 20 P 16
Ravières [F] 19 L 16
Ravna Dubrava [YU] 22 X 18
Rawa Mazowiecka [PL] 17 V 13
Rawicz [PL] 16 T 13
Δ Raxalpe [A] 21 T 16
Δ Raz, Pointe du — [F] 12 F 15
Ražanj [YU] 22 X 18
≈ Razelm, Lacul — [RO] 23 Zb 16
Razgrad [BG] 23 Za 18
Razlog [BG] 22 Y 19
Δ Ré, Île de — [F] 18 H 16
Reading [GB] 13 J 13
Δ Reales [E] 25 C 22
Réalmont [F] 19 K 18
Δ Rebbenesøy [N] 2 S 1
≈ Rebnesjaure [S] 2 S 4
Rebordelo [P] 24 C 19
Recanati [I] 21 R 18
Recaş [RO] 22 W 17
Recess [IRL] 10 D 11
Recey-sur-Ource [F] 19 M 16
Recklinghausen [D] 15 N 13
Recogne [B] 14 M 14
Recz [PL] 16 S 12
Reda [PL] 7 U 11
Redcar [GB] 11 J 11
Rédics [H] 21 T 16
Redon [F] 18 H 15
Redondela [E] 24 B 18
Redondo [P] 25 B 20
Redruth [GB] 12 F 13
Redstone Cross [GB] 12 G 13
Rees [D] 15 N 13
Refsnes [N] 2 R 2
≈ Rega [PL] 16 S 12
Regalbuto [I] 29 T 22
Regen [D] 16 R 15
≈ Regen [D] 15 Q 15
Regensburg [D] 16 Q 15
Règgio di Calàbria [I] 29 T 22
Règgio nell'Emìlia [I] 20 P 18
Reghin [RO] 22 Y 16
Regna [S] 7 S 8
Regozero [SU] 3 X 3
Reguengos de Monsaraz [P] 25 B 21
Reichenbach/Vogtland [DDR] 15 Q 14
Reigate [GB] 13 J 13
Reigi [SU] 8 V 8
Reims [F] 14 L 15
Reinosa [E] 18 E 18
Δ Reinøy [N] 2 S 1
Δ Reinøy [N] 3 U 1
≈ Reisa [N] 2 T 2
Reisjärvi [SF] 9 V 5
Reit im Winkl [D] 21 R 16
Reitmehring [D] 20 Q 15
Δ Rekarne [S] 7 S 8
Rekovac [YU] 22 X 18
Rekuby [SF] 9 V 7
Remiremont [F] 20 N 16
Remscheid [D] 15 N 13
Rena [N] 4 Q 7
≈ Rena [N] 4 Q 7
Renda [SU] 8 V 9
Rendina [GR] 30 Y 21
Rendina [GR] 31 Z 20
Renesse [NL] 14 M 13
Reni [SU] 23 Zb 16
Rennerod [D] 15 O 14
Rennes [F] 13 H 15
Δ Rennesøy [N] 6 N 8
≈ Reno [I] 20 Q 18
Rensburg [D] 6 P 11
Réole, la — [F] 18 H 17
≈ Replotfjärd [SF] 9 U 5
Reposaari [SF] 9 U 7
Repvåg [N] 3 U 1
Requena [E] 26 G 21
Requista [F] 19 K 18
Reşadiye [TR] 31 Zc 22
Δ Reschenpaß = Passo di Résia [A, I] 20 P 16
Resen [YU] 30 X 20
Reşeti [SU] 8 Y 9
Rëshen [AL] 30 W 19
Δ Résia, Passo di — [A, I] 20 P 16
Reşiţa [RO] 22 X 17
Reszel [PL] 8 V 11
Δ Retezat, Munţii — [RO] 22 X 17
Rethel [F] 14 M 14
Rethimnon [GR] 32 Za 23
Retournac [F] 19 L 17
Reus [E] 27 J 20
≈ Reuss [CH] 20 O 16
Reutlingen [D] 15 P 15
Reval = Tallinn [SU] 9 W 8
Revel [F] 19 K 18
Δ Revellata, Pointe de — [F] 28 O 19
Δ Revermont [F] 19 M 17
Revničov [CS] 16 R 14
≈ Revnsbotn [N] 3 U 1
Reze [F] 18 H 16
Rēzekne [SU] 8 Y 9
≈ Reznas ezers [SU] 8 Y 9
Rezovo [BG] 23 Zb 18
Rhayader [GB] 13 H 12
Rheda-Wiedenbrück [D] 15 O 13
≈ Rhein [CH, D] 20 O 15
Rheine [D] 15 O 13
Rheinfelden (Baden) [D] 20 O 16
Δ Rheinisches Schiefergebirge [D] 15 N 14
Rheinsberg (Mark) [DDR] 16 R 12
Rhenen [NL] 15 N 13
≈ Rhinkanal [DDR] 15 Q 12
Rhinow [DDR] 15 Q 12
Rho [I] 20 O 17
Δ Rhön [D] 15 P 14
Rhondda [GB] 12 G 13
≈ Rhône [CH, F] 19 M 17
≈ Rhône au Rhin, Canal du — [F] 20 N 15
Δ Rhonegletscher [CH] 20 O 16
Rhune, la — [E, F] 18 G 18
Rhyl [GB] 13 H 12
Riaño [E] 24 E 18
Rians [F] 19 M 18
≈ Riansares, Río — [E] 26 F 20
Δ Rías Gallegas [E] 24 B 18
Riaza [E] 26 F 19
Ribadavia [E] 24 C 18
Ribadeo [E] 24 D 17
≈ Ribadeo, Ría de — [E] 24 D 17
Ribadesella [E] 24 E 18
Ribaforada [E] 26 G 19
Δ Ribagorza [E] 26 H 19
Ribarska Banja [YU] 22 X 18
Ribas de Freser [E] 27 K 19
Δ Ribatejo [P] 25 A 20
Ribe [DK] 6 O 11
≈ Ribe Å [DK] 6 O 11
Ribeira [E] 24 B 18
Ribera [I] 29 S 22
Ribérac [F] 19 J 17
Ribnica [YU] 21 S 17
Ribnitz-Damgarten [DDR] 6 Q 12
Riccia [I] 29 S 20
Riccione [I] 21 R 18
Riceys, les — [F] 19 M 15
Richelieu [F] 19 J 16
Riec-sur-Belon [F] 12 G 15
Ried im Innkreis [A] 21 R 15
Riedlingen [D] 20 P 15
Riego de la Vega [E] 24 D 18
Riesa [DDR] 16 R 13
Riesi [I] 29 S 22
Rietavas [SU] 8 V 10
Rieti [I] 29 R 19
Rieumes [F] 19 H 18
Rievaulx Abbey [GB] 11 J 11
Riez [F] 19 M 18
Riga [SU] 8 W 9
≈ Rīgas Jūras Līcis [SU] 8 V 9
Δ Rigi [CH] 20 O 16
Riguldi [SU] 8 V 8
Riihimäki [SF] 9 W 7
Riihivaara [SF] 9 X 5
Riipi [SF] 3 V 3
Riistavesi [SF] 9 X 5
Rijeka [YU] 21 S 17
Riksgränsen [S] 2 S 2
Δ Rila [BG] 22 Y 19
Rilski manastir [BG] 22 Y 19
Rimavská Sobota [CS] 17 V 15
Rimbo [S] 5 T 8
Rimforsa [S] 7 S 9
Rìmini [I] 21 R 18
Rîmnicu de Jos [RO] 23 Zb 17
Rîmnicu Sărat [RO] 23 Za 16
Rîmnicu Vîcea [RO] 22 Y 17
Rincón de la Victoria [E] 25 D 22
Rinda [SU] 8 V 9
Rindal [N] 4 P 6
Ringarum [S] 7 S 9
Ringe [DK] 6 P 11
Δ Ringerike [N] 4 P 8
Ringerike-Hønefoss [N] 4 P 8
Ringkøbing [DK] 6 O 10
≈ Ringkøbing Fjord [DK] 6 O 10
Δ Ringsö [S] 7 T 9
Ringsta [S] 5 R 6
Ringsted [DK] 6 Q 11
Δ Ringvassøy [N] 2 S 1
Ringwood [GB] 13 H 13
Δ Rinia [GR] 31 Za 21
Rinteln [D] 15 P 13
≈ Río Grande [E] 26 G 21
Δ Rioja, La — [E] 18 F 19
Riom [F] 19 L 17
Rio Maior [P] 25 A 20
Riom-ès-Montagnes [F] 19 K 17
Rion [GR] 30 Y 21
Rionero in Vùlture [I] 29 T 20
Riós [E] 24 C 18
Ripoll [E] 27 K 19
Ripon [GB] 11 J 11
Riqueval [F] 14 L 14
Riš [BG] 23 Zb 18
Risan [YU] 22 V 19
Risbäck [S] 5 R 5
Risca [GB] 13 H 13
Riscle [F] 18 H 18
≈ Risle [F] 14 J 15
Δ Risnjak [YU] 21 S 17
Rîşnov [RO] 23 Z 16
Risør [N] 6 P 9
Rissa [N] 4 P 6
Risti [SU] 8 W 8
Risti [SU] 9 W 8
Ristijärvi [SF] 3 W 4
Δ Ristna [SU] 8 V 8
Risträsk [S] 5 S 5
Risudden [S] 3 U 4
Δ Ritakorkia [SF] 3 W 3
Ritjemjåkk [S] 2 S 3
Riva del Garda [I] 20 Q 17
Rivanazzano [I] 20 O 18
Rivarolo Canavese [I] 20 O 17
Rive-de-Gier [F] 19 M 17
Rivergaro [I] 20 P 18
Rives [F] 19 M 17
Rivesaltes [F] 19 K 19
Rìvoli [I] 20 N 17
Rjukan [N] 4 O 8
Roanne [F] 19 L 17
Roavvegiedde [N] 3 V 1
Röbel [DDR] 15 Q 12
Robertsfors [S] 5 T 5
Robla, La — [E] 24 D 18
Robledo [E] 26 F 21
Robledo de Chavela [E] 26 E 20
Roca de la Sierra, La — [E] 25 C 20
Rocamadour [F] 19 K 17
Roccadàspide [I] 29 T 20
Roccastrada [I] 20 Q 19
Δ Rocciamelone [I] 20 N 17
Rochdale [GB] 11 H 12
Δ Roche, Cabo — [E] 25 C 22
Roche-Bernard, la — [F] 18 G 15
Roche-Chalais, la — [F] 19 J 17
Rochechouart [F] 19 J 17
Roche-de-Rame, la — [F] 20 N 18
Rochefort [B] 14 M 14

ochefort [F] 18 H 17
ochefort-en-Terre [F] 18 G 15
ochefoucauld, la — [F] 19 J 17
ochelle, la — [F] 18 H 16
oche-Posay, la — [F] 19 J 16
ochester [GB] 13 K 13
oche-sur-Foron, la — [F] 20 N 17
oche-sur-Yon, la — [F] 18 H 16
ochlitz [DDR] 16 R 14
ochmojva, gora — [SU] 3 W 3
ocío, El — [E] 25 C 21
ociu [RO] 23 Z 17
ocroi [F] 14 M 14
oda, La — [E] 26 F 21
oda de Andalucía, La — [E] 25 D 22
ødberg [N] 4 P 8
ødby Havn [DK] 6 Q 11
ødding [DK] 6 P 11
odel [GB] 10 G 9
odewisch [DDR] 15 Q 14
odez [F] 19 K 18
odi Garganico [I] 29 T 19
oding [D] 16 R 15
odna [RO] 22 Y 15
Δ Rodna, Munţii — [RO] 17 Y 15
Δ Rodopi [BG] 31 Z 19
odos [GR] 32 Zd 22
Δ Rodos [GR] 32 Zd 22
≈ Rodou, Stenon — [GR] 32 Zd 22
oermond [NL] 15 N 13
oeselare [B] 14 L 14
Δ Rofflaschlucht [CH] 20 P 16
ogač [YU] 21 T 18
Δ Rogaland [N] 6 N 9
ogatica [YU] 22 V 18
ogatin [SU] 17 Y 14
≈ Rogen [S] 4 Q 6
ogliano [F] 28 P 19
ognan [N] 2 R 3
ogowo [PL] 16 T 12
Δ Rogozna [YU] 22 W 18
ogoznica [YU] 21 T 18
ogoźno [PL] 16 T 12
ohrbach an der Lafnitz [A] 21 T 16
ohrbach in Oberösterreich [A] 21 S 15
ohuküla [SU] 8 V 8
Δ Roi, Bois du — [F] 19 L 16
≈ Roine [SF] 9 V 7
oja [SU] 8 V 9
okiškis [SU] 8 X 10
okosov [SU] 17 X 15
okycany [CS] 16 R 14
Δ Rolla [N] 2 R 2
olle [CH] 20 N 16
Δ Rolvsøy [N] 3 U 1
oma [I] 29 R 19
Δ Romagna [I] 20 Q 18
omagnano Sesia [I] 20 O 17
omakloster [S] 7 T 9
oman [BG] 22 Y 18
oman [RO] 23 Za 15
omânaşi [RO] 22 X 16
omanshorn [CH] 20 P 16
omans-sur-Isère [F] 19 M 17
oman Wall [GB] 11 H 11
Δ Romdalshorn [N] 4 O 6
Δ Romeleåsen [S] 7 R 11
Δ Romerike [N] 4 Q 8
omilly-sur-Seine [F] 14 L 15
Δ Romø [DK] 6 O 11
omorantin-Lanthenay [F] 19 K 16
Δ Romsdal [N] 4 O 6
≈ Romsdalsfjord [N] 4 O 6
omsey [GB] 13 H 13
oncesvalles [E] 18 G 18
onco Scrivia [I] 20 O 18
onda [E] 25 D 22
Δ Ronda, Sierra de — [E] 25 C 22
ønde [DK] 6 P 10
Δ Rondeslottet [N] 4 P 7
öngu [SU] 8 X 8
ønne [DK] 7 S 11
onneby [S] 7 S 10
ønningen [N] 4 P 5
önnöfors [S] 5 R 5
önnskär [S] 5 U 5
onquillo, El — [E] 25 C 21
onse [B] 14 L 14
oosendaal en Nispen [NL] 14 M 13
opeid [N] 6 N 8
oquefort [F] 18 H 18
oquefort-sur-Soulzon [F] 19 K 18
oquemaure [F] 19 M 18
oquevaire [F] 19 M 18
øra [N] 4 Q 5
örbäcksnäs [S] 4 Q 7
øros [N] 4 Q 6
orschach [CH] 20 P 16
ørvig [DK] 6 Q 10
ørvik [N] 4 Q 5
≈ Rosa [N] 2 R 4
osal de la Frontera [E] 25 B 21
≈ Rosarito, Pantano de — [E] 25 D 20
osarno [I] 29 T 21
osas [E] 27 K 19
≈ Rosas, Golfo de — [E] 27 K 19
oscoff [F] 12 G 15
Ros Comáin = Roscommon [IRL] 10 E 11
Roscommon [IRL] 10 E 11
Roscrea [IRL] 10 E 12
Ros Cré = Roscrea [IRL] 10 E 12
Rosehall [GB] 11 H 9
Rosenheim [D] 20 Q 16
Roşia [RO] 22 X 16
Roşia-Jiu [RO] 22 Y 17
Rosica [BG] 23 Za 18
Rosice [CS] 16 T 15
Roşiorii de Vede [RO] 23 Z 17
Roskilde [DK] 6 Q 11
Ros Láire = Rosslare [IRL] 12 F 12
Δ Roslangen [S] 5 T 8
Ros Mhic Treoin = New Ross [IRL] 12 F 12
Røsnæs [DK] 6 Q 11
Rosolini [I] 29 T 22
Rosporden [F] 12 G 15
Rossano [I] 29 U 21
Roßdorf [D] 15 O 14
Rosslare [IRL] 12 F 12
Roßlau/Elbe [DDR] 15 Q 13
Rossnes [N] 4 N 7
Ross-on-Wye [GB] 13 H 13
Røssvassbukt [N] 2 R 4
≈ Røssvatn [N] 2 R 4
≈ Rostaelv [N] 2 T 2
≈ Rostavatn [N] 2 S 2
Rostock [DDR] 15 Q 12
Rostonga [S] 7 R 10
Rostrenen [F] 12 G 15
Rostuša [YU] 30 W 19
Røsvik [N] 2 R 3
Rosvik [S] 3 U 4
Rota [E] 25 C 22
≈ Rotälven [S] 5 R 7
Rotenburg/Wümme [D] 15 P 12
Roth [D] 15 Q 15
Rothbury [GB] 11 J 10
Rothenburg ob der Tauber [D] 15 P 15
Rotherham [GB] 13 J 12
Rothesay [GB] 10 G 10
Δ Rotondo, Mont — [F] 28 O 19
≈ Rott [D] 16 R 15
Rotterdam [NL] 14 M 13
Rottneros [S] 4 Q 8
Δ Rottumeroog [NL] 15 N 12
Δ Rottumerplaat [NL] 15 N 12
Rottweil [D] 20 O 15
Rötz [D] 16 R 15
Roubaix [F] 14 L 14
Rouen [F] 14 K 14
Rougemoent [F] 20 N 16
Rouillac [F] 19 J 17
Rountzenheim [F] 15 O 15
Δ Rousay [GB] 11 J 8
Δ Roussillon [F] 19 K 19
Rovaniemi [SF] 3 V 3
≈ Rovdefjord [N] 4 N 6
Rove, le — [F] 19 M 18
Rovereto [I] 20 Q 17
Rovigo [I] 20 Q 17
Rovinari [RO] 22 Y 17
Rovinj [YU] 21 R 17
≈ Roxen [S] 7 S 9
Royal Tunbridge Wells [GB] 13 J 13
Royan [F] 18 H 17
Roye [F] 14 L 14
Røykenes [N] 2 R 2
Røykenvik [N] 4 P 7
Røyrvik [N] 4 Q 5
Royston [GB] 13 J 13
Roza [BG] 23 Za 18
Rožaj [YU] 22 W 19
Rózan [PL] 17 V 12
Rozeni [SU] 8 W 9
Rožmitál pod Třemšínem [CS] 16 R 14
Rožňava [CS] 17 V 15
Rožnov pod Radhštěm [CS] 16 U 14
Rozogi [PL] 17 V 12
Δ Roztocze [PL] 17 W 13
Δ Rtanj [YU] 22 X 18
Rúa, La — [E] 24 C 18
Rubio, El — [E] 25 D 22
Δ Rubio [E] 26 F 19
Rucava [SU] 8 V 10
Ruda [S] 7 S 10
Rüdersdorf bei Berlin [DDR] 16 R 13
Δ Rudha Hunish [GB] 10 G 9
Rūdiškės [SU] 8 X 11
Rudki [SU] 17 X 14
Rudkøbing [DK] 6 P 11
Rudna [PL] 16 T 13
Rudnik [BG] 23 Zb 18
Rudo [YU] 22 V 18
Rudolstadt [DDR] 15 Q 14
Rudozem [BG] 31 Z 19
Rue [F] 14 K 14
≈ Ruecas, Río — [E] 25 D 20
Rueda [E] 26 E 19
Ruelle [F] 19 J 17
Δ Ruen [BG, YU] 22 Y 19
Ruffec [F] 19 J 17
Rugāji [SU] 8 Y 9
Rugby [GB] 13 J 12
Rugeley [GB] 13 H 12
Δ Rügen [DDR] 7 R 11
Δ Ruhner Berge [DDR] 15 Q 12
Δ Ruhnu [SU] 8 W 9
Ruhpolding [D] 21 R 16
Δ Ruj [YU] 22 Y 18
Δ Rujen [YU] 22 X 19
Rūjiene [SU] 8 X 9
Δ Rum [GB] 10 G 9
Ruma [YU] 22 W 17
Rumburk [CS] 16 S 14
Δ Rumelija [BG] 23 Z 18
Rumilly [F] 19 M 17
Rumšiškės [SU] 8 X 11
Rundhaug [N] 2 S 2
Δ Rundhøgda [N] 4 P 6
Rundvik [S] 5 T 5
Δ Runmarö [S] 7 T 8
≈ Runn [S] 5 S 7
Δ Runnö [S] 7 S 10
≈ Ruotjajaure [S] 2 S 3
≈ Ruotsalainen [SF] 9 W 6
Ruovesi [SF] 9 V 6
Rupa [YU] 21 S 17
Rupea [RO] 23 Z 16
≈ Rur [D] 15 N 14
Ruse [BG] 23 Za 17
Ruşeţu [RO] 23 Za 17
Rushden [GB] 13 J 12
Rusinowo [PL] 16 T 12
Ruskele [S] 5 T 5
Rüsselsheim [D] 15 O 14
Russenes [N] 3 U 1
Rust [A] 21 T 16
Rustefjelbma [N] 3 V 1
Ruszki [PL] 17 V 13
Ruszów [PL] 16 S 13
Rute [E] 25 D 22
Δ Ruten [N] 4 P 6
Δ Ruten [N] 4 P 7
Ruthin [GB] 13 H 12
Ruurlo [NL] 15 N 13
Ruuvaoja [SF] 3 W 2
Δ Ruven [N] 6 O 8
≈ Ruvozero [SU] 3 X 3
Ružany [SU] 17 X 12
Ružomberok [CS] 17 V 15
Rybačij [SU] 8 V 11
Δ Rybačij, poluostrov — [SU] 3 W 1
Rybnik [PL] 16 U 14
Rychnowo [PL] 17 V 12
Rychwał [PL] 16 U 13
Ryd [S] 7 R 10
Ryde [GB] 13 J 13
Rye [DK] 6 P 10
Rye [GB] 13 K 13
Δ Ryfjället [S] 2 R 4
Ryhope [GB] 11 J 11
Ryki [PL] 17 W 13
Rýmařov [CS] 16 T 14
Rymättylä [SF] 9 V 7
Rypin [PL] 16 U 12
Rytinki [SF] 3 W 4
Rzeczenica [PL] 16 T 12
Rzeszów [PL] 17 W 14

S

Sääksjärvi [SF] 9 V 7
≈ Saale [DDR] 15 Q 14
Saalfeld/Saale [DDR] 15 Q 14
Saanen [CH] 20 N 16
Saarbrücken [D] 15 N 15
Saarburg [D] 15 N 14
Δ Saaremaa [SU] 8 V 9
Saarenkylä [SF] 3 V 3
Saarenpää [SF] 2 T 2
Saarijärvi [SF] 9 W 6
Saarikoski [SF] 2 T 2
Δ Saariselkä [SF] 3 V 2
Saarivaara [SF] 3 X 4
Saarlouis [D] 15 N 15
Šabac [YU] 22 V 17
Sabadell [E] 27 K 19
Săbăoany [RO] 23 Za 15
Δ Sabatini, Monti — [I] 29 R 19
Sabaudia [I] 29 R 20
Sabile [SU] 8 V 9
Sabiñánigo [E] 26 H 19
Δ Sabini, Monti — [I] 29 R 19
Sabla [BG] 23 Zb 17
Sables-d'Olonne, les — [F] 18 H 16
Sablé-sur-Sarthe [F] 19 J 15
Saboia [P] 25 A 21
≈ Sábor, Rio — [P] 25 C 19
Sabres [F] 18 H 18
Sabugal [P] 25 C 19
Săcel [RO] 17 Y 15
Săcele [RO] 23 Z 16
Δ Sachsen [DDR] 16 R 14
Sachsenburg [A] 21 R 16
Sacile [I] 21 R 17
Säckingen [D] 20 O 16
Sacu [RO] 22 X 17
Sádaba [E] 26 G 19
Sadala [SU] 9 X 8
≈ Sado, Rio — [P] 25 A 20
≈ Sado, Rio — [P] 25 A 21
Sadova [RO] 22 Y 18
Sädvaluspen [S] 2 S 4
Sæbø [N] 4 O 6
Sæby [DK] 6 P 10
Saelices [E] 26 F 20
Šafárikovo [CS] 17 V 15
Säffle [S] 6 Q 8
Saffron Walden [GB] 13 K 13
≈ Sagany, ozero — [SU] 23 Zc 16
Sagan = Żagań [PL] 16 S 13
Sagard [DDR] 7 R 11
Sågen [S] 5 R 8
≈ Sagfjord [N] 2 R 3
Sagone [F] 28 O 19
≈ Sagone, Golfe de — [F] 28 O 19
Δ Sagra, La — [E] 26 F 21
Sagres [P] 25 A 21
Sagunto [E] 26 H 20
Sagu = Sauvo [SF] 9 V 7
Sahagún [E] 24 E 18
Šahy [CS] 17 V 15
Saillans [F] 19 M 18
≈ Saimaa [SF] 9 X 6
Saint-Affrique [F] 19 K 18
Saint-Agrève [F] 19 L 17
Saint-Aignan [F] 19 K 16
Saint Albans [GB] 13 J 13
Saint-Amand-les-Eaux [F] 14 L 14
Saint-Amand-Mont-Rond [F] 19 K 16
Saint-André-de-Cubzac [F] 18 H 17
Saint Andrews [GB] 11 J 10
Saint-Angel [F] 19 K 17
Saint-Antonin [F] 19 K 18
Saint-Aubin-du-Cormier [F] 13 H 15
Saint-Aulaye [F] 19 J 17
Saint Austell [GB] 12 F 13
Saint-Avold [F] 15 N 15
Δ Saint-Barhélemy, Pic de — [F] 19 J 19
Saint-Béat [F] 19 J 19
Saint-Benoît-du-Sault [F] 19 K 16
Saint-Benoit-en-Woëvre [F] 15 N 15
Saint-Bertrand-de-Comminges [F] 19 H 18
Saint Boswells [GB] 11 J 10
Saint-Brévin-les-Pins [F] 18 G 16
Saint-Brieuc [F] 12 G 15
Saint-Calais [F] 19 J 15
Saint-Céré [F] 19 K 17
Saint-Chamond [F] 19 L 17
Saint-Chély-d'Apcher [F] 19 L 17
Saint-Chinian [F] 19 K 18
Saint-Cirq-Lapopie [F] 19 K 18
Saint-Claude [F] 19 M 17
Saint Clears [GB] 12 G 13
Saint-Cyprien [F] 19 K 19
Saint David's [GB] 12 F 12
Δ Saint David's Head [GB] 12 F 12
Saint-Dié [F] 20 N 15
Saint-Dizier [F] 14 M 15
Sainte-Adresse [F] 14 J 14
Δ Sainte Baume, Chaîne de la — [F] 19 M 18
Sainte-Énimie [F] 19 L 18
Sainte-Foy-la-Grande [F] 19 J 17
Sainte-Gauburge-Sainte-Colombe [F] 14 J 15
Sainte-Hélène [F] 18 H 17
Sainte-Hermine [F] 18 H 16
Sainte-Éloy-les-Mines [F] 19 K 17
Sainte-Maure-de-Touraine [F] 19 J 16
Sainte-Maxime [F] 20 N 19
Sainte-Menehould [F] 14 M 15
Saint-Émilion [F] 18 H 17
Saintes [F] 18 H 17
Sainte-Savine [F] 19 L 15
Sainte-Sévère-sur-Indre [F] 19 K 16
Saintes-Maries-de-la-Mer [F] 19 L 18
Saint-Étienne [F] 19 L 17
Saint-Florent [F] 28 P 19
≈ Saint-Florent, Golfe de — [F] 28 O 19
Saint-Florentin [F] 19 L 15
Saint-Florent-sur-Cher [F] 19 K 16
Saint-Flour [F] 19 L 17
Saint-Gaultier [F] 19 K 16
≈ Saint George's Channel 12 F 12
Saint-Georges-d'Oléron [F] 18 H 16
Saint-Germain-du-Plain [F] 19 M 16
Saint-Germain-en-Laye [F] 14 K 15
Saint-Gervais-d'Auvergne [F] 19 K 17
Saint-Gervais-les-Bains [F] 20 N 17
Saint-Gilles [F] 19 L 18
Saint-Girons [F] 19 J 19
Saint-Gorgon-Main [F] 20 N 16
Δ Saint Govan's Head [GB] 12 G 13
Saint Helens [GB] 11 H 12
Saint Helier [GB] 13 H 14
Saint-Hilaire-du-Harcouët [F] 13 H 15
Saint-Hippolyte [F] 20 N 16
Saint-Hippolyte-du-Fort [F] 19 L 18
Saint Ives [GB] 12 F 13
Saint-Jean-d'Angély [F] 18 H 17
Saint-Jean-de-Bournay [F] 19 M 17
Saint-Jean-de-Luz [F] 18 G 18
Saint-Jean-de-Maurienne [F] 18 G 16
Saint-Jean-de-Maurienne [F] 20 N 17
Saint-Jean-Pied-de-Port [F] 18 G 18
Saint-Junien [F] 19 J 17
Saint Just [GB] 12 F 14
Saint-Just-en-Chaussée [F] 14 L 14
Saint-Just-Saint-Rambert [F] 19 L 17
Saint-Laurent-de-la-Salanque [F] 19 K 19
Saint-Laurent-en-Grandvaux [F] 19 M 16
Saint-Laurent-et-Benon [F] 18 H 17
Saint-Léonard-de-Noblat [F] 19 K 17
Saint-Lizier [F] 19 J 18
Saint-Lô [F] 13 H 14
Saint-Loup-sur-Semouse [F] 20 N 16
Saint-Maixent-l'École [F] 19 J 16
Saint-Malo [F] 13 H 15
≈ Saint Malo, Golfe de — [F] 12 G 15
Saint-Mamet-la-Salvetat [F] 19 K 17
Saint Marcel [F] 19 M 16
Saint-Marcellin [F] 19 M 17
Saint Margaret's Hope [GB] 11 J 8
Saint-Martin-de-Londres [F] 19 L 18
Saint-Martin-de-Ré [F] 18 H 16
Saint-Martin-du-Var [F] 20 N 18
Saint-Martin-Vésubie [F] 20 N 18
Saint-Martory [F] 19 J 18
Saint-Mathieu [F] 19 J 17
Δ Saint-Mathieu, Pointe — [F] 12 F 15
Saint-Maximin-la-Sainte-Baume [F] 19 M 18
Saint-Méen-le Grand [F] 13 H 15
Δ Saint Michael's Mount [GB] 12 F 14
Δ Saint Michel, Mont — [F] 12 G 15
Saint-Michel-de-Maurienne [F] 20 N 17
Saint-Michel-en-l'Herm [F] 18 H 16
Saint-Mihiel [F] 14 M 15
Saint-Nazaire [F] 18 G 15
Saint-Nectaire [F] 19 L 17
Saint Neots [GB] 13 J 13
Saint-Omer [F] 14 L 14
Δ Saintonge [F] 18 H 17
Saint-Palais [F] 18 H 18
Saint-Pardoux-la-Raivière [F] 19 J 17
Saint-Paul-de-Fenouillet [F] 19 K 19
Saint-Paulien [F] 19 L 17
Saint-Paul-lès-Dax [F] 18 H 18
Saint-Peray [F] 19 M 17
Saint Peter Port [GB] 13 H 14
Saint-Pierre-d'Oléron [F] 18 H 16
Saint-Pierre-Église [F] 13 H 14
Saint-Pierre-le-Moutier [F] 19 L 16
Saint-Pierre-sur-Dives [F] 14 J 15
Saint-Pol-de-Léon [F] 12 G 15
Saint-Pol-sur-Ternoise [F] 14 L 14
Saint-Pons [F] 19 K 18
Saint-Pourcain-sur-Sioule [F] 19 L 17
Saint-Quay-Portrieux [F] 12 G 15
Saint-Quentin [F] 14 L 14
Saint-Raphaël [F] 20 N 18
Saint-Renan [F] 12 F 15
Δ Saint Rigaud, Mont — [F] 19 M 17
Saint-Sauveur-en-Puisaye [F] 19 L 16
Saint-Sauveur-sur-Tinée [F] 20 N 18
Saint-Savin [F] 19 J 16
Saint-Sernin-sur-Rance [F] 19 K 18
Saint-Sever [F] 18 H 18
Saint-Sulpice [F] 19 J 18
Saint-Symphorien [F] 18 H 17
Saint-Thégonnec [F] 12 G 15
Saint-Tropez [F] 20 N 19
Saint-Ursanne [CH] 20 N 16
Saint-Vaast-la-Hougue [F] 13 H 14
Saint-Valéry-en-Caux [F] 14 K 14
Saint-Vallier [F] 19 M 17
Saint-Venant [F] 14 L 14
Saint-Vincent-de-Tyrosse [F] 18 G 18
Saint-Vit [F] 19 M 16
Saint-Vith [B] 15 N 14
Saint-Vivien-de-Médoc [F] 18 H 17
Saint-Yrieix-la-Perche [F] 19 J 17
Saivomuotka [S] 3 U 2
Sájószentpéter [H] 17 W 15
Šakiai [SU] 8 W 11
Sakskøbing [DK] 6 Q 11
Säkylä [SF] 9 V 7
Sala [S] 5 S 8
≈ Salace [SU] 8 W 9
Sala Consilina [I] 29 T 20
Salahmi [SF] 9 W 5
Salamajärvi [SF] 9 V 5
Salamanca [E] 25 D 19
Δ Salamis [GR] 31 Z 21
Salån [S] 5 R 8
Salantai [SU] 8 V 10
Salaora [GR] 30 X 21
Salardú [E] 27 J 19
Salas [E] 24 D 18
Salaš [YU] 22 X 18
Salas de los Infantes [E] 26 F 19
Salbris [F] 19 K 16
Salces [F] 19 K 19
Saldaña [E] 24 E 18
Saldus [SU] 8 V 10
Salemi [I] 29 R 22
Salen [S] 5 R 7
Salen [Island of Mull] [GB] 10 G 9
Salen [Schottland] [GB] 10 G 9
Δ Salentina [I] 29 U 20
Salernes [F] 20 N 18
Salerno [I] 29 S 20
≈ Salerno, Golfo di — [I] 29 S 20
Salers [F] 19 K 17
Salford [GB] 13 H 12
Salgótarján [H] 22 V 15
Salies-de-Béarn [F] 18 H 18
Salignac [F] 19 J 17
Δ Salina, Isola — [I] 29 T 21
Δ Salinas, Cabo de — [E] 27 K 21
Salisbury [GB] 13 H 13
Sălişte [RO] 22 Y 16
Salla [SF] 3 W 3
Sallanches [F] 20 N 17
Sallent de Gállego [E] 18 H 19
Salles [F] 18 H 17
Δ Salling [DK] 6 O 10
Salmerón [E] 26 F 20
Saló [I] 20 P 17
Salo [SF] 9 V 7
Salobreña [E] 26 E 22
Salon-de-Provence [F] 19 M 18
Salonta [RO] 22 W 16
≈ Salor, Río — [E] 25 C 20
Salorno [I] 20 Q 17
Δ Salou, Cabo de — [E] 27 J 20
Δ Salpausselkä [SF] 9 W 7
≈ Salso [I] 29 S 22
Saltash [GB] 12 G 13
Saltdal [N] 2 R 3
Δ Saltdal [N] 2 R 3
Δ Salten [N] 2 R 3
≈ Saltfjord [N] 2 R 3
Saltfleet [GB] 13 K 12
Δ Saltholm [DK] 7 R 11
≈ Salto, Lago del — [I] 29 R 19
Saltsjöbaden [S] 7 T 8
≈ Saltstraumen [N] 2 R 3
Saltvik [SF] 9 U 7
Salurn = Salorno [I] 20 Q 17
Saluzzo [I] 20 N 18
Salva [RO] 22 Y 15
Salvaterra de Magos [P] 25 A 20
Salvatierra [E] 18 G 18
Salvetat-sur-Agout, la — [F] 19 K 18
Salviac [F] 19 J 17
Salzburg [A] 21 R 16
Δ Salzburg [A] 21 R 16
Salzgitter [D] 15 P 13
Δ Salzkammergut [A] 21 R 16
Salzwedel [DDR] 15 Q 12
Samatan [F] 19 J 18
Sambor [SU] 17 X 14
≈ Sambre [B] 14 M 14
Samedan [CH] 20 P 16
Samer [F] 14 K 14
Sami [GR] 30 X 21
Samnanger [N] 4 N 8
Samobor [YU] 21 T 17
Samokov [BG] 22 Y 19
Samora Correia [P] 25 A 20
Samorín [CS] 21 U 15
Samos [GR] 31 Zb 21
Δ Samos [GR] 31 Zc 21
Samothraki [GR] 31 Za 20
Δ Samothraki [GR] 31 Za 20
Sampeyre [I] 20 N 18
Δ Samsø [DK] 6 P 10
≈ Samsø Bælt [DK] 6 P 10
≈ San [PL] 17 W 14
≈ Sana [YU] 21 U 18
San Antonio Abad [E] 27 J 21
San Bartolomeo in Galdo [I] 29 T 20
San Benedetto del Tronto [I] 21 S 19
San Benedetto Po [I] 20 Q 17
Δ San Bernardino, Passo di — [CH] 20 P 17
San Bonifácio [I] 20 Q 17
San Carlos [E] 27 J 21
San Cataldo [I] 29 S 22
San Cataldo [I] 30 V 20
San Celoni [E] 27 K 19
Sancerre [F] 19 L 16
San Clemente [E] 26 F 21
Sancoins [F] 19 L 16
San Cristóbal de Cea [E] 24 C 18
Δ San Croce, Capo — [I] 29 T 22
Sancti-Spíritus [E] 25 C 19
Δ Sancy, Puy de — [F] 19 K 17
Sand [N] 6 N 8
Sandane [N] 4 N 7
Sandanski [BG] 30 Y 19
Sandared [S] 6 Q 9
Δ Sanday [GB] 11 J 8
≈ Sanddøla [N] 4 Q 5
Sande [N] 6 P 8
Sandefjord [N] 6 P 8
Sandeid [N] 6 N 8
Δ Sandhammaren [S] 7 R 11
Δ Sandhornøy [N] 2 R 3
Sandmo [N] 4 Q 5
Sandnäset [S] 5 S 6
Sandnes [N] 6 N 8
Sandnessjøen [N] 2 Q 4
Δ Sandö [SF] 9 V 7
Sandomierz [PL] 17 W 13
Δ San Domino, Isola — [I] 29 T 19
Δ Sandön [S] 3 U 4
San Donà di Piave [I] 21 R 17
Δ Sandøy [N] 2 S 1
Δ Sandøy [N] 4 N 7
Sandringham Hall [GB] 13 K 12
Sandset [N] 2 R 2
Sandsjö [S] 5 R 7
Δ Sandskär [S] 3 U 4
Sandslån [S] 5 S 6
Δ Sandsøy [N] 2 R 2
Sandstad [N] 4 P 6
Sandvika [N] 4 P 8
Sandvika [N] 4 Q 5
Sandviken [S] 5 S 7
Sandwich [GB] 13 K 13
Δ Sandžak [YU] 22 V 18
San Esteban de Gormaz [E] 26 F 19
San Esteban del Valle [E] 25 D 20
San Felice sul Panaro [I] 20 Q 18
San Feliú de Guixols [E] 27 K 19
San Fernando [E] 25 C 22
Δ Sånfjället [S] 5 R 6
San Francisco Javier [E] 27 J 21
San Fratello [I] 29 T 22
Sangerhausen [DDR] 15 Q 13
San Gimignano [I] 20 Q 18
Sanginkylä [SF] 3 W 4
San Giórgio di Nogaro [I] 21 R 17
San Giovanni di Sinis [I] 28 O 21
San Giovanni in Fiore [I] 29 U 21
San Giovanni in Persiceto [I] 20 Q 18
San Giovanni Rotondo [I] 29 T 19
Sangis [S] 3 U 4
≈ Sangis älv [S] 3 U 4
≈ Sangro [I] 29 S 19
Δ Sanguinaires, Îles — [F] 28 O 19
San Ignacio de Loyola [E] 18 G 18
San Ildefonso [E] 26 E 19
San Javier [E] 26 G 22
≈ San Jorge, Golfo de — [E] 27 J 20
San Juan Bautista [E] 27 J 21
San Juan de Alicante [E] 26 G 21
San Juan de la Peña [E] 26 H 19
San Juan de las Abadesas [E] 27 K 19
San Juan del Puerto [E] 25 B 21
Δ San Just, Sierra de — [E] 26 G 20
Sankt Anton am Arlberg [A] 20 P 16
Sankt Gallen [CH] 20 P 16
Sankt Gilgen [A] 21 R 16
Sankt Goarshausen [D] 15 O 14
Δ Sankt Gotthard [CH] 20 O 16
Sankt Johann am Tauern [A] 21 S 16
Sankt Johann im Pongau [A] 21 R 16
Sankt Johann in Tirol [A] 21 R 16
Sankt Leonhard am Forst [A] 21 S 15
Sankt Michael in Obersteiermark [A] 21 S 16
Sankt Michel = Mikkeli [SF] 9 X 6
Sankt Moritz [CH] 20 P 17
Sankt Peter-Ording [D] 6 O 11
Sankt Pölten [A] 21 T 15
Sankt Veit an der Glan [A] 21 S 16
Sankt Wolfgang im Salzkammergut [A] 21 R 16
Δ San Lorenzo, Sierra de — [E] 26 F 19
San Lorenzo del Escorial [E] 26 E 20
San Lorenzo del Escorial, Monasterio de — [E] 26 E 20
Sanlúcar de Barrameda [E] 25 C 22
Sanlúcar la Mayor [E] 25 C 21
San Marcello Pistoiese [I] 20 Q 18
San Marco Argentano [I] 29 U 21
San Marino [RSM] 21 R 18
San Martín de Unx [E] 18 G 19
San Martín de Valdeiglesias [E] 26 E 20
San Mateo [E] 26 H 20
San Michele [F] 28 P 19
San Miguel de Salinas [E] 26 G 22
Δ San Millán [E] 26 F 19
San-Nicolao [F] 28 P 19
Sanniki [PL] 17 V 13
Sanok [PL] 17 W 14
Δ San Pedro, Sierra de — [E] 25 C 20
San Pedro del Pinatar [E] 26 G 22
Δ San Pietro, Isola di — [I] 28 O 21
San Pietro Vernótico [I] 30 V 20
Sanquhar [GB] 11 H 10
San Rafael [E] 26 E 20
San Remo [I] 20 O 18
San Roque [E] 25 C 22
San Salvador [E] 27 K 21
San Salvo [I] 29 S 19
San Saturnino [E] 24 C 17
San Sebastián [E] 18 G 18
Sansepolcro [I] 20 Q 18
San Severino Marche [I] 21 R 19
San Sèvero [I] 29 T 19
Sanski Most [YU] 21 T 17
Santa Bárbara [E] 26 H 20
Δ Santa Bárbara [E] 26 E 22
Santa Caterina Villarmosa [I] 29 S 22
Santa Comba [E] 24 B 18
Santa Cruz [P] 25 A 20
Santa Cruz de Moya [E] 26 G 20
Santa Cruz de Mudela [E] 26 E 21
Santa Cruz de Retamar [E] 26 E 20
Santadi [I] 28 O 21
Santa Elena [E] 26 E 21
Santa Eufemia [E] 25 D 21
Santa Eulalia del Río [E] 27 J 21
Santafé [E] 26 E 22
Sant'Ágata di Militello [I] 29 T 22
Santa Luzia [P] 25 A 21
≈ Santa Manza, Golfe de — [F] 28 P 20
Santa Margherita Ligure [I] 20 P 18
≈ Santa Maria, Ría de — [E] 24 C 17
Δ Santa Maria, Cabo de — [P] 25 B 21
Santa María de Huerta [E] 26 F 19
Santa María del Páramo [E] 24 D 18
Δ Santa Maria di Leuca, Capo — [I] 30 V 21
Santa Maria di Pomposa [I] 21 R 18
Santa María la Real de Nieva [E] 26 E 19
Santa Marta [E] 25 C 21
Santander [E] 18 F 18
Sant'Angelo Lodigiano [I] 20 P 17
Sant' Antíoco [I] 28 O 21
Δ Sant' Antíoco, Isola di — [I] 28 O 21
Santañy [E] 27 K 21
Santa Olalla [E] 26 E 20
Santa Olalla del Cala [E] 25 C 21
Santa Pola [E] 26 G 21
Δ Santa Pola, Cabo de — [E] 26 G 21
Sant' Arcángelo [I] 29 U 20
Santarcángelo di Romagna [I] 21 R 18
Santarém [P] 25 B 20
Santas Creus, Monasterio de — [E] 27 J 20
Santas Martas [E] 24 E 18
Santa Teresa di Riva [I] 29 T 22
Santa Teresa Gallura [I] 28 O 20
≈ Sant' Eufemia, Golfo di — [I] 29 T 21
Santhià [I] 20 O 17
Santiago de Compostela [E] 24 B 18
Santiago de la Espada [E] 26 F 21
Santiago do Cacém [P] 25 A 21
Santiago do Escoural [P] 25 B 20
Δ Säntis [CH] 20 P 16
Sant Julià [AND] 27 J 19
Santo Comba Dão [P] 25 B 19
Santo Domingo de la Calzada [E] 18 F 19
Santo Domingo de Silos [E] 26 F 19
Santomera [E] 26 G 21
Δ Santorin = Thira [GR] 31 Zb 22

Sofporog [SU] 3 X 13
Søgne [N] 6 O 9
≈ Sognefjord [N] 4 N 7
≈ Sognesjø [N] 4 N 7
Søholt [N] 4 O 6
Soignies [B] 14 M 14
Soini [SF] 9 V 6
Δ Soisalo [SF] 9 X 5
Soissons [F] 14 L 15
Sokal' [SU] 17 X 13
Söke [TR] 31 Zc 21
Soko Banja [YU] 22 X 18
Sokółka [PL] 8 W 12
Sokolov [CS] 16 R 14
Sokołów Podlaski [PL] 17 W 12
Sokolozero [SU] 3 X 3
Sokoły [PL] 17 W 12
Solana, La — [E] 26 E 21
Δ Sølandsfjell [N] 4 P 8
Solares [E] 18 F 18
Solbad Hall in Tirol [A] 20 Q 16
Solberg [S] 5 S 5
≈ Solbergfjord [N] 2 S 2
Sölden [A] 20 Q 16
Solenzara [F] 28 P 19
Solferino [I] 20 P 17
Δ Solfonn [N] 4 O 8
Solheim [N] 4 N 7
Solheimsvik [N] 6 N 8
Solihull [GB] 13 H 2
Solin [YU] 21 T 18
Solingen [D] 15 N 13
Sollefteå [S] 5 S 6
Sollentuna [S] 5 T 8
Sóller [E] 27 K 21
Søllerød [DK] 6 Q 11
Sollerön [S] 5 R 7
Sollia [N] 4 P 7
Δ Søln [N] 4 Q 7
Δ Sølnkletten [N] 4 P 7
≈ Sølnsjø [N] 4 Q 7
Δ Sologne [F] 19 K 16
Δ Solør [N] 4 Q 7
Solothurn [CH] 20 O 16
Solsona [E] 27 J 19
Solstad [N] 4 Q 5
Solt [H] 22 V 16
Δ Šolta [YU] 21 T 18
Soltau [D] 15 P 12
Sölvesborg [S] 7 R 10
≈ Solway Firth [GB] 11 H 11
Soma [TR] 31 Zc 20
Sombor [YU] 22 V 17
Somero [SF] 9 V 7
≈ Somes [RO] 17 X 15
Δ Somesan, Podisul — [RO] 22 X 16
≈ Somme [F] 14 K 14
Sommelsdijk [NL] 14 M 13
Sommen [S] 7 R 9
≈ Sommen [S] 7 S 9
Sommepy-Tahure [F] 14 M 15
Sömmerda [DDR] 15 Q 13
Sommerset [N] 2 R 3
Sommesous [F] 14 M 15
Sommières [F] 19 L 18
Sømna [N] 4 Q 4
Somogybabod [H] 21 U 16
Somogyszob [H] 21 U 16
Δ Somontano [E] 26 H 19
Δ Somosierra, Puerto de — [E] 26 E 19
Sompolno [PL] 16 U 13
Δ Somport, Puerto de — [E, F] 18 H 19
Son [E] 24 B 18
Son [GR] 23 Za 19
Son [N] 6 P 8
Sønderborg [DK] 6 P 11
Sønder Omme [DK] 6 O 10
Sondershausen [DDR] 15 Q 13
Søndersø [DK] 6 P 11
Søndervig [DK] 6 O 10
Sondrio [I] 20 P 17
Sonkajärvi [SF] 9 W 5
Sonneberg [DDR] 15 Q 14
Sonseca con Casalgordo [E] 26 E 20
Sonthofen [D] 20 P 16
Soorts-Hossegor [F] 18 G 18
Sopoćani [YU] 22 W 18
Sopot [PL] 7 U 11
Sopron [H] 21 T 16
≈ Sor, Rio — [P] 25 B 20
Sora [I] 29 S 20
Sorbas [E] 26 F 22
Δ Sørdalen [N] 2 S 2
Sore [F] 18 H 18
Soresina [I] 20 P 17
≈ Sørfjord [N] 4 N 8
≈ Sørfolda [N] 2 R 3
Sörfors [S] 5 T 5
Sorgono [I] 28 O 21
Sorgues [F] 19 M 18
Soria [E] 26 F 19
Sørkjosen [N] 2 T 1
Sørli [N] 5 R 5
Sorø [DK] 6 Q 11
Δ Soro, Monte — [I] 29 T 22
≈ Sørøsund [N] 2 T 1
Δ Sørøy [N] 2 T 1
Δ Sørøyane [N] 4 N 6
≈ Sorraia, Rio — [P] 25 B 20
Sørreisa [N] 2 S 2
Sorrento [I] 29 S 20
Δ Sorsatunturi [SF] 3 W 2
≈ Sorsavesi [SF] 9 X 6
Sorsele [S] 2 S 4
Sørsjona [N] 2 Q 4
Sort [E] 27 J 19
Sortino [I] 29 T 22
Sortland [N] 2 R 2
Sørvær [N] 2 T 1
Sörvattnet [S] 4 Q 6
Sörve [SU] 8 V 9
Δ Sõrve säär [SU] 8 V 9
Sørvika [N] 4 Q 6
Sörviksnäset [S] 5 S 5
Sösdala [S] 7 R 10
Sosenka [SU] 8 Y 11
Δ Sösjöfjällen [S] 4 Q 5
Sośnice [PL] 16 U 14
Sosnowiec [PL] 16 U 14
Sospel [F] 20 N 18
Šoštanj [YU] 21 S 17
Sotillo de la Adrada [E] 26 E 20
Sotkamo [SF] 9 X 5
Δ Sotra [N] 4 N 8
≈ Sottern [S] 7 S 8
Soual [F] 19 K 18
≈ Soudas, Ormos — [GR] 32 Za 23
Souflion [GR] 31 Za 19
Souillac [F] 19 J 17
Soulac-sur-Mer [F] 18 H 17
Sounion [GR] 31 Za 21
Δ Sounion, Akrotirion — [GR] 31 Za 21
Sourpi [GR] 30 Y 21
Sousel [P] 25 B 20
Soustons [F] 18 G 18
Souterraine, la — [F] 19 K 16
Southam [GB] 13 J 12
Southend on Sea [GB] 13 K 13
Δ Southern Uplands [GB] 11 G 10
Southampton [GB] 13 H 13
South Molton [GB] 12 G 13
Southport [GB] 11 H 11
Δ South Ronaldsey [GB] 11 J 8
South Shields [GB] 11 J 11
Δ South Uist [GB] 10 F 9
Southwold [GB] 13 K 13
Souvigny [F] 19 L 16
Sovajari [SU] 3 W 3
Sovata [RO] 23 Z 16
Soverato [I] 29 U 21
Sovetsk [SU] 8 V 11
Sozopol [BG] 23 Zb 18
Spalato = Split [YU] 21 T 18
Spalding [GB] 13 J 12
Δ Spanda, Akrotirion — [GR] 32 Za 23
Δ Spanish Head [GB] 10 G 11
Spåre [SU] 8 V 9
Sparta = Sparti [GR] 30 Y 22
Δ Spartel, Cap — [MA] 25 C 22
Sparti [GR] 30 Y 22
Δ Spartivento, Capo — [I] 28 O 21
Spasovo [BG] 23 Zb 17
Spean Bridge [GB] 11 H 9
≈ Sperillen [N] 4 P 7
Δ Spessart [D] 15 P 14
Δ Spetse [GR] 31 Z 22
≈ Spey, River — [GB] 11 H 9
Speyer [D] 15 O 15
Spèzia, La — [I] 20 P 18
Spezzano Albanese [I] 29 U 21
Δ Spiekeroog [D] 15 O 12
Spiez [CH] 20 O 16
Δ Spildra [N] 2 T 1
Spileon [GR] 30 X 20
Spilimbergo [I] 21 R 17
Spilion [GR] 32 Za 23
Spilsby [GB] 13 K 12
Spinazzola [I] 29 T 20
Spinus [RO] 22 X 16
Spiralen [N] 4 P 8
Spišská Nová Ves [CS] 17 V 15
Spišské Podhradie [CS] 17 W 15
Spittal an der Drau [A] 21 R 16
Split [YU] 21 T 18
Splügen [CH] 20 P 16
Δ Splügen [CH, I] 20 P 17
Spodsbjerg [DK] 6 Q 11
Spogi [SU] 8 Y 10
Spoleto [I] 29 R 19
Spøttrup [DK] 6 O 10
≈ Spreča [YU] 20 V 18
≈ Spree [DDR] 16 R 13
Spremberg [DDR] 16 S 13
Sprendingen [D] 15 O 14
Spresiano [I] 21 R 17
Δ Spùlico, Capo — [I] 29 U 21
≈ Squillace, Golfo di — [I] 29 U 21
Sraith Salach = Recess [IRL] 10 D 11
Srath an Urláir = Stranorlar [IRL] 10 F 10
Srbica [YU] 22 W 19
Δ Srbija [YU] 22 W 17
Srbobran [YU] 22 V 17
Središte [BG] 23 Zb 17
Δ Sredna gora [BG] 23 Z 18
Sredneje [SU] 17 X 15
Śrem [PL] 16 T 13
Δ Srem [YU] 22 V 17
Sremska Mitrovica [YU] 22 V 17
Sremski Karlovci [YU] 22 W 17
Δ Srnetica [YU] 21 T 18
Srnice [YU] 22 V 17
Δ Srnopas [YU] 21 T 18
Środa Wielkopolski [PL] 16 T 13
Srokowo [PL] 8 V 11
≈ Stabburselv [N] 3 U 1
Δ Stack Skerry [GB] 11 H 8
Stade [D] 15 P 12
Δ Stådjan [S] 4 Q 7
Δ Stadland [N] 4 N 6
Stafford [GB] 13 H 12
Stakčin [CS] 17 W 14
Stallvika [N] 4 Q 5
Stamford [GB] 13 J 12
Stamsund [N] 2 Q 3
Stâncuța [RO] 23 Zb 17
Stange [N] 4 Q 7
Stănilești [RO] 23 Zb 15
Stanke Dimitrov [BG] 22 Y 19
Stanorlar [IRL] 10 F 10
Stanos [GR] 30 X 21
Stans [CH] 20 O 16
Stara L'ubovňa [CS] 17 V 14
Stara Novalja [YU] 21 S 18
Stara Pazova [YU] 22 W 17
Δ Stara Planina [BG] 22 Y 18
Stara Reka [BG] 23 Za 18
Stara Titovka [SU] 3 W 1
Stara Zagora [BG] 23 Za 18
Stargard in Pommern = Stargard Szczeciński [PL] 16 S 12
Stargard Szczeciński [PL] 16 S 12
Stari Bar [YU] 30 V 19
Starigrad [YU] 21 T 18
Stari Grad [YU] 21 T 18
Starnberg [D] 20 Q 16
≈ Starnberger See [D] 20 Q 16
Starogard Gdański [PL] 7 U 12
Starokazačje [SU] 23 Zc 15
Starý Smokovec [CS] 17 V 15
Staszów [PL] 17 W 14
Stathelle [N] 6 P 8
Stavanger [N] 6 N 8
Stavelot [B] 15 N 14
Stavenhagen [DDR] 16 R 12
Staveren [NL] 14 M 12
Δ Stavros [GR] 31 Zb 22
Stavroupolis [GR] 31 Z 19
Stawiszyn [PL] 16 U 13
Steenbergen [NL] 14 M 13
Steenwijk [NL] 15 N 12
Stefan Karadža [BG] 23 Zb 17
Δ Stefleşti [RO] 22 Y 17
Stege [DK] 6 Q 11
Stegeborg [S] 7 S 9
Δ Steiermark [A] 21 S 16
Δ Steigerwald [D] 15 P 15
Steinach [A] 20 Q 16
Steinestø [N] 4 N 7
Δ Steinfeld [A] 21 T 16
Steinfurt [D] 15 O 13
≈ Steinhuder Meer [D] 15 P 13
Steinkjer [N] 4 Q 5
Steinlløysa [N] 4 O 6
Steki [SU] 8 X 9
Δ Stello [F] 28 P 19
Δ Stèlvio, Passo dello — [I] 20 P 16
Stenay [F] 14 M 15
Stendal [DDR] 15 Q 13
Stende [SU] 8 V 9
≈ Stende [SU] 8 V 9
Steneby [S] 6 Q 8
Stensele [S] 5 S 4
Δ Stenshuvud [S] 7 R 11
Stensträsk [S] 2 T 4
Stenudden [S] 2 S 4
Stepojevac [YU] 22 W 17
Šternberg [DDR] 15 Q 12
Šternberk [CS] 16 T 14
Sterzing = Vipiteno [I] 20 Q 16
Stęszew [PL] 16 T 13
≈ Stettiner Haff [DDR, PL] 16 R 12
Stettin = Szczecin [PL] 16 S 12
Δ Stevns [DK] 6 Q 11
Δ Stevns Klint [DK] 6 Q 11
Steyr [A] 21 S 15
Δ Stiavnické pohorie [CS] 16 U 15
Stigamodal [S] 7 R 9
Stigen [S] 6 Q 9
Stigliano [I] 29 U 20
Stiklestad [N] 4 Q 5
Stilis [GR] 30 Y 21
Δ Stilo, Punta — [I] 29 U 21
Štimlje [YU] 22 X 19
Δ Stînişoara, Culmea — [RO] 23 Z 15
Stintino [I] 28 O 20
Ştio [I] 29 T 20
Štip [YU] 30 Y 19
Štipoklasy [CS] 16 S 14
Stirling [GB] 11 H 10
Δ Stjernøy [N] 2 T 1
≈ Stjernsund [N] 2 T 1
Stjørdal [N] 4 P 6
Δ Stjørdal [N] 4 Q 6
≈ Stjørnfjord [N] 4 P 5
Støa [N] 4 Q 7
Stobi [YU] 30 X 19
≈ Stochod [SU] 17 Y 13
Stockbridge [GB] 13 H 13
Stockerau [A] 21 T 15
Stockholm [S] 7 T 8
Stockport [GB] 13 H 12
Stockton-on-Tees [GB] 11 J 11
Stoczek Łukowski [PL] 17 W 13
Stöde [S] 5 S 6
Stoke on Trent [GB] 13 H 12
Stokksund [N] 4 P 5
Stokmarknes [N] 2 R 2
Stolac [YU] 21 U 18
Stolbcy [SU] 8 Y 11
Stolberg/Erzgebirge [DDR] 16 R 14
Stolp = Słupsk [PL] 7 T 11
Stolzenau [D] 15 P 13
Stömsbruk [S] 5 S 7
Ston [YU] 21 U 19
Stone [GB] 13 H 12
Stonehaven [GB] 11 J 9
Stonehenge [GB] 13 H 13
Stonglandet [N] 2 S 2
Stopnica [YU] 233 V 14
≈ Storå [DK] 6 O 10
Δ Stora Askö [S] 7 S 9
≈ Stora Blåsjön [S] 4 R 5
Δ Stora Brändön [S] 3 U 4
≈ Stora Bygdeträsk [S] 5 T 5
≈ Stora Gla [S] 6 Q 8
Storå = Isojoki [SF] 9 U 6
Δ Stora Karlsö [S] 7 T 9
≈ Stora Le [S] 6 Q 8
≈ Stora Lule älv [S] 2 T 3
≈ Stora Lulevatten [S] 2 T 3
Storås [N] 4 P 6
≈ Stora Sjöfallet [S] 2 S 3
≈ Stora Sjöfallets nationalpark [S] 2 S 3
Δ Stord [N] 4 N 8
Stordal [N] 4 O 6
≈ Store Bælt [DK] 6 Q 11
Store Heddinge [DK] 6 Q 11
Stor-Elvdal [N] 4 Q 7
Store Molvik [N] 3 V 1
Støren [N] 4 P 6
≈ Storfjälen [S] 4 Q 7
Storfjord [N] 2 S 2
≈ Storfjord [N] 4 O 6
Storfors [S] 7 R 8
Storforshei [N] 2 R 4
≈ Storfoss [N] 3 U 2
≈ Storglåmvatn [N] 2 R 4
Δ Storhø [N] 4 O 6
Δ Storhøgd [N] 4 Q 7
≈ Storjorm [S] 5 R 5
≈ Storsjø [N] 4 Q 8
Δ Storjungfrun [S] 5 S 7
≈ Stor-Laisan [S] 2 S 4
Storlien [S] 4 Q 6
Stornoway [GB] 10 G 8
Storoddan [N] 4 P 6
≈ Storrensjön [S] 4 Q 5
Δ Storrustefjell [N] 4 P 8
Storsjö [S] 4 Q 6
≈ Storsjø [N] 4 Q 7
≈ Storsjön [S] 5 R 6
≈ Storsjön [S] 5 S 5
Δ Storskär [SF] 5 U 6
Δ Storskavl [N] 4 Q 7
Δ Storsteinfjell [N] 2 S 2
Storsteinnes [N] 2 S 2
Storsund [S] 2 T 4
Δ Stortervo [SF] 9 V 7
Storuman [S] 5 S 4
≈ Storuman [S] 5 S 4
Δ Storvigelen [N] 4 Q 6
Storvik [S] 5 S 7
≈ Storvindeln [S] 2 S 4
Δ Stöttingfjället [S] 5 S 5
Stožer [BG] 23 Zb 17
Strabane [GB] 10 F 10
Stradella [I] 20 P 17
Strakonice [CS] 16 R 15
Stralsund [DDR] 7 R 11
Strand [N] 4 Q 7
Stranda [N] 4 O 6
Strängnäs [S] 7 S 8
Stranraer [GB] 10 G 11
Strasbourg [F] 15 N 15
Strasburg [DDR] 16 R 12
Strašeny [SU] 23 Zb 15
Straßwalchen [A] 21 R 16
Stratford on Avon [GB] 13 H 12
Strathaven [GB] 11 H 10
Δ Strathmore [GB] 11 H 10
Stråtjära [S] 5 S 7
Stratoniki [GR] 31 Z 20
Straubing [D] 16 R 15
Straumen [N] 4 Q 5
≈ Straumsfjorden [N] 2 S 2
Straumsjøen [N] 2 R 2
Straumsnes [N] 2 S 2
Strausberg [DDR] 16 R 13
Δ Straža [YU] 22 X 19
Δ Stražov [CS] 16 U 15
Δ Strážovská hornatina [CS] 16 U 15
Streatley [GB] 13 J 13
≈ Strednji kanal [YU] 21 S 18
Strehaia [RO] 22 Y 17
Strelča [BG] 23 Z 18
Stresa [I] 20 O 17
Stříbro [CS] 16 R 14
Střílky [CS] 16 T 15
Strimasund [S] 2 R 4
≈ Strimon [GR] 31 Z 19
Δ Strofades [GR] 30 X 22
Strofilia [GR] 31 Z 21
Δ Strómboli, Isola — [I] 29 T 21
Stromeferry [GB] 10 G 9
Strömfors [SF] 9 V 7
Strömnäs [S] 5 R 5
Stromness [GB] 11 J 8
Stromstad [S] 6 Q 8
Strömsund [S] 2 S 4
Strömsund [S] 5 R 5
Δ Stronghili [GR] 31 Za 22
Stróngoli [I] 29 U 21
Δ Stronsay [GB] 11 J 8
Stroud [GB] 13 H 13
Struer [DK] 6 O 10
Struga [YU] 30 X 20
Strugi Krasnyje [SU] 8 Y 8
≈ Struma [BG] 30 Y 19
Strumica [YU] 30 Y 19
Strumień [PL] 16 U 14
Stryj [SU] 17 X 14
≈ Stryj [SU] 17 X 14
Stryn [N] 4 O 7
≈ Strynsvatn [N] 4 O 7
Strzegom [PL] 16 T 14
Strzehlin [PL] 16 T 14
Strzelce Krajeńskie [PL] 16 S 12
Strzelce Opolskie [PL] 16 U 14
Strzelno [PL] 16 U 12
Strzyżów [PL] 17 W 14
Stubbekøbing [DK] 6 Q 11
Δ Stubbenkammer [DDR] 7 R 11
Studenica [YU] 22 W 18
Studsviken [S] 5 T 5
Stugun [S] 5 R 6
Stuhlweißenburg = Székesfehérvár [H] 21 U 16
Stuljgiai [SU] 8 W 10
Δ Stuorajavrre [N] 2 T 2
Δ Sturkö [S] 7 S 10
Šturminster [GB] 13 H 13
Šturovo [CS] 21 U 15
Stuttgart [D] 15 P 15
Δ Styrsö [S] 6 Q 9
Δ Suajo, Serra do — [P] 24 B 18
Subata [SU] 8 X 10
Subiaco [I] 29 R 19
Subotica [YU] 22 V 16
Sučeviči [YU] 21 T 18
Sucha Beskidzka [PL] 17 V 14
Suchorze [PL] 7 T 11
Suchowola [PL] 8 W 12
Sućuraj [YU] 21 U 18
Sudbury [GB] 13 K 13
Δ Sudety [CS, PL] 16 S 14
Sueca [E] 26 H 21
Şugag [RO] 22 Y 16
≈ Suhalu [RO] 23 Za 16
≈ Suha reka [BG] 23 Zb 17
Suhl [DDR] 15 P 14
Δ Suido, Sierra del — [E] 24 C 18
Suippes [F] 14 M 15
Sujica [YU] 21 U 18
Sukeva [SF] 9 W 5
Süköśd [H] 22 V 16
Δ Sula Sgeir [GB] 10 G 8
≈ Suldalsvatn [N] 6 O 8
Sulechów [PL] 16 S 13
Sulejów [PL] 17 V 13
Suleskar [N] 6 O 8
Δ Sule Skerry [GB] 11 H 8
Sulina [RO] 23 Zc 16
≈ Sulina, Bratul — [RO] 23 Zc 16
Sulingen [D] 15 O 13
Sulitjelma [N] 2 R 3
Δ Sulitjelma [N] 2 R 3
Sully-sur-Loire [F] 19 K 16
Sulmona [I] 29 S 19
Sulstua [N] 4 Q 5
Sultanhisar [TR] 32 Zd 21
Sulzbach-Rosenberg [D] 15 Q 15
Δ Šumadija [YU] 22 W 17
Sumartin [YU] 21 U 18
Sümeg [H] 21 U 16
Šumen [BG] 23 Za 18
Šumperk [CS] 16 T 14
Sumsa [SF] 3 X 4
Sundbyberg [S] 7 T 8
Sunderland [GB] 11 J 11
Sundre [N] 4 O 7
Sundre [S] 7 T 10
Sunds [DK] 6 P 10
Sundsvall [S] 5 S 6
≈ Sundsvalls bukten [S] 5 S 6
Sunndal [N] 4 N 7
Δ Sunndal [N] 4 P 6
≈ Sunndalsfjord [N] 4 O 6
Sunndalsøra [N] 4 O 6
Sunne [S] 5 R 8
Sunnersta [S] 5 T 8
Δ Sunnfjord [N] 4 N 7
Δ Sunnhordland [N] 4 N 8
Δ Sunnmøre [N] 4 O 6
≈ Sunnylvsfjord [N] 4 O 6
Suntazi [SU] 8 X 9
Δ Suokon mäki [SF] 9 V 6
Suolovuobme [N] 3 U 1
Δ Suomenlinna [SF] 9 W 7
≈ Suomujoki [SF] 3 V 2
Suomussalmi [SF] 3 X 4
Suonenjoki [SF] 9 W 6
≈ Suonne [SF] 9 W 6
≈ Suonteenselkä [SF] 9 W 6
Δ Suorsapää [SF] 3 V 2
Suorva [S] 2 S 3
Supetar [YU] 21 U 18
Supuru-de-Jos [RO] 22 X 15
Şupuru-de-Sus [RO] 22 X 15
Šurany [CS] 21 U 15
Surduc [RO] 22 X 15
Δ Surduc, Pasul — [RO] 22 Y 17
Surdulica [YU] 22 X 18
Surgères [F] 18 H 16
Suria [E] 27 J 19
Δ Sur-Sari [SU] 9 X 7
Susa [I] 20 N 17
Δ Sušac [YU] 21 U 19
Δ Susak [YU] 21 S 18
Δ Susendal [N] 2 R 4
Sušice [CS] 16 R 15
≈ Susita [RO] 23 Za 16
Δ Suspiro del Moro, Puerto de — [E] 26 E 22
Δ Sussex [GB] 13 J 13
Susurluk [TR] 31 Zc 20
Susz [PL] 16 U 12
Şuţeşti [RO] 23 Za 16
Δ S'utk'a [BG] 23 Z 19
Sutme [S] 5 R 5
Süttö [H] 21 U 15
Suure-Jaani [SU] 8 W 8
≈ Suur väin [SU] 8 V 8
Δ Suva gora [YU] 30 X 19
Δ Suva planina [YU] 22 X 18
Suva Reka [YU] 22 X 19
≈ Suvasvesi [SF] 9 X 5
Suwałki [PL] 8 W 11
Svabensverk [S] 5 S 7
Δ Sværholthalvøya [N] 3 U 1
≈ Svågan [S] 5 S 6
Sval'ava [SU] 17 X 15
Svaneke [DK] 7 S 11
Svanesund [S] 6 Q 9
Δ Svanhågna [S] 4 Q 6
Svansele [S] 5 T 4
Svanstein [S] 3 U 3
Svanvik [N] 3 W 1
Svappavaara [S] 2 T 3
Svärdsjä [S] 5 S 7
Svartå [S] 7 R 8
Δ Svartisen [N] 2 R 4
Svartnäs [S] 5 S 7
Svartnes [N] 3 W 1
Svätý Beňadik [CS] 16 U 15
Δ Svealand [S] 4 Q 8
Svedasai [SU] 8 X 10
Sveg [S] 5 R 6
Sveingardsbotn [N] 4 O 7
Svelgen [N] 4 N 7
Şvenarum [S] 7 R 9
Švenčionys [SU] 8 X 10
Svendborg [DK] 6 P 11
Svenljunga [S] 7 R 9
Svenningdal [N] 2 Q 4
Δ Svenningdal [N] 4 Q 4
Svensby [N] 2 S 2
Svensbyn [S] 2 T 4
Δ Svenska Högarna [S] 5 U 8
Şveredžius [SU] 8 W 11
Şvėkšna [SU] 8 V 10
Δ Svetac [YU] 21 T 19
Sveti Djordje [YU] 22 X 19
Sveti Jovan Bigorski [YU] 30 X 19
Sveti Nikola [YU] 30 V 19
Δ Sveti Nikola [YU] 22 X 18
Sveti Nikole [YU] 30 X 19
Sveti Stefan [YU] 30 V 19
Svetlogorsk [SU] 8 U 11
Svetogorsk [SU] 9 X 6
Svetozarevo [YU] 22 X 18
Svidník [CS] 17 W 14
Δ Svilaja [YU] 21 T 18
Svilengrad [BG] 23 Za 19
Svir' [SU] 9 Y 10
Svištov [BG] 23 Z 18
≈ Svitava [CS] 16 T 14
Svitavy [CS] 16 T 14
Svodje [YU] 22 X 18
Svoge [BG] 22 Y 18
Svolvær [N] 2 R 3
Svor [CS] 16 S 14
Svrljig [YU] 22 X 19
Δ Svrljiške planine [YU] 22 X 18
Svulryra [N] 4 Q 8
Swaffham [GB] 13 K 12
Swansea [GB] 12 G 13
Swarzędz [PL] 16 T 13
Świdnica [PL] 16 T 14
Świdwin [PL] 16 S 12
Świebodzice [PL] 16 T 14
Świebodzin [PL] 16 S 13
Świecie [PL] 16 U 12
Δ Świetej Anny, Góra — [PL] 16 U 14
Δ Świętokrzyskie, Góra — [PL] 17 V 13
Swindon [GB] 13 H 13
Swinoujście [PL] 16 R 12
Sycow [PL] 16 T 13
Sydänmaa [SF] 9 V 6
Sydänmaa [SF] 9 W 5
Syke [D] 15 O 12
Sykkylven [N] 4 O 6
Δ Sylarna [S] 4 Q 6
Δ Sylt [D] 6 O 11
Sylte [N] 4 O 6
Syltefjord [N] 3 W 1
≈ Syltefjord [N] 3 W 1
Δ Synhovd [N] 4 O 8
Δ Synnfjell [N] 4 P 7
Sysmä [SF] 9 W 6
Δ Sysmond's Yat [GB] 13 H 13
≈ Syväri [SF] 9 X 5
Syvde [N] 4 N 6
≈ Syv Søstre [N] 4 O 6
Syysjärvi [SF] 3 V 1
Szabadka = Subotica [YU] 22 V 16
Szadek [PL] 16 U 13
Szalánta [H] 21 U 17
Szamotuły [PL] 16 T 12
Szápár [H] 21 U 16
Szarvas [H] 22 W 16
Δ Szátmarisikság [H] 17 X 15
Szczecin [PL] 16 S 12
Szczecinek [PL] 16 T 12
Szczekociny [PL] 17 V 14
Szczerców [PL] 16 U 13
Szczucin [PL] 17 W 14
Szczuczyn [PL] 8 W 12
Szczytno [PL] 17 V 12
Szécsény [H] 22 V 15
Szederkeny [H] 22 V 17
Szeged [H] 22 W 16
Szeghalom [H] 22 W 16
Δ Szekelyföld [RO] 23 Z 16
Székesfehérvár [H] 21 U 16
Szekszárd [H] 22 V 16
Szendrö [H] 17 W 15
Szentendre [H] 22 V 16
Szentes [H] 22 W 16
Δ Szeskie Wzgorza [PL] 8 W 11
Szigetvár [H] 21 U 17
Szin [H] 17 W 15
Szlichtyngowa [PL] 16 T 13
Szolnok [H] 22 V 16
Szombathely [H] 21 T 16
Szprotawa [PL] 16 S 13
Sztum [PL] 7 U 12
Sztutowo [PL] 7 U 11
Szubin [PL] 16 T 12

T

Taavetti [SF] 9 X 7
Tábara [E] 25 D 19
Tabarka [TN] 28 O 22
Δ Taberg [S] 7 R 9
Tabernas [E] 26 F 22
Taboada [E] 24 C 18
Tábor [CS] 16 S 15
T'ačev [SU] 17 X 15
Tachov [CS] 16 R 14
Tadcaster [GB] 11 J 11
Tafalla [E] 18 G 19
Taga [RO] 22 Y 16
Tagliacozzo [I] 29 R 19
Δ Tagomago, Isla de — [E] 27 J 21
Δ Tahkuna [SU] 8 V 8
Δ Taibilla, Sierra de — [E] 26 F 21
Δ Taïghetos Oros [GR] 30 Y 22
Δ Taillefer [F] 19 M 17
Tain [GB] 11 H 9
Tain-l'Hermitage [F] 19 M 17
Taipale [SF] 9 X 5
Taipaleenkylä [SF] 3 V 3
Tairbeart = Tarbert [IRL] 12 D 12
Taivalkoski [SF] 3 W 4
Δ Taivaskero [SF] 3 U 2
Taivassalo [SF] 9 U 7
Tajbola [SU] 3 X 2
≈ Tajo, Río — [E] 26 E 20
≈ Tajuña, Río — [E] 26 F 20
≈ Tåkern [S] 7 R 9
Talavera de la Reina [E] 25 D 20
Talavera la Real [E] 25 C 20
Δ Talayón [E] 26 F 22
Δ Talayuelo [E] 26 F 20
Talence [F] 18 H 17
Talgarth [GB] 13 H 13
Δ Talkkunapää [SF, SU] 3 W 2
Tallinn [SU] 9 W 8
Talmăciu [RO] 22 Y 16
Talmont-Saint-Hilaire [F] 18 H 16
Talpaki [SU] 8 V 11
Δ Tal'šem-Tundra [SU] 3 X 2
Talsi [SU] 8 V 9
≈ Tam, River — [GB] 12 G 13
Tamames [E] 25 D 19
Tamarite de Litera [E] 26 H 19
Tamasi [H] 21 U 16
≈ Tambre, Río — [E] 24 B 18
≈ Tâmega, Rio — [P] 25 C 19
Δ Taminaschlucht [CH] 20 P 16
≈ Tamiš [YU] 22 W 17
Tammerfors = Tampere [SF] 9 V 6
Tammisaari = Ekenäs [SF] 9 V 7
≈ Tämnaren [S] 5 S 8
Tamnay-en-Bazois [F] 19 L 16
Tampere [SF] 9 V 6
Tamsweg [A] 21 R 16
Tamworth [GB] 13 J 12
≈ Tana [N] 3 V 1
Tana bru [N] 3 V 1
≈ Tanafjord [N] 3 V 1
Δ Tanahorn [N] 3 V 1
Δ Tanargue [F] 19 L 18
≈ Tànaro [I] 20 O 18
Tăndărei [RO] 23 Zb 17
Tandsjöborg [S] 5 R 7
Tangen [N] 4 Q 7
Tangermünde [DDR] 15 Q 13
Tanger = Tanja [MA] 25 C 22
Tanhua [SF] 3 V 2
Tanja [MA] 25 C 22
Tanján [H] 21 U 16
Tännäs [S] 4 Q 6
≈ Tännforsen [S] 4 Q 6
Tannière, la — [F] 13 H 15
≈ Tannis Bugt [DK] 6 P 9
Tanum [S] 6 Q 9
Tanvald [CS] 16 S 14
Taormina [I] 29 T 22
Tapa [SU] 9 X 8
Tapia de Casariego [E] 24 D 17
Tápiósüly [H] 22 V 16
Tápiószele [H] 22 V 16
Tapolca [H] 21 U 16
≈ Tara [YU] 22 V 18
Taraklija [SU] 23 Zb 15
Taraklija [SU] 23 Zb 16
Δ Taran, mys — [SU] 7 U 11
Tarancón [E] 26 F 20
Taranto [I] 29 U 20
≈ Táranto, Golfo di — [I] 29 U 20
Tarare [F] 19 L 17
Tarascon [F] 19 L 18
≈ Taravo [F] 28 O 19
Tarazona de Aragon [E] 26 G 19

Tarazona de la Mancha [E] 26 F 21
Tarbert [GB] 10 G 10
Tarbert [GB] 10 G 9
Tarbert [IRL] 12 D 12
Tarbes [F] 18 H 18
△ Tarcău, Munţii — [RO] 23 Z 16
Tarcento [I] 21 R 17
Tarčin [YU] 22 V 18
△ Ţarcu, Munţii — [RO] 22 X 17
Tărendö [S] 3 U 3
Tarifa [E] 25 C 22
Tarm [DK] 6 O 10
≈ Tarn 19 K 18
△ Tarn, Gorges du — [F] 19 L 18
Tärnaby [S] 2 R 4
Tärnet [N] 3 W 1
Tarnobrzeg [PL] 17 W 14
Tarnogród [PL] 17 X 14
Tarnów [PL] 17 W 14
△ Taro [I] 20 P 18
Tarouca [P] 25 C 19
Tarragona [E] 27 J 20
△ Tarrakoski [S] 2 T 2
Tarrasa [E] 27 J 19
Tàrrega [E] 27 J 19
Tartas [F] 18 H 18
Tărtăşeşti [RO] 23 Z 17
Tartu [SU] 8 X 8
Tarutino [SU] 23 Zb 16
Tarvisio [I] 21 R 16
△ Tåsinge [DK] 6 P 11
Tåsjö [S] 5 R 5
≈ Tåsjön [S] 5 R 5
Taşnad [RO] 22 X 15
Tata [H] 21 U 16
Tatabánya [H] 21 U 16
Tătărăştii de Sus [RO] 23 Z 17
Tatarbunary [SU] 23 Zc 16
△ Tatry [CS, PL] 17 V 14
Tau [N] 6 N 8
Tauberbischofsheim [D] 15 P 14
△ Tauerntunnel [A] 21 R 16
Taunton [GB] 12 G 13
△ Taunus [D] 15 O 14
Tauragė [SU] 8 V 10
Taurianova [I] 29 U 22
≈ Taurion [F] 19 K 17
△ Tausa [N] 2 R 3
Tauste [E] 26 G 19
Tavajärvi [SU] 3 X 3
△ Tavastehus = Hämeenlinna [SF] 9 W 7
△ Tavastland = Häme [SF] 9 V 7
△ Tavätno [S] 2 T 2
Tavira [E] 25 B 21
Tavistock [GB] 12 G 13
Tavola [SF] 9 V 7
△ Tavolara, Isola — [I] 28 P 20
△ Tavoliere [I] 28 T 19
Täxan [S] 5 S 5
≈ Tay, Firth of — [GB] 11 H 10
Tazoghrane [TN] 28 Q 22
≈ Tea, Río — [E] 24 B 18
Teaca [RO] 22 Y 16
Teampall Mór = Templemore [IRL] 10 E 12
Tébourba [TN] 28 P 22
≈ Tech [F] 19 K 19
Tecuci [RO] 23 Za 16
Teeriranta [SF] 3 X 4
≈ Tees, River — [GB] 11 J 11
Tegelträsk [S] 5 S 5
Tegernsee [D] 20 Q 16
Tehumardi [SU] 8 V 9
Teignmouth [GB] 12 G 13
Teil, le — [F] 19 M 18
Teisko [SF] 9 W 7
Teius [RO] 22 Y 16
△ Teixeira, Sierra de — [E] 25 D 22
Tejo, Rio [P] 25 A 20
Teke burnu [TR] 31 Zb 20
△ Teke burnu [TR] 31 Zb 21
Telciu [RO] 22 Y 15
Teleč [CS] 16 S 15
Telechany [SU] 17 Y 12
△ Telemark [N] 6 O 8
△ Teleno, El — [E] 24 D 18
Telese [I] 29 S 20
Telford [GB] 13 H 12
Telfs [A] 20 Q 16
Telgte [D] 15 O 13
Telirdağ [TR] 31 Zb 19
Telšiai [SU] 8 V 10
△ Teltow [DDR] 16 R 13
Tembleque [E] 26 E 20
Templemore [IRL] 10 E 12
Templin [DDR] 16 R 12
Tenala [SF] 9 W 7
△ Tenaron, Akrotirion — [GR] 31 Z 22
Tenay [F] 19 M 17
Tenby [GB] 12 G 13
Tence [F] 19 L 17
△ Tenda, Colle di — [F. I.] 20 N 18
Tende [F] 20 N 18
Tenhola = Tenala [SF] 9 W 7
Tennevoll [N] 2 S 2
≈ Tenniojoki [SU] 3 W 3
≈ Tenniojoki [SF] 3 W 3
≈ Tenojoki [SF] 3 V 1
Tenterden [GB] 13 K 13
Tepasto [SF] 3 U 2
Tepelenë [AL] 30 W 20
Teplice [CS] 16 R 14
≈ Ter, Río [E] 27 K 19
△ Tera, Rio — [P] 25 B 20
Téramo [I] 29 S 19
Teregova [RO] 22 X 17
Terespol [PL] 17 X 12
Terezín [CS] 16 R 14
≈ Terges, Rio — [P] 25 B 21
Tergnier [F] 14 L 14
Termas de Monfortino [P] 25 C 20
Términi Imerese [I] 29 S 22
≈ Términi Imerese, Golfo di — [I] 29 S 22
△ Termillo, Monte — [I] 29 R 19
Térmoli [I] 29 T 19
Terneuzen [NL] 14 M 13
Terni [I] 29 R 19

Terracina [I] 19 R 20
Terrasson-laVilledieu [F] 19 J 17
△ Terschelling [NL] 14 M 12
Tertenia [I] 28 P 21
Teruel [E] 26 G 20
Tervel [BG] 23 Zb 17
Tervete [SU] 8 W 10
Tervola [SF] 3 V 4
Tešanj [YU] 21 U 18
Teskraia [TN] 28 P 22
Teslić [YU] 21 U 18
≈ Teslui [RO] 23 Z 17
Tesside [GB] 11 J 11
Teste, la — [F] 18 H 17
Teterow [DDR] 15 Q 12
Teteven [BG] 23 Z 18
Tetovo [YU] 30 X 19
△ Teugmo [SF] 9 U 5
Teulada [I] 28 O 21
△ Teulada, Capo — [I] 28 O 21
Teurajärvi [S] 3 U 3
△ Teutoburger Wald [D] 15 O 13
Teuva [SF] 9 U 6
≈ Tèvere [I] 29 R 19
△ Texel [NL] 14 M 12
Thalwil [CH] 20 O 16
Thame [GB] 13 J 13
≈ Thames, Mouth of the — [GB] 13 K 13
≈ Thames, River — [GB] 13 H 13
Thassos [GR] 31 Z 19
△ Thassos [GR] 31 Za 19
△ Thau, Bassin de — [F] 19 L 18
≈ Themse = River Thames [GB] 13 H 13
Thenon [F] 19 J 17
Theologos [GR] 31 Za 20
Thera [GR] 31 Zb 22
≈ Thermaikos Kolpos [GR] 30 Y 20
Thermon [GR] 30 Y 21
△ Thermopile [GR] 30 Y 21
△ Thessalia [GR] 30 Y 21
Thessaloniki [GR] 30 Y 20
≈ Thessalonikis, Kolpos — [GR] 30 Y 20
Thetford [GB] 13 K 12
Theth [AL] 30 W 19
Thienen [B] 14 M 14
Thiermais [E] 18 G 19
Thierp [S] 5 T 7
Thiers [F] 19 L 17
Thillot, le — [F] 20 N 16
Thionville [F] 14 N 15
Thira [GR] 31 Zb 22
△ Thira [GR] 31 Zb 22
△ Thirassia [GR] 31 Zb 22
Thirsk [GB] 11 J 11
Thisted [DK] 6 O 10
Thive [GR] 31 Z 21
Thiviers [F] 19 J 17
Thizy [F] 19 L 17
Thônes [F] 20 N 17
Thonon-les-Bains [F] 20 N 17
Thorame-Haute [F] 20 N 18
Thornbury [GB] 13 H 13
Thorne [GB] 11 J 12
Thornhill [GB] 11 H 10
Thouars [F] 19 J 16
≈ Thrakikon Pelagos [GR] 31 Z 20
Thun [CH] 20 O 16
≈ Thuner See [CH] 20 O 16
≈ Thuringen [DDR] 15 P 14
△ Thüringer Wald [DDR] 15 P 14
△ Thurn, Paß — [A] 21 R 16
Thurso [GB] 11 J 8
Thury-Harcourt [F] 14 J 15
Thusis [CH] 20 P 16
△ Ţibana [RO] 23 Za 15
Tibava [CS] 17 W 15
△ Tibles, Munţii — [RO] 17 Y 15
Tibro [S] 7 R 7
Tichtozero [SU] 3 X 3
△ Ticino [CH] 20 O 17
△ Ticino [I] 20 O 17
△ Ticino [CH] 20 O 17
Tidaholm [S] 7 R 9
Tiebas-Muruarte de Reta [E] 18 G 19
Tiefencastel [CH] 20 P 16
Tiel [NL] 14 M 13
Tiemblo, El — [E] 26 E 20
△ Tierra del Pan [E] 24 D 18
△ Tierra del Vino [E] 25 D 20
△ Tiétar, Río — [E] 25 D 20
Tigu Bujor [RO] 23 Zb 16
Tihany [H] 21 U 16
△ Tikšozero [SU] 3 X 3
Tilburg [NL] 14 M 13
Tilbury [GB] 13 K 13
△ Tilos [GR] 31 Zc 22
Tilsit = Sovetsk [SU] 8 V 11
Timbakion [GR] 32 Zb 23
Timiş [RO] 22 X 18
Timişoara [RO] 22 W 17
Timmendorfer Strand [D] 15 P 12
≈ Timok [YU] 22 X 18
Timrå [S] 5 S 6
Tinca [RO] 22 X 16
Tindari [I] 29 T 22
≈ Tinée [F] 20 N 18
Tineo [E] 24 D 18
Tinglev [DK] 6 P 11
Tingsryd [S] 7 S 10
Tingstäde [S] 7 T 8
Tingvoll [N] 4 O 6
△ Tinnsjø [N] 4 P 8
Tinos [GR] 31 Za 21
△ Tinos [GR] 31 Za 21
△ Tiñosa, La — [E] 25 D 22
△ Tiñoso, Cabo — [E] 26 G 22
Tinţăreni [RO] 22 Y 17
Tinténiac [F] 13 H 15
Tintern Abbey [GB] 13 H 13
Tiobraid Árann = Tipperary [IRL] 12 E 12
Tipperary [IRL] 12 E 12
Tirana = Tiranë [AL] 30 W 19
Tiranë [AL] 30 W 19
Tirano [I] 20 P 17
Tiraspol [SU] 23 Zb 15
△ Tireia [GR] 10 G 9
≈ Tiree Passage [GB] 10 F 9
Trgoviște [YU] 23 Z 17
Tírgu Cărbuneşti [RO] 22 Y 17

Tîrgu Frumos [RO] 23 Za 15
Tîrgu Jiu [RO] 22 Y 17
Tîrgu Lăpuş [RO] 22 Y 15
Tîrgu Mures [RO] 22 Y 16
Tîrgu Neamt [RO] 23 Z 15
Tîrgu Ocna [RO] 23 Za 15
Tîrgu Secuiesc [RO] 23 Z 16
Tirins [RO] 31 Z 21
Tîrkšliai [SU] 8 V 10
Tirnaveni [RO] 22 Y 16
Tirnavos [GR] 30 Y 20
△ Tirol [YU] 21 R 16
Tirrènia [I] 20 P 18
Tirstrup-Fuglslev [DK] 6 P 10
≈ Tisa [SU] 17 X 15
≈ Tisa [YU] 22 W 17
Tismana [RO] 22 Y 17
≈ Tisnaren [S] 7 S 8
≈ Tistelsöfjärden [S] 3 U 4
≈ Tisza [H] 22 W 16
Tiszaczege [H] 22 V 16
Tiszafölvár [H] 22 V 16
Tiszaföred [H] 22 V 16
Tiszakécske [H] 22 V 16
Tiszavasvári [H] 17 W 15
Titaguas [E] 26 G 20
Titel [YU] 22 W 17
Titisee-Neustadt [D] 20 O 16
Titograd [YU] 22 W 19
Titova Korenica [YU] 21 T 18
≈ Titovka [SU] 3 W 1
Titovo Uzice [YU] 22 W 18
Titov Veles [YU] 30 X 19
△ Titov vrh [YU] 30 X 19
Titran [N] 4 O 5
Tittelsnes [N] 4 N 8
Tivat [YU] 30 V 19
Tiverton [GB] 12 G 13
Tivoli [I] 29 R 19
Tjällmo [S] 7 S 9
Tjämotis [S] 2 S 3
Tjautjas [S] 2 T 3
≈ Tjeggelvas [S] 2 S 4
Tjeldnes [N] 2 R 2
△ Tjeldøy [N] 2 R 2
Tjöck [SF] 9 U 6
Tjolöholm [S] 6 Q 9
△ Tjörn [S] 6 Q 9
Tjøtta [N] 2 Q 4
△ Tjurkö [S] 7 S 10
Tkon [YU] 21 T 18
Tobar an Choire = Tubbercurry [IRL] 10 E 11
Tobarra [E] 26 F 21
Tobermory [GB] 10 F 9
Toblach = Dobbiaco [I] 20 Q 16
≈ Toce [I] 20 O 17
Tocha [P] 25 B 19
Töcksfors [S] 6 Q 8
Todi [I] 29 R 19
Todireşti [RO] 23 Za 15
Todtnau [D] 20 O 16
Toftlund [DK] 6 P 11
△ Tohnin mäki [SF] 9 V 6
Toholampi [SF] 9 V 5
Toijala [SF] 9 V 7
≈ Toisvesi [SF] 9 V 6
Toivola [SF] 9 V 7
Tokaj [H] 17 W 15
≈ Toke [N] 6 P 8
Tobuhin [BG] 23 Zb 17
Tolastadh [GB] 11 G 8
Tolbuhin [BG] 23 Zb 17
Toledo [E] 26 E 20
△ Toledo, Montes de — [E] 25 D 20
Tolentino [I] 21 R 19
Tolga [N] 4 Q 6
Tolkmicko [PL] 7 U 11
Tollånes [N] 2 R 3
Tolmezzo [I] 21 R 17
Tolmin [YU] 21 R 17
Tolna [F] 22 V 17
Tolosa [E] 18 G 18
△ Tolox, Sierra de — [E] 25 D 22
≈ Tolvand, ozero — [SU] 3 X 3
Tolve [I] 29 T 20
Tomar [P] 25 B 20
Tomaševka [SU] 17 X 13
Tomaszów Lubelski [PL] 17 X 13
Tomaszów Mazowiecki [PL] 17 V 13
Tomelilla [S] 7 R 11
Tomelloso [E] 26 F 21
Tomintoul [GB] 11 H 9
△ Tømma [N] 2 Q 4
△ Tomtabacken [S] 7 R 9
Tôň [CS] 21 U 15
Tone [I] 27 K 19
Tonbridge [GB] 13 J 13
Tønder [DK] 6 O 11
Tongeren [B] 14 M 14
Tongue [GB] 11 H 8
Tonnay-Charente [F] 18 H 17
Tonneins [F] 19 J 18
Tonnerre [F] 19 L 16
Tønsberg [N] 6 P 8
Tonstad [N] 6 N 9
Toomebridge [GB] 10 F 11
Topliţa [RO] 22 Y 16
Topoj-Qerim [AL] 30 W 20
Topola [YU] 22 W 18
Topola [S] 6 Q 9
Topolčani [CS] 16 U 15
Topolovgrad [BG] 23 Za 18
Topolovgrad [BG] 23 Zb 17
Topraisar [RO] 23 Zb 17
Topusko [YU] 21 T 17
Torà [E] 27 J 19
△ Torbalı [TR] 31 Zc 21
Torbay [GB] 12 G 13
Törberget [N] 4 Q 7
Tordesillas [E] 26 E 19
Töre [S] 3 U 4
Toreboda [S] 7 R 9
Torekov [S] 6 Q 10
Toreno [E] 24 D 18
Torestorp [S] 6 Q 9
Torgau [DDR] 16 R 13
Torgelow [DDR] 16 R 12
△ Torghatten [N] 2 Q 4
Torhamn [S] 7 S 10
Torhop [N] 3 V 1
Torì [SU] 8 W 8
Torigini-Sur-Vire [F] 13 H 15
Torija [E] 26 F 20

△ Toriñana, Cabo — [E] 24 B 18
Torino [I] 20 O 17
≈ Tormes, Río — [E] 25 D 19
≈ Torne älv [S] 2 T 3
≈ Torne älv [S] 3 U 3
≈ Torne Lappark [S] 2 T 2
△ Torneträsk [S] 2 S 2
Tornio [SF] 3 V 4
≈ Torniojoki [SF] 3 U 3
Toro [I] 25 D 19
△ Toro [E] 27 L 21
△ Toró [S] 7 T 8
Toroiaga [RO] 17 Y 15
Törökszentmiklós [H] 22 W 16
Torpa [S] 7 R 9
Torpshammar [S] 5 S 6
Torquemada [E] 26 E 19
Torralba de Calatrava [E] 26 E 21
Torrão [S] 25 B 21
Torre Annunziata [I] 29 S 20
Torreblanca [E] 26 H 20
Torrecilla en Cameros [E] 26 F 19
Torre del Greco [I] 29 S 20
Torredembarra [E] 27 J 20
Torre de Moncorvo [P] 25 C 19
Torredonjimeno [E] 26 E 21
Torrejoncillo [E] 25 C 20
Torrejón de Ardoz [E] 26 E 20
Torrelaguna [E] 26 E 20
Torrelavega [E] 18 F 18
Torrelodones [E] 26 E 20
△ Torre Maggiore, Monte — [I] 29 R 19
Torremegia [E] 25 C 20
Torremolinos [E] 25 D 22
Torrente [E] 26 G 21
Torre Pèllice [I] 20 N 18
Torreperogil [E] 26 F 21
Torres Novas [P] 25 B 20
Torres Vedras [P] 25 A 20
Torrevieja [E] 26 G 22
Torríglia [I] 20 O 18
Torrijos [E] 26 E 20
Tørring [N] 4 P 6
Torroella de Montgrí [E] 27 K 19
≈ Torröjen [S] 4 Q 5
Torsåker [S] 5 S 6
Torsborg [S] 5 R 6
Torsby [S] 4 Q 8
Torsfjärden [S] 5 R 5
△ Torsön [S] 7 R 9
Torsvåg [N] 2 S 1
Tortolì [I] 28 P 21
Tortona [I] 20 O 18
Tortorici [I] 29 T 22
Tortosa [E] 26 H 20
△ Tortosa, Cabo de — [E] 27 J 20
Toruń [PL] 16 U 12
Torup [S] 7 R 9
△ Tôrva [SU] 8 X 9
Torvsjö [S] 5 S 5
≈ Tory Island [IRL] 10 F 10
≈ Torysa [CS] 17 W 14
Torzym [PL] 16 S 13
≈ Tosas, Puerto de — [E] 27 K 19
Tosbotn [N] 4 Q 4
△ Toscana [I] 20 P 18
△ Toscano, Appennino — [I] 20 P 18
Tosen [N] 4 Q 4
≈ Tosenfjord [N] 4 Q 5
Tossa [I] 27 K 19
≈ Totak [N] 6 O 8
Totana [E] 26 F 22
Tôtes [F] 14 K 14
Tótkomlós [H] 22 W 16
Tøtlandsvik [N] 6 N 8
Totnes [GB] 12 G 13
Toucy [F] 19 L 16
Toul [F] 15 N 15
Toulon [F] 19 M 19
△ Toulousain [F] 19 J 18
Toulouse [F] 19 J 18
Touquet-Paris-Plage, le — [F] 14 K 14
△ Touraine [F] 19 J 16
Tour-du-Pin, la — [F] 19 M 17
Tournai [B] 14 L 14
Tournon [F] 19 M 17
Tournus [F] 19 M 16
Tours [F] 19 J 16
Tourves [F] 19 M 18
Toury [F] 14 K 15
Tovarnik [YU] 22 V 17
Towcester [GB] 13 J 13
Töysä [SF] 9 V 6
≈ Tozal de Guara [E] 26 H 19
Tozew [RO] 22 V 16
Trabazos [E] 25 D 19
≈ Trænfjord [N] 2 Q 4
△ Trafalgar, Cabo de — [E] 25 C 22
△ Tráighlí = Tralee [IRL] 12 D 12
Traiguera [E] 26 H 20
Traisen [A] 21 T 15
Traiskirchen [A] 21 T 15
Trakai [SU] 8 X 11
△ Trakijska nizina [BG] 23 Z 19
Trakošćan [YU] 21 T 17
△ Trakya [BG, GR, TR] 31 Za 19
Tralee [IRL] 12 D 12
≈ Tralee Bay [IRL] 12 D 12
Trần [BG] 22 Y 18
Tranås [S] 7 S 9
Tranche, la — [F] 18 H 16
≈ Tranco, Pantano del — [E] 26 F 21
Tranemo [S] 7 R 9
Trångsviken [S] 5 R 6
Trani [I] 29 U 20
△ Transilvania [RO] 22 X 16
△ Transilvaniei, Cîmpia — [RO] 22 Y 16
△ Transilvaniei, Podişul — [RO] 22 Y 16
Trápani [I] 29 R 22
Tráryd [S] 7 R 10
△ Trascău, Munţii — [RO] 22 Y 16
≈ Trasimeno, Lago — [I] 29 R 19
△ Trás-os-Montes e Alto Douro [P] 25 C 19
Traun [A] 21 S 15
Traunstein [D] 21 R 16
Tråvad [S] 7 R 9
Travemünde [D] 15 Q 12
Travers [F] 20 N 16
Tr'avna [BG] 23 Za 18
Travnik [YU] 21 U 18
Trbovlje [YU] 21 S 17

Trebič [CS] 16 T 15
Trebinje [YU] 22 V 19
Trebisacce [I] 29 U 21
Treblinka [PL] 17 W 12
Trebnje [YU] 21 S 17
Třeboň [CS] 16 S 15
Trecate [I] 20 O 17
Tredegar [GB] 13 H 13
Tregaron [GB] 12 G 12
△ Trégastel [F] 13 G 15
△ Trégorrois [F] 12 G 15
Tréguier [F] 12 G 15
Trehörningsjö [S] 5 T 5
Treignac [F] 19 K 17
Trekljano [BG] 22 Y 19
Trelleborg [S] 7 R 11
≈ Tremadoc Bay [GB] 12 G 12
Tremblade, la — [F] 18 H 17
△ Trèmiti, Ìsole — [I] 29 T 19
Tremp [E] 27 J 19
Trenčianske Teplice [CS] 16 U 15
△ Trenčín [CS] 16 U 15
△ Trent, River — [GB] 13 J 12
Trento [I] 20 Q 17
Trepča [YU] 22 X 18
≈ Treska [YU] 30 X 19
Trespaderne [E] 18 F 18
△ Tresta [YU] 22 X 18
Trets [F] 19 M 18
Tretten [N] 4 P 7
Treuenbrietzen [DDR] 16 R 13
Treungen [N] 6 O 8
Trevi [F] 19 M 18
Trèvi [I] 29 R 19
Treviglio [I] 20 P 17
Treviso [I] 21 R 17
Trévoux [F] 19 M 17
Trgovište [YU] 23 Y 19
Trhové Sviny [CS] 16 S 15
Triana [E] 28 Q 19
≈ Tria Nissia [GR] 31 Zc 22
△ Tribeč [CS] 16 U 15
Tribsees [DDR] 7 R 12
Tricárico [I] 29 T 20
Tricase [I] 29 U 21
≈ Trichonis, Limni — [GR] 30 Y 21
Trie [F] 19 J 18
Trieben [A] 21 S 16
Trier [D] 15 N 14
Trieste [I] 21 R 17
≈ Trieste, Golfo di — 21 R 17
△ Triglav [YU] 21 R 17
Trikala [GR] 30 Y 20
Trikerion [GR] 31 Z 21
Trimouille, la — [F] 19 J 16
Trinità di Dèlia [I] 29 R 22
Trinité-Porhoët, la — [F] 12 G 15
Trino [I] 20 O 17
Trípolis [GR] 30 Y 22
Trivento [I] 29 S 19
Trnava [CS] 16 U 15
Tródje [S] 5 S 7
Trofors [N] 2 Q 4
Trogir [YU] 21 T 18
△ Troglav [YU] 21 T 18
Tröia [I] 29 T 20
Troina [I] 29 T 22
≈ Trois Cornes [F] 19 K 16
△ Trois Seigneurs, Pic des — [F] 19 J 19
Troizkoje [SU] 23 Zc 15
Trojan [BG] 23 Z 18
△ Trojanski prohod [BG] 23 Z 18
Troja = Truva [TR] 31 Zb 20
Trollhättan [S] 6 Q 9
△ Trollheimen [N] 4 P 6
△ Trolltinder [N] 4 O 6
△ Tromsdalstind [N] 2 S 2
Tromsø [N] 2 S 2
△ Tron [N] 4 P 6
Tronche, la — [F] 19 M 17
≈ Trondheimsfjord [N] 4 P 6
≈ Trondheimsleden [N] 4 O 6
Trones [N] 4 Q 5
△ Tronto [I] 21 R 19
Tropea [I] 29 T 21
Tropojë [AL] 30 W 19
Trosa [S] 7 T 8
Trowbridge [GB] 13 H 13
Troyes [F] 14 L 15
Trpanj [YU] 21 U 19
Trstenik [YU] 22 W 18
Trstín [CS] 16 U 15
Trubia las Caldas [E] 24 D 18
Trügi [SU] 8 V 8
Trujillo [E] 25 D 20
Truskava [SU] 8 W 10
Trutnov [CS] 16 T 14
Truva [TR] 31 Zb 20
≈ Truyère [F] 19 K 17
△ Trysilelv [N] 4 Q 7
△ Trysilfjell [N] 4 Q 7
Tryškiai [SU] 8 W 10
Trzcianka [PL] 16 T 12
Trzciel [PL] 16 S 13
Trzebiatów [PL] 7 S 12
Trzebnica [PL] 16 T 13
△ Tsăktso [S] 2 T 2
Tsangarada [GR] 31 Z 20
≈ Tsovietonen [S] 3 V 3
Tuaim = Tuam [IRL] 10 E 11
Tuam [IRL] 10 E 11
Tubbercurry [IRL] 10 E 11
Tubilla del Agua [E] 18 F 18
Tübingen [D] 15 O 15
≈ Tude, Rochers de la — [F] 19 L 18
Tudela [E] 26 G 19
Tudela del Duero [E] 26 E 19
△ Tudia, Sierra de — [E] 25 C 21
Tudu [SU] 9 X 8
≈ Tuela, Rio — [P] 24 C 19
Tufjord [N] 3 U 1
Tuft [N] 6 P 8
≈ Tukka = Tjöck [SU] 9 U 6
Tükums [S] 8 W 9
Tulach Mhór = Tullamore [IRL] 10 F 11

Tulach Ua bhFeidhlimidh = Tullow [IRL] 12 F 12
Tulare [YU] 22 X 18
Tulcea [RO] 23 Zb 16
Tulghes [RO] 23 Z 15
Tullamore [IRL] 10 F 11
Tulle [F] 19 K 17
Tulleng [N] 2 S 2
Tullgarn [S] 7 T 8
Tullins [F] 19 M 17
Tulln [A] 21 T 15
Tullow [IRL] 12 F 12
≈ Tuloma [SU] 3 X 1
Tulppio [SF] 3 W 2
Tumba [S] 7 T 8
△ Tumča [SU] 3 W 2
Tuna-Hästberg [S] 5 R 8
△ Tunnevik [N] 4 O 8
Tunis [TN] 28 P 22
≈ Tunis, Golfe de — [TN] 28 P 23
Tunnsjø [N] 4 Q 5
≈ Tunnsjøen [N] 4 Q 5
Tuntsa [SF] 3 W 2
Tuohikotti [SF] 9 X 7
Tuolluvaara [S] 2 T 3
Tupicyno [SU] 8 Y 8
≈ Turawskie, Jezioro — [PL] 16 U 14
△ Turbacz [PL] 17 V 14
△ Turbino, Pico — [E] 24 E 18
Turda [RO] 22 Y 16
Turec [SU] 8 Y 11
Turégano [E] 26 E 19
Turek [PL] 16 U 13
Turenne [F] 19 K 17
Turgutlu [TR] 31 Zc 21
Túri [SU] 8 W 8
≈ Turia, Río — [E] 26 G 20
Turis [E] 26 G 21
△ Turismaa [SF] 9 W 7
Türje [H] 21 U 16
Turka [SU] 17 X 14
Türkismühle [D] 15 N 15
Turku [SF] 9 V 7
Turlava [SU] 8 V 10
Turmantas [SU] 8 Y 10
Turnhout [N] 14 M 13
Turnov [CS] 16 S 14
Turnu Măgurele [RO] 23 Z 18
△ Turnu Roşu, Pasul — [RO] 22 Y 16
△ Turopolje [YU] 21 T 17
Turriff [GB] 11 J 9
Tursi [I] 29 U 20
△ Turtojva, gora — [SU] 3 X 3
Turtola [SF] 3 V 4
Turzno [PL] 16 U 12
Turzovka [CS] 16 U 14
Tusby = Tuusula [SF] 9 W 7
△ Tustna [N] 4 O 6
Tutin [YU] 22 W 18
Tutrakan [BG] 23 Za 17
Tuttlingen [D] 20 O 16
Tuusniemi [SF] 9 X 5
Tuusula [SF] 9 W 7
Tuxford [GB] 13 J 12
Tüy [E] 24 B 18
Tuzla [RO] 23 Zb 17
Tuzla [YU] 22 V 18
Tuzly [SU] 23 Zc 16
Tvärälund [S] 5 T 5
Tväräträsk [S] 5 S 4
△ Tvårdica [BG] 23 Za 18
△ Tvårdiški prohod [BG] 23 Za 18
Tvedestrand [N] 6 P 9
Tvrdošín [CS] 17 V 14
Twardogóra [PL] 16 T 13
≈ Tweed, River — [GB] 11 H 10
Twimberg [A] 21 S 16
△ Ty [DK] 6 O 10
Tyborøn [DK] 6 O 10
Tychy [PL] 16 U 14
Tydal [N] 4 Q 6
Tyfors [S] 5 R 8
Tyin [N] 4 O 7
≈ Tyin [N] 4 O 7
Tylawa [PL] 17 W 14
Tyldal [N] 4 P 6
Tylösand [S] 6 Q 10
Tymbark [PL] 17 V 14
Tyndrum [GB] 11 H 10
Tynemouth [GB] 11 J 11
Tyngsjö [S] 5 R 8
Tynkä [SF] 9 V 5
Tyn nad Vltavou [CS] 16 S 15
Tynset [N] 4 P 6
Tyrjärvi [SF] 3 W 4
△ Tyrävaara [SF] 3 W 4
△ Tyrifjord [N] 4 P 8
Tyrnävä [SF] 3 V 4
△ Tysfjord [N] 2 R 3
△ Tysnesøy [N] 4 N 8
Tysse [N] 4 N 8
Tyssedal [N] 4 O 8
△ Tyssestrenge [N] 4 O 8
Tywyn [GB] 12 G 12

U

Uachtar Ard = Oughterard [IRL] 10 E 11
Ub [YU] 22 W 18
Úbeda [E] 26 E 21
Überlingen [D] 20 P 16
△ Ubiña, Peña — [E] 24 D 18
△ Uckermark [DDR] 16 R 12
Uckfield [GB] 13 J 13
Udbina [YU] 21 T 18
Uddeholm [S] 5 R 8
Uddevalla [S] 6 Q 9
≈ Uddjaur [S] 2 S 4
Udine [I] 21 R 17
Udovo [YU] 30 Y 19
△ Udvoj [BG] 23 Za 18
≈ Uecker [DDR] 16 R 12
Ueckermünde [DDR] 16 R 12
Uelzen [D] 15 P 12
Uffenheim [D] 15 P 15
Ug [SU] 17 X 14
Ugäle [SU] 8 V 9
Ugeny [SU] 23 Za 15
Ugljan [E] 26 E 22
Ugine [F] 20 N 17
△ Ugljan [YU] 21 S 18

herské Hradiště [CS] 16 U 15
herský Brod [CS] 16 U 15
ig [GB] 10 G 9
ithuizen [N] 15 N 12
jście [PL] 16 T 12
kmerge [SU] 8 X 10
Ukrainskaja SSR [SU] 17 Y 13
cani [RO] 23 Z 16
ćinj [YU] 30 W 19
leåborg = Oulu [SF] 3 V 4
lefoss [N] 6 P 8
lfborg [DK] 6 O 10
libice [CS] 16 S 14
ljanovo [SU] 8 V 11
ljma [YU] 22 W 17
≈ Ulla, Río — [E] 24 C 18
llånger [S] 5 T 6
llapool [GB] 11 H 9
llared [S] 6 Q 10
llatti [S] 2 T 3
llava [SF] 9 V 5
lldecona [E] 26 H 20
llfors [S] 5 S 8
≈ Ullsfjord [N] 2 S 2
≈ Ullvettern [S] 7 R 8
lm [D] 20 P 15
lmen [D] 15 N 14
log [YU] 22 V 18
Δ Uløy [N] 2 T 1
lricehamn [S] 7 R 9
lsberg [N] 4 P 6
lsteinvik [N] 4 N 6
Δ Ulster [GB, IRL] 10 F 10
≈ Ulster Canal [IRL] 10 F 11
lsvåg [N] 2 R 3
≈ Ulvå [N] 4 Q 7
lvik [N] 4 O 7
Δ Ulvoarna [S] 5 T 6
mag [YU] 21 R 17
mbertide [I] 21 R 19
Δ Umbria [I] 20 Q 19
Δ Umbro-Marchigiano, Appennino — [I] 21 R 18
mbukta [N] 2 R 4
meå [S] 5 T 5
≈ Ume älv [S] 5 T 5
mfors [S] 2 R 4
mka [YU] 22 W 17
Δ Ummanz [DDR] 7 R 11
mnäs [S] 2 R 4
murbey [TR] 31 Zb 20
murga [SU] 8 W 9
≈ Una [YU] 21 T 17
naja [SF] 9 U 7
nari [SF] 3 V 3
≈ Unarijärvi [SF] 3 V 3
≈ Unden [S] 7 R 9
ndenäs [S] 7 R 9
ndersåker [S] 4 Q 6
ndersvik [S] 5 S 7
Δ Undva neem [SU] 8 V 8
nichowo [PL] 7 T 11
ničov [CS] 16 T 14
niejów [PL] 16 U 13
Δ Unije [YU] 21 S 18
nión, La — [E] 26 G 22
nirea [RO] 22 Y 17
nirea [RO] 23 Zb 17
Δ Universales, Montes — [E] 26 G 20
≈ Unnukka [SF] 9 X 6
nquera [E] 24 E 18
≈ Unstrut [DDR] 15 P 14
Δ Unterfranken [D] 15 P 14
pesgrīva [SU] 8 W 9
ppingham [GB] 13 J 12
Δ Uppland [S] 5 S 8
ppsala [S] 5 T 8
≈ Ura [SU] 3 X 1
ra-Guba [SU] 3 X 1
ras [I] 28 O 21
rbània [I] 21 R 18
rbino [I] 21 R 18
Δ Urbión, Sierra de — [E] 26 F 19
rçay [F] 19 K 16
Δ Urddevarre [N] 2 T 2
Δ Uredahkefjället [S] 5 R 5
Δ Urgel, Llanos de — [E] 26 H 19
rjala [SF] 9 V 7
rk [NL] 15 N 12
rla [TR] 31 Zb 21
rlingford [IRL] 12 E 12
rnes [N] 4 O 7
rošević [YU] 22 X 19
≈ Ursfjord [N] 4 Q 4
rshult [S] 7 S 10
Δ Ursu [RO] 22 Y 17
rsus [PL] 17 V 13
rziceni [RO] 23 Za 17
sagre [E] 25 C 21
sče [YU] 22 W 18
Δ Usedom [DDR] 16 R 12
singen [D] 15 O 14
skedal [N] 4 N 8
sküdar [TR] 23 Zc 19
≈ Usmas ezers [SU] 8 V 9
ssel [F] 19 K 17
st'čorna [SU] 17 Y 15
ster [CH] 20 O 16
≈ Ustevatn [N] 4 O 8
stikolina [YU] 22 V 18
stí nad Labem [CS] 16 R 14
stí nad Orlicí [CS] 16 T 14
stjoki [SF] 3 V 1
stka [PL] 7 T 11
stronie Morskie [PL] 7 S 11
strzyki Dolne [PL] 17 X 14
strzyki Gorne [PL] 17 X 14
tajärvi [SF] 3 W 4
tåker [N] 4 N 8
tansjö [S] 5 S 6
tena [SU] 8 X 10
tiel [E] 26 G 20
Δ Utlängen [S] 7 S 10
Δ Utö [S] 7 T 8
trecht [NL] 14 M 13
trera [E] 25 C 22
Δ Utrera, Peña — [E] 25 C 21
trillas [E] 26 G 20
≈ Utroja [SU] 8 Y 9
ttoxeter [GB] 13 H 12
tvik [N] 4 O 7
tvorda [N] 4 P 5
ulu [SU] 8 W 8
urainen [SF] 9 W 6
usikaarlepyy = Nykarleby [SF] 9 U 5
usikaupunki [SF] 9 U 7
Δ Uusimaa [SF] 9 W 7
Uutela [SF] 3 V 2
Uvdal [N] 4 O 8
Užava [SU] 8 V 9
Uzerche [F] 19 K 17
Uzès [F] 19 L 18
Užgorod [SU] 17 X 15
Δ Uzlomac [YU] 21 U 17
Uzunköprü [TR] 31 Zb 19
Užventis [SU] 8 W 10

V

Vääksy [SF] 9 W 7
Vaala [SF] 9 W 4
Vaalajärvi [SF] 3 V 3
Vaalimaa [SF] 9 X 7
≈ Väänajõgi [SU] 9 W 8
Vaaraslahti [SF] 9 W 5
Vaasa [SF] 9 U 6
Vabalninkas [SU] 8 X 10
Vác [H] 22 V 15
≈ Vaccarès, Étang de — [F] 19 L 18
Vacha [DDR] 15 P 14
Δ Väddö [S] 5 T 8
Vadheim [N] 4 N 7
Vadna [H] 17 W 15
Vado Ligure [I] 20 O 18
≈ Vadozero [SU] 3 X 2
Vadsø [N] 3 W 1
Vadstena [S] 7 R 9
Vaduz [FL] 20 P 16
Δ Værøy [N] 2 Q 3
Δ Værøy [N] 4 N 7
Vågåmo [N] 4 P 7
≈ Vågåvatn [N] 4 O 7
Vaggeryd [S] 7 R 9
≈ Vaggetemjavrre [N] 3 W 1
Vagnhärad [S] 7 T 8
≈ Vågsfjord [N] 2 R 2
Vägsjöfors [S] 4 Q 8
≈ Váh [CS] 21 U 15
Vähäkyrö [SF] 9 U 6
Vaiges [F] 14 J 15
Väike Marja [SU] 9 X 8
Vailly-sur-Sauldre [F] 19 K 16
Vaison-la-Romaine [F] 19 M 18
Vaiste [SU] 8 W 8
Vajdaguba [SU] 3 W 1
Vakarel [BG] 22 Y 18
Vålådalen [S] 4 Q 6
Δ Valaisannes, Alpes — [CH] 20 N 17
Δ Valamarës, Mali i — [AL] 30 W 20
Valašské Meziříčí [CS] 16 U 14
Δ Valaxa [GR] 31 Za 21
Valdagno [I] 20 Q 17
≈ Valdavia, Río — [E] 24 E 18
Δ Valdavia, Valle de — [E] 24 E 18
Valdealgorfa [E] 26 H 20
Δ Valdecebollas [E] 24 E 18
Valdemarsvik [S] 7 S 9
Δ Val Dèmone [I] 29 S 22
Valdepeñas [E] 26 E 21
≈ Valderaduey, Río — [E] 25 D 19
Val-d'Isère [F] 20 N 17
Valdobbiadene [I] 20 Q 17
Δ Valdosa [E] 26 F 19
Δ Valdres [N] 4 P 7
Våle [S] 5 R 6
Valea-lui-Mihai [RO] 22 X 15
Valea Mărului [RO] 23 Za 16
Vålebru [N] 4 P 7
Valença [P] 24 B 18
Valençay [F] 19 K 16
Valence [F] 19 J 18
Valence [F] 19 M 17
Valencia [E] 26 H 21
≈ Valencia, Golfo de — [E] 26 H 21
Δ Valencia [E] 26 G 21
Valencia de Alcántara [E] 25 C 20
Valencia de las Torres [E] 25 C 21
Δ Valencia Island [IRL] 12 D 12
Valenciennes [F] 14 L 14
Vălenii de Munte [RO] 23 Za 17
Valenza [I] 20 O 17
Våler [N] 4 Q 7
Valetta [M] 30 V 22
Valga [SU] 8 X 9
Δ Válico [I] 20 Q 18
≈ Valinco, Golfe de — [F] 28 O 20
Valjevo [YU] 22 W 18
Valjok [N] 3 U 1
Valkeakoski [SF] 9 V 7
Valkenswaard [NL] 14 M 13
Valkolanmäki [SF] 9 X 6
Valladolid [E] 26 E 19
Vallata [I] 29 T 20
Valldemosa [E] 27 K 21
Valle [N] 6 O 8
Valleraugue [F] 19 L 18
Vallet [F] 19 H 16
Δ Vallgrund = Raippaluoto [SF] 9 U 5
Vallon-Pont-d'Arc [F] 19 L 18
Vallorbe [CH] 20 N 16
Vallrun [S] 5 R 5
Valls [E] 27 J 20
Vallsta [S] 5 S 7
Valmaseda [E] 18 F 18
Valmiera [SU] 8 X 9
Δ Valnera, Monte — [E] 18 F 18
Valnesfjord [N] 2 R 3
Valognes [F] 13 H 14
Valongo [P] 25 B 19
Valpaços [P] 24 C 19
Valréas [F] 19 M 18
Vals-les-Bains [F] 19 L 18
Δ Valsoarna [SF] 5 U 5
Valta [GR] 31 Z 20
≈ Valtavaara [SF] 3 W 3
Δ Valtellina [I] 20 P 17
Val-Thorens [F] 20 N 17
Valtimo [SF] 9 X 5
Valverde de Júcar [E] 26 F 20
Valverde del Camino [E] 25 C 21
Vamberk [CS] 16 T 14
Vamdrup [DK] 6 P 11
Vammala [SF] 9 V 7
Vamos [GR] 32 Za 23
Vampula [SF] 9 V 7
≈ Vanajan selkä [SF] 9 V 7
Vandra [SU] 8 W 8
≈ Vänern [S] 6 Q 9
Vänersborg [S] 6 Q 9
Vang [N] 4 O 7
Vånga [S] 7 R 10
Vangsnes [N] 4 O 7
Vännacka [S] 6 Q 8
Vännäs [S] 5 T 5
Vannes [F] 18 G 15
Δ Vannøy [N] 2 S 1
Vans, les — [F] 19 L 18
Vansbro [S] 5 R 7
Vantaa [SF] 9 W 7
≈ Vanylvsfjord [N] 4 N 6
≈ Var [F] 20 N 18
Vara [S] 6 Q 9
≈ Vara [I] 20 P 18
Varades [F] 18 H 16
Varakļāni [SU] 8 X 9
Varallo [I] 20 O 17
Varangerbotn [N] 3 V 1
≈ Varangerfjord [N] 3 V 1
Δ Varangerhalvøya [N] 3 V 1
≈ Varano, Lago di — [I] 29 T 19
Varaždin [YU] 21 T 17
Varazze [I] 20 O 18
Varberg [S] 6 Q 10
Vărbica [BG] 23 Za 18
Vărbica [BG] 31 Za 19
Varby [S] 7 T 8
Varda [GR] 30 X 21
≈ Vardar [YU] 30 X 19
Varde [DK] 6 O 11
≈ Varde Å [DK] 6 O 11
Vardi [SU] 9 W 8
Varel [D] 15 O 12
Varėna [SU] 8 X 11
Δ Värend [S] 7 S 10
Varennes-en-Argonne [F] 14 M 15
Varennes-sur-Allier [F] 19 L 16
Vareš [YU] 22 V 18
Varese [I] 20 O 17
Vårgårda [S] 6 Q 9
Vargön [S] 6 Q 9
Δ Vargön [S] 3 U 4
Varhaug [N] 6 N 9
Varilhes [F] 19 J 18
≈ Väringen [S] 7 S 8
Varkaus [SF] 9 X 6
≈ Värmeln [S] 6 Q 8
Δ Värmland [S] 4 Q 8
Δ Värmlandsnäs [S] 6 Q 8
Varna [BG] 23 Zb 18
Värnamo [S] 7 R 10
Varnhem [S] 7 R 9
Varniai [SU] 8 V 10
Városlöd [H] 21 U 16
Varpaisjärvi [SF] 9 W 5
Várpalota [H] 21 U 16
≈ Värriojoki [SF] 3 W 2
Δ Vars, Col de — [F] 20 N 18
Δ Varsinais Suomi [SF] 9 U 7
Vartalambi [SU] 3 X 3
Vartdal [N] 4 N 6
≈ Vartdalsfjord [N] 4 N 6
Δ Vartsala [SF] 9 U 7
Varvarin [YU] 22 X 18
Varzi [I] 20 P 18
Varzo [I] 20 O 17
Varzy [F] 19 L 16
Vasaraperä [SF] 3 W 3
Vásárosnamény [H] 17 X 15
Vasa = Vaasa [SF] 9 U 6
Väsby [S] 5 T 8
≈ Vascão, Ribeira do — [P] 25 B 21
Vaşcău [RO] 22 X 16
Vasilovci [BG] 22 Y 18
≈ Vaskivesi [SF] 9 V 6
≈ Vaskojoki [SF] 3 V 2
Vaslui [RO] 23 Za 15
≈ Väsman [S] 5 R 8
Δ Vassdalseggi [N] 4 O 8
Vasse [GR] 30 Y 22
Vassilika [GR] 30 Y 20
Vassmolösa [S] 7 S 10
Västansjö [S] 2 R 4
≈ Vastenjaure [S] 2 R 3
Västerås [S] 5 S 8
Δ Västerbotten [S] 5 T 5
≈ Västerdalälven [S] 5 R 7
Västergarn [S] 7 T 9
Δ Västergötland [S] 6 Q 9
Västermyrriset [S] 5 S 5
Δ Västerö [SF] 9 U 5
Västervik [S] 7 S 9
Δ Västmanland [S] 7 S 8
Vasto [I] 29 S 19
≈ Västra Kvarken [S] 5 U 5
≈ Västra Lägern [S] 7 S 9
≈ Västra Silen [S] 6 Q 8
Vasvár [H] 21 T 16
Vát [H] 21 T 16
Vatan [F] 19 K 16
Δ Vaticano, Capo — [I] 29 T 21
≈ Vätö [S] 5 T 8
Vatolakkos [GR] 30 X 20
Vatra Dornei [RO] 23 Z 15
Δ Vätskär [SF] 9 W 7
≈ Vättern [S] 7 R 9
Vattholma [S] 5 T 8
Vauclaix [F] 19 L 16
≈ Vaucluse, Fontaine de — [F] 19 M 18
Δ Vaucluse, Monts de — [F] 19 M 18
Vaucouleurs [F] 14 M 15
Vauvert [F] 19 L 18
Vaux-le-Vicomte [F] 14 L 15
Vaxholm [S] 7 T 8
Växjö [S] 7 R 10
Våxtorp [S] 7 R 10
Väyrylä [SF] 3 W 4
Vebomark [S] 5 U 5
Večäki [SU] 8 W 9
Vechta [D] 15 O 12
Vecilla, La — [E] 24 E 18
Vecmuiža [SU] 8 W 10
Veddige [S] 6 Q 10
≈ Vedea [RO] 23 Z 17
Vedevåg [S] 7 S 8
Vedjeön [S] 5 R 5
Δ Vedrà, Isla del — [E] 27 J 21
≈ Vefsna [N] 2 Q 4
≈ Vefsnfjord [N] 2 Q 4
Δ Vega, La — [E] 25 D 22
Δ Vega [N] 2 Q 4
Vegadeo [E] 24 D 18
Vega de Valcarce [E] 24 C 18
≈ Vegafjord [N] 2 Q 4
≈ Vegår [N] 6 O 9
Vegårshei [N] 6 P 9
Vegeriai [SU] 8 W 10
Veggli [N] 4 P 8
Veghel [NL] 15 N 13
≈ Vegoritis, Limni — [GR] 30 X 20
Vegset [N] 4 Q 5
Vehmaa [SF] 9 U 7
≈ Veitastrandsvatn [N] 4 O 7
Vejen [DK] 6 P 11
Vejer de la Frontera [E] 25 C 22
Vejle [DK] 6 P 11
≈ Vejle Fjord [DK] 6 P 11
Vejva [SU] 8 X 9
Velagići [YU] 21 U 18
Vela Luka [YU] 21 U 19
Δ Velay, Monts du — [F] 19 L 17
Velbert [D] 15 N 13
Velden am Wörther See [A] 21 S 16
Δ Velebit [YU] 21 S 17
≈ Veleka [BG] 23 Zb 18
≈ Velencei tó [H] 21 U 16
Δ Veleš, Mali i — [AL] 30 W 19
Velestinon [GR] 30 Y 20
Vélez de Benaudalla [E] 26 E 22
Vélez-Málaga [E] 25 D 22
Vélez Rubio [E] 26 F 22
Velfjord [N] 2 Q 4
≈ Velfjord [N] 2 Q 4
Velika [YU] 21 U 17
Δ Velika Golija [YU] 21 U 18
≈ Velikaja [SU] 8 Y 9
Velika Kladuša [YU] 21 T 17
Velika Plana [YU] 22 W 18
Velike Lašče [YU] 21 S 17
Δ Veliki Drvenic [YU] 21 T 18
Velikij Byčkov [SU] 17 Y 15
≈ Veliki kanal [YU] 22 V 17
Δ Veliki Krš [YU] 22 X 17
Velikodolinskoje [SU] 23 Zc 15
Veliko Gradište [YU] 22 X 17
Veliko Tarnovo [BG] 23 Za 18
Veli Lošinj [YU] 21 S 18
Velingrad [BG] 23 Z 19
Δ Velino, Monte — [I] 29 R 19
Veljki [SU] 8 X 9
Velká Bíteš [CS] 16 T 15
Δ Veľká Fatra [CS] 16 U 15
Δ Veľká Javořina [CS] 16 U 15
Veľké Kapušany [CS] 17 W 15
Velké Losiny [CS] 16 T 14
Velké Meziříčí [CS] 16 T 15
Velletri [I] 29 R 20
Vellinge [S] 7 R 11
Δ Velopoula [GR] 32 Z 22
Velsen [NL] 14 M 13
Velten [DDR] 16 R 12
≈ Veman [S] 5 R 6
Vemdalen [S] 5 R 6
Vemeiro [P] 25 B 20
Δ Ven [S] 6 Q 10
Vena [S] 7 S 9
Venaco [F] 28 O 19
Venafro [I] 29 S 20
Venaria [I] 20 N 17
Vence [F] 20 N 18
Vendargues [F] 19 L 18
Vendas Novas [P] 25 B 20
Vendays-Montalivet [F] 18 H 17
Δ Vendée [F] 18 H 16
Vendesund [N] 4 Q 4
Vendeuvre-sur-Barse [F] 19 M 15
Vendôme [F] 19 K 15
Vendrell [E] 27 J 20
Δ Vendsyssel [DK] 6 P 10
Veneheitto [SF] 9 W 4
Venèzia [I] 21 R 17
≈ Venèzia, Golfo di — 21 R 17
Δ Vengsøy [N] 2 S 1
Venjan [S] 5 R 7
≈ Venjansjön [S] 5 R 7
Δ Venjekula [N] 6 N 9
Venlo [NL] 15 N 13
Venna [GR] 31 Za 19
Vennesla [N] 6 O 9
Venosa [I] 29 T 20
Δ Venosta, Val — [I] 20 P 16
Venraij [NL] 15 N 13
≈ Venta [SU] 8 V 9
Ventas de Zafarraya [E] 25 D 22
≈ Ventilegne, Golfe de — [F] 28 O 20
Ventimiglia [I] 20 N 18
Ventnor [GB] 13 J 14
Δ Ventoux, Mont — [F] 19 M 18
Ventspils [SU] 8 V 9
Venzone [I] 21 R 17
Vera [E] 26 F 22
Δ Vera, La — [E] 25 D 20
Vera de Moncayo [E] 26 G 19
Verbània [I] 20 O 17
Vercelli [I] 20 O 17
≈ Verchneje Kujto, ozero — [SU] 3 X 4
Verchne Sinevidnoy [SU] 17 X 14
Verchnetulomskij [SU] 3 X 2
Δ Vercors [F] 19 M 18
Verdal [N] 4 Q 5
Δ Verdal [N] 4 Q 5
Δ Verde, Col de — [F] 28 P 19
Verden (Aller) [D] 15 P 12
≈ Verdon [F] 19 M 18
Δ Verdon, Grand Canyon du — [F] 20 N 18
Verdon-sur-Mer, le — [F] 18 H 17
Verdun [F] 14 M 15
Veren [N] 4 Q 5
Vergato [I] 20 Q 18
Vergel [E] 26 H 21
Veria [GR] 30 Y 20
Verín [E] 24 C 18
Verlaicene [SU] 8 X 9
Vermenton [F] 19 L 16
Vermeș [RO] 22 X 17
Vernár [CS] 17 V 15
Verneuil-sur-Avre [F] 14 K 15
Vernon [F] 14 K 15
Verona [I] 20 Q 17
Verpillière, la — [F] 19 M 17
Verrès [I] 20 O 17
Versailles [F] 14 K 15
Δ Vértes [H] 21 U 16
Δ Vertiskos Oros [GR] 30 Y 19
Vërtop [AL] 30 W 20
Veruela [E] 26 G 19
Verviers [B] 15 N 14
Vervins [F] 14 L 14
Vesanto [SF] 9 W 5
Vescovato [F] 28 P 19
Veselí nad Moravou [CS] 16 U 15
≈ Vesijärvi [SF] 9 W 7
Vesoul [F] 20 N 16
Vestbygd [N] 6 N 9
Δ Vesterålen [N] 2 R 2
≈ Vesterålsfjord [N] 2 R 2
≈ Vesterelv [N] 3 V 1
≈ Vestfjorden [N] 2 Q 3
Vestre Gausdal [N] 4 P 7
Δ Vestvågøy [N] 2 Q 3
Δ Vesuvio [I] 29 S 20
Veszprém [H] 21 U 16
Veszprémvarsány [H] 21 U 16
Vetlanda [S] 7 S 9
Vetralla [I] 28 Q 19
Vetren [BG] 23 Z 19
Vetrino [BG] 23 Zb 18
Vettasjärvi [S] 2 T 3
≈ Vettisfoss [N] 4 O 7
Δ Vettore, Monte — [I] 21 R 19
Veurne [B] 14 L 13
Vevey [CH] 20 N 17
Vevi [GR] 30 X 20
Veynes [F] 19 M 18
Vézelay [F] 19 L 16
Vezins [F] 18 H 16
Véztő [H] 22 W 16
Δ Via Mala [CH] 20 P 16
Viana [E] 18 G 19
Viana del Bollo [E] 24 C 18
Viana do Alentejo [P] 25 B 21
Viana do Castelo [P] 24 B 18
Vianden [L] 15 N 14
≈ Viar, Río — [E] 25 C 21
Viarèggio [I] 20 P 18
Viborg [DK] 6 P 10
Vibo Valèntia [I] 29 U 21
Vibraye [F] 19 J 15
Vibyggerå [S] 5 T 6
Vic-en-Bigorre [F] 18 H 18
Vicenza [I] 20 Q 17
Vic-Fézensac [F] 19 J 18
Vich [E] 27 K 19
Vichy [F] 19 L 17
Vic-le-Comte [F] 19 L 17
Vico [F] 28 O 19
Vic-sur-Cère [F] 19 K 17
Victoria [M] 30 V 22
Victoria [RO] 23 Z 16
Vidago [P] 24 C 19
Vidauban [F] 20 N 18
Videbæk [DK] 6 O 10
Videle [RO] 23 Z 17
Vidigueira [P] 25 B 21
Vidin [BG] 22 Y 18
Δ Vidio, Cabo — [E] 24 D 18
Δ Vidlič [YU] 22 Y 18
Vidml'a [SU] 17 X 12
Δ Vidojevica [YU] 22 X 18
Vidra [RO] 23 Za 16
≈ Vidraru, Lakul — [RO] 23 Z 17
Vidsel [S] 2 T 4
≈ Vidskärsfjärd [SF] 9 U 8
Vidsmuiža [SU] 8 Y 9
Δ Vidzeme [SU] 8 W 9
Vidzy [SU] 8 Y 10
Vieille-Lyre, la — [F] 14 J 15
Vieira do Minho [P] 24 B 19
≈ Viekijärvi [SF] 9 X 5
Viekšniai [SU] 8 V 10
Viella [E] 27 J 19
Vielsalm [B] 15 N 14
Vienne [F] 19 M 17
≈ Vienne [F] 19 J 16
Vieremä [SF] 9 W 5
Viersen [D] 15 N 13
Vierumäki [SF] 9 W 7
Δ Vierwaldstätter Alpen [CH] 20 O 16
≈ Vierwaldstätter See [CH] 20 O 16
Vierzon [F] 19 K 16
Viesīte [SU] 8 X 10
Vieste [I] 29 T 19
Vievis [SU] 8 X 11
Vif [F] 19 M 17
Vig [DK] 6 Q 10
Vigan, le — [F] 19 L 18
Vigeland [N] 6 O 9
Vigevano [I] 20 O 17
Vignola [I] 20 Q 18
Vigo [E] 24 B 18
≈ Vigo, Ría de — [E] 24 B 18
Vigo di Fassa [I] 20 Q 17
Vihanti [SF] 9 V 5
Vihiers [F] 18 H 16
Δ Vihorlat [CS] 17 W 15
Δ Vihren [BG] 30 Y 19
Vihtari [SF] 9 X 6
≈ Vihterpalu laht [SU] 8 V 8
Vihti [SF] 9 W 7
Viiala [SF] 9 V 7
≈ Viinijärvi [SF] 9 X 5
Viitamäki [SF] 9 W 5
Viitasaari [SF] 9 W 5
Vika [S] 5 R 7
Vikan [N] 2 S 1
Vike [N] 4 N 7
Vikebukt [N] 4 O 6
Viken [N] 4 N 7
≈ Viken [S] 7 R 9
Vikersund [N] 4 P 8
Vikna [N] 4 P 5
Viksjö [S] 5 S 6
≈ Vil [BG] 23 Z 18
Vila Boim [P] 25 B 20
Vila da Igreja [P] 25 C 19
Vila do Bensafrim [P] 25 A 21
Vila do Conde [P] 25 B 19
Vila Flor [P] 25 C 19
Vila Franca de Xira [P] 25 A 20
≈ Vilaine [F] 18 G 15
Viļaka [SU] 8 Y 9
Vilaller [E] 27 J 19
Vila Nova da Barquinha [P] 25 B 20
Vila Nova da Cerveira [P] 24 B 18
Vila Nova de Famalição [P] 24 B 19
Vila Nova de Gaia [P] 25 B 19
Vila Pouca de Aguiar [P] 25 C 19
Vila Pouca de Aguiar [P] 25 C 19
Vila Real [P] 25 C 19
Vila Real de Santo António [P] 25 B 21
Vilar Formoso [P] 25 C 19
Vila Verde [P] 24 B 19
Vila Verde de Ficalho [P] 25 B 21
Vila Viçosa [P] 25 B 20
Δ Vîlcan, Munţii — [RO] 22 X 17
Vilches [E] 26 E 21
Vilejka [SU] 8 Y 11
Vilémov [CS] 16 S 14
Vilēni [SU] 8 Y 9
Vilhelmina [S] 5 S 5
≈ Vilija [SU] 8 X 11
Δ Viljakansaari [SF] 9 X 6
Viljandi [SU] 8 X 8
Vilkaviškis [SU] 8 W 11
Vilkija [SU] 8 W 11
Vilkovo [SU] 23 Zc 16
Δ Villa, Campo de la — [E] 24 E 18
Villablino [E] 24 D 18
Villacañas [E] 26 E 20
Villacarlos [E] 27 L 21
Villacarrillo [E] 26 E 21
Villacastín [E] 26 E 19
Villach [A] 21 S 16
≈ Villachica, Lago de — [E] 24 D 18
Villacidro [I] 28 O 21
Villada [E] 24 E 19
Villa de Don Fadrique, La — [E] 26 E 20
Villa del Río [E] 25 D 21
Villadiego [E] 18 E 18
Villadòssola [I] 20 O 17
Villafranca del Bierzo [E] 24 D 18
Villafranca de los Barros [E] 25 C 21
Villafranca del Panadés [E] 27 J 20
Villafranca di Verona [I] 20 Q 17
Villagarcía de Arosa [E] 24 B 18
Villahermosa [E] 26 F 21
Villaines-la-Jubel [F] 14 J 15
Villajoyosa [E] 26 H 21
Villalba [E] 24 C 18
Villalón de Campos [E] 24 E 19
Villamañán [E] 24 D 18
Villamanrique de la Condesa [E] 25 C 21
Villamartín [E] 25 C 22
Δ Villano, Cabo — [E] 24 B 17
Villanova Monteleone [I] 28 O 20
Villanúa [E] 18 H 19
Villanubla [E] 26 E 19
Villanueva de Alcolea [E] 26 H 20
Villanueva de Alcorón [E] 26 E 21
Villanueva de Alcorón [E] 26 F 20
Villanueva de Córdoba [E] 25 D 21
Villanueva de Gállego [E] 26 H 19
Villanueva de la Jara [E] 26 F 21
Villanueva de la Serena [E] 25 D 20
Villanueva de la Sierra [E] 25 C 20
Villanueva del Fresno [E] 25 B 21
Villanueva de los Castillejos [E] 25 B 21
Villanueva del Río y Minas [E] 25 C 21
Villanueva y Geltrú [E] 27 J 20
Villapando [E] 25 D 19
Villarasa [E] 25 C 21
Villarcayo [E] 18 F 18
Villar de Peralonso [E] 25 D 19
Villarejo de Salvanés [E] 26 E 20
Villarente [E] 24 D 18
Villares del Saz [E] 26 F 20
Villargordo del Cabriel [E] 26 G 20
Villarosa [I] 29 S 22
Villarreal de Álava [E] 18 F 18
Villarreal de los Infantes [E] 26 H 20
Villarrobledo [E] 26 F 21
Villarroya de la Sierra [E] 26 G 19
Villars-les-Dombes [F] 19 M 17
Villa San Giovanni [I] 29 T 22
Villa Santina [I] 21 R 17
Villasimius [I] 28 P 21
Villatobas [E] 26 E 20
Villava [E] 18 G 18
Villaverde [E] 26 E 20
Villaviciosa [E] 24 E 18
Villé [F] 20 N 15
Villedieu-les-Poêles [F] 13 H 15
Villefagnan [F] 19 J 17
Villefranche [F] 20 N 18
Villefranche-de-Conflent [F] 19 K 19
Villefranche-de-Lauragais [F] 19 J 18
Villefranche-de-Rouergue [F] 19 K 18
Villefranche-sur-Cher [F] 19 K 16
Villefranche-sur-Saône [F] 19 M 17
Villel [E] 26 G 20
Villena [E] 26 G 21
Villeneuve-de-Marsan [F] 18 H 18
Villeneuve-sur-Lot [F] 19 J 18
Villeneuve-sur-Yonne [F] 19 L 15
Villeréal [F] 19 J 17
Villers-Bocage [F] 14 J 15
Villers-Carbonnel [F] 14 L 14
Villers-Cotterêts [F] 14 L 15
Villeurbanne [F] 19 M 17
Villingen-Schwenningen [D] 20 O 15
Villoldo [E] 24 E 19
Vilnius [SU] 8 X 11
Vilppula [SF] 9 V 6
≈ Vils [D] 16 R 15
Vilsbiburg [D] 16 R 15
Vilshofen [D] 16 R 15
Viluse [YU] 22 V 19
Vimianzo [E] 24 B 18
Vimmerby [S] 7 S 9
Vimoutiers [F] 14 J 15
Vimpeli [SF] 9 V 5
Vimperk [CS] 16 R 15
Vinaixa [E] 27 J 19
Vinaroz [E] 26 H 20
Vînători [RO] 23 Z 16
Vindala = Vimpeli [SF] 9 V 5
≈ Vindelälven [S] 2 R 4
≈ Vindelälven [S] 5 T 5
Vindeln [S] 5 T 5
Vinderup [DK] 6 O 10
Δ Vindö [S] 7 T 8
Vinga [RO] 22 W 16
Vingåker [S] 7 S 8
Vinhais [P] 24 C 19
Δ Vinho, País do — [P] 25 C 19
Vinje [N] 4 N 7
Vinje [N] 4 P 6
Vinje [N] 6 O 8
≈ Vinjefjord [N] 4 P 6
Vinju Mare [RO] 22 Y 17
Vinkovci [YU] 22 V 17
Vinnelys [N] 2 T 1
Vinon-sur-Verdon [F] 19 M 18
≈ Vinsteren [N] 4 P 7
Vinstra [N] 4 P 7
Vinterbru [N] 4 P 8

Vintjärn [S] 5 S 7
Δ Vintschgau = Val Venosta [I] 20 P 16
Vipiteno [I] 20 Q 16
Δ Vir [YU] 21 S 18
Vire [F] 13 H 15
Vireši [S] 8 X 9
Vrřurile [RO] 22 X 16
Virgen de la Cabeza, Santuario de la — [E] 26 E 21
Virihaure [S] 2 R 3
≈ Virmasvesi [SF] 9 W 5
≈ Virmo = Vehmaa [SF] 9 U 7
Virmutjoki [SF] 9 X 6
Virojoki [SF] 9 X 7
Virovitica [YU] 21 U 17
Virrat [SF] 9 V 6
Virserum [S] 7 W 12
Virtaniemi [SF] 3 V 2
Virton [B] 14 M 14
Virtsu [SU] 8 W 8
Virttaa [SF] 9 V 7
Virzapar [YU] 30 V 19
Vis [YU] 21 T 19
Δ Vis [YU] 21 T 19
Visby [S] 7 T 9
Visè [B] 15 N 14
Višegrad [BG] 23 Za 19
Višegrad [YU] 22 V 18
Viseu [P] 25 B 19
Viseu-de-Sus [RO] 17 Y 15
Visingsö [S] 7 R 9
Δ Visk'ar'l'ulin [BG] 22 Y 18
Δ Viški kanal [YU] 21 T 19
Vislanda [S] 7 R 10
Višnevo [S] 8 Y 11
Viso, El — [E] 26 D 21
Δ Viso, Monte — [I] 20 N 18
Δ Visočica [YU] 22 V 18
Visoki Dečani [YU] 22 W 19
Visoko [YU] 22 V 18
Visp [CH] 20 O 17
Vissefjärda [S] 7 S 10
Visso [I] 21 R 19
Vistheden [S] 2 T 4
Δ Vištyneckoje, ozero — [SU] 8 W 11
Viterbo [I] 29 R 19
Vithkuq [AL] 30 X 20
Vitigudino [E] 25 C 19
Vitina [SU] 30 Y 22
Vitolište [YU] 30 X 19
Vitoria [E] 18 F 18
Δ Vitorog [YU] 21 U 18
Δ Vitoša planina [BG] 22 Y 18
Vitré [F] 13 H 15
Vitry-le-François [F] 14 M 15
Δ Vitsion Oros [GR] 30 X 20
Vittangi [S] 2 T 3
Vitteaux [F] 19 M 16
Vittòria [I] 29 S 22
Vittório Vèneto [I] 21 R 17
Vittråsk [S] 2 T 4
Vitvattnet [S] 3 U 4
Δ Vivarais [YU] 19 L 18
Δ Vivarais, Monts du — [F] 19 L 18
Vivaro [F] 28 O 19
Viver [E] 26 G 20
Vivero [E] 24 C 17
Δ Vivero, Ría de — [E] 24 C 17
Viviers [F] 19 M 18
Vivonne [F] 19 J 16
Vize [TR] 23 Zb 19
Vizille [F] 19 M 17
Viziru [RO] 23 Zb 16
Vizovice [CS] 16 U 15
Vizzavona [F] 28 O 19
Vizzini [I] 29 T 22
≈ Vjóse [AL] 30 W 20
Δ Vlǎdeasa [RO] 22 X 16
Vladičin Han [YU] 22 W 17
Vladimirci [YU] 22 W 17
Vladimir-Volynskij [SU] 17 X 13
Vlasenica [YU] 22 V 18
Δ Vlašić [YU] 21 U 18
Δ Vlašić [YU] 22 V 18
Vlašim [CS] 16 S 14
Vlasotince [YU] 22 X 18
Δ Vlieland [NL] 14 M 12
Vlissingen [NL] 14 L 13
Vlorë [AL] 30 W 20
Δ Vlorës. Gjiri i — [AL] 30 W 20
≈ Vltava [CS] 16 S 15
Voćin [YU] 21 U 17
Vodica [BG] 23 Za 18
Vodňany [CS] 16 S 14
Vodnjan [YU] 21 S 17
Δ Vogelsberg [D] 15 P 14
Voghera [I] 20 O 17
≈ Võhandu [SU] 8 X 9
Võhma [SU] 8 X 8
Void [F] 14 M 15
Voiron [F] 19 M 17
Voise [F] 14 K 15
≈ Voiviis, Limni — [GR] 30 Y 20
Vojakkala [SF] 3 U 4
Vojakkala [SF] 9 V 7
Vojens [DK] 6 P 11
Vojnić [YU] 21 T 17
Vojnica [SU] 3 X 4
≈ Vojnica [SU] 3 X 4
Δ Vojvodina [YU] 22 W 17
Volary [CS] 16 R 15
Volda [N] 4 N 6
Volime [GR] 30 X 22
Völkermarkt [A] 21 S 16
Volkolata [SU] 8 Y 10
Volkovysk [SU] 17 X 12
Volontirovka [SU] 23 Zb 15
Volos [GR] 30 Y 20
Volovec [SU] 17 X 15
Voložin [SU] 8 Y 11
Volterra [I] 20 Q 18
Voltri [I] 20 O 18
Voltti [SF] 9 U 6
≈ Volturno [I] 29 S 20
Δ Volvi, Limni — [GR] 31 Z 20
Võma [SU] 8 V 8
Vonitsa [GR] 30 X 21
Vorá [SF] 9 U 5
Δ Voras Oros [GR] 30 X 20
Vorderrhein [CH] 20 O 16
Vordingborg [DK] 6 Q 11
Vorë [AL] 30 W 19
Voreppe [F] 19 M 17

Δ Vorii Sporades [GR] 31 Z 20
Δ Vormsi [SU] 8 V 8
Vorn'any [SU] 8 Y 11
Vorpommern [DDR] 16 R 12
Δ Vorterøy [N] 2 T 1
≈ Võrts järv [SU] 8 X 8
Võru [SU] 8 X 9
Δ Vosges [F] 20 N 16
Voskopojë [AL] 30 X 20
Voss [N] 4 N 7
Votice [S] 16 S 14
≈ Vouga, Rio — [P] 25 B 19
Voulte-sur-Rhône, la — [F] 19 M 18
Δ Vourinos Oros [GR] 30 X 20
Δ Voutsikaki [GR] 30 Y 21
Vouzela [P] 25 B 19
Vouziers [F] 14 M 15
Voxna [S] 5 R 7
≈ Voxna älv [S] 5 R 7
Vöyri = Vörå [SF] 9 U 5
Vrå [S] 7 R 10
Δ Vráble [S] 16 U 15
≈ Vrancea, Munții — [RO] 23 Za 16
Δ Vranica [YU] 21 U 18
Vranje [YU] 22 X 19
Vranjska Banja [YU] 22 X 19
Vrapče Polje [YU] 22 W 18
≈ Vrbanja [YU] 21 U 18
≈ Vrbas [YU] 21 U 18
Vrbové [CS] 16 U 15
Vrbovec [YU] 21 T 17
Vrbovsko [YU] 21 S 17
Vrchlabí [CS] 16 S 14
Vresthena [GR] 30 Y 22
Vretakloster [S] 7 S 9
Vrgin Most [YU] 21 T 17
Vrigstad [S] 7 R 9
Vríssia [GR] 30 Y 21
Vrlika [YU] 21 T 18
Vrnjačka Banja [YU] 22 W 18
Vrondou [GR] 30 Y 20
Vrpolje [YU] 22 V 17
Vršac [YU] 22 W 17
Vrsar [YU] 21 R 17
Δ Vrška Čuka [YU] 22 X 18
Vsetín [CS] 16 U 15
Δ Vtáčnik [CS] 16 U 15
Δ Vuba [SU] 3 W 2
Δ Vučjak [YU] 21 U 17
≈ Vuka [YU] 22 V 17
Vukovar [YU] 22 V 17
Δ Vulcano, Ìsola — [I] 29 T 22
Vulok [SU] 17 X 15
≈ Vulturești [YU] 22 Y 17
≈ Vuohijärvi [SF] 9 W 6
Vuojärvi [SF] 3 V 3
Vuokatti [SF] 9 W 5
Δ Vuokatti [SF] 9 W 5
Δ Vuokki [SF] 9 X 4
≈ Vuokkijärvi [SF] 3 X 4
Vuolijoki [SF] 9 W 5
Vuollerim [S] 2 T 4
≈ Vuolvojaure [S] 2 S 4
Vuorijarvi [SU] 3 X 3
≈ Vuosjärvi [SF] 9 W 5
≈ Vuotjärvi [SF] 9 X 5
Vuotso [SF] 3 V 2
Vurpăr [RO] 22 Y 16
≈ Vyborgskij zaliv [SU] 9 X 7
Vyšgorodok [SU] 8 Y 9
Vyškov [CS] 16 T 15
Vysokoje [SU] 17 X 12
Vyžkov [SU] 17 X 15
Δ Vyžkovskij, pereval — [SU] 17 X 15
Vyžuonos [SU] 8 X 10

W

≈ Waal [NL] 14 M 13
Waalwijk [NL] 14 M 13
Wąbrzeżno [PL] 16 U 12
Δ Wachau [A] 21 S 15
≈ Waddenzee [NL] 14 M 12
Wadebridge [GB] 12 F 13
Wadowice [PL] 17 V 14
Δ Wagram [A] 21 T 15
Wągrowiec [PL] 16 T 12
Waiblingen [D] 15 P 15
Waidhaus [D] 16 R 14
Waidhofen an der Thaya [A] 21 S 15
Waidhofen an der Ybbs [A] 21 S 16
Wakefield [GB] 11 J 12
Wałbrzych [PL] 16 T 14
Wałcz [PL] 16 T 12
Waldbröl [D] 15 O 14
Waldenburg [DDR] 16 R 14
Waldenburg (Schlesien) = Wałbrzych [PL] 16 T 14
Waldshut [D] 20 O 16
Δ Waldviertel [A] 21 S 15
≈ Walensee [CH] 20 P 16
≈ Wales [GB] 12 G 12
Wallasey [GB] 11 H 12
Walldürn [D] 15 P 15
Wallingford [GB] 13 J 13
Δ Wallis [CH] 20 N 17
Δ Walney Island [GB] 11 H 11
Walsall [GB] 13 J 12
Walsrode [D] 15 P 12
Walton on the Naze [GB] 13 K 13
Wangen im Allgäu [D] 20 P 16
Δ Wangerooge [D] 15 O 12
Wantage [GB] 13 J 13
Wareham [GB] 13 H 13
Waremme [B] 14 M 14
Waren [DDR] 16 R 12
Warendorf [D] 15 O 13
Warka [PL] 17 V 13
≈ Warmia [PL] 7 U 11
Warminster [GB] 13 H 13
Warnemünde [DDR] 6 Q 11
≈ Warnow [DDR] 15 Q 12
Warrington [GB] 11 H 12
Warszawa [PL] 17 V 11
Δ Warta [PL] 16 S 13
≈ Warta [PL] 16 S 12
Warth [A] 20 P 16

Warwick [GB] 13 J 12
≈ Wash, the — [GB] 13 K 12
Wasselonne [F] 14 N 15
Wassen [CH] 20 O 16
Wasserburg am Inn [D] 20 Q 15
≈ Wasserkuppe [D] 15 P 14
Waterford [IRL] 12 E 12
Waterloo [B] 14 M 14
Wattwil [CH] 20 O 16
Watzelsdorf [A] 21 T 15
Wavre [B] 14 M 14
≈ Wdzydze, Jezioro — [PL] 7 T 12
Wearhead [GB] 11 J 11
≈ Węchadłow [PL] 17 V 14
Weert [NL] 15 N 13
Węgorzewo [PL] 8 V 11
Węgorzyno [PL] 16 S 12
Węgrów [PL] 17 W 12
Wegscheid [D] 16 R 15
Weiden in der Oberpfalz [D] 15 Q 14
Weilburg [D] 15 O 14
Weilheim in Oberbayern [D] 20 Q 16
Weimar [DDR] 15 Q 14
Weingarten [D] 20 P 16
Weinheim [D] 15 O 15
Weinsberg [D] 15 P 15
Δ Weinviertel [A] 21 S 16
Weißenbach am Lech [A] 20 P 16
Weißenburg in Bayern [D] 15 Q 15
Weißenfels [DDR] 16 Q 13
Weißwasser [DDR] 16 S 13
Weitenegg [A] 21 S 15
Weitra [A] 21 S 15
Weiz [A] 21 T 16
Wejherowo [PL] 7 T 11
Wellingborough [GB] 13 J 12
Wellington [GB] 13 H 12
Wells [GB] 13 H 13
Wells next the Sea [GB] 13 K 12
Wels [A] 21 S 15
Welshpool [GB] 13 H 12
Wem [GB] 13 H 12
≈ Wendland [D] 15 Q 12
Werdohl [D] 15 O 13
Werfen [A] 21 R 16
Werl [D] 15 O 13
Wernberg [D] 15 Q 15
Werneck [D] 15 P 14
Wernigerode [DDR] 15 Q 13
≈ Werra [DDR] 15 P 14
≈ Wertach [D] 20 P 15
Wertheim [D] 15 P 14
Wesel [D] 15 N 13
≈ Weser [D] 15 P 12
≈ Weserbergland [D] 15 P 13
West Calder [GB] 11 H 10
≈ Westerems [D, NL] 15 N 12
Westerland [D] 6 O 11
Δ Westerwald [D] 15 O 14
Δ Westfriesland [NL] 14 M 12
West Linton [GB] 11 H 10
Weston-super-Mare [GB] 13 H 13
Westport [IRL] 10 E 11
≈ Westray [GB] 11 J 8
Wetzlar [D] 15 O 14
Wexford [IRL] 12 F 12
Weymouth [GB] 13 H 13
Δ Whernside [GB] 11 H 11
Whitby [GB] 11 J 11
Whitchurch [GB] 13 H 12
Whitchurch [GB] 13 J 13
Whitehaven [GB] 11 H 11
Whithorn [GB] 10 G 11
Whitstable [GB] 13 K 13
Wick [GB] 11 J 8
≈ Wicklow Mountains [IRL] 12 F 12
Wicko [PL] 7 T 11
Więcbork [PL] 16 T 12
Wiedenbrück, Rheda— [D] 15 O 13
Wielbark [PL] 17 V 12
Wieleń [PL] 16 T 12
Wieliczka [PL] 17 V 14
≈ Wielimie, Jezioro — [PL] 16 T 12
Wieluń [PL],16 U 13
Wien [A] 21 T 15
Wiener Neustadt [A] 21 T 16
≈ Wienerwald [A] 21 T 15
≈ Wieprz [PL] 17 W 13
≈ Wieprza [PL] 7 T 11
Wierden [NL] 15 N 13
Wies [A] 21 S 16
Wiesbaden [D] 15 O 14
Wieselburg = Mosonmadyaróvár [H]
Wiesloch [D] 15 O 15
Wiesmoor [D] 15 O 12
Δ Wiezyca [PL] 17 T 11
Wigan [GB] 11 H 12
≈ Wight, Isle of — [GB] 13 H 14
≈ Wigry, Jezioro — [PL] 8 W 11
Wigton [GB] 11 H 11
Wigtown [GB] 10 G 11
Wil [CH] 20 O 16
Wilczęta [PL] 7 U 11
Wilczków [PL] 16 T 13
Δ Wildspitze [A] 20 P 16
Wilhelmshaven [D] 15 O 12
Wilhering [A] 21 S 15
Willenberg = Wielbark [PL] 17 V 12
Wilnsdorf [D] 15 O 14
Δ Wilseder Berg [D] 15 P 12
Wilton [GB] 13 H 13
Wimbledon [GB] 13 J 13
Wimborne Minster [GB] 13 H 13
Wimmenau [F] 15 N 15
Wincanton [GB] 13 H 13
Winchcomb [GB] 13 J 13
Winchester [GB] 13 J 13
Windermere [GB] 11 H 11
≈ Windermere [GB] 11 H 11
Windischgarsten [A] 21 S 16
Windsor [GB] 13 J 13
Winklern [A] 21 R 16
Winschoten [NL] 15 N 12
Wińsko [PL] 16 T 13
Winterberg [D] 15 O 14
Winterthur [CH] 20 O 16
Wisbech [GB] 13 K 12
≈ Wisła [PL] 17 W 14
≈ Wiślany, Zalew — [PL, SU] 7 U 11
Wisłok [PL] 17 W 14
Wismar [DDR] 6 Q 11
Wissant [F] 14 K 14
Wissembourg [F] 15 O 15

Wisznice [PL] 17 X 13
Withernsea [GB] 11 K 12
Witney [GB] 13 J 13
Witnica [PL] 16 S 12
Wittau [A] 21 T 15
Witten [D] 15 O 13
Wittenberge [DDR] 15 Q 12
Wittenburg [DDR] 15 Q 12
Wittingen [D] 15 P 12
Wittlich [D] 15 N 14
Wittmund [D] 15 O 12
Δ Wittow [DDR] 7 R 11
Wittstock [DDR] 15 Q 12
Witzenhausen [D] 15 P 13
Władysławowo [PL] 7 T 11
Włocławek [PL] 16 U 12
Δ Włodawa [PL] 17 X 13
Włoszczowa [PL] 17 V 13
Wodzisław [PL] 17 V 14
Wokingham [GB] 13 J 13
Wolbrom [PL] 17 V 14
Woldegk [DDR] 16 R 12
Wolfenbüttel [D] 15 P 13
Wolfhagen [D] 15 P 13
Wolfratshausen [D] 20 Q 16
Wolfsberg [A] 21 S 16
Wolfsburg [D] 15 Q 13
Wolgast [DDR] 7 R 12
Δ Wolin [PL] 16 R 12
Δ Wólka [PL] 16 T 13
Wolkenstein = Selva di Val Gardena [I] 20 Q 16
Wołów [PL] 16 T 13
Wolsztyn [PL] 16 T 13
Wolverhampton [GB] 13 H 12
Wolverton [GB] 13 J 13
Wooler [GB] 11 J 10
Worbis [DDR] 15 P 13
Worcester [GB] 13 H 12
Wörgl [A] 20 Q 16
Workington [GB] 11 H 11
Worksop [GB] 13 J 12
Worms [D] 15 O 14
Wörrstadt [D] 15 O 14
Worthing [GB] 13 J 13
Wragby [GB] 13 J 12
Wrangle [GB] 13 K 12
Δ Wrath, Cape — [GB] 11 H 8
Wrexham [GB] 13 H 12
Wriezen [DDR] 16 R 12
Wrocław [PL] 16 T 13
Września [PL] 16 T 13
Wschowa [PL] 16 T 13
Wunsiedel [D] 15 Q 14
Wunstorf [D] 15 P 13
Δ Weserbergland [D] 15 P 13
Wuppertal [D] 15 N 13
Würzburg [D] 15 P 14
Wurzen [DDR] 16 R 13
Δ Wustrow [DDR] 6 Q 12
≈ Wye, River — [GB] 13 H 12
Wyk [D] 6 O 11
Wylatowo [PL] 16 U 12
Wymondham [GB] 13 K 12
Wyrzysk [PL] 16 T 12
Wyszków [PL] 17 V 11
Wyszogród [PL] 17 V 12
Wyszyna [PL] 17 V 14
Δ Wyżyna [PL] 17 V 13
Δ Wyżyna Lubelska [PL] 17 W 13

X

Xanthi [GR] 31 Za 19
Xilagani [GR] 31 Za 19
Xilokastron [GR] 30 Y 21
Xilopolis [GR] 30 Y 19
Δ Xodoton, Akrotirion — [GR] 31 Zb 22

Y

Yassiören [TR] 23 Zc 19
Yatagan [TR] 2 Zd 21
Yébenes, Los — [E] 26 E 20
Yecla [E] 26 G 21
≈ Yeda, Pantano de — [E] 18 G 19
Δ Yeguas, Sierra de — [E] 25 D 22
Yenice [TR] 31 Zb 20
Yenipazar [TR] 2 Zd 21
Yenne [F] 19 M 17
Yeovil [GB] 13 H 13
Yerville [F] 14 K 14
Ygrande [F] 19 L 16
Ylakiai [SU] 8 V 10
Ylämaa [SF] 9 X 7
Yläne [SF] 9 V 7
Ylihärmä [SF] 9 U 5
Ylikärppä [SF] 3 V 4
Ylikiiminki [SF] 3 V 4
≈ Ylikitka [SF] 3 W 3
Yli-Ii [SF] 3 V 4
Ylimarkku = Övermark [SF] 9 U 6
≈ Ylisuolijärvi [SF] 3 W 3
Ylitornio [SF] 3 U 3
Ylivieska [SF] 9 V 5
Δ Yllästunturi [SF] 3 U 3
≈ Yngaren [S] 7 S 8
≈ Yonne [S] 19 L 16
York [GB] 11 J 11
Δ York [GB] 11 J 11
Youghal [IRL] 12 E 12
Yppäri [SF] 9 V 5
Yssingeaux [F] 19 L 17
Ystad [S] 7 R 11
Ytredal [N] 4 O 6
Ytre Laksvatn [N] 2 S 2
Ytterhogdal [S] 5 R 6
Yttermalung [S] 5 R 7
Yuste [E] 25 D 20
Yverdon [CH] 20 N 16
Yvetot [F] 14 K 14
≈ Yxern [S] 7 S 9
Δ Yxlö [S] 5 T 8
≈ Yxnö [S] 7 S 9

Z

Zaanstad [NL] 14 M 13
≈ Zăbala [RO] 23 Za 16
Žabalj [YU] 22 W 17
Žabari [YU] 22 X 17
Žabje [SU] 17 Y 15
Žabljak [YU] 22 V 18
Zabok [YU] 21 T 17
Δ Zabrdje [BG, YU] 22 Y 18
Zabrze [PL] 16 U 14
Zabrzeź [PL] 17 V 14
Zacharo [GR] 30 Y 22
Zadar [YU] 21 T 18
≈ Zadarski kanal [YU] 21 T 18
≈ Zadorra, Río — [E] 18 F 18
Zafirovo [BG] 23 Z 18
Žagań [PL] 16 S 13
Zagora [A] 21 T 18
Δ Zagora [YU] 21 T 18
Δ Zagorodje [SU] 17 X 12
Zagreb [YU] 21 T 17
Zagubica [YU] 22 X 18
Zahrádky [CS] 16 S 14
Zajanje [SU] 8 Y 8
Zaječar [YU] 22 X 18
Zakinthos [GR] 30 X 22
Zakinthos [GR] 30 X 22
Zakopane [PL] 17 V 14
Zakroczym [PL] 17 V 12
Zakros [GR] 32 Zc 23
≈ Zala [H] 21 U 16
Zalaegerszeg [H] 21 T 16
Zalalövö [H] 21 T 16
Zalamea de la Serena [E] 25 D 21
Zalamea la Real [E] 25 C 21
Zalău [RO] 22 X 16
Zales'e [SU] 8 V 11
Zalewo [PL] 7 U 12
Założcy [SU] 17 Y 14
Δ Zamkowa, Góra — [PL] 17 V 14
Zamora [E] 25 D 19
Zamość [E] 17 X 13
≈ Záncara, Río — [E] 26 F 21
Zandvoort [NL] 14 M 13
≈ Zapadnaja Dvina [SU] 8 Y 10
≈ Zapadnaja Lica [SU] 3 W 1
Δ Zapadni Rodopi [BG] 23 Z 19
≈ Zapatón, Río — [E] 25 C 20
Zapere [SU] 8 W 8
Zapol'arnyj [SU] 3 W 1
Zappion [GR] 30 Y 20
Zaragoza [E] 26 G 19
Zarakes [GR] 31 Za 21
Zărand [RO] 22 W 16
Δ Zarand, Munții — [RO] 22 X 16
Zarasai [SU] 8 X 10
Zarauz [E] 18 G 18
Zara = Zadar [YU] 21 T 18
Zarečensk [SU] 3 X 3
Žarki [PL] 17 V 14
Žärnešti [RO] 23 Z 16
Žárnovica [CS] 16 U 15
Žarošice [CS] 16 T 15
Zarza la Mayor [E] 25 C 20
Zašejek [SU] 3 X 2
Zaskoviči [SU] 8 Y 11
Zasliai [SU] 8 X 11
Žatec [CS] 16 R 14
Zatoka [SU] 23 Zc 16
≈ Zatoka Pucka [PL] 7 U 11
Zator [PL] 17 V 14
Zău-de-cîmpie [RO] 22 Y 16
Zawadzkie [PL] 16 U 14
Zbąszyń [PL] 16 S 13
Zbąszynek [PL] 16 S 13
Zblewo [PL] 7 U 12
Zborov [PL] 17 Y 14
Zbrachlin [PL] 16 U 12
Žďár nad Sázavou [CS] 16 T 14
Zdice [CS] 16 R 14
Zdirek nad Doubravou [CS] 16 T 14
Zdunje [YU] 30 X 19
Zebreira [P] 25 C 20
Δ Zečije [YU] 21 S 18
Zeebrugge [B] 14 L 13
Zehdenick [DDR] 16 R 12
Zeitz [DDR] 15 Q 14
Zejtun [M] 30 V 22
Zelenogradsk [SU] 8 V 11
Železnik [YU] 22 W 17
Železniki [YU] 21 S 17
Železnodorožnyj [SU] 8 V 11
Zelina [YU] 21 T 17
Zella-Mehlis [DDR] 15 P 14
Zell am See [A] 21 R 16
Želva [SU] 8 X 10
Zemblak [AL] 30 X 20
Δ Zembra, Île — [TN] 28 Q 22
Zemītė [SU] 8 W 9
Δ Zemlandskij poluostrov [SU] 8 V 11
Zenia [GR] 32 Zb 23
Zenica [YU] 21 U 18
Žepče [YU] 21 V 18
Zerbst [DDR] 15 Q 13
Zerf [D] 15 N 14
Zerind [RO] 22 W 16
Zermatt [CH] 20 O 17
Zernez [CH] 20 P 16
Zerqan [AL] 30 W 19
Zettlitz [D] 15 Q 14
Zeven [D] 15 P 12
Zevenbergen [NL] 14 M 13
≈ Žèzere, Rio — [P] 25 B 20
Zgierz [PL] 16 U 13
Žiar nad Hronom [CS] 16 U 15
Zicavo [F] 28 O 19
Zidani Most [SU] 21 S 17
Zielona Góra [PL] 16 S 13
Ziesar [DDR] 15 Q 13
Žilina [CS] 16 U 15
Zillertaler Alpen [A. I] 20 Q 16
Zilupe [SU] 8 Y 9
Zimbor [RO] 22 X 16
Zimnicea [RO] 23 Z 18
Zinal [CH] 20 O 17

Zingst auf Darß [DDR] 6 Q 11
Zinnowitz [DDR] 7 R 12
Zirç [H] 21 U 16
Zirl [A] 20 Q 16
Ziros [GR] 32 Zc 23
Zistersdorf [A] 21 T 15
Δ Žitni Potok [YU] 22 X 18
Zitsa [GR] 30 X 20
Zittau [DDR] 16 S 14
Δ Zlarin [YU] 21 T 18
Zlatar [YU] 21 T 17
Δ Zlatarsko jezero [YU] 22 W 18
Zlatica [BG] 23 Z 18
Δ Zlatijata [BG] 22 Y 18
Zlatna [RO] 22 Y 16
Zlatna Panega [BG] 23 Z 18
Zlatni Pjasăci [BG] 23 Zb 18
Zlékas [S] 8 V 9
Zletovo [YU] 30 X 19
Δ Zljeb [YU] 30 W 19
Złoczew [PL] 16 U 13
Złotoryja [PL] 16 S 13
Złotów [PL] 16 T 12
Žmigród [PL] 16 T 13
Žnin [PL] 16 U 12
Znojmo [CS] 16 T 15
Žodiški [SU] 8 Y 11
Zogno [I] 20 P 17
Zollhaus [D] 15 O 14
Zoločev [SU] 17 Y 14
Zonza [F] 28 P 20
Zorianos [GR] 30 Y 21
Zorita [E] 25 D 20
Zornica [BG] 23 Zb 18
Žory [PL] 16 U 14
Zossen [DDR] 16 R 13
Zovka [SU] 8 Y 8
Zrenjanin [YU] 22 W 17
Δ Zrinjska gora [YU] 21 T 17
Zsámbék [H] 21 U 16
Δ Zselic [H] 21 U 16
Zuera [E] 26 H 19
Zug [CH] 20 O 16
≈ Zuger See [CH] 20 O 16
Δ Zugspitze [D] 20 Q 16
Zújar [E] 26 E 22
≈ Zújar, Pantano del — [E] 25 D 21
≈ Zújar, Río — [E] 25 D 21
Zülpich [D] 15 N 14
Zumaia [E] 18 G 18
Županja [YU] 22 V 17
Žuravno [SU] 17 Y 14
Zürich [CH] 20 O 16
≈ Zürichsee [CH] 20 O 16
Žuromin [SU] 17 V 12
Zurrieq [M] 30 V 22
Δ Žut [YU] 21 T 18
Zutphen [NL] 15 N 13
Zvårde [SU] 8 V 10
Zvezdec [BG] 23 Zb 18
Zvolen [YU] 17 V 15
Zvornik [YU] 22 V 18
Zweibrücken [D] 15 N 15
Zweisimmen [CH] 20 N 16
Zwettl Stadt [A] 21 S 15
Zwickau [DDR] 16 R 14
Zwoleń [PL] 17 V 13
Zwolle [NL] 15 N 13
Żyrardów [PL] 17 V 13
Żywiec [PL] 17 V 14

Europa · Eurooppa · Europe · Εὐρώπη · Avrupa
1 : 800.000

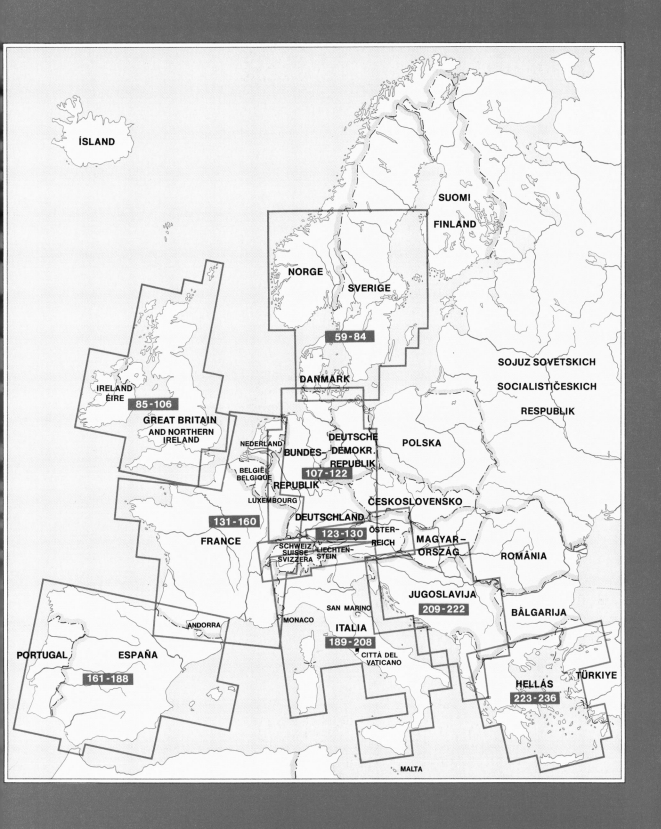

ÍSLAND

SUOMI
FINLAND

NORGE

SVERIGE

59-84

DANMARK

IRELAND
ÉIRE

85-106

GREAT BRITAIN
AND NORTHERN
IRELAND

SOJUZ SOVĚTSKICH

SOCIALISTIČESKICH

RESPUBLIK

NEDERLAND

DEUTSCHE
DEMOKR.
REPUBLIK

POLSKA

BUNDES

BELGIË
BELGIQUE

107-122

REPUBLIK

LUXEMBOURG

ČESKOSLOVENSKO

DEUTSCHLAND

131-160

123-130

ÖSTER-
REICH

MAGYAR-
ORSZÁG

FRANCE

SCHWEIZ
SUISSE
SVIZZERA

LIECHTEN-
STEIN

ROMÂNIA

JUGOSLAVIJA

209-222

BÂLGARIJA

SAN MARINO

ANDORRA

MONACO

ITALIA

189-208

PORTUGAL

ESPAÑA

CITTÀ DEL
VATICANO

TÜRKIYE

161-188

HELLÁS

223-236

MALTA

Distans · Distanser · Etäisyydet · Distancer · Distances · Entfernungen · Afstanden · Distancias · Distanze · Αποθτάθεις · Mesafeleri

Europa Eurooppa Europe Ευρώπη Avrupa	Zürich	Wien	Warzawa	Trondheim	Tromsø	Trieste	Torino	Stuttgart	Strasbourg	Stockholm	Sevilla	Salzburg	Roma	Praha	Paris	Palermo	Oslo	Nürnberg	Nice	Napoli	München	Milano	Marseilles	Madrid	Lyon	Luxembourg	London	Lisboa	Leipzig	København	Köln	Helsinki	Hannover	Hamburg	Göteborg	Genève	Frankfurt a.M.	Firenze	Edinburgh	Calais	Budapest	Bruxelles	Bordeaux	Bern	Berlin	Beograd	Basel	Barcelona	Athenai	Amsterdam
Amsterdam	854	1156	1218	1848	3142	1397	1152	632	656	1361	2304	1006	1742	945	502	2766	1290	665	1334	1960	856	1141	1171	1765	869	402	482	2304	658	740	267	1528	395	428	952	994	457	1439	1126	366	1404	198	1064	876	676	1798	768	1533	2979	
Athenai	2527	1823	2284	3983	5277	1809	2360	2392	2534	3413	4354	2038	2519	2135	3069	-	3425	2337	2525	-	2172	2227	2744	3815	2692	2709	3213	4501	2392	2877	2761	3996	2822	2967	3087	2549	2591	2216	3857	3097	1575	2926	3250	2562	2486	1181	2594	3261		2979
Barcelona	1085	1839	2503	3310	4604	1452	891	1309	1143	2823	1160	1546	1468	1924	1031	2492	2752	1489	736	1686	1401	1024	571	621	699	1208	1422	1265	1783	2202	1400	2951	1749	1890	2414	808	1392	1210	2066	1306	2036	1335	600	965	1945	2080	1061		3261	1533
Basel	86	846	1338	2249	3543	768	465	268	147	1763	2129	545	974	708	492	1998	1691	428	672	1192	395	376	664	1590	362	343	808	2160	722	1141	501	1929	688	829	1353	266	331	671	1452	692	1094	560	898	108	884	1413		1061	2594	768
Beograd	1346	642	1103	2802	4096	628	1179	1211	1353	2232	3173	857	1338	954	1888	2362	2244	1156	1344	1556	991	1046	1563	2634	1511	1528	2032	3320	1211	1696	1580	2815	1641	1786	1906	1368	1410	1035	2676	1916	394	1745	2069	1381	1305		1413	2080	1181	1798
Berlin	846	663	582	1497	2791	1147	1190	633	777	927	2871	756	1576	351	1061	2600	939	441	1395	1794	592	1046	1548	2332	1246	764	1065	2871	185	391	572	1094	285	290	601	1150	558	1273	1709	949	911	885	1631	992		1305	884	1945	2486	676
Bern	120	876	1540	2357	3651	759	357	344	242	1871	2057	586	942	960	561	1966	1799	527	570	1160	436	341	569	1518	316	451	907	2114	830	1249	609	2037	796	937	1461	158	467	639	1551	791	1124	668	874		992	1381	108	965	2562	876
Bordeaux	993	1756	2420	2966	4260	1441	890	1080	919	2479	1240	1443	1611	1552	562	2635	2408	1272	879	1829	1293	1034	714	701	558	903	926	1240	1620	1858	1095	2646	1395	1546	2070	716	1083	1353	1570	810	2004	866		874	1631	2069	898	600	3250	1064
Bruxelles	646	1100	1412	2000	3294	1295	936	544	426	1514	2106	904	1534	889	304	2558	1442	609	1136	1752	754	933	973	1567	671	217	322	2106	828	892	313	1680	532	580	1104	678	503	1231	966	206	1348		866	668	885	1745	560	1335	2926	198
Budapest	1007	248	709	2408	3702	584	1135	919	1038	1838	3129	541	1294	560	1511	2318	1850	739	1300	1512	691	1002	1519	2590	1446	1228	1732	3276	817	1302	1137	2421	1220	1365	1512	1288	957	991	2376	1616		1348	2004	1124	911	394	1094	2036	1575	1404
Calais	778	1306	1509	2164	3458	1466	1025	790	603	1678	2050	1075	1666	1095	275	2690	1606	815	1215	1884	925	1065	1055	1511	750	388	116	2050	1034	1056	519	1844	738	744	1268	767	597	1363	760		1616	206	810	791	949	1916	692	1306	3097	366
Edinburgh	1538	2066	2269	-	-	2226	1785	1475	1363	2438	2810	1835	2426	1855	1035	3450	-	1575	1975	2644	1685	1825	1815	2271	1510	1148	644	2810	1794	1816	1279	2604	1498	1504	-	1527	1357	2123		760	2376	966	1570	1551	1709	2676	1452	2066	3857	1126
Firenze	604	842	1565	2895	4189	407	430	844	975	2409	2303	696	303	1081	1129	1327	2337	845	474	521	680	298	693	1764	762	1014	1479	2409	1112	1787	1172	2575	1350	1475	1999	626	998		2123	1363	991	1231	1353	639	1273	1035	671	1210	2216	1439
Frankfurt a.M.	417	709	1077	1923	3217	970	824	195	230	1437	2323	569	1301	495	570	2325	1365	215	1003	1519	419	700	995	1784	693	290	713	2323	395	815	190	1603	351	503	1027	597		998	1357	597	957	503	1083	467	558	1410	331	1392	2591	457
Genève	277	1040	1704	2515	3809	740	258	501	400	2029	1899	747	930	1116	503	1954	1957	684	485	1148	593	328	411	1360	158	492	883	1956	988	1407	767	2195	954	1095	1619		597	626	1527	767	1288	678	716	158	1150	1368	266	808	2549	994
Göteborg	1439	1264	1190	861	2155	1860	1917	1216	1251	497	3310	1469	2302	986	1408	3326	338	1150	2025	2520	1319	1726	2017	2771	1715	1157	1384	3310	850	278	965	664	737	524		1619	1027	1999	-	1268	1512	1104	2070	1461	601	1906	1353	2414	3087	952
Hamburg	915	1117	872	1420	2714	1336	1393	692	727	933	2786	945	1778	645	884	2802	862	626	1501	1996	795	1202	1493	2247	1191	633	860	2786	382	312	441	1100	156		524	1095	503	1475	1504	744	1365	580	1546	937	290	1786	829	1890	2967	428
Hannover	770	972	813	1576	2870	1191	1248	547	582	1081	2635	800	1653	526	779	2677	1009	476	1360	1871	650	1061	1352	2096	1050	482	854	2635	269	459	290	1248		156	737	954	351	1350	1498	738	1220	532	1395	796	285	1641	688	1749	2822	395
Helsinki	2015	1757	1712	894	1390	2436	2493	1792	1827	167	3966	2045	2878	1479	1984	3902	727	1726	2601	3096	1885	2302	2593	3347	2291	1733	1960	3866	1345	789	1541		1248	1100	664	2195	1603	2575	2604	1844	2421	1680	2646	2037	1094	2815	1929	2951	3996	1528
Köln	587	889	1099	1861	3159	1130	966	365	400	1375	2335	739	1475	678	489	2499	1303	398	1267	1693	589	874	1003	1796	701	192	635	2335	515	753		1541	290	441	965	767	190	1172	1279	519	1137	313	1095	609	572	1580	501	1400	2761	267
København	1227	1054	990	1174	2468	1648	1705	1004	1039	622	3098	1257	2090	776	1196	3114	616	938	1813	2308	1107	1514	1805	2559	1503	945	1172	3098	572		753	789	459	312	278	1407	815	1787	1816	1056	1302	882	1858	1249	391	1696	1141	2202	2877	740
Leipzig	662	569	682	1746	3040	973	1030	473	619	1178	2860	582	1415	257	1004	2439	1188	281	1235	1633	432	886	1399	2321	1084	685	1150	2860		572	515	1345	269	382	850	988	395	1112	1794	1034	817	828	1620	830	185	1211	722	1783	2392	658
Lisboa	2233	2996	3422	4206	5500	2692	2130	2428	2159	3720	405	2700	2667	2792	1802	3691	3648	2512	1935	2885	2533	2274	1770	645	1798	2143	2166		2860	3098	2335	3866	2635	2786	3310	1956	2323	2409	2810	2050	3276	2106	1240	2114	2871	3320	2160	1265	4501	2304
London	894	1422	1625	2280	3574	1582	1141	831	719	1794	2166	1191	1782	1211	391	2806	1722	931	1331	2000	1041	1181	1171	1627	866	504		2166	1150	1172	635	1960	854	860	1384	883	713	1479	644	116	1732	322	926	907	1065	2032	808	1422	3213	482
Luxembourg	429	980	1394	2053	3347	1078	750	327	209	1567	2211	687	1317	764	346	2341	1495	484	972	1535	537	716	811	1672	509		504	2143	685	945	192	1733	482	633	1157	492	290	1014	1148	388	1228	217	903	451	764	1528	343	1208	2709	402
Lyon	436	1198	1727	2611	3905	883	332	659	444	2125	1790	905	1065	1097	475	2083	2053	817	465	1283	752	476	302	1251		509	866	1798	1084	1503	701	2291	1050	1191	1715	158	693	762	1510	750	1446	671	558	316	1246	1511	362	699	2692	869
Madrid	1637	2400	3121	3667	4961	2006	1512	1861	1620	3181	539	2144	2022	2253	1263	3046	3109	1973	1290	2240	1953	1639	1125		1251	1672	1627	645	2321	2559	1796	3347	2096	2247	2771	1360	1784	1764	2271	1511	2590	1567	701	1518	2332	2634	1590	621	3815	1765
Marseilles	688	1383	2047	2622	3916	418	144	912	811	2429	1664	1050	951	1427	777	1975	2355	1147	219	1169	982	528		1125	302	811	1171	1770	1399	1805	1003	2593	1352	1493	2017	411	995	693	1815	1055	1519	973	714	569	1548	1563	664	571	2744	1171
Milano	306	815	1479	2913	4207	935	384	530	525	2136	2178	522	601	868	871	1625	2064	619	349	819	454		528	1639	476	716	1181	2274	886	1514	874	2302	1061	1202	1726	328	700	298	1825	1065	1002	933	1034	341	1046	1046	376	1024	2227	1141
München	316	443	1044	2215	3509	527	598	220	363	1729	2492	150	983	414	820	2007	1657	165	803	1201		454	982	1953	752	537	1041	2533	432	1107	589	1885	650	795	1319	593	419	680	1685	925	691	754	1293	436	592	991	395	1401	2172	856
Napoli	1125	1363	2086	3416	4710	928	951	1365	1496	2930	2779	1217	218	1602	1651	806	2858	1366	950		1201	819	1169	2240	1283	1535	2000	2885	1633	2308	1693	3096	1871	1996	2520	1148	1519	521	2644	1884	1512	1752	1829	1160	1794	1556	1192	1686	-	1960
Nice	655	1164	1874	2921	4215	716	222	879	819	2435	1829	871	732	1217	983	1756	2363	966		950	803	349	219	1290	465	972	1331	1935	1235	1813	1267	2601	1360	1501	2025	485	1003	474	1975	1215	1300	1136	879	570	1395	1344	672	736	2525	1334
Nürnberg	381	491	910	2046	3340	692	763	192	338	1560	2512	315	1148	280	784	2172	1488		966	1366	165	619	1147	1973	817	484	931	2512	281	938	398	1726	476	626	1150	684	215	845	1575	815	739	609	1272	527	441	1156	428	1489	2337	665
Oslo	1777	1602	1528	558	1852	2198	2255	1554	1589	560	3648	1807	2640	1323	1746	3664		1488	2363	2858	1657	2064	2355	3109	2053	1495	1722	3648	1188	616	1303	727	1009	862	338	1957	1365	2337	-	1606	1850	1442	2408	1799	939	2244	1691	2752	3425	1290
Palermo	1931	2169	2892	4222	5516	1734	1757	2171	2302	3736	3585	2023	1024	2408	2457		3664	2172	1756	806	2007	1625	1975	3046	2083	2341	2806	3691	2439	3114	2499	3902	2677	2802	3326	1954	2325	1327	3450	2690	2318	2558	2635	1966	2600	2362	1998	2492	-	2766
Paris	578	1263	1588	2304	3598	1260	761	604	457	1818	1802	970	1433	1064		2457	1746	784	983	1651	820	871	777	1263	475	346	391	1802	1004	1196	489	1984	779	884	1408	503	570	1129	1035	275	1511	304	562	561	1061	1888	492	1031	3069	502
Praha	661	312	630	1881	3175	727	1012	472	618	1312	2792	369	1384		1064	2408	1323	280	1217	1602	414	868	1427	2253	1097	764	1211	2792	257	776	678	1479	526	645	986	1116	495	1081	1855	1095	560	889	1552	960	351	954	708	1924	2135	945
Roma	907	1145	1868	3198	4492	710	733	1147	1278	2712	2561	999		1384	1433	1024	2640	1148	732	218	983	601	951	2022	1065	1317	1782	2667	1415	2090	1475	2878	1653	1778	2302	930	1301	303	2426	1666	1294	1534	1611	942	1576	1338	974	1468	2519	1742
Salzburg	466	293	957	2365	3659	391	666	370	500	1879	2683		999	369	970	2023	1807	315	871	1217	150	522	1050	2144	905	687	1191	2700	582	1257	739	2045	800	945	1469	747	569	696	1835	1075	541	904	1443	586	756	857	545	1546	2038	1006
Sevilla	2176	2939	3660	4206	5500	2545	2051	2400	2159	3720		2683	2561	2792	1802	3585	3648	2512	1829	2779	2492	2178	1664	539	1790	2211	2166	405	2860	3098	2335	3866	2635	2786	3310	1899	2323	2303	2810	2050	3129	2106	1240	2057	2871	3173	2129	1160	4354	2304
Stockholm	1849	1590	1526	886	1778	2270	2327	1625	1661		3720	1879	2712	1312	1818	3736	560	1560	2435	2930	1729	2136	2429	3181	2125	1567	1794	3720	1178	622	1375	167	1081	933	497	2029	1437	2409	2438	1678	1838	1514	2479	1871	927	2232	1763	2823	3413	1361
Strasbourg	220	806	1248	2147	3441	890	612	161		1661	2159	500	1278	618	457	2302	1589	338	819	1496	363	525	811	1620	444	209	719	2159	619	1039	400	1827	582	727	1251	400	230	975	1363	603	1038	426	919	242	777	1353	147	1143	2534	656
Stuttgart	224	671	1102	2112	3406	761	656		161	1625	2400	370	1147	472	604	2171	1554	192	879	1365	220	530	912	1861	659	327	831	2428	473	1004	365	1792	547	692	1216	501	195	844	1475	790	919	544	1080	344	633	1211	268	1309	2392	632
Torino	432	959	1623	2813	4107	551		656	612	2327	2051	666	733	1012	761	1757	2255	763	222	951	598	144	384	1812	332	750	1141	2130	1030	1705	966	2493	1248	1393	1917	258	824	430	1785	1025	1135	936	890	357	1190	1179	465	891	2360	1152
Trieste	718	494	1158	2756	4050		551	761	890	2270	2545	391	710	727	1260	1734	2196	692	716	928	527	935	418	2006	883	1078	1582	2692	973	1648	1130	2436	1191	1336	1860	740	960	407	2226	1466	584	1295	1441	759	1147	628	768	1452	1809	1397
Tromsø	3629	3454	3304	1294		4050	4107	3406	3441	1778	5500	3659	4492	3175	3598	5516	1852	3340	4215	4710	3509	4207	3916	4961	3905	3347	3574	5500	3040	2468	3159	1390	2870	2714	2155	3809	3217	4189	-	3458	3702	3294	4260	3651	2791	4096	3543	4604	5277	3142
Trondheim	2335	2160	2086		1294	2756	2813	2112	2147	886	4206	2365	3198	1881	2304	4222	558	2046	2921	3416	2215	2913	2622	3667	2611	2053	2280	4206	1746	1174	1861	894	1576	1420	861	2515	1923	2895	-	2164	2408	2000	2966	2357	1497	2802	2249	3310	3983	1848
Warzawa	1291	684		2086	3304	1158	1623	1102	1248	1526	3660	957	1868	630	1588	2892	1528	910	1874	2086	1044	1479	2047	3121	1727	1394	1625	3422	682	990	1099	1712	813	872	1190	1704	1077	1565	2269	1509	709	1412	2420	1540	582	1103	1338	2503	2284	1218
Wien	759		664	2160	3454	494	959	671	806	1590	2939	293	1145	312	1263	2169	1602	491	1164	1363	443	815	1383	2400	1198	980	1422	2996	569	1054	889	1757	972	1117	1264	1040	709	842	2066	1306	248	1100	1756	876	663	642	846	1839	1823	1156
Zürich		759	1291	2335	3629	718	432	224	220	1849	2176	466	907	661	578	1931	1777	381	655	1125	316	306	688	1637	436	429	894	2233	662	1227	587	2015	770	915	1439	277	417	604	1538	778	1007	646	993	120	846	1346	86	1085	2527	854

Syd-Skandinavia · Sydskandinavien · Skandinavia eteläosa
South Scandinavia · Südskandinavien · Zuid-Skandinavië
Scandinavie du Sud · Escandinavia meridional
Scandinavia meridionale · Νοτιος Σκανδιναβία · Güney İskandinavya

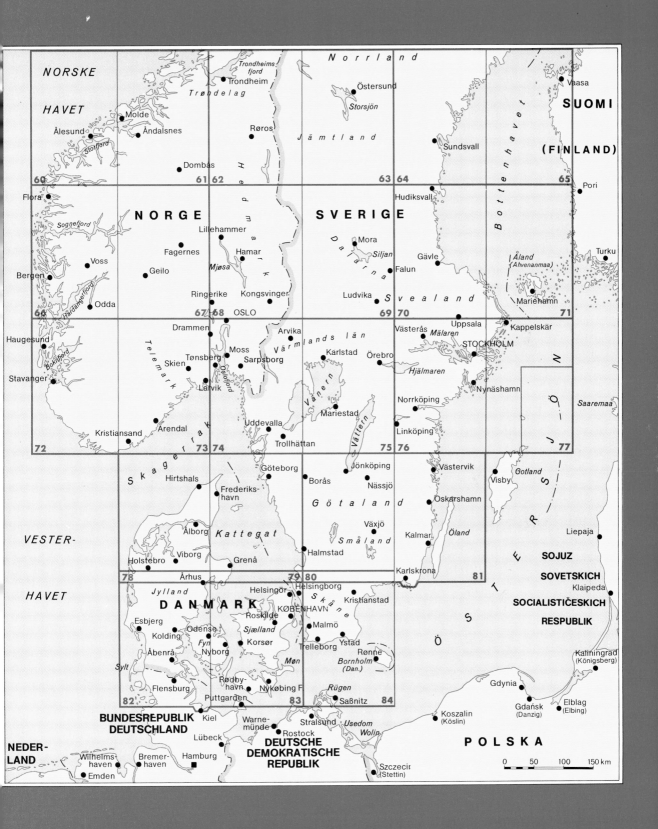

N O R S K E H A V E T

Kråksund
Bjørnsund
Ona
Sandøy
Go

Harøya
Fjørtoft
Ulla fyr Flem
Haramsøya Flemsøya
Hellevik fyr Austnes Hildrestranda
Lepsøya Roald Vigra
Erkna fyr Vigra
Alnes Giske Valderøy
Godøy Ålesund
Gjuv Borgund

Midsund Otrø
Mia 729
Fiksdal
Brattvåg Skærjngen 661
Sävik 659 1062
Hamnsund 17 Vatne 661
Skodje
658 10 Mev
Sjøholt
Spjelkavik Brusdal
E69 Ørskog
Blindhm. 12 60 Magerholm Vagsvik
Emlein Klokk Ramstad
Festøy Sykkylven Fjellseter hot.
Barstadvik Hundeidvik Bergheim
Trollkyrkja

Rundøy fyr Grœsøyane fyr
Rundøy Breisund
Brandal
Nerlandsøy Flø
Leinestrand Hareid- Sula
Fosnavåg Ulsteinvik landet Sulesund Sulø
Svinøy fyr Herøy Hareid Solvåg
654 Hjørungavåg
Sande 61 Alme Vartdal
Kwamsøy Gurskøy Gursken 653 Rjånes Buset Romedalshorn
496 Sande Leikanger Berknes 14 1460 Standalshytta
Larsens Vollnes Skrede 1303 Ørsta Storestandel
Ervik Åram Årvik Ørsta Hjørundfjord Urke Engeset
Stadlandet 599 Koparnes Rovde Asen Søbø Stogjen
Hoddevika Leikanger 38 Fiskå Eidsås 971 Lauvstad 655 Øye Hotell 1588
620 Dalsfjord Volda Bondalseidet Storhorn
Sildegapet Syvde 651 Folkestad 1546 Storfjorden Viddal 655
Krakenes Skorgenes Selje Vanylven Dale Austefjord Bjørke
fyr St. Synneva (Hove) 1285 Straumshamn Tussavaten Hellesy
Kloster 619 Aheim Volda Sunn
Nord-Vågsøy Bårmen Bjørkedal Kalvatn Tryggestad
618 Almklov Steinsvik 4.2 60
Vagsøy 617 Bryggja 61 Maurstad 13 Kjølsdal 54 Stårheim 21 Navelesaker Hornindal
Måløy Deknepollen Totland Haus 15 Hjelle Stigedalen Grodås Hornindal
Husevagoy Rugsund Davik Nordfjordeid Eid Skrede 5/s Lunde
Bremangerlandet Isane Torheim Nor 14 1270 Langeset Nedstryn
Bremanger Berle Langesi Ålfoten 14 Lote Glittereggja 16 Stryn Oppst
616 Frøya Fræya Aksla Hestenesøyri 41 (377m) Randabygd 613 17 Loen
Kalvåg 592 Svelgen Kleppenes Nolfjorden 8 Innvik 60
Kvannhovden fyr Midtgulen Bremanger 612 Vereide Utvik 61 Olden Bø
Hovden Ålfotbreen Straume Gjemmestad Hjelmsminne Bødal
614 1630 Hyen Holme Sandane 14 17 Stryn
Grøfjellet 615 Gloppen Breim Byrkjelo Mykland Oldevatnet
697 Norddal Gröndal Storvaten 39 Egge Snønipa Briksdalsbre
Lykkjebø Hjortset Breimsvaten 1827 Briksdal
Skorpa Flora Brandsøy Flora Gjengedal Blåfjellet Bogstad Hotell Melkevoll
Kinnakyrhia Indre 5 Emhjella 1390 20 Ămot
Eikefjord Endestadvaden Eimhjellvaten Mykland Grovebreen
Stavøy 29 Nes Naustdal Førde 1636 Suphellenipa
Askrova Vallestad Osøyra Vonevs Helgheim Klakegg
Svanøy Stavang Vadsetet 80 Øybost Aksla Skei Hotell Lunde
Vevring Blåfjell Horstad 52 Ålhus Suphellenipa
Grimeli Hegrenes 791 Naustdal 611 Jølstraholmen 188 Grovebreen
609 Redals- grend Vassenden Grøning Bøyumseter
Stongfjord Løvik Ervik Førde 14 Mundal Hotell
Herland Grimeli Moskog 5 Holsen Fjærland
Værlandet Askvoll Holmedal Eikenes Førde Haukedal
Atløy Bygstad o r d Etterli Haukedalsvaten
Vilnes Dale Eidevik Storehaug
Fysse 57 Viksdalen
20 14

66 Borgund

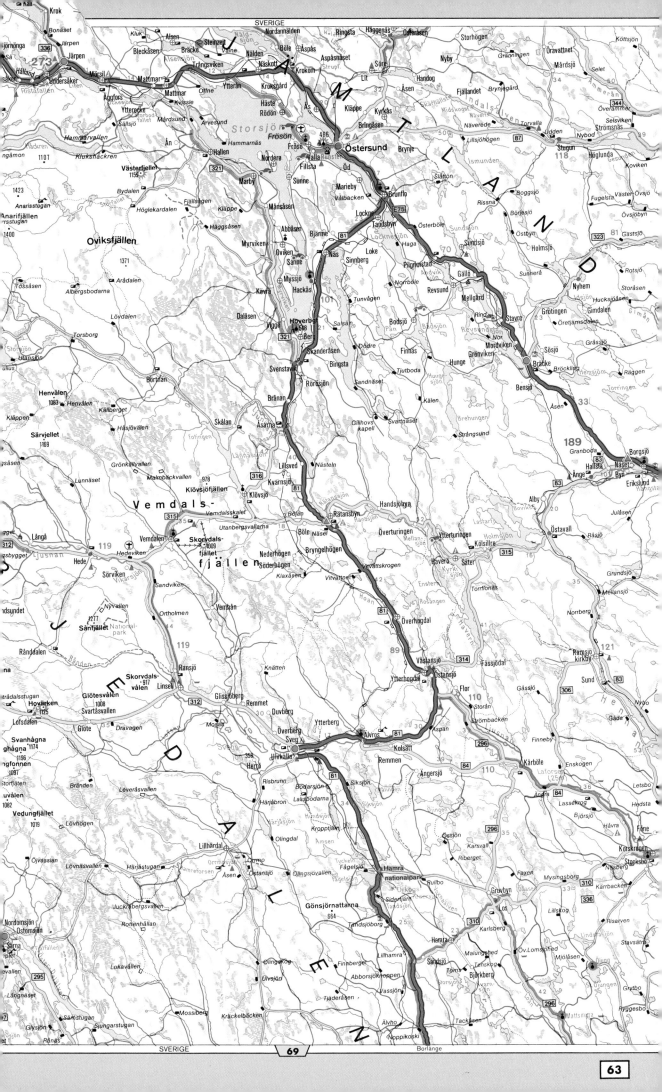

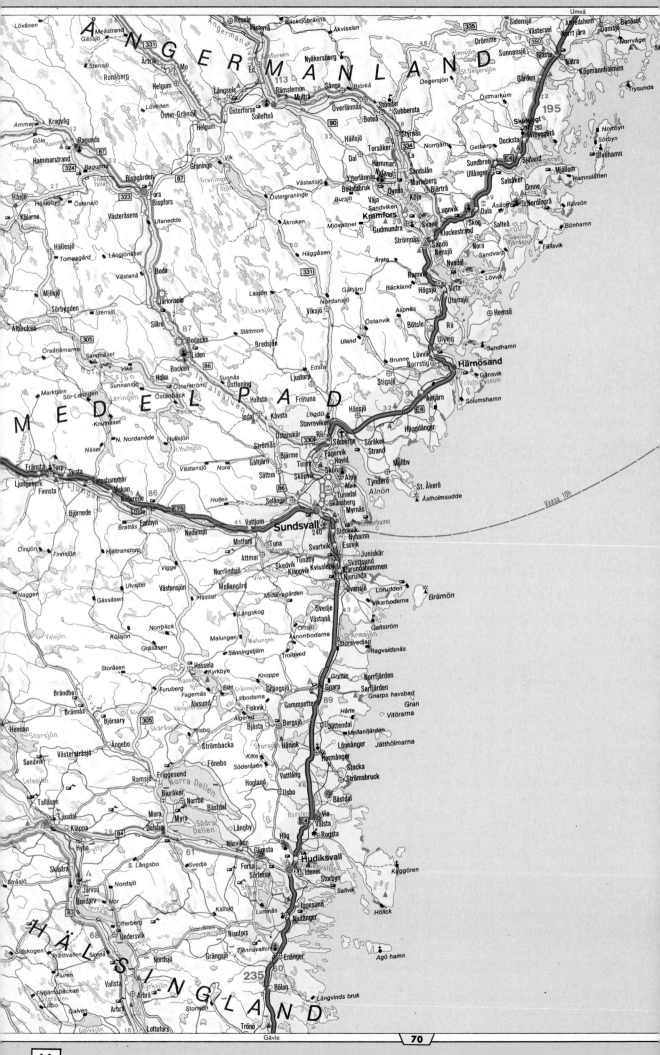

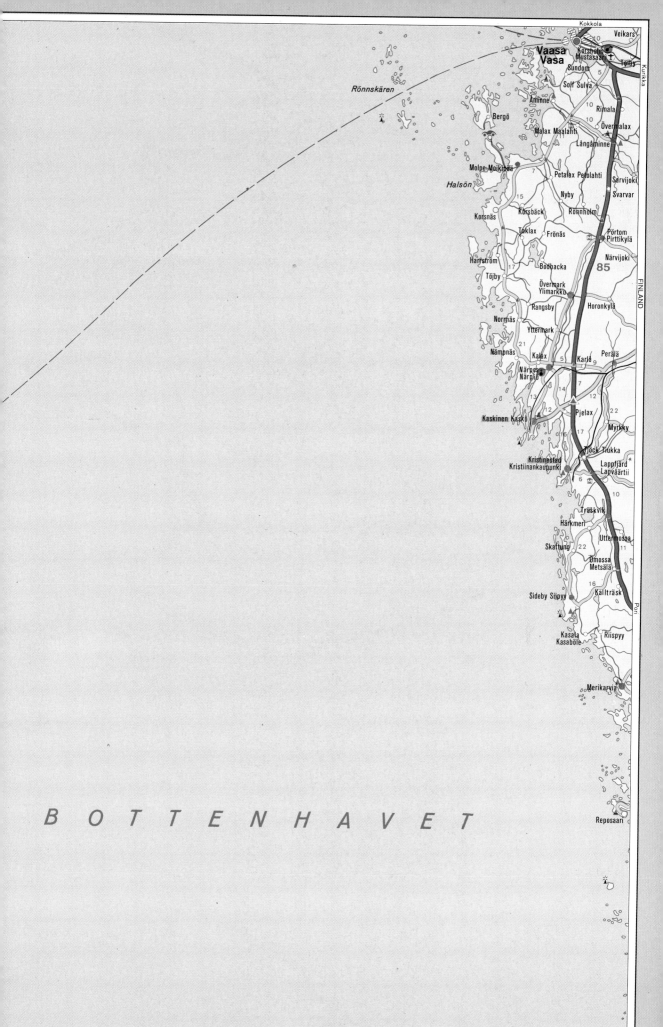

Kokkola

Veikars

Vaasa
Vasa

Korsholm
Mustasaari

Tölby

Kurikka

Sundom

Solf Sulva

Aminne

Rimala

Bergö

Malax Maalahti

Övermalax

Långåminne

Molpe Moikipää

Petalax Petolahti

Sarvijoki

Halsön

Nyby

Svarvar

Korsbäck

Rönnholm

Korsnäs

Pörtom
Pirttikylä

Taklax

Frönäs

Närvijoki

Harrström

Bodbacka

85

Töjby

Övermark
Ylimarkku

FINLAND

Rangsby

Horonkylä

Norrnäs

Yttermark

Nämpnäs

Perälä

Kalax

Karla

Närpes
Närpiö

Pjelax

Myrkky

Kaskinen Kaskö

Tjöck Tiukka

Kristinestad
Kristiinankaupunki

Lappfjärd
Lapväärtii

Träskvik

Härkmeri

Uttermossa

Skaftung

Ömossa
Metsälä

Pori

Sideby Siipyy

Källträsk

Kasala
Kasaböle

Riispyy

Merikarvia

BOTTENHAVET

Reposaari

Rönnskären

Florø Øybost Aksla Stryn

Skudeneshavn 72

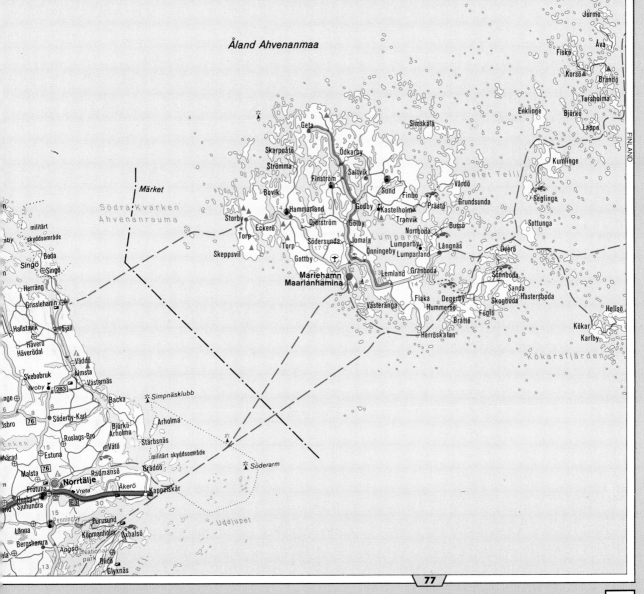

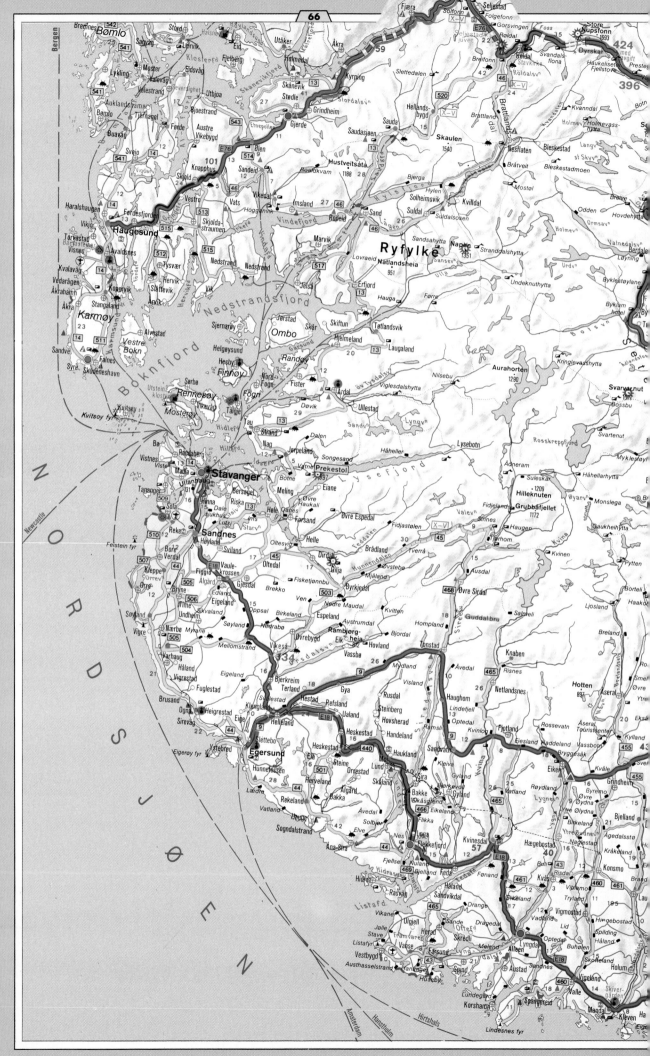

SKAGERRAK

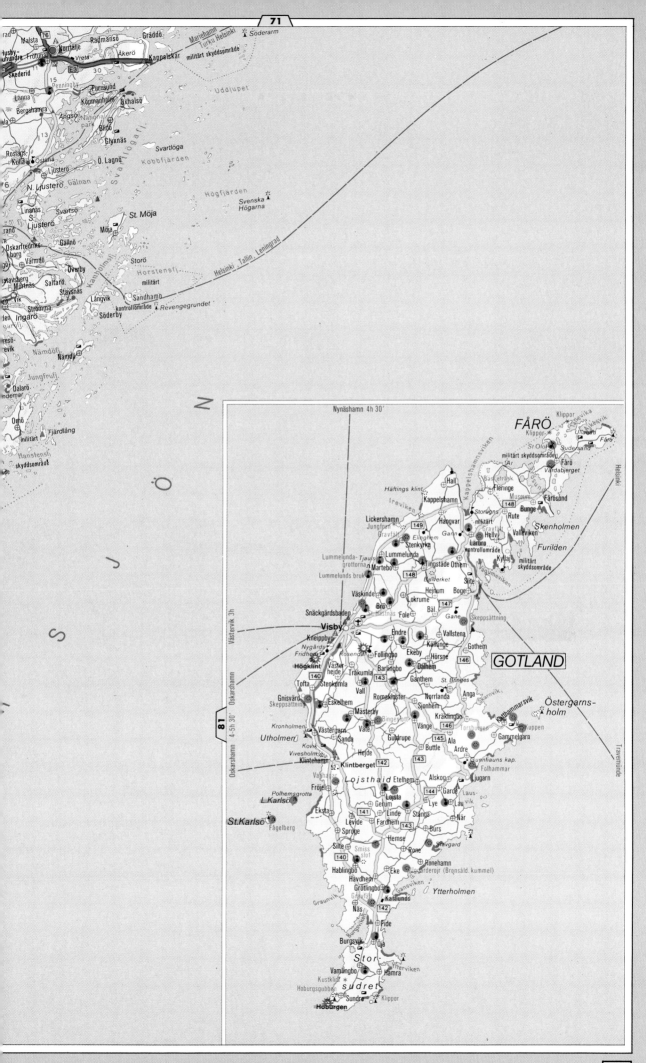

S K A G E R R A K

Kristiansand
Stavanger 11h   4h 30'

Egersund 7h 30'

Tórshavn 3th

Felixtowe- Göteborg

Tannis B

Jammerbugt

Hirtshals   Tannisby
                   Uggerby
                   Mos
Skallerup-   Bjergby
Klit   Sinda
Lønstrup   Hjørring
Mårup
Rubjerg 14 Knude   Ugilt
Gølstrup 21   Rakkeby   Ilbro   Tårs
Lyngby   Vrejlev-
Løkken   Børglum   kloster
              Borglum-   Serritslev   Øster
              kloster   Vendsys 47   Jerslev
Ingstrup   Øster
              Vester   Brønderslev Helli
44   Hjermitslev Brønderslev
      55   Hune   Klokkerholm
Blokhus   13
         Pandrup   Tylstrup Ajstrup
                          Vadum   Hammer   Dronning
Lildstrand Tranumstrand 11   20   Bakken   Horsens
Bulbjerg   Svinkløv   Lindholm
47   Slettestrand Åbybro Bratsk Nørresundby Vester
Hanstholm Vester Torup Hjortdal Tranum 15 Lindholm (Wikmenst) Hassing
         Vust Frøstrup Fjerritslev Svenstrup Gjøl Ø
Vigsø   Bjerget   20   15 Brovst Øland Oksholm
Ræhr   Skræm   Kokkedal Tørslev
         Hjardemål Gøttrup Haverslev   Nørhalne Ålborg
Klitmøller 29 Kastrup   26   Farstrup Sebbersund
Nors 26   Øsløs   Aggersborg Aggersund Nibe Sønderholm Sønder
Vester Vandet   Østerild Arup   Lundby Vokslev Tranders Klarup
  Vandet Sø   Løgstør Skarp Borup Øster Svenstrup Sejlflod
Nørre Skinnerup   Salling Bislev Hornum Lindenborg Gudumholm
Vorupør Sjørring Thisted   Ranum Vindblæs 29 Ellidshøj Nørre Kongerslev Vårst
Røsvang Hundborg   Ejerslev Livø Gundersted Vegger Støvring Volstad Kongerslev Lille
Stenbjerg Thy Sejlbjerg Livø Bredning Flejsborg 23 Blenstrup Gammel Lyngby
Snedsted Skjoldborg 89 24 Vitskøl Hornum Suldrup Skørping Skørping Torup
Lyngby Sønder Salgjerhøj Øster Jølby Trend Bjørnsholm Blære Giver Rebild Rold Bakker Terndrup
Svindborg Dråby Skyum 19 Tæbring Nederby Ertebølle Havbro   Års Arestrup Rold Skov Nat. Park Solbjerg
Lodbjerg Hassing Koldby Tedsø 26 Nykøbing Strandby Sønder Nørlund Astrup
Bedsted Mors Dueholm Selde Farsø Borremose Haverslev Rold Vilhestrup Rostrup
Agger Visby Karby Glyngøre Durup Torum Vognsild Østrup Ravnkilde Arden Øster Visbor Hadsund
Vesterivig Heltborg Legind Hvalpsund Thise Ullits Vester Kongens Simested Øster Doense Ove Vive
Helligsø Ydby Bjerge Haltrø Rosløv Fovlum Bøll Tisted Nørager Rørbæk Hadsund
Thyborøn Øster Legind Ø Øster Grinderslev Alstrup Vester 110 Hørby Assens Havn
Hurup Hvidbjerg Hessel Gedsted Bølle Simested Stenild Hobro Mariager Kastbjerg
Limfjorden Agerø Øster Assels Vester Fjelsø Hvam Snæbum Øls Fyrkat Dalbyover
Nissum Bredning Bøddum Grønning Lovns Bredning Ulbjerg Vester 81 Vester Tørslev Kærby
Harboør Lyngs Jegind Rødding Oddense Lyby Testrup Møldrup Gassum
Odby Hvidbjerg Jegind Ø Sønder Hem Øxslev Kloster 13 Glenstrup Hald Gje
Nissumby Spøttrup Balling Krabbesholm Sundstrup Klejtrup Borup
Oddesund Olhme Lem Højslev Nørre Kvols Låstrup Mellerup Tvede
Lemvig Nord Kås Veno By Stby Ørum Lynderup Handest Harridslev E3
Hove Bjerge 34 Skive Kobberup Vester Nørre Øster Borup
Ferring 12 Veno Ranbjerg Vorde Rødding Vinge Vorning Ørum 40 Randers
Bovbjerg Lemvig Resen Estvad Fiskbæk Romlund Tjele Vammen Hammershøj Randers
Fjaltring 45 Struer Sahl Vinderup Nørre Borris 26 Vester Velling Hvorslev Øst
Ramme 28 Bugt Den gamle Kirke Vroue Mønsted Vester Vinkel Skjern kirke Ulstrup 46 Laurbjerg Lime
Bøvlingbjerg Vejrum Kirkeby Vandsby Freiluftmus. Fly Stoholm 51 Ravnstrup Asmild Kloster Bjerringbro Langå Lerbjerg Øst 36
Vemb Flynder Kirke Linde Sevel Rydhave Borbjerg Dåsbjerg Finderup Vejrum Vinge Houlbjerg Hadsten E3
Bækmarksbro Møborg Asp Handbjerg Mønsted 71 Resen Kongenshus Haldrum Gullev Halling
Nees By Navr Hjerm 18 Haderup Hodsager Bakken Dollerup Rødkærsbro Tange Aidt Haldum Sperring
Bur Idum 16 Tvis Over Grove Frederiks Amsstrup Sjørslev Lysgård 38 Torning Kjellerup Hinge Farvang 65 Trige
Staby Råsted Kirke Vind Holstebro Felding Simmelkær Karup Løvring Ans Hammel Todbe
Ulfborg Ulfborg Vinding 12 Ilskov 201 Kjellerup Grøn Thorsø Frijsenborg Vokby
Vedersø Tihøje Ørre 34 Vinderslev Tvilum Hinge Lemming 52 Gjern 20 Sabro 26
Vedersø Klint 111 Øre Stora Sunds 13 Kragelund Voel Sørring Silkeborg Låsby ÅRHUS
Sønderby Torsted Kirke Vildbjerg Sinding Navling Bording 46 Graballe 15 53
Stadil Ørnhøj 32 Trehøje 18 Timring Kirke kast Engesvang Gjellerup Silkeborg 14 Lasby
Hee Hover 11 103 Herning Gjellerup

S Vemb Stora

Ringkøbing Esbjerg Ringkøbing Vejle 82 Vejle

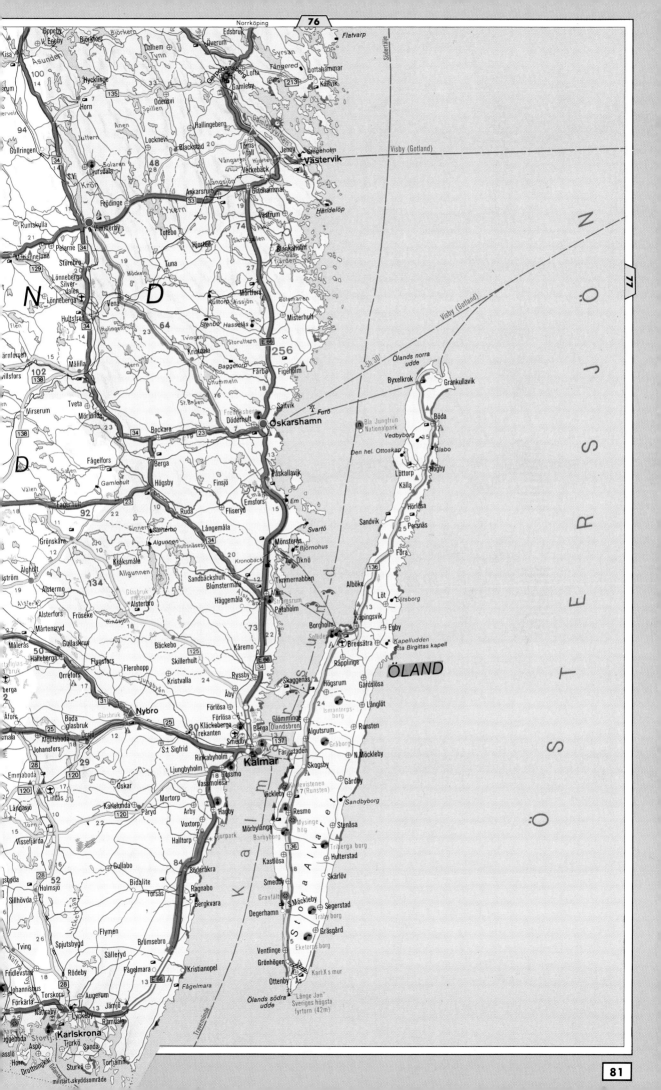

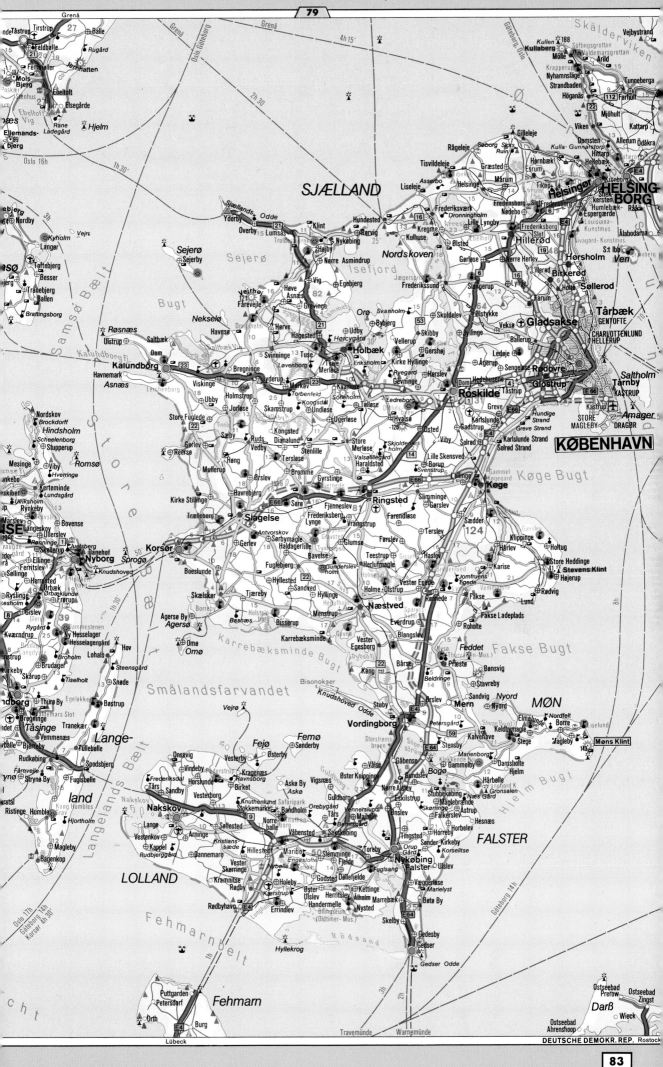

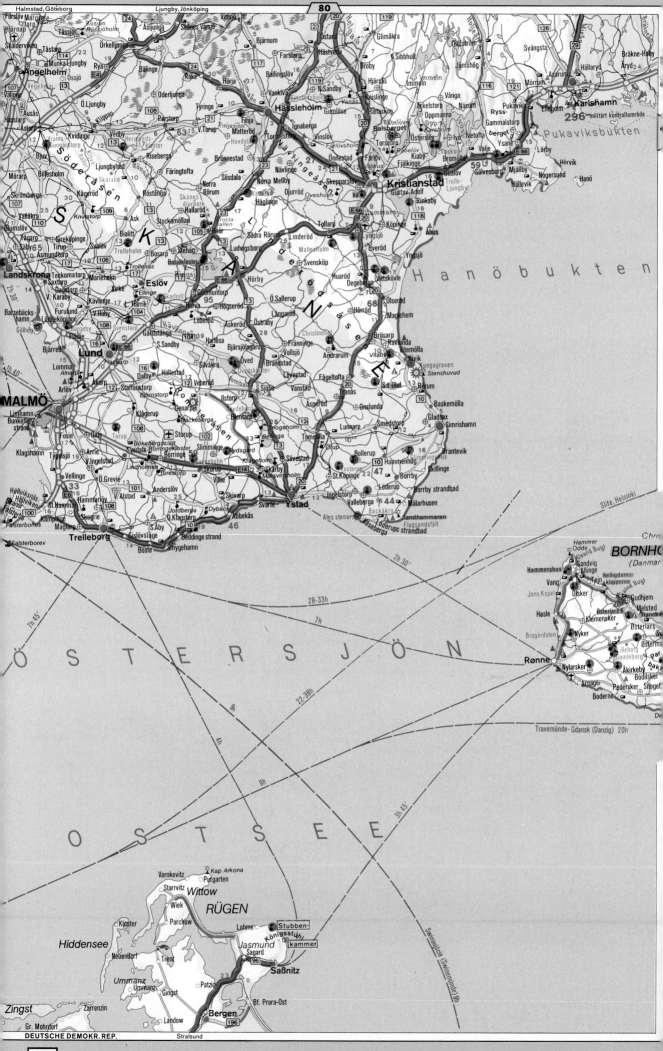

Förslöv Margrete-
torp
Skälderviken
Angelholm
Vejeholm
E4
Vallinge
Munka-Ljungby
Ausås
Hasslarp
Mörarp
Skromberga
Billesholm
Vallåkra
Glumslöv
Säby
Asmundtorp
Landskrona
Barsebäcks-
hamn
Gillhög
Bjärred
Lomma
Alnarp
Arlöv

MALMÖ
Limhamn
Bunkeflo-
strand
Klagshamn
Tygelsjö
Vellinge
Ö. Grevie
Hällviksnäs
Höllviken
Skanör
Falsterbo
Falsterborev

Trelleborg
Smygehamn

Tåstarp
Rya
Örkelljunga
Åsljunga
Skånes Värsjö
Vittsjö
Östanå
Glimåkra
Öström
Svängsta
Bräkne-Hoby
Åryd

Hjärnap
Roston
Rössjöholm
24
Bjärnum
Farstorp
Hästveda
Broby
Sibbhult
Jämshög
Hällaryd

Örkened
Oderljunga
Bällingslöv
N.Sandby
Hjärsås
Immeln
Vånga
Näsum
Mörrum
Karlshamn
296
militärt kontrollområde

Hässleholm
Gumlösa
Hanaskog
Arkelstorp
Österslöv
Pukavik
Gammalstorp
berget
Pukaviksbukten

Kristianstad
Gustav Adolf
Rinkaby
Åhus

H a n ö b u k t e n

Ö S T E R S J Ö N

O S T S E E

BORNHOLM
(Danmark)
Hammershus
Sandvig
Allinge
Hasle
Rønne
Nylarsker
Arnager
Boderne

Kap Arkona
Varnkevitz
Putgarten
Starrvitz
Wittow
Wiek
Parchow
RÜGEN
Kloster
Hiddensee
Neuendorf
Trent
Ummanz
Gingst
Patzig
Lohme
Jasmund
Sagard
Saßnitz
Stubben-
kammer
Bf. Prora-Ost

Zingst
Gr. Mohrdorf
Zarrenzin
Landow
Bergen

Great Britain, Ireland
Storbritannia, Irland · Storbritannien, Eire · Englanti, Irlanti
Storbritannien, Irland · Großbritannien, Irland
Groot-Brittannië, Ierland · Grande-Bretagne, Irlande
Gran Bretaña, Irlanda · Gran Bretagna, Irlanda
Μεγαλη Βρεταννία, Ιρλανδία · Büyük Britanya, İrlanda

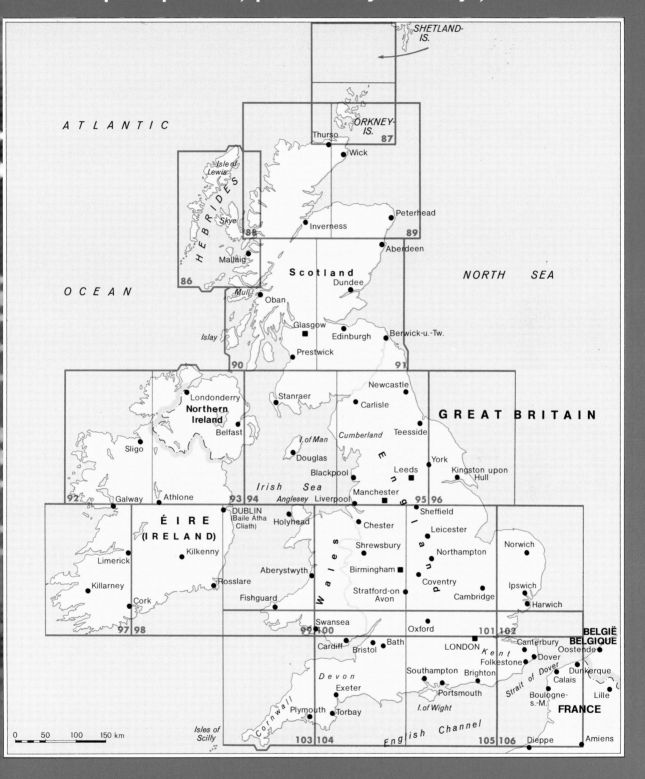

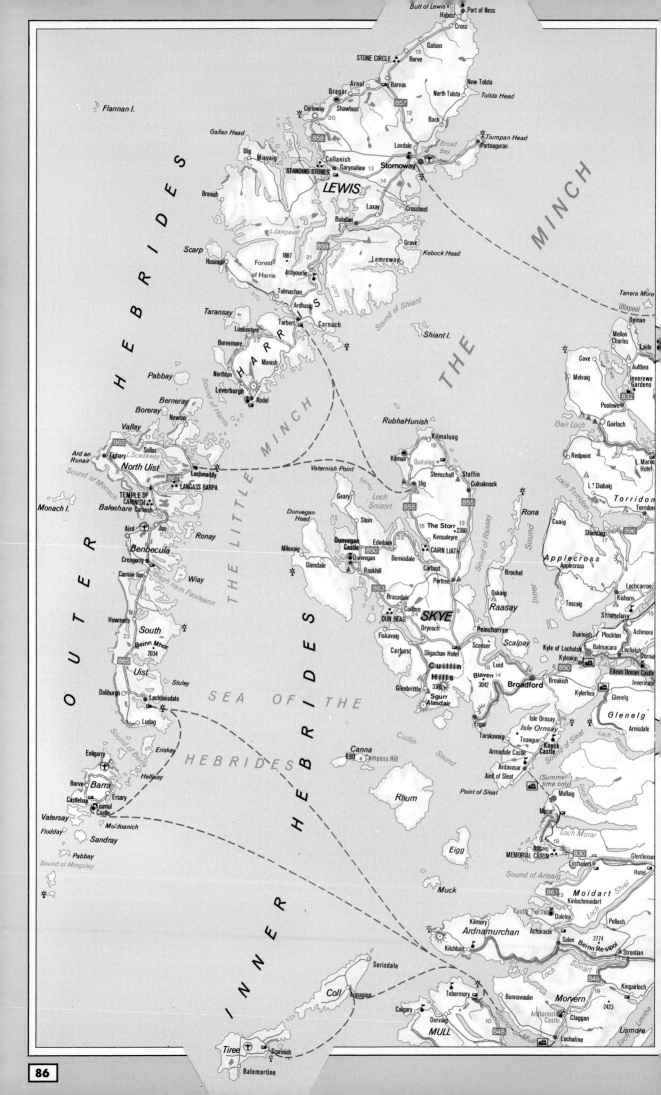

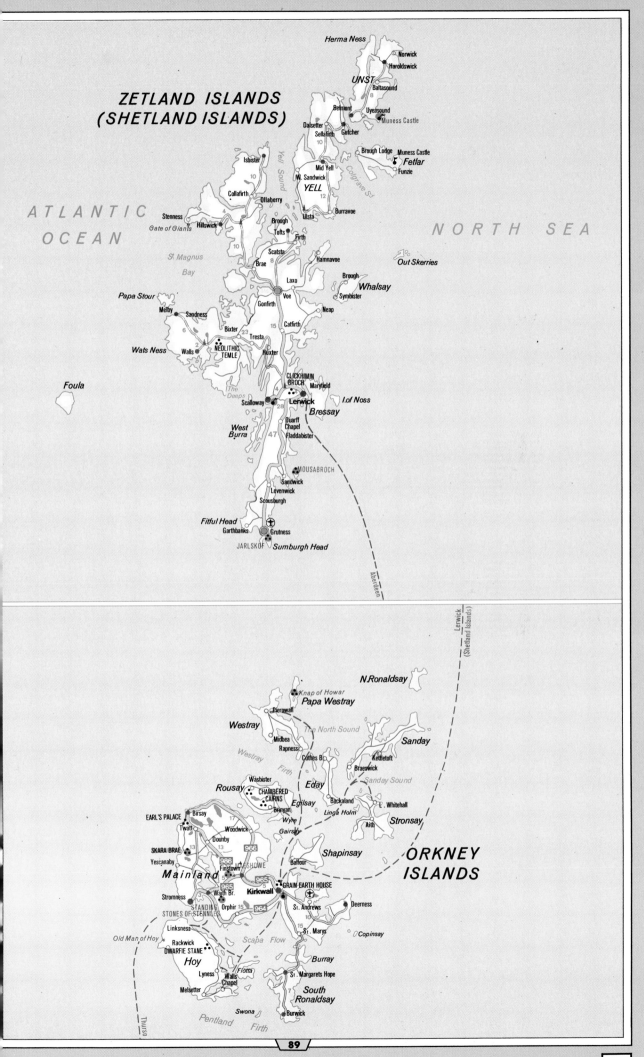

ZETLAND ISLANDS (SHETLAND ISLANDS)

ATLANTIC OCEAN

NORTH SEA

Herma Ness

Norwick
Haroldswick

UNST

Baltasound
8

Belmont
Uyeasound

Muness Castle

Dalsetter
Sellafirth
Gutcher

10

Brough Lodge
Muness Castle

Fetlar

Isbister
Mid Yell
Funzie

10
W. Sandwick

YELL

Collafirth
Ollaberry
12

Stenness
Ulsta
Burravoe

Gate of Giants
Hallswick

Brough
Tofts
Firth

St. Magnus Bay
Scatsta
8
Hamnavoe

Out Skerries

Brae
Laxo
Brough

Voe
Whalsay

Symbister

Papa Stour
Gonfirth
Neap

Melby
Sandness
15
Catfirth

Bixter
The Deeps

Tresta

Wats Ness
Walls
2
NEOLITHIC TEMLE
Huxter

Foula

CLICKHIMIN BROCH
Maryfield

4
Scalloway
I. of Noss

28
Lerwick
Bressay

West Burra
Ouarff
Chapel
47
Fladdabister

MOUSABROCH

Sandwick
Levenwick
Scousburgh

Fitful Head
Garthbanks
Grutness

JARLSKOF
Sumburgh Head

Aberdeen

Lerwick (Shetland Islands)

N.Ronaldsay

Knap of Howar
Papa Westray

Pierowall

Westray
The North Sound

Midbea
Sanday

Rapness
Kettletoft

Westray Firth
Cothes B.
Braeswick

Sanday Sound

Washbister
Backaland
E. Whitehall

Rousay
Eday
Linga Holm
Stronsay

CHAMBERED CAIRNS
Egilsay
Aith

EARL'S PALACE
Birsay
Brinyan
Wyre
Gairsay

Twatt
Woodwick

SKARA BRAE
Dounby
13
Shapinsay

Yescanaby
966
Balfour

Mainland
986
Finstown
GRAIN EARTH HOUSE

965
Kirkwall

ORKNEY ISLANDS

Stromness
Wasth Br.
5

STANDING STONES OF STENNESS
Orphir
15
964
St. Andrews

Deerness

Linksness
St. Marys

Old Man of Hoy
Copinsay

Rackwick
Scapa Flow

DWARFIE STANE
Burray

Hoy
Lyness
Flotta
St. Margarets Hope

Walls
Chapel
7
South Ronaldsay

Melsetter
Swona
Burwick

Pentland Firth

Thurso

ATLANTIC OCEAN

THE MINCH

Cape Wrath
Strathy Point
Thorshavn (seasonal)

Aghleam
Balnakeil
Eilean nan Ron
Sheigra
Durness
Smoo Cave
Strathan
Armadale
Strathy
Reay
Reay Bridge
Forss W.
Portskerra
Melness
Coldbackie
Hope Lo.
Bettyhill
Golval
838
Eriboll
Tongue
Dalhalvaig
Kinlochbervie
28
836
Altnabreac
19
Rhiconich
Loch Loyal
Strath Naver
21
897
Dion ard
Laxford Bridge
Altnacaillich
DUN DORNAIGIL BROCH
17
Loch nan Cuinne
Forsinard Hotel
Scourie
L.Stack
Reay
L.Meadie
Loch Choire Lodge
Baddanloch
Clutt Lodge
Achfary
18
Forest
Kinbrace
Kildonan
Berriedale W.
Kylestrome
838
37
Altnaharra
Loch nan Clar
17
Culkein
Drumbeg
L.Naver
Torrish Lo.
Clashnessie
Quinag 2653
Unapool
The Crask Inn
Loch Choire
Balnacoil Lodge
Ben Uarll 2046
Lochinver
Inchnadamph
Overscaig Hotel
Loch Shin
Shinness
11
9
Inverkirkaig
15
L.Assynt 19
Canisp 2779
Ben More Assynt 3773
Duchally
KINTRADWELL
130
Crackaig
Rubha Coigach
Enard Bay
Inverpolly
Ledmore Lo.
Glen Cassley
Lairg
Pittentrail
L.Brora
Brora
9
Reiff
Elphin
Almacealgach Hotel
836
21
Golspie
Summer Isles
L. Lurgain
835
Rosehall
839
14
Dunrobin Castle
Coigach
Tanera Mor
837
20
1408
Oykel Bridge
9
Altassmore
836
113
Embo
DUN CANNA BROCH
Strath Oykel
10
Culrain
Carbisdale Castle
Invershin
Birichen
Poles
Achiltibuie
Culnacraig
Strathkanaird
Croick
Bonar Bridge
Clashmore
Dornoch
Opinan
Ardmair
Rhidorroch Old Lodge
1650
Ardgay
15
Skibo Castle
Dornoch Firth
Tarbat Ness
Mellon Charles
Badluchrach
Ullapool
Carron
Kincardine
Spinningdale
Edderton
Portmahomack
Cove
Laide
Gruinard
Ardcharnich
Inverlael
Deanich Lodge
Gleann Mor
Kildermorie Lodge
Aultnamain Inn
11
Tain
Inver
Melvaig
Aultbea
Little Gruinard
39
Dundonnell Hotel
Loch na Sealga
12
Beinn Dearg 3547
Braemore
L.Morie
Ardross
9
Fearn
Balintore
Inverewe Gardens
Fionn Loch
835
Corrieshalloch Gorge Falls of Measach
Wyvis Lodge
836
15
Barbaraville
Nigg
832
Poolewe
Strathnasheallag
Loch Vaich
Strathvaich Lodge
L.Glass
Eileanach Lodge
Alness
Invergordon
Cromarty
Gair Loch
Gairloch
Sgurr Mor 3637
20
Altguish Inn
Inchbae Lo.
8
Evanton
Balblair
Moray Firth
Letterewe
L. Maree Hotel
Fannich Lodge
Loch Fannich
Foulis Castle
Tulloch Castle
832
Rosemarkie
Fort George
Nairn
Redpoint
L.Maree
Kinlochewe
Achnasheen
832
Strath Bran
Loch Luichart
Contin
Dingwall
Black Isle
Fortrose
Avoch
Ardersier
Auldearn
96
38
Loch Maree
Beinn Eighe 3309
Meig
Strathpeffer
832
Conon Bridge
Munlochy
939
Cawdor
Torridon
Torridon
896
Glencarron Lodge
Scardroy Lodge
Orrin Res.
Muir of Ord
New Kessock
CLAVA STONES
Croy
Ferness
23
Cuaig
Ben Damph
890
Achnashellach Lodge
18
Beauly
862
10
INVERNESS
Shieldaig
Carron
Glen
L.Monar
Orrin Res.
Davion
Dearn
Applecross
Applecross
Lochcarron
Strathcarron
Inchvuilt
Farrar
Struy
Dores
Moy
Lochindorb
Kishorn
Glass
Glen Convinth
82
18
Grantown-on-Spey
Toscaig
Ling
Cozae Lodge
Cannich
CHAMBERED CAIRN
Drumnadrochit
Freeburn Hotel
Dulnain Bridge
31
Strathcarron
Achmore
L.Mullardoch
3773
Duthil
10
Stromeferry
Glen Cannich
Bearnock
Urquhart Castle
Torness
Tomatin
Carrbridge
Duirinish
Plockton
Carnach
Loch Ness
12
Kyle of Lochalsh
Balmacara
Lochalsh
Dornie
Carn Eige 3877
Affric Lodge
Glen Affric
13
Errogie
Carn Odhar 2618
L.Spey
850
Kyleakin
Eilean Donan Castle
Invermoriston
Inverfarigaig
Coignafearn Lodge
Boat of Garten
Broadford
Kylerhea
Glenelg
Shiel Bridge
Falls of Glomach
White Bridge Hotel
Strath Findhorn

90

Fort William, Glasgow
Pass of Killiecrankie, Perth

88

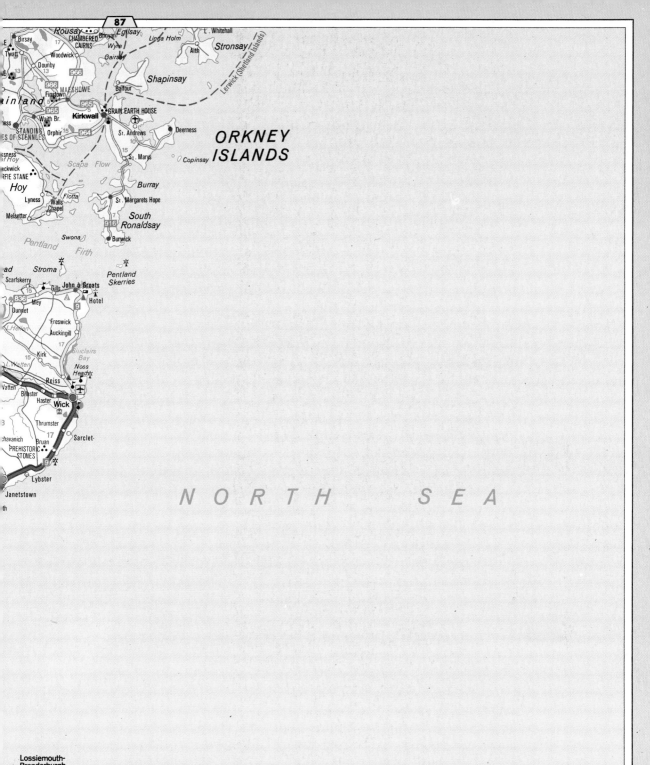

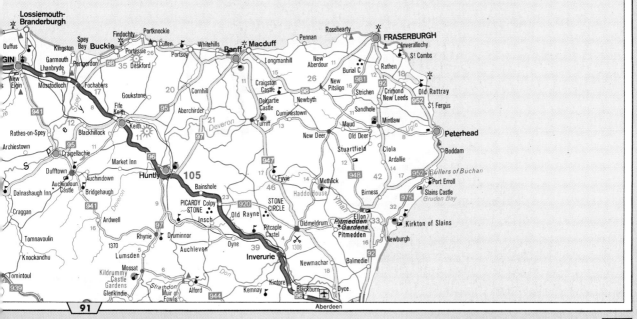

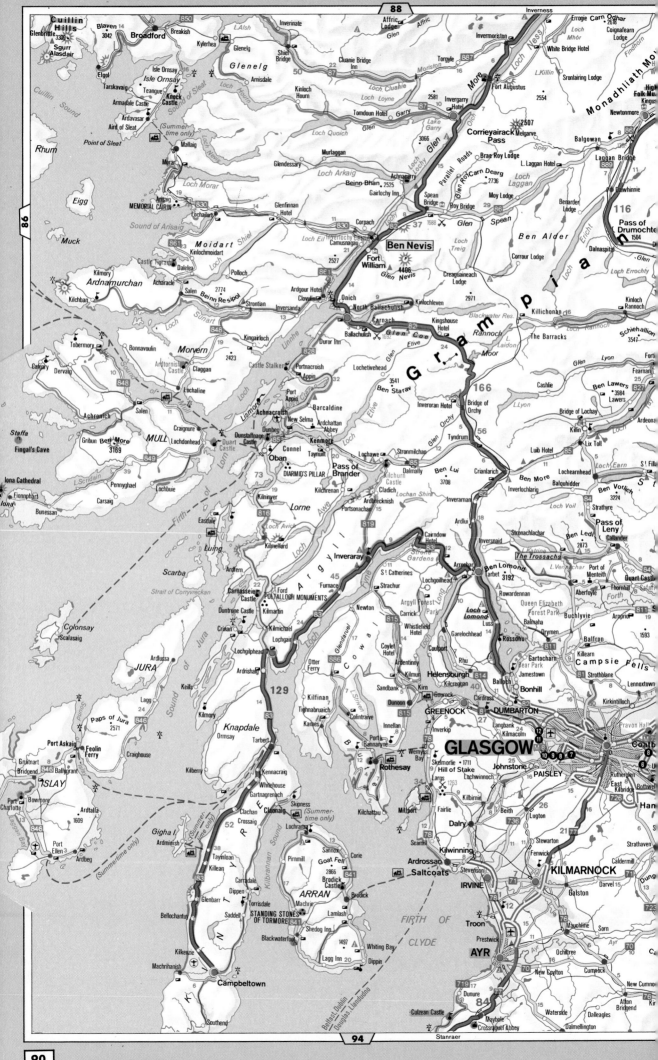

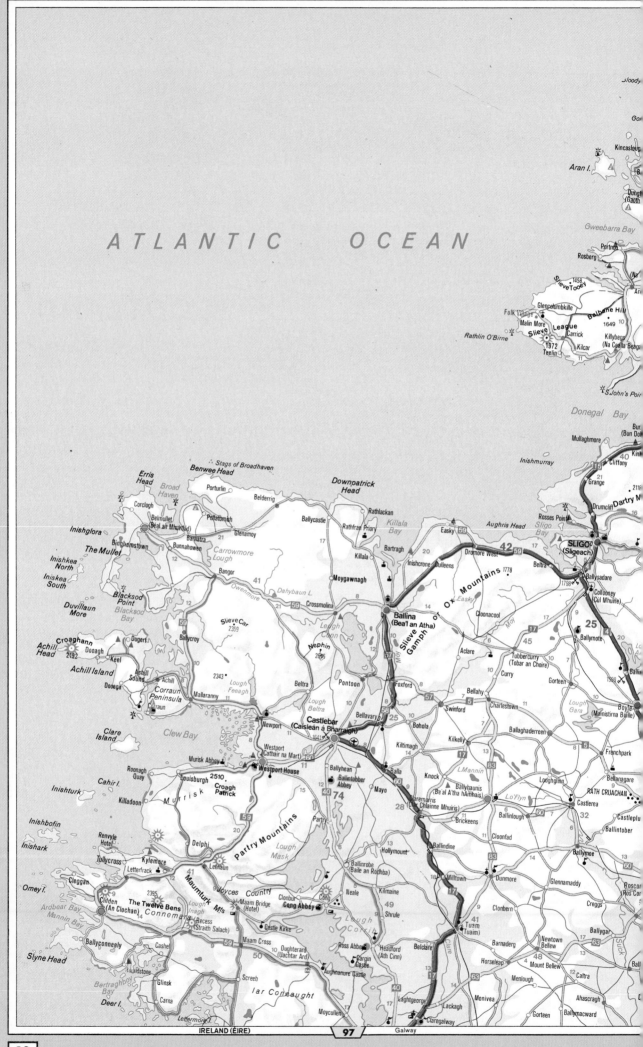

ATLANTIC OCEAN

KINTYRE
Southend
Mull of Kintyre   Sanda

Ayr, Glasgow

Culzean Castle   719   77
Maybole
Turnberry
Crossraguel
Abbey
New Dailly
Girvan

Waterside   Dalleagles
Kirkconnel   Sanquhar
Green-Lowther 2403
702
Enterkinfoot
Carronbridge   Drumlanrig Castle
Penpont   Thornhill
Closeburn

Straiton   Dalmellington
Alhang 2100
713
Loch Doon Castle   Carsphairn
Tynron   Moniaive   76
15

Ailsa Craig

51
Lendalfoot   New Dailly
Barr
Polmaddie Hill   1281
Merrick 2764
Carrick
Galloway
Corserine 2668
Rinns of Kells
Castlefern   Dalry   702
Dunscore
Balmaclellan   New Bridge
DUMFRIES
75
Crocketford
Springholm   711

Colmonell
Ballantrae   Glennap Castle Gardens   77
Benera ird 1435

19

Barrhill   22
Bargrennan
714
Forest Park
68
New Galloway
712
Parton
713
1150   Corsock   Shawhead
762
DRUMCOLTRAN TOWER   New Abbey
Dalbeattie
Criffel 1866
12

Cairn Ryan
Kirkcolm
Loch Ryan
Stranraer
Castle Kennedy Gardens
75

The Moors
New Luce
Barlae   15
Newton Stewart
Cairnsmore of Fleet 2331
Creetown
Laurieston   Dee
Gatehouse of Fleet   Cardoness
109
Castle Douglas
Palnackie
Auchencairn   Douglas Hall

The Rinns of Galloway
Innermessan
Whitehill
Dunragit
Glenluce   Kirkcowan
746
Wigtown
CAIRN HOLY   75
75
Tongland
Macfellans Castle   Kirkcudbright   Dundreman

Portpatrick
Sandhead
KIRKMADDINE STONES   716
Logan Gardens
Restricted area
Luce Bay
Chapel Finian
DRUCHTAG MOTEHILL
747
Port William
Sorbie
BIG BALCRAIG MARKED STONES
Whithorn
Garlieston
Barharrow
Borgue   Dirk Hatteraick's Cave
Restricted area
Wightown Bay

LARNE   12   The Maidens

CHANNEL

Drummore
St Niman's Cave
St Ninian's Chapel   Isle of Whithorn
Burrow Head
Mull of Galloway

NORTH

Island Magee
The Goblins   Gransha
Eden   2
Carrickfergus
Carrickfergus Castle
Belfast
Whitehead
Holywood
Bangor
Dundonald   Newtownards
Comber   Mt Stewart Gardens
Greyabbey Abbey
Kircubbin   Ballywalter
Ballygowan   Ballyhalbert
Saintfield   Gardens of Rowallane
Crossgar   Killyleagh   Kearney
Downpatrick   Portaferry
Strangford
Kilclief
Clough   Jordan's Castle   Ardglass
Tyrella   Killough
Dundrum Bay

Mewl I.
Copeland I.
Donaghadee
Millisle
Ards Peninsula
Strangford Lough
Cloghy
Ardkeen

MA
WORKINGT
WHITEHAVEN
St Bees Head
St Bee
E

Point of Ayre
Bride
Jurby   13
Ramsey Bay
Ramsey
Ballaugh
Kirkmichael   Wildlife Park
18   2
Snaefell 2036
Carraghan   1640
Laxey
Maughold

ISLE OF MAN

Peel Castle
Peel
Corrin's Tower
Dalby
Crosby
Foxdale   1
Lady Isabella
DOUGLAS

Milner Tower   Port Erin
MEAYL CIRCLE
Calf of Man   Manx Village Folk Museum
Chicken Rock
Ballasalla
Castletown   Rushen
Langness Point

(Belfast 11)
(4)

I R I S H   S E A

Dublin
Dublin
Llandudno

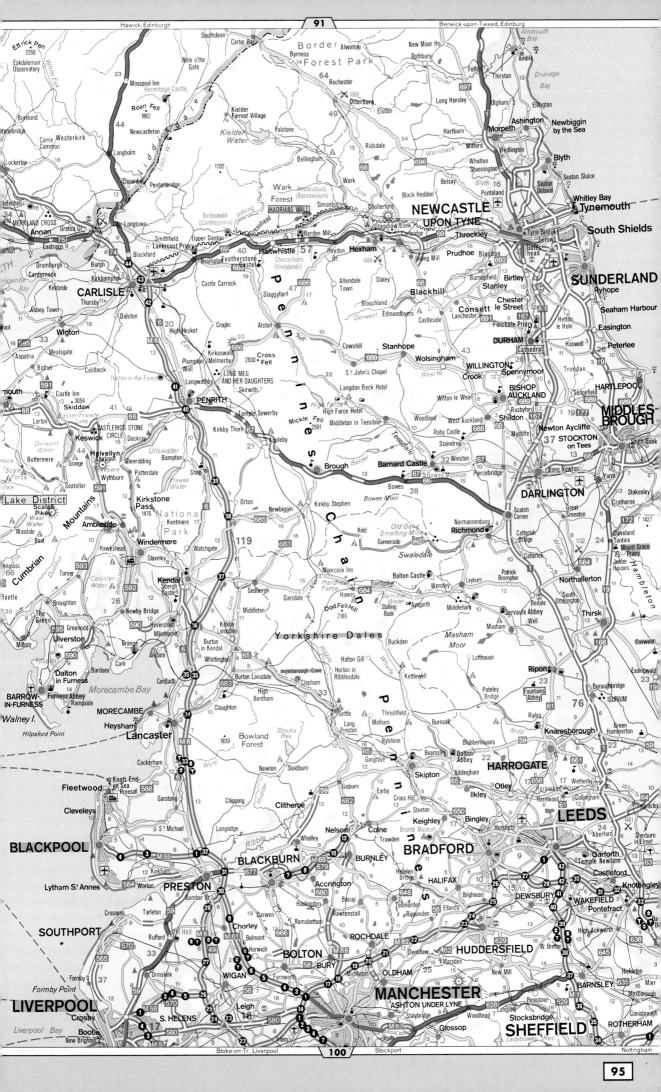

N O R T H   S E A

Göteborg Esbjerg

Redcar
Marske
Salzburn
Loftus   174   Boulby
6   Cliffs   Runswick Bay
Guisborough   Hinderwell   16
33   Sandsend
22   Whitby
Sealing Res.
Egton   Sleights   Robin Hood's Bay
Castleton   Goathland   171
Chop   North   York   20   Ravenscar
Gate   169
Rosedale   Saltersgate
Abbey
Cleveland   National   Park   Cloughton
Hills   44   SCARBOROUGH
Rievaulx   Kirkbymoorside   West Ayton   7
Abbey   27   Allerston   170   Pickering   7
Rievaulx   Helmsley   Pickering   Staxton   18   Filey
170   170   Vale   64   Hunmanby   Reighton
Rye   8   West   165   11
Hovingham   of   Heslerton   Foxholes   Flamborough Head
Malton   41   W   Rudston   Flamborough
Stillington   Castle   o   Langtoft   Carnaby   BRIDLINGTON
Howard   Sledmere   l   Burton Agnes   12   Bridlington
Wharram   d   Hall   166   Bay
Strensall   18   Barton Hill   le Street   s   Great Driffield   Lissett
64   41   Fridaythorpe   Wetwang   16   Skipsea
Shipton   19   Sledmere   North   15   Cranswick   165
New Earwick   166   Dalton   Middleton   30   Hornsea
Stamford Bridge   163   on the Wolds   13   Leven
1066   1079   Pocklington   37   Holderness
YORK   Elvington   18   Market   Burton   Aldbrough
14   Hayton   Weighton   1079   Minster   Constable
Escrick   Holme   11   Beverley   14   Sproatley
19   62   Newbald   Skidby   11   Kingston upon
Cawood   Bubwith   614   St Cave   HULL   Roos   Withernsea
Selby   Abbey Church   63   Howden   63   12   Hedon   6
Hambleton   Booth   37   47   Hessle   New   Patrington   4
9   Rawcliffe   36   Goole   Tollbridge   Holland   Easington
34   645   7   Snaith   13   Barton   Thornton   160   Kilnsea
M62   35   M 18   12   Winterton   Abbey
6   Thorne   11   Immingham   ENGLAND
Askern   5   1   18   Crowle   Amcotts   14   Dock   Spurn Head
Tatfield   13   614   SCUNTHORPE   5   GRIMSBY
10   M180   Althorpe   3   Messingham   Keelby   Cleethorpes
DONCASTER   2   Epworth   Brigg   16   Irby
3   Blaxton   14   Haxey   Redbourne   Caistor   46   18   N. Coates
Wadworth   638   Misterton   Blyton   Kirton   38   Binbrook   Ludborough   29   N. Somercotes
Maltby   Bawtry   Grinnley   Waddingham   Lincoln   16   Saltfleet
Tickhill   on the Hill   15   Caenby   1103   Wolds
Gainsborough   631   Corner   Market Rasen

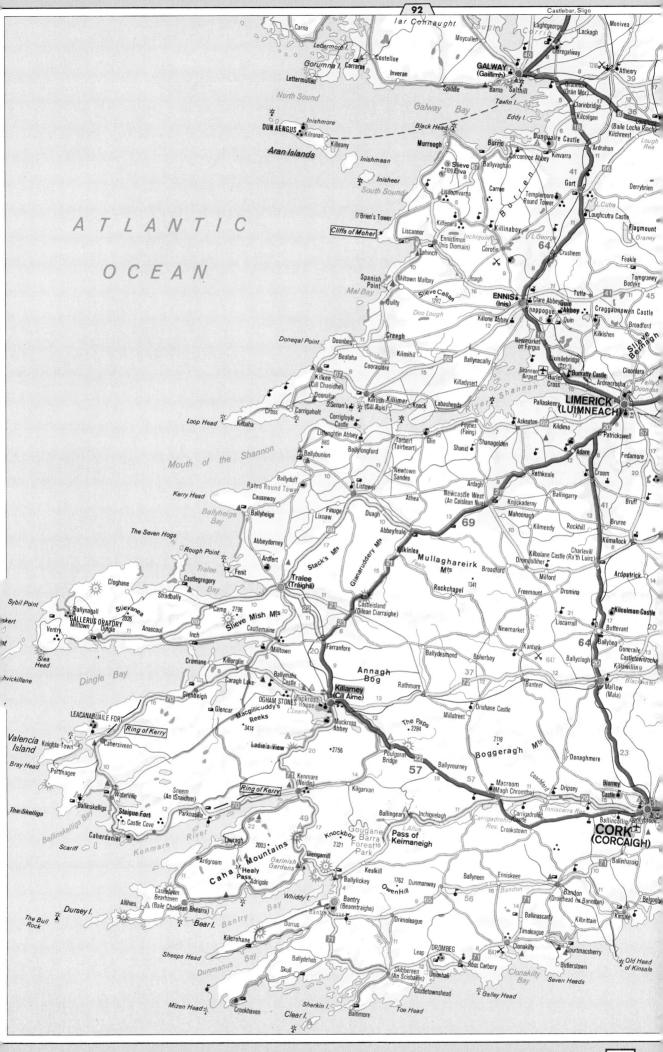

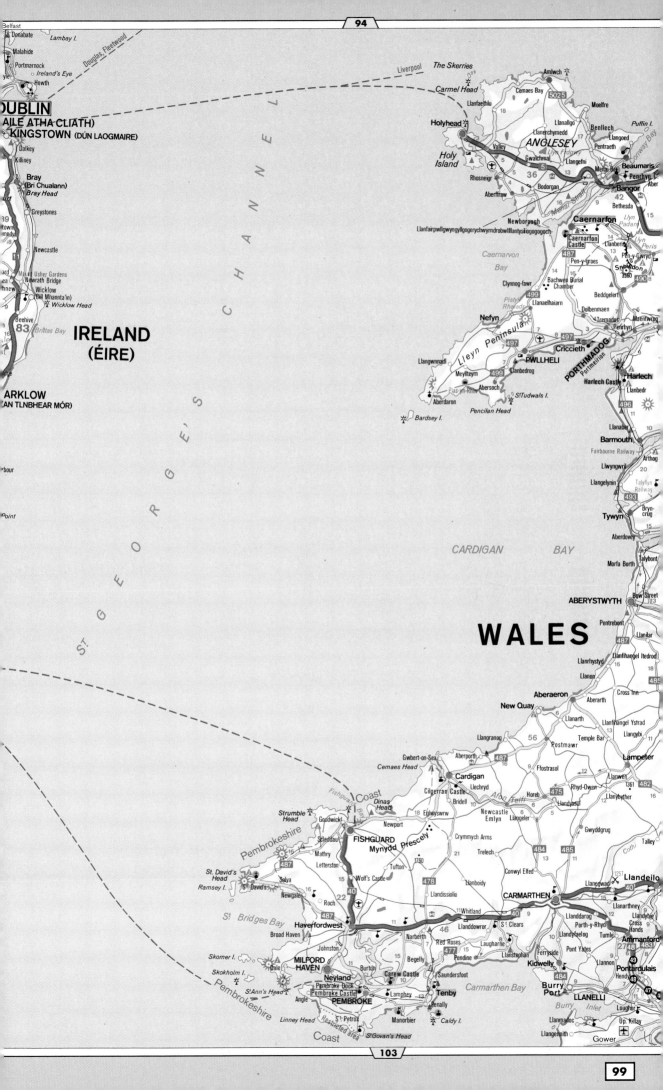

Belfast
Donabate
Lambay I.
Malahide
Portmarnock
Ireland's Eye
Howth
yle

OUBLIN
AILE ATHA CLIATH)
KINGSTOWN (DÚN LAOGMAIRE)

Dalkey
Killiney

Bray
(Brí Chualann)
Bray Head

Greystones

39
town
enedy
11
Newcastle

ard
Mount Usher Gardens
Newrath Bridge
nnew
Wicklow
(Cill Mhannta'in)
Wicklow Head

Beehive
83   *Brittas Bay*

16

IRELAND
(ÉIRE)

ARKLOW
AN TLNBHEAR MÓR)

rbour

Point

ge

ST. GEORGE'S CHANNEL

Liverpool
Douglas, Fleetwood
Carmel Head
The Skerries
Amlwch
Cemaes Bay   5025

Llanfaethlu   18
Holyhead
Valley   **ANGLESEY**
Llanerchymedd   17
Llanallgo   Moelfre
Benllech   *Puffin I.*
Llangoed
Pentraeth

Holy Island
Gwalchmai   Llangefni
5   36
13
Rhosneigr   Bodorgan   **Beaumaris**
Menai Br.   **Penrhyn C.**
Bangor   Aber
42
Newborough   9   Bethesda
Llanfairpwllgwyngyllgogerychwyrndrobwllllantysiliogogogoch   15
Caernarfon   *Llyn Padarn*
Caernarfon Castle   14
Llanberis   13
Pen-y-Gwryd
487   Pen-y-groes   Pen-y-Pass
Snowdon   3560
Clynnog-fawr   Bachwen Burial Chamber   190
Beddgelert
Pistyll   Dolbenmaen
499   Llanaelhaiarn   Tremadoc   Maentwrog
Rhaiadr   7   Penrhyn
Nefyn   8   497   3
497   **Criccieth**   **PORTHMADOG**
Llangwnnadl   **PWLLHELI**   Portmeirion
Meyllteyrn   499   Llanbedrog   7   **Harlech**
Abersoch   **Harlech Castle**   Llanbedr
Aberdaron   *St Tudwals I.*   496
Bardsey I.   *Pencilan Head*
Llanaber   10
Barmouth
Fairbourne Railway
Llwyngwril   Arthog
20
Llangelynin   Talyllyn Railway
493
Bryn-   15
crûg
Tywyn
Aberdovey   15

CARDIGAN   BAY
Morfa Borth   Talybont
Bow Street
ABERYSTWYTH   113

WALES
Pentrebont

Llanilar
487   Llanfihangel Itedrod
Llanrhystyd   485
Llanon   Cross Inn
Aberaeron   Aberarth
New Quay   Llanarth   Llanfihangel Ystrad   Llangybi
Llangranog   56   Temple Bar   11
Postmawr   **Lampeter**
Gwbert-on-Sea   Aberporth   Ffrostrasol   Llanwen   1361
Cemaes Head   487   9   482
Cardigan   Rhyd-Owen   Llanybyther
Cilgerran Castle   Llechryd   Horeb   Llandyssul   16
Fishguard Coast   Bridell   *Afon Teifi*
Dinas Head   Newcastle   Llangeler   Gwyddgrug
Strumble   18   Eglwyswrw   Emlyn   Talley
Head   Goodwick   Newport   Crymmych Arms   484   485
Scleddau   Crymmych Arms   Trelech   Colhi
Pembrokeshire   **FISHGUARD**   21   1760
Mathry   Mynydd Prescely   Conwyl Elfed   Llanegwad   **Llandeilo**
Letterston   Tufton   1257   40
St. David's   487   15   Wolf's Castle   Llandissiliogo   **CARMARTHEN**   Llanarthney
Head   478   Llanboidy   Llanddarog   Llandybie
Ramsey I.   **St. David's**   Roch   11 Whitland   40   Porth-y-Rhyd   Cross Hands
Newgale   46   S! Clears   Tumle   **Ammanford**
St. Bridges Bay   22   40   Red Roses   Llanddowror   Llandyfaelog   27 48 483
Haverfordwest   11   Narberth   Laugharne   Pont Yates
Broad Haven   477   15   Llanstephan   Ferryside   Llannon   49
Johnston   Begelly   Pendine   **Kidwelly**   Hendy   48
Skomer I.   Dale   Burton   11   Saundersfoot   Llannon   Pontardulais   47
Skokholm I.   **MILFORD HAVEN**   Carew Castle   *Carmarthen Bay*   **Burry Port**   Up. Killay
Neyland   Lamphey   **Tenby**   **LLANELLI**   Loughor
Pembroke Dock   Penally   Llanmadoc   *Burry Inlet*
St. Ann's Head   **Pembroke Castle**   Caldy I.   Llangennith   Gower
Angle   **PEMBROKE**
Linney Head   St Petrox   Manorbier
Restricted area   St Govan's Head
Pembrokeshire
Coast

NORTH SEA

Brancaster Holkham Holkham Wells-next-the-Sea Sheringham Cromer
Burnham Stiffkey Blakeney Cley Weybourne
Burnham Market 52 Binham Holt Thorpe Mundesley
Docking Walsingham 148 Edgefield Green Blickling Hall Roughton Market Bacton Happisburgh
Fakenham Saxthorpe 149 North Walsham Palling
Briston Ingworth Stalham Waxham
Harpley 148 1065 Aylsham Marsham Catfield Norfolk Winterton
Hillington Great Massingham Guist Cawston 23 Horstead Broads 14 Filby Caister-on-Sea
Gayton Brisley Reepham 23 Wroxham 149 Caister Castle
N. Elmham Bawdeswell Norfolk Wildlife Park 140 25 Acle GREAT
Castle Acre Newton Litcham Attlebridge Drayton Easton Blofield 57 19 YARMOUTH
Narborough 47 Wendling East Dereham Hockering Honingham NORWICH Trowse Gorleston
Swaffham Necton 43 Shipdham Newton 143
Watton Caston Kimberley Hethersett Reedham Hopton Corton
Hilborough Hingham Swardeston Swainsthorpe 146 Haddiscoe 20 12
Methwold Mundford 134 G. Ellingham Wymondham Loddon LOWESTOFT
Feltwell Croxton Larling Attleborough New Buckenham 140 Long Stratton Hempnall 7 Beccles Pakefield
Brandon Thetford E. Harling Bressingham Hall Gardens Bungay Mettingham 146 N. Cove Kessingland
Lakenheath 1065 Elveden Garboldisham Kenninghall Diss Pulham Homersfield Suffolk Wildlife and Country Park Covehithe
Mildenhall 11 Euston 1036 Scole Dickleburgh Harleston Brampton Wenhaston Southwold
134 Botesdale Waveney Fressingfield Walpole Halesworth Blythburg
Ingham 143 Stradbroke Laxfield Bramfield Yoxford Dunwich
Lackford Ixworth Stanton Eye Hevening ham 54
BURY Thwaite 43 Dennington 12 Westleton
Kentford 45 ST. EDMUNDS Debenham Saxmundham Leiston
Ickworth House Beyton Woolpit Framlingham Farnham Thorpeness
Bradfield Combust Stowmarket 140 Wickham Market Aldeburgh
143 G. Finborough 26 45 Tunstall Orford
19 Needham Market Claydon Utford
Alpheton 134 Lavenham Bildeston G. Blakenham Woodbridge Sandlings Göteborg
Clare Long Monks Eleigh IPSWICH Brightwell Kristiansand
Baythorn End Melford Hadleigh Hintlesham Alderton Esbjerg (19)
Sudbury 32 Boxford Copdock 45 Bawdsey
Castle Hedingham 48 Bures Nayland Stratford St. Mary Trimley Bremerhaven (16)
Finchingfield 43 131 Wakes Stoke FELIXSTOWE Hamburg (21)
Swan Street Halstead 133 Colne Ardleigh Manningtree Dovercourt HARWICH Hoek van Holland (6)
Gosfield 120 Wix
BRAINTREE Earls Colne Weeley
Rayne 120 Mark's Tey COLCHESTER Thorpe Walton-on-the-Naze
131 Coggeshall Kelvedon Brightlingsea G. Clacton Frinton
Witham 22 Tiptree Abberton Zeebrugge-Rotterdam
Broomfield 76 Tolleshunt d'Arcy Mersea I. St. Osyth CLACTON-on-Sea
Hatfield Peverel West Mersea
Maldon Tollesbury Bradwell on Sea
Chelmsford Blackwater
130 Cold Norton
Stock Althorne Southminster
Rettendon Burnham-on-Crouch Crouch Foulness Pt. Restricted area
Nevendon 20 Rayleigh Rochford
BASILDON SOUTHEND-ON-SEA
Vange Pitsea Wakering
Hadleigh 13 Leigh Canvey on Sea Shoeburyness
Coryton Thames Allhallows Oostende
Stanford le Hope

106

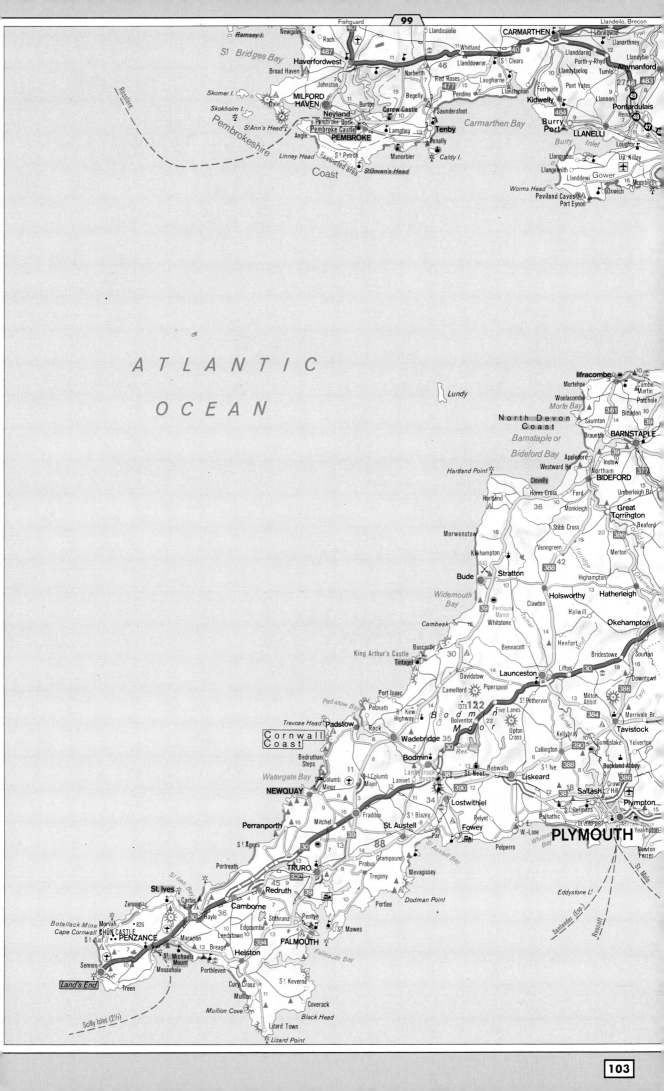

OXFORD
AYLESBURY
Blenheim Palace
Kidlington
Oakley
Oakley
Witney
Lynsham
Thame
Tring
Waterend
HEMEL
HEMPSTEAD
Harpenden
St.
Albans
Hatfield House
Hatfield
Hertford
HARLOW
Writtle
Stoke
Mandeville
Wendover
Berkhamsted
Chesham
King's Langley
Potters Bar
Cheshunt
Hoddesdon
Epping
Chipping
Ongar
Ingatestone
Billericay
Princes
Risborough
G. Missenden
Amersham
Chenies
S. Mimms
Waltham
Abbey
BRENTWOOD
Horndon
Romford
Nuneham
Stadhampton
Stokenchurch
W. Wycombe
HIGH
WYCOMBE
Beaconsfield
Rickmansworth
WEMBLEY
TOTTENHAM
BARKING
Grays
Thurrock
Tilbury
ABINGDON
Wallingford
Marlow
Cliveden
MAIDENHEAD
SLOUGH
Denham
Uxbridge
LONDON
GREENWICH
Dartford
Gravesend
Erith
Shillingford
Didcot
Stonor
Nettlebed
Henley-
on-Thames
Twyford
Caversham
Reading
Windsor Castle
WINDSOR
Heathrow
Airport
Kew Gardens
KINGSTON
RICHMOND
WIMBLEDON
Orpington
Eynsford
Meopham
Kingsdown
Harwell
Wantage
Blewbury
Pangbourne
Ascot
STAINES
Hampton Court
CHEAM
CROYDON
Farnborough
Seal
SEVENOAKS
Borough Gn.
W. Shefford
Hungerford
NEWBURY
Thatcham
Theale
Wokingham
Bracknell
Chertsey
Weybridge
Esher
Hook
Epsom
Caterham
Godstone
Oxted
Westerham
Knole House
TONBRIDGE
Shalbourne
Highclere
Newtown
Aldermaston
SILCHESTER
Riseley
Common
Eversley
Camberley
Chobham
Ripley
Leatherhead
Chiddingstone Castle
Edenbridge
ROYAL
TUNBRIDGE
WELLS
Burbage
Kingsclere
Tadley
Sherfield
WOKING
Cobham
BASINGSTOKE
Hook
FARNBOROUGH
ALDERSHOT
Merrow
E. Horsley
Dorking
REIGATE
Redhill
Horley
Collingbourne
Kingston
Ludgershall
Overton
Odiham
Micheldever
FARNHAM
Elstead
Godalming
Guildford
Gatwick
Airport
East
Grinstead
Forest Row
ANDOVER
Herriard
Alton
Preston
Candover
Milford
Bramley
Cranleigh
Ockley
Capel
CRAWLEY
Crowborough
Wher Well
New Alresford
Kingsley
Hindhead
Liphook
Hascombe
Chiddingfold
Alfold
Warnham
HORSHAM
Cuckfield
Haywards
Heath
Maresfield
Mayfield
WINCHESTER
Cheriton
Bramdean
Ropley
Selborne
Greatham
Haslemere
Bucks
Green
Billingshurst
Handcross
Balcombe
Uckfield
Heathfield
Dunbridge
Hursley
Twyford
W. Meon
George Inn
Rogate
Fernhurst
Wisborough
Green
Buck
Barn
Cowfold
Burgess
Hill
North
Common
Halland
Herstmonceux
Whiteparish
Romsey Abbey
Chandler's
Ford
Upham
Bishops
Waltham
Petersfield
Midhurst
Petworth
Pulborough
Storrington
Hurstpierpoint
Hentfield
Westmeston
LEWES
Ringmer
Dicker
Eastleigh
SOUTHAMPTON
St Harting
Up. Waltham
Singleton
Washington
Pycombe
BRIGHTON
Ower
Botley
Wickham
Mid-Lavant
Arundel
Arundel Castle
Findon
Sompting
Shoreham
Rottingdean
NEWHAVEN
SEAFORD
Eastbourne
Beachy Head
Cadnam
Totton
Hythe
Waterlooville
HAVANT
Emsworth
CHICHESTER
Sidlesham
Felpham
Littlehampton
WORTHING
New Forest
Nettley Abbey
Ramble
FAREHAM
GOSPORT
Exbury Gardens
PORTSMOUTH
SOUTHSEA
South
Hayling
West
Wittering
Selsey
BOGNOR
REGIS
Lymington
Cowes
E. Cowes
Pushbourne
RYDE
Selsey Bill
Yarmouth
The Needles
Freshwater
NEWPORT
Carisbrooke
Castle
Blackwater
S! Helen's
Bembridge
Sandown
Isle of Wight
Shanklin
Chale
Niton
Ventnor
S!Catherine's Point
Cherbourg, St. Malo
Cherbourg, Le Havre
Dieppe

C H A N N E L

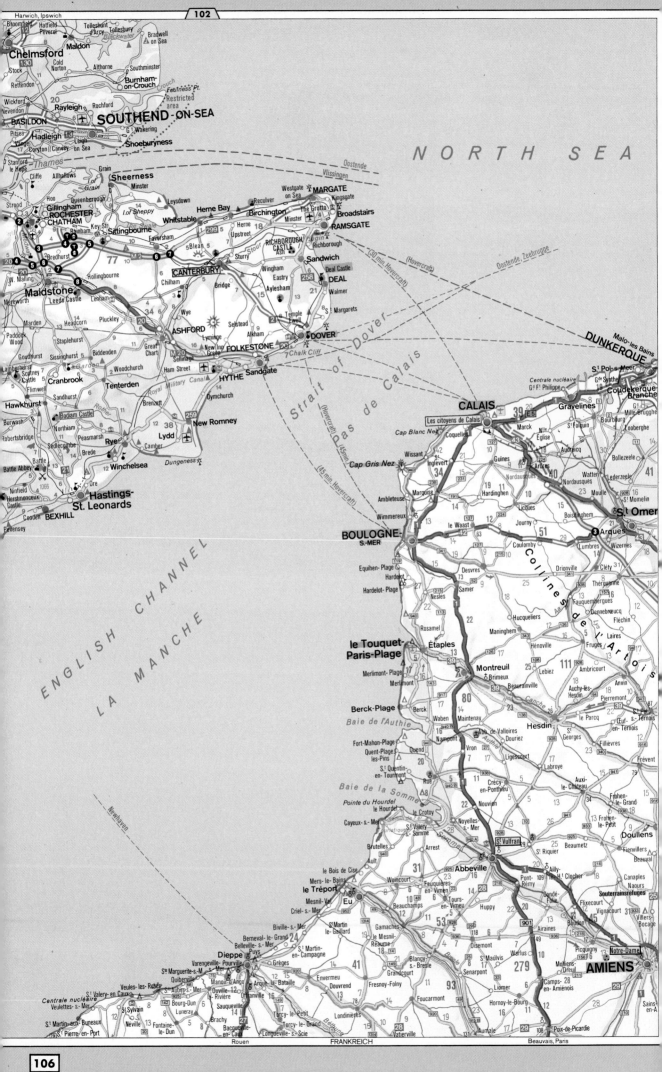

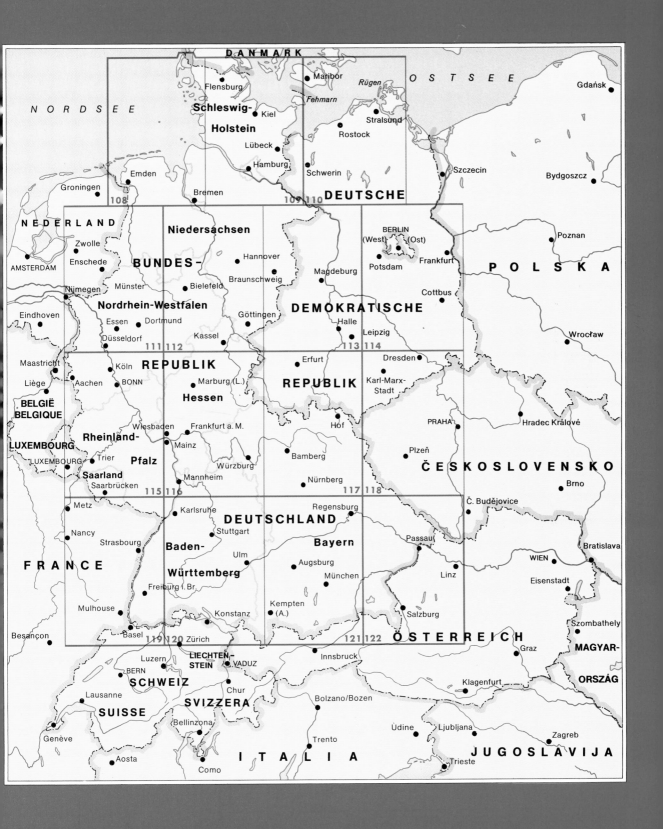

Deutschland
Tyskland · Saksa · Germany · Duitsland · Allemagne · Alemania
Germania · Γερμανία · Almanya

DANMARK

OSTSEE

NORDSEE

Flensburg

Maribor

Rügen

Fehmarn

Gdańsk

Schleswig-

Kiel

Holstein

Stralsund

Lübeck

Rostock

Schwerin

Szczecin

Bydgoszcz

Hamburg

Emden

Groningen

Bremen

108

109 110

DEUTSCHE

NEDERLAND

Niedersachsen

BERLIN

Poznan

Zwolle

(West) (Ost)

POLSKA

Enschede

BUNDES-

Hannover

Magdeburg

Frankfurt

AMSTERDAM

Münster

Braunschweig

Potsdam

Nijmegen

Bielefeld

Cottbus

Eindhoven

Nordrhein-Westfalen

Göttingen

DEMOKRATISCHE

Essen

Dortmund

Halle

Leipzig

Wrocław

Düsseldorf

Kassel

111 112

113 114

Maastricht

REPUBLIK

Erfurt

Dresden

Liège

Köln

Marburg (L.)

Karl-Marx-

Aachen

BONN

REPUBLIK

Stadt

BELGIË

Hessen

PRAHA

Hradec Králové

BELGIQUE

Wiesbaden

Frankfurt a. M.

Hof

LUXEMBOURG

Rheinland-

Mainz

Plzeň

LUXEMBOURG

Trier

Pfalz

Bamberg

ČESKOSLOVENSKO

Saarland

Würzburg

Saarbrücken

Mannheim

Nürnberg

Brno

115 116

117 118

Metz

Karlsruhe

Regensburg

Č. Budějovice

DEUTSCHLAND

Nancy

Stuttgart

Bayern

Passau

Bratislava

Strasbourg

Baden-

WIEN

FRANCE

Ulm

Augsburg

Linz

Eisenstadt

Württemberg

München

Freiburg i. Br.

Mulhouse

Kempten

Konstanz

(A.)

Salzburg

Szombathely

Besançon

Basel

119 120

Zürich

121 122

ÖSTERREICH

MAGYAR-

Luzern

LIECHTEN-

Innsbruck

Graz

BERN

STEIN

VADUZ

ORSZÁG

SCHWEIZ

Chur

Klagenfurt

Lausanne

SVIZZERA

Bolzano/Bozen

Genève

SUISSE

Bellinzona

Üdine

Ljubljana

Zagreb

Trento

Aosta

ITALIA

JUGOSLAVIJA

Como

Trieste

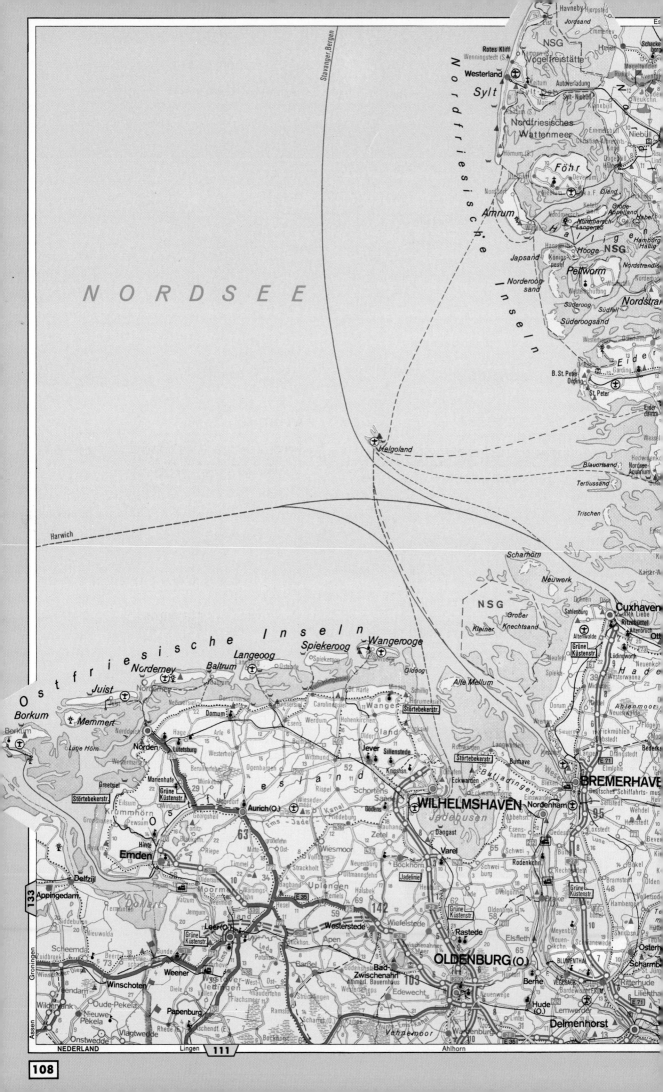

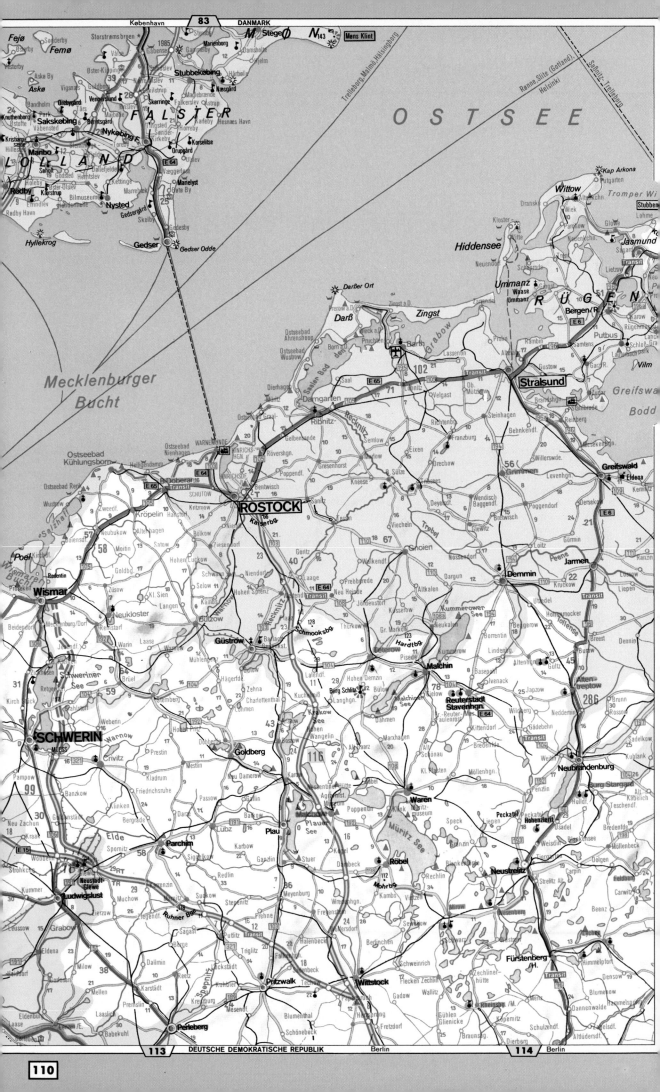

Schweiz, Österreich
Sveits, Østerrike · Schweiz, Österrike · Sveitsi, Itävalta
Schweiz, Østrig · Switzerland, Austria · Zwitserland, Oostenrijk
Suisse, Autriche · Suiza, Austria · Svizzera, Austria
Ελβετία, Αυστρία · İsvicre, Avusturya

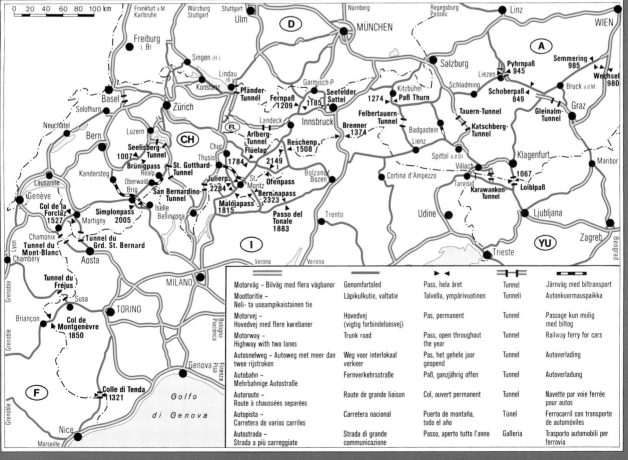

Motorväg - Bilväg med flera vägbanor	Genomfartsled	Pass, hela året	Tunnel	Järnväg med biltransport
Moottoritie - Neli- ta useampikaistainen tie	Läpikulkutie, valtatie	Talvella, ympärivuotinen	Tunneli	Autonkuormauspaikka
Motorvej - Hovedvej med flere kørebaner	Hovedvej (vigtig forbindelsesvej)	Pas, permanent	Tunnel	Passage kun mulig med biltog
Motorway - Highway with two lanes	Trunk road	Pass, open throughout the year	Tunnel	Railway ferry for cars
Autosnelweg - Autoweg met meer dan twee rijstroken	Weg voor interlokaal verkeer	Pas, het gehele jaar geopend	Tunnel	Autoverlading
Autobahn - Mehrbahnige Autostraße	Fernverkehrsstraße	Paß, ganzjährig offen	Tunnel	Autoverladung
Autoroute - Route à chaussées séparées	Route de grande liaison	Col, ouvert permanent	Tunnel	Navette par voie ferrée pour autos
Autopista - Carretera de varios carriles	Carretera nacional	Puerto de montaña, todo el año	Túnel	Ferrocarril con transporte de automóviles
Autostrada - Strada a più carreggiate	Strada di grande comunicazione	Passo, aperto tutto l'anno	Galleria	Trasporto automobili per ferrovia

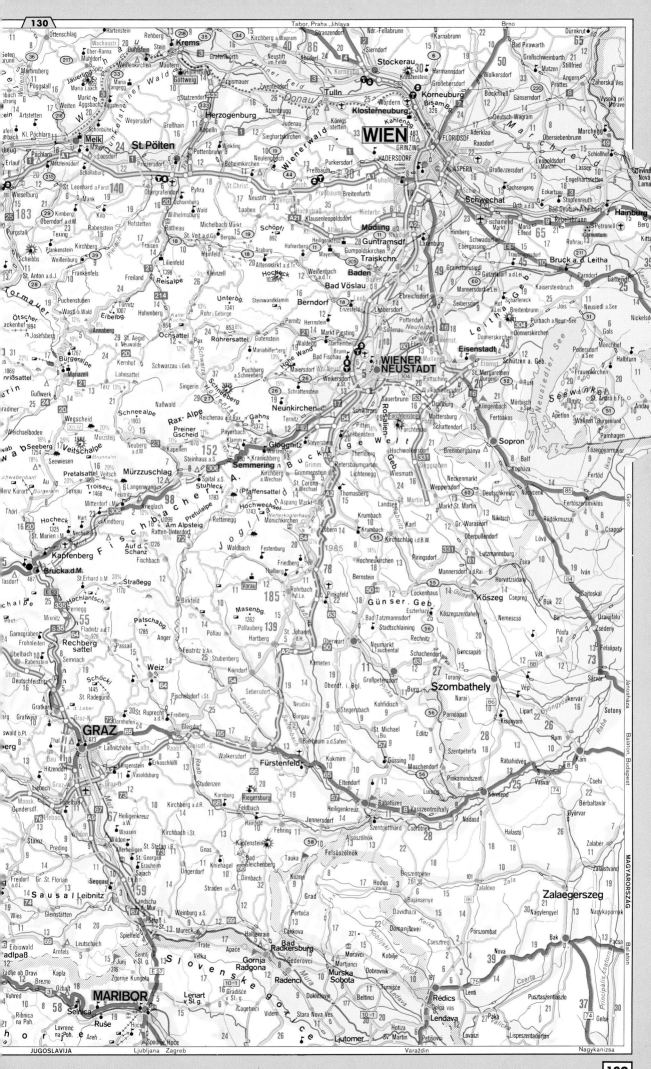

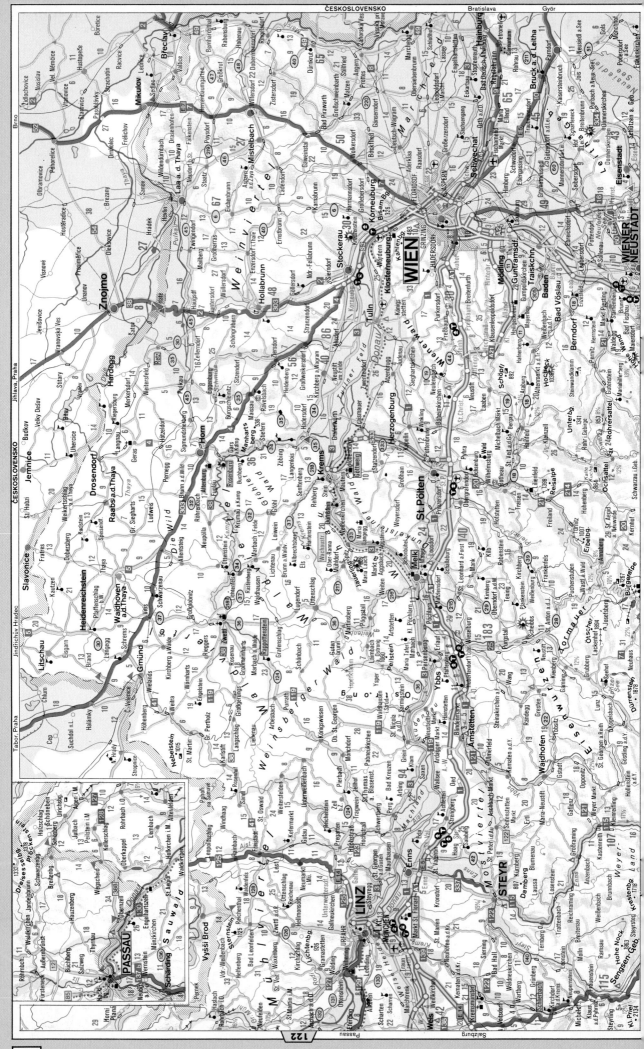

Benelux, France
Benelux, Frankrike · Benelux, Ranska · Benlux, Frankrig
Benelux, Frankreich · Benelux, Frankrijk · Benelux, Francia
Μπενελουξ, Γαλλία · Benelüx, Fransa

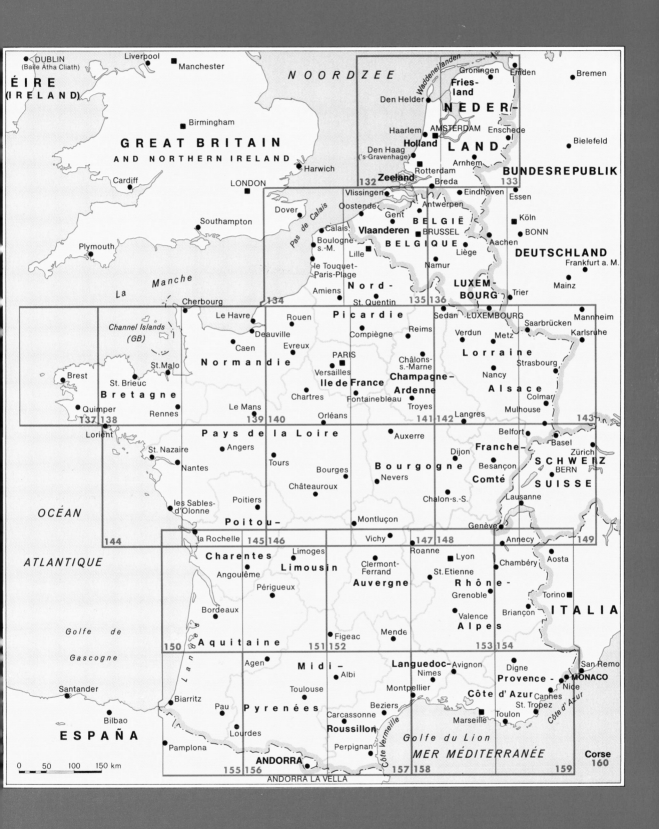

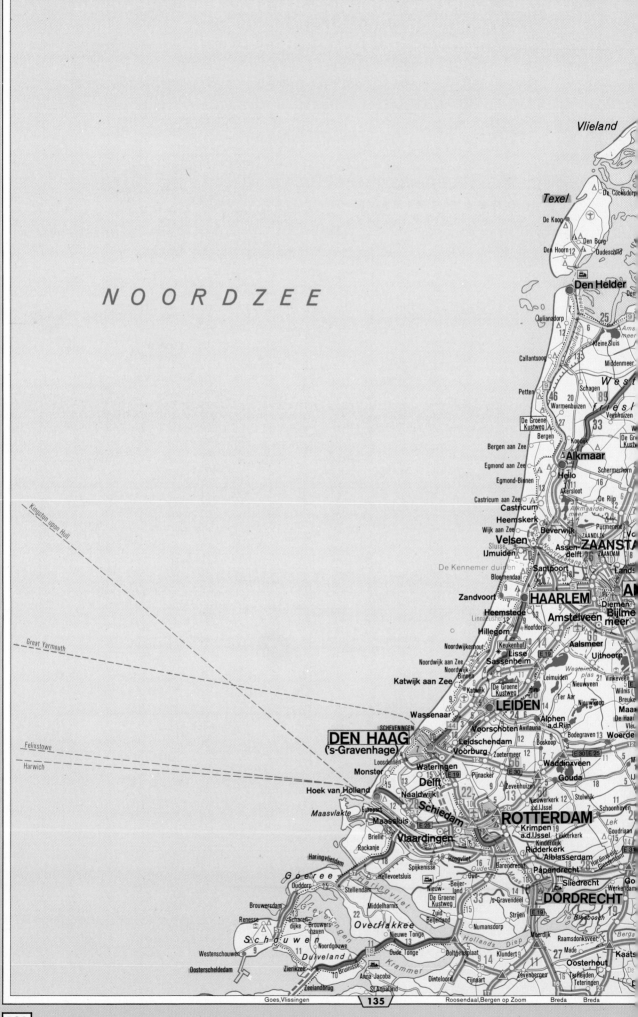

Vlieland

Texel
De Cocksdorp

De Koog
Den Burg
Den Hoorn 12   Oudeschild

Den Helder   Den

Julianadorp
Kleine Sluis   25   9
Callantsoog   Middenmeer

West
Schagen   89
Petten   9   46   20   *friesl*
Warmenhuizen
Veenhuizen   33
De Groene
Kustweg   27   De Groe
Bergen   Kustw
Bergen aan Zee   Koedijk
Alkmaar
Egmond aan Zee   Schermerhorn
Heiloo   16
Egmond-Binnen   Akersloot   De Rijn
Castricum aan Zee   *Alkmaardermeer*   24
Castricum   *Purmerend*
Heemskerk
Wijk aan Zee   **Beverwijk**   ZAANDIJK   Vc
Velsen   Assen   **ZAANST**
Sluise   delft   ZAANDAM
IJmuiden   Woordzekanaal   10
De Kennemer duinen   **Santpoort**   **Lands**
Bloemendaal
HAARLEM   **A**
Zandvoort   9   Diemen
Heemstede   **Amstelveen**   **Bijlme**
Linnaeushof   **meer**
Hillegom   Hoofddorp   66
Noordwijkerhout   **Keukenhof**   14   **Aalsmeer**
Noordwijk aan Zee   *Lisse*   E 19   **Uithoorn**
Noordwijk-Binnen   Sassenheim   *Westein*   Vinkeveen
Katwijk aan Zee   Leimuiden   21   Wilnis   Breuke
Katwijk   *plas*   Nieuwveen   Nieuwkoop
De Groene   Ter Aar   De Haar
Kustweg   Maa
Wassenaar   **LEIDEN**   Alphen
Avifauna   a.d.Rijn
SCHEVENINGEN   **Voorschoten**   Bodegraven   **Woerde**
DEN HAAG   **Leidschendam**   Boskoop
('s-Gravenhage)   **Voorburg**   Zoetermeer   E 30 E 25
Loosduinen   Waddinxveen
Wateringen   Pijnacker   E 30   **Gouda**
Monster   E 19   Zevenhuizen   18
Hoek van Holland   **Delft**   Stolwijk   11
Naaldwijk   22   Nieuwerkerk 12   Schoonhoven
Maasvlakte   Europad   a.d.IJssel
Maassluis   **Schiedam**   *Lek*   Goudriaan
Brielle   E 25   **ROTTERDAM**   15   14
Rockanje   **Vlaardingen**   Krimpen   Lekkerkerk
a.d.IJssel
Hoogvliet   Kinderdijk   Harding
Haringvlietdam   Spijkenisse   **Ridderkerk**   28
Helvoetsluis   Barendrecht   **Alblasserdam**
Goeree   Nieuw-   16   **Papendrecht**
Ouddorp   Beijer-   Oude   *Maas*
Stellendam   land 20   **Sliedrecht**   Go
Brouwersdam   De Groene   33   's-Gravendeel   **DORDRECHT**   Werker
Renesse   Schaaren   Kustweg   E 19   19
dijke   Middelharnis   Zuid   Biesbosch
Brouwers-   22   Beijerland   Strijen   *Bergs*
Schouwen   haven   *Overflakkee*   Nieuwe Tonge   Numansdorp   Raamsdonksveer
Noordgouwe   11   Moerdijk   Made   Kaats
Westenschouwen   9   Oude-Tonge   *Holland's Diep*   Oosterhout
Oosterscheldedam   *Duiveland*   Ooltgensplaat   14   Zevenbergen   16   Terheijden
Bruinisse   9   Klundert   27   Teteringen
Zierikzee   70   Anna Jacoba   *Krammer*
Zeelandbrug   Dinteloord   Fijnaart
St Annaland   **135**   Roosendaal,Bergen op Zoom   Breda   Breda
Goes,Vlissingen

NOORDZEE

Kingston upon Hull

Great Yarmouth

Felixstowe
Harwich

132

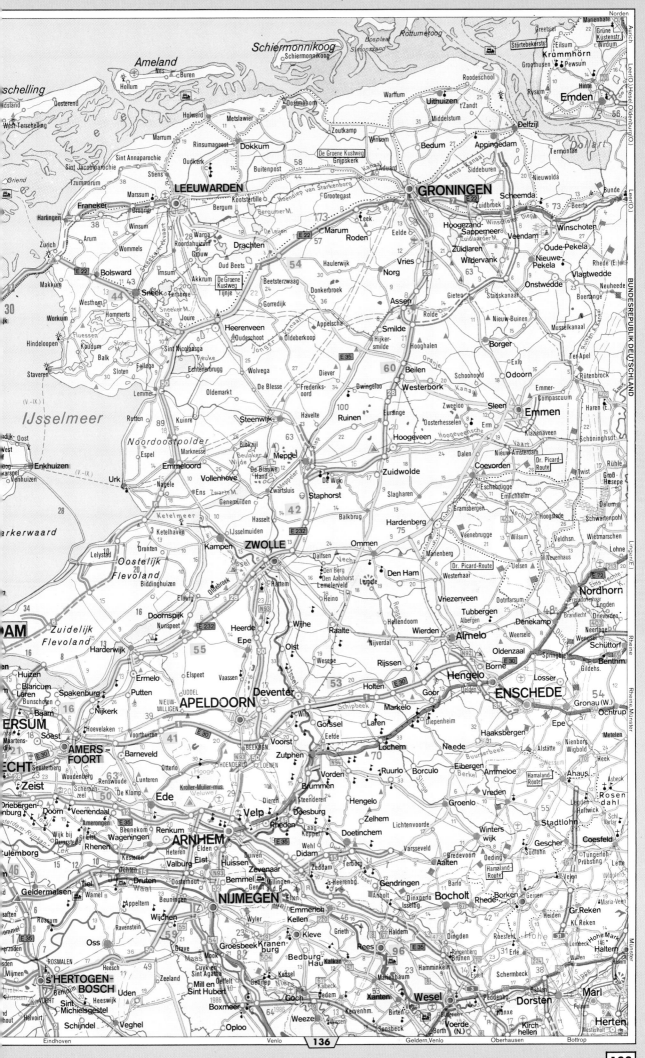

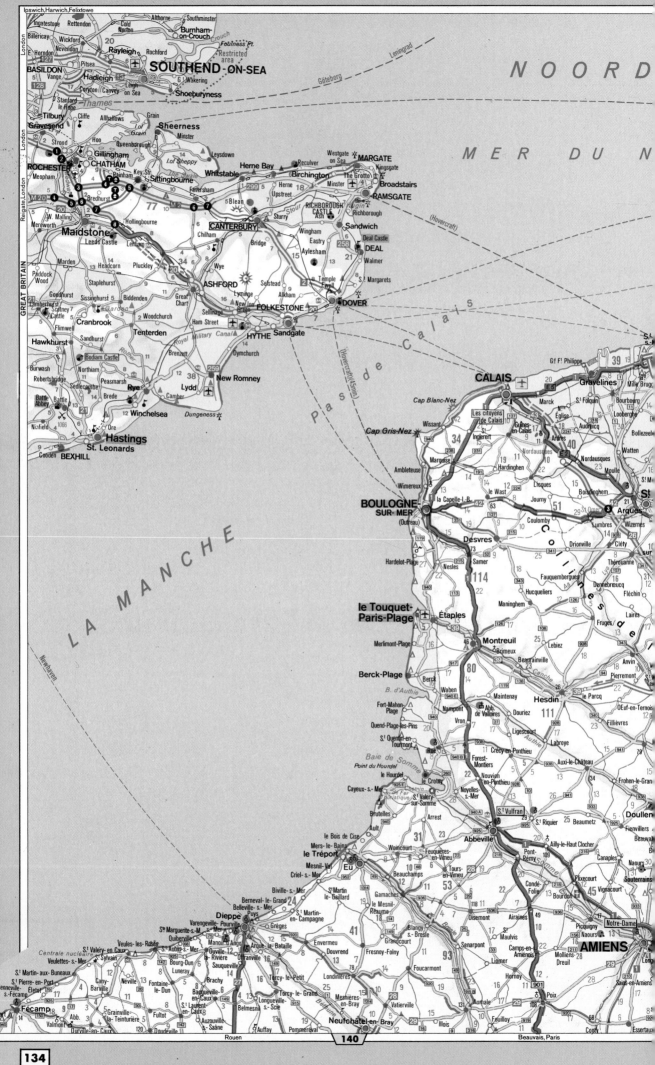

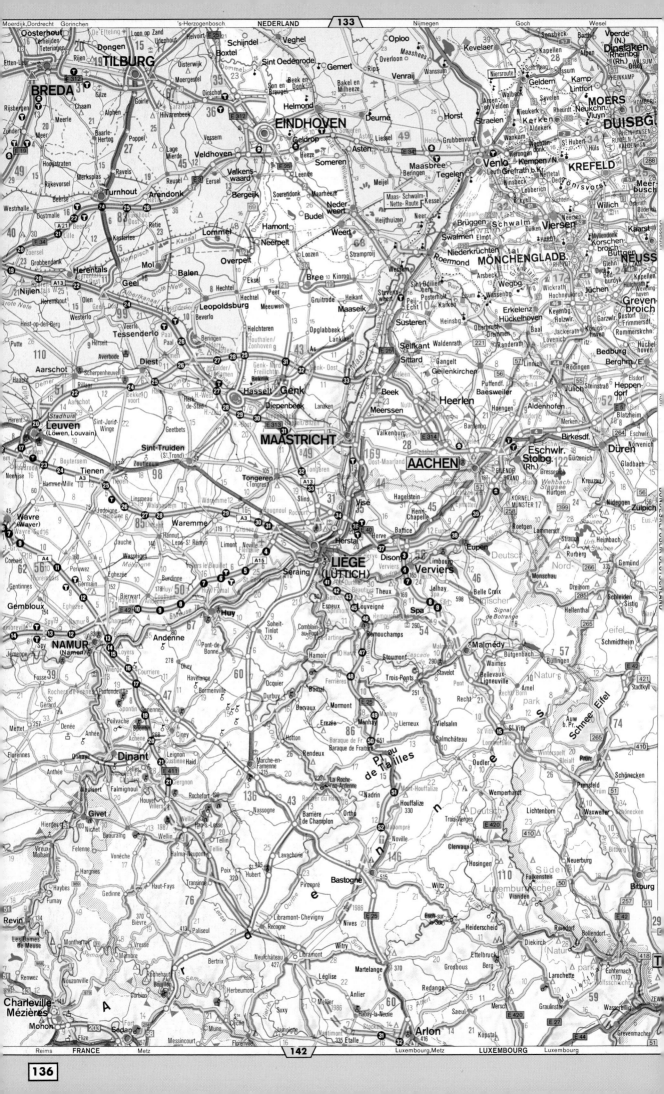

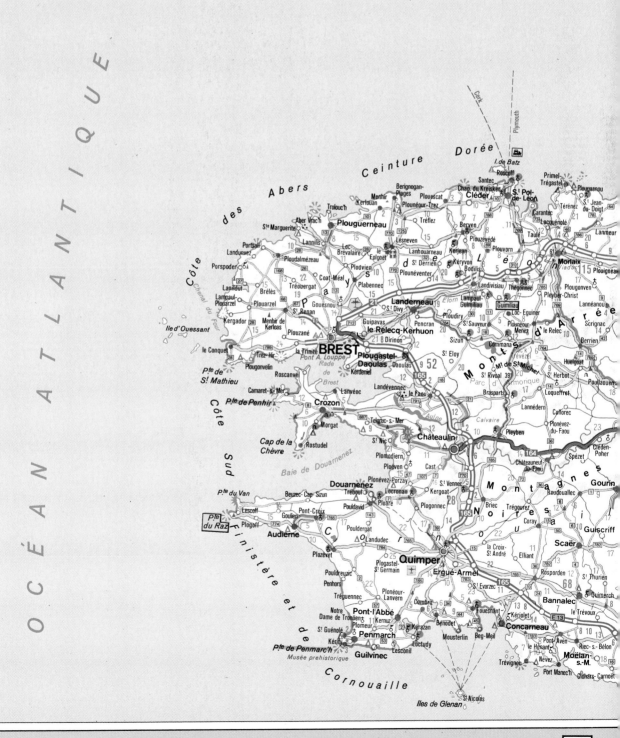

LA MANCHE

OCÉAN ATLANTIQUE

Ceinture Dorée

Côte des Abers

Côte Sud

Finistère et de

Cornouaille

Cork
Plymouth

I. de Batz
Roscoff
Primel-
Trégastel
Santec
Chap. du Kreisker
Plougasnou
Cléder
S.t Pol-
de-Léon
S.t Jean-
du-Doigt
Térénez
Menhir
Bérignogan-
Plages
Plouescat
Carantec
Lanmeur
Kerfouan
Plounéour-Trez
Locquénolé
Trolouc'h
Tréflez
Berven
Taulé
S.te Marguerite
Aber Vrac'h
Lesneven
Plouzévédé
Plouvorn
Morlaix
Plouigneau
Portsall
Lannilis
Loc-
Brévalaire
Lanhouarneau
Kerjean
Plougonven
Landunvez
l'Epipet
Kéryvon
Bodilis
Pleyber-Christ
Lannéanou
Ploudalmézeau
Plodvien
S.t Derrien
Landivisiau
Thégonnec
Porspoder
Coat-Méal
Plounéventer
Guimiliau
Loc-Eguiner
Plabennec
Landerneau
Ploudiry
Scrignac
Lampaul-
Ploudalzarel
Brélès
Tréouergat
Landivy
S.t Divy
Pencran
S.t Sauveur
Plounéour-
Menez
Berrien
Kergador
Plouarzel
Gouesnou
Guipavas
le Relecq-Kerhuon
Sizun
Commana
M.t de S.t Michel
S.t Herbot
Huelgoat
Poullaouen
S.t Renan
Menhir de
Kerloas
Plouzané
Dirinon
S.t Eloy
S.t Rivoal
391
Parc d'Armorique
Loqueffret
Ile d'Ouessant
le Conquet
la Trinité
BREST
Plougastel-
Daoulas
Daoulas
Brasparts
Lannédern
Collorec
Trez-Hir
Pont A. Louppe
Rade
Kerdeniel
Landévennec
le Faou
Plonévez-
du-Faou
P.te de
S.t Mathieu
Plougonvelin
Roscanvel
Lanvéoc
Châteauneuf-
du-Faou
Cléden-
Poher
Spézet
Camaret-s.-Mer
Crozon
Telgruc-s.-Mer
Pleyben
Châteaulin
164
P.te de Penhir
Morgat
S.t Nic
Calvaire
Gourin
Cap de la
Chèvre
Rostudel
Baie de Douarnenez
Plomodiern
Roudouallec
Ploéven
Cast
Châteauneuf-
P.te du Van
Beuzec-Cap-Sizun
Tréboul
Plonévez-Porzay
S.t Vennec
Briec
Trégourez
Coray
Guiscriff
Lescoff
Pont-Croix
Locronan
Kergoat
Plogonnec
Scaër
P.te
du Raz
Plogoff
Pouldavid
Ploaré
la Croix-
S.t André
Elliant
Audierne
Pouldergat
Landudec
Quimper
Rosporden
S.t Thurien
Plozévet
Ergué-Armel
S.t Evarzec
Quimerc'h
Pouldreuzic
Plogastel-
S.t Germain
Combrit
Bannalec
Penhors
Plonéour-
Lanvern
le Trévoux
Tréguennec
Kériolet
Quimerc'h
Notre
Dame de Tronoën
Pont-l'Abbé
Kernuz
Bénodet
Fouesnant
Concarneau
Riec-s.-Bélon
S.t Guénolé
Plomeur
Kérazan
Beg-Meil
Port Aven
Ploudy
Penmarch
Mousterlin
Moëlan
s.-M.
Kérity
Loctudy
Névez
Trévignon
Port Manec'h
Clohars-Carnoët
P.te de Penmarc'h
Guilvinec
Lesconil
Musée préhistorique

Iles de Glénan
S.t Nicolas

137

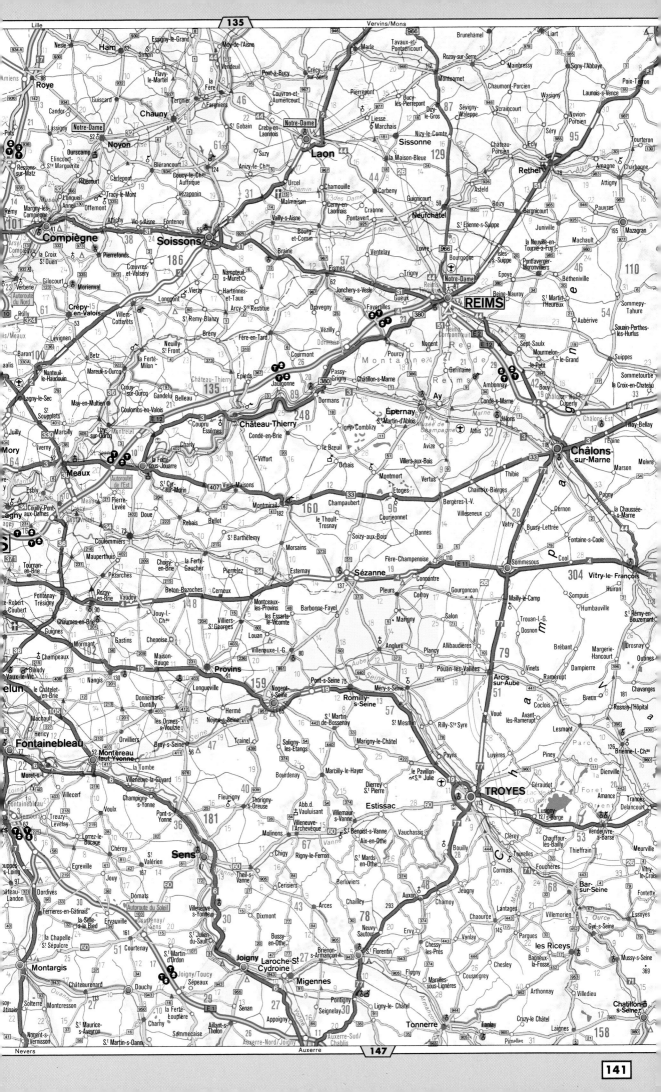

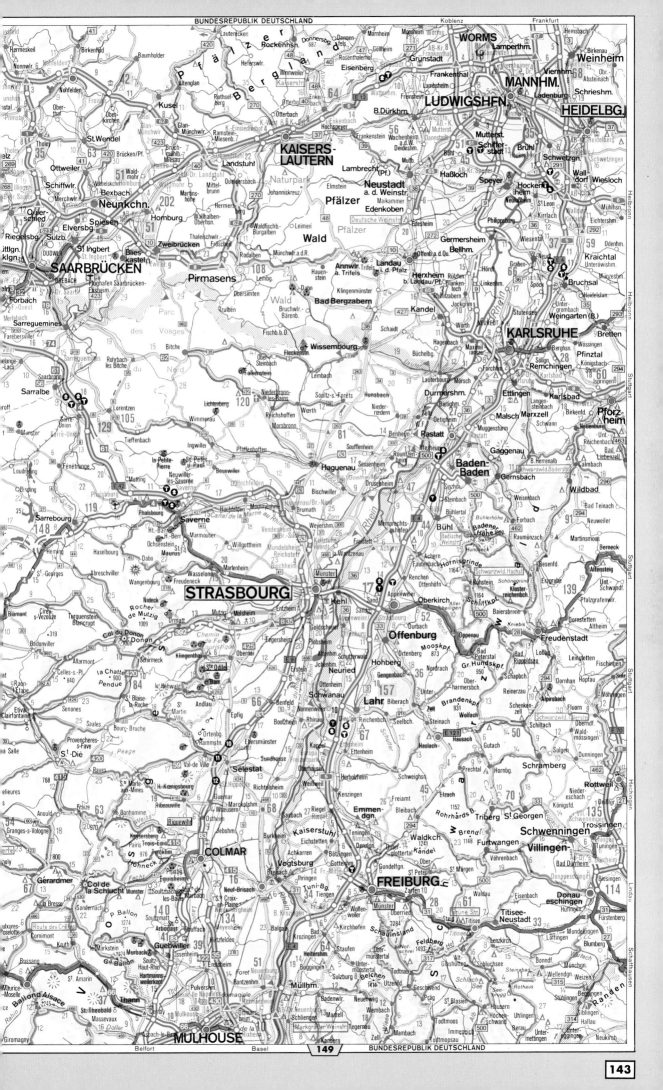

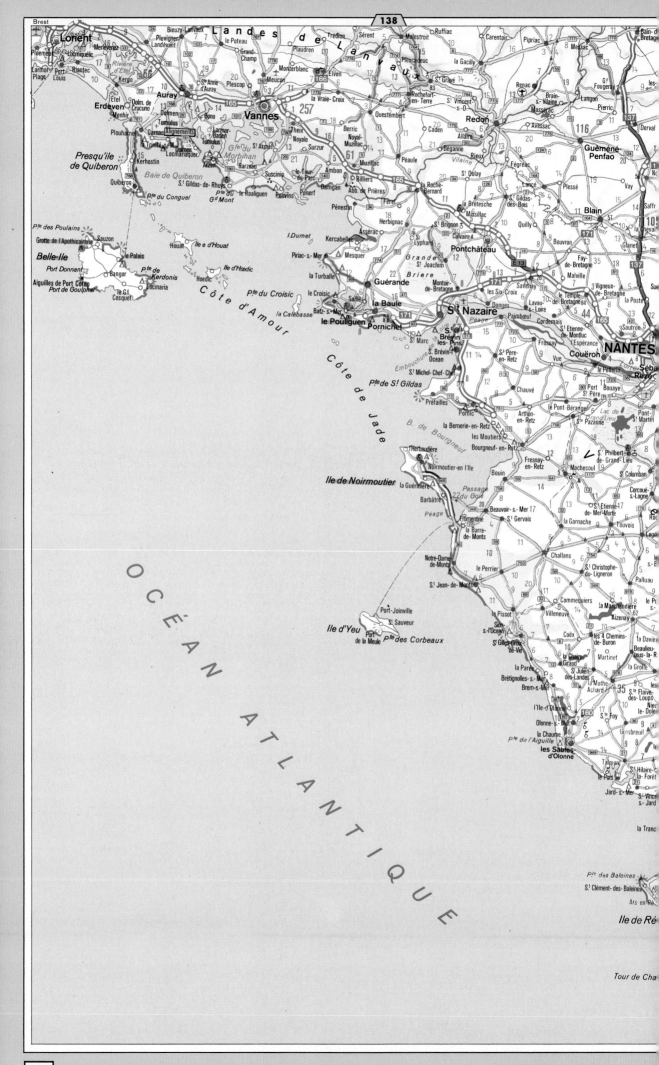

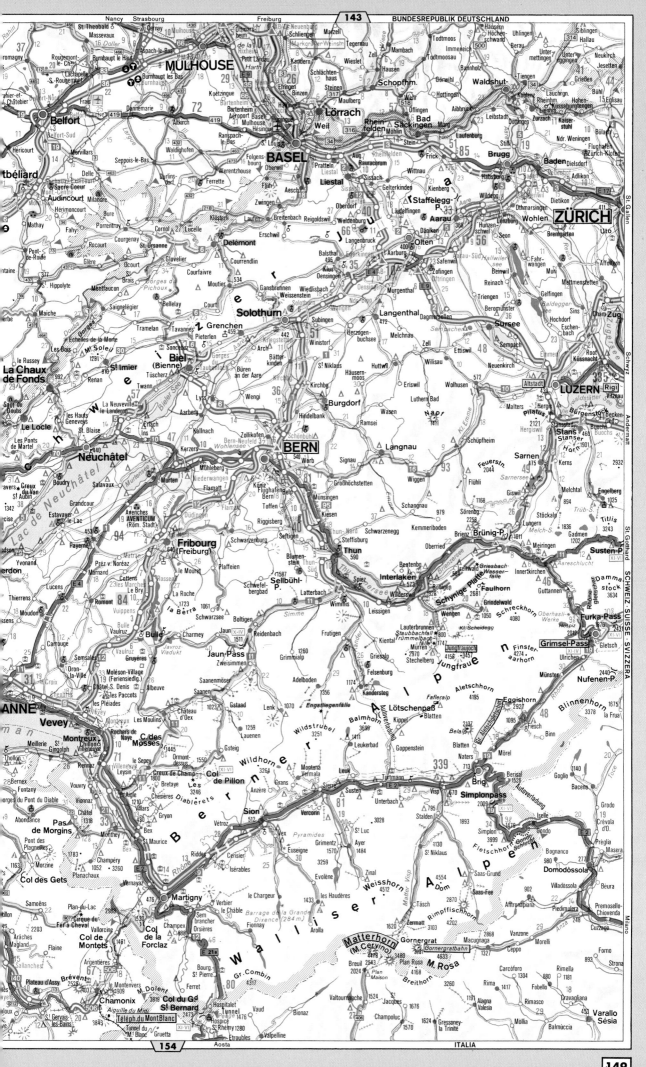

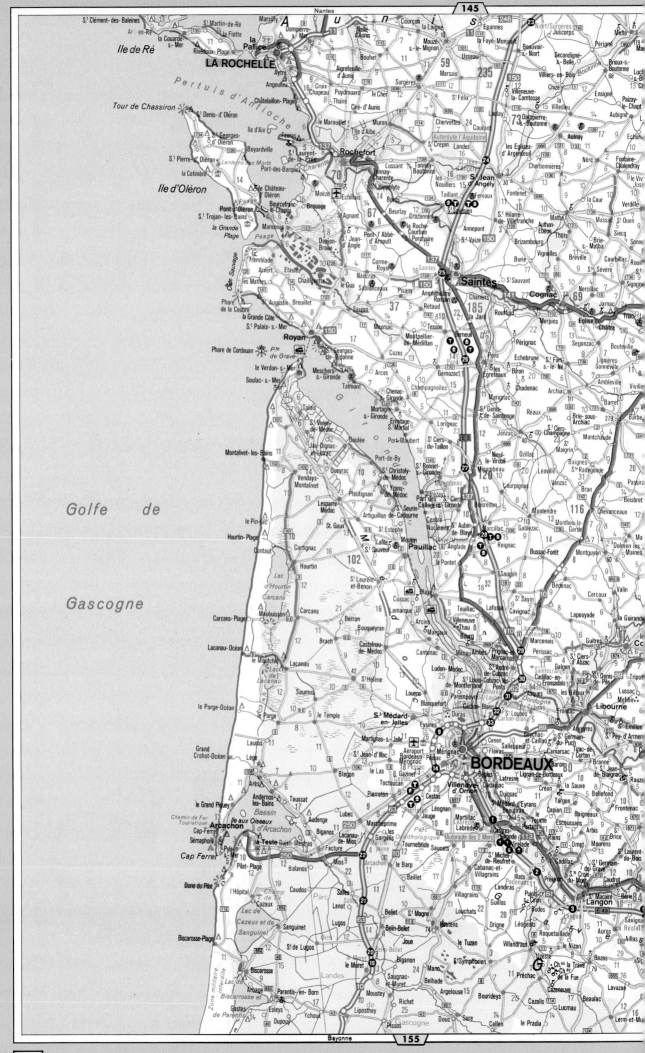

Bordeaux   Cahors

ESPAÑA

España, Portugal
Spania, Portugal · Spanien, Portugal · Espanja, Portugali
Spain, Portugal · Spanje, Portugal · Espagne, Portugal
Spagna, Portogallo · Ισπανία, Πορτογαλλία · İspanya, Portekiz

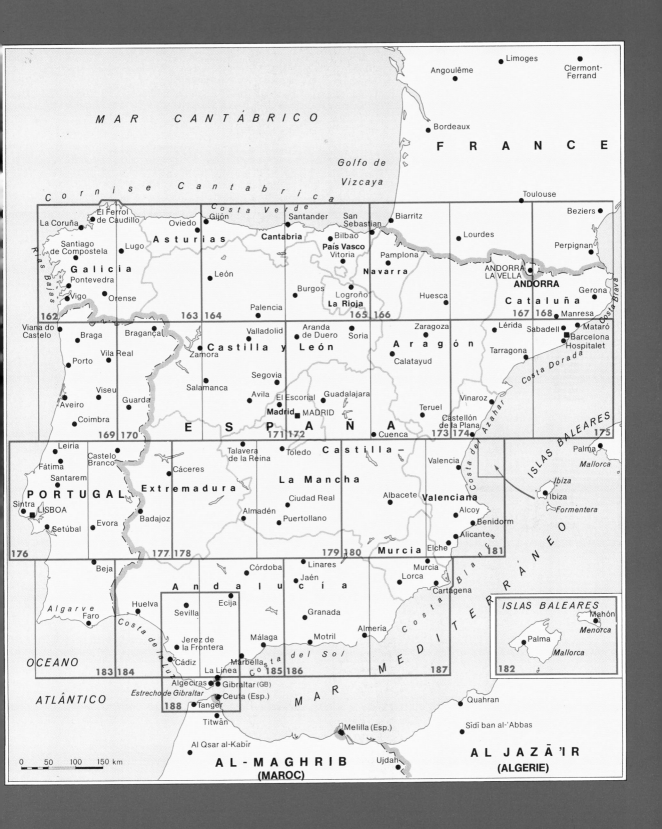

MAR CANTÁBRICO

Golfo de Vizcaya

FRANCE

Cornise Cantabrica

Costa Verde

Limoges
Clermont-Ferrand
Angoulême
Bordeaux
Toulouse
Beziers
Perpignan
Lourdes
Biarritz
San Sebastian
Santander
Gijón
La Coruña
El Ferrol de Caudillo
Oviedo
Santiago de Compostela
Lugo
Bilbao
Vitoria
Pamplona
Huesca
ANDORRA LA VELLA
ANDORRA
Gerona
Manresa
Sabadell
Mataró
Barcelona
Hospitalet
Lérida
Zaragoza
Soria
Aranda de Duero
Valladolid
Bragança
Braga
Vila Real
Viana do Castelo
Porto
Zamora
Tarragona
Calatayud
Segovia
Salamanca
Avila
El Escorial
Guadalajara
Teruel
Vinaroz
Castellón de la Plana
Madrid
MADRID
Cuenca
Viseu
Guarda
Aveiro
Coimbra
Leiria
Fátima
Santarem
Castelo Branco
Cáceres
Talavera de la Reina
Toledo
Valencia
Ibiza
Formentera
Mallorca
Palma
Sintra
LISBOA
Setúbal
Evora
Badajoz
Almadén
Puertollano
Ciudad Real
Albacete
Alcoy
Benidorm
Alicante
Elche
Murcia
Lorca
Cartagena
Beja
Córdoba
Linares
Jaén
Murcia
Huelva
Ecija
Sevilla
Jerez de la Frontera
Cádiz
Granada
Motril
Almería
Mahón
Menorca
Palma
Mallorca
Faro
Marbella
La Línea
Algeciras
Gibraltar (GB)
Ceuta (Esp.)
Tanger
Titwān
Al Qsar al-Kabir
Melilla (Esp.)
Quahran
Sìdî ban al-'Abbas
Ujdah

Asturias
Cantabria
País Vasco
Navarra
La Rioja
Galicia
Pontevedra
Vigo
Orense
León
Burgos
Logroño
Palencia
Cataluña
Costa Brava
Aragón
Castilla y León
Costa Dorada
ESPAÑA
Castilla-La Mancha
Valenciana
ISLAS BALEARES
Costa del Azahar
Costa Blanca
PORTUGAL
Extremadura
Murcia
Andalucía
Algarve
Costa de la Luz
Costa del Sol
MEDITERRÁNEO
OCEANO
ATLÂNTICO
MAR
ISLAS BALEARES
Estrecho de Gibraltar

AL-MAGHRIB (MAROC)
AL JAZĀ'IR (ALGERIE)

162 163 164 165 166 167 168
169 170 171 172 173 174 175
176 177 178 179 180 181
183 184 185 186 187 182
188

0 50 100 150 km

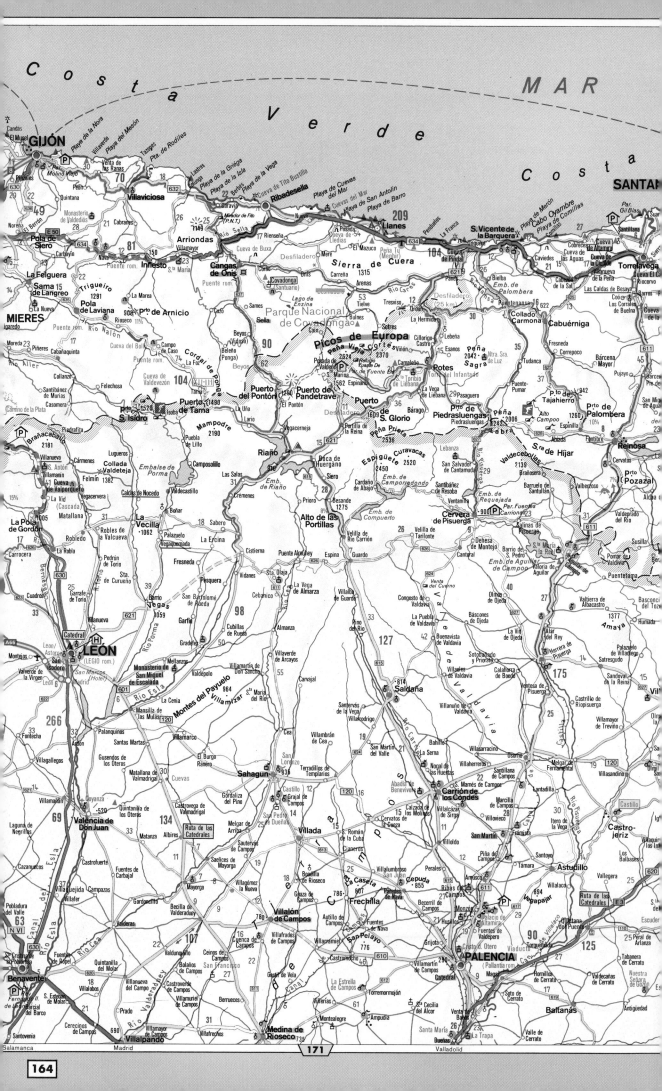

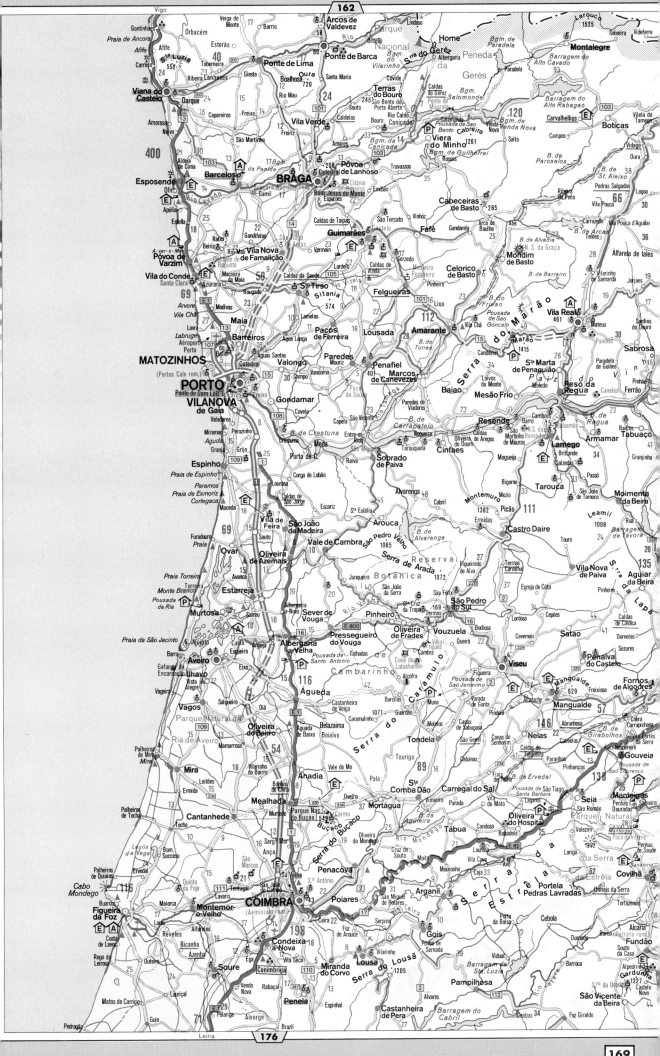

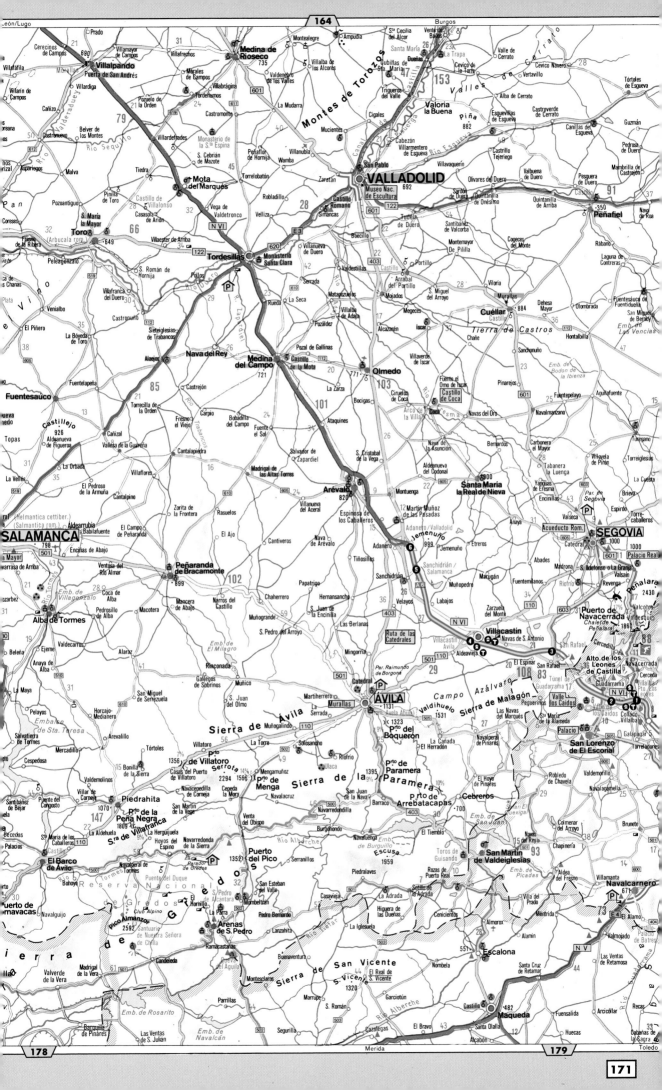

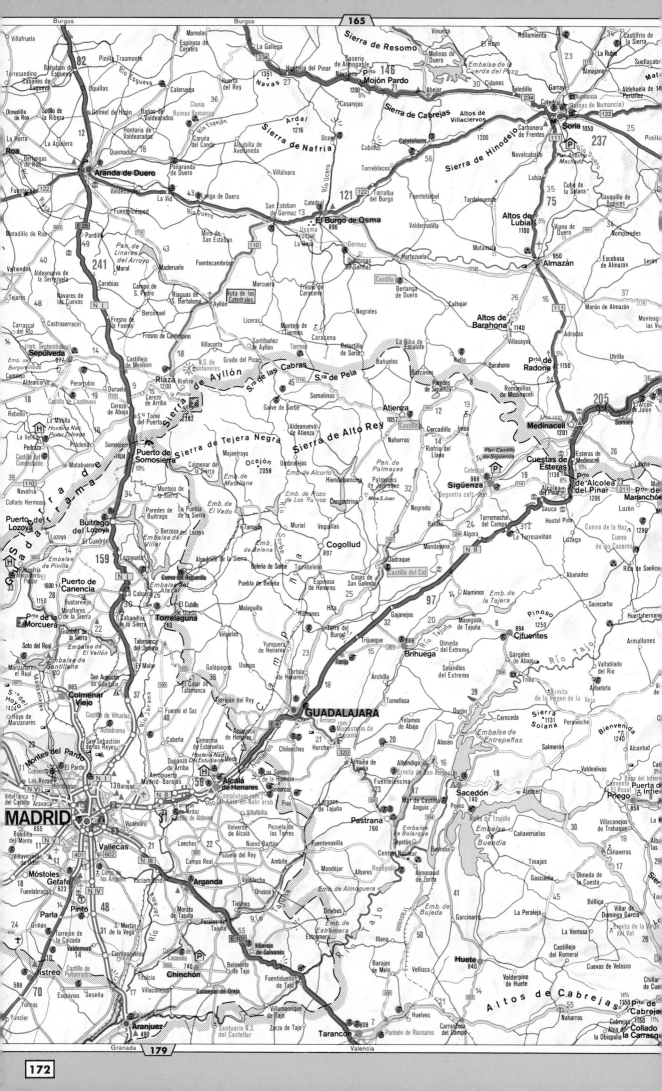

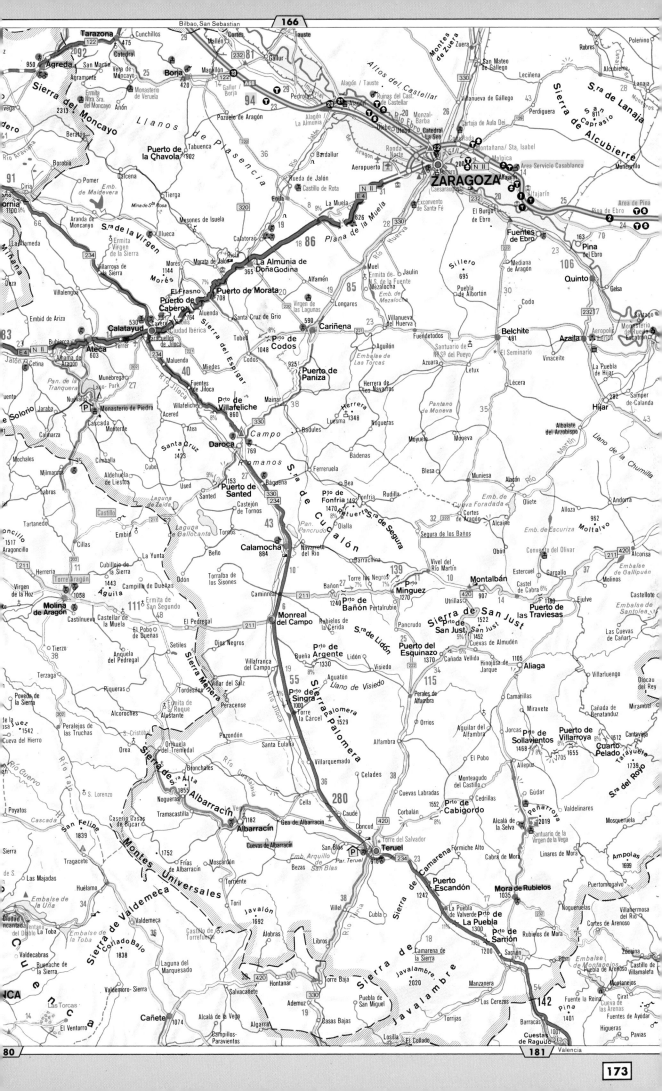

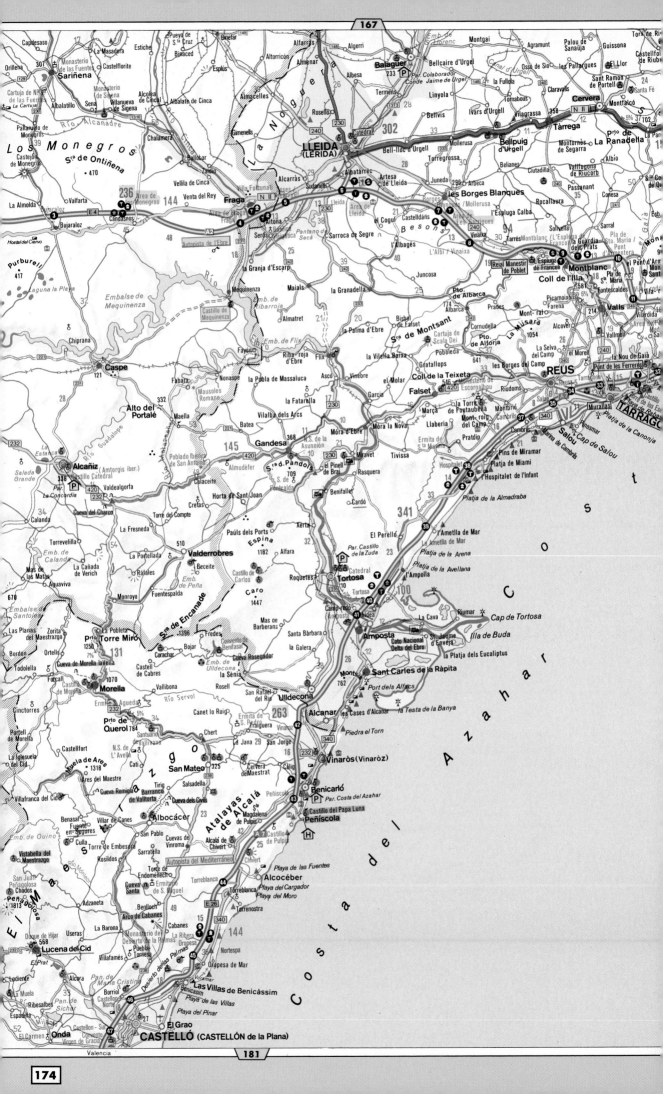

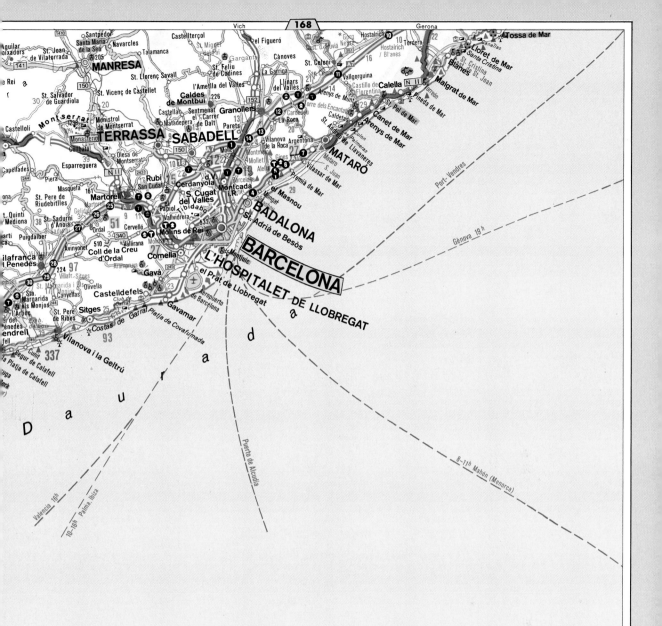

MANRESA

TERRASSA SABADELL

BARCELONA

L'HOSPITALET DE LLOBREGAT

BADALONA

MATARO

Calella

Malgrat de Mar

Lloret de Mar

Tossa de Mar

Blanes

Sitges

Vilanova i la Geltrú

D   a   u   r   a   d   a

Port-Vendres

Génova 19 h

8–11h Mahón (Menorca)

Valencia 16h

10–16h Palma Ibiza

Puerto de Alcudia

MAR MEDITERRÁNEO

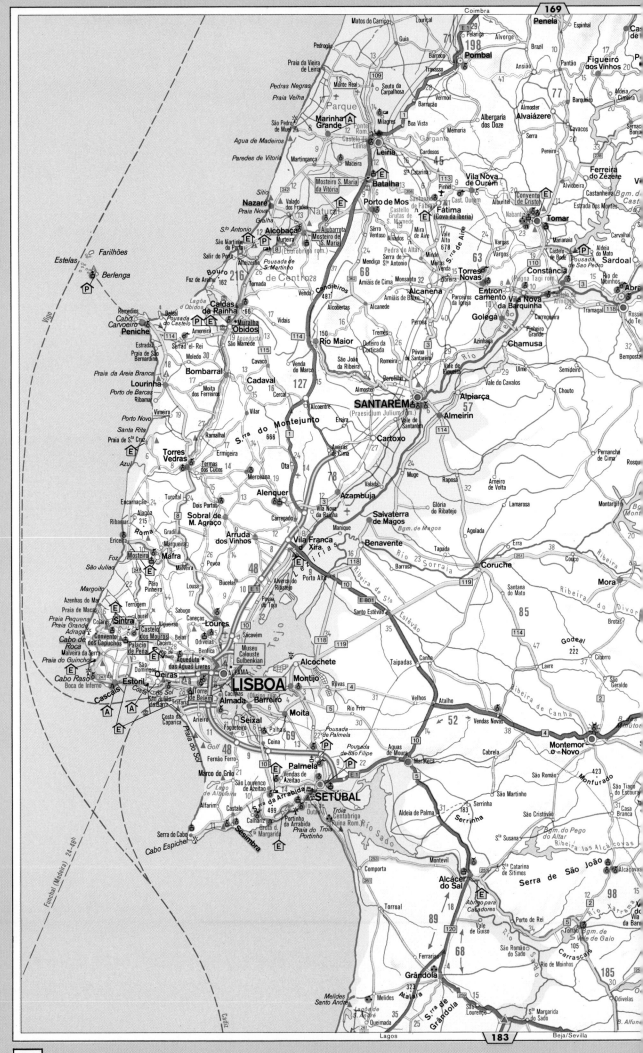

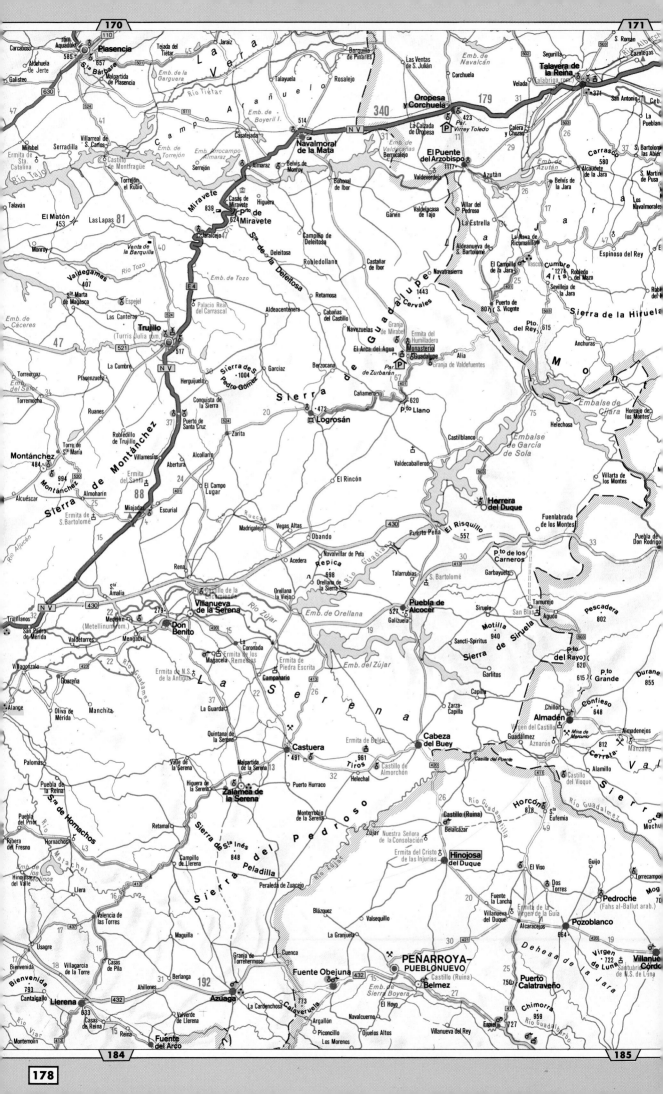

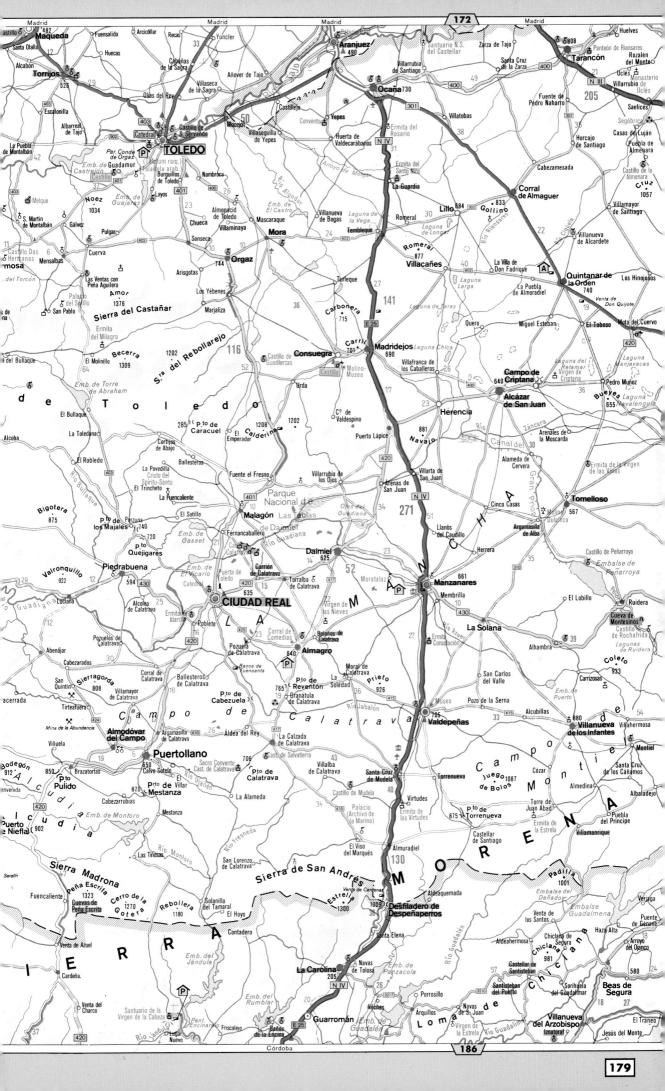

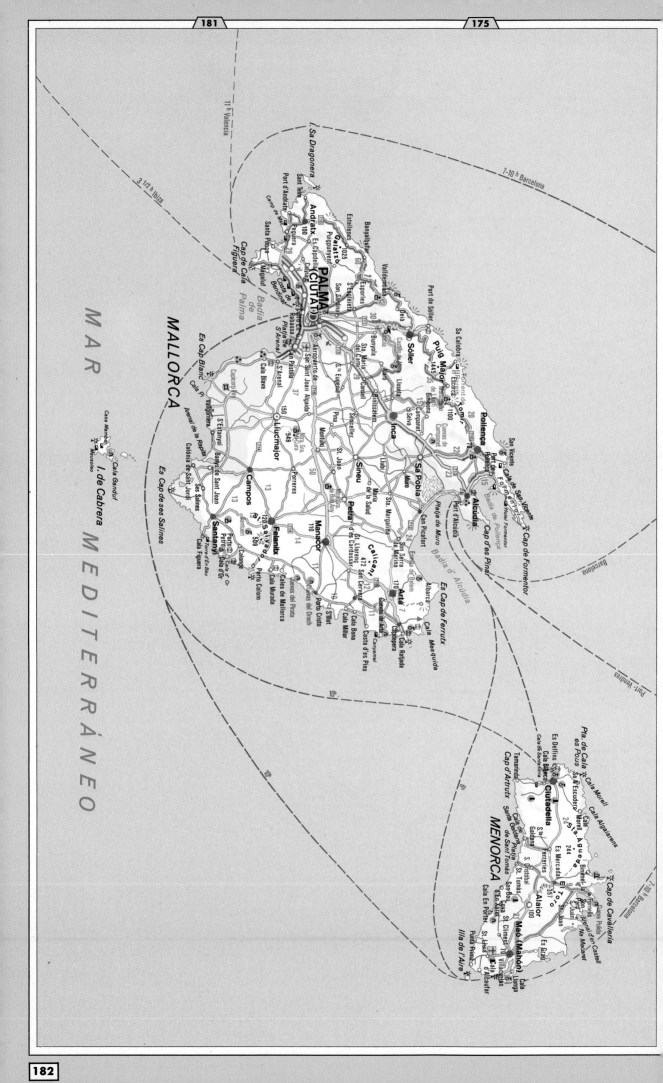

O C E A N O   A T L Â N T I C O

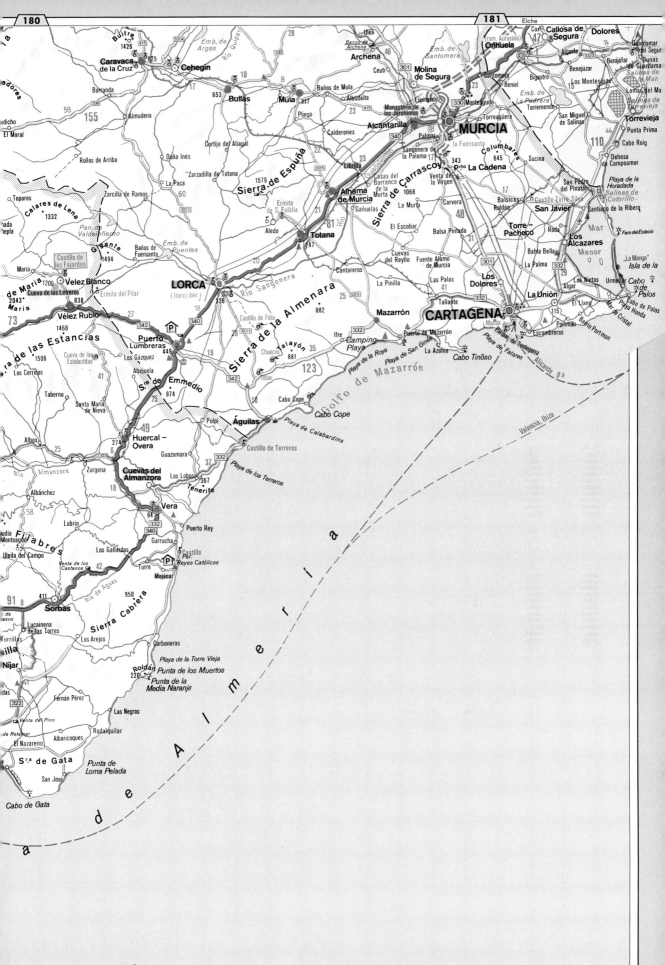

Buitre
1426
Caravaca
de la Cruz
415
625
Cehegin
Ulea
Baños de
Archena
Archena
(rom. Aurasiola)
Oríhuela
Cox
Callosa de
Segura
Dolores
47
Guardamar
del Segur
Dunas de
Guardama
Salinas de
la Mati
Barranda
3314
Emb. de
Argos
Río Quípar
28
Ceuti
Molina
de Segura
301
Santomera
Santomera
17
23
Bigastro
Benejúzar
Los Montesinos
3323
14
Emb. de
la Pedrera
Torremendo
415
10
8
Baños de Mula
Albudeite
330
Monteagudo
343
645
Benijófar
Algorfa
Benjel
San Miguel
de Salinas
15
Lomas del Ma
Salinas de
Torrevieja
Torrevieja
155
653
Bullas
Mula
317
Pliego
MURCIA
la Fuensanta
Punta Prima
El Moral
Almudena
Cortijo del Aliagal
Calderones
Monasterio de
los Jerónimos
Alcantarilla
Palmar
340
Sangónera la
Paloma
Columbares
Sucina
110
Cabo Roig
Dehesa
de Campoamor
Doña Inés
Zarzadilla de Totana
Sierra de Espuña
1579
Casas del
Barranco
de la
Murta
415
Sangónera de
la Paloma
Carrascoy
Prio La Cadena
Venta de
la Virgen
San Pedro
del Pinatar
Playa de la
Horadada
Salinas de
Cotorillo
Rollos de Arriba
La Paca
60
3315
Alhama
de Murcia
La Murta
1068
Corvera
Balsicas
Roldán
17
Castillo Torre Silla
San Javier
Santiago de la Ribera
Topares
Zarcilla de Ramos
Ermita de
S. Eulalia
Gañuelas
El Escobar
48
Torre
Pacheco
Roda
Los
Alcazares
Faro del Estacio
Calares de Lena
1332
3211
81
Río
Totana
247
Aledo
Balsa Pintada
Cuevas
del Reyllo
Fuente Álamo
de Murcia
31
Bahía Bella
La Palma
332
29
Mar
Menor
"La Manga"
Isla de la
de Maria
Castillo de
los Fajardos
Pan de
Valdepñierro
Baños de
Fuensanta
Emb. de
Puentes
LORCA
(Ilorci iber.)
326
Río Sangonera
Cántareros
La Pinilla
Las Palas
41
Los
Dolores
301
La Unión
El Llano
Los Nietos
Algar
"La Manga"
Maria
Gigante
1494
18
340
Castillo de Félix
882
25
3315
Mazarrón
Tallante
332
CARTAGENA
Urmeon
Cabo
de
Palos
Cabo de Palos
Playa Honda
2043
Maria
Cueva de los Letreros
Vélez Blanco
838
Ermita del Pilar
P
Puerto
Lumbreras
449
Sierra de la Almenara
28
3211
Talayón
881
Chuecos
Ifre
332
Camping
Playa
Puerto de Mazarrón
La Azohia
Cabo Tiñoso
Mastía
Parque de Tentegorra
Escombreras
Baño Portman
73
Vélez Rubio
1468
27
342
35
123
Tébar
10
Cabo Cope
Playa de la Roya
Playa de San Ginés
Golfo de Mazarrón
ra de las Estancias
1506
Cueva de las
Estalactitas
Los Gázquez
Abejuela
S·ª de Emmedio
974
342
Cabo Cope
Águilas
Playa de Calabardina
Cabo Cope
Valencia, Ibiza
Taberno
41
Santa María
de Nieva
25
Pulpi
Playa de los Terreros
Golfo de Mazarrón
Alicante g h
Albox
25
274
323
6
49
Huercal–
Overa
Guazamara
37
332
Castillo de Terreros
Río Almanzora
Zurgena
Cuevas del
Almanzora
Los Lobos
367
Tenerife
Playa de los Terreros
Albánchez
18
dia
Monteagud
Uleila del Campo
58
Lubrin
Los Gallardos
Vera
94
332
340
Sierra de
Cabrera
950
Puerto Rey
Garrucha
Castillo
Reyes Católicos
Sorbas
91
411
Lucainena
de las Torres
Los Arejos
Río de Aguas
42
Venta de los
Castanos
Turre
P
Pºz
Castillo
Reyes Católicos
Mojácar
Filabres
Nijar
322
Fernán Pérez
Roldán
220
Carboneras
Playa de la Torre Vieja
Punta de los Muertos
Punta de la
Media Naranje
de Almería
41
Venta del Pino
de Retamar
El Nazareno
Albaricoques
Las Negras
Rodalquilar
S·ª de Gata
Punta de
Loma Pelada
San José
Cabo de Gata

TERRÁNEO

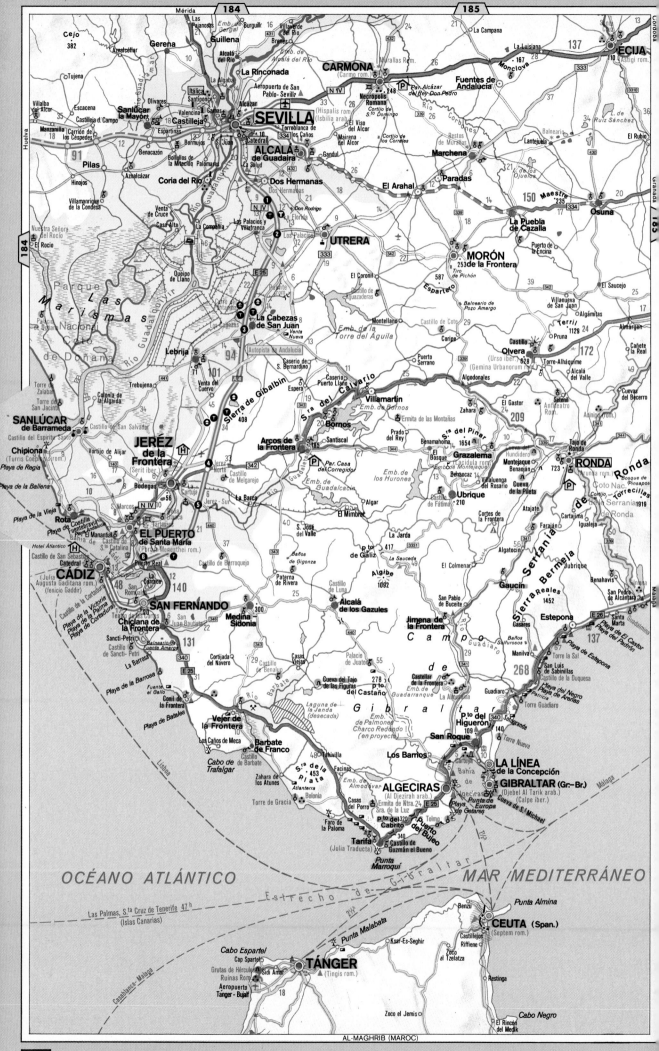

OCÉANO ATLÁNTICO

MAR MEDITERRÁNEO

AL-MAGHRIB (MAROC)

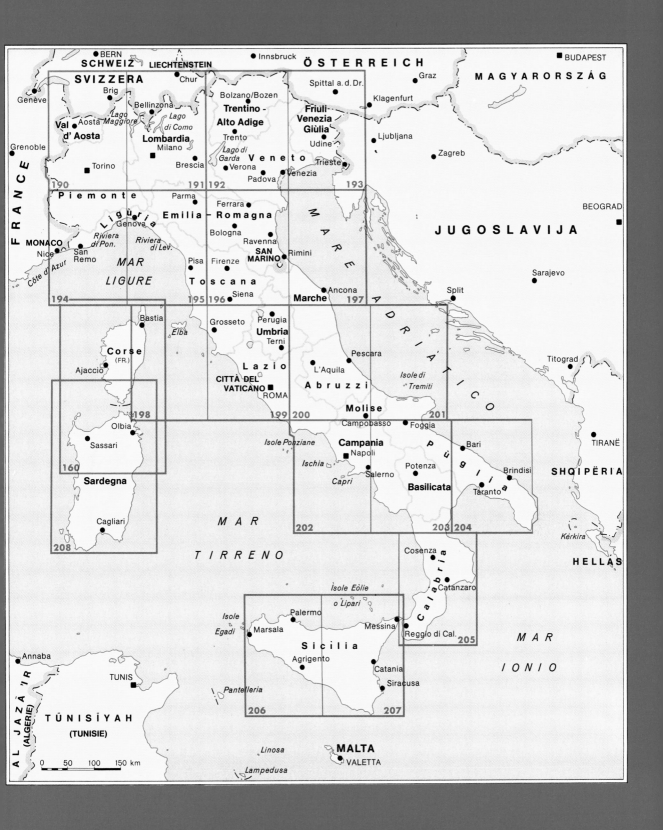

Italia
Italien · Italy · Italie · Italië · Ιταλία · İtalya

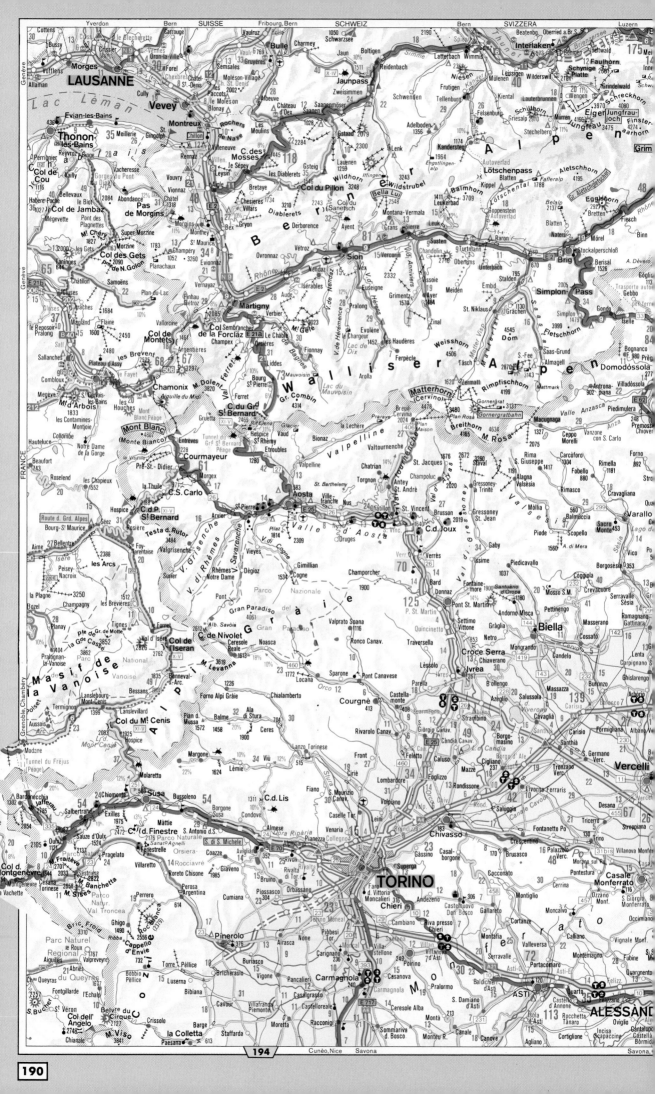

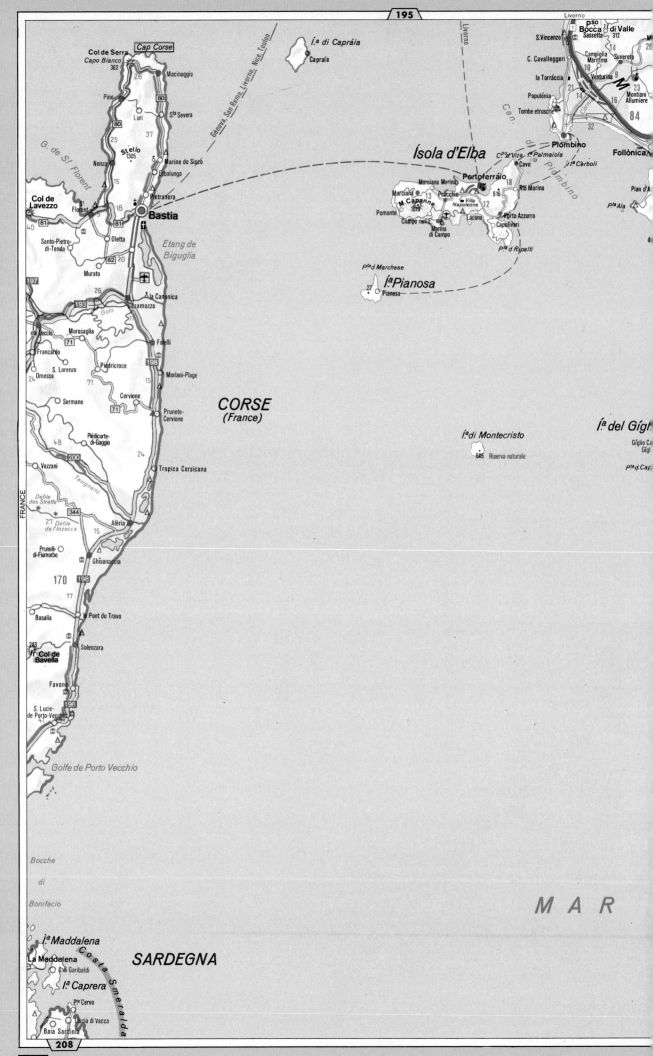

Livorno

Pso Bocca di Valle
S.Vincenzo   Sassetta   312

Col de Serra   *Cap Corse*
Capo Bianco
362
Macinaggio
Pino
80
Luri   Sta Severa

C. Cavalleggeri
Campiglia
Marittima
la Torràccia   Venturina
Populónia
Tombe etrusche
Píombino
Follònica

Í.a di Capráia
Capraía

Génova San Remo Livorno, Nice, Toulon

G. de St Florent
Nonza
Stello
1305
Marine de Sisço
Erbalunga
Pietranera
Bastia

Ísola d'Elba
Cpo d.Vita Í.a Palmaiola
Cavo
Rio Marina
Marciana Marina
Marciana   Procchio
M.Capanne   Villa
1019   Napoleone
Pomonte   Lacona
Campo nell'E.   Porto Azzurro
Marina   Capoliveri
di Campo
Pta d.Ripalti
Pta d.Cèrboli
Pian d.

Col de
Lavezzo
40   81   81
Santo-Pietro-
di-Tenda   Oletta
82   20
Murato
197
26
193   Casamozza
Morosaglia   Golo
71   Folelli
Francardo
S. Lorenzo   Piedricroce
Omessa   198
Sermano   Cervione
71   Moriani-Plage
Prunete-
Cervione
Pédicorte-
di-Gaggio
200   24
Vezzani
Tropica Corsicana

Etang de
Biguglia

la Canonica

CORSE
(France)

Pta d.Marchese
27   *Í.a Pianosa*
Pianosa

Í.a di Montecristo
645   Riserva naturale

Í.a del Gígl
Gíglio C
Gígl
Pta d.Cap

FRANCE

Défile
des Strette
344
27 Défile
de l'Inzecca
15   Alèria
Prunelli-
di-Fiumorbo
Ghisonaccia
170   198
17
Basalla   le Pont du Travo
243
**Col de
Bavella**   Solenzara
Favone
S. Lucie-
de Porto-Vecchio
198

Golfe de Porto Vecchio

M A R

Bocche
di
Bonifacio

Í.a Maddalena
La Maddalena   C.di Garibaldi
Í.a Caprera   **SARDEGNA**
Ptª Cervo
Liscia di Vacca
Baia Sardinia   Costa Smeralda

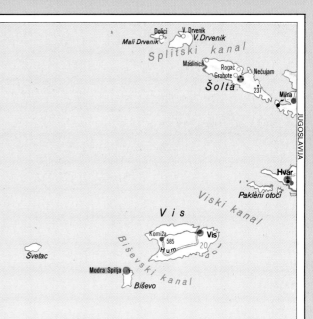
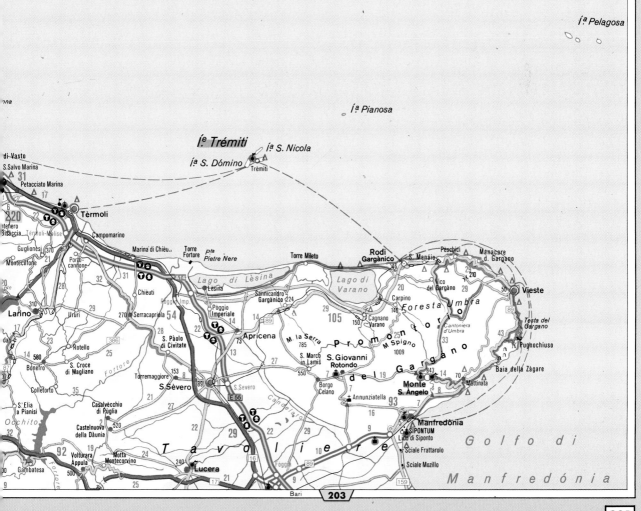

Roma | Isèrnia | Isèrnia | Tèrmoli

Priverno
Amaseno
Grotte di Pàstena
S. Giovanni Incàrico
Pontecorvo
519
Abbàzia di Montecassino
Cassino
Venafro 220
Cantalupo nel Sànnio 587
Vinchiaturo 625

Faìti 150
Monti Ausoni
Abb. di Fossanova
Vallecorsa
Ponte corvo
S. Vittore
Cassano
S. Vittore
Mignano Mte. Lugno
Capriati a Volturno
Mt. d. Matese 488
Boiano
14
A

Pontinia
Sonnino 1090
M. delle Fate 565
23 350
Lènola
Pico 16
Esperia 521
S. Giorgio a Liri
6
Pratella
Psо di Miralago 1080
Campitello Matese
Sella d. SAEPINUM 88
16

Parco Naz. Circeo
Galeria di M. Orsa
M. Petrella
45
Fondi 8
7
Monti Aurunci
Ausònia
Terme di Sùio
Roccamonfina
Caianello
E 45
Alife
Piedimònte Matese
M. Mutria 1823
Sèpino

Lºdi Sabaudia
Tempio di Giove Anxur
Terracina
36 242
CASTAGNETO
Fòrmia
MAMURRANO
Minturno 140
Terme di Sùio
Cascano
Teano
Dragoni
S. Angelo d'Alife 186
Alvignano
Gioia Sannitica
Morcone
Pontelandolfo 83

M. Circeo
S.Felice Circeo
Sperlonga
Grotta di Tiberio
Itri
Tomba di Cicerone
Sessa Aurunca
203
Pignataro Maggiore
Capua
Bellona
Caiazzo
Cerreto Sannita
S. Salvatore Telesino
Guàrdia Sanframondi

Gaeta
Bàia Domizia
Carinola 99
Sparanise
22
Vitulano 500
Solopaca
Vituláno 30

Golfo
di Gaeta
Mondragone
27 73
Cancello ed Arnone
Grazzanise
S. Maria Càpua Vetere
Càpua
200
Frasso Telesino

Isole Ponziane
Ia Zannone
Ia Palmarola
Ponza
Ia di Ponza
Castel Volturno
S. Cipriano d'A.
Succivo
S. Angelo in For.
Caserta Vècchia
Caserta
Maddaloni
Airola
Montesárchio

BENEVENTO
Apollosa
Bonea
S. Agata de' Goti

Aversa
Caivano
Cìcciano
Nola
Cervinara
Baiano
Pietrastornina

Ia di Ventotene
Ventotene
Scoglio S. Stefano
Qualiano
Marano di Napoli
Aeroporto Napoli
Pomigliano d'Arco
Somma Ves.
Palma Campania
Monteforte Irpino
Avellino

NAPOLI
CUMA
Pozzuoli
Lºdel Fusaro
Aquae Tre. Gaveta Baia
Bàcoli
Solfatara
C.º Miseno
Ercolano
Pòrtici
Osservatorio
Vesuvio 1277
S. Anastasia
S. Giuseppe Vesuviano
Sarno

Lacco Ameno
Casamicciola Terme
Ia di Prócida
Prócida
Forio
Pòrto
Ponte
Ischia
ERCOLANO
TORRE D.GRECO
TORRE ANNUNZIATA
POMPEI 33
Angri
Nocera Inferiore
Baronissi

Ìsola d'Íschia
Sp.gia di Citara
Barano d'Ischia
Lido di Maronti
Sant'Angelo
CASTELLAMMARE DI STABIA
Gragnano
Valico di Cava de' Tirreni
Maiori
SALERNO

Gfo
di
Napoli
Vico Equense
M. Faito
Agerola
Ravello
Amalfi
Grotta Pandona
Grotta Smeralda

Grotta Azzurra
Sorrento
Massa Lubrense
Grotta delle Sirene
S. Agata sui due Golfi
Positano
Praiano
Anacapri
Villa di Tiberio
Grotta di Regina Giovanna
Pta. Campanella

Capri
Ia di Capri
Gfo di Salerno

Cagliari

Palermo

Stromboli Messina

MAR TIRRENO

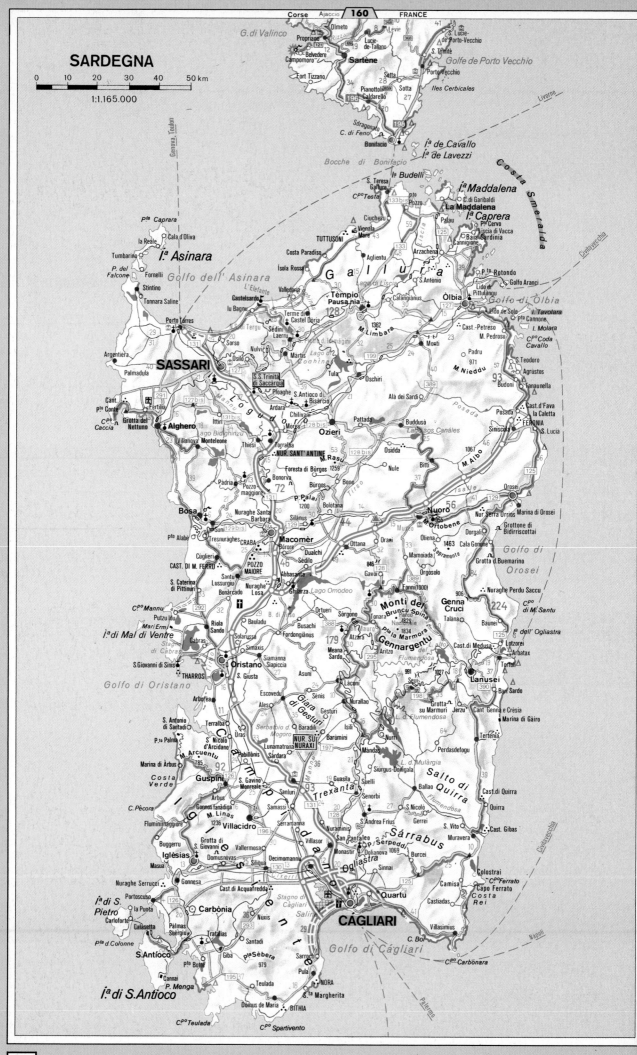

SARDEGNA

0 10 20 30 40 50 km

1:1.165.000

Jugoslavija
Jugoslavia · Jugoslavien · Yugoslavia · Jugoslawien · Joegoslavië
Yougoslavie · Iugoslavia · Γουγκσλαβία · Yugoslavya

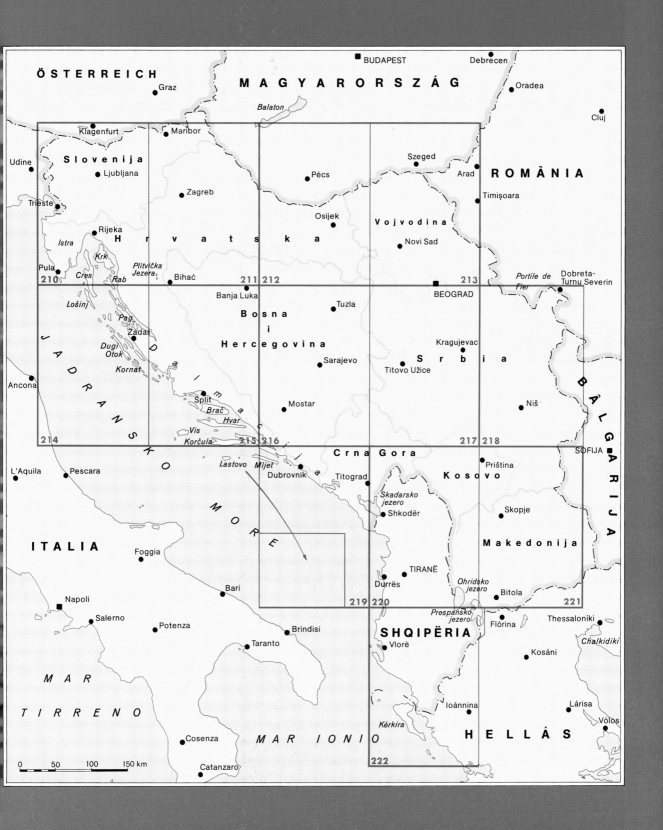

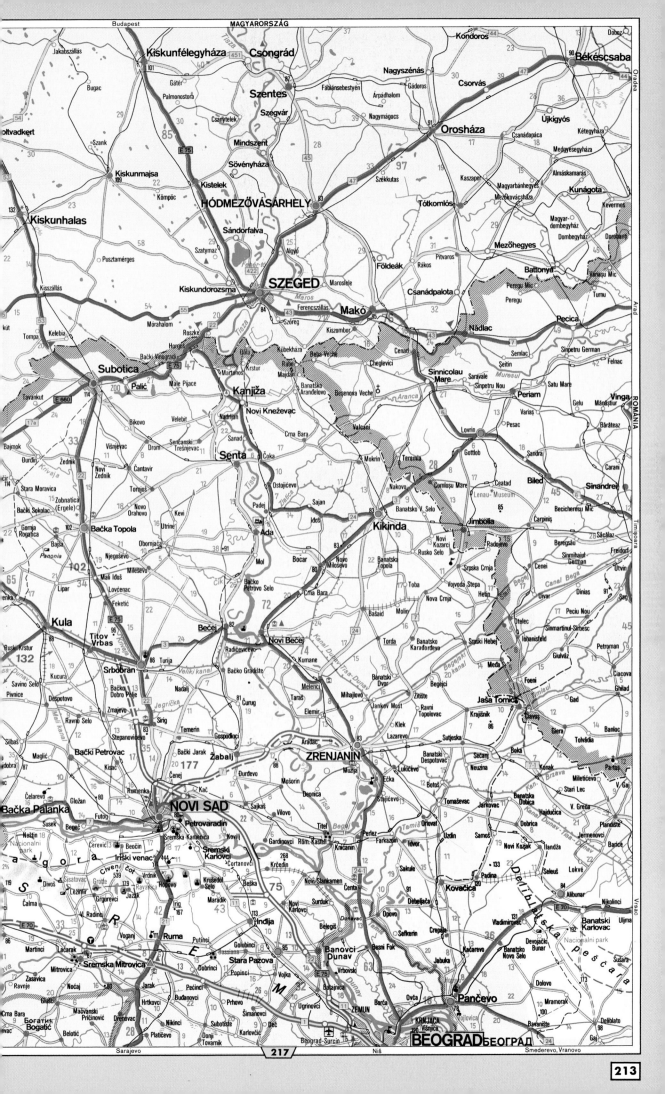

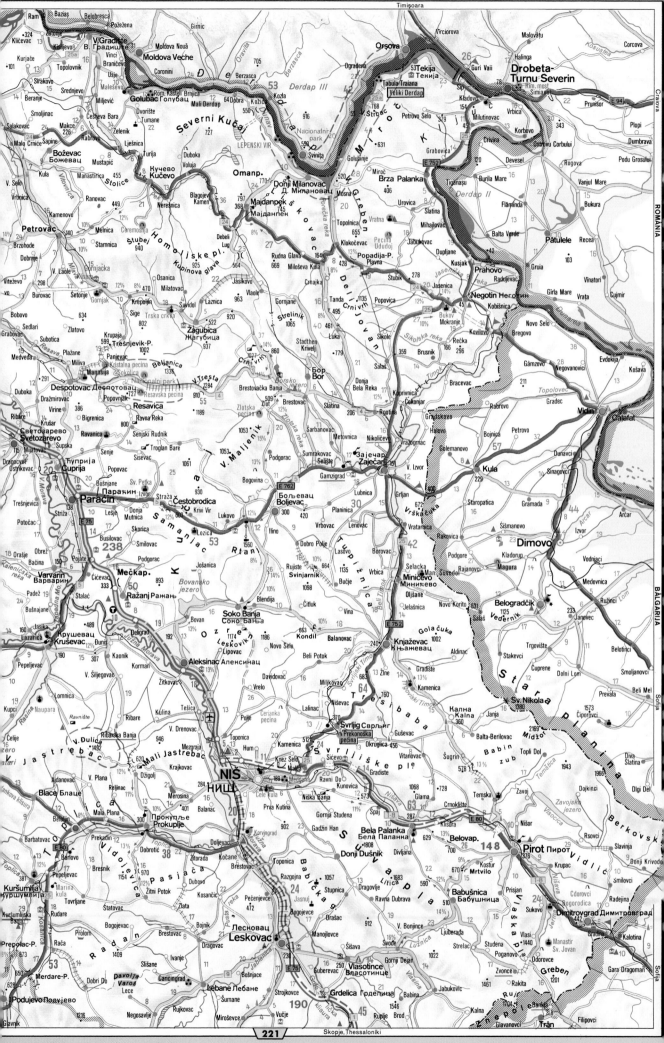

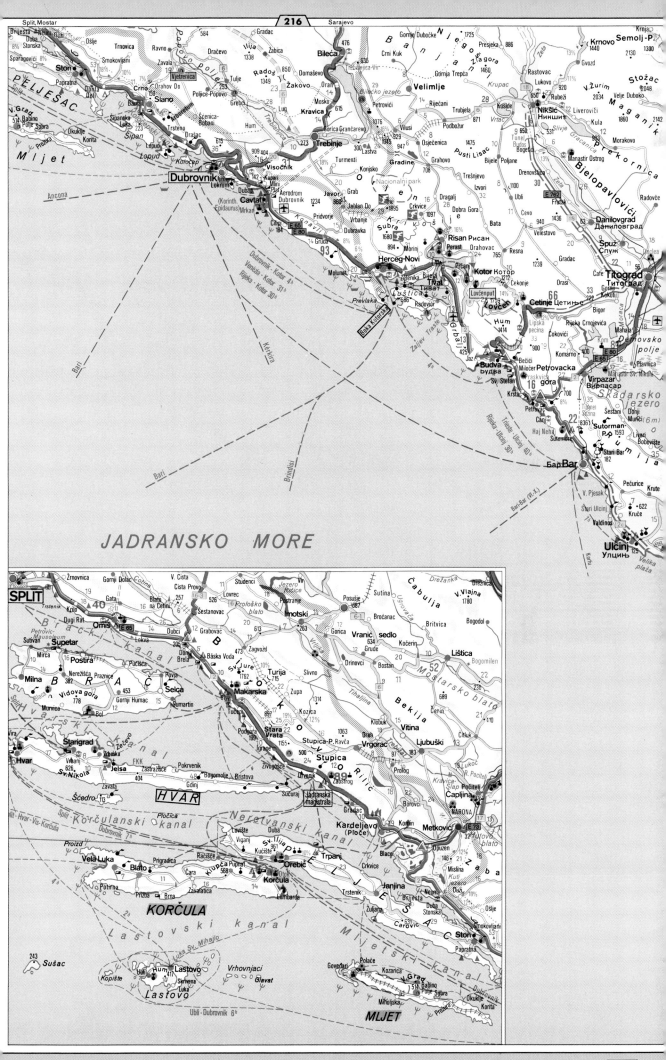

JADRANSKO MORE

PELJEŠAC

Mljet

SPLIT

BRAČ

HVAR

KORČULA

Lastovo

MLJET

SHQIPËRIA

Lushnja

Beléshi

Dharzeza

Hodoništa

Sv. Zaum

Otešovo

Trpejca

Carina

Sv. Naum

Lubanište

Stenje

Pogradeci

Peshkepi

Zervaska

14

Alarupi

Collomboci

Bishqethmi

Tunja

Grámshi

Trebinja

2073

1351

1884

Kushova

Kokla

Pirgu

Poiani

Pusteci

Podgori

2035

Poshnja

Kumani

Berati

2417

Cëvica

Moglica

Loshani

Maliqi

Vinçani

29

Zvezda

1770

Korça

Mova

Fieri

Pojani

APOLLONIA

31

15

Mjeta

2061

Voskopoja

Voskopi

1649

Dërsniku

Dvorani

12

1675

Zemblaku

Bilisti

Gryka

Novosela

Patosi

39

24

Ballshi

Paraspuari

Bargullas

Çorovoda

Gramshi

2396

Treska

Qafëzezi

1196

Lofka

1879

Trilofon

Ruins

Bozhigradi

Ballabani

1248

Lapani

Frashëri

1365

Luarasi

Qinami

2253

Plikátion

2070

ISH. SAZANIT

Narta

Panaja

Selenica

Peshkëpia

Gilava

226

Memaliaj

Vajza

70

42

Parakastra

Tepelena

18

Hoshteva

2050

Petrani

Dhembeli

Nemercka

2486

60

Radanj

Leskoviku

2041

Amárantos

Pírgos

179

Smólikas

2637

Eléftheron

Kep i Gjuhëzës

Vlora (Valona)

364

24

29

7

Rradhima

Gjormi

AMANTIA

1870

94

86

Gusmari

Griba

Shushica

Kosina

Vinjaki

Përmeti

M. i Postenanit

Kávassila

Exochi

Eléftheron

Kónitsa

2022

Timfi

2497

Laïsta

Logara-Paß

1055

Dhermiu

1672

Kuçi

Kolonia

Patakastra

Poliçani

Suha

Libohova

1763

Yeroplátanos

Vissani

Doliana

30

Kalpákion

Pápigon

Vitsa

Kipi

Negádes

Fragádes

Shën Theodor

Himara

Borshi

Qeparol

1842

Gjirokastra

M. i Gjërë

Dhuvjani

Pontikáte

Delvinákion

Dolianá

Vikos

Zagoriá

Monodéndrion

Asprángeli

Kaminiá

Kefali

Piqerasi

35

Shënvasija

PHÖNIKE

Jergucati

Kakavi

16

32

Theollogu

Charavyi

Peristérion

Kastani

Ieromnimi

Gitsa

Mitsikéli

62

Kourendon

Asfáka

Eleoúsa

Perama

Saranda

Dhrovjani

Konispoli

Theollogu

Tsamántas

Liá

Lista

Achoúria

Vaveúriou

Aetópetra

1329

Ag. Ilías

Souliópoulon

Klimatiá

Mármara

Ioánnina

Erikoússa

Akr. Ag. Ekaterinis

Kassiópi

Roda

Perithía

Pantokrátor

914

Butrinti

Pandelejmoni

Av. Nikólaos

Keramitsa

23

Pléssion

1240

Vrossina

Pónte Ekklissiés

1172

Grammenón

76

Pedini

Kastrítsa

Óthoni

Avlióte

Karoussádes

Nimfe

Spartilas

BUTHROTON

Çifliku

Konispoli

Ciñku

Ay. Nikólaos

Eleftherochórion

Dodóni

DODONA

Pérdika

Mathrákion

Ay. Stefanos

Makradés

Páyi

40

600

Korakiána

Ipsos

Gouvia

Kérkira (Corfu)

Sayiáda

Filiáte

Parapótamos

GUMANI

657

Paramithiá

Salonki

Ménina

15

509

Tomaros

Varyiádes

Pérdika

65

Térovon

75

N. KÉRKIRA (CORFU)

Angelokastron

Paleokastritsa

Liápades

26

13

Kanóni

Achilleion

Pélekas

576

Sinarades

Kynopiáste

Igoumenítsa

100

Grekochórion

Prodrómion

1615

Tsangárion

Assos

1332

Ay. Górdios

Vouniatádes

Ay. Matthéos

Strongilí

Moraitika

Chlomós

330

Arvirádes

Akr. Lefkímnis

Platariá

957

Masarákia

745

Karvounárion

47

Dervisiána

1553

Mon. Metám. S. Remanou

Gardikion

Nikólitsion

Gorgómilos

1274

Lefkimmi

Dragotiná

Kávos

Sívota

Pérdika

14

Margaritíon

Chóika

Vrissoúla

Filippiás

Áno Lefkími

Arkoudila

Akr. Asprókavos

Ayiá

927

Mórfion

1082

Messopótamon

Thesprotikón

Ióníon Pélagos

Paxí

N. ΠΑΞΟΙ

Lákka

Párga

NEKROMANTEÍON

Skepastón

Loútsa

Kató Despotikó

43

27

Oropós

Stefáni

Antípaxi

Kamarína

773

Kastrossíkia

Archángelos

Néa Sampsoús

Michalítsion

Salaóra

Kassópi

Strongili

Ráchi

Anesa

Ελλάς
Hellás · Grekland · Kreikka · Grækenland · Greece · Griechenland
Griekenland · Grèce · Grecia · Yunanistan

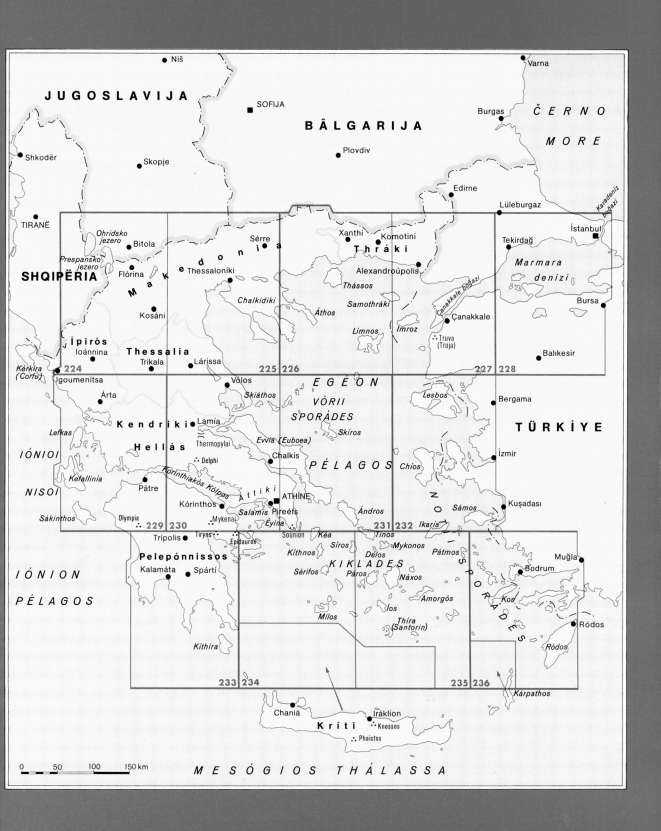

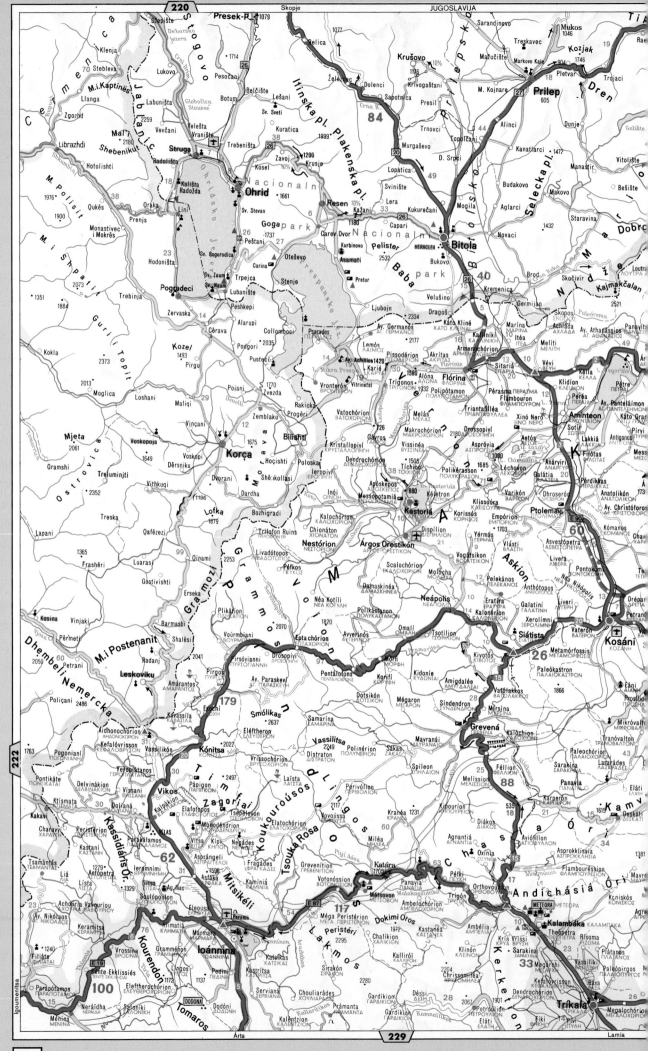

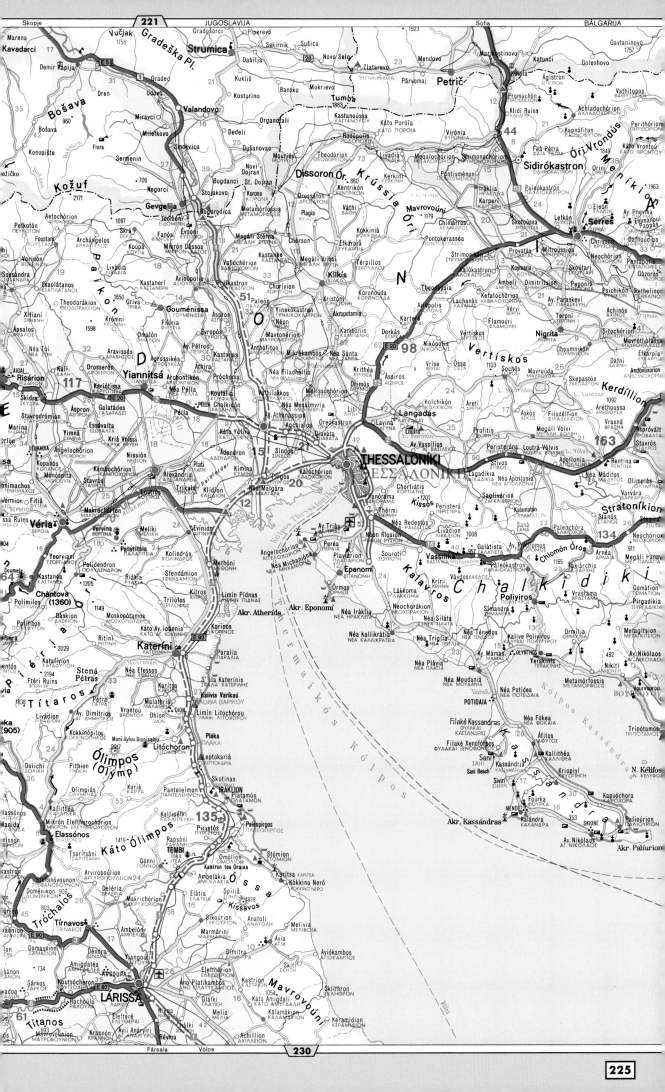

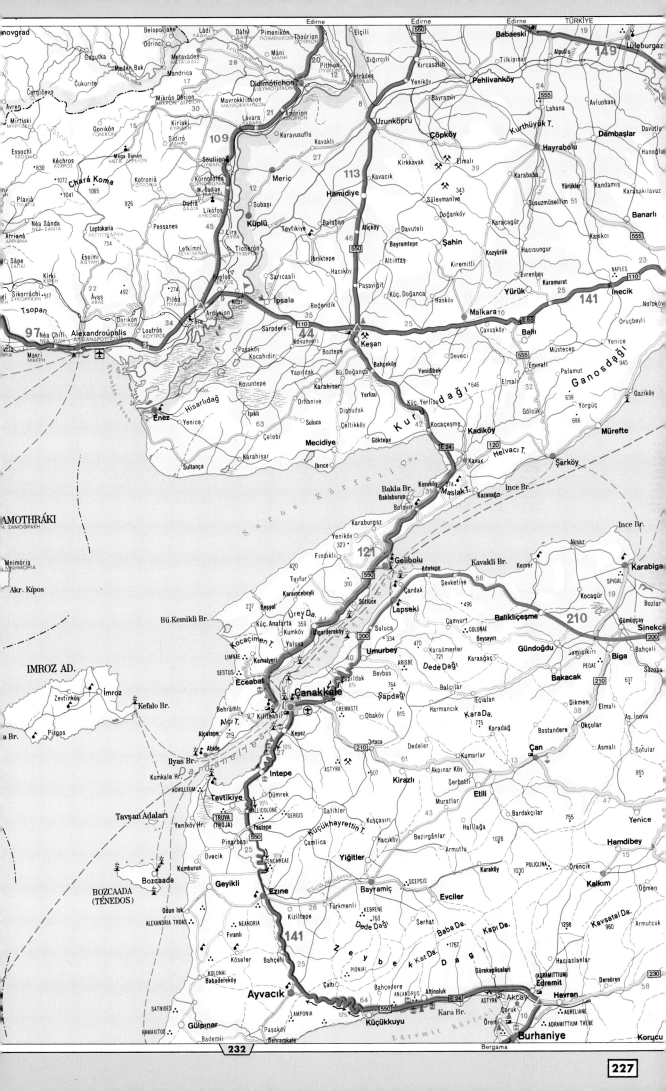

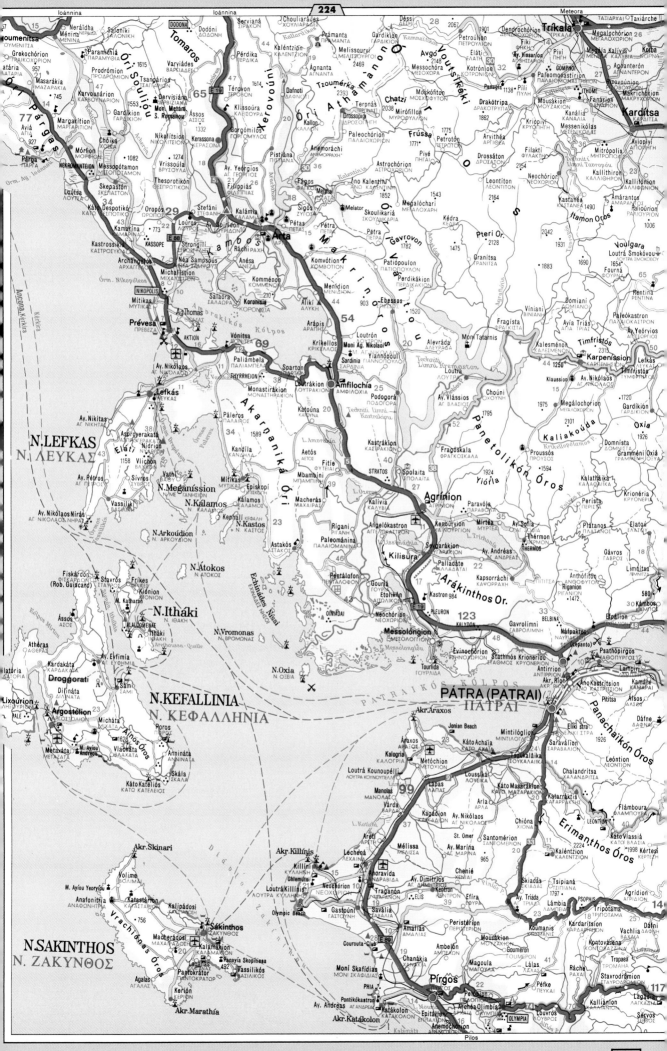

N. Limnos
N. Ay. Apóstoli
Ν. ΑΓ. ΑΠΟΣΤΟΛΟΙ
Ay. Efstrátios
ΑΓ. ΕΥΣΤΡΑΤΙΟΣ
N. Roúmnos
Ν. ΡΟΥΜΝΟΣ

Áy. Nikólaos
ΑΓ ΝΙΚΟΛΑΟΣ
● 303
N. Ay. Efstrátios
Ν. ΑΓ. ΕΥΣΤΡΑΤΙΟΣ

N. Psathoúra
Ν. ΨΑΘΟΥΡΑ

N. Míga
Ν. ΜΥΓΑ

N. Yioúra
Ν. ΓΙΟΥΡΑ
570

N. Prásson
Ν. ΠΡΑΣΣΟΝ

N. Pipérion
Ν. ΠΙΠΕΡΙΟΝ

N. Kirá Panayiá
(Pélagos)
Ν. ΚΥΡΑ ΠΑΝΑΓΙΑ
(ΠΕΛΑΓΟΣ)
290

E G É O N

S P O R Á D E S

N. Lechoússa
Ν. ΛΕΧΟΥΣΑ

N. Peristéra
Ν. ΠΕΡΙΣΤΕΡΑ
456

N. Adelfópoulo
Ν. ΑΔΕΛΦΟΠΟΥΛΟ
N. Adelfí
Ν. ΑΔΕΛΦΟΙ

N. Skántzoúra
Ν. ΣΚΑΝΤΖΟΥΡΑ

N. Skantílion
Ν. ΣΚΑΝΤΗΛΙΟΝ
N. Kórakas
Ν. ΚΟΡΑΚΑΣ

368
Ólimpos
Skíros
ΣΚΥΡΟΣ

N. Skiropoúla
Ν. ΣΚΥΡΟ ΠΟΥΛΑ

Linariá
ΛΙΝΑΡΙΑ

N. SKÍROS
Ν. ΣΚΥΡΟΣ

N. Erinía
Ν. ΕΡΗΝΙΑ

N.Valaxa
Ν. ΒΑΛΑΞΑ

Akr. Lithári

N. ÉVVIA- EUBOEA
Ν.ΕΥΒΟΙΑ

N.Sarakinón
Ν. ΣΑΡΑΚΗΝΟΝ

Metóchion
ΜΕΤΟΧΙΟΝ
Kími
ΚΥΜΗ
Akr. Kímis

Taxiárche
ΤΑΞΙΑΡΧΑΙ
24
Paralía
ΥΠΑΡΑΛΙΑ
21

Vríssi
ΒΡΥΣΗ

Ochthoniá
ΟΧΘΟΝΙΑ

Akr.Ochthoniá

Chánia
ΧΑΝΙΑ
12
Neochórion
ΟΝΕΟΧΩΡΙΟΝ

Ay. Loukás
ΑΓ. ΛΟΥΚΑΣ
M. Ay. Nikólaou
Alivérion
ΑΛΙΒΕΡΙΟΝ
Lépoura
ΛΕΠΟΥΡΑ
Akr. Pounta
árindos
35 44

Milákion
ΜΥΛΑΚΙΟΝ

L. Distos
DYSTOS

41
Almiropótamos
ΑΛΜΥΡΟΠΟΤΑΜΟΣ

Messochória
ΜΕΣΟΧΩΡΙΑ

Kapandrítion
ΚΑΠΑΝΔΡΙΤΙΟΝ
N. Kavalliani
ΚΑΒΑΛΛΙΑΝΗ
RAMNOUS
Ag. Marina
ΑΓ. ΜΑΡΙΝΑ
20
Grammatikón
ΓΡΑΜΜΑΤΙΚΟΝ
Néa Stíra
ΝΕΑ ΣΤΥΡΑ
10

Marathón
ΜΑΡΑΘΩΝ
N. Stíra
Ν. ΣΤΥΡΑ
Venus Beach
Stíra
ΣΤΥΡΑ

MARATHON
Yiannitsion
ΓΙΑΝΝΙΤΣΙΟΝ
Kalérgon
ΚΑΛΕΡΓΟΝ

Akr. Kafiréfs

ssiá
Dióniss os
Néa Mákri
ΝΕΑ ΜΑΚΡΗ
Marmárion
ΜΑΡΜΑΡΙΟΝ
Óchi Óros
1398
Kómiton
ΚΟΜΙΤΟΝ
Platanistós
ΠΛΑΤΑΝΙΣΤΟΣ

15
Limin
ΛΙΜΗΝ
32

PENTELI
SION
allíni
ΑΛΛΗΝΗ
Rafína
ΡΑΦΗΝΑ
Níssi Petalii
ΝΟΙ ΠΕΤΑΛΙΟΙ
**Megalónissos
Petalíon**
ΜΕΓΑΛΟΝΗΣΟΣ
ΠΕΤΑΛΙΩΝ
Káristos
ΚΑΡΥΣΤΟΣ

P É L A G O S

N. Antipsara
Ν. ΑΝΤΙΨΑΡΑ

Spáta
ΣΠΑΤΑ
Loútsa
ΛΟΥΤΣΑ
BRAURON (VRAVRON)
Órmos
Karistou
N. Mandílou
Ν. ΜΑΝΔΗΛΟΥ

Akr. Kambanós

N. ÁNDROS
Ν. ΑΝΔΡΟΣ

A
Markópoulon
ΜΑΡΚΟΠΟΥΛΟΝ
Limin Messoyéas
ΛΙΜΗΝ ΜΕΣΟΓΕΙΑΣ
(Porto Rafti)
Kalivárion
ΚΑΛΥΒΑΡΙΟΝ
Gávrion
ΓΑΥΡΙΟΝ
Argás
ΑΡΓΑΣ
994

HAGNUS
Kouvaras
Kouvaras
ΚΟΥΒΑΡΑΣ
Moni Sotiros
ΜΟΝΗ ΣΩΤΗΡΟΣ
Akr. Strongiló
Mbatsion
ΜΠΑΤΣΙΟΝ
Ándros
ΑΝΔΡΟΣ
ANDROS
Paleópolis
ΠΑΛΑΙΟΠΟΛΙΣ

KEPHALE
Keratéa
ΚΕΡΑΤΕΑ
Paralias
ΠΑΡΑΛΙΑΣ
40
Kaki Thálassa
ΚΑΚΗ ΘΑΛΑΣΣΑ
Akr.Tripití
Órmos
Kórthi
ΚΟΡΘΙ

PHREARRION
Ag. Konstantinos
ΑΓ. ΚΩΝΣΤΑΝΤΙΝΟΣ
Thorikón
ΘΟΡΙΚΟΝ
Lávrion
ΛΑΥΡΙΟΝ

Paléa Fókea
ΠΑΛΑΙΑ ΦΩΚΑΙΑ
N. Makrónissos
Ν. ΜΑΚΡΟΝΗΣΟΣ
Korissia
ΚΟΡΗΣΙΑ
N. KÉA
Ν. ΚΕΑ
Akr. Steno
N. TÍNOS
Ν. ΤΗΝΟΣ

Legrena
ΛΕΓΡΕΝΑ
Káto
Soúnion
ΣΟΥΝΙΟΝ
Akr.
Agálistros
JULIS
Kéa
ΚΕΑ
N. Yíaros
Ν. ΓΥΑΡΟΣ
N. Síros
Pánormos
ΠΑΝΟΡΜΟΣ
Istérnia
ΙΣΤΕΡΝΙΑ

POSEIDON
Kap Soúnion

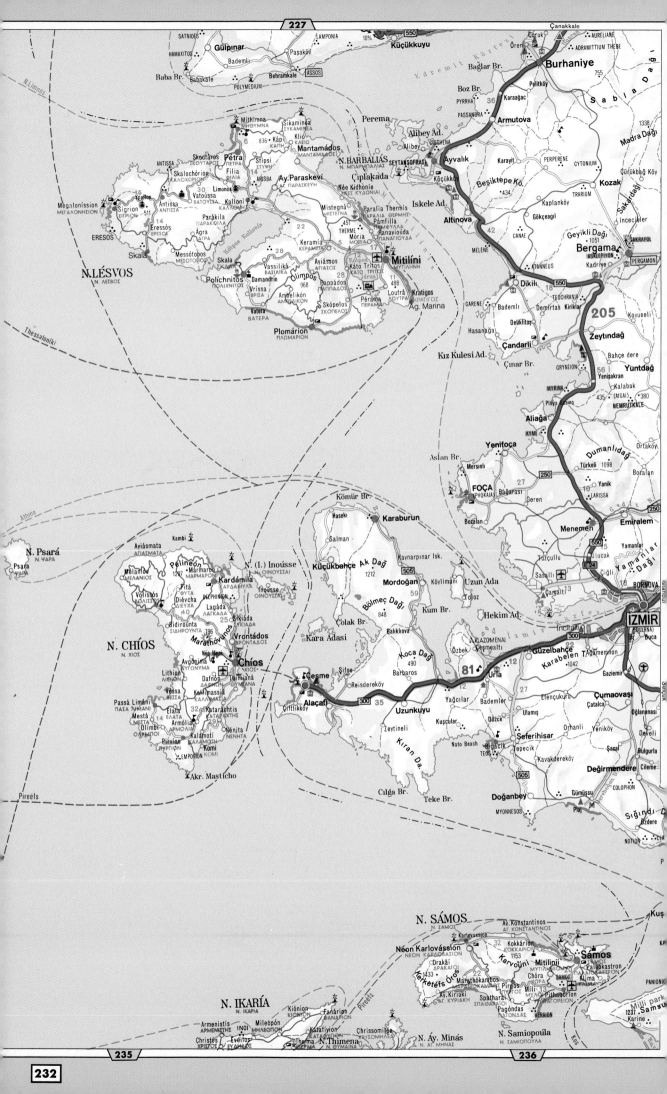

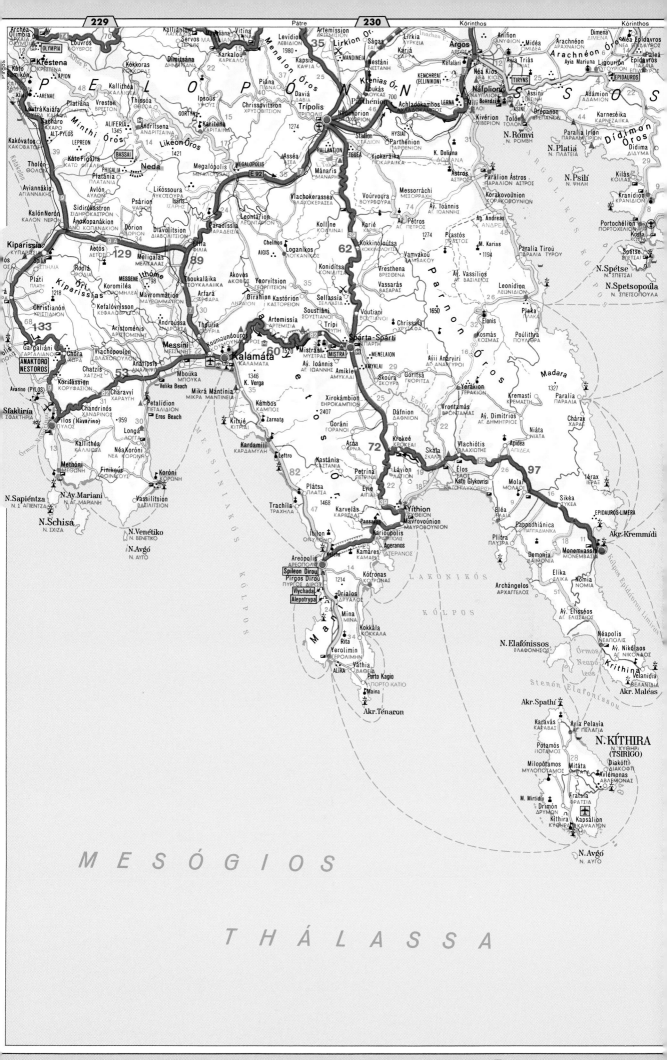

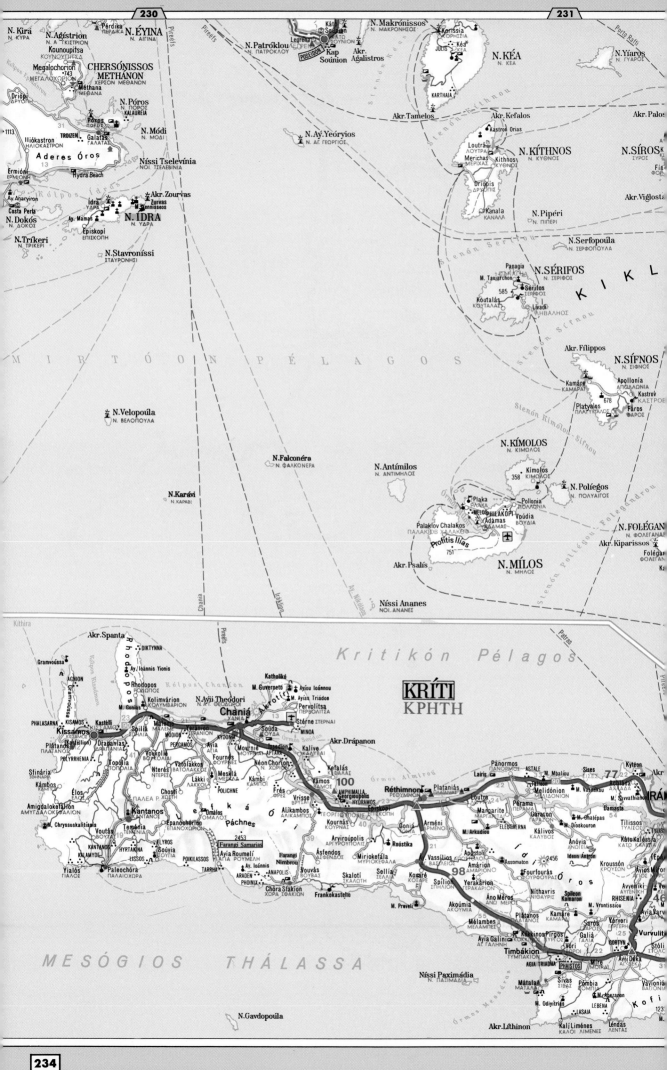

N. Kirá
Ν. ΚΥΡΑ

N. Agístrion
Ν. ΑΓΚΙΣΤΡΙΟΝ

Pérdika
ΠΕΡΔΙΚΑ

N. ÉYINA
Ν. ΑΙΓΙΝΑ

Kounoupítsa
ΚΟΥΝΟΥΠΙΤΣΑ

Megalochorion =743
ΜΕΓΑΛΟΧΩΡΙΟΝ

CHERSÓNISSOS
METHÁNON
ΧΕΡΣΟΝΗΣΟΣ
ΜΕΘΑΝΩΝ

Driópi
ΔΡΥΟΠΗ

Méthana
ΜΕΘΑΝΑ

Káto
Soúnion

N. Makrónissos
Ν. ΜΑΚΡΟΝΗΣΟΣ

Korissía
ΚΟΡΗΣΣΙΑ

N. KÉA
Ν. ΚΕΑ

N. Ýaros
Ν. ΥΑΡΟΣ

Legrená
POSEIDON
Kap
Soúnion

Akr.
Agálistros

JULIS

KARTHAIA

N. Póros
Ν. ΠΟΡΟΣ

N. Patróklou
Ν. ΠΑΤΡΟΚΛΟΥ

N. Módi
Ν. ΜΟΔΙ

N. SÍROSK
Ν. ΣΥΡΟΣ

1113

Iliókastron
ΗΛΙΟΚΑΣΤΡΟΝ

TROIZEN
Galatás

Póros
ΠΟΡΟΣ
KALAUREIA

N. Aý. Yeóryios
Ν. ΑΓ. ΓΕΩΡΓΙΟΣ

Kastron Orias

Loutrá
ΛΟΥΤΡΑ
Merichas
ΜΕΡΙΧΑΣ

N. KÍTHNOS
Ν. ΚΥΘΝΟΣ

Akr.Tamelos

Akr. Kefalos

Akr. Palos

Aderes Óros
13

Nissi Tselevínia
ΝΟΙ ΤΣΕΛΕΒΙΝΙΑ

31

Aý. Anarýiron

Idra
ΥΔΡΑ

Akr. Zourvás
ΑΚΡ. ΖΟΥΡΒΑΣ

Zurvás
Μ. ΞΕΝΙΣSEOS

Kithnos
ΚΥΘΝΟΣ

Driópis
ΔΡΥΟΠΙΣ

N. Pipéri
Ν. ΠΙΠΕΡΙ

Akr. Viglosta

Fin
ΦΟ

Ermíoni
ΕΡΜΙΟΝΗ

Hydra Beach

N. ÍDRA
Ν. ΥΔΡΑ

Kanala
ΚΑΝΑΛΑ

N. Serfopoúla
Ν. ΣΕΡΦΟΠΟΥΛΑ

Costa Perla

Aý. Mamás

N. DOKÓS
Ν. ΔΟΚΟΣ

Episkopí
ΕΠΙΣΚΟΠΗ

Panagia
Μ. ΤΑΞΙΑΡΧΟΝ

N. SÉRIFOS
Ν. ΣΕΡΙΦΟΣ

K I K L

N.Tríkeri
Ν. ΤΡΙΚΕΡΙ

N.Stavroníssi
ΣΤΑΥΡΟΝΗΣΙ

585

Sérifos
ΣΕΡΙΦΟΣ

Koutalás
ΚΟΥΤΑΛΑΣ

Livadi
ΛΙΒΑΔΙ

Akr. Fílippos

N. SÍFNOS
Ν. ΣΙΦΝΟΣ

M I R T Ó O N   P É L A G O S

Kamáre
ΚΑΜΑΡΑΙ

Apollonía
ΑΠΟΛΛΩΝΙΑ

Kastrov
ΚΑΣΤΡΟΕ

678

Fáros
ΦΑΡΟΣ

N.Velopoúla
Ν. ΒΕΛΟΠΟΥΛΑ

Platyalos
ΠΛΑΤΥΓΙΑΛΟΣ

Stenón Kimólou-Sífnou

N. KÍMOLOS
Ν. ΚΙΜΟΛΟΣ

N.Falconéra
Ν. ΦΑΛΚΟΝΕΡΑ

N. Antímilos
Ν. ΑΝΤΙΜΗΛΟΣ

358

Kímolos
ΚΙΜΟΛΟΣ

N. Políegos
Ν. ΠΟΛΥΑΙΓΟΣ

N.Karávi
Ν. ΚΑΡΑΒΙ

Plaka
ΠΛΑΚΑ

Pollonia
ΠΟΛΛΩΝΙΑ

N. FOLÉGAN
Ν. ΦΟΛΕΓΑΝΔ

MELOS PHILAKÓPI

Voúdia
ΒΟΥΔΙΑ

Akr. Kiparissos

Folég
ΦΟΛΕΓΑΝ

Palakióv Chalakos
ΠΑΛΑΙΟΒ ΧΑΛΑΚΟΣ

Adámas
ΑΔΑΜΑΣ

Profítis Ilías
751

Akr. Psalís

N. MÍLOS
Ν. ΜΗΛΟΣ

Níssi Ananes
ΝΟΙ. ΑΝΑΝΕΣ

Kithira

Akr.Spanta

DIKTYNNA

Kritikón   Pélagos

Patras

Gramvoússa

Rhodopos
ΡΟΔΟΠΟΣ

Aý. Ioánnis Yionis

Katholikó

Μ. Guvernéto

Ayíou Ioánnou

KRÍTI
ΚΡΗΤΗ

PHALASARNA
ΦΑΛΑΣΑΡΝΑ

Gramvoússa

M. Gonias

Rhodopos
ΡΟΔΟΠΟΣ

Kolimvárion
ΚΟΛΥΜΒΑΡΙΟΝ

N. Aýii Theódori
Ν. ΑΓΙΑ ΘΕΟΔΩΡΑ

Μ. Ayías Triádos

Pervolítsa
ΠΕΡΒΟΛΙΤΣΑ

Akrotíri

Kolpos Kissamou

Chaniá
ΧΑΝΙΑ

Stérne ΣΤΕΡΝΑΙ
MINOA

Kastélli
ΚΑΣΤΕΛΛΙ

Soúlia
ΣΟΥΛΙΑ

Maleme
ΜΑΛΕΜΕ

MODION

Soúda
ΣΟΥΔΑ

Kissamos
ΚΙΣΣΑΜΟΣ

Drápanias
ΔΡΑΠΑΝΙΑΣ

PERGAMÓS

KYDONA

Kalíve
ΚΑΛΥΒΑΙ

Akr. Drápanon

Plátanos
ΠΛΑΤΑΝΟΣ

POLYRRHENIA

Topólia
ΤΟΠΟΛΙΑ

Voukoliá
ΒΟΥΚΟΛΙΑΙ

Ayía
ΑΓΙΑ

Mournié
ΜΟΥΡΝΙΑ

Néon Chorion
Ν. ΧΩΡΙΟΝ

Kefalás
ΚΕΦΑΛΑΣ

Pánormos
ΠΑΝΟΡΜΟΣ

ASTALE

Μ. Mbaliou

Sises

Kytéon

Akr

Sfinária
ΣΦΗΝΑΡΙΑ

Vatólakkos
ΒΑΤΟΛΑΚΚΟΣ

Nterés
ΝΤΕΡΕΣ

Fournés
ΦΟΥΡΝΕΣ

Meskiá
ΜΕΣΚΛΑ

100

Vámos
ΒΑΜΟΣ

AMPHIMALLA
Georgioupolis
ΝΥΔΡΑΜΟΣ

Réthimnon
ΡΕΘΥΜΝΟΝ

Plataniás
ΠΛΑΤΑΝΙΑΣ

Lairis

Melidónion
ΜΕΛΙΔΟΝΙΟΝ

Μ. Vasaeou

Achláda

77

Kámbos
ΚΑΜΠΟΣ

Élos
ΕΛΟΣ

Chosti
ΧΩΣΤΗ

Kámbi
ΚΑΜΠΙ

Frés
ΦΡΕ

Vrisse
ΒΡΥΣΣΕ

Episkopí
ΕΠΙΣΚΟΠΗ

Loutra
ΛΟΥΤΡΑ

Perama
ΠΕΡΑΜΑ

Margarite
ΜΑΡΓΑΡΙΤΑ

Garason

Μ. Chalépas

Damastas

IRÁK

Amigdalokefálion
ΑΜΥΓΔΑΛΟΚΕΦΑΛΙΟΝ

Μ. Chryssoskalítissis

Voutás
ΒΟΥΤΑ

Kantanos
ΚΑΝΤΑΝΟΣ

Temenía
ΤΕΜΕΝΙΑ

Epanochórion
ΕΠΑΝΟΧΩΡΙΟΝ

Umalos
ΟΜΑΛΟΣ

Páchnes

Pelká
ο

ς

Alikambos
ΑΛΙΚΑΜΠΟΣ

Vrisse

Gonía
ΓΟΝΙΑ

Argiroúpolis
ΑΡΓΥΡΟΥΠΟΛΙΣ

Roústika
ΡΟΥΣΤΙΚΑ

Apostoli
ΑΠΟΣΤΟΛΙ

Μ. Arkadíou

Kálivos
ΚΑΛΥΒΟΣ

Eleútherna
ΕΛΕΥΘΕΡΝΑ

Μ. Dioskouron

Anóyia
ΑΝΩΓΙΑ

Ideon Antron

Μ. Savvathianón

2456

54

TYLISC

KÁNTANOS
ΚΑΝΤΑΝΟΣ

19

Hyrtakina
ΥΡΤΑΚΙΝΑ

Temenía
ΤΕΜΕΝΙΑ

2453
Farangi Samarias

Ayía Rouméli
ΑΓΙΑ ΡΟΥΜΕΛΗ

Vrisse

Asfendos
ΑΣΦΕΝΔΟΣ

Miriokefála
ΜΥΡΙΟΚΕΦΑΛΑ

Vassilios
Μ. ΒΑΣΙΛΕΙΟΥ

Amárion
ΑΜΑΡΙΟΝ

Fourfourás
ΦΟΥΡΦΟΥΡΑΣ

98

Kroussón
ΚΡΟΥΣΩΝ

Ayios Miro

RHISENIA

46

Yialós
ΓΙΑΛΟΣ

Paleochóra
ΠΑΛΑΙΟΧΩΡΑ

Souía
ΣΟΥΓΙΑ

Ayía Ioánnis

Μ. Preveli

Anapolis
ΑΝΑΠΟΛΙΣ

Vouvás
ΒΟΥΒΑΣ

Skalotí
ΣΚΑΛΩΤΗ

Sellía
ΣΕΛΛΙΑ

Yerakárion
ΓΕΡΑΚΑΡΙΟΝ

Spílion
ΣΠΗΛΙΟΝ

Nithavris
ΝΙΘΑΥΡΙΣ

Spileon
Kamaron

Ayía Varva

KÁNTANOS

KALAMYD

LISSOS

POIKILASSOS

TARRHA

ARADEN
PHOINIX

Chóra Sfakíon
ΧΩΡΑ ΣΦΑΚΙΩΝ

Frankokastello

Akoúmia
ΑΚΟΥΜΙΑ

Áno Méros
ΑΝΩ ΜΕΡΟΣ

Plátanos
ΠΛΑΤΑΝΟΣ

Kamáre
ΚΑΜΑΡΕ

Kamáre

Sarós

Várveri
ΒΑΡΒΕΡΙ

Vurvulit

Mélambes
ΜΕΛΑΜΠΕΣ

Ayía Galíni
ΑΓΙΑ ΓΑΛΗΝΗ

Kókkinos Pírgos
ΚΟΚΚΙΝΟΣ

Galiá
ΓΑΛΙΑ

GORTYN
ΓΟΡΤΥΝ

Stóli

Ayía
Avenéki

Yiánnis
Μ. VRANIS

M E S Ó G I O S   T H Á L A S S A

Timbákion
ΤΥΜΠΑΚΙΟΝ

Vóri
ΒΩΡΟΙ

Mire

PHAISTOS

GALIA

Aýii Déka
ΑΓΙΟΙ ΔΕΚΑ

AGIA TRIADNA

Níssi Paximádia
ΝΟΙ ΠΑΞΙΜΑΔΙΑ

Sívas
ΣΙΒΑΣ

Pómbia
ΠΟΜΠΙΑ

Vaýioni

N.Gavdopoúla
Ν. ΓΑΥΔΟΠΟΥΛΑ

Mátala
ΜΑΤΑΛΑ

Μ. Apezanon

Ko fi

Akr. Líthinon

Μ. Odiýitrias

Kalí Liménes
ΚΑΛΟΙ ΛΙΜΕΝΕΣ

LEBENA

Léndas
ΛΕΝΤΑΣ

123

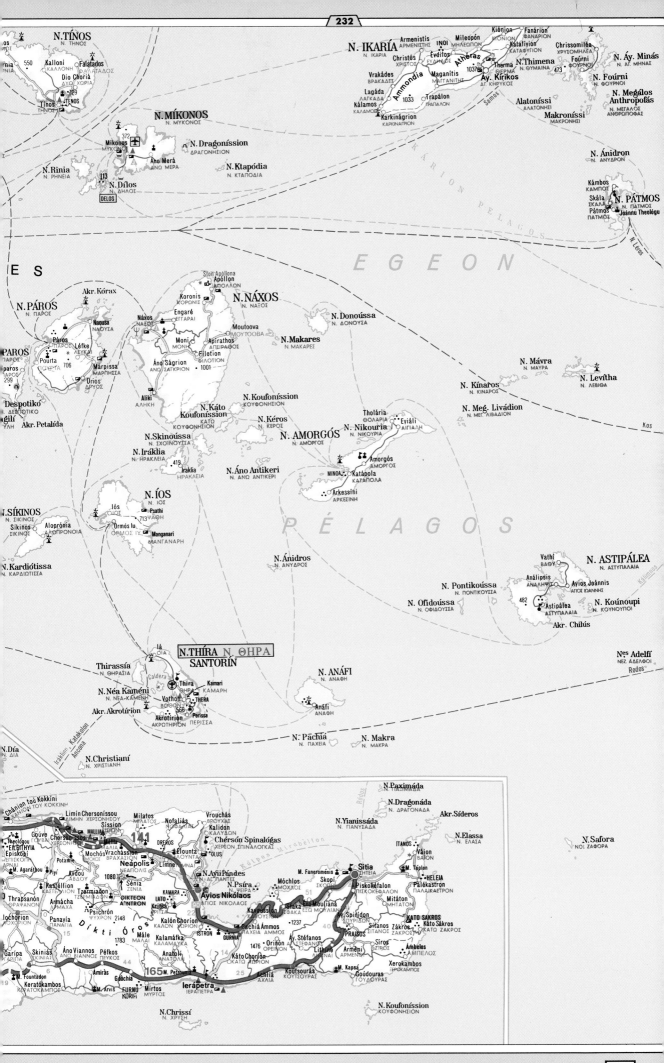

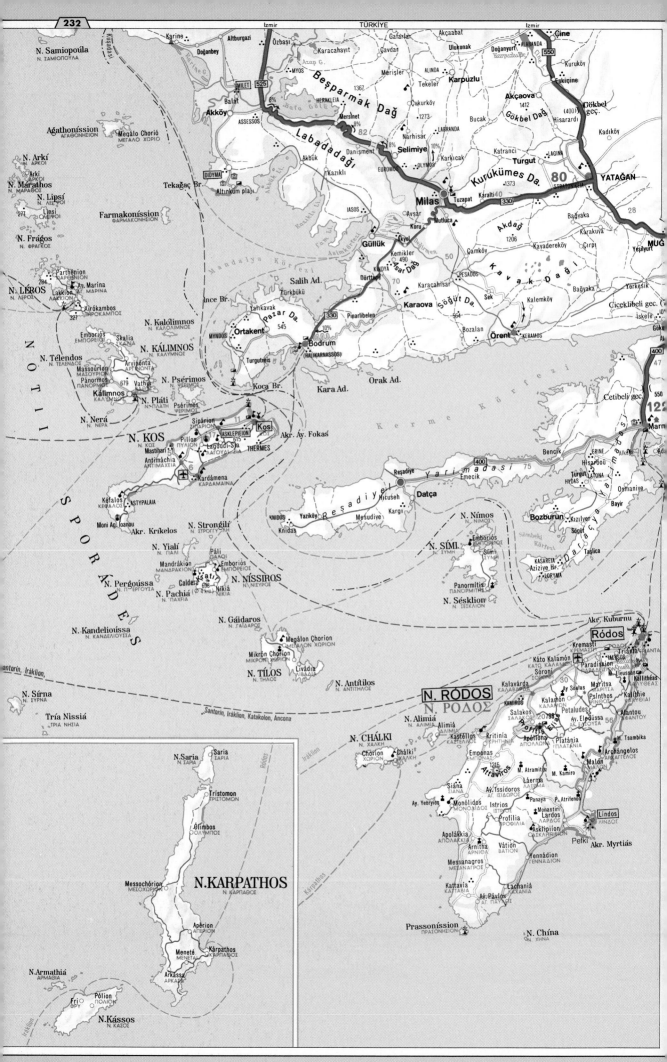

Bykart · Stadplaner · Kaupungien kartat · Byplaner · Town plans · Stadtpläne · Stadsplattegronden · Plans de villes · Planos de ciudades · Piante di città · Σχεδιαγράμματα τών πόλεων · Şehir haritaları

ÍSLAND

NORGE

SVERIGE

SUOMI
FINLAND

Helsinki
239

Oslo
238

Stockholm
238

DANMARK

København
239

SOJUZ SOVETSKICH
SOCIALISTIČESKICH
RESPUBLIK

GREAT BRITAIN
AND NORTHERN IRELAND

IRELAND
ÉIRE

NEDERLAND
Amsterdam
245

DEUTSCHE
DEMOKR.

Berlin
241

POLSKA

London
240

BUNDES-

REPUBLIK

BELGIË
BELGIQUE
Brussel

Bruxelles/
Brussel
245

Bonn
242

Praha
243

ČESKOSLOVENSKO

LUXEM-
BOURG 247

DEUTSCHLAND

Paris
246

Strasbourg
247

München
242

Wien
243

MAGYAR-
ORSZÁG

251
Budapest

ROMÂNIA

FRANCE

SCHWEIZ
SUISSE
SVIZZERA

Zürich
244

LIECHTEN-
STEIN

ÖSTER-
REICH

Bern
244

Milano
249

JUGOSLAVIJA

Bucureşti
251

SAN MARINO

BÂLGARIJA

PORTUGAL

ANDORRA

MONACO

ITALIA

Istanbul
252

Barcelona
248

CITTÀ
DEL
VATICANO

Roma
250

TÜRKIYE

Madrid
248

Lisboa
249

ESPAÑA

HELLÁS

Athinai
252

0   200   400   600 km

MALTA

Oslo

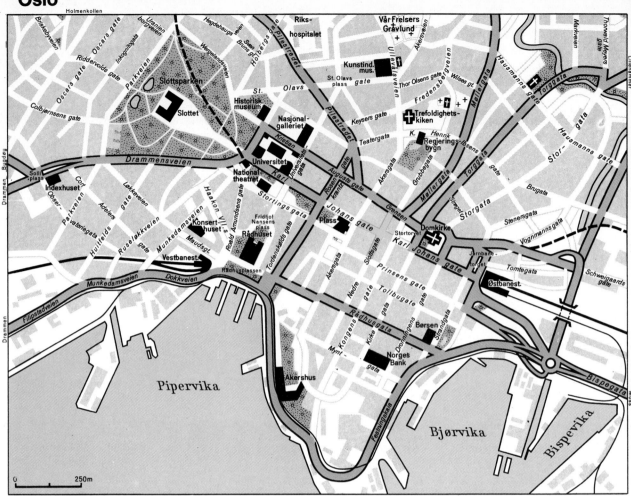

Holmenkollen · Uranien borgveien · Birkelunveien · Oscars gate · Hegdehaugsveien · Riks-hospitalet · Vår Frelsers Gravlund · Thowald Meyers gate · Markveien

Oscars gate · Inkognitogata · Parkveien · Slottsparken · St. Olavs gate · Kunstind. mus. · Ullevålsveien · Thor Olsens gate · Wilses gt. · Akersveien · Hausmanns gate · Lilleakern

Ridderveldts gate · Slottet · Historisk museum · St. Olavs plass · Keysers gate · Fredensborgveien · Trefoldighets-kiken · K. · Hausmanns gate

Colbjørnsens gate · Drammensveien · Nasjonal-galleriet · Teatergata · Akersgata · Regjerings bygn · Møllergata · Storgata

Drammen · Bygdøy · Solli plass · Indexhuset · Obser- · Universitet · National-theatret · Haakon VII's gate · Stortings gata · Johans gate · Plass · Domkirke · Stortorvet · Storgata · Brugata · Stenersgata · Vognmannsgata

Lekkeveien · Adelers gate · Munkedamsveien · Konsert-huset · Fridtjof Nansens plass · Rådhuset · Karl Johans gate · Jernbane-torget · Tomtegata · Schweigaards gate

Hutfields · Ruseløkkveien · Maudsgt. · Vestbanest. · Rådhusplassen · Prinsens gate · Tollbugate · Østbanest. · Bispegata · Voss

Munkedamsveien · Dokkveien · Rådhusgata · Nedre · Kongens gate · Kirke gata · Børsen · Strandgata

Filipstadveien · Drammen · Mynt · Norges Bank · Akershus

Pipervika · **Bjørvika** · **Bispevika**

0 — 250m

Stockholm

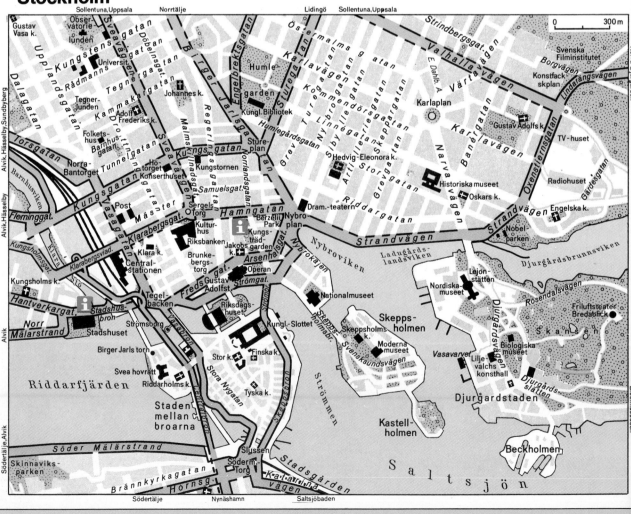

Sollentuna, Uppsala · Norrtälje · Lidingö · Sollentuna, Uppsala · 0 — 300 m

Gustav Vasa k. · Obser-vatorie lunden · Sveavägen · Döbelnsgatan · Östermalms gatan · Strindbergsgat.en · Valhallavägen · Svenska Filminstitutet

Upplandsgatan · Kungstens-gatan · Universit. · Rådmanns · Humle · Karlavägen · Borgvägen · Konstfack-skplan · Linderängsvägen

Dalagatan · Tegnérgatan · Kammakargatan · Adolf Frederiks k. · Johannes k. · garden · Kommendörsgatan · Karlaplan · Gustav Adolfs k. · TV-huset

Alvik, Hässelby, Sundbyberg · Tegnér-lunden · Drottninggatan · Birger Jarlsgatan · Kungl. Bibliotek · Humlegårdsgatan · Skeppargatan · Karlavägen · Oxenstiernsgatan · Radiohuset

Torsgatan · Folkets-hus · Barnhus-gatan · Stureplan · Hedvig-Eleonora k. · Narvavägen · Historiska museet · Gärdesgatan

Alvik, Hässelby · Barnhusviken · Norra Bantorget · Tunnelgatan · Sveavägen · Hö-torget · Konserthuset · Kungstornen · Storgatan · Historiska museet · Oskars k. · Engelska k.

Fleminggat. · Kungsgatan · Vasagatan · Mäster · Samuelsgat. · Sergels · Dram.-teatern · Riddargatan · Strandvägen · Nöbel-parken

Kungsholmsgatan · Klara · Post · Klarabergsgatan · Torg · Kultur-hus · Berzelii Parki · Nybro-plan · Nybroviken · Strandvägen · Djurgårdsbrunnsviken

Kungsholms k. · Klarabergsviad. · Klara k. · Riksbanken · Kungs-träd-garden · Jakobs k. · Ladugårds-landsviken · Lejon-stätten · Nordiska-museet · Rösendalsvägen

Hantverkargat. · Central-stationen · Brunke-bergs-torg · Arsenali · Gustav Adolfst. · Strömgat. · Operan · Nationalmuseet · Nordiska-museet · Friluftsteater Bredablick

Norr Mälarstrand · Stadshus-bron · Tegel-backen · Freds · Kungl.-Slottet · Skepps-holmen · Skeppsholmskyrkan · Djurgårdsvägen · Biologiska museet · Djurgårds-slätten

Alvik · Stadshuset · Strömsborg · Riksdags-huset · Moderna museet · Vasavarvet · Lilje-valchs konsthall · Skansen

Birger Jarls torn · Stor k. · Finska k. · Svenksundsvägen · Kastell-holmen

Söndertälje, Alvik · Svea hovrätt · Riddarholms k. · Stora Nygatan · Tyska k. · Strömmen

Riddarfjärden · Staden mellan broarna · Slussen · **Skeppsholmen** · Beckholmen

Söder Mälarstrand · Söderm. Torg · Stadsgården · **Saltsjön**

Skinnaviks-parken · Brännkyrkagatan · Hornsg. · Karlavägen

Söndertälje · Nynäshamn · Saltsjöbaden · Djurgårdstaden

238

Helsinki

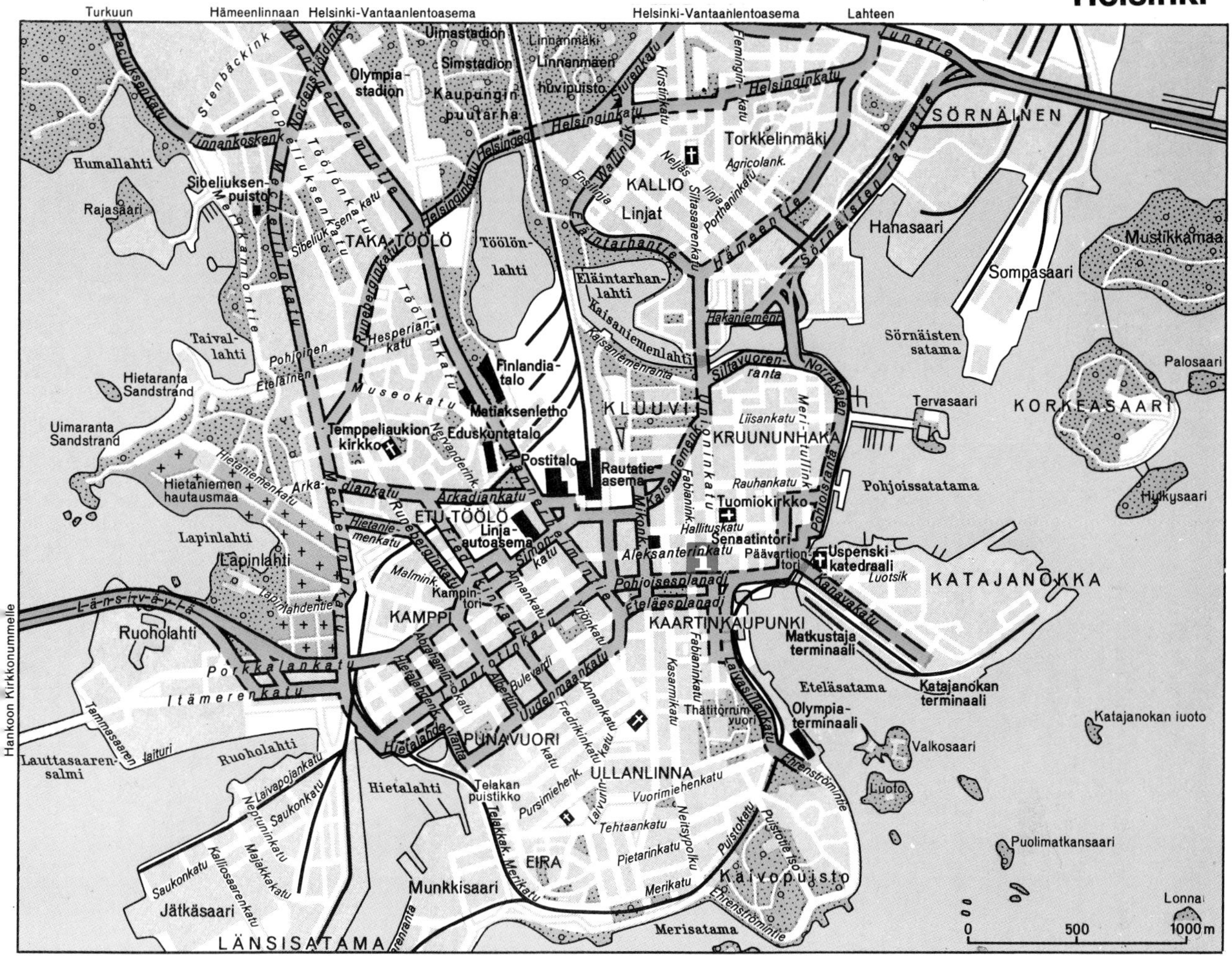

Turkuun Hämeenlinnaan Helsinki-Vantaanlentoasema Helsinki-Vantaanlentoasema Lahteen

SÖRNÄINEN

Uimastadion
Olympia-stadion
Simstadion
Linnanmäki
Linnanmäen huvipuisto
Kaupungin puutarha
Humallahti
Rajasaari
Mustikkamaa
Torkkelinmäki
Agricolank.
KALLIO
Linjat
Hanasaari
Sompasaari
Sibeliuksen-puisto
TAKA-TÖÖLÖ
Töölön-lahti
Eläintarhan-lahti
Korkeasaari
Taival-lahti
Hesperian-katu
Kaisaniemenlahti
Palosaari
Hietaranta Sandstrand
Pohjoinen Eläinen
Finlandia-talo
Museokatu
KLUUVI
Sörnäisten satama
Liisankatu
Uimaranta Sandstrand
Temppeliaukion kirkko
Matiaksenietho
Eduskuntatalo
KRUUNUNHAKA
Tervasaari
Hietaniemen hautausmaa
Postitalo
Rautatie-asema
Rauhankatu
Tuomiokirkko
Pohjoissatama
Lapinlahti
Arkadiankatu
ETU-TÖÖLÖ
Hallituskatu
Sensaatintori
Uspenski-katedraali
Hiukysaari
Läpinlahti
Linja-autoasema
Aleksanterinkatu
Päävartion tori
Luotsik
KATAJANOKKA
Ruoholahti
KAMPPI
Kampintori
Pohjoisesplanadi
KAARTINKAUPUNKI
Matkustaja terminaali
Katajanokan iuoto
Porkkalankatu
Itämerenkatu
PUNAVUORI
Fabianinkatu
Kasarmikatu
Tähtitorninvuori
Etelässatama
Olympia-terminaali
Katajanokan terminaali
Ruoholahti
Hietalahti
Telakan puistikko
ULLANLINNA
Vuorimiehenkatu
Valkosaari
Lauttasaaren salmi
Laivapojankatu
Tehtaankatu
Luoto
EIRA
Pietarinkatu
Puolimatkansaari
Munkkisaari
Jätkäsaari
Merikatu
Kaivopuisto
Lonnai
LÄNSISATAMA
Merisatama

0   500   1000 m

København

0   200   400m

Hillerød, Helsingør   Helsingør

Østre
Hirschsprungske Malerisamling
Statens Museum f. Kunst
Anlæg
Frihedsmus.
Kommune Hospital
Palmehus
Mineralog. Mus.
Tekniske Højskole
Kunstindustri-museet
Blågårds-pl.
Botanisk Have
Rosenborg
Botan. Mus.
Kongens Have
Frederiks-kirke
Amalienborg
Amalie-haven
Oddfellow Palæt
Ørsteds-parken
Nørreport-Station
Hauser-pl.
Kultorvet
Rundetårn
Garnisons-K.
Kongens Nytorv
St.Petri Kirke
Universitetet
Vor Frue Kirke
Helligånds-kirken
Charlottenborg
Nyhavn
Kgl. Teater
Domhuset
Nikolai-K.
Thorvaldsen Mus
Rådhus-pl.
Holmenskirke
Børsen
Rådhuset
Christiansborg
Tivoli
National Museet
Glyptoteket
Kgl. Bibl.
Hoved banegård
Vesterport-Station
Christianshavn
Vor Frelsers Kirke

Køge   Københavns Lufthavn

239

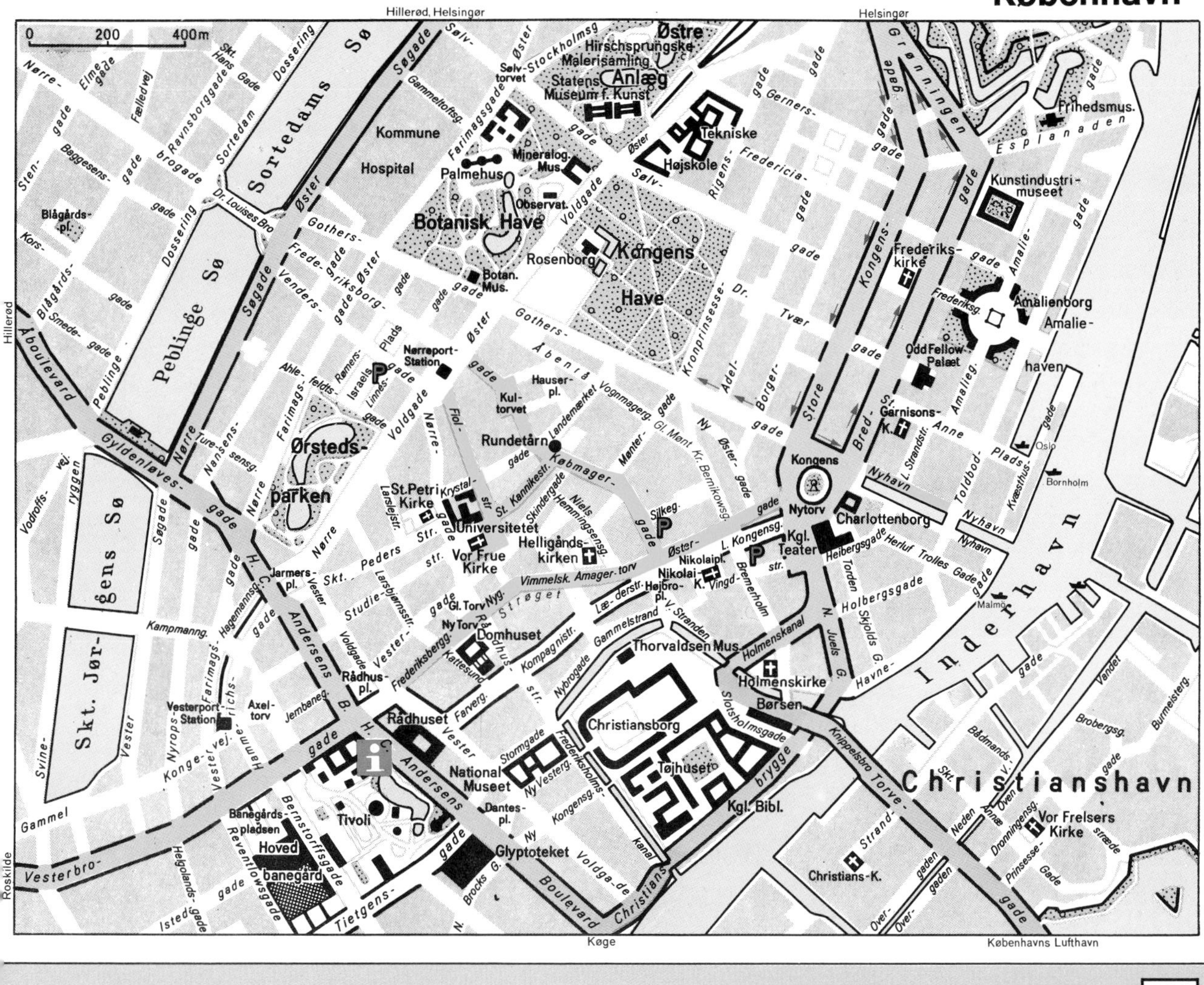

London

① Tower Bridge
② Tower
③ Monument
④ Bank of England
⑤ Stock Exchange
⑥ Royal Exchange
⑦ Mansion House
⑧ Mithras Temple
⑨ Guildhall
⑩ St.Paul's Cathedral
⑪ Old Bailey
⑫ St.Bride's Church
⑬ Dr.Johnson's House
⑭ The Temple
⑮ Staple Inn
⑯ Lincoln's Inn
⑰ Gray's Inn
⑱ Royal Courts of Justice
⑲ St.Clement Danes
⑳ St.Mary-le-Strand
㉑ Somerset House
㉒ Royal Opera House
㉓ St.Paul's Church
㉔ Cleopatra's Needle
㉕ Nelson's Column
㉖ St.Martin-in-the-Fields
㉗ National Gallery
㉘ Admiralty Arch
㉙ Admiralty
㉚ Horse Guards
㉛ Downing Street No.10
㉜ The Cenotaph
㉝ Houses of Parliament
㉞ Westminster Abbey
㉟ Queen Victoria Memorial
㊱ Buckingham Palace
㊲ Lancaster House
㊳ St.James's Palace
㊴ Marlborough House
㊵ British Museum
㊶ University of London
㊷ Dickens' House

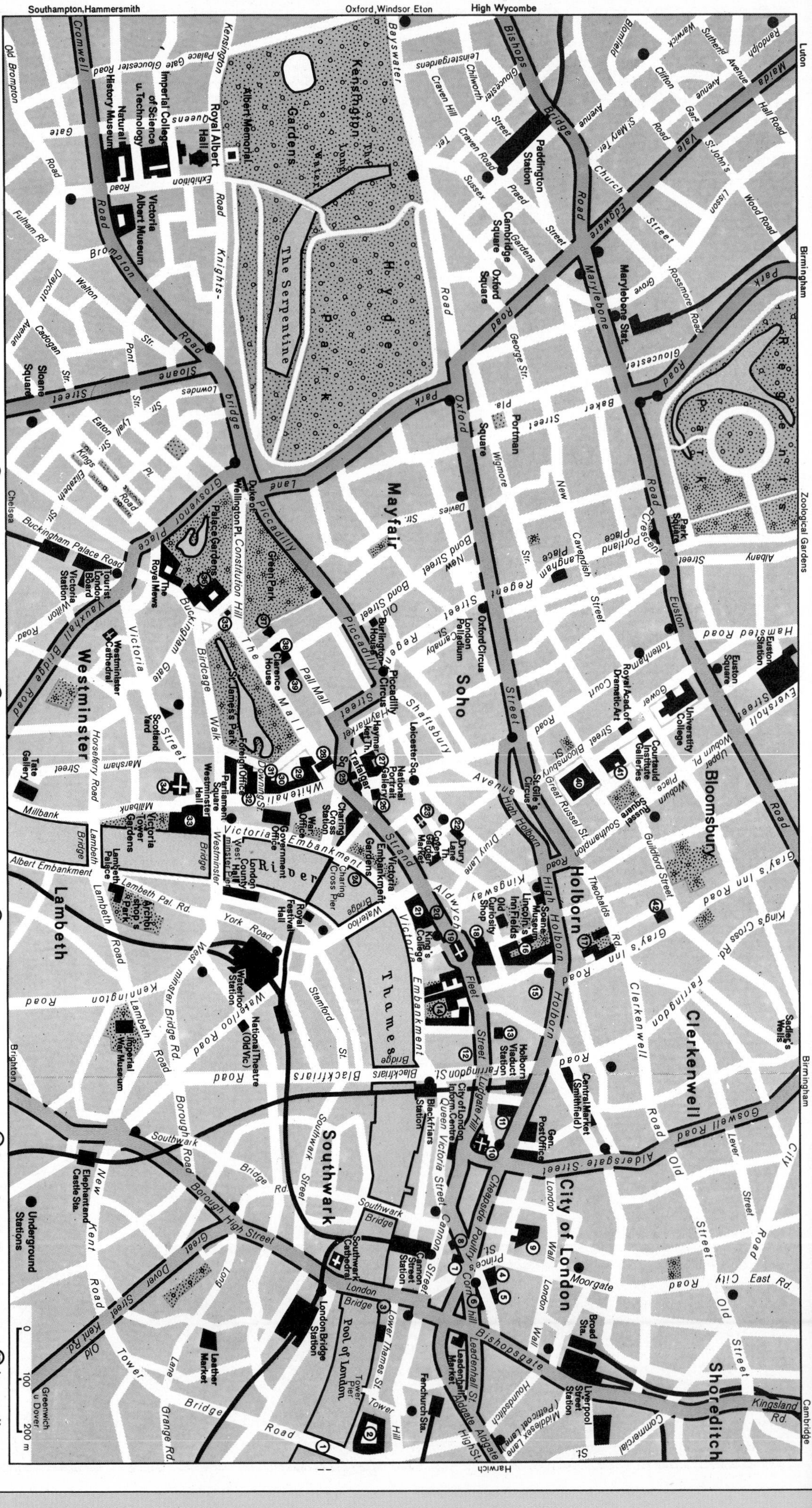

• Underground Stations

Bonn

1 Bundesmin. f. Post- u. Fernmeldewesen
2 Bundestag u. Bundesrat
3 Presse- u. Informationsamt der Bundesregierung

4 Alter Zoll
5 Rathaus
6 Beethovenhaus
7 Verkehrsamt
8 Hauptpost
9 Altes Stadthaus

München

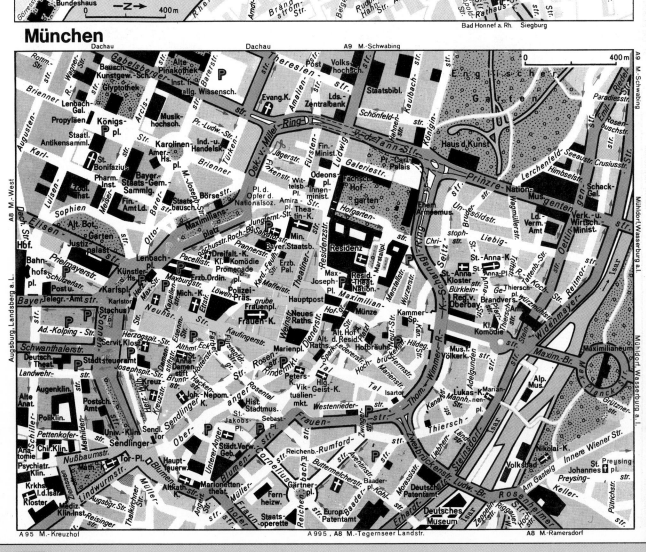

Wien

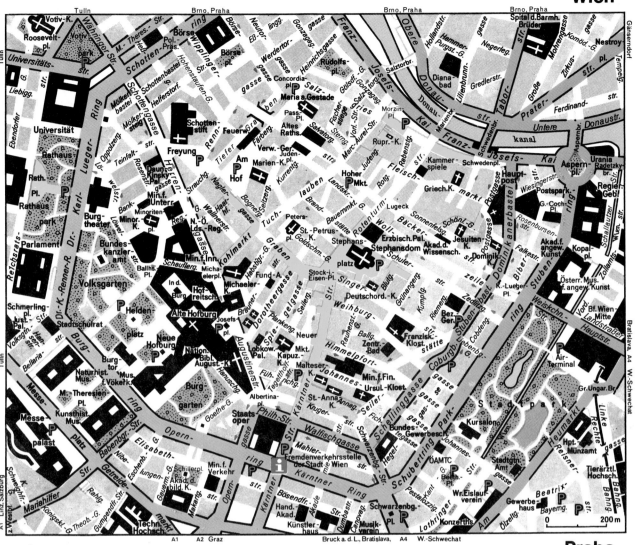

Praha

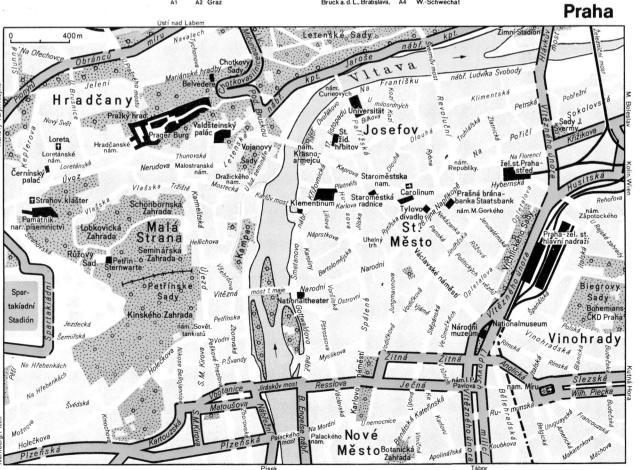

Zürich

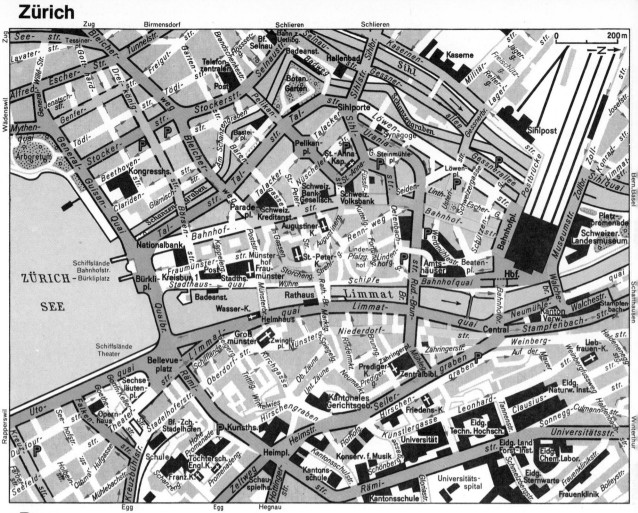

Bern

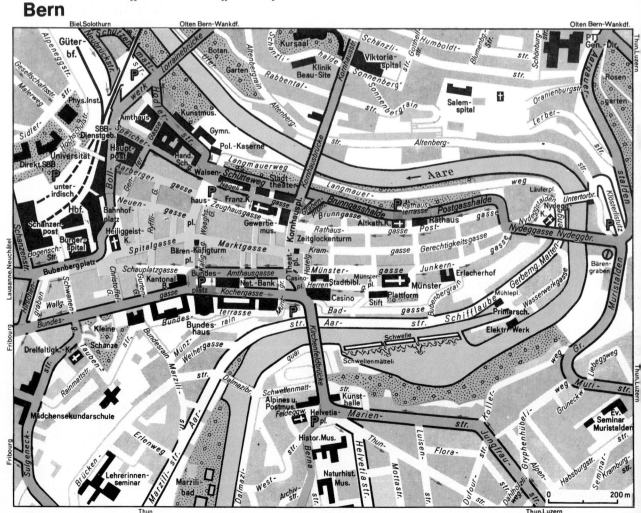

Amsterdam

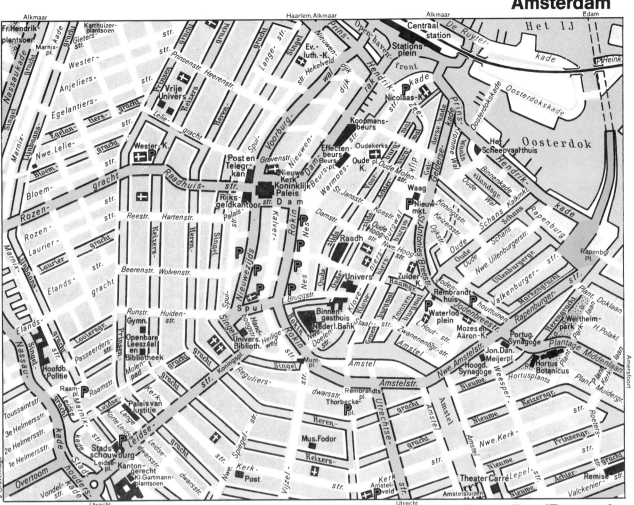

Bruxelles/Brussel

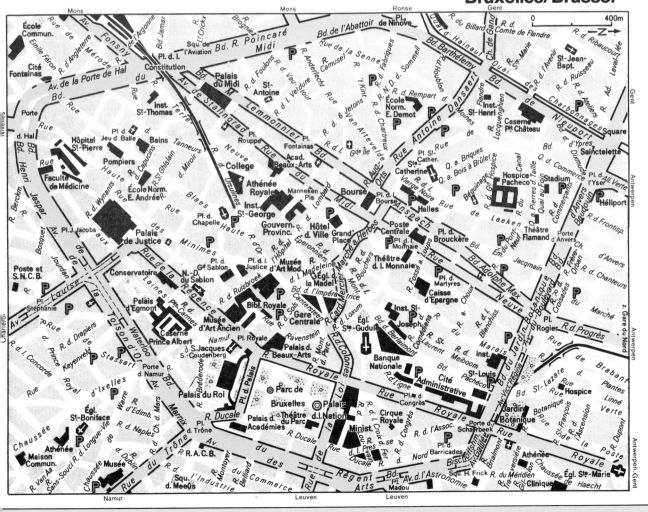

Paris

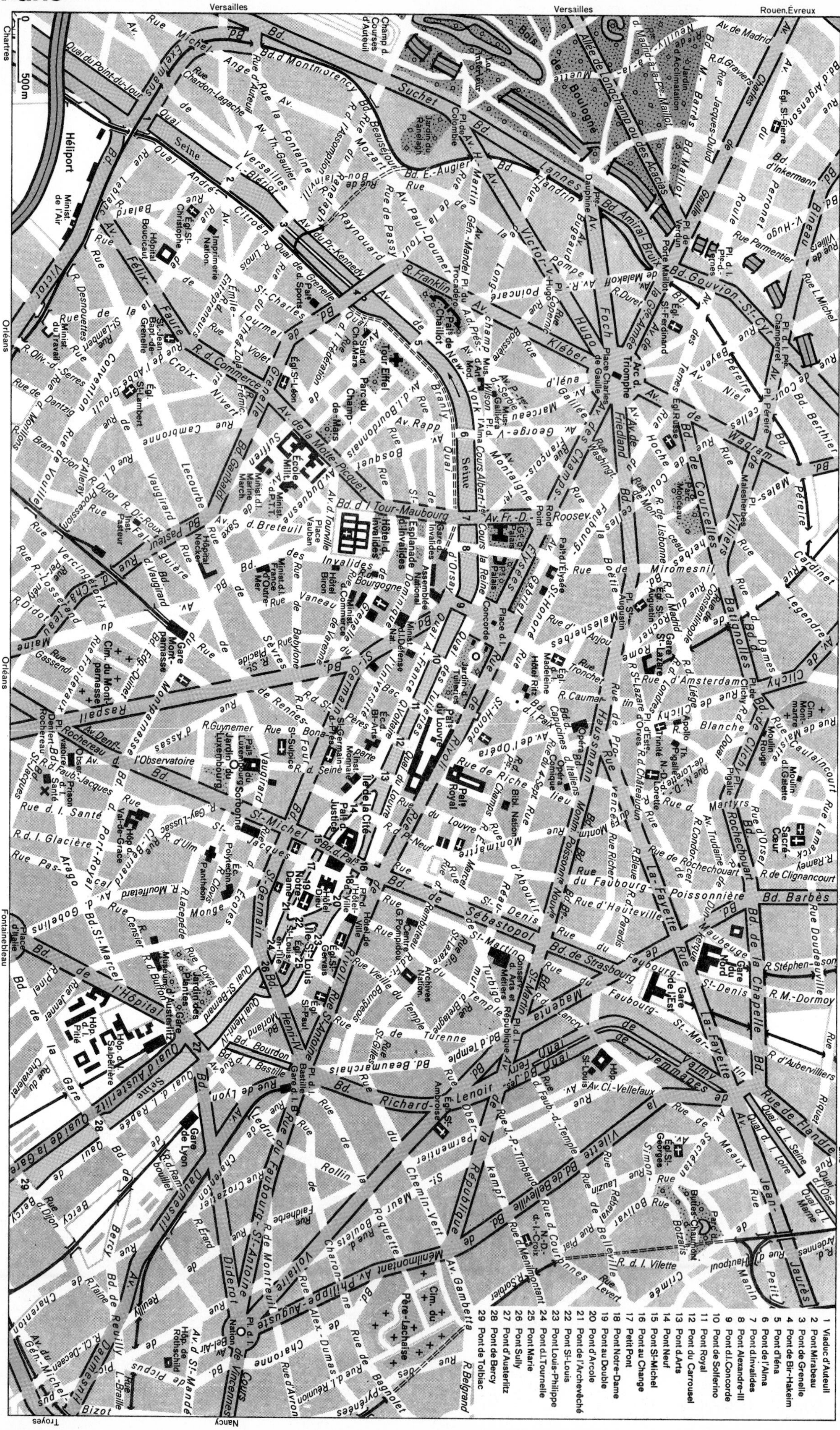

1 Viaduc d'Auteuil
2 Pont Mirabeau
3 Pont de Grenelle
4 Pont de Bir-Hakeim
5 Pont d'Iéna
6 Pont de l'Alma
7 Pont des Invalides
8 Pont Alexandre-III
9 Pont de la Concorde
10 Pont de Solférino
11 Pont Royal
12 Pont du Carrousel
13 Pont des Arts
14 Pont Neuf
15 Pont St-Michel
16 Petit Pont
17 Pont Notre-Dame
18 Pont au Change
19 Pont au Double
20 Pont d'Arcole
21 Pont de l'Archevêché
22 Pont St-Louis
23 Pont Louis-Philippe
24 Pont Marie
25 Pont de Sully
26 Pont d'Austerlitz
27 Pont de Bercy
28 Pont de Tolbiac
29 Pont Belgrand

Luxembourg

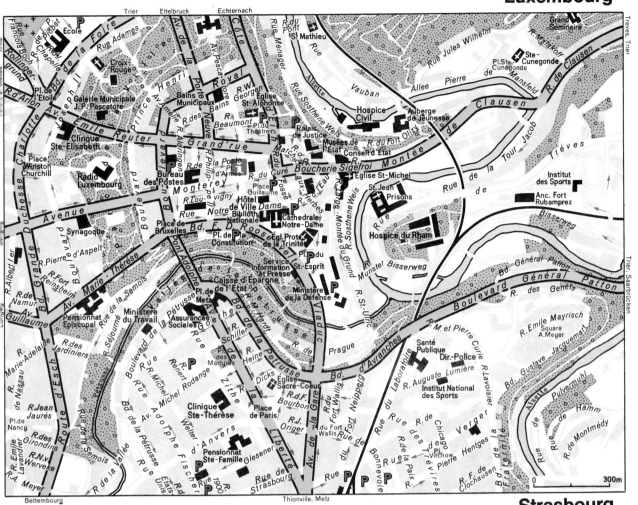

Strasbourg

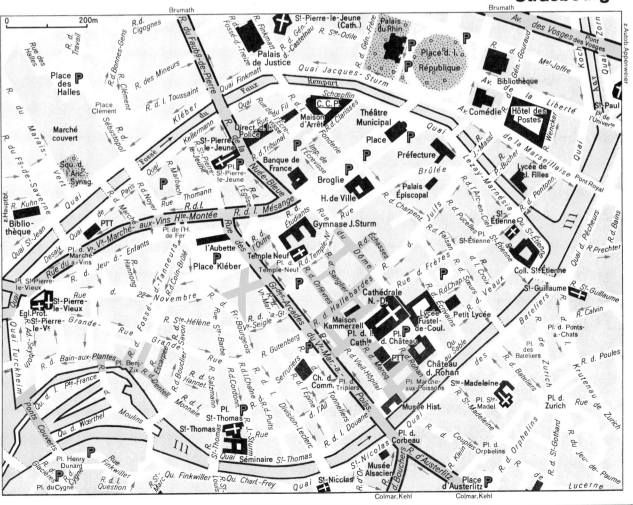

Madrid

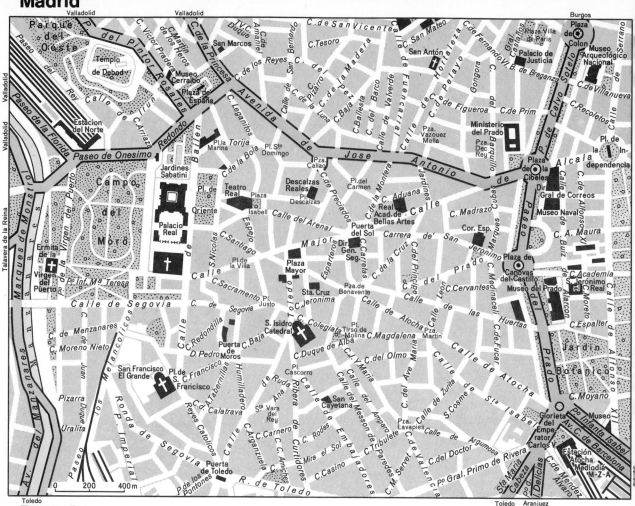

Barcelona

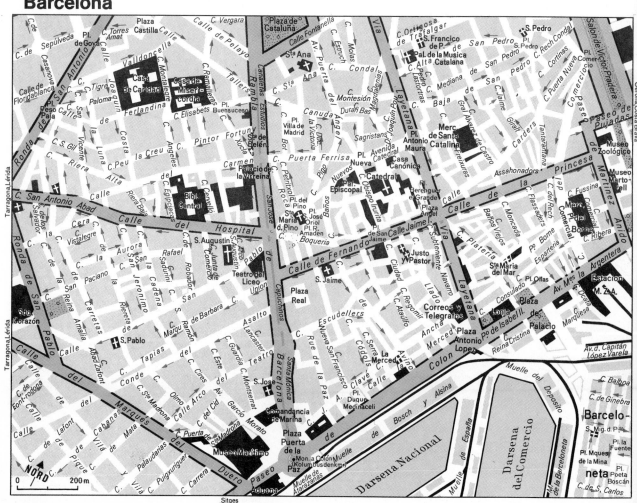

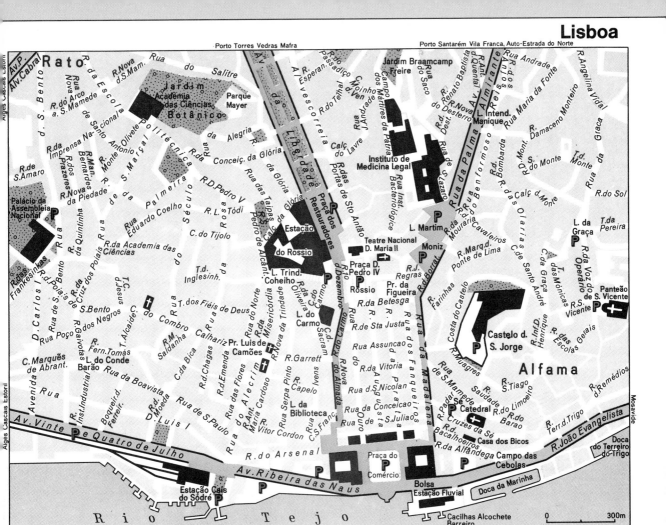

Milano

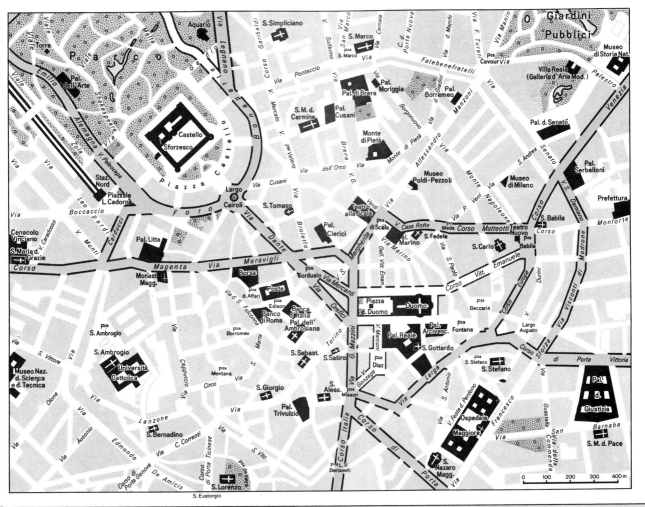

Roma

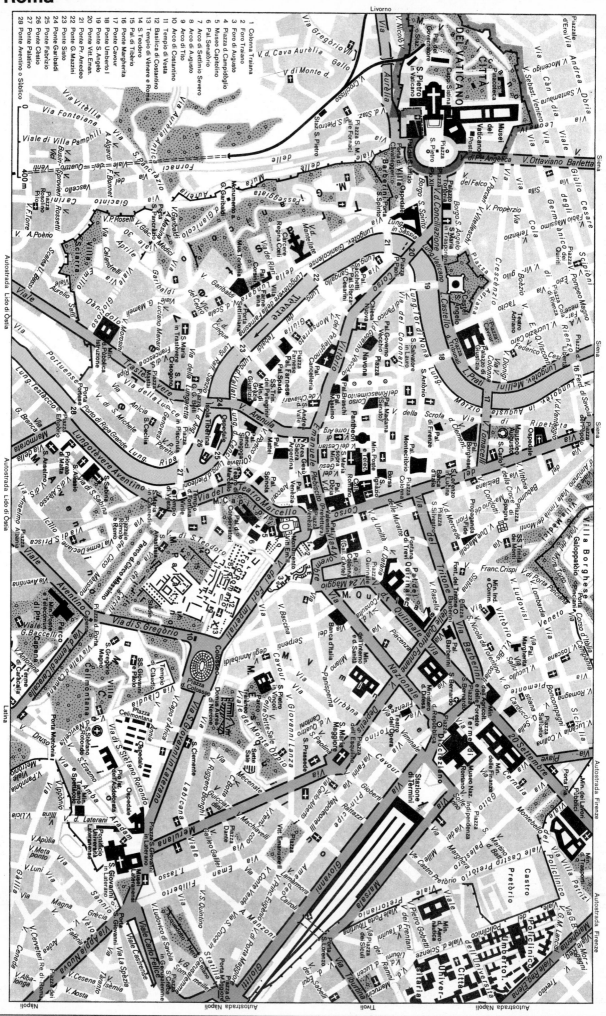

1 Colonna Traiana
2 Foro Traiano
3 Foro di Augusto
4 Piazza di Campidoglio
5 Museo Capitolino
6 Pal. Senatorio
7 Arco di Settimio Severo
8 Arco di Augusto
9 Arco di Tito
10 Arco di Costantino
11 Tempio di Vesta
12 Basilica di Costantino
13 Tempio di Vènere e Roma
14 S. Teodoro
15 Pal. di Tiberio
16 Ponte Margherita
17 Ponte Cavour
18 Ponte Umberto I
19 Ponte S. Angelo
20 Ponte Vitt. Eman.
21 Ponte Pr. Amedeo
22 Ponte G. Mazzini
23 Ponte Sisto
24 Ponte Garibaldi
25 Ponte Fabrizio
26 Ponte Cestio
27 Ponte Palatino
28 Ponte Aventino o Sùblicio

Budapest

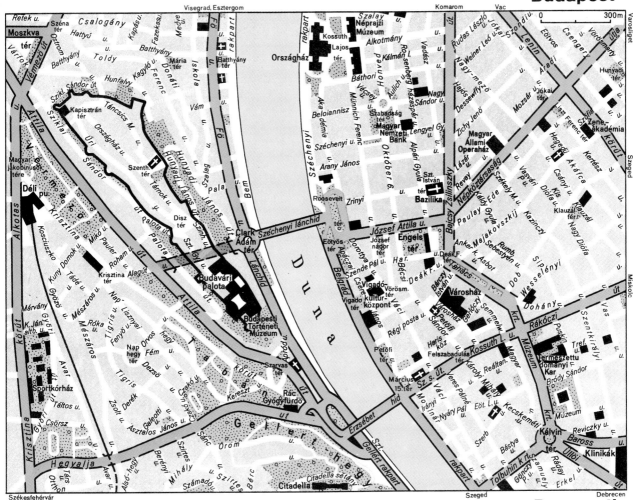

Bucureşti

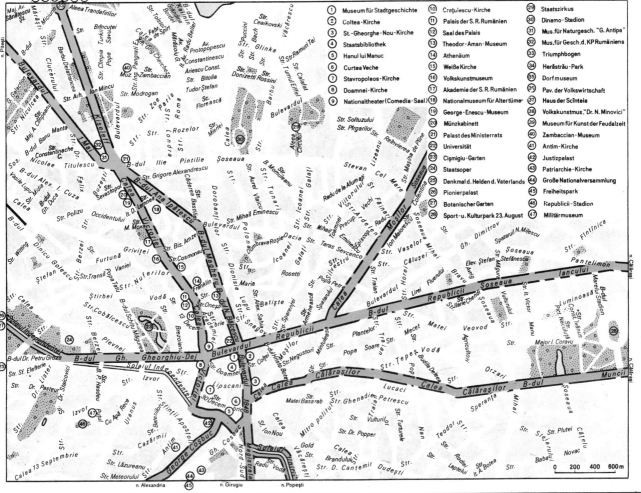

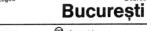

1	Museum für Stadtgeschichte
2	Coltea-Kirche
3	St.-Gheorghe-Nou-Kirche
4	Staatsbibliothek
5	Hanul lui Manuc
6	Curtea Veche
7	Stavropoleos-Kirche
8	Doamnei-Kirche
9	Nationaltheater (Comedia-Saal)
10	Creţulescu-Kirche
11	Palais der S. R. Rumänien
12	Saal des Palais
13	Theodor-Aman-Museum
14	Athenäum
15	Weiße Kirche
16	Volkskunstmuseum
17	Akademie der S. R. Rumänien
18	Nationalmuseum für Altertümer
19	George-Enescu-Museum
20	Münzkabinett
21	Palast des Ministerrats
22	Universität
23	Cişmigiu-Garten
24	Staatsoper
25	Denkmal d. Helden d. Vaterlands
26	Pionierpalast
27	Botanischer Garten
28	Sport-u. Kulturpark 23. August
29	Staatszirkus
30	Dinamo-Stadion
31	Mus. für Naturgesch. "G. Antipa"
32	Mus. für Gesch. d. KP Rumäniens
33	Triumphbogen
34	Herăstrău-Park
35	Dorfmuseum
36	Pav. der Volkswirtschaft
37	Haus der Scînteia
38	Volkskunstmus. "Dr. N. Minovici"
39	Museum für Kunst der Feudalzeit
40	Zambaccian-Museum
41	Antim-Kirche
42	Justizpalast
43	Patriarchie-Kirche
44	Große Nationalversammlung
45	Freiheitspark
46	Republicii-Stadion
47	Militärmuseum

Athenai

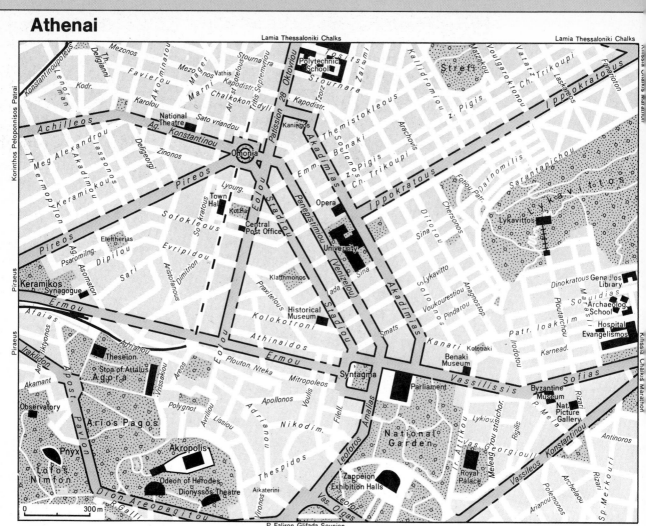

İstanbul

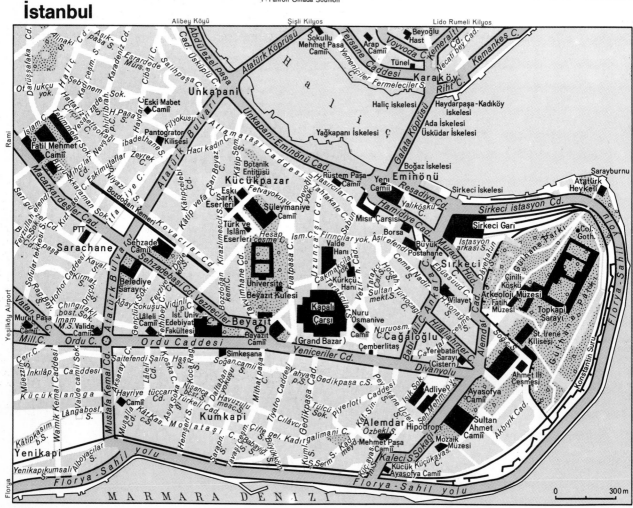